KU-751-759

22 C   d Way
am
E
Tel: 081 891 3302

Annabel Skinner

TANZANIA
& ZANZIBAR

'An entire afternoon might be spent
searching for a glimpse of a leopard,
to find instead a vision of migrating
wildebeest jostling at a crocodile-
infested waterhole, or a herd of impala
poised like dancers in a sunlit glade.'

CADOGANguides

1 Beach, Zanzibar

3

4

2 Beach hut dining
3 Emerson and Green Hotel, Stone Town,
  Zanzibar
4 Beach scene, southeast coast, Zanzibar

5 Chimpanzee, Gombe Stream
  National Park
6 Red colobus monkey, Jozani Forest
7 Cheetah, Serengeti National Park

9

10

8 Bridge of God, Uporoto Mountains
9 Sisal plantations, Morogoro
10 Mount Kilimanjaro

11 Black rhinos, Ngorongoro Crater
12 Giraffes near the shore of Lake Natron
13 Maasai in traditional dress

14 Woman selling rice cakes, Pangani
15 Carved Zanzibari doorway

16 Street scene, Stone Town, Zanzibar
17 House of Wonders, Stone Town, Zanzibar
18 Kariakoo Market, Dar es Salaam
19 Spice market, Mtwara

16

17

18

20 Old Dhow Harbour, Stone Town, Zanzibar
21 Sailing dhows, Zanzibar coast

21

About the author

This book is the culmination of a long-term interest in Tanzania. Over the years, author **Annabel Skinner** has seen this part of East Africa from many different perspectives: her early travels in the country soon developed into extended stays until a series of articles commissioned on the subject of Tanzania led, somewhat obliquely, to a stint as a travel consultant. Drawing on her experiences as a national newspaper journalist and seeking a greater challenge, Annabel felt that writing this guide book was the next logical step.

Annabel currently lives in small half-finished house in London, with a big husband, two small babes and a little dog. In order to use and develop the experience and information gathered in collating this updated guide she is keen to advise and be advised – please e-mail any queries or updates to her on *info@cadogantanzania.com*.

Author's acknowledgements

Without the help of the following people this guide would not be; so grateful thanks to **Charlotte Wilcox** for her massive updating expedition for this second edition, **Julian Carter-Manning** from **Tanzania Odyssey** and **Mark Rolfe** for his Udzungwa Mountains insights. Many thanks too to **Susan D'Costa** of **Roy Safaris** for providing information and answers to endless queries for both editions, and to **Charles Dobie** of **Selous Safari Company**, **Tim Hendricks** of **Ras Nungwi Beach Hotel** (still 'arguably the best' beach on Zanzibar), and **Nicola Colangelo** of **Coastal Travels** for his invaluable assistance on the ground and off it. Also thanks to **Peter Byrne** of **Kinasi Lodge** on Mafia Island for his assistance, advice and opinions along the way, and to **Peter Lindstrom** and his team at **Hoopoe Adventure Tours**, Arusha, for so many magical days in the Northern Parks. **Joseph Lengai** and **Tumaini** deserve a special mention for being such amusing, informative and long-suffering travelling companions over many long days. On Zanzibar, thanks to **Antonella** for letting me stay for so many fun nights, and to **Maya Tours**, **Natalie** at **Breezes Beach Club** and **Georges** at **Sunrise**. The same to **Abdul** and those at **Flycatcher Safaris** for helping me to get to Rubondo Island, **Bettie Loibookie** of **TANAPA**, **Martin** and **Christina** in **Mikindani** and **Mtwara**, **Cliff de Souza** of **Savannah Tours**, and to **Neema** and **Mrs Kambona** for much-needed warm welcomes in Dar es Salaam.

Special thanks to **Chris Fox** of **Mwagusi Luxury Camp** in Ruaha, aka the elephant whisperer of Tanzania, for contributing such extensive and fascinating information to the Wildlife chapter, and **Vica Irani** for contributing first-hand information about Zoroastrianism.

For support at home, thanks to **Emma** and **Andy** for gaining me access to the excellent libraries at SOAS and VSO, and to **Miranda and Mark Harvie-Watt** for donating computer space, phone lines and plenty of coffee in the corner of their office.

But most thanks must go to **Marc**, my wonderful husband and funniest friend, who continues to support, encourage and inspire through good times and bad; the one I abandoned to a life of frozen pizzas and lonely DIY just weeks after marrying, the most handsome tour operator to specialize in Tanzania, and inspiration enough for a lifetime.

Contents

Introducing 08

Reference

Publisher's acknowledgements

Many thanks to **Nasor Malik** for his observations on Tanzanian history and politics. Thanks too to **Tony Janes**, a former VSO field director of Tanzania, who now runs the the **Simply Tanzania Tour Company**, for his comments on conservation issues and ways to be a 'responsible tourist' in Tanzania.

Cadogan Guides
2nd Floor, 233 High Holborn, London WC1V 7DN
info@cadoganguides.co.uk
www.cadoganguides.com

The Globe Pequot Press
246 Goose Lane, PO Box 480, Guilford,
Connecticut 06437–0480

Copyright © Annabel Skinner 2001, 2005

Cover design by Sarah Gardner
Cover photographs: front © Flo Montgomery
back Alan Montgomery
Photo essay: © pp.2–3 Peter Adams Photography/
Alamy; p.4 Nicholas Pitt/Alamy; p.5 Images of
Africa Photobank/Alamy, Nicholas Pitt/Alamy; p.6
Norman Tomalin/Alamy; p.7 Alan Montgomery,
Craig Lovell/Eagle Visions Photography/Alamy;
p.8 Annabel Skinner; p.9 Alan Montgomery,
Robert Harding Picture Library Ltd/Alamy; p.10
Westend61/Alamy , Craig Lovell/Eagle Visions
Photography/Alamy; pp.11–12 Annabel Skinner;
pp.13–15 Flo Montgomery, Annabel Skinner;
p.16 Kicca Tommasi
Maps © Cadogan Guides, drawn by Maidenhead
Cartographic Services Ltd
Managing Editor: Natalie Pomier
Editor: Linda McQueen
Editorial Assistant: Nicola Jessop
Proofreading: Alison Copland
Indexing: Isobel McLean

Printed in Italy by Legoprint
A catalogue record for this book is available
from the British Library
ISBN 1-86011-216-1

The author and publishers have made every effort to ensure the accuracy of the information in this book at the time of going to press. However, they cannot accept any responsibility for any loss, injury or inconvenience resulting from the use of information contained in this guide.

Please help us to keep this guide up to date. We have done our best to ensure that the information in this guide is correct at the time of going to press. But places and facilities are constantly changing, and standards and prices in hotels and restaurants fluctuate. We would be delighted to receive any comments concerning existing entries or omissions. Authors of the best letters will receive a copy of the Cadogan Guide of their choice.

All rights reserved. No part of this publication may be reproduced, stored in a retrieval system, or transmitted, in any form or by any means, electronic or mechanical, including photocopying and recording, or by any information storage and retrieval system except as may be expressly permitted by the UK 1988 Copyright Design & Patents Act and the USA 1976 Copyright Act or in writing from the publisher. Requests for permission should be addressed to Cadogan Guides, 2nd Floor, 233 High Holborn, London, WC1V 7DN, in the UK, or The Globe Pequot Press, 246 Goose Lane, PO Box 480, Guilford, Connecticut 06437–0480, in the USA.

Introduction

A Guide to the Guide 4

How to describe the extraordinary nature of the land that is Tanzania? Its diverse and dramatic landscape was wrought by the fluctuations of the earth's plates, to create, in the shadow of the Great Rift Valley, a realm of volcanic mountains, craters and lakes, ancient forests and rolling, open plains where wild creatures roam. Some of these beasts are far greater than humans in size, others more beautiful, agile, elegant or ugly, and many more ancient by far, but all may be found in the unspoilt wilderness of the Tanzanian landscape in a world that is truly their own.

This vast landmass brims with exuberant life under the constant spectre of death, a land of plenty, with gold and mineral seams and a diversity of crops, yet fighting a constant battle against extreme poverty, corrupt politics and the wild forces of equatorial nature. Its people have gathered through centuries, from all regions of the African continent, and by sea from Persia, Arabia, India and Europe; now they are joined in the modern United Republic of Tanzania and mostly speak the Swahili language as fluently as their original tongues.

And this same country is fringed by hundreds of kilometres of idyllic coastline and myriad islands, lapped by the startlingly clear azure waters of the Indian Ocean. All along these coral sandy shores, in the shade of coconut palms and sewn dhow sails, are the signs and remnants of the history that shaped both land and people. This coastline, the destination of ancient trade routes from far-distant foreign lands, was the crossroads for luxury goods so highly prized that sailors would risk their lives to reach them, then wait half the year for monsoon winds to bear them home. In the wake of these early traders the fine warm sands are punctuated with ruins to inspire dreams of the past, while the present day adds possibilities of diving, swimming, fishing and sailing in the clear waters and coral reefs nearby.

While historically the interior of Tanzania has confounded scientists and broken the bravest explorers, now the way is open for travellers to investigate at their leisure. Those with a whim to conquer the snow-capped peaks of Mount Kilimanjaro, the continent's highest mountain, now have a fair chance to try; and on offer everywhere are extraordinary experiences: trekking in the ancient forests of the Eastern Arc Mountains or tracking chimpanzees through the sheltered woodlands of Mahale Mountains and Gombe Stream, following the trail of an elusive leopard through the little-known wilderness of Ruaha or lying beneath the pale billowing sails of a wooden dhow on the aquamarine waters of the coast. There are endless possibilities for wildlife safaris and the exploration of an unspoilt wilderness by car or boat, on foot or on horseback, from a camel, a balloon or a bus. Whether you choose the open expanse of the Serengeti, so beloved by film-makers and wildlife documentarists, or the lesser-known sanctuaries of Ruaha, Katavi or Selous, there is exceptional range and scope for wildlife-watching in privacy, comfort and peace.

Travellers will find that this incredible land can seem to open up before them, and vast, changing distances can be happily covered against all the odds of poorly maintained roads, agonizingly slow railways and overcrowded ferries. Somehow there is always a means, a vehicle, eventually, be it car, truck, train or bicycle, and invariably a willing companion to while away hours in storytelling or conversation at your side. Those who live here must work hard for the luxuries of life, but relish them

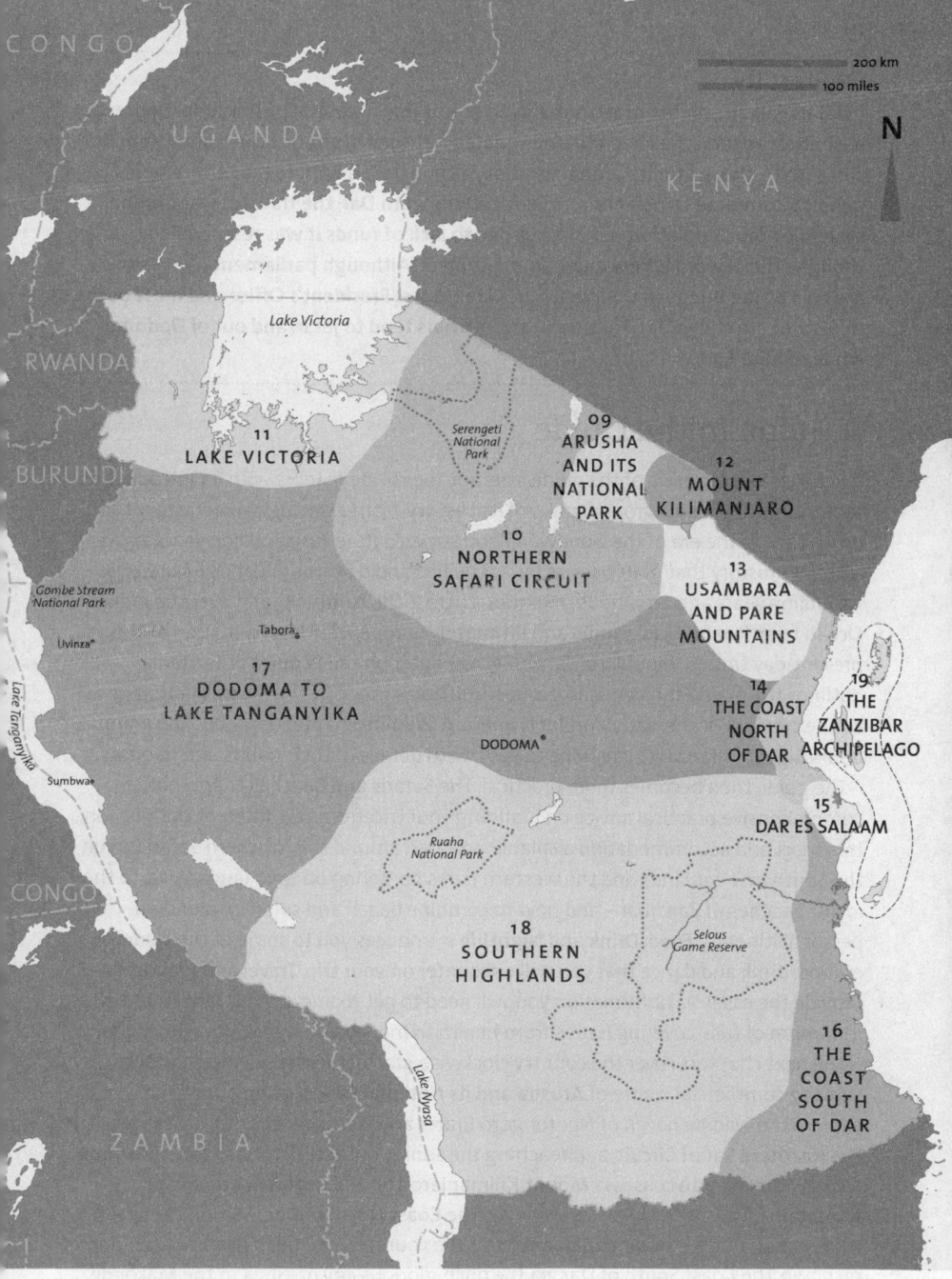

CONGO

UGANDA

KENYA

200 km

100 miles

N

RWANDA

Lake Victoria

BURUNDI

Serengeti National Park

11 LAKE VICTORIA

09 ARUSHA AND ITS NATIONAL PARK

12 MOUNT KILIMANJARO

Gombe Stream National Park

Uvinza

Tabora

10 NORTHERN SAFARI CIRCUIT

13 USAMBARA AND PARE MOUNTAINS

Lake Tanganyika

17 DODOMA TO LAKE TANGANYIKA

DODOMA

14 THE COAST NORTH OF DAR

19 THE ZANZIBAR ARCHIPELAGO

Sumbwa

Ruaha National Park

15 DAR ES SALAAM

CONGO

18 SOUTHERN HIGHLANDS

Selous Game Reserve

16 THE COAST SOUTH OF DAR

Lake Nyasa

ZAMBIA

when they are won. Visitors are welcomed with wide smiles and a vitality that is invariably infectious. With the help of the people you meet, and of course of this guide, whatever your personal interests, the chances are you will be inspired, exhilarated, and rewarded by the fulfilment of your most idyllic dreams.

Capital City

Dar es Salaam, on the coast, remains the commercial capital of Tanzania. Dodoma, in central Tanzania, has been the 'designated national capital' of the United Republic since 1973 – chosen for its central location, although it is hard to reach. It remains pending complete transfer of official functions from Dar; the transfer was originally scheduled for completion in 1990, but due to lack of funds it was rescheduled, though official word is very quiet on the subject. Although parliamentary sessions are held at the Bunge in Dodoma, the State House, President's Office and most of the ministries are still in Dar. Politicians and officials tend to jet in and out of Dodoma when required.

A Guide to the Guide

The first five chapters of the guide attempt to provide readers with an **Introduction** to Tanzania and a background grasp of its **History**, from a geological prehistory that dates back to the era of the Gondwanaland supercontinent 150 million years ago, and a human history that goes back as far as the hominoid footprints of Olduvai Gorge 3.5 million years ago, to various migrations across the continent and over the Indian Ocean from Persia, Arabia, India and ultimately Europe, until the formation of the present-day United Republic of Tanzania. A chapter on the **Peoples** of Tanzania outlines the main ethnic African groups, unified as much by the Swahili language as by the creation of the nation under Nyerere. A **Wildlife** chapter describes the animals a safari-goer in Tanzania can hope to spot, with details of their habits and habitats.

The guide then becomes more practical. The **Safaris and Beaches** chapter offers comprehensive practical advice on planning your trip, from the different options for transport and accommodation available on safari around the Northern Safari Circuit, the Southern Highlands and the western parks bordering on Lake Tanganyika, to the idyllic beaches of Zanzibar – and how to combine beach and safari in your own personal itinerary. **Food, Drink and Nightlife** introduces you to some of the traditions of food, drink and dance that you will encounter on your trip. **Travel** and **Practical A–Z** provide the essential information you will need to get to and around Tanzania with a minimum of fuss, covering issues from health to money and travelling with children.

The next chapters cover the country clockwise, starting in the northeast at the thriving commercial centre of **Arusha and its National Park**, setting out from there to explore the wildlife haven of Ngorongoro Crater and the expanses of the Serengeti in the **Northern Safari Circuit**, and reaching the shores of **Lake Victoria** before returning to the Indian Ocean coast via **Mount Kilimanjaro** and the **Usambara and Pare Mountains**. The guide then travels down **The Coast North of Dar**, visiting the grand ruins of Bagamoyo, to **Dar es Salaam** itself, the country's capital in all but name, and on down **The Coast South of Dar** via the once-glorious city of Kilwa to the Makonde Plateau. The guide skips across the country from **Dodoma to Lake Tanganyika**, with visits to the chimp havens of Gombe Stream and Mahale Mountains, down through the **The Southern Highlands** of Selous and Ruaha to Lake Nyasa, before going on a detailed tour of **The Zanzibar Archipelago**, the islands of Zanzibar, Pemba and Mafia.

History

What you see in Tanzania today is the result of an unusually long and varied history. Human life in the United Republic of Tanzania and Zanzibar has evolved over thousands of millennia: Olduvai Gorge, in the north of the country, is the site of the earliest ever excavated evidence of human existence – 3.5 million-year-old hominoid footprints. Since then, more than 120 tribes have migrated and settled here from overland, and trading peoples have frequented the Indian Ocean coast and islands since the time of the ancient Egyptians. Arab traders first settled here around 1,000 years ago, followed by Portuguese, German and British explorers, who rediscovered this land, plundered, colonized and attempted to convert it. Since the 1960s Tanzania and Zanzibar have been united, independent, self-governing and largely democratic, achieving a remarkable degree of national cohesion despite the ethnic mix. It remains, however, one of the five poorest nations in the world.

Tanzania's history has been pieced together from archaeological remains, oral traditions – tribal story-telling and explorers' tales – and written accounts dating back as far as the 1st century AD, describing life on the coast and islands. Fossil evidence has been found of life many thousands of years earlier: evidence of some of the earliest known proto-human ancestors have earned Tanzania the name 'Cradle of Mankind'.

Prehistory

Africa is geologically ancient: the vast continent was once a major component of the **Gondwanaland** supercontinent that drifted apart in the Mesozoic period 100–150 million years ago. The ancient rock strata of Tanzania contain petrified evidence of dinosaurs, such as the giant brachiosaurus and tiny kentrosaurus found on Tendaguru Mountain in the region of Lindi in southeast Tanzania in 1912 (now in the Natural Museum of Humboldt). One of the oldest known examples of bipedal hominids, immortalized in a pair of fossilized footprints – dating back 3.5 million years – were found at Olduvai Gorge in northern Tanzania. Throughout Tanzania many remains have been unearthed from the Stone Age, between 5,000 and 3,000 years ago: the site at Isimila, in the Mbeya region, is one of the most notable.

These earliest civilizations are thought to be direct ancestors of the **bushmen tribes** still, just, in evidence in Tanzania today – notably the **Hadzabe** tribe now clustered around Lake Eyasi, west of the Serengeti. Hunter-gatherers, they have left a legacy of rock paintings, covering over a thousand sites: the best of them can be seen at Kondoa in Kola, Cheke and Kisese.

A Steady Migration of Peoples

From around 1000 BC, pastoral and agricultural **Cushitic-speakers** from the north-eastern regions of Africa (now Ethiopia and Somalia) began migrating south. These early pastoralists were responsible for the first food production in Tanzania, and have left evidence of cattle-herding and irrigation techniques, including the advanced systems excavated at Engakura in the north. The Iraqw people of northern Tanzania and the Mbulu, Burungi and Gorowa are descended from these Cushitic immigrants.

Around 500 BC the **Iron Age** emerged at Buhaya in Tanzania, spreading across the northern reaches of the interior. The most important Iron Age sites are around Lake

Victoria, notably Urewe in the Kagera region, from where techniques used to create pottery later spread throughout east and southern Africa. Iron Age tools and hand-axes have been found in abundance at Isimila near Iringa, and Katuruka, near Bukoba.

The Cushitic tribes were joined around AD 500 by tribes of **Bantu-speaking people** who moved in from west Africa, and in the 2nd and 3rd centuries AD there was an influx of pastoral **Nilotic tribes** into the northwestern regions. The influx of migratory tribes has been constant since then: the infamous Maasai did not arrive until the 1800s, when they cut a swath through the northern plains, raiding cows, women and land. The Maasai's progress was thwarted north of Dodoma by a combination of sickness and combat with the Hehe tribe. Like many immigrants they were hit by the tsetse fly, carrier of the sleeping sickness *trypanosomiasis*, which can kill cattle and badly affect people.

Assimilation and Interaction

As displaced tribes from north and west Africa settled, for reasons of war, famine, disease, drought and a constant quest for pastures new, clans were divided or absorbed into other clans, or displaced by the arrival of other peoples. This ebb and flow of life encouraged trade, as each group brought new skills, ideas and foodstuffs. A barter economy developed. The most valuable of these commodities, notably salt, iron hoes and livestock, became a form of currency as a network of trading paths developed in response to demand for items between the interior and the coast.

And Sailors to the Shores

More than 4,000 years ago the first traders are known to have arrived on the East African coast by sea. Evidence of these early sailing ventures is carved into the stone monuments of the **ancient Egyptians**, who navigated the Horn of Africa and carried on south to trade incense and myrrh for spiritual ceremonies, ivory, tortoiseshell, ebony, ambergris and palm oils. Their carvings give some indication of the wealth of resources abundant on the coastline of East Africa, and include many of the items that have continued to draw sailors to these shores since. The Temple of Thebes at Karnak was inscribed in 2050 BC with the voyage of a man named Seneb to this coast, known for its exotic fragrances even 1,000 years earlier. Queen Hatshepsut's temple near Luxor tells of a journey in 1493 BC that brought back shiploads of luxuries. The Greek historian Herodotus records an expedition in 600 BC, of **Phoenician sailors** who sailed down the Red Sea, rounded the Cape, and returned to the Mediterranean through the Straits of Gibraltar – 'the Pillars of Hercules'.

The Greek geographer Ptolemy's 2nd century AD *Guide to Geography* is one of the earliest written records of the East African coast, referring to an offshore island called Menouthias in the Indian Ocean which may have been Zanzibar. Trading connections with Arabia and Europe were well established, as recorded in the *Periplus of the Erythraean Sea*, a guide to the trading ports of Arabia, East Africa and India written at the end of 1st century AD by a Greek merchant. The account describes the thriving trade capital of 'Azania', called Rhapta, in the middle of the current Tanzanian coast-line. Rhapta's remains have not, however, been discovered, and remain a mystery.

Influence of Arabia, Blown to Azania on the Monsoon Winds

Growing geographical awareness and the abundance of natural goods attracted another, more distant civilization, from the eastern shores of the Indian Ocean, in the 1st century AD. Maritime expertise had developed enough to trust sailors to the monsoon winds, which carried their crafts from the Arabian Peninsula to the shores of Azania. By AD 700, **Arabian merchants** began to appreciate the benefits of the offshore islands, landing places and climate of the Azania coastline, and shifted the focus of their trade southwards from the coast of Somalia. They brought cargoes of copper, tin, cloaks and cloth, daggers, hatchets and glass, in exchange for aromatic gums, coconut oil, tortoiseshell, ivory and slaves. These early sailors recorded their findings: early Arab geographers described the coast as 'Zenj' – Arabic for 'black'.

Soon traders started to settle too. Archaeological evidence suggests that the first significant migration to the Zanzibar archipelago occurred in AD 750, coinciding with political and religious strife in the Persian Gulf on the death of Prophet Mohammed. As Islam reached the Gulf, the rulers of Persia were not keen for converts among their people. Immigrants came from both sides: many followed the ancient Zoroastrian faith and fled persecution as a result of the rise of Islam, but many Muslims migrated to East Africa too. Entire families relocated to the palm-fringed climes of Zenj at this time. The immigrant settlers described themselves as **Shirazi**, and all determined to establish themselves as ruling sheikhs, whether they were or not. This was the start of a continuous stream of immigration from the 8th to 11th centuries. By the 9th century Arabic records mention a civilization on an island called Quanbalu – present-day Pemba – where Arab inhabitants ruled the native population.

Development of the Gold Trade, and Swahili City States

The centuries between AD 1200 and AD 1500 saw Indian Ocean trade between East Africa, Persia, Oman, India and China reach an all-time high, with trading posts along the coast prospering as a result. They exported ivory to India and China, leopard skins and ambergris, mangrove poles to Arabia for building houses, tortoiseshell, but the greatest wealth was from the gold trade, which from AD 1200 began to follow an overland route from Zimbabwe to Sofala in Mozambique, from where the gold was transferred up the coast by sea to Kilwa, 'Rhapta', Mafia and Pemba and on to India and the Gulf, where it was exchanged for textiles and porcelain from China – the china in such quantities that it was used to decorate the new mosques. The island of Kilwa was the southernmost point that Arab dhows could reach on the monsoon winds, so became a crucial port. By the 15th century it had overtaken Mogadishu as the centre of the gold trade, and the population was several thousand – huge for sub-Saharan Africa at the time. With its vast stone palaces, houses and mosques, the town became known as 'the last outpost of the civilization of Islam'.

The Advent of the Portuguese

This lavish lifestyle could not continue unchallenged by other Arab settlements and native islands, and the prosperity of the trading towns swung about. Finally, at the end of the 15th century, the first European ships sailed around the Cape of Good Hope to discover the eastern shores of Africa. The first ship was captained by the infamous Portuguese sailor, **Vasco da Gama**, who docked in Malindi on the Kenyan coast in 1498. His travels had taken him past Kilwa, Mafia and Zanzibar and alerted him to the flourishing trading possibilities in gold, ivory, spices, slaves and much else besides. Da Gama sent emissaries to Portugal for gunboats and forced the Sheikh of Kilwa to bow to Portuguese sovereignty in 1502, sacking the island in 1505. He went on to subjugate the island states of Zanzibar, and Lamu and Pate in Kenya.

The Portuguese stronghold was Mombasa, where the garrison was housed within the walls of Fort Jesus. From there they undermined a number of Shirazi dynasties and cowed others with demands for regular tribute, making clear that the alternative was destruction. Their aim was gain: they creamed off every form of economic exchange within their asserted jurisdiction, and controlled the trade routes.

But their ascendancy too could not go unchallenged. The **Persians** took back Hormuz in 1622, and **Omani Arabs** took control of Muscat in 1650. In 1652 the Omanis sent ships to Zanzibar and Pate to rid the islands of their Portuguese incumbents – at the request of local rulers, who then found themselves dominated once more, by the Omanis. The Europeans retained some strongholds along the coast, notably in Mombasa, until 1698, when Fort Jesus fell to the Imam, Sayf bin Sultan. A short period of respite followed among the different factions along the East African coast.

Arab Control and Rule from Muscat: the 1800s

Persian-Omani power struggles continued through the 1800s, with parallel wrangles in East Africa. Here the **Mazrui dynasty**, whose allegiance to Muscat was tenuous, was on the rise. The Mazruis had been appointed governors of Mombasa by the Imam of Oman in 1698 and managed the volatile situation there until the early 1800s, when they dominated a large region extending south to the Pangani River. Zanzibar and Kilwa, prominent again, offered allegiance to the Sultan of Muscat, the Mazruis' rival. The island states reinstated trade with the interior after the Portuguese era, thriving on imports of cloth, arms and ammunition and exports of ivory, until around 1730, when the export of slaves increased, especially to French colonies such as Mauritius and Réunion where they were put to work on the sugar plantations.

Aware of the economic potential of the area, the Sultan of Muscat appointed a new Omani governor of Kilwa in 1784. His navy developed its power along the coast, and made Zanzibar its central stronghold. He annexed Pemba in 1822 and took Mombasa in 1837. Export profits grew rapidly, especially for ivory: between 1820 and 1850 the price of ivory doubled, then trebled again by 1890. It was exported to the West, for knife handles and piano keys, and to India for ivory bangles.

Trade Routes and Coastal Kingdoms

The Arab trade network relied on the co-operation of tribes in the interior and spread wealth through Azania. A complex network of tribal or clan strongholds had developed between Lakes Victoria, Albert and Tanganyika since the 1500s. Accounts tell of around 200 small chiefdoms led by a tribal chief, known as **Ntemi**, who, with the aid of a council, ruled around 1,000 subjects. These 'kingdoms' evolved out of a need for political control extending beyond family ties as the population grew. Later, in the case of the Kilindi kingdom in the Usambara Mountains of northern Tanzania, this system became a defence against the invasion of warrior-like migrating tribes, such as the Maasai. Tribes united against slave raiders with firearms from the coast.

But while Arab, French and Swahili slave-traders threatened tribes in the interior, some chiefs – such as Fundikira of the Nyamwezi around Tabora, the Gogo from central Tanzania, and Yao chiefs from Kilwa – seized on foreign trade. They organized their people as porters, carrying goods hundreds of miles on foot and earning relative wealth (coastal traders kept the real wealth for themselves). Some tribes demanded 'hongo', a toll on trade caravans. By the mid-1800s, the interior had evolved into a small number of larger tribal empires around centralized, fortified villages.

Resistance to Arab Control

Not all African chiefs were able to profit from trade, and some attempted to resist Arab control. The great **Chief Mirambo**, who ruled west of Tabora, a permanent Arab stronghold and collection point at the end of the 19th century, built a fortified empire in the middle of the trade routes, forcing the caravans to pay tributes. Chief Mirambo united the Nyamwezi clans into a powerful kingdom after 1850, continuing to seek military alliances with neighbouring clans to the east, south, north and west. His empire thrived from the 1860s until the 1880s, earning him the nickname 'Napoleon of East Africa', initially coined by foreign correspondent Henry Morton Stanley.

The Omani Heyday in Zanzibar

Back on the coast, **Sayyid Said bin Sultan**, the Sultan of Oman signed a treaty with the chief of the Hadimu, the **Mwinyi Mkuu**, to colonize the island in 1828. The Omanis took the best land on the western side of the island, leaving the less fertile stretch to the east for the hapless Hadimu. The Sultan exploited all economic possibilities from ivory- and slave-trading to clove plantations; cloves were first brought to the island in 1813, when the sultan insisted that all his subjects plant cloves beside their coconut trees. Said's domain soon rivalled the power of Mombasa; in 1832 he transferred his capital from Muscat to Zanzibar and by 1837 he spotted a weakness in the Mazrui stronghold and extended his own, thus ruling his momeland from afar for 50 years.

India had always traded with Zanzibar, but under the sultan more Indian merchants settled on Zanzibar. The Indian population grew from 215 in 1810 to 5,000 just 50 years later. Indians provided credit, financed expeditions into the interior and collected taxes on behalf of the sultan. After 1827, an Indian merchant family rose to prominence alongside the sultan as the wealthiest and most powerful in Zanzibar. The British later exploited the Indians, technically citizens of British India, to intervene in Zanzibari trading laws and limit the sultan's power.

The first Westerners to deal with the sultan were in fact Americans, who spotted the trade potential, negotiated a deal in 1833, and in 1837 sent the first foreign consul to Zanzibar. They supplied cheap cotton cloth so successfully that all cloth became known as 'Amerikani'. The British devised a trade agreement with the sultan in 1839, and set up a consul in 1841, followed by the French and Germans. The range of items traded expanded. The sultan soon came under intense pressure, however, over one 'commodity' – slaves, as the British tried to curtail the slave trade. In 1822 they drew up the Moresby Treaty prohibiting the sale of slaves to Christian countries, and in 1845 the Hamerton Treaty attempted to ban the slave trade to Muslim territories too. However, the slave market in Zanzibar continued trading until 1873.

Missionaries and Explorers

Geographical maps of the African continent were a point of great debate in Britain in the early years of the 19th century, mainly due to the large blank area that filled the centre, labelled 'Unknown Parts'. The Association for Promoting the Discovery of the East African Interior was formed in Britain in 1788, later joining the Royal Geographical Society in a quest to solve the riddle. The coastline had been known for centuries, and the north and south were charted, but the centre remained a mystery, with just a few clues pieced together from Ptolemy's *Geography* and Arab manuscripts. What lay in those parts was a source of academic argument and interest.

While the geographical societies theorized, another society was sending explorers to the continent. The Church Mission Society in London posted the first white missionary explorer to East Africa. The intrepid man was **Johann Ludwig Krapf**, a Protestant doctor of divinity from Germany. Krapf arrived in Zanzibar – the starting point for any journey to the interior – with his wife in January 1844, and set off equipped with porters and guides. Despite his enthusiasm at finding 'innumerable heathens' to convert, the way ahead was arduous, not least because of malaria. Two years later the CMS sent the Swiss missionary **Johannes Rebmann** to join him. Their travels brought them to the mystical mountain of the Djagga, or 'Mountain of the Moon', described by Ptolemy and hotly debated in London academic circles. Rebmann reported that he had seen a snow-covered peak on the equator; his report reached the geographical societies, and was dismissed as the mad rantings of an unhinged mind. The missionaries' reports nonetheless fuelled the arguments about the existence of Kilimanjaro. Fellow missionary **Jakob Erhardt** produced a map of the lakes in the northern regions, on the basis of reports from Arab traders along the caravan routes, showing a large body of water that was probably Lakes Victoria, Albert and Tanganyika all running into one. Despite being called 'the slug map' after the shapeless blob of water, it further incited the geographers to ascertain the truth.

The RGS finally decided to have a look for itself. In 1856 the society funded an expedition led by a 'clever and adventurous Captain', **Richard Francis Burton**, accompanied by **John Hanning Speke**, to find Mount Kilimanjaro and determine the source of the Nile. Burton and Speke set out from Bagamoyo in 1857 following the trade caravan route south towards Lake Tanganyika. Leaving Burton sick near Tabora, Speke reached Lake Victoria alone, convinced he had found the source of the Nile. He returned in 1860 to verify his theory, this time in the company of **J.A. Gant**.

The already famous explorer and missionary **Dr David Livingstone**, who had made two previous expeditions into southern Africa, soon followed the first explorers. The RGS and the British Foreign Office raised capital for him to continue the exploration, and he agreed to go, 'not as a simple geographer, but as a missionary, and to do geography on the way'. Livingstone was also driven by a desire to put an end to the slave trade, the horrors of which he had witnessed on his earlier expeditions. When he arrived in Zanzibar in 1866 for what turned out to be his last journey, to Lake Nyasa, the traffic in slaves was between 80,000 and 100,000 people a year. Journalist and explorer **Henry Morton Stanley** arrived on a boat from Bombay in 1871, in hot pursuit of his idol, whose disappearance on the Dark Continent had become a *cause célèbre*.

As the frenzy of explorers abated following Livingstone's death on the shores of Lake Tanganyika, Christian missions continued to brave the African continent. Roman Catholic missionaries arrived in Zanzibar in 1860, and settled in Bagamoyo in 1868, and were followed by Anglo-Catholic, Anglican, and Catholic White Fathers, who worked their way along the trade routes from Zanzibar to Lake Tanganyika.

Tribal Movement and Change

Life among the fiefdoms of the interior continued to evolve. Populations grew in fertile agricultural regions and tribes continued to migrate, often leading to conflict. During the 1800s, warrior-like tribes such as the nomadic **Maasai** moved into the foothills of Mount Meru in the north, and the south was prey to constant attacks from the Ngoni tribe, and the Ngindo, Mwera and Makonde. The southern tribes were pushed northwards by the skilled fighters of the southern African Zulu tribe, learning a few tricks for survival and attack as they retreated. Tribes became adept at defending their settlements, and when the first Europeans ventured inland in the 1880s, they found that 'everywhere people had withdrawn to fortified villages, and concluded that the land was freely available for European settlement'.

German Intervention: 1885 Onwards

Germany's 'Iron Chancellor' Bismarck aggressively sought colonial expansion in the mid 19th century. The German imperialists realized that although the Sultan claimed nominal hold over the interior, he was a world apart from the African chiefs who actually ruled there. The sultan cared only for the fruits of the caravan routes. Ambitious young Germans such as **Carl Peters** and colleagues Count Joachim Pfeil and Karl Juhlke avoided the sultan's coastal ports and ventured directly into the bush, where they signed 12 treaties with individual chiefs who were persuaded to hand over territories to the pale-skinned newcomers. The treaties concerned the sultan's land, but, when Bismarck ordered five warships to the shores of Zanzibar, the sultan was persuaded to accept the German purchase offer of 400,000 marks.

Through the 1880s the imperialists pushed inland, following established routes, and in 1885 Bismarck claimed a central portion of the interior as a German protectorate, under the rule of the **German East Africa Company**, headed by Carl Peters. The strength of tribal resistance led to the army being called in, earning Peters the Swahili epithet '*Mkono wa damu*' – 'Him with blood-stained hands'. By 1890, the protectorate extended as far as Mwanza and Bukoba. In this year the British and Germans began establishing the boundaries of German East Africa to include what is now mainland Tanzania, Rwanda and Burundi. It seems likely that the Europeans acquired the name of '*Mzungu*' at this point: it translates as 'he who goes around'.

Resistance to German Control

Between 1888 and 1896, 54 military conflicts were recorded as 'resistance to colonial control'. The first rebellion in 1888, described by Germans as the '**Arab Rebellion**', began on the coast, led by **Bushiri bin Salim** (enemy of Sultan Said) and Zigua chief **Bwana Heri** (who had resisted Omani control of Saadani). They amassed widespread support on the coast and inland, initially overcoming German firearms by guerrilla tactics – ambush from the bush – but the German troops responded with a 'scorched earth' policy, burning crops, destroying villages and confiscating cattle. By 1889 the Germans triumphed: when Bwana Heri surrendered as a result of widespread hunger and famine in 1890, he was followed by troops of Zigua people, Nyamwezi, Arabs, Indians, and slaves. Nyamwezi Chief Siki blew himself up in his ammunition store to evade capture by the Germans when they besieged his fortress at Tabora.

The German troops also met with strong resistance from the military state of the Hehe tribe in the Southern Highlands, based around an impressive central fortress, under the formidable warrior **Chief Mkwawa**. The Hehe had been forced to adopt a militaristic strategy in response to invasion by the Ngoni tribe from southern Africa, themselves being pushed north by the Zulu. Clashes around the Iringa Plateau forced tribes to unite, and led to the emergence of leaders such as Munyigumba and his son Mkwawa, who led the tribe victorious through a bloody five-year war with the Ngoni (1878–82). So when a German military expedition met with Mkwawa's troops in 1891 it faced a highly organized military system. The Hehe were rumoured to have taken only 15 minutes to kill 290 members of the colonial forces. Three years later the Germans had their revenge: pounding Mkwawa's fort with grenades, they overcame the tribe by firepower. Mkwawa escaped, but, having evaded capture for four years, he refused to be taken alive and took his life with a bullet through his own skull.

The Maji Maji Rebellion

The German colonialists continued to face problems subduing the southern tribes, most notably in the Maji Maji rebellion that began in 1905 – the most widespread, united resistance to colonial rule anywhere in Africa. The rebellion started west of Kilwa and spread across the country until nearly all the southern tribes were allied, given strength by the belief that the tribes had access to magic water that would shield them from German bullets. The united front, sure of its safety, confronted the German military forces with bravado, until thousands were machine-gunned to death trying to storm the fort at Mahenge. More than 75,000 people died in two years; their resistance finally broke in 1907, when famine swept the land as a direct result of the Germans' scorched earth policy of retaliation (*see* p.282).

German Consolidation

The German colonial grasp was considerably strengthened by imported diseases that severely weakened the rural population. In 1890 a devastating outbreak of rinderpest wiped out 90 per cent of cattle; other diseases, such as jiggers and smallpox, also entered the country at this time. The pastoral communities in the north, such as the Maasai, suffered a severe blow to their military strength and standing. As a result, when German and British settlers came to the grazing lands around the Rift Valley and slopes of Kilimanjaro at this time, they claimed that they were uninhabited. By 1896 the Germans had constructed forts in most key areas, and enforced a number of unpopular taxes, such as taxes on huts. They preferred the cooler mountain climate of the north, where the land was better suited to crops and where divisions among the chiefdoms meant that they found some allies: **Rindi of Moshi** welcomed them, in return for their support in putting down nearby chiefs Sina and Marealle of Marangu.

The Europeans made Tanga their base on the coast, with settlements in the cool foothills of the nearby Usambaras, where they sought to develop coffee and sisal plantations, encouraging chiefs and akidas to follow. The first 62 sisal plants were illegally imported from Brazil in 1892, yet by 1910 there were 54 plantations, exporting thousands of tons a year. A railway was built from Tanga to Mombo, Kilimanjaro and Meru before the great rebellion of 1905. Lines were extended to Tabora in 1912, and Kigoma by 1914, just before the outbreak of the First World War. The Germans devised a system of authority based on the sultan's. Each major town was governed by a *liwali*, aided by *akidas* and *jumbes*, or headmen, who collected tax. These posts were gradually filled by German officials and students of the German-Swahili schools, of which a number were created to teach literacy and groom African administrators; they had a reputation for forced attendance and corporal punishment.

The British Protectorate

By the 1890s, British colonialists were increasingly nervous about the encroaching power of the Germans, and persuaded the **Sultan of Zanzibar** to sign a treaty that made the islands of Zanzibar and Pemba a British protectorate. A marginal chapter of the First World War was played out on East African soil and, following Germany's defeat in the war, German East Africa was renamed **Tanganyika**, and governed by the British until 1961, initially under a mandate from the League of Nations. The name Tanganyika has two possible sources: either it is a combination of the Swahili words *tanga* – sail – and *nyika* – the dry expanse of the interior – or it comes from *Mchanganyiko* – a group of 120 linguistic peoples.

The new British administration set out to implement a policy of 'indirect rule', encouraging rule through individual chiefs under the jurisdiction of British district commissioners. The Prince of Wales made a popular tour of Tanganyika in 1928. City streets were filled with shiny motor cars and the following year the *Daily Mail* called Dodoma 'Clapham Junction-in-the-Bush'. The population of Dar es Salaam was estimated in British papers to be about 25,000 Africans, 5,000 Indians and 1,200 Europeans (120 Germans, a few Greeks, a handful of Syrians and the rest British).

German property was confiscated and estates auctioned off in 1922, when many smaller properties were bought by Greeks and Asians. Sisal exports recovered and the new settlers made good money, but many farms were neglected. The war had sapped energy and finances, and the Great Depression of the 1930s hit before the country had recovered. Real investment in Tanganyika only really occurred during the last 15 years of British occupation. By 1945, however, Tanzania and Zanzibar were once again part of the world economy as exporters of raw materials and importers of manufactured goods. This moment of relative prosperity was short-lived: after the war the colonies became less economically viable, and the Independence struggle began.

Towards Independence

Opposition to British rule emerged in several forms, which involved forces aligned with traditional tribal authority and those opposed to both British and traditional indigenous power. Resistance to colonial and traditional tribal authority developed first among co-operative farmers, members of the colonial bureaucracy, and an emerging trade union movement. The **Tanganyika African Association (TAA)**,was established in 1929 to give a forum to trade unionists and cooperative farmers who opposed British rule. Other opposition movements developed in response to specific

The First President: Julius Nyerere

Julius Kambarage Nyerere headed Tanzania for nearly a quarter of a century, as president of the one-party state of Tanganyika after Independence in May 1961, and then as president of the United Republic of Tanzania after unification in 1964. He resigned in 1985 and died on 14 October 1999. Nyerere is remembered as 'Mwalimu', meaning 'Teacher', a reflection of his attitude to the governance of the people. His leadership earned him the accolades *Baba wa Taifa* – 'Father of the Nation', 'The Father of Authentic African Socialism', and 'The Conscience of Africa'. His model for African socialism united the disparate tribes and religions of the country, creating a strong national identity, but led the country into devastating economic decline.

Julius was born in 1922, the son of Nyerere Burito, an aristocratic, illiterate chief of the small Zanaki tribe and led a traditional rural tribal life until he was 12 years old. Educated initially at the Native Authority school in Musoma, he came top of the class at a British-run Roman Catholic secondary school, where he converted to Catholicism. After attending Makerere university in Kampala he taught for three years – later saying that he was a schoolmaster by choice and a politician by accident. In 1949 he won a scholarship to to study history, politics and law at Edinburgh University, becoming the first Tanzanian graduate of a British university. Nyerere was influenced by Fabian socialists there, developing his concept of grafting socialism on to African communal existence; he later claimed that he formed his whole political philosophy then. Nyerere also translated two Shakespeare plays into Swahili – *Julius Caesar* and *The Merchant of Venice*. In 1953 he married Maria Magige, and the couple subsequently had five sons and two daughters. In 1954 he formed the Tanganyikan African National Union (TANU), supported by a growing group of educated Africans committed to achieving independence. Nyerere was elected to the legislative council of the former British colony of Tanganyika in 1958, the first time that blacks were represented, became leader of the opposition, chief minister in 1960 and prime minister of the newly independent country in 1961. Nineteen months later, when the constitution was amended to make Tanganyika a republic, Julius Nyerere was elected as president and TANU was declared the only legal political party. The slogan *'Uhuru na Umoja'* – 'Freedom and Unity' – adopted in 1954, became the motto of the country.

colonial policies. In 1951 British authorities began to implement a programme to remove African homesteaders to make way for post-war British settlers, a policy that swelled an incipient nationalist movement. In 1953 **Julius Nyerere**, Tanzania's first president (*see* box, p.15), was elected president of the TAA, soon to be renamed the **Tanganyika African National Union** or **TANU**.

Zanzibar Independence, Constitution and Unity

The British Parliament approved a new constitution for Zanzibar in 1960. The transition was uneasy: the first elections in January 1961 ended in a deadlock, and further elections in June of that year were accompanied by rioting and casualties, but resulted in a coalition of the **Zanzibar Nationalist Party (ZNP)** and **Zanzibar and Pemba People's Party (ZNPP)**. The ZNPP was a splinter group from the **Afro-Shirazi Party**, which largely represented indigenous people, especially the Shirazi people of Pemba. Most members of the ZNP were local Africans, although the party had a significant number of Arab members, some of whom were in the leadership, laying the party open to accusations of representing the Arab minority (around 17 per cent of the population of Zanzibar and Pemba). The ZNP had been founded in 1955 as a continuation of the **National Party of Subjects of the Sultan of Zanzibar**, which had rapidly developed from a league of rural African peasants. Around the time of the formation of the NPSSZ, the Arab Association had fallen into the hands of progressive young elements with strong socialist leanings, one of whose aims was to do away with racial representation and communal division as under British colonial rule. Their policy agreed with the aims of the NPSSZ, so they supported it, leading to the formation of the ZNP.

Self-government followed in June 1963; **Independence** was achieved in December. Just before the 1963 election another new party was formed, the **Zanzibar People's Party**, or Umma party. This was a ZNP splinter party, which eventually collaborated with the Afro-Shirazi Party in the revolution, and many members of its leadership became members of the Revolutionary Council of Zanzibar. Immediately after Independence, however, it was the perception of many Zanzibaris that the old Arab families had hung on to power, and 'Field Marshal' **John Okello** led a revolution that overthrew the government. Many Arabs were killed in ensuing riots and many fled for their lives before the sultan was deposed, and Zanzibar was proclaimed a republic. Okello fled. **Sheikh Abeid Amani Karume** was installed as president of the People's Republic of Zanzibar and Pemba, at the helm of the Afro-Shirazi Party.

An army mutiny on the mainland in 1964 forced Julius Nyerere to call for British military assistance and led to the restructuring of the army, with Tanganyikans replacing British officers. Military security became a huge concern. East Germans, Russians and Chinese were shipped in to train the army. Zanzibar and Tanzania united in 1964, eventually becoming the **United Republic of Tanzania**. A joint constitution was approved in 1977, when TANU joined with the Afro-Shirazi Party of Zanzibar to form the **Revolutionary Party Chama Cha Mapinduzi** (CCM). Nyerere remained president of the Republic and commander in chief of the armed forces, with President Karume of Zanzibar as vice president. The islands have, however, retained a large degree of autonomy from the mainland, with a separate constitution, approved in 1979, elected president, cabinet and parliament dealing with justice in Zanzibar. Unity was never smooth: in the early days Nyerere found it impossible to intervene in the dictatorship of Karume in Zanzibar, until the military assassinated Karume in 1972. Zanzibari factions continue to lobby for greater autonomy, but the islands are increasingly dependent on the mainland for utilities such as electricity and water supplies.

An Independent Republic

The Tanzanian constitution created a one-party state. Nyerere sought to make it a socialist one, without racism, tribalism or class. It ended up being paternalistic-cum-autocratic, on the grounds that the majority was too ill-educated to know what was best. A harsh **Preventative Detention Act** allowed for the imprisonment of the regime's opponents. The state controlled all media, banned opposition groups, ran the unions and prohibited strikes. After Karume's assassination, the number of political prisoners placed Tanzania high on Amnesty International rankings: more than a thousand people were detained, 81 of whom were convicted a year later, on the grounds of confession after torture.

State rule became even clearer, if more benign, in the years that followed: in 1973 all western clothing was forbidden. Tight trousers, mini-skirts, wigs and make-up (notably skin-lighteners) were all banned. Police were expected to uphold the rules by inserting a bottle into men's trouser legs to ensure that they were wide enough.

A Model for African Socialism?

While Nyerere himself stuck to the principles of a socialist leader, accepting only an annual salary of £4,000, the same could not be said of many of his fellow senior ministers, civil servants and leaders of TANU, who were caught in the thrall of a lust for wealth. In the mid-1960s the British *Daily Telegraph* reported on the era of 'a new and all-powerful tribe in Tanzania ... the WaBenze, "the people of the Mercedes Benz".' This fast-expanding group was seen as 'the new rich of a new nation', who were making the most of their influential positions. Nyerere was disappointed by the reception he received on a tour of Tanzania in 1966–7, and he realized that the majority was disenchanted with the unfulfilled promises of Independence. He retired into solitude on completion of the tour, emerging with a plan for the new future of Tanzania – embodied in the **Arusha Declaration** of 1967.

Nationalization and Self-Reliance

The Arusha Declaration aimed to restrict the greed and corruption of the 'WaBenze'. It decreed that ministers must rely only on their salaries, and could not own more than one house or accept jobs in private companies. The declaration also determined a policy of self-reliance for Tanzania, which was no longer to remain dependent on foreign aid. Banks and large companies were nationalized. The immediate impact was disastrous: businesses stood still for 10 days and had only recovered 20 per cent of volume by the end of the first month. But the main focus for development was agriculture, with the introduction of the '*Ujamaa*' policy: rural production was to be organized into cooperative villages so that crops could be grown in 'collectives' (*see* p.18).

Ujamaa

The Arusha Declaration had an extreme and lasting effect on the rural population, much of which was required to move into 'cooperative villages' in order to develop agricultural collectives and pool services like schools and clinics. This was the essence of the policy known as 'Ujamaa', literally 'familyhood', which inspired the development of 8,000 co-operative villages and the resettlement of more than 13 million Africans in the decade following the 1967 declaration. The Ujamaa policy was deeply controversial, but the re-villageization concept was born of the best intentions: the general lack of infrastructure made it difficult to provide community education and health schemes for the disparate small, rural communities, so drastic action was required. However the failings of this enforced policy soon emerged.

The implementation of Ujamaa was heavy-handed. Nyerere stated that the re-villageization process was to be voluntary, but villages were burned and their inhabitants forced to move; the president desparately tried to distance himself from the violent methods used to carry out his policies in remote areas, especially the far south and north. Whatever the methods, the results were drastic. Entire villages and rural regions suffered extreme poverty and near starvation as the people were forced to leave the land that had provided their subsistence to establish new crops on unknown land. The policy for agricultural collectives suffered because the 8,200 Ujamaa villages were reliant on the hand-hoe, meaning that group action had little effect, and many farmers were reduced to subsistence farming again in overcrowded conditions. The sisal plantations, previously a highly developed industry, suffered from mismanagement and cashew farmers were moved so far from their crops that they abandoned them. The real effects of Ujamaa on the economy helped to reduce Tanzania's financial standing to being ranked as one of the poorest countries in the world. The Arusha Declaration's proclamation that Tanzania would continue without foreign aid was put to the test when nearly all aid was withdrawn.

Foreign Aid, Pan-Africanism and Idi Amin

Tanzania's foreign policy was officially non-aligned, but the new republic became reliant on its socialist models, finding assistance in Chinese, Russian and East German governments. When the West rejected plans for a railway linking Tanzania and Zambia, on account of Tanzania's dismissal of Britain's role in Rhodesia and disapproval of the supply of arms to South Africa, China financed the route with an interest-free loan. A British press report from Dar es Salaam in 1969 reported that it was 'not unusual to find a Chinese behind every palm tree along Tanzania's palm-fringed shores', following the arrival of the Yao Hua steamship, which had dispatched nearly 1,000 engineers. The Chinese were angling for a means through East Africa into central and southern Africa, and the Russians were interested in helping the East Germans block the Chinese. President Nyerere happily discovered that the Americans were content to support any aid that might thwart the influence of either the Chinese or the Russians.

Nyerere was also committed to African liberation movements. In 1961 he denounced the racist policies of South Africa, and stated that Tanzania would not join the Commonwealth if the apartheid regime remained in it: South Africa withdrew its membership. Nyerere's Tanzania later played host to the African National Congress (ANC) and the Pan-African Congress (PAC) of South Africa in exile. He also welcomed the Samora Machel's Frelimo freedom-fighters, battling against the Portuguese in Mozambique, and Robert Mugabe's Zanla forces, which opposed colonial rule in the Southern Rhodesia. He broke off relations with Britain, the country's principal aid donor, after its failure to use force when Ian Smith declared UDI in 1965 – earning himself a description by Smith as the 'evil genius' behind the ensuing guerrilla war.

In another example of Nyerere's tendency to put principles before advantage, he took an uncompromising stand against the brutal regime of Idi Amin in Uganda in the late 1970s. When the dictator's armies crossed Tanzania's northern borders in 1978 Nyerere not only drove back the invaders, but rallied all his resources to topple the invading regime. Kampala fell in 1979, with its residents lining the streets chanting the name of the Tanzanian leader. The war was, however, financially ruinous to Tanzania, emptying the state's coffers of an estimated £250 million.

Economic Crisis

By the 1980s Tanzania's economic state was dire. The country was reliant on imported cereals. Rationing was introduced. Corruption was widespread. Industry was working to only 30 per cent capacity. Nearly half of the 330 farms taken over by the state went into liquidation. In 1985 global oil prices rose, and Tanzania, already stretched to the limit, suffered further. Prices for the cash crops that the *Ujamaa* collective farms and villages grew fell, and regions of rural farmers came close to starvation again owing to lack of maize. Food shortages were terrible, the shops in Dar es Salaam were bare, and the country suffered a desperate lack of currency.

Years of harsh and dogmatically enforced socialist policies had left Tanzania one of the world's poorest countries, and utterly dependent on aid from the West. Although Nyerere had tried to make Tanzania politically independent of the developed world, he was forced to leave it one of the most aid-dependent nations. In his last year as president, Nyerere denationalized the sisal plantations and began to devalue the currency, before handing over to his successor, President Ali Hassan Mwinyi of Zanzibar, to negotiate further structural reforms and devaluation in order to gain aid from the International Monetary Fund (IMF).

After Nyerere

Nyerere stepped down in 1985, in an unprecedented step becoming the first African leader to voluntarily resign his position. At the height of the bleakest years of Tanzanian economy, he declared that 'although socialism has failed in Tanzania, I will remain a socialist because I believe socialism is the best policy for poor countries like Tanzania.' His successors decided otherwise, embracing capitalism and the free market: the full results have yet to be seen. Some believe that *Ujamaa* failed largely because it was often enforced by officials who lacked the insight and integrity of Nyerere. But the economic crisis of the 1970s was to a considerable extent caused by the falling commodity prices, rising oil prices and the war to remove Amin, which was morally supported by the West but for which Tanzania bore the cost. Nyerere saw that the impact of IMF 'structural adjustment' would be to destroy many of the great achievements in education and healthcare, and to worsen the plight of the poorest. He has not yet been proved wrong. After 32 years of authoritarianism, Nyerere and his supporters continued to defend the one-party state on the basis that it had developed a homogenous society and a strong national unity. After resigning as president, Nyerere continued to take an advisory role in Tanzanian and African politics, mediating peace agreements between neighbouring east and southern African countries such as Zambia and Burundi. When Nyerere died in 1999, Tanzania mourned the leader who had led the country to Independence and united the nation. No music other than tributes was played in public places and shops were closed as a mark of respect to 'Mwalimu'. Hundreds of new kangas were printed with Nyerere's image and that of reigning President Mkapa alongside. A line of African and Western leaders gathered to pay their respects at his funeral.

The constitution was amended in 1984 to include a bill of rights, direct elections to the National Assembly with allocated seats for women, union representatives and the president's nominees. In November 1985, **President Ali Hassan Mwinyi**, president of Zanzibar, succeeded President Nyerere as president of the United Republic. His appointment temporarily quelled dissent from Zanzibar. In 1992 the constitution was amended to establish a multi-party political process, ending the dominion of the CCM in all aspects of political life. By the time of the first multi-party elections in 1995, more than a dozen opposition political movements were officially registered. Out of these, three main opposition parties have crystallized. The most colourful and renowned politician on the scene is a former Nyerere protégé, the maverick, unpredictable **Augustine Mrema**, who was adopted as presidential candidate of the NCCR–Mageuzi Mageuzi Party. Despite the choice of Mrema by the oppositon, the CCM remained in power. President Mwinyi stood for two consecutive five-year terms after Nyerere stepped down. He was replaced by **President Mkapa**, who has an impressive reputation as the 'Mr Clean' of Tanzanian politics.

However, it seems as though the hegemony of the CCM may be near an end. The president is near to the end of his second term, and will step down at the upcoming 2005 elections in October. Meanwhile, opposition parties, including CUF, have formed a political alliance that aims to divest the ruling CCM of its majority. The question of Zanzibari sovereignty continues to bubble away; a concession made in April 2004 granted the island its own flag, but it remains to be seen if this will satisfy the separatists. Whatever happens, there is no doubt that Tanzanian nationals will attempt to conserve their image as one nation, or two, of democracy and stability; this is an aid requirement, and donor contributions constitute close to 40 per cent of the Tanzanian economy. Tanzania remains the UK's largest development programme in Africa, and the present government's efforts to fight corruption and lift the economy have made it a rare success story. Primary school enrolment has risen from 53 per cent in 1999 to 91 per cent in 2004, and Lord Triesman, Minister for Africa recently described the country as 'a beacon of stability in Africa'. That said, Tanzania is still one of the poorest in the world; there is a long way to go to fight the desperate spread of HIV/AIDS, and recent efforts for international debt relief are sorely needed.

Peoples

The last census in Tanzania, in 1997, reckoned the population to be 29,646,753. The true figure today is probably closer to 40 million, with an annual growth of more than three per cent a year; the birth rate is 46 per 1,000 population, the death rate 15 per 1,000. Average life expectancy is 49 years: 47 for men, 50 for women. Most Tanzanians – around 95 per cent – are of African Bantu origin. Other groups include Cushitic speakers of Nilotic origins, and the last few descendants of hunter-gatherer bushmen tribes who inhabited the land undisturbed until 1,000 BC, when Cushitic speakers and Bantu tribes moved south and east into this region. The hunter-gatherers are closely associated by physiognomic, cultural and linguistic similarities with the Khoisan (bushmen) of southern Africa; the Hadzabe and Sandawe tribes are the last of them here. The remaining two per cent of the population dates from more recent migrations and is made up of Arabic, Asian and European inhabitants. The numbers of these minority groups have dropped since Independence.

Language and Ethnic Distinction

As a result of its unusual combination of peoples, Tanzania has the greatest linguistic diversity in the whole of the African continent, with four major African language bases, ranging from Bantu, Cushitic and Nilotic languages to the less often spoken Khoisan or 'click' languages of the bushmen. Within these broad language groups the people of Tanzania are of hugely mixed racial origins, defined by language, with around 129 ethnic sub-groups, within the main groups. It is questionable how many of these were recognized as such before Western colonialists categorized them. The differences between 'tribes' range from obvious to indistinct.

Bantu is the main language as well as ethnic group. The second most important is the Nilotic group, which can be divided into the plains Nilotic or Maasai, the highland Nilotic, who bear close ancestral similarities to the Barbaig of north-central Tanzania, and the river-lake Nilotic who immigrated from Kenya and Uganda to settle on the eastern shores of Lake Victoria as the Luo tribe. The Cushitic language has evolved from the negroid caucasoid group known as Cushites who migrated south to Tanzania as Mbulu or Iraqw nomadic pastoralists. These people now farm the fertile volcanic northern highlands of the Great Rift Valley escarpment around Ngorongoro.

It was one of the founding directives of the Republic that no ethnic group should dominate, made easier by the fact that none of the 129 tribes and sub-tribes exceeds 10 per cent of the population. Attempts to reduce tribal distinctions continue, as chiefdoms are superseded by the boundaries and requirements of national politics; there have been directives to ban tribal clothing and to insist that citizens register a permanent residence. There are, however, many minority tribal groups still living in rural isolation who continue to speak their own languages and live according to tribal traditions. The most successful unifying factor in Tanzania is the national language of Swahili, enabling peoples to mix on the basis of one language.

Closer proximity to other groups of peoples means that many Tanzanians now speak a number of languages, indicating a general softening of 'tribal' distinctions and reflecting a very mixed culture. In most cases, distinctive tribal practices are becoming more or less historic, often mixed with newer Christian and Islamic beliefs.

Swahili: a National Language for All Peoples of Tanzania

With such diverse people contained within the boundaries of Tanzania, nothing could bring about such a strong sense of nationality and identity as the growth of Swahili as a national language. The language originated in the coastal regions and Zanzibar from one of the original Bantu languages, as a language of trade and exchange with Arabic-speaking sailors. Its name evolved from the Arabic word *sahil*, meaning coast. It has since developed to include vocabulary from all foreign settlers, especially Persian, Arabic, Indian, Portuguese, German and English, with words from each of these often reflecting the traces of those cultures left on this African land.

Words such as *chai* (tea), *achari* (pickle) and *serikali* (government) are derived from Farsi, the Persian language. *Sheha* (village councillor) has Arabic origins. *Pesa* (money) is a Hindi term, as is *gari* (car). The Portuguese left a legacy of words such as *leso* (handkerchief), *meza* (table) and *mvinyo* (Portuguese for wine). The English words used by Swahili are mostly to do with machines, money or control, words like *baiskeli* (bicycle), *basi* (bus), *penseli* (pencil), *mashine* (machine), *kompyuta* (computer), *risiti* (receipt) and *jela* (prison). Just a few German words are found in Swahili, words like *shule* for school.

There are around 20 dialects of Swahili, the language showing great variations in its widespread usage throughout Tanzania and Kenya. The most common dialects are Kimbita of Mobasa, Kiamu of Lamu and Kiunguja of Zanzibar Stone Town. By the 19th century the Swahili spoken in Zanzibar had become established as a *lingua franca* along the trade routes from the coast to the interior, and became widespread among the different tribes. Subsquent colonial rulers standardized it and used it for their administration: Swahili became the official language of the German colonial government from 1885 to 1917. The Germans used a Roman script to write it in, taught it to their colonial subjects in schools, and printed books in it. The British continued this practice after 1918, as they sought to unify the disparate territory of Tanganyika.

Swahili was adopted as a national language after Tanzanian Independence. When the socialist policy of '*ujamaa*' was introduced in the 1970s (*see* **History**, p.18), a shared language was required to carry the message to all the different tribes in the new nation, and Swahili was the perfect vehicle. It became a political language to erode tribal differentiation so that the country might be united. The success of its spread in East Africa has acted as an incentive to make Swahili the *lingua franca* of the African continent.

While modern linguistic orthodoxy does not believe that one language or dialect is superior to others as long as it meets the social needs of its speakers, the different dialect groups still enjoy mocking each other. Coastal people speak more rapidly and use more slang in their speech. In rural areas Swahili reflects the local vernacular: the Sukuma around Lake Victoria employ very emphatic tones, and the Ha on the shores of Lake Tanganyika speak slowly and carefully. Nationalistic Tanzanians regard their use of Swahili as more polite than that of the Swahili-speaking people of Kenya!

Many individuals will explain their parentage to be of mixed ethnic origin, as inter-marriage between tribes is widespread. Nevertheless, almost everyone will be very clearly able to tell you his or her tribal lineage. The following is not a comprehensive list of all 129 individual tribes, but instead bears reference to the largest or most well known ethnic groups that travellers in Tanzania may encounter, or hear about.

Sukuma

Considerably the largest ethnic group is the Sukuma, whose people make up 10–13 per cent of the population and inhabit the regions around Lake Victoria in northern Tanzania. The importance of the tribe has evolved since the small, independent chiefdoms in this region were grouped together in one unit under the British colonial government of Tanzania in 1946. The **Sukuma Museum** near Mwanza (*see* pp.153–6) has gathered together memorabilia from the tribal past, including a huge map of the distinct Sukuma regions, and tall ornamental spinning drums showing different forms of counting required by boys, girls, shepherds and elders. The centrepiece of the museum is a pavilion containing vast tribal drums for each chiefdom; other pavilions show the paraphernalia of witch doctors and the costumes for traditional dance groups. The Sukuma dance with snakes, which they regard as an important spiritual omen, and often keep snakeskins hanging inside their double-walled round huts. Much of their culture is centred around the large round boulders that dominate the landscape of Lake Victoria, used by women to grind corn, and by men to peek over the top and spy out the strongest unmarried girl to choose as a wife.

Haya

The Haya people of the Kagera Region in northwest Tanzania are a sizeable tribe, of Bantu origin, most closely allied with Bantu tribes to the north and west of them. The Haya were traditionally divided into 130 distinct patrilineal clans, in turn organized into eight small sub-states ruled by a *mukama* chief. These broad clans include the pastoral **Hima** people, and the more agricultural **Iru**.

Nyamwezi

The Nyamwezi number more than 400,000 and inhabit the central regions around Tabora. They rose to prominence working as long-distance porters and trading salt and slaves along the caravan routes during the 19th century, when they challenged the commercial power even of the Arabs with their flair for trade across the interior. They organized themselves into a powerful warrior state under the rule of their first warrior chief **Mirambo**, between 1870 and 1884. Their Swahili name, derived from their appearance to early traders out of a desolate landscape, translates as 'People of the Moon'. Their tribal structure developed a hierarchy of aristocracy and slaves, and relied on frequent readings by the *mfumi* spirit diviner and spiritual initiation rites. The Nyamwezi share cultural and linguistic similarities with the Sukuma people.

Maasai

The Maasai tribe were originally Nilotic pastoralists, who migrated into Tanzania along the course of the Nile from southern Sudan. They speak Maa, similar to the language of Sudan; *maasai* in Amharic means 'like me', and the Maa word *sidan*, like

Sudan, means 'beautiful'. Maasai tribal factions migrated into Tanzania in the 17th century, having occupied East African lands further north since the 14th century.

Around 12 distinct groups of Maasai remain in the world, the largest of which now lives in Tanzania. They call themselves *Otunlangana loo Ngishu*, the 'People of the Cattle', and have made enemies as a result of their fundamental belief that all the cows in the world were given to them as a right by god. The Maasai adhere to very strict social structures and regulations, in deference to the *Olaibon*, the highest-ranking member of the tribe, who mediates between the people and the ancestral spirits. *Olaibon* is a hereditary title, and he is responsible for solving conflicts within his clan. He is the tribal healer, with the greatest knowledge of plant remedies upon which people rely for survival in the bush. He also oversees the rites of passage of the tribal age sets to which every Maasai male belongs. These work on a seven-year scale: the first is *Engayok*, young children at home; the second *Layooni*, uncircumcised boys who learn about cattle-herding; the third *Sikoliyo*, the newly circumcised boys awaiting the cleansing ceremony which will make them a Maasai *Murran* – a warrior. A boy remains *Sikoliyo* for up to three months, during which time he will dress in black robes and adorn his face with patterns of white chalk and soot, take an arrow and venture into the bush to kill birds and use the plumage to adorn his head. After seven years as *Murran*, protecting the community, he becomes *Orpaiyan*, a married man with children; he is expected to marry numerous wives. Much later he becomes an elder, or *Ilmoruak*, responsible for making wise decisions about the clan's future.

Most Maasai remain true to traditional religious beliefs, based on the god Engai and his messiah, Kindong'oi, from whom their priests descend. Worship is done under 'holy' fig trees, or at Ol Doinyo Lengai, the 'Mountain of God'. Maasai people do not believe in life after death. The Maasai adhere to a strict diet consisting only of cow's milk, blood and meat, and wear a red cloth rubbed with fat for warmth, called *shuka*. Such strict tribal regulations have made the conversion to modern living hard for Maasai, as they have to continue a pastoral nomadic existence among an increasing population with tight boundaries. Some Maasai have changed over to cultivation. Many are highly educated and have demonstrated qualities of leadership that have afforded them important positions in government.

Barbaig

The Barbaig are one of the largest sub-tribes of the broader Datoga ethnic group. Their language has evolved from eastern Sudanic roots, and they have a Nilotic appearance that once physically distinguished them from neighbouring tribes such as the Nyaturu, Nywamba, Hadzabe and Sandawe. The tribe used to practice scarification, marking cuts around each eye and down each cheek with soot from burnt wood, and would pierce earlobes much like the Maasai. Neither of these practices is considered relevant to life today. The Barbaig were once enemies of the Maasai tribe, owing to their remarkably similar lifestyles; they too herded (zebu-humped) cattle southwards along the course of the Nile. They share a recipe for a strong alcoholic drink made from aloe roots and wild honey. The two tribes fought a deciding battle over who should inhabit the lush lands of the Ngorongoro Highlands:

the Maasai arrived to find the Barbaig already settled there, but took the land. The tribes still regard each other as 'respected enemies', and Barbaig elders return to the graves of their ancestors in Ngorongoro Crater. The **Maasai Wars** were ended by the intervention of the German military, and the British administration later put large numbers of the Barbaig on trial. They now live a quiet life in the region around Mount Hanang, north of Dodoma, combining pastoralism with crop cultivation.

The Barbaig have, however, maintained traditional beliefs in the power of spirits, for good or evil, but also in an afterlife which is a more pleasant and better version of this one, without such destructive enemies as lion, elephant, rhino, cape buffalo, spirits in the form of snakes and invincible alien tribes. Like the Maasai, the Barbaig practise polygamous marriages with girls aged between 13 and 14; there were once said to be no unmarried women in the tribe. The marriage ceremony requires the suitor to capture his bride in the cow kraal. The end of her residence in her father's house is shown by her husband placing a string of beads around her neck. The ceremony often took place with a struggle, the bride trying to fight away the bridegroom with a large stick – as well she might: her marriage means the complete severance of relations with girls of her age, who gather at her home to mourn. After the marriage she, her children, house and belongings belong to her husband. If they divorce, she leaves with nothing. Women wear a special pleated leather skirt, known as *hananywend*, symbolically representing Udameselgwa, the female deity and patroness of Barbaig women.

Sandawe and Hadzabe or Hadzapi

The Sandawe and Hadzabe or Hadzapi are distinct tribes but usually classed together, both being widely held to have the most ancient history of all the tribes, and to represent the last remaining ancestors of the first hunter-gatherer tribes. They speak a language closely related to the 'click' language of the southern African Khoisan bushmen. The **Sandawe** occupy an area of northern central Tanzania and are generally more assimilated with surrounding tribes, while the **Hadzabe** remain distinct hunter-gatherers, keeping to the rural regions around Lake Eyasi in the north, subsisting on roots and plants, or by bow and arrow during the dry season; their requirements have barely changed from the Palaeolithic era. However, the lifestyle of the Hadza is suffering from the encroachment of other peoples, whose cattle scatter the game and pollute their water sources, and the growth of conservation areas, such as Ngorongoro, which diminish their hunting grounds. The Hadzabe have developed a number of ingenious methods of attracting game closer to their arrows, including placing the horns of a slain impala on their heads and bobbing around in the bush imitating the actions of a live one, an age-old act of impressionism that attracts passing impala straight into the cooking pot. An alternative method is to cover themselves with an animal skin and lie in wait for hungry vultures; as a bird swoops to land the Hadza hunter can grab it in his hand; one bird then attracts others, and so the tribe is fed. The diet is supplemented with wild honey, a commodity hard to obtain, but useful for trading with other tribes when arrowheads or tobacco run out. Both the Hadzabe and the Sandawe have an ancestral tradition of rock paintings, such as those in the Kondoa area between Dodoma and Arusha.

Iraqw or Mbulu

Also with an ancient history, the Iraqw or Mbulu who now cultivate the highlands on the Great Rift Valley escarpment of northern Tanzania are linguistically defined by their rare southern Cushitic language. They are thought to have occupied the lands around Lakes Natron, Manyara and Eyasi since ancient times, perhaps since the Upper Palaeolithic period.

The caucasoid origins of the Iraqw suggest that they were the first immigrants to produce food in East Africa during the 1st millennium, introducing the advanced irrigation systems such as those at Engakura in northern Tanzania – although evidence such as later pottery styles found at the site suggest that this settlement achieved greater significance in the middle of the 2nd millennium.

Hehe

The Hehe are Bantu-speaking corn and cattle farmers, settled predominantly in the Southern Highlands around Iringa. This disparate cluster of patrilineal clans shares a similar language and culture. They were among the first to unite in a single political state in the mid-19th century under **Munyigumba**, head of the Muyinga family. Such organization was necessary at this time, to protect against the Ngoni tribe who were violently raiding southern Tanzanian tribes.

When Munyigumba died in 1879, his tribal respect was passed down to his son, **Mkwawa**, who adopted Ngoni-style military tactics, and expanded his people's domain. The tribe is renowned for its fierce warrior-like reputation: the origins of the name have been attributed to a weird and terrifying battle cry, although elders claim the name has ancestral connections.

The Hehe were subdued by German forces in 1898, but only after seven years of resistance, which culminated in the German forces bombarding Mkwawa's large mud fortress, he committed suicide to avoid capture (*see* p.297). The paramount tribal chief was restored in 1926, and the heads of the peoples reinstated as sub-chiefs.

Hehe religion focuses upon the cult of ancestors, but recently many Hehe people have been converted to Christianity and Islam. The old caravan routes passed through their lands, leading to Kilwa and the coast from the interior, and the Hehe exploited the trade, creating wealth by dealing in ivory. Subsequently the Hehe have made the most of education and Western ways.

Ngoni

The Ngoni are said to have fled from Zululand in southern Africa following the force of King Shaka's Zulu wars, and reached southern Tanzania in 1840, searching for new lands. In around 1845 their main party was broken up at the northern end of Lake Nyasa, and some groups splintered off towards Songea further east, while others continued north to Lake Victoria. Their strict internal military organization and raiding techniques encouraged surrounding immigrant tribes to organize themselves into more politically defined leaderships. These southern tribes and the Ngoni later stopped fighting among themselves in order to put up a fierce resistance to German occupation. The Ngoni were defeated in 1910 after a bloody and hard-fought fight.

Makonde

The Makonde people are of Bantu origin, and although they continue to live on both sides of the southern Tanzanian border with Mozambique, they remain one of the five most populous tribes in Tanzania. The Makonde migrated north across the Ruvumu River to the Makonde Plateau, now in the region of Mtwara, and this region has taken on a great significance for the tribe, whose creation story tells of nomadic beginnings followed by settling on higher ground. The legend tells of a being that was neither man nor animal, which wandered the land alone. One night it carved the figure of a woman from a tree. It left the carving outside its dwelling while it slept. The next morning, as the sun dawned on the carving, the female figure came to life. This first woman became this first being's wife, and soon the couple conceived and bore a child. But three days after the child was born, it died. The new wife suggested moving to higher ground, and when they did she conceived once again. Again a child was born to them, but again, after three days the child died. 'Let us move higher still, to where the thick bush grows,' the wife said. So once again they moved. A third time a child was born, and this time the child survived and this was the first Makonde.

This story has many elements that reflect the traditions and beliefs of the Makonde people, particularly their widely renowned talent for wood carving, but also their passion for stories and legends; it also shows the origins of their belief in a matriarchal society in which women lead and advise their men. Makonde men carved wooden female figures for protection when they made a journey, and continue to represent the mother figure in their ebony carvings today. These carvings also represent external influences on their lives, including the family, shetani spirits, dreams and more abstract images, such as cloud formations. The Makonde responded strongly to the influx of Christian missionaries; the majority has converted to Christianity.

The tribe used to practise distinctive tribal markings, notably small scarification marks around the face and extended earrings and lip-plugs for women, which meant that the top two front teeth had to be removed. While it is still common to see Makonde women with these distinctions today, the practice is dying out among younger generations. The Makonde are also famous for their dramatic Sindimba dance, in which performers move and twist with superb agility on high wooden stilts, their heads and faces covered with emotive decorated masks.

Chagga

The Chagga, Chaga or Shaka are Bantu-speaking people living on the fertile volcanic slopes of Kilimanjaro. The tribe is descended from immigrants of various groups who settled on the once forest-covered foothills. Of the 400 main clans most are of Kamba origin, mixed with Teita, Maasai and other peoples. 'Chaggaland' was divided into a number of politically independent chiefdoms, which vied for supremacy over each other and gradually over the whole tribe. In the mid-18th century, the great Chagga chief, **Horombo**, nicknamed Kilimia – 'the Conqueror'– was close to uniting the tribe and reigning as a paramount chief. He inspired respect and command throughout the whole Kilimanjaro region, and would very likely have succeeded but was killed in his prime by Maasai warriors, his policy of unification dying with him.

The rivalry between the more powerful tribal chiefs reached a peak at the latter end of the 19th century when **Rindi of Moshi** and **Sina of Marangu** were at the height of their power, and played each other off against the influx of German colonials. Rindi was astute and recognized opportunities for treaties and negotiations with wealthy foreigners. When the slave and ivory trade was at its peak in Zanzibar, Rindi worked to ensure that Moshi was an important staging post for both, and later, in 1885, he signed a treaty with the Germans, allowing them to use Moshi as their central headquarters. Sina, on the other hand, ruled his empire with his indomitable army, with which he terrorized surrounding clans with cattle raids. There remained, however, no paramount chief until **Marealle of Marangu** was established in that position by the colonial administration in 1893.

The fertile nature and high-altitude climate of the Chagga homelands around Kilimanjaro is perhaps the force behind the success of the Chagga people, who have developed a reputation for being among the wealthiest and most highly organized of African peoples. Whether this is true or not, they have had to develop their methods of cultivation to support an ever-increasing population, making the Kilimanjaro region an area of intensive methods of agricultural irrigation, permanently cultivated by means of fertilizers and crop circulation. They have been forced to widely adopt the policy of 'zero-grazing', bringing grass to the animal rather than taking the animal to the grass, as pastures have given way to crops and the national park.

Perhaps most significantly, the Chagga have realized the benefits of farming cash crops alongside those grown as staples: they are responsible for producing the greatest quantity of aromatic Arabica coffee from the Kilimanjaro region for worldwide sale. Their position at the base of the equatorial mountain of Africa has ensured that the Chagga have had more than their share of international visitors, from the first missionaries, geographers and colonists who found respite from the equatorial sun on the cooler mountain slopes to today's endless stream of climbers.

The Chagga are keen to claim that they have established a relatively egalitarian society, although it remains patrilineal in rules of descent and inheritance, and polygamous marriages still occur, if less commonly. One poignant aspect of their marriage ceremony is to wrap the mother of the bride in a large blanket, given by the invited guests, to show that she will now feel the cold without her daughter beside her at night. The Chagga have traditionally worshipped a great god called Ruwa, who resides in the sky, and to whom they offer animal sacrifices, but they also hold great regard for the spirits of the dead, believing them to return to earth in different forms. However many of the Chagga now follow Christianity, and have been widely receptive to the teaching offered by different denominations of missionaries in the region.

Perhaps this open-minded attitude to new ideas is one of the reasons behind the widely recognized success of the Chagga as a people, but their enterprise has not always found a welcome reception within their own country. Many Chagga have moved away from the Kilimanjaro region to set up businesses throughout Tanzania, and many have found great success as entrepreneurs. They have experienced much non-constructive discrimination and adverse local feeling, which appears to stem from resentment of their successes.

Island Groups

There are several groups of Africans on the islands, nearly one-third of whom are recent arrivals from the mainland. Indigenous Bantu groups, consisting of the **Pemba** in Pemba and the **Hadimu** and **Tumbatu** in Zanzibar, have absorbed the settlers who came from Persia between the 8th and 11th centuries. These groups call themselves **Shirazi**. There are also small enclaves of **Comorans** and **Somalis**. **Arab** settlements were established early, and intermarriage with the local people took place. Later Arab arrivals came from Oman and constituted an élite (*see* **History**, pp.8–11). The poorer recent immigrants from Oman are known as **Manga**. **Asians**, forming a very small minority of recent arrivals, may be divided into Muslim and non-Muslim groups.

Wildlife and Conservation

04

Herbivores

Antelope; Family Antilopinae

Any safari-goer needs to know his or her antelope. But this is easier said than done, given the incredible diversity of these horned, hoofed creatures, which range from tiny, sprightly dik diks to the larger, horse-like eland.

Duikers; Tribe Cephalophini

Duikers are small to medium-sized. The **common duiker** (Swahili: *ndsya*) is the most widespread in Tanzania, although **red** and **blue duikers** are also occasionally spotted. All duikers are reticent creatures that favour covered woodland habitats and are buff-coloured to blend in with their surroundings. They live in clearly marked and defended small territories in monogamous pairs, although the male is not above taking advantage of any female that wanders through his territory. Families engage in plenty of tactile communication such as head-nibbling and licking. When threatened, duikers are able to freeze in mid-stride, then sink or slink to nearby cover. When captured, their distinctive bleating alerts other duikers – and predators – to their plight.

Hunters often stick the web of a parchment spider over the open end of a duiker's horn, and carve a groove into the other end to form a trumpet, which they use to call up leopard and antelope, imitating with incredible accuracy the sounds of duiker in distress. Many a hunter has been forced to take refuge up a tree from the attack of a duiker moved by the distress call to defend its family. There are two rare and endangered species of duiker in Tanzania: **Ader's duiker** is confined to Zanzibar; the larger **Abbott's duiker** lives in the mountain forests around Kilimanjaro.

Dwarf Antelope; Tribe Neotragini

The most common dwarf antelopes to be seen in Tanzania are **Kirk's dik dik**, *Madoqua kirkii* (Swahili: *digi digi*), the **klipspringer**, *Oreotragus oreotragus*, the **oribi**, *Ourebia ourebia*, and the **suni antelope**, *Neotragus moshatus*. All members of the smallest family of antelope, they vary in size, but are all small enough to require advanced 'nasal panting' techniques to keep their body temperature low.

Kirk's dik diks and **suni antelopes** both have rabbit-like limb proportions, with much longer back legs than forelegs, resulting in more of a bounding spring than a run. Dik diks are monogamous and are most often seen in pairs, as they move together from territory to territory throughout their lives. Family members call to each other with a soft whistle, but use a loud, breathy 'zik zik' alarm when threatened, giving them their name. On average only 35–43cm high, dik diks are threatened by around 20 different predators, including vultures and eagles when young. They remain in peak condition at all times, are able to reach top speed within a couple of bounds and always know of a hiding place nearby. Like the duiker, they freeze at the first sign of trouble, and then either leap to safety with loud whistles of alarm (most often a duet between the pair) or sink silently to the ground.

While dik diks favour wooded areas and *kopjes*, their larger cousin, the **klipspringer**, is far better adapted to springing over high rocky outcrops and escaping out of the range of most predators. Klipspringers have specially adapted hooves to help them bound over the rocks, and have been spotted at a height of 4,500m, at the peak of Mount Meru in northern Tanzania. The **oribi** is the largest of this tribe, up to 67cm tall with more 'gazelle-like' proportions. Oribis have a white rump and belly similar to a tommy (*see* below) but a black tail and a black beauty spot on the cheek beneath each ear. They are said to be monogamous, but they all seem to be unfaithful!

Gazelles; Tribe Antilopini

Gazelles are perhaps the most numerous of all the antelope commonly spotted on safari, and tend to herd together in elegant groupings. Social organization varies from herd to herd, depending on the strength of the territorial male: females move at will between herds, but males may be actively evicted by the territorial male. Gazelles are among the fastest of all fast-running mammals (just outpaced by the cheetah) and can attain speeds of 82kph at full pace. When in danger, they will bound high in the air in order to enable those behind to see them and keep with the herd, especially in long grass and in flight from predators – a trick known as 'stotting'.

Thompson's Gazelle, *Gazella thompsonii*

Thompson's gazelles (Swahili: *swala*) are more widely known as 'tommies'. The tommy flourishes in abundance on the short grass plains of the Serengeti; it once roamed across all the African plains. Males are prone to extensive duelling and some-times fatal fights to earn the right to a herd of females, resorting to forming bachelor herds when thwarted. A duel may last longer than an hour, as they often graze intermittently while in combat, until one or both graze their way out of the 'fight ring'. The most characteristic distinction of a tommy is its wagging black tail across its white rump, contrasting with the white tail of the Grant's gazelle.

Grant's Gazelle, *Gazella granti*

Grant's gazelles (Swahili: *swala granti*) are larger and paler than tommies, elegantly proportioned with long, ringed horns. They try to migrate through different pastures than tommies, but herds will often mingle in small groups in the same area. Grant's gazelles seem to be a little braver than Thompson's, moving out of the Ngorongoro Crater into the highlands in search of better pastures.

Gerenuk, *Litocranius walleri*

A less commonly seen antelope is the sinuous **gerenuk**, found in northwest Tanzania. Its Swahili name is *swala twiga*, which translates as 'impala giraffe'. Curiously, the gerenuk has evolved the ability to browse leaves while standing on its back legs to reach higher; its image is immortalized in stone on the walls of Ancient Egyptian tombs. While often wandering alone, gerenuks also group into small, loose collectives. They tend to be fairly sedentary, rarely move territories and prefer freezing to fleeing, an effective tactic that means they are easily overlooked by predators.

Reedbuck and Waterbuck; Tribe Reducini

Medium- to large-sized antelope that favour areas where there is an abundance of water, these buck are found in the greatest numbers on flood plains. All three types of **reedbuck**, *Redunca redunca*, can be found in Tanzania, in different areas. The **bohor reedbuck** is the most widespread. While the **mountain reedbuck** is found only in the northerly mountains, the **common reedbuck** is seen only around central and southern Tanzania. The reedbuck is medium-sized with a thick reddish to grey-brown coat and pale whitish belly, a ring of white around the eyes and short ringed horns curving forwards in a hook at the top. They are unsociable with each other if there is shade and cover, but gather into groups if there is none, becoming the easy and preferred prey of leopard and cheetah during the dry season, as they lack endurance and natural fighting defences. If they sense a threat they pretend to eat, skulk into the shadows and finally dart off at speed with a distinctive rocking canter, giving a whistle-like alarm call. Once disturbed, the reedbuck can keep up its whistling for half an hour.

The rather shaggy-looking **waterbuck**, *Kobus ellipsiprymnus*, is a distinctive, stocky antelope with bodily markings that must have inspired the *Far Side* cartoon by Gary Larson: 'Bummer of a birthmark, Hal'. The **common waterbuck** has a ring on its rump, while its cousin the **defassa waterbuck** has a narrow white collar around its throat. Waterbuck need green grass, which in the dry season lies around permanent water, as they are the most susceptible of all antelope to dehydration. This need to linger around waterholes makes waterbuck very vulnerable to ambush from predators. As a defence, when waterbuck are attacked a toxin is released into the muscles, probably triggered by increased adrenaline, which makes the meat taste unpalatable. This toxic release mechanism has probably saved the species.

Horse Antelope; Tribe Hippotragini

Roan, *Hippotragus equinus*

Roan are the fourth largest, and now very rare as a result of poaching and of diminishing habitat, but still found in the south of Tanzania. Roans prefer open grasslands near water with cover close by. These animals are big bruisers: a large bull might weigh up to 280kg, and a female up to 260kg. Both sexes have tufty manes and extraordinarily long ears – up to 30cm long and flopping forwards – and backward-curling horns similar to the sable, but shorter. The roan's face has dark tribal features, with a white snout, semicircles around the eyes and a black 'mask' over the rest of the head. Its body is usually grey to brown in colour – roan, even – with darker legs.

Sable, *Hippotragus niger*

With horns like huge scimitars, a black- and white-striped face-mask and horse-like mane, the sable is regarded as Africa's finest large antelope. In a corner, a sable can become a fearsome adversary, as many a lion has found to its cost. Both female and male sables are born a reddish-brown colour, but after long and bloody battles to gain control of territory, the new territorial male turns a jet-black colour – probably due to exceptionally high levels of testosterone. Very few sights are more rewarding than that of a magnificent, cautiously defiant bull moving down from the hills to water, where he drops on to his front knees to drink. Female sable and immature bull sable wander through the territories of three different territorial males, unlike the roan antelope, whose dominant bull fights for control and then moves with his herd.

Oryx, *Gazella callotis*

Of all the different species of oryx, the **fringe-eared oryx** is most common to the acacia bush of Tanzania, such as that of the Serengeti. This oryx is an antelope with incredible powers of endurance, energy and strength, able to wander for long distances across arid savannah where few others of its kind could survive. It carries a straight, stocky grey-tan body on long, thin legs and its short, blunt face is framed by tall, subtly curved horns up to 75cm long. These are a formidable weapon in combat, and used with a ferocious stabbing action during affirmations of hierarchy within the herd. The fringe-eared oryx has black markings on the forehead and face, leading down the chest and tops of the legs to form a diamond shape on the rump.

Hartebeest, Topi and Wildebeest; Tribe Alcelaphini

These, too, are all medium- to large-sized antelope with prominent humps on their forequarters and sloping backs, generally a dark colour with white tufts and short, ringed, curving horns.

Hartebeest, *Alcelaphus buselaphus*

Hartebeest (Swahili: *kongoni*) are especially high shouldered with strangely twisted 'S'-shaped horns. Both **Coke's hartebeest** and **Lichtenstein's hartebeest** are found in Tanzania, with Coke's preferring open savannah and Lichtenstein's happier near to miombo woodland. They range in colour from tawny to chocolate-brown.

Topi, *Damaliscus lunatus*

Topi (Swahili: *nyamera*) are similar to hartebeest but are much darker and often smaller, with a very close-cropped, dark brown shiny coat, a thin blue-black face and matching haunch markings. They have adapted to survive in arid conditions, so that although they drink regularly when possible, they can also go without water for up to one month. They have an odd habit while resting in a herd of standing in serried ranks, nodding at each other with their eyes apparently closed.

Wildebeest, *Connochaetes taurinus*

The wildebeest found in Tanzania is the **common wildebeest** or **gnu**, broad-shouldered with sloping hindquarters, horns similar to a cow's and a short glossy coat. The gnu also has a broad cow-like muzzle for cropping short grasses. But do not be fooled into thinking that the gnu's grazing process is random: bulls challenge each other daily for territory by initially grazing another bull's patch; the challenge is followed by a range of horn-rubbing and head-to-head grazing tactics, and some disrespectful tail-swinging, intended to provoke the rival. Wildebeest need to drink every day, and so aim to remain always within a 15km range of water. To achieve this

Conservation Issues

The conservation of African wildlife has inspired European concern for centuries: in AD 77, when the Roman Senate was built with benches of pure ivory, Pliny issued a rallying cry for the preservation of elephants in his *Natural History*. The **ivory trade** continued, however, for nearly two thousand years; serious efforts to curtail it were made only when the elephant population was reduced to near-extinction – in the last 50 years. While the West did its best to decimate animal populations in East Africa with colonial-era **big-game shoots** (*see* 'The History of Safaris', pp.56–7), before becoming set on a course of wildlife protection, local African communities have forever relied on wild animals and the land for their survival through hunting and farming – a fact that early foreign conservationists were long reluctant to recognize.

In the past large numbers of **people** – most famously the Maasai pastoralists – have been **evicted** from the hunting grounds and free-ranging pastures of the national parks, game reserves and conservation areas in order to conserve tracts of land as 'primeval wilderness' – disregarding the fact that this same wilderness was the traditional home of nomadic tribes who had long lived in harmony with it. The dispossessed peoples have found themselves squeezed into confined areas where they have been forced to over-utilize natural resources, with detrimental effects on the environment. As populations have grown rapidly in villages on the outskirts of protected areas, they have been forced to rely on wild animals for food, and to kill them when they threaten crops and livestock. The meat of animals such as buffalo is sold from some hunting reserves at far lower prices than farmed meat, but freely hunted still prevails over cheap when serious **rural poverty** is so prevalent.

Indigenous people's needs for water, food and fuel and a say in the management of their own territory are now widely recognized as key elements in the conservation equation, but bitterness towards conservationists has often been the net result of their well-meaning interference. Moreover, the profits to be made from trading **ivory**, **rhino horn** and the **skins** of animals such as leopard often, unsurprisingly, still outweigh conservation dilemmas in Tanzania, one of the world's poorest countries; **poaching** has become one of the few options for survival. Although the ivory trade has been outlawed and the dangerously depleted black rhino population is constantly monitored, illegal hunting continues to be a real problem.

Attitudes and approaches to conservation are constantly being re-evaluated. There is now a growing awareness that throwing people off the land does not encourage them to care about the animals preserved with apparently far greater regard than themselves on their old homelands. Effective conservation has to benefit local communities if it is to be successful. This realization has sparked a drive among international aid and development groups to communicate with locals, to understand and meet their requirements even if land is appropriated for wildlife conservation.

The migratory ecosystem of the northern **Serengeti** region, long recognized as a unique and important wildlife region of world importance, has set precedents for other parks to either follow or dismiss depending on their success. Great attention has been paid to the long-term conservation development of the northern parks.

The **Tanzania National Parks Association** (TANAPA) and international conservation organizations including the **World Conservation Union** (IUCN), **Norwegian Agency for International Development** (NORAD) and **Frankfurt Zoological Society** (FZS), were among the first to articulate the 'primeval wilderness' concept and to publicize the wildlife preservation in this region. Having understood from early on the need for education and improved living standards in outlying villages, however, they were unable to foresee all the consequences of their intervention: as new schools and business ventures were set up in outlying villages, they inadvertently encouraged immigration into the region, and the local population doubled as outsiders moved in to share the benefits of development. Problems of sufficiency then arose once more, as demand for resources again strained the local environment, and the most hard-to-manage small-time poaching began again.

As a result the **Serengeti Regional Conservation Strategy** (SRCS) was formed in 1985 to integrate conservation practices in the massive Serengeti-Mara ecosystem, although it still only covers the conservation areas on the Tanzanian side of the border with Kenya. This mosaic of national parks, wildlife reserves and communally and privately owned lands covers 30,000 square kilometres, and makes up one of the most important wildlife areas in the world, but is also home to native tribes such as the Maasai, Sukuma, Datoga, Ikoma, Isenye and Chagga (*see* **Peoples**, pp.21–30). The strategy focuses particularly on integrating local people's needs with natural resource conservation, with distinct reference to land-use conflicts and poaching.

In another case, in the region around **Udzungwa Mountains National Park**, **deforestation** has been a serious problem as wood is used for fuel. Conservation organizations are now providing seedlings for reforestation beyond the boundaries of the park; in the meantime locals still gather wood from the forest as long as it is not cut from living trees. Alongside wood-collection issues there are issues of food, pasture for grazing livestock, fresh water sources, fertile farming land, living spaces, education, health, and so on in and around the parks. Some community tourism and development schemes have attempted to address these issues.

In further acknowledgement of the need for balance the Maasai people have now been 'granted' grazing rights around **Ngorongoro Crater**. In the **Ugalla River Game Reserve**, near Tabora, honey collectors are allowed into the reserve at certain times of year to continue their traditional collection of wild honey – a change to the original rules of the reserve, which prohibited any access other than for permitted hunting. Conflicts have for the time being been resolved less successfully at the **Mikomazi Black Rhino Project**, where local people have had their grazing rights restricted in the game reserve; there is resentment at the money being spent on an expensive high-quality electric rhino-proof fence when the people themselves are denied access.

In **Ruaha National Park**, the morale of state-funded rangers was at a rock-bottom low after years of under-funding by the economically crippled government. There was little incentive for the rangers, who did not even have boots, to battle poachers equipped with the latest hi-tech weapons. A pressure group called the **Friends of Ruaha** raised morale by paying cash incentives to catch poachers, providing fuel, a river-crossing, radios and ultimately a plane for patrols and emergency evacuations. Similarly, a controlled hunting area adjoining the park was long plagued by illegal hunting by Iringa residents. A Ruaha Conservation Group, with the backing of the 'friends', now manages this **Mkupule block**, employing and equipping four local game scouts. The area is now home to an abundance of freely roaming animals that have crossed the river from the national park.

The Ruaha area is in fact a microcosm of the conservation dilemmas afflicting Tanzania. The primary need for local people is to be self-sufficient in food production, but more intensive farming easily upsets the ecological balance, affecting wildlife. A classic example of the conflicts that arise can be seen in the case of the **Usangu Flats** and the **Great Ruaha River**. The river is the lifeblood of the region's animals at the end of the dry season, when its tributaries become sand rivers. The main catchment area of the river is the Usangu Flats; a rice-growing project has been established here, increasing the off-take of water from the river. This demand for water has been compounded by increased cattle-grazing in the swamps; soil compaction and removal of vegetation decrease the land's water-holding capability, leading to flash flooding and drought, a problem so acute that the not-so-Great Ruaha River dried up for the first time in living memory in 1993, and has done so every dry season since. Crocodiles, hippopotami and catfish crowd into ever smaller pools, while buffalo and elephant fight over the remaining waterholes. In addition, the river is meant to fuel the Matera hydroelectric dam. A British-funded research project on the 'Sustainable Development of the Usangu Wetland and Catchment Area', aiming to find a solution to the problems, has run aground on the sand banks of politics and vested interests.

In addition to economic and ecological issues, it has become clear that much greater efforts to involve and **educate** local people in conservation must be made for projects to be sustainable. Most Tanzanian children have never seen their country's native animals in the wild and few ever get the chance to visit the national parks. Unless the new generation appreciates the importance of the parks to Tanzania, their future will be uncertain, especially in times of population pressure.

Development projects are beginning to tackle these issues. Near Kilimanjaro, the **Village Education Project**, an NGO set up to improve primary education in the Marangu area, has linked up with Guerba, a travel company, to provide annual outings for local children to the national parks in the region; these visits have been an unqualified success. In the Ruaha area, a vet from Iringa, Dr Dulle, has started a **Village Schools Conservation Project**. The project focuses on villages close to the national park, with a Tanzanian team educating a new generation about the delights of the wildlife around them and the need to conserve their part of Tanzania.

Tensions remain today between the exploitation of natural resources for survival, profit and tourism and the preservation of unique wildlife, biodiversity and precious ecosystems. As in so much of the world, there are more questions than answers – but, to end on a positive note, there may be hope for the future if local people have access to education about conservation, become involved in the management of national parks, can benefit from employment and can access resources in a sustainable way.

Conservation Organizations

Wildlife Conservation Society of Tanzania (WCST), 28 Garden Avenue, PO Box 70919, Dar es Salaam, t (022) 2112518, f (022) 2124572, *wcst@africaonline.co.tz*. A non-profit, non-government organization, established in June 1988, which carries out numerous conservation projects in Tanzania, including a nationwide programme of awareness and advocacy. It has set up wildlife clubs and coastal forest education schemes, publishes information materials and holds seminars, workshops and meetings. WCST encourages woodland conservation and has planted thousands of seedlings in deforested areas.

Tanzanian Wildlife Protection Fund, Ivory Room, Nyerere Road, PO Box 1994, Dar es Salaam, t (022) 2866377, f (022) 2863496. Has supported management and development of wildlife resources since 1978, appliying conservation research and education projects. The TWPF is also a non-profit NGO.

Sand Rivers Selous Rhino Project, c/o Nomad Safaris, Sand Rivers Selous, PO Box 1344, Dar es Salaam, t (022) 2862173, f (022) 2617060, *sand-rivers@twiga.com*. Concerned with protecting the ecosystem of the Selous Game Reserve. Specifically aims to provide security and surveillance for monitoring and assessing black rhino in this region.

WWF Tanzania, Plot no. 350, Regent Estate, Mikocheni, PO Box 63117, Dar es Salaam, t (022) 2700077, f (022) 275535, *www.wwf.org*, *www.panda.org*, *WWFTPO@raha.com*. Tanzanian branch of the World Wildlife Fund for Nature. Particularly involved in black rhino conservation in the Selous Game Reserve, and in elephant conservation.

Roots and Shoots, c/o JGI-Tanzania, PO Box 1182, Kigoma, Tanzania, *www.janegoodall.org*. Established by Gombe Stream chimp observer Jane Goodall in 1991, Roots and Shoots is focused towards conservation, environmental research and education.

From its base in Dar es Salaam, the group has established youth 'clubs' in 45 schools in the area and more than 300 schools in Tanzania as a whole, and promotes care and concern for the environment, teaching each club that the actions of an individual can make a difference however hard their personal circumstances.

Wildlife Conservation Society, 200 Southern Boulevard, Bronx, New York 10460, t (718) 220 5100, *www.wcs.org/home/wild/Africa/2937*. Founded in 1895 by the New York Zoological Society at the Bronx Zoo, the WCS has run field conservation programmes around the world since the 1950s. Projects in Tanzania include research into the effects of poaching on elephant social systems in Tarangire National Park, and studies of cheetah, amphibians and lion.

Friends of Ruaha Society, PO Box 2369, Ruaha National Park, Iringa, *wwwfriendsofruaha.org*. A pressure group concerned with preserving the Ruaha ecosystem as a whole. Funds wildlife rangers, in collaboration with the Ruaha Conservation Group, to patrol and protect the area from indiscriminate hunting. Also lobbies for greater awareness of the environmental effects of new farm schemes affecting the Great Ruaha River flow, and supports conservation education for local primary school children.

Tony Fitzjohn/George Adamson African Wildlife Preservation Trusts, 301 North A Street, PO Box 5352, Oxnard, CA 93031-5352, USA, *www.mkomazi.com*. Manages the Mkomazi Game Reserve in the northeast of the country, which runs a black rhino sanctuary and seeks to protect elephant, African hunting dog and other animals too, along with education and outreach projects.

Tusk Trust, 116 Battersea Business Centre, 103–9 Lavender Hill, London SW11 5QL, UK, t (020) 7978 7100, f (020) 7223 251, *www.tusk.org*. Aims to help the conservation of all wildlife, notably elephant, African wild dog, cheetah, rhino and chimpanzee.

they migrate from regions of seasonal drought. How far they travel and how numerous the herds are depend on the environment, their initial location and the annual situation; their movement is dictated by rainfall, available pastures and unexpected events such as bushfires. Some herds are able to remain resident in one area, while others are forced to follow an entirely nomadic lifestyle. The Serengeti and Maasai Mara herds travel more than 800km annually, in columns of animals up to 40km long. All wildebeest are territorial and gather in vast, mobile herds to follow the same migratory routes year after year; it is estimated that around 1.6 million wildebeest make the great migration across northern Tanzania and southern Kenya. Wildebeest have specially adapted nostrils to filter out dust kicked up by their migrating fellows in the herds.

Wildebeest sleep lying down in lines of between a hundred and a thousand beasts, leaving a safe distance of one or two metres between them so that the entire herd can jump safely to its feet to avoid attack. When the dry season ends, the need for larger herd aggregations also diminishes and herds break back down into localized groupings. Wildebeest also follow an unusually strict timetable for calving, ensuring that calves are born in a three-week window before the long rains.

Impala, *Aepyceros melampus*

While Grant's and Thompson's gazelle are the bread and butter of the plains, **impala** (Swahili: *swala pala*) are more at home in bush and wooded countryside and thrive in very high numbers across the East African savannah. The male fights hard for his territory and rarely holds on to it for more than two years. Contrary to popular belief he does not run a harem; instead he has to struggle to keep the females within his territory for long enough to serve as many as possible. If they start to wander off, he fakes an alarm call, signalling attack by a predator, and he can often be seen chasing errant females back into the herd. The female's territory covers three times that of the territorial male. Impala are often found with baboons: with the impala's great sense of smell and the baboon's ability to climb, they make life difficult for prowling predators.

Bushbuck, Kudu and Eland; Tribe Tragelaphini

Eland (Swahili: *pofu*) domesticate well, and are the farmed wild animal of choice, yet in the wild they take forever to habituate. Their very efficient sense of sight and smell and their instinct to run instead of to freeze or hide make them very difficult to approach. They are always the last animals to settle comfortably around safari vehicles. They can run great distances without rest, jump easily over fences 3m high, and their horns can run through the body of a car as though it were paper. Many Africans love the taste of eland more than any other meat, but African hunters believe to kill one will bring them very bad luck.

Buffalo; Tribe Bovini

African Cape buffalo (Swahili: *nyati*) may conjure up images of stupid, smelly cows, but the Cape buffalo also causes more injuries to humans than all of Africa's other wild animals put together. Just as with the lone bull in a field, it is the solitary buffalo bull that is the most dangerous. Old, cranky, sick and injured, he cannot keep up with the others and benefit from the relative safety in numbers, and his defence is to hide in thick bush and to attack rather than to run.

Buffalo receive help from an unexpected quarter: small birds with red and yellow beaks are attracted to the thousands of bloodsucking ticks that pester them day and night. Ticks spread diseases; some even have specially adapted chemical sensors on their front legs, which they wave about in the air to help them seek out sick animals from afar. The oxpecker birds help to keep the number of ticks to a minimum, so helping to keep their host healthy. They also warn the buffalo herds of danger by flying up in the air and calling loudly in alarm. The buffalo have learned to heed this warning; so too has the experienced safari guide. All too often it is the only sound that betrays the presence of a cranky bull, hidden in nearby thick bush.

In the dry season, when water is limited, and prides of lion wait in ambush, the buffalo herds (usually no more than 2–300 in number) come together, forming huge groups of up to 5,000. They move together in their own cloud of dust, a seemingly never-ending line, with the pathfinders ahead probing cautiously for the safest route. The strongest buffaloes form a protective flank around the young and vulnerable, ready to swing out and face any threat to the herd. Even the boldest lion can be forgiven for being intimidated by a wall of a thousand horns! The weak and sick struggle to keep up, however, and it is these which lion pick off in the confusion and panic of the initial stampede.

With the onset of rain, ticks breed more profusely and, with water now readily available everywhere and the increased threat of tick-borne disease, the herds split up and go their separate ways, to fatten up ready for the next dry season. Few experiences can be more dramatic than to see rivers turn black with buffalo, and to watch the way a handful of lions can single out and kill from a stampeding herd of thousands – a battle which does not always end cleanly for the hunter either.

Hippopotamus; Family Hippopotamidae

The common hippopotamus, *Hippopotamus amphibius* (Swahili: *kiboko*), likes to spend its day almost entirely submerged in water, with just eyes, ears and occasionally mouth exposed to the sun. Adults can spend up to five minutes entirely submerged and baby hippos are able to suckle underwater as well as on land. Hippos swim by 'galloping' underwater, and bounce along the bottom of a pool with surprising grace. Any such elegance deserts them on land, where they tend to move at a slower pace, occasionally building up to a frisky trot and only gearing up to their 30kph limit in absolute emergencies. Their apparently sociable daytime habits of languishing semi-submerged in large groups are entirely changed after dark, as by night each animal leaves the water to engage in impressively anti-social eating habits, cruising defiantly alone or with their calves if nursing. Much is still being discovered about how hippopotami communicate above and below water.

Their muscular lips are usually up to 50cm wide, well adapted for grazing a broad path through short grasses, and they can consume up to 40kg of grass a night within a five- or six-mile range. Their large, well-developed incisor teeth are rarely used for eating, and more commonly used for fighting among themselves.

More people are killed or injured by buffalo than any other animal in Africa, but you have less chance of surviving a hippo attack, and the injuries for anyone who does are likely to be far more serious. It is not uncommon for a man to be bitten in half, or to have his legs bitten off. They leave huge deep holes with great risk of infection. Never allow yourself to come between a hippo and water!

Rhinoceros; Family Rhinocerotidae

The rhinoceros is one of the last remaining examples of similarly jointed massive mammals, and, with its apparently armour-plated bulk and strangely prehistoric features, it even looks like an ancient relic from a previous era. These creatures used to roam freely throughout Asia, North America and Africa, but now all are dangerously threatened due to demand for rhino horn, for which many thousands of animals have been hunted and killed to the point of near-extinction (*see* below). Both the African species of black and white rhino are now protected. Only the **black rhinoceros**, *Diceros bicornis*, has family members still surviving in sparse pockets of Tanzania, most commonly visible in the Ngorongoro Crater. The small, puffy eyes set back in the head are pretty useless for seeing; the rhino relies instead on its acute sense of smell and

Black Rhino Conservation

During the 1970s, when Tanzania was at its poorest and rhino horn became worth its weight in gold, black rhinos suffered an even worse fate than elephants at the hands of hunters, and were almost entirely eliminated from the country. In Africa as a whole the population of these extraordinary prehistoric animals, which have roamed the earth for 60 million years, has fallen from 65,000 to fewer than 2,700 in a few decades. In Tanzania there are only 32 known rhinos left. Rhinos are prized by poachers for the horn on their nose, especially valued in China for its supposed aphrodisiac and analgesic properties and in Yemen to make coming-of-age dagger handles for boys.

Great efforts are now being made to reverse this near-extinction. The remaining animals are policed in their natural environment and in reserves, with expensive 24hr surveillance required as a result of the continuing black market trade – a single horn can fetch $85,000 in Yemen. Rhinos still roam in secret areas of the **Serengeti** inaccessible to tourists, but there is a slim chance of glimpsing one in **Ngorongoro Crater**, and an even slimmer one in the dense bush of the **Selous**.

The **Black Rhino Project** at **Mkomazi Game Reserve** (*see* pp.176–7) in the northeast has ambitious aims to relocate rhinos that are under threat elsewhere in Africa to the sanctuary of Mkomazi, which is securely fenced and guarded. In the late 1960s, 250 rhinos roamed wild in this area; by the late 1980s there were none; now there are four – at a an annual cost of $90,000 per animal per year. The **Sand Rivers Selous Rhino Project** provides security and surveillance for black rhinos in its area, where the population fell from 2,000 to fewer than 150 rhinos between 1970 and 1996.

hearing. Rhinos are able to charge at up to 50kph but usually prefer more sedentary, solitary activity, although the black rhino is considerably more aggressive and dangerous than the **white rhino**. The black rhino is distinguished from its relative by its prehensile upper lip and slightly smaller size – there is actually very little difference in colour.

Giraffe; Family Giraffidae

The giraffe, *Giraffa camelopardis* (Swahili: *twiga*) is the world's tallest animal. The male giraffe usually tops around 5.5m, and the female around 4m. Their unusual necks have seven vertebrae, like other mammals, except that each of the giraffe's has become greatly elongated to gain a 2m browsing advantage over all other tree- and shrub-eaters, except elephants. Its height does present disadvantages, such as the problem of having to straddle its legs or kneel to drink, at which time the giraffe is at its most vulnerable to attack. Not only are the neck and legs exceptionally long, but so is the giraffe's tongue, which extends a full 45cm. The tongue is designed to pluck juicy leaflets selectively from thorny growth without harm, and the long, narrow lips can strip a bough bare. Female giraffes tend to browse for longer periods, taking time to select more nutritious leaves, while males eat more quickly and wander further. They often lie down at night, and may even curl up to sleep for short periods. They have only two speeds, walking or galloping, both of which require a certain rhythmic co-ordination; although a giraffe can achieve speeds of up to 60kph it may still appear to be moving in slow motion as a result of its attenuated limbs. Female giraffes rarely have more than one calf at a time, and tend to take the calf away from a group to remain sheltered in the company of other females. The mothers often leave their offspring in a 'crèche' with others the same age while they find food. While grown giraffes are rarely easy prey for lion, young must be protected; a female giraffe may attack a lion with her hooves if her calf is threatened.

Zebra; Family Equidae

Two kinds of zebra are commonly seen in Tanzania, the **Grevy's zebra**, *Equus grevyi*, which has thinner stripes and a broader head than its smaller relative, and the **plains zebra**, *Equus burchelli*, which also lacks the Grevy's concentric circle pattern on the rump. Both stay mainly in herds, maintaining peaceful equanimity most of the time, and generally accept a new natural leader without a fight when the original stallion is injured, sick or too old. Groups are either composed of a 'harem' of about five or six mares led by a stallion, which would have been started by a stallion bold enough to abduct a filly from her herd, or a smaller number of bachelor males, but these groups band together during the dry season. Herds are not closely defined, and animals will join and depart herds of both types of zebra quite freely, but will always provide excellent group defence against predators. They will surround young and move away as a group, and act as a crèche if a mother has to move away to find water during a drought. A herd will always have at least one animal posted as 'lookout' while the other animals are sleeping, even at night.

Zebras have been reclassified according to when they were discovered. Since the first of its species to be recorded was the now extinct **quagga** (the last known quagga died in captivity in London Zoo at the end of the 19th century) all subspecies related to the quagga are now recorded as *Equus quagga burchelli*, *Equus quagga boems* or *Equus quagga crawshayii*, the zebra common to the Ruaha area. From the DNA of that last specimen, which now resides in the Natural History Museum in London, some researchers believe that through a process of crossbreeding it would be possible to breed the original quagga back into existence in six generations.

Elephant; Order Proboscidea; Family Elephantidae

Elephants (Swahili: *tembo*) are highly intelligent, complex creatures with close social structures and relationships. Family groups are led by an adult matriarch, often accompanied by closely related females and their offspring, with males forming separate herds or wandering alone. Young males reach adolescence at about 12 years old, and are then likely to leave the matriarchal herd to join up with groups of other

Elephant Conservation

The world trade in ivory has been the root of many evils. Ivory has been a valuable commodity for many centuries, dating back to the earliest trade between the Tanzanian interior and the coast, and pre-dating the trade in slaves, which actually began as a by-product of the ivory trade: the huge tusks of the elephants that were once common across the wild reaches of Africa weighed up to 500kg each, and the slaves required to carry them to the coast for sale could also be sold on arrival.

Despite its long history, the ivory trade's most critical period was very recent. In the mid-20th century the price of ivory rocketed upwards, reaching $60 per kilo in 1979, and increasing fivefold in the following decade. To meet this demand, most of the big-tusked male elephants were wiped out, and ivory-hunters resorted to killing younger, smaller-tusked elephants to produce the same weight to trade. Around 100,000 elephants were killed for their tusks in the 1980s, and the African elephant population has fallen from 1.5 million 20 years ago to roughly 650,000 today.

The massacre of so many animals has had a lasting effect on the species, reducing the genetic diversity that produced the enormous tusks now more often seen in early photographs and museums than on elephants in the wild. The tragic elimination of so many thousands of animals has not only affected the elephant population in numerical terms but has also had an impact on the social organization of the herds. On a more optimistic note, however, the devastating effects of the ivory trade have brought about a sea-change in attitudes, at least in the West. Efforts taken to reduce the international value of ivory and, more importantly, to protect these animals in their natural habitat, have had a beneficial effect on the elephant population, which is now showing signs of recovery in most of the Tanzanian national parks.

young bulls. The bulls can travel thousands of kilometres in range, while recent research shows the female range to be quite limited. The bulls fight each other and the strongest will mate. Often there is a peak of mating activity in the middle of the rainy season when herds aggregate to over 300 in number. 'Musth', when bull elephants feel a strong hormonal drive to mate, is strong at this time and this brings many bulls together into these aggregations. The mating process appears quite distressing to the herd, with a huge, well-endowed bull raging through the bush after a terrified and squealing female, amid deafening trumpeting and stomach-rumbling from the other protective members of the herd. It is during musth that even the most tame elephant can become 'testy' and consequently aggressive, unpredictable and dangerous. It is nearly always a mistake to run from a charging elephant unless you are sure to make good your escape – they become more serious if they feel they have the upper hand. A top Nairobi surgeon has recounted that only two accident victims involving elephant had ever reached him alive.

Elephants generally show great affection for one another, however, and are commonly protective towards smaller or older members of the herd. If a herd grows too big, the herd will split in two, but the elephants remain on close and friendly terms and always greet emphatically if they have been parted. They rally around to support each other, to the extent that if a matriarch is injured the herd will gather around her to try to lift her and help her walk supported between two others, and will rarely move away if she has been shot by poachers.

Elephants were once the most widespread of all large mammals. Evidence in Neolithic rock paintings shows that they existed in the Sahara before it became desert. When once allowed to range freely, elephants were the natural gardeners of the African bush. There is no subtlety about the path of elephants through the bush – their progress is often marked by a trail of apparent sheer destruction. Once they turned over the soil and trees in their path and contributed to the greater diversity of the landscape, but now, frequently confined to much smaller areas, their tendency to uproot trees may convert limited woodland to grassland, and leave them little to forage. In recent years their population has been diabolically reduced by human slaughter, with an estimated depopulation of up to 80 per cent in East Africa between the years of 1980 and 1990 alone.

Hyrax; Order Hyracoidea; Family Procaviidae

Through the process of evolution the number of toes and the intestines do not change. It is on this basis that the hyrax (Swahili: *pimbi*) is considered to be the nearest living relative to the elephant. It evolved 40 million years ago from a species that ranged in size from a giant forest hog to the size of the ones you see now – lap-dog-sized, rodent-like creatures. Over the intervening millions of years only the ones that could climb to feed off the leaves of trees, and live in small crevices in rocks and trees, survived. The **rock hyrax** and **bush hyrax** are often seen around the Serengeti lodges, and are quite tame. There is a nocturnal **tree hyrax**, which is less common but can be heard shrieking in the night. Hyraxes work well together in defence, pooling their sense of smell and sight, with a system of lookouts. Their shrill squeals often betray the presence of a leopard. They have very poor thermo-regulation and, like reptiles, have to go out in the sun to warm up and retreat into the dark to cool down.

Swine; Family Suidae

The **warthog** (Swahili: *ngiri*) is a distinctive creature commonly spotted on safari, but not widely noted for its beauty. Males have prominent tusks and a tendency to facial warts and the warthog body is generally a mass of hairless grey skin, topped by a bristly mane around the neck and shoulder, but colours can change depending on how much mud-wallowing is available to the individual.

Many visitors talk of the warthog as the ugliest of Africa's wild animals and yet it is also many people's favourite. The male, with all his warts, and the young at play, spinning in tight mad circles, seemingly bursting with the joy of life and completely unable to control themselves, are fantastic entertainment. They reverse awkwardly into their holes ready to charge out in a cloud of dust and rip apart any threat with their lethal tusks. It is for good reason that wild dogs will often steer a wide berth around warthogs. The warthog's tail automatically sticks up vertically when the animal begins to trot at speed, perhaps as a type of antenna for other family members to follow.

Carnivores

Genets, Civets and Mongooses; Family Viverridae

This is the largest family of carnivores, the most varied and the most primitive. Genet and civet skeletons and teeth have barely altered in the last 40–50 million years; the earliest similar mongoose skull is 30 million years old.

Genet, *Gennetta spp.*

A small but vicious carnivore, which prefers to carry out its deadly deeds under the cover of darkness, particularly in the first hours of the night. Genets have a lithe, feline appearance, with a long bushy tail that fluffs up when the animal wishes to seem more frightening. The coat is usually tawny with black spots or stripes. Nocturnal leanings lead them to spend much of the day in burrows or hollows in trees, and they are as keen climbers as ground-dwellers. They are fairly indiscriminate in their diet, finding protein in prey from insects such as grasshoppers to reptiles and amphibians such as lizards, snakes and frogs. Genets also spot the easy pickings available around safari lodges, and have earned a bad name for devouring poultry stocks. Anyone travelling to Ndutu Lodge on the borders of the Serengeti stands a high chance of witnessing fine examples of genet agility, when the local cats scout the rafters of the restaurant for titbits left out for them.

African Civet, *Civettictis civetta*

The civet is larger than the genet. Its stocky, furry body resembles a raccoon, with long legs. Civets' colouring is paler grey, with black blotches and lines and very distinct black 'panda' eyes, which provide an easy means to recognize each other in the dark. They too prefer nocturnal foraging, but unlike the genet, which stalks and chases like a cat, the civet snuffles along using its highly developed sense of smell and hearing to unearth prey in their burrows, and then pounces. The musk extracted from captive civets is called 'civetone' and was once used to 'fix' the expensive fragrances in floral perfumes, although a chemical substitute is now more common.

Mongooses

As the name suggests, the **slender mongoose**, *Herpestes sanguineus,* is the thinnest and longest-bodied of the mongoose family, and most closely resembles a weasel. The coat is among the sleekest of its family. Colour varies depending on the habitat, with lighter brown shadings common in the open savannah and darker browns likely if the animal lives in forests; most though have red eyes and a black tip to their long, tapering tail. They move with a rippling motion, and are able to shin up and down trees with squirrel-like prowess, but spend as much time on the ground, where they are able to stand on their hind legs and watch over long grass for prey or predators. The slender mongoose is an especially playful species, keen on pretend stalking and picking up eggs and objects and throwing them against rocks. They also chase and play with squirrels, monkeys and hyraxes, apparently simply for the sake of it.

Another mongoose common in Tanzania is the **ichneumon**, **grey** or **Egyptian mongoose**, *Herpestes ichneumon*, a rather fatter version of the slender mongoose, whose name derives from the Greek word meaning 'tracker'. These mongooses are far more sociable than their slender cousins, especially when food is abundant; they have a tendency to look after their offspring together, leaving the young with 'babysitters'.

Another large mongoose is the **white-tailed mongoose**, *Ichneumia albicauda*, with a fluffy white tail to distinguish it. It is rarely seen on safari, however, owing to its strict nocturnal habit of emerging a clear half-hour after sunset and disappearing before the sun rises.

More otter-like in appearance, the **marsh mongoose**, *Atilax paludinosus,* tends to spend its life in close proximity to water; its legs are much shorter and paws much broader as a result. It is supposedly nocturnal, but might be seen scouting about during daylight hours, seeking out the snails, crabs and fish that distinguish its diet.

The most numerous of all in this group is the **dwarf mongoose**, *Helogale pavula*, a squirrel-sized carnivore with a taste for termites and tree-dwelling insects along with small birds and rodents. These most commonly seen mongooses are extremely sociable and tend to stay together in groups averaging about nine animals, sharing the upbringing of their young with an advanced degree of community spirit including suckling, playing with and foraging for others' offspring. They also have achieved an impressive rapport with a number of birds much larger than them, such as bush hornbills, and beat through the bush together finding food and sharing each other's predator responses.

The **banded mongoose,** *Mungos mungo,* favours even larger packs and is distinguished by the blackish bands along its grizzled grey-brown back. They are commonly seen in daylight, flowing along in packs looking for food – invertebrates, small reptiles and roots – or squatting on their hindquarters scouting for danger. While sociable within their pack, they will firmly defend their territory against others.

Cats; Family Felidae

Serval, *Felis serval*
Tall, slender and small with very long legs, the serval has spots on its legs and stripes on its back. It stalks mainly high grass areas and pounces on small prey like rodents, but with such quick reactions that it has been known to catch birds in mid-air.

Caracal, *Felis caracal*
The caracal has tufted, pointed ears and a plain, tawny, much bulkier body than the serval. It is most at home in arid bush. The size of its prey has been noted to increase in areas where there are few other competing carnivores – extending to include antelope such as impala and even young kudu – but more usually the caracal will eat smaller mammals such as monkeys, jackals and birds.

Leopard, *Panthera pardus*
The leopard (Swahili: *chui*) is one of the most elusive of the cats seen on safari, and yet is said to be one of the most ubiquitous worldwide after the domestic cat, despite being so threatened by hunters for its fantastically spotted coat. One reason is its rare stealth and ability to survive on a very varied protein diet ranging from beetles and birds to larger mammals such as wildebeest and zebras, so that it can cope in diverse conditions. They are essentially solitary cats, but mothers will reunite with their adult cubs after they have gone their separate ways, and they may share prey until the children are fully self-reliant. A leopard's innate feline skills enable it to stalk and ambush prey with sheer surprise tactics, creeping as close as possible before pouncing, and rarely chasing if the quarry escapes, although it is thought they can accelerate to up to 60kph. They prefer hunting at night, and spend most of the day languishing in the dappled light of trees, where they can be impressively camouflaged even at a very close distance. Trees provide a fine hiding place from other predators, especially other cats that lack their climbing agility and hyenas, who will otherwise attempt to steal the leopard's kill. Leopards commonly drag even quite large prey into a nook in a tree to consume over time.

There is a Muslim belief that cats can take food from your hand and be thinking how to kill you at the same time. This is true of no cat more than the leopard, renowned for its unpredictability, for turning on and killing handlers. They have very little bond with one another, preferring to lead solo lives, and unrelated adults are rarely seen together. The leopard is living proof that beauty runs only skin-deep!

Masters of camouflage and concealment, leopards are definitely the most efficient hunters in Africa. You can stand inches above them and know they are there, yet still be unable to see them. They know, intimately, every bush, gully, hill, cave, hole, dip in the ground, riverbed – every square inch of their small territory – giving them full advantage over intruders or prey. They appear, and disappear, like magic, and they know how to move over difficult terrain with absolute stealth and silence. You can live among them oblivious to their presence. This mysterious and breathtakingly beautiful animal is the single most sought-after animal in all Africa, by hunters and tourists alike. All want to possess it, either in trophy or in photograph; few can just watch and leave the experience to memory.

Lion, *Panthera leo*

The lion (Swahili: *simba*) is the largest African carnivore and again used to be far more numerous before the effects of hunting greatly reduced the lion population across the continent. Yet lions continue to thrive in good natural conditions, despite the unusual evolutionary twist that has led the male lion to require so impressive a mane and stature to attract a mating partner that he has forfeited his abilities to hunt – leaving the hardest work to the females. Lions tend to be more sociable with the same sex, and make lifelong companions – particularly mothers and daughters – although males that leave their pride together will often remain together. Males have just a few good years of sexual prowess in which they may lead a pride, peaking between the years of five and six but potentially continuing until they are about nine, and after this time they are ousted by another, younger competitor. The newcomer will then attempt to catch and kill any cubs under a year old, which allows the mothers to mate again within a few days, although it takes much longer for them to actually become fertile again. Lionesses tend to nurture cubs at the same time, raising their cubs cooperatively. They hunt most productively as a pack and stalk their prey until as close as possible before chasing for a short distance, while the males tend to wait until the quarry is killed before demanding the first bite. All lions spend an average of 20 hours each day resting, and when the time is right for copulation enjoy four days at an average of 2.2 times each hour, although the male might increase his abilities to 3.5 times each hour if he is with two different females. A female will accept any male when she is ready to mate, but she is a formidable partner, and continually snarls and snaps throughout.

Cheetah, *Acinonyx jubatus*

Cheetahs (Swahili: *duma*) are lithe and light with long, thin legs, a spotted coat and a small, flat face with distinctive 'tear-stains' around and beneath the eyes. They are not only the fastest cat but the fastest mammal, reaching a top speed of between 90 and 112kph, and are therefore able to prey on the quickest antelope, or in times of need a speedy hare. But the effort of speed has a depleting effect on stamina, and if a chase fails the cat must rest for at least half an hour before attempting again. Cheetahs particularly favour daytime hunting, and prefer open savannahs with grassy cover from which to watch and stalk their prey, such as the plains of the Serengeti.

They are mainly solitary; after a mother and cub divide they seldom reunite, though they may keep overlapping territories. The more delicate frame of a cheetah compared to the other large cats reflects a similar difference in disposition; they tend to steer clear of other predators, who frequently steal their prey, and aim to remain as inconspicuous as possible. The hundreds of wildlife films on plain-dwelling cheetah belie the fact that they are just as comfortable in woodland. Their very specialized way of hunting, the fact that, unlike leopard and lion, they don't scavenge, and the frequency with which they are chased off their kills by a multitude of other stronger predators, all combine to limit the numbers of cheetah a habitat can sustain.

Hyena and Aardwolf; Family Hyaenidae

Hyenas (Swahili: *fisi*) are medium-sized, dog-like carnivores with unusually large heads for their sloping bodies. They are able to digest the skin and bones of prey and regurgitate balls of undigested hair, like an owl, making them natural scavengers, although they will kill too. The **spotted hyena**, *Crocuta crocuta,* is the most common, largest member of its family, and the most able to kill and eat larger prey, while the more solitary **striped hyena**, *Hyaena hyaena,* will settle for more scraps and the **brown hyena** is somewhere in the middle. Hyenas hunt and kill effectively in a pack. They may shake their prey to death or bite indiscriminately to end its life. Hyena can be aggressive enough to rob leopards and cheetahs of their prey, but tend to wait a while before approaching feeding lion.

Aardwolf, *Proteles cristatus,* look like small striped hyenas, but dine on termites. They have evolved over time to obtain their protein in such a way as not to compete with the multitude of stronger predators. With an incredibly acute sense of hearing and using ears like radar they can hear the munching of harvester termites from up to 500m away and in a night they can consume more than 200,000 termites. Aardwolf have good sight and smell, but their specialized diet and small body size have cost them their ability to defend themselves: with no need to tear meat or crunch bone, their teeth are weak. For defence, aardwolf have evolved a long silky grey dorsal mane extending the full length of their body; they can erect part or all of it and, fully extended, the mane gives the illusion that the animal is 75 per cent bigger. They also bare their teeth, but they will run before they are challenged to fight. They are nocturnal, rarely appearing from their burrows before 10pm.

Foxes, Jackals and Dogs; Family Canidae

Bat-eared Fox, *Otocyon megalotis*

The bat-eared fox is easily recognized by its bat-like ears, which are also essential to its survival. The foxes mostly eat scorpions and beetle larvae, putting their big ears to the ground and listening for movement underground, before tapping with their paws. This tapping tricks insects into thinking that it is raining, so that they crawl up to the surface into the waiting jaws of the cunning old fox!

Jackal, *Canis spp.*

There are three kinds of jackal in East Africa, all scavenging fox-like animals which will also hunt insects, rodents and even small gazelles and supplement their diet with wild fruit. The **golden jackal**, *Canis aureus*, is the most common carnivore seen in open savannah, despite its name often tending to a silvery-grey colour. The **silver-backed** jackal, *Canis mesomelas*, a night scavenger, and the **side-striped jackal**, *Canis adustus*, are less commonly seen. All jackals form pair bonds. The female gives birth to up to four cubs, and a female cub of the previous litter may remain with her mother to help raise the next. If she does, they can bring twice the number of young to adulthood.

Wild Dog, or African Hunting Dog, *Lycaon pictus*

Wild dogs share a similar social structure with dwarf mongoose. A female and male will meet and bond and then beat their respective siblings into submission. Only the 'alpha' male and female will breed; the rest will have subservient roles raising the young and finding food. The alpha female will kill any offspring from other females should they disobey these rules. It is said that the alpha female will pine and starve herself to death if the alpha male loses interest. It is a sad sight to watch her waste away as siblings and offspring try to feed, groom and encourage her not to give up.

Hunting dogs, which can be recognized by their 'painted' coats, are most active in the evenings, when they wake up to ritual territory marking and play-fighting. The dogs run, fan out, stop to listen, run again in perfect formation, each instinctively picking up the intentions of the others. When they see, hear, or pick up the scent of prey, they sweep through the area, spreading pandemonium before them, hooting to maintain contact with each other. Never will you see such panic: antelope will throw themselves off cliffs into crocodile-infested torrents just to get away; they will not stop running, such is the fear of wild dogs. When the dogs catch something, they rip it apart and eat it in seconds, carrying meat in their stomachs and regurgitating it later to feed other members of the pack. In the confusion of the hunt, they often lose each other and are chased off their prey before other dogs have had a chance to catch up. They literally wolf the meat down. Sometimes they even regurgitate meat to bury underground for later.

When they mate and give birth, known as 'denning', the dogs' range becomes more limited, and consequently they can be easier to find. There will always be 'nannies' left behind to take care of the pups while the others are out hunting. They often hunt by the light of the full moon.

Primates

In the great order of primates there are at least 185 species, divided into 11 different families. The four main divisions within the order include prosimians, said to be 'almost monkeys', such as the bushbaby or galago, new world monkeys, old world monkeys and hominoids, which include apes and humans.

Bushbabies; Family Lorisinae

Bushbabies, also called **galago**, are small primates with big claws on the end of agile insect-catching hands. They have wide eyes facing forwards and bat-like ears, and range from 12–40cm in size depending on the type. Bushbabies tend to sleep curled up in nest groups by day but forage alone at night, and call to each other with such high frequency that the sound can carry over 250m. While the different species of bushbabies have individual sounds, they all share the same squeak of distress, which brings others to the rescue – but also alerts predators to their plight. When not in distress, they can cover 4–5m in a single long-jump, and prepare for such a feat by rotating their heads a full 180 degrees to check all angles first. The species you are most likely to come across in Tanzania are the **lesser bushbaby**, *Galago senegalensis*, **greater bushbaby**, *Otolemur crassicaudatus*, and **Zanzibari bushbaby**, *Galago zanzibaricus* – particularly at Manta Reef Lodge on the northernmost tip of Pemba Island.

Old World Monkeys; Family Cercopithecidae

Blue or Sykes Monkey, *Cercopithecus mitis*

This forest-dweller is more common in southern Africa but can be found in areas of Tanzania such as around Kilimanjaro and in the Udzungwa Mountains. It is a big, chunky monkey with a bluish-black coat, silvery tufty ears and a monobrow over very close amber eyes, although the same species on Mount Kenya has a redder coat and white collar. The monkey eats a forest diet of berries and fruit, supplemented with birds' eggs and insects, and steers clear of direct sunlight whenever it can.

Vervet Monkey, *Cercopithecus aethiops*

The vervet monkey is a more common sight, its slender, agile form distinguished by a black face with a furry white 'eskimo' hood and an olive-grey body with a long, thin tail dipped in black at the tip. They are gregarious, living in groups of between 10 and 50 or more, and communicating loudly among themselves. Babies attract the attention of other females for long sessions of playing, grooming and cuddling. A broad, omnivorous diet leads them to take advantage of whatever may be found, and this, along with their prolific distribution, has made them a crop pest, like their cousin the **savannah baboon**, *Papio cynocephalus*, a huge ground-dwelling monkey with a pointed dog-like snout and sharp pointed teeth. Of the four sub-species of baboon the **yellow baboon**, *Papio cynocephalus cynocephalus*, is most commonly seen in Tanzania. A slighter example of its species, with close-set amber eyes and pinkish eyelids – one of the most expressive forms of communication after vocalization – they are highly sensitive and able to communicate subtle mood-swings. They look out for those with whom they may have distinct social bonds, even to the extent of fostering children of their close associates when required. Baboons also practise advanced methods to ensure survival of the fittest – while only the alpha male may mate with females during the peak of their cycle, the rest are free to have a go at any other time.

Colobus Monkeys, *Colobus guereza* or *angolensis*

Two species of colobus monkey are found in Tanzania. The reddish coloured **eastern colobus**, *Colobus guereza*, is found in the north of the country, and the black and white **western colobus**, *Colobus angolensis*, is more common in coastal regions. With their flowing white manes and fleece-tipped tails, colobus monkeys look and act as if they are the most regal of species, and behave with considered deliberation and concentration in their branch-focused world. Their days follow a distinctly relaxed pattern: they usually leave their sleeping nests around dawn and climb to the highest tree-tops to greet the morning and any other passing troops. After an hour or so of sociable grooming they move back down towards food. Their agility in the trees is impressive, especially jumps to distant lower branches, which may cover drops of up to 15m to avoid predators, but they are not as happy on the ground. Their numbers have dropped dramatically with along with deforestation across the continent.

Chimpanzees, Pan troglodytes; Family Pongidae

Chimpanzees are the most humanoid of the hominoids – our closest relations – and among the smallest of the great apes, reaching an average of about 150cm high. They are the most vocal of all the primates, very territorial and at home up a tree or on the ground. They build a new nest each night. The amazing research of the Jane Goodall Research Institute at Gombe Stream (*see* p.266) has demonstrated how chimpanzees use tools to fish for insects, to eat, and to clean themselves, as well as using certain leaves for medicines. They often stand on two feet in order to survey their surroundings and walk short distances, but never far before pushing off with knuckles again, in their more habitual four-legged gait. To most observers' surprise, chimpanzees supplement their normal diet of leaves, gruit and termites by hunting, in a slightly opportunistic manner – such as stealing piglets and running up trees with them.

Insects

Termites

Tiny termites make their presence known across the landscape by gathering in vast colonies, all strictly governed by a hierarchical order headed by a queen, then a king, followed by soldiers and workers. Inside the mound, which is constructed from whatever soil is available in that region, a complicated maze of pathways, tunnels, and 'fungus gardens' provides a diverse living space and regulates the temperature of their food stores.

Termite mounds have been likened to big cities, with more than three million inhabitants in each, living very closely together in perfectly synchronized harmony. The temperature and humidity of each 'city' is precisely regulated through a system of ventilation shafts, and with water carried up by individual termites from wells, which are sometimes hundreds of feet underground. They cultivate and irrigate a fungus in special chambers, which is tended to by workers. They can live off this fungus, which grows on their excrement, for up to two months until the 'recycled' effect of the fungus becomes too toxic. Considering the fact that half of annual plant growth is eaten by ungulates such as buffalo, and the other half by termites, one can imagine the effects on the termite population of bush-fires, which rage through vast areas every dry season. Even when the flames of these fires lick against its walls, the temperature and humidity inside the 'city' remain exactly the same; and although the food supply outside is cut off, inside the 'city' walls it's business as usual.

Inside one chamber lives the huge, fat, bloated and pulsating queen, and, beside her, a smaller king. She is fed and cleaned by workers, and it is with the food carried to her by each worker, and through chemical secretions collected by workers from her abdomen, that she receives and sends the information needed to regulate her 'city'. She lays 30,000 eggs a day, each egg individually carried, by workers, to special 'nursery' chambers which are tended by more workers. From the information fed to her she knows, and regulates by birth, the proportion of her subjects – which are to be workers, soldiers, or future kings and queens.

The soldiers exist to protect the city and its inhabitants, defending the city from invaders and escorting the foraging parties out of the city. They travel through subterranean tunnels, which radiate out from the city to places where there is food. No worker is allowed to return empty-handed, so they must return to the 'city' with food, or die in the process. Each soldier is armed with a large pair of pincers, and on its forehead is a spray nozzle to squirt out a noxious poison. If the foraging party is attacked, the workers flee into tunnels, and are quickly reinforced by more soldiers. Where the threat is big, such as an aardwolf, aardvark or pangolin, which can eat up to 200,000 termites a night, the soldiers use the spray in their nozzles. Soon the taste of termites becomes unpalatable, and the predator moves away. They use their pincers to fight off the warlike **matabele ants**, which raid the city at the same time every day and carry off more than 6,000 termites in one raid.

There is one time in the year that millions of workers and soldiers break through the city walls, to remove every blade of grass from the outer surface, and polish it smooth. Then, usually at night, and just after rain, when it is humid and cool outside, a remarkable event occurs. All of the city's 20,000 virgins (both male and female reproducers, known as allates), with their very delicate shiny wings, take to the air on a journey that, for them, will never again repeat itself. Their wings will break off soon after they land, and many will die; but a few, perhaps even only two, will find each other, and burrow underground, to live together side by side as king and queen and a new city will be born, one that may last another twenty years.

Termites are often also called 'white ants', but are more closely related to cockroaches; their nutritional value is widely appreciated by humans and wildlife alike.

Safaris and Beaches

Safaris

'Safari' is a Swahili word that evolved from the Arabic *safariya*, meaning a voyage or expedition. Although it is used to describe the undertaking of a journey of any kind, for most people these days the word has one specific meaning: travelling to watch wildlife in the African bush, for sheer interest and enjoyment. The main attraction of the vast protected reaches of the Tanzanian safari landscape is its wild nature: each day sees animal instinct focused entirely on survival, life reduced to its most basic impulses – the absolutes of killing, feeding and reproduction. Yet there is no guarantee that a safari-goer will experience this raw life. Spotting different animals and birds is a matter of diligence, some knowledge of their preferred habitats – and luck; often your most breathtaking moments will be the least expected. An entire afternoon might be spent searching for a glimpse of a leopard, to find instead a vision of migrating wildebeest and zebra jostling for precious, dangerous minutes at a crocodile-infested waterhole, or a herd of impala poised like dancers in a sunlit glade. One enduring truth of safaris – whether you are a novice or an old-timer, or even if you spend every day of the year guiding people through the passions and pathways of the bush – is that every safari is different. Each venture into the bush brings new experiences, sights, sounds and smells, and always the possibility that you may be in the right place at the right time to witness something marvellous.

The History of Safaris

The word 'safari' was introduced into English by the 19th-century explorer and linguist Sir Richard Francis Burton, who was fluent in 29 languages including Arabic and Swahili. In his day safaris meant dangerous expeditions into the African interior, to plunder ivory and slaves for trade or to go on hunting sprees. But changing attitudes over the past 200 years have irrevocably altered the definition of safari. Now the images conjured by the word, aside from khaki cotton suits with pockets, are of trips into the African bush to see animals in the wild. Safaris are now focused on conservation not on conquest, except for the capture of wildlife on film.

The change in attitude began in the late 19th century, in the era of the first expeditions undertaken by international geographers, naturalists (Birchell, Harry Johnston), and hunters (Cornwallis Harris, Frederick Courtney Selous), who began to realize the need for conservation of African wildlife. East Africa became the focal point for such safaris, not least because the southern African wildlife had suffered such decimation at the hands of early hunters. Around this time too, more people began to travel for travel's sake, to feed their curiosity and need for adventure, inspired by the writings and information filtering back from the African continent. Some of the greatest proponents of adventurous travel at this time were women. Among those who demonstrated notable spirit were the flamboyant feminist American Mary French Sheldon, who single-handedly ran a 150-porter trek from Zanzibar to Kilimanjaro in 1891, and the impressive Mary Hall, who made a successful trek from Cape Town to Cairo at 50. (Mary French Sheldon published a revealing, still-readable account of her trip: *Sultan to Sultan: Adventures among the Maasai and other tribes of East Africa*.)

If you count all of its national parks, game reserves, conservation areas and marine parks, Tanzania has set aside over a third of its overall landmass for conservation protection. It is an impressive expanse: the Serengeti alone, just one of the national parks, is 7,000 square kilometres – comparable in size to Wales, Belgium or the state of Ohio; the Selous Game Reserve – one-fifth of Tanzania's territory – encompasses a greater region for conservation than any other in Africa. From east to west and south to north, the landscapes and ecosystems vary dramatically within the different conservation areas to provide an Incredible range of possible safaris.

Organizing a Safari

Safaris are expensive: air fares into Tanzania, transport around the country, accommodation, national park fees and guides' salaries, taking in food and equipment – all add up to a high minimum. Any extended trip into the wilderness of the African bush is a costly venture, but over the last 10 years it has become less so, as the safari market has developed different levels to suit differing budgets. A greater range of choice and style has become available, from fly-in opulence to simple budget camping, with operators appealing to widely different tastes. The methods and means of safari travel have diversified too, so that you can choose to watch wildlife

However, as writings and news of the African colonies and protectorates drifted back to Europe and America, hunting safaris developed a glamorous appeal once more. They remained the widely reported fun of the rich and famous, of film stars, aristocrats, the monarchy, or any millionaire. Theodore Roosevelt's safari in 1909 – during which an estimated 5,000 animals, including nine white rhinos (which were already virtually extinct), 4,000 birds, 500 fish and 2,000 reptiles were also killed – became one of the most famous African safaris in history, especially after Roosevelt's own account of the trip, *African Game Trails*, was published in 1910. This popular jaunt cost £15,000, and no doubt others succeeded in spending even more.

At the turn of the 20th century any safari into the bush required hundreds of porters to carry a vast cargo of goods for elaborate camping, every single item carried on foot. Even the white 'masters' would frequently be carried, borne between the shoulders of four men on a palanquin, a shady canvas 'box' contrived to rest on two long poles. The safari industry was born in those days, existing solely to cater to the demands of high-rolling and demanding adventurers. The invention of the motor car in the early 20th century considerably reduced the cost of such East African adventures, and hunting as the primary aim of safari was gradually superseded by a greater interest in wildlife and travel. Other modes of transport also became popular, including hot air balloons, following the Boyce Balloonograph Expedition of 1909, masterminded by a Chicago newspaper. The newly possible photographic safaris were well publicized by Martin and Osa Johnson when they embarked on a five-year film trip in the 1920s, funded by George Eastman of Eastman-Kodak. The African wildlife safari was fast developing an ever-closer association with conservation.

from a specially adapted safari vehicle, a balloon, a boat, a horse or, in the tradition of old, close-up and personal – on foot. Itineraries suitable for all budgets and ambitions are available. The key is in preparation, and in choosing the right combination.

There are basically two ways of organizing your safari. The first is to arrange the whole thing through a tour operator before you leave your own country (*see* **Travel** for a list of UK and US tour operators). This is by far the easiest way – your operator will arrange everything for you, saving you time and hassle once you arrive in Tanzania – and should cost no more than arranging the safari direct with an operator or lodge in Tanzania, since all operators take their cut from the lodges directly. Alternatively, you can arrange your own transport to Tanzania, and organize your safari through a local operator once you get there, which can be cheaper, at the bottom end of the market – especially if you join a 'set-date departure' trip where the operator is looking to fill the last space. It is quite difficult to organize an entirely independent safari, whatever your resistance to organized travel: it requires a lot of planning, and can easily end up costing more. If you leave the preparation to an experienced operator, you need only worry about spotting the animals and loading your camera film.

Most people trying to arrange a safari on arrival will end up doing it from Arusha, the main base for the more accessible Northern Circuit, or from Moshi, Mwanza or even Dar es Salaam. The southern and western parks are far more difficult to get to without prior planning. If arranging your safari trip from Arusha, you are likely to be besieged by local tour operators offering you deals (*see* pp.122–4 for Arusha operators). When selecting your safari, err on the side of caution and don't necessarily go for the cheapest deal. Choose a company with a well-established office and find out exactly what the price quoted includes: it should cover a vehicle with driver and guide, fuel, accommodation, camping equipment, camping and park entrance fees, and meals. The details – what kind of vehicle you travel in, how many people are in your group, whether you stay in a national park or just outside it – can all affect your experience considerably; if there is any way you can afford to spend a little more to travel in a Land Rover with fewer people and stay in better locations, for example, it will be well worthwhile. There will inevitably be an element of compromise in most people's planning, but try to decide what price bracket you come under and then go for the best within it – you're better off with top-end fly-camping than with a bottom-end lodge-based safari travelling in a minibus with strangers.

Transport Options

Driving Safaris

If you are travelling as a couple or in a small group, the ideal option is a **private safari** with your own driver-guide. This allows each person a decent window seat, and the freedom to spend the day searching for or watching the wildlife of your choice at leisure. Your itinerary can be tailor-made to include any combination of accommodation in lodges and camping alternatives you prefer.

If you are travelling alone, or if you wish to experience luxury tented camping (*see* p.63), which may be prohibitively expensive if there are just one or two of you, then consider a **set-date departure safari**, in which you join up with a group on a pre-determined itinerary. These may be in a convoy of Land Rovers, which is preferable, or, more likely, in a minibus. The latter can provide a level of air-conditioned comfort, and it costs around a third less per person to go in a group of four or more, but the downside is an irritating lack of freedom. A photographer keen to capture every quiver of a sleeping lion's ears at dawn, a twitcher who prefers to stop and identify every coloured wing or a family with young children can cause friction among a group with mixed ambitions for their trip. The minibus option feels more like a package tour, and less like a wilderness experience.

Independent Self-drive Safaris

A minority prefer to go it alone, especially those who have their own 4x4 vehicle in the country, as car hire tends to be expensive (*see* **Travel** for details). The advent of well-appointed lodges in the distant reaches of the parks and reserves has made independent self-drive safaris a more viable option, but there are still major drawbacks: life on the African continent, and significantly in Tanzania, is a far cry from the developed western world. Vast areas remain almost entirely in their wild and natural state. Roads are often dirt tracks, and as such are frequently churned into terribly rutted and occasionally undriveable routes after the rains in April and May; even vehicle owners may find it beneficial to take a local guide on board for the first few days' driving in order to get to know the roads at a particular time of year. Drivers should equip themselves with a fully prepared 4x4 vehicle – punctures are a common occurrence, as are breakdowns as a result of wear and tear – and before taking to the dirt tracks may also need basic training in how to handle skids, dust clouds, wandering animals, thundering trucks and so on. There are few good maps of the parks: some have been spotted in the hands of park rangers, but these are not usually accessible to casual tourists. International border crossings may not be passable to tourists, even if they are marked on maps (currently the case for the Tanzania–Kenya crossing at the Bologonja Gate between the Serengeti and Maasai Mara). Communications are frequently difficult, relying on often unreliable radio frequencies. Petrol is a limited resource in the northern parks: drivers should carry their own supplies and not rely on the pumps in remote regions being stocked.

The easiest (or least problematic) regions for independent or self-drive safaris include **Mikumi National Park** (*see* pp.288–9), a half-day journey from Dar es Salaam on the well-surfaced Tanzam highway, and **Arusha National Park** (*see* pp.113–16), a half-hour drive from Arusha town centre. Both of these provide a wild environment and 'soft' safari experience, with plenty of wildlife (although these parks are not ideal for spotting predators) and excellent scenery. Each has good accommodation and campsites. **Lake Manyara National Park** (*see* pp.126–30) and **Tarangire National Park** (*see* pp.147–50) are easy to navigate and less difficult to manage than the Serengeti.

Down south, **Ruaha National Park** (*see* pp.298–303) is still open to self-drive travellers, although there is a move to stop this, as petrol is scarce, the roads can be bad and there have been problems. It is also possible to drive to lodges in the **Selous Game Reserve** (*see* pp.279–87), although these roads really are bad, and it is presently only accessible from the eastern, coastal route (estimate more than 7hrs' drive from

Dar es Salaam), as the road from Mikumi remains impassable under an unfulfilled promise of renewal. Driving into these last two parks is entirely at the driver's risk, and is generally not encouraged by the lodges in each park. If you are determined to drive in, it is often worthwhile to park up for the duration of your stay and join safari expeditions with local guides. You can also drive to the park gates of the new **Udzungwa National Park** (*see* pp.290–94), but, as there are no driving routes at all within this conservation region, you will then have to get out and walk and climb!

Fly-in Safaris

This option allows you to fly directly to the distant reaches of a park and be met by a private driver-guide, attached either to a tour company or to the lodge at which you are staying. This option is useful to those who are restricted by time limitations or who may find the long drives uncomfortable. Alternatively, you can complete half of the driving circuit and then fly out. Fly-in is more developed in the **southern parks**, where many lodges are really only accessible by air, though in the northern circuit Coastal and Regional Air's scheduled flights and the advent of certain lodges (e.g. CC Africa, Elewana, Sanctuary) running their own safari vehicles with driver-guides has opened up new possibilities. A fly-in (and/or fly-out) private safari with your choice of camping or lodge accommodation can be arranged with most tour operators.

Boating Safaris

Boating safaris are mainly available in the **Selous Game Reserve** (*see* pp.279–87). The pace is gentle and allows for a close-up view of riverine wildlife and birds. The river attracts all kinds of colourful, long-legged or fast-diving water birds; there are grunting hippos and stealthy crocodiles, and you may see other animals, such as elephants, buffalo, giraffes and occasionally lions, in the lush greenery at the water's edge. Boats are generally simple, flat-bottomed aluminium motor boats with a sunshade, just large enough for a couple of couples, a boatman and guide. Not only do the waterways of the Selous provide the best environment for boating safaris, but the better lodges here are adept at organizing picnic breakfasts or sundowners on the beaches and banks, and may equip the boats with fishing lines if required. These same operators can also organize fly-camping excursions to distant locations only accessible by boat. Camping costs more than the price of a room due to the extra staff and organization required, but all forms of safari transport, including boat trips, are included in the price of the accommodation.

Boat safaris are also just becoming a viable option at **Saadani Game Reserve** (*see* pp.199–200), on the coast north of Dar es Salaam and Bagamoyo. Although not quite as adventurous or as rich in animal life as the Selous, boat safaris in Saadani are a fun means of game-viewing, highlighted by flocks of thousands of vibrant pink flamingos. Other watery adventures on boats can be arranged through the ocean-like waters of Lake Victoria that surround **Rubondo Island National Park** (*see* pp.156–8), where crocodiles and hippopotami reside, but the birds, especially cormorants and fish eagles, are a more evident attraction. There are also boating possibilities on the waters of Lake Tanganyika from **Mahale Mountains National Park** (*see* pp.268–71).

Walking Safaris

Tanzania's rolling unspoilt landscapes provide plenty of opportunities to get even closer to the raw nature of sky and sun and earth and bush on a walking safari. Casual walking safaris – an hour, a morning, or a full day with a picnic – are worthwhile for all ages and abilities, even for those who regard walking as a curse suffered by those without a car. Exploring on foot affords a chance to sense the smaller details and aromatic freshness of the landscape at a more relaxed pace, and to feel yourself in sharp perspective and proportion to the surrounding wildlife, as they scent your presence on the wind and flee in alarm or simply turn and watch. Walking safaris accompanied by an armed ranger are always on the agenda in the **southern parks and reserves**, where rules are less stringent than in the north. Walking is the only means of transport in **Udzungwa National Park** (*see* pp.290–94), **Mahale Mountains National Park** (*see* pp.268–71) and **Rubondo Island National Park** (*see* pp.156–8), although you can also take boat trips around Mahale (Lake Tanganyika) and Rubondo (Lake Victoria). Foot safaris are one of the attractions of the Selous and Ruaha.

Northern Circuit rules prohibit walking within the national park boundaries. Nevertheless there are plenty of opportunities to explore the landscape just beyond the parks. Good tour operators specializing in walking and camping trips can organize superb 'off the beaten track' hikes though absolutely unspoilt landscapes. Arusha-based safari operators take hiking expeditions as far as Mount Hanang or the regions around Ngorongoro, and also arrange superb walking and camping safaris across the wildly beautiful and sparsely populated reaches of the Maasai plains, and in the realms of the Hadzabe or Hadzapi hunter-gatherers around Lake Eyasi. Walks around the smaller craters and rolling highlands of the Ngorongoro Conservation Area, where the national park rules do not apply, are very rewarding (although no walking is allowed inside Ngorongoro Crater, unless you are Maasai).

Kirurumu Tented Lodge (*see* p.127) and **Gibb's Farm** (*see* p.128), both between Lake Manyara and the Ngorongoro Conservation Area, have devised walking routes around their properties. Kirurumu specializes in 'ethno-botanic' or bird walks accompanied by a Maasai guide. Gibb's Farm walks lead you to caves though the forests around the Ngorongoro Highlands. **Tamarind Tented Camp** and **Tarangire Treetops** (*see* pp.148–9) both arrange guided walks in outlying bush around Tarangire National Park, and **Klein's Camp** (*see* p.147), just beyond the very northern reaches of the Serengeti, runs walking safaris through a private reserve (*see* pp.122–4 for northern tour operators).

Mountain Treks

Scenic mountain treks can be arranged in **Kilimanjaro National Park** (*see* pp.162–70) and to the peaks of **Mount Meru** in **Arusha National Park** (*see* pp.113–16): routes and details of climbs and walks on each are discussed at length in the relevant chapters. You can trek up the smaller but steeper volcanic cone of **Ol Doinyo Lengai** in the **Ngorongoro Conservation Area** (*see* p.130), or the least-visited, ninth-highest East African peak, the 'forgotten mountain' of **Mount Hanang** in **Babati Region** (*see* p.149).

The most recent national park in Tanzania is a ranging mountainous forest rich in indigenous wildlife, which remains largely undiscovered by tourists. **Udzungwa**

Mountains National Park (*see* pp.290–94) is a dream location for serious hikers seeking a challenging and yet more rewarding venture into the Tanzanian landscape The terrain can be hard going and demands quite intensive climbing at times, but views from the top and hidden waterfalls make all such efforts worthwhile. There is no accommodation inside the park, but there are a number of campsites that you will probably have to yourselves, and a decent, inexpensive lodge close to the park gates.

Wonderfully scenic walking opportunities requiring little or no pre-planning are abundant in the often less-visited rural mountain areas, such as the regions around the **Usambara Mountains** in the northwest (*see* pp.181–8), or the ranges around **Mbeya** in the far south (*see* pp.307–11). The picturesque towns and villages in the dramatic regions around **Lushoto** in the Usambaras can be visited in the course of a short stay in the area. Day walks or longer itineraries are easily devised on arrival with local guides from the Lushoto tourist information centre or through the tourist facilities provided in the surrounding old colonial lodges. There are numerous interesting focal points for walks in the **Mbeya**, **Uporoto** and **Livingstone Mountains** around Mbeya town, where these three ranges meet on an uncertain fault in the earth's crust and volcanoes, crater lakes and waterfalls punctuate the landscape.

Horse-riding and Camel Safaris

The terrible tsetse fly makes it difficult to keep domestic animals such as horses in many regions of Tanzania, but horses do thrive in the cooler mountainous regions around Arusha. A good centre is at **Uto Farm** on the slopes of **Mount Meru** (*see* 'Arusha', p.105). It is also possible to take an extended trek on a camel with Maasai guides from the camel village at **Mkuru**. Contact the Cultural Tourism Office in Arusha (*see* p.113).

Accommodation Options

Lodges

One alternative for accommodation is to stay in one of the many lodges dotted around the parks, especially in the north. Staying in lodges is the most popular option for fly-in safaris, the obvious advantages being a roof over your head, restaurant food, comfort and ease; the equally obvious disadvantages are that you are a step away from nature and you share your stay with other tours. It can, however, be cheaper to stay in a lodge than in a tent! The **northern parks** are the fiefdoms of four major hotel chains, all specializing in safari lodges that are easily characterized and fall into distinct price brackets. At the top end, **Conservation Corporation Africa**, a South African company, runs stylish lodges that charge around $600 per person per night all-inclusive. The **Serena** chain specializes in individual, eco-friendly, locally designed lodges too, and charges around half the price of CCA. The **Sopa** chain was built in the 1980s with a nostalgia for the 1970s that shows in the style of its lodges, which cost slightly less than the Serenas. The formerly government-owned **TAHI Wildlife** lodges were always rather spartan, despite occupying, more often than not, the best settings. However, they have been privatized and are now enjoying a renaissance under the care of Hotels and Lodges, the management company. To date, the consensus is that little has changed. Tour operators often have special rates and arrangements that can result in minimal price differences over a seven-day itinerary, and you will find that any one operator may deal exclusively with one hotel chain (*see* pp.121–2 for details of the chains, and individual parks for lodges). There are also a handful of extremely good small **independent lodges dotted** around the circuit, with more individual character and design. There is little choice in the western parks.

Camping Trips

For many, the ultimate safari experience is the incomparable situation of being under canvas in the wild seclusion of the bush at dusk and dawn. Camping trips also afford the freedom to mix and match possibilities, combining a couple of nights' camping with other nights elsewhere. The choice for tented accommodation ranges from the luxurious, all-mod-cons **permanent tented camps**, through slightly less extravagant **semi-permanent tented campsites** in secluded locations to the ultimate camping experience, a **mobile camp** that sets up in a different place each night.

At the top end of the mobile camping scale is **luxury tented camping** at private campsites, in vast canvas 'beach and bush' tents, large enough to stand up comfortably inside (about 3m high) – and accommodate good-sized wooden beds with proper mattresses while leaving enough space to manoeuvre around the sides. Each tent has its own shower and toilet facilities at the back; water for washing and showering is poured into vast containers rigged up behind the tent. A separate dining tent can be opened at either end or entirely opened out; this will house a long table laden with bush cuisine prepared in a separate kitchen tent. The standards and prices of luxury (or special) tented camping trips vary; allow $400–500 per person per night.

Adventure or **standard camping** is slightly less expensive, with lighter, smaller tents, camp cots rather than full-sized wooden beds, and washing facilities in smaller separate tents, either private or shared. There will be a separate kitchen and dining tent, with less smart wooden furniture and accessories. There will still, however, be camp staff, cook and bottle-washer. Adventure camping is a fine alternative, suitable for those who still wish to adventure in comfort and style. The price per person per night is generally in the region of $200–300, again decreasing if the party is larger.

More adventurous camping trips are available for budget travellers, who tend to find themselves more at one with the bush than those who pay for greater luxury. The least expensive form in the north is **fly-camping**, under lightweight fly tents which act as a simple canvas shade over a low camp bed. A camp cook will generally prepare the food outdoors over a lightweight African cooking stove, and meals are enjoyed around an easy folding table under the stars. Fly-camping is less expensive, usually around $150 per person per night, as less equipment and fewer porters, cooks and other staff are needed to join you on your jaunt to the distant reaches of the bush or plains. It is also possible to arrange very adventurous fly-camping excursions from the better lodges in the Selous, but these have reached a very high premium.

Campsites

Whether you go for organized luxury or spartan independence, the regulations governing campsites are the same: it is forbidden to pitch camp anywhere other than designated camping grounds. Spaces are best reserved in advance, as they are often completely booked up during the busy seasons, especially in the private sites. There is an extra charge for camping on top of the daily park fee, generally $25 per night for public sites, $50 for private sites. **Public campsites** have rudimentary, often not very pleasant facilities, and are open to everyone: often you will share the space with an overland truck. A private campsite is reserved for your group only, and can be hard to distinguish from the surrounding bush. **Private campsites** have no facilities: campers must bring everything they need, including water. All safari-goers, independent or guided, should adhere to conservation and preservation rules as laid down by each park and region (*see* 'The Parks', below); a more complete instruction is available at each park gate when you pay your entry fees. A popular conservationists' rule applies to all, and that is to 'take only photographs, and leave only footprints'.

The Parks

Northern Circuit Safaris

See pp.117–50 for full description and listings.

Safaris in the north of Tanzania are distinct from any other because of the range and variety of national parks and conservation areas in relative proximity. These are all accessible on a driving route with very long distances, averaging four hours, between each safari centre, linking some of the most renowned and important conservation areas in the world, including the **Serengeti**, **Lake Manyara** and **Tarangire** national parks and the rolling highlands and craters of the **Ngorongoro Conservation Area**.

The rules for the northern parks decree that all vehicles must be closed-sided, although vehicles with sunroofs and pop-top Land Rovers are allowed and are the most popular choice of transport. The three national parks prohibit any walking within the park boundaries. It is possible to trek and walk within the Ngorongoro Conservation Area (though not in the crater) and at some camps situated just beyond the boundaries of the national parks. In the near future it is possible that the government will bend to the pressure of the hotel chains in the north, and allow walking safaris, as well as night drives. The debate continues, since conservationists and anti-poaching experts argue this could be detrimental (*see* 'Walking Safaris' p.61).

Mobile safari itineraries in the north usually include a combination of some or all of the Northern Circuit parks and reserves, often beginning and ending in Arusha and incorporating one or more nights in each area. The distances between each park and lodge are often a good morning's or afternoon's drive. A rough idea of the timings:

Arusha to Manyara	2 hours
Manyara to Ngorongoro	2 hours
Ngorongoro to Seronera (with excellent game-viewing in the Serengeti, and a detour to Olduvai Gorge)	4–5 hours

Seronera to Grumeti River and the Western Corridor	3 hours
Seronera to the Lobo region	3–4 hours
Manyara to Tarangire	2–3 hours

Most Northern Circuit safaris are heavily vehicle-based, requiring perhaps six or seven days on the road, so the choice of vehicle (usually between a Land Rover or Land Cruiser or a 4x4 minibus, all open-topped) is of great importance. That choice may be made for you according to the kind of safari you select (see 'Driving Safaris', pp.58–9).

Fly-in safaris in the Northern Circuit are limited to the particular camps that have developed their own game-viewing facilities. These follow the example of the top-of-the-range flying circuit offered by the South African-based hotel chain Conservation Corporation Africa (CCA), which runs immaculate, stylish and individual safari lodges in the northern and western reaches of the Serengeti, Lake Manyara and the Ngorongoro Crater, as well as a resort on Mnemba Island, just off Zanzibar, all of which can be linked mainly by air. The safari properties all run their own vehicles and guests will probably share a guide among a small group, with the chance to return to their lodge for lunch. The Elewana and Sanctuary lodges have recently begun to provide their own vehicles and drivers to support fly-in safaris too.

Southern Highlands Safaris

See pp.273–312 for full description and listings.

The lodges and camps in the southern and western reaches of Tanzania are almost entirely small, independent, well-run and utterly reliant on fly-in safaris, as the driving routes in can be extremely tough. The real appeal of these parks is their extreme under-development, which guarantees an unspoilt wilderness experience even as their attractions become better known. The lodges that exist in these areas are too small to support the numbers that visit the north, and are situated at great enough distances from each other that safari vehicles' paths rarely cross. Their distant locations make these parks less touristy; beyond the Selous they become increasingly expensive to reach, but all the more worthwhile. It is national policy to encourage tourism in the southern parks, for revenue and to draw the crowds from the north as tourism in the country develops. It is felt that the Ministry of Natural Resources has a sufficiently strong mandate to ensure that tourism development is done thoughtfully and incrementally, so the joy of the southern parks should not be lost.

In the **Selous Game Reserve** (named after 'great white hunter' Frederick Courtney Selous and pronounced 'seloo') and **Ruaha National Park**, the individual lodges run their own specially adapted safari vehicles and employ their own drivers and guides, who generally have notable expertise and knowledge of their local area. These parks do not have such strict regulations regarding the nature of the vehicles, thus the lodges here tend to use vast open-sided vehicles with up to three long seats raised up behind the driver. This allows for an often exciting, breezy drive, with ample opportunities for photographs, and sometimes a slightly more sociable safari, as guests tend to group in three pairs for each excursion. But you are not stuck with the same group for days, and can choose the pace and nature of your game-viewing

Responsible Tourism

While tourism is widely seen as economically beneficial to Tanzania, as to other developing countries, there is increasing awareness worldwide that the benefits of tourism may not always reach local people. In general, it is unclear how much of the profit from tourism remains in tourist destination countries and 'trickles down' to local communities; a large proportion of the income generated by the industry remains in the hands of Western-based companies, a phenomenon known by development organizations as 'leakage' of profits. The World Bank has estimated that on average 55 per cent of what you spend on a holiday in a developing country returns to the West. Of the rest, most goes to people at the top of the business hierarchy. Tourism workers tend to be badly paid.

Tanzania is one of the world's poorest countries. Around half of the population lives below the poverty line, one in six children dies before the age of five, and almost one-third of the population will not live until the age of forty – the culmination of two decades of slow growth and under-investment in social services. Economic reform programmes have raised growth rates during the 1990s, winning praise from the IMF and World Bank; there is, however, little evidence of the benefits trickling down to the rural and urban poor. Like so many developing countries, Tanzania is plagued by debt. On a per capita basis, Tanzania spends nine times as much on debt servicing as on basic health, and four times as much on debt as on primary education – spending patterns inconsistent, in the eyes of many, with sustained recovery and human development. Although the country has undertaken one of the most far-reaching adjustment programmes in sub-Saharan Africa, including trade and exchange rate liberalization and privatization, it fails to qualify for Highly Indebted Poor Country (HIPC) debt relief schemes that might aid its full recovery.

In tourism, this economic situation translates into an inherent conflict between government aims and objectives and a desire to see the benefits of tourism trickle down. The Tanzanian Government's five-year plan for tourism seeks to encourage 'high yield, low volume tourism' – in other words to encourage fewer, wealthier tourists, who will bring in the cash direly needed by the country to pay off its debt. In one sense this is a good thing: the debt needs to be paid, investment is good and companies involved in providing upmarket facilities tend to be mindful of the need to provide high-quality, environmentally friendly facilities. But these companies also tend to be the foreign-owned ones, a larger proportion of whose profits is 'leaked' back to the West. They are also the companies most likely to bring in Western managers and staff, to offer Western cooking, and to import food supplies.

One approach to spreading the benefits of tourism more widely has been the development of 'community tourism' – often with the aid of international organizations and usually hand in hand with sustainable development schemes – which aim to involve local people. The benefits are two-fold: more of the income from tourism is channelled directly to local people or infrastructure projects, while tourists get a chance to be involved in the culture of the country they are visiting. The Netherlands Development Organization (SNV) in partnership with local people has initiated a number of **Cultural Tourism Programmes**, mainly in the north of Tanzania, but also in the Pare Mountains and around Mbeya. Started in 1995, these projects give tourists the opportunity of a cultural experience, and provide people in the area with a new means of income. Both tours and development projects have been designed by local groups individually, according to their culture and requirements, and include rural walks and camel rides with guides who know the land, gathering honey, fetching water 'the Barbaig way', birdwatching with local experts and a chance to discuss local ways of life, rituals and beliefs. In addition, tourists see demonstrations of the developments that have been afforded by the new revenue – visits to irrigation, farming and education projects. Some tours are described in detail in the text (see pp.111–13).

Another initiative encourages Maasai people to work as guides around the Northern Safari Circuit; their local knowledge is, after all, second to none. It is already possible to climb Ol Doinyo Lengai, the Maa 'Mountain of God', and to visit the ruins of Engakura with knowledgeable local guides. Individual tour operators have also realized the benefits of employing tribal guides in their local regions, enabling tourists to enjoy unique experiences such as hunting with Hadzabe hunter-gatherers or exploring the caves around Kilimanjaro with local Chagga people. Interaction between groups such as the Hadzabe and tourists does, however, raise complex issues. In one respect their traditional lifestyle is already so severely threatened by displacement from the land that they can no longer exist on hunted game and must seek other forms of sustenance, but cash payments are frequently spent on alcohol – further destroying the traditional way of life; it is worth considering alternative forms of barter payment and gifts (kangas, arrow heads or goats).

While community tourism is growing, it is still a very small percentage of total tourism and likely to remain so. Research by the pressure group Tourism Concern, Stapleton House, 277–281 Holloway Rd, London N7 8HN, UK, t (020) 7753 3330, info@ tourismconcern.org.uk, www.tourismconcern.org.uk, indicates that most tourists only participate in it for a small part of their trip; that said, it is often the highlight. It can provide a more meaningful experience and raise awareness of development issues. Tourists are delighted to see the fees they pay for a day visit to a village community handed over directly to the village committee for all the visitors to witness – a direct relationship and transaction between the tourist and the local community.

There is much to be said for independent tourism too, using local tour operators, staying in locally owned hotels, eating in local restaurants and using local buses and trains. From the tourist's point of view, it is cheaper, and, while it may take longer, there's more chance of meeting local people and getting a feel for life in Tanzania – and most money spent remains in the local economy. There has been a recent growth in local hotels of good quality offering excellent value across the country: one night at a luxury hotel could buy you 30 at a more basic one nearby, with a clean self-contained room, mosquito netting, ample hot and cold water, good security and breakfast. Added to this, three or four bus companies offer safety above speed, and the TAZARA Railway provides excellent service at reasonable rates. In using such facilities the tourist is not only getting value for money, but also backing the region.

activities. These parks also offer guided walking safaris with an armed ranger, and boating safaris along the river courses through the Selous, which can be combined with walking or driving game-drives, and fly-camping overnight safaris.

The Western Parks

See pp.262–72 for full description and listings.

The western parks of **Gombe Stream**, **Mahale Mountains** and **Katavi** are the most distant gems; exceptionally expensive to reach by air and extremely arduous to access by car or train. Gombe Stream National Park is home to a famous, well-studied chimpanzee population, and is predominantly a research station that allows tourists to visit, rather than specifically designed with facilities for tourists. The wild plains of Katavi are absolutely under-discovered, and provide a superbly rich wildlife landscape for those who are dedicated enough to make the trip. Plans are afoot to open the park up; there is a government strategy to encourage luxury, high-income tourism. Where once only the gilded few such as Robbie Williams trod, in the future more will follow; plans are to build an additional four permanent camps within the park.

Expeditions to Katavi are often combined with Mahale Mountains National Park, where cool forests and beaches form a unique environment in which to enjoy the finest safari chic or adventurous pioneer camping expeditions. This car-free environment is unique for its 1,000-strong chimpanzee population (five times the population of Gombe Stream).

Both Mahale Mountains and Gombe Stream border on the shores of Lake Tanganyika and provide snorkelling refreshment, but Gombe's proximity to local farms and habitation makes the possibility of bilharzia more acute (*see* p.88).

Beaches

One of the great attractions of Tanzania is its location as an unspoilt safari destination which also has a fantastic coastline, so that a safari can easily be combined with a stunning beach holiday. As with safaris, there is a great range of beach accommodation. The following are recommended options according to different priorities.

Best Beaches

The sands of **Mnemba Island** (off Zanzibar, *see* p.369) and Mesali Island (off Pemba) are the best the country offers – pure white coral sand lapped by the Indian Ocean. The beaches of **Ras Nungwi** and **Kendwa Rocks** on Unguja (*see* pp.364–8) are the finest on the island, each with long, shallow stretches of sand extending to a distant reef, shining with clean and clear sea and sand. The tidal east coast beaches are almost as superb, a little more wild and windswept. The southeast is shallower, with a greater distance to the reef. The mainland beach of **Ras Kutani** (*see* p.236) just south of Dar is pounded by real waves at certain times of day, good enough for boogie-boarding. The sand here lies in plump drifts that separate the sea from a freshwater

Best Fine Cuisine

Mnemba Island Lodge, on Mnemba Island off the northeast of Zanzibar (*see* p.369).
Ras Kutani, on the mainland south of Dar es Salaam (*see* pp.234–5).
Amani Beach Club, on the mainland, south of Dar es Salaam (*see* p.235).
Matemwe Bungalows, on the northeast coast of Zanzibar (*see* pp.369–70).

Best for Diving

Kinasi Lodge, the archipelago of Mafia Island, south of Zanzibar (*see* pp.392–3).
Fundu Lagoon, the west coast of Pemba Island, in the Pemba Channel (*see* pp.382–3).
Mnemba Island Lodge, for Mnemba Atoll off the northeast of Zanzibar (*see* p.369).
Ras Nungwi Beach Hotel, on Zanzibar's northern peninsula (*see* p.365).

Best for Robinson Crusoe-style Holidays

Mnemba Island (*see* p.369).
Ras Kutani, south of Dar es Salaam (*see* pp.234–5).
Matemwe Bungalows, on the northeast coast of Zanzibar, is no longer strictly
   isolated, but the lodge has hammocks and a personal feel (*see* pp.369–70).
Chumbe Island Coral Park and Lodge, Zanzibar's first marine park and eco-resort,
   surrounded by a shallow reef alive with 200 species of coral (*see* pp.358–60).

Best Range of Activities

Kinasi Lodge (*see* pp.392–3) in the Mafia Archipelago provides daily dhow trips
   around nearby islands, with options for snorkelling, diving, sailing and watersports,
   deep sea fishing, exploring ruins and historic sites, bird and nature walks through
   the mangroves and island forests and extended camping trips to deserted beaches.

Best Value for Money

Breezes Beach Club (*see* p.374) on the east coast of Zanzibar – among all the choices
   for luxury beach accommodation, this provides the best food, beach and activities –
   from disco to watersports – for the most reasonable price.

lagoon. Even with areas of rocky reef just below the tide line and a tendency to
seaweed deposits, this beach is idyllic.

Itineraries

Overleaf are some popular itineraries to help with planning your trip. The first is a
classic 'Northern Circuit Safari' of Ngorongoro and the Serengeti, taking in a few days'
relaxing on a beach in Zanzibar at the end. The second is a more off-the-beaten-track
'Southern Highlands Safari' exploring the lesser-known reaches of the Selous and
Ruaha parks. The third is a full 'Beaches and Islands' holiday on Zanzibar and Mafia.
These are just a very few ideas; the best option is to discuss your interests with a tour
operator before you go, and use this book to devise your own itinerary.

Northern Circuit Safari and Zanzibar

Day 1: From a start in Arusha, perhaps spend one night in the beautiful mountain region around the town. In the top range the best choices are the Moivaro Coffee Plantation Lodge or Mountain Village Lodge.

Day 2: Met early by your safari operators for the start of a six-night safari. Just a few hours' drive through Maasailand brings you to Lake Manyara for an afternoon game-drive and overnight at Kirurumu Tented Lodge or the Manyara Serena Lodge.

Day 3: Drive into the Serengeti, afternoon game-drive around Seronera. Overnight at the Serengeti Serena Lodge.

Days 4–5: Full day exploring the Serengeti, possibly moving north to see the migration, depending on season. Overnight at the Serengeti Serena Lodge again.

Day 6: Morning game-drive in the Serengeti followed by a drive to the Ngorongoro Crater. Overnight at the Ngorongoro Serena Lodge.

Day 7: Full day in the crater, overnight at the Ngorongoro Serena Lodge again.

Days 8–9: Drive back to Arusha and fly to Zanzibar. Overnight at the Tembo House Hotel in Stone Town for two nights (on a bed-and-breakfast basis).

Days 10–12: Transfer to Ras Nungwi Beach Hotel in the north of the island for your final three nights. Stay in luxury, enjoying all the water sports, diving, fishing and relaxation that the Indian Ocean has to offer.

Day 13: Fly from Zanzibar to Dar es Salaam.

This itinerary would cost around $4,500 per person, including a full safari for four people in a 4x4, and on a full-board basis with all internal flights.

Southern Highlands Safari

Days 1–3: Fly from Zanzibar or Dar es Salaam to the Selous Game Reserve, staying at the Selous Safari Camp. Each day includes activities from game-drives, game-walks and game-viewing by boat. Alternatively, stay at Sand Rivers Selous.

Days 4–8: Take a short flight to Ruaha National Park. Overnight at Mwagusi, which is one of Tanzania's best small lodges. Enjoy full game-viewing activities by vehicle or on foot in this remote, game-packed location. Otherwise stay at Ruaha River Lodge.

This itinerary would cost around $3,200 per person, including full safari, internal flights and full-board lodgings.

Beaches and Islands

Days 1–5: On arrival in Zanzibar, travel to Ras Nungwi Beach Hotel in the north of the island. Enjoy snorkelling, diving and beaches at one of Zanzibar's best locations. Alternative accommodation includes Breezes Beach Club or Matemwe Bungalows.

Days 6–8: Drive from Nungwi to the east coast and travel to Mnemba Island by boat. Spend three nights at Mnemba Island Lodge, drinks and diving included.

Days 9–13: Return to Zanzibar airport for a short flight to Mafia Island. Transfer to Kinasi Lodge for five nights on a full-board basis.

The itinerary outlined above would cost approximately $3,850 per person staying on a full-board basis, and includes internal flights.

Food, Drink and Nightlife

06

Food and Drink

Local Specialities

Local food tends to be simple, emphasizing caught or locally grown produce over culinary prowess. The diet tends to be much higher in **carbohydrates** than most westerners are used to: large amounts of rice or corn-meal (*ugali*) are served with every meal. Accompanying **protein** might be fish or meat – *nyama* – or beans – *maharagwe*. Chicken and chips are often available in tourist areas. Carnivores should look out for *nyama choma* – 'hot meat' – a popular bar food: chunks of beef are grilled over a barbecue, and may be served with chapati. An alternative is *mishkaki*, barbecued beef kebabs on a skewer. Other common roadside **snacks** are samosas, roast cassava, and hard-boiled eggs – *mayai*.

Breakfast foods are variations on the chapati, or *mandazi*, a doughnut-like bread or cake that is especially delicious when cooked with honey. Rice flour and honey cakes are well recommended too, and are best enjoyed with a generous mug of hot *chai* – Indian-style spiced tea. Omelettes frequently feature on the breakfast menu.

The variety and freshness of local **fruits** is a joy, with a surfeit of seasonal items. Mango season coincides with Christmas, with some varieties available earlier in the year. Sweet oranges come into their own in June. Bananas, grapes, pineapples, paw-paw, jack fruit and custard apples are also grown, along with huge avocados, tomatoes and sweet potatoes. All of the above are quite safe to eat if you stick to the popular travellers' adage: 'Boil it, cook it, peel it – or forget it.' Attractive salads or unpeeled fruits should be left untouched unless you have copious quantities of mineral water to wash them thoroughly first.

Eating Out

Restaurant prices tend to be very reasonable in all but the most upmarket international hotels and lodges. In many local establishments it is possible to eat for a couple of dollars. We have applied similar price categories to our restaurant listings as to hotels. For restaurant price ranges used in this book, *see* p.98.

If you fancy a change from the local cuisine, the range of international cooking styles continues to increase, with expats of Australian, British, Italian, South African, American, Indian and Chinese origins all maintaining their own country's cuisine. A number of Asian restaurants are opening up across Tanzania, with good curry and rice dishes on the menu.

Drinks

It is not advisable to drink **tap water**. If you do, use purifying tablets such as iodine, or boil it first (*see* 'Health', p.88). Some tourist hotels have their own water filters, but

Some Food Vocabulary

to eat *kula*
to drink *kunywa*
food/meal *chakula*
a drink *kinywaji*
water *maji*
I am very hungry *Nasikia njaa sana*
Bring me a cold drink, please *Nipatie kinywaji baridi, tafadhali*
I am very thirsty *Nasikia kiu sana*
rice *wali*
bread *mkate*

meat *nyama*
fish *samaki*
chicken *kuku*
goat *mbuzi*
eggs *mayai* (one egg *yai*)
potatoes *viazi*
fruits *matunda*
coconut *nazi*
bananas *ndizi*
coffee *kahawa*
tea *chai*
milk *maziwa*
sugar *sukari*

check first and be wary. **Ice** should be avoided, and **ice cream** may have melted in a power cut and been refrozen. **Mineral water** is widely available; keep a bottle with you, as you should drink plenty of water in the hot, dry climate.

Fizzy **soft drinks** are easy to find, especially Coca-Cola and Fanta, which comes in a range of flavours, among them passion fruit, blackcurrant, lemon and orange. Soda and tonic waters are common too, but there are no diet varieties. Sometimes you may come across **fresh fruit drinks**. Again, watch out for these being mixed with local water or dirty blocks of ice, common practice at street stalls where sugar cane is pressed and mixed with ice chips – a delicious concoction if you can mix the pure sugar-cane pulp with mineral water instead. An excellent thirst-quencher most often found in coastal areas is coconut *madafu*, the fresh juice of a green coconut, drunk straight from the shell and accessible only with the firm stroke of a *panga* knife. When you have drunk your fill you can use a small shard of the coconut shell to eat the soft jelly-like fruit inside.

Beer is on sale in most towns and villages, with good local brands from Tanzanian or Kenyan breweries the best value at $2–3 for a decent-sized bottle. 'Kilimanjaro' is refreshing and not very strong, 'Safari' is even more popular and slightly stronger; there is a growing trend for seriously strong beers in the wake of the 'Kibo Gold' brand's popularity. Imported South African beers can be found, and occasionally European beers for about three times the price of the local brew.

Wine is mostly imported from South Africa and is expensive at $10–20 a bottle. European imports cost more, and are ever-increasing. Be aware in coastal areas and the islands that Islam forbids alcohol; this evil is still quite a novelty in some rural towns, so be sensitive about public drinking, and don't encourage local friends to drink to excess.

Coffee, in this land of coffee plantations, is usually instant, often the ubiquitous 'Africafé', but you may come across a street *baraza*, where fresh, local Arabica coffee is served in tiny espresso cups, strong and black with lots of sugar. You can smell the aroma before you spot the seller; the price is often nominal – 5¢. *Chai* is a popular alternative – tea mixed with milk, sugar and sometimes cardamom and cinnamon, or otherwise black and sometimes mixed with ginger, called *chai tangawizi*.

Traditional Dance

Known as *'ngoma'* in Swahili, referring to the single most all-important drum at the heart of each, many traditional dances have become sadly dissociated from the ceremonial events that they celebrate. These days dances are more often performed as entertainment in international hotels or can be seen during cultural evenings at the Old Fort in Stone Town, but the adrenaline, energy and verve required to dance never fail to be drummed up when the music takes a hold. *Ngomas* represent all manner of day-to-day activities, customs and special occasions. With the drum there may be instruments including whistles, xylophones, animal-horn trumpets, the marimba, the banjo or even mango stones tied to dancers' legs. Coastal musicians in Zanzibar beat rhythms on upturned buoys, and when there is no other instrument they clap and beat the rhythm with their hands.

Different tribes and peoples have distinct dance styles. The Makonde are known for their dramatic **Sindimba**, in which dancers vibrate their bottoms in an ever-increasing frenzy, and perform on stilts in formidable costumes. The Zaramo bounce in undulating processions in their **Mdundiko**, and Maasai men leap high in the air while their women undulate and flash their elaborate beaded jewellery to rhythmic chanting of voices. The Sukuma are famed for their **Gobogobo**, so competitive that dancers traditionally carry magic charms to protect them from harm while they dance; certain dancers perform a dance with a live snake.

Entertainment and Nightlife

If you are seeking nightlife in the conventional form of bars and nightclubs, you will find a choice in the major cities, such as Dar es Salaam, Arusha, Tanga, Iringa, and Stone Town in Zanzibar. Most clubs hold their most popular nights on Fridays and Saturdays. There are excellent live bands, which are advertised in the local press or in the *What's On* and *What's Happening in Dar es Salaam* guides, available free in most hotel foyers, although the best approach is usually to ask around.

Occasionally you will find local dance groups putting on shows in nightclubs and other venues. The best places to look are the Village Museum and the Karibu Art Gallery, both on Bagamoyo Road in Dar, or the Bagamoyo Arts College, where a select few talented students study traditional dance (*see* box, above). There are also troupes in Arusha. The Cultural Tourism Programmes in the South Pare Mountains invite visitors to request dance performances.

Travel

Getting There

By Air

Tanzania has three international airports: Dar es Salaam airport (DAR), which handles most international flights, Kilimanjaro airport (JRO) and Zanzibar airport (ZNZ). Consider also flying to Nairobi or Johannesburg, from where you can transfer by air or road to Tanzania.

Bargain flights to Tanzania are not easy to come by. Try the ads in the travel pages of Sunday newspapers and magazines, or contact a travel agent for special offers.

There is a departure tax of $20 if you are taking an international flight out of Tanzania, which is sometimes included in your ticket.

From the UK and Europe

A few European airlines fly into Dar es Salaam with varying regularity – usually three times a week; see box, below. Prices tend to be around £500 return, increasing to as much as £800 in peak season.

Airline Carriers

UK and Ireland

British Airways, Waterside, PO Box 365, Harmondsworth UB7 0GB, t 0870 850 9850, www.ba.com. Direct London to Dar es Salaam flights three times a week.

Egyptair, 29–31 Piccadilly, London W1J 0LF, t (020) 7734 2395, www.egyptair.com. London to Dar es Salaam via Cairo.

Emirates Airlines, 95 Gloucester Park, Cromwell Road, London SW7 4DL, t (020) 7808 0033. London to Dar es Salaam via Dubai.

Ethiopian Airlines, Room 238, Terminal 3, Camberley Road, Heathrow Airport, Hounslow, Middlesex TW6 1JT, t (020) 8745 4234, www.flyethiopian.com. London to Dar es Salaam, Kilimanjaro and Zanzibar via Addis Ababa.

Gulf Air, 10 Albermarle Street, London W15 4BL, t 0870 777 1717, www.gulfairco.com. London to Dar es Salaam and Zanzibar via Muscat (Masqat), Oman.

Kenya Airways, Cirrus House, Bedford Road, Heathrow Airport, Staines, Middlesex TW19 7NR, t (01784) 888260, f (01784) 888299, www.kenya-airways.com. Flights from London to Dar es Salaam, Kilimanjaro and Zanzibar, via Nairobi.

KLM, Endeavour House, Stansted Airport, Stansted, Essex CM24 1RS, t 0870 507 4074, www.klm.com. Daily flights from London to Dar es Salaam and Kilimanjaro via Amsterdam. Also daily London to Nairobi.

South African Airways (SAA), St George's House, 61 Conduit Street, London W1R 0NE, t (020) 7312 5000, f (020) 7312 5009,
www.flysaa.com. Regular flights from London to Johannesburg, and Jo'burg to Dar.

Swissair, 313 Regent Street, London W1B 2HP, t 0845 601 0956, www.swiss.com. London to Dar, via Zürich, three times a week.

Africa

Kenya Airways, PO Box 19002, Nairobi, Kenya, t (+254) 2 823 000, www.kenya-airways.com. Daily flights to Dar es Salaam from Nairobi.

South African Airways (SAA), Raha Towers Building, PO Box 5182, Dar es Salaam, t (022) 2220058, f (022) 2244031, or international number t (+27) 11 722 24800, www.flysaa.com. Flights three times a week to Dar es Salaam from Johannesburg.

Linhas Aereas De Mocambique, www.lam.co.mz. Fly from Dar to Pemba in Mozambique in a daily service, $200 per person each way.

USA and Canada

Air France, 125 West 55th Street, New York NY 10019-5384, t 800 237 2747, www.airfrance.com. Frequent flights from major US cities to Paris, and daily flights from Paris to Johannesburg.

British Airways, t 800 AIRWAYS, www.ba.com. Flights from many US cities to London, and London Gatwick to Dar es Salaam three times a week.

KLM, Northwest Airlines/KLM, Central Airline Terminal, 100 East 42nd Street, 2nd Floor, New York NY 10017, t 1 800 447 4747, www.nwa.com. Flights from most major US cities, via Amsterdam, to Johannesburg daily.

South African Airways (SAA), PO Box 25578, Los Angeles, CA 90025-0578, t (310) 478 3585, www.saa.co.za. Flights from most major cities in the USA to Johannesburg.

From Africa

Dar es Salaam is served by Kenya Airways, South African Airways, and other African airlines from their respective countries. Travellers from Europe or the USA might consider flying to Nairobi or Johannesburg and on from there. Kenya Airways is the only company that flies into Dar es Salaam daily, also flying into Zanzibar and Kilimanjaro.

Air Tanzania also has an (unreliable) service to and from other African countries including Kenya, South Africa and Zambia.

From the USA

There are no direct flights from the United States into Tanzania. The easiest connections are through Europe: flights from London (on BA) and Amsterdam (on KLM) tend to be the cheapest, although any major airline will get you to Europe.

Another possibility for travellers from North America is to fly direct to Johannesburg and catch an onward flight to Dar es Salaam on South African Airways.

Students, Discounts and Special Deals

Agencies specializing in advice on low-cost travel include the following; see also 'Internet Travel', below.

UK and Ireland

Bridge the World, 47 Chalk Farm Road, Camden, London NW1 8AJ, t 0870 444 7474, f (020) 7813 3350, www.bridgetheworld.com.

Flight Centre, Head Office, Broadway House, Wimbledon SW19 1RL, t 0870 499 0040, f (020) 8541 5120, and branches across the UK, www.flightcentre.co.uk.

Quest Worldwide, 4–10 Richmond Road, Kingston-upon-Thames, Surrey KT2 5HL, t 0870 442 3542, travel@qww.co.uk, www.questtravel.com. Competitive air fares.

STA Travel, 6 Wright's Lane, London W8 6TA, t (020) 7361 6161, general enquiries t 08701 600599, enquiries@statravel.co.uk, www.statravel.co.uk. Also have offices in Bristol, Leeds, Manchester and elsewhere.

Trailfinders, 194 Kensington High Street, London W8 7RG, t (020) 7938 3939, f (020) 7938 3305, www.trailfinders.com.

USIT Campus Travel, 52 Grosvenor Gardens, London SW1W 0AG, t (020) 7730 3402, www.usitcampus.co.uk. Branches at most UK universities.

USA and Canada

Airtech, 584 Broadway, Suite 1007, New York, NY 10012, t 800 575 TEC, t (212) 219 7000, fly@airtech.com, www.airtech.com.

Council Travel, 205 East 42nd Street, New York, NY 10017, t 800 743 1823, t (212) 822 2700, www.counciltravel.com. Specializing in student flights; branches across the USA.

STA Travel, 10 Downing Street (6th Avenue and Bleecker), New York, NY 10014, t (212) 627 3111, t 800 777 0112, f (212) 627 3387; on the West Coast: 120 Broadway 108, Santa Monica, Los Angeles, CA 90401, t (310) 394 5126, f (310) 394 4041. Branches US-wide.

Internet Travel

There are many travel agents, airlines and bargain flight companies who operate websites. The usefulness of these really depends upon your requirements. If you're hunting for a cheap or last-minute deal, then, rather than readying yourself for a quick surf, prepare yourself for what might be a doggy-paddle. As well as the websites for companies listed above, try the following, a mere selection of those available in cyberspace.

UK websites include:
www.airtickets.co.uk
www.cheapflights.com
www.expedia.co.uk
www.lastminute.com
www.opodo.co.uk
www.skydeals.co.uk
www.sky-tours.co.uk
www.thomascook.co.uk
www.travelocity.com
www.travelselect.com

For US-orientated websites, try:
www.air-fare.com
www.expedia.com
www.flights.com
www.travellersweb.ws
www.travelocity.com

By Road

There is a good paved road from the Kenyan capital, **Nairobi**, to Arusha, which crosses the border at the Namanga border post. A number of shuttle buses follow this route. The trip takes around 4–6 hours, and costs around $30. Tour operators can arrange this journey, or call Devanu Shuttle on **t** (027) 2504311 in Arusha or **t** (+254) 2 222002 in Nairobi for times and tickets. Another bus route is from **Mombasa** to Tanga along the coast (about 4 hours).

You could travel either of these routes independently in a 4x4. Although a road continues from the Serengeti into the Maasai Mara in Kenya, this border is closed to tourists.

From the south the road from **Malawi** enters Tanzania at Karonga before continuing to Mbeya. There are no viable bus services on this route. It is possible to cross the border from **Uganda** at the Mutukula border post, but again transport options are limited. Overland routes from northern and western Africa are not currently feasible due to conflicts – in Sudan and the Congo, to name just two.

By Boat

Fishing and cargo **dhows** ply the coastline from **Mombasa** in Kenya to Dar es Salaam and the Zanzibar archipelago. It is actually illegal for Tanzanian dhows to take tourists as passengers, probably owing to poor safety record: the dhows frequently capsize or sink. For determined sea adventurers it may, however, be possible to hitch a lift on a motorized or sailing dhow from Mombasa to Zanzibar. This is a long journey that takes at least a couple of days, depending on winds, with no shade, no toilets, and sacks of rice or vegetables to sleep on. Dhows can be found in Tanga and Zanzibar Stone Town too.

More reliable and methods of boat travel arrival are by **sea and lake ferry**, ranging from the ancient MV *Liemba*, which has steamed its way around Lake Tanganyika since before the First World War, to the high-speed ferries that travel to Zanzibar. The tragic sinking of the MV *Bukoba* on Lake Victoria in 1996 has probably improved boat safety overall.

There is a port tax of $5 for all ferry and boat services entering the country.

By Lake

The rusty MV *Liemba* steams around **Lake Tanganyika**, connecting Kigoma with Mpulungu in **Zambia**, and Bujumbura in **Burundi**. It does the circuit twice weekly, departing Kigoma on Wednesdays and Sundays (*see* pp.263 for times). It is wise to take your own food and water supplies. A ticket in a **first class cabin** with two bunks costs $55, in a **second class cabin** with four bunks and poor ventilation $45, and a **third class seat** $40 – try to get a place on deck. The MV *Mwongoza* sometimes supplements or replaces it. Cargo boats sometimes carry passengers from Kigoma to Kalemie in the Democratic Republic of Congo; ask at the port.

The Tanzanian ferry MV *Iringa* sails **Lake Nyasa** between Mbamba Bay, Tanzania, and Nkhata Bay, in **Malawi**, weekly. Another ferry, the MV *Songea*, has also been known to sail the route, but is currently out of service. The Malawian ferry MV *Ilala* sails between Nkhata Bay and Mbamba Bay twice a week, but the timetable is known to be erratic (*see* p.304).

The MV *Victoria* crosses **Lake Victoria** from Kampala (Port Bell) in **Uganda** to Mwanza once a week (18 hours), leaving Mwanza late on Sundays and Kampala late on Mondays. it also stops at Kisumu in **Kenya**, a route also plied by the MV *Serengeti*. The Kampala–Mwanza route is a major cargo route, taking goods to and from landlocked Uganda to the sea via the lake and Tanzanian Railways; you may be able to get a passage on a cargo boat (*see* p.154).

By Sea

The Sepideh service connects Mombasa in **Kenya** with Tanga, Pemba, Zanzibar and Dar es Salaam once a week, leaving Tanga on Wednesdays and returning on Thursdays. Contact Mega Speed Liners in Dar es Salaam, **t** (022) 2110807/**t** (0741) 326414, Zanzibar, **t** (024) 2232423, Pemba, **t** (024) 2456100.

By River

Mozambique is just a river-crossing away from Tanzania. A new **car ferry service** crosses the Ruvuma River from Mwambo, a short drive south of Mtwara, to Nachindundo, every day at high tide for $7.50 per vehicle. At low tide you can walk across, or at other times there is a passenger ferry (*see* p.2515).

Specialist and Safari Tour Operators

The following companies can provide travellers with good, up-to-date information and advice on planning holiday itineraries in Tanzania. The majority of them have wide-ranging expertise throughout Africa; specialist Tanzania operators such as Tanzania Odyssey (www.tanzaniaodyssey.com) are very rare. Most operators offer a combination of wildlife safaris, trekking and beach stays in Zanzibar. While a few offer set, scheduled routes, most can arrange tailor-made tours to meet the specific requirements of a group. Trips typically start from around £2,000, but can range as high as £6,000 per person for the utmost in Tanzanian luxury.

An increasing number of operators are attempting to ensure that the trips they offer are environmentally sustainable, offer inter-action with local people and benefit the communities visited too (see pp.111–13).

A list of tour operators recommended by the Tanzanian Tourist Board can be found on the TTB website, www.tanzania-web.com, www.tanzaniatouristboard.com.

UK

Abercrombie and Kent, Sloane Square House, Holbein Place, London SW1W 8NS, t (01242) 547700, www.abercrombiekent.co.uk. This long-established company offers luxurious tailored fly-in safaris with travel in customized 4x4s and trekking with expert guides, sleeping in luxury walk-in tents and three-course dining in a 'colonial' safari atmosphere.

Africa Archipelago, 6 Redgrave Road, Putney, London SW15 1PX, t (020) 8780 5838, www.africaarchipelago.com. Specialize in person-alized trips to East and southern Africa. Years of experience organizing luxury or budget safari trips to all the Tanzanian

national parks, which can be combined with beach holidays in fine locations on Zanzibar, Pemba and Mafia, or in other Indian Ocean and African countries.

Africa Travel Centre, 21 Leigh Street, London WC1H 9EW, t (020) 7387 1211, www.africatravel.co.uk. Individual and specialized travel itineraries. Ideas include classic safari and beach holidays, or a 'Kilimanjaro and the Crater' tour; trips tailored to suit budgets. Accommodation is high-class: luxury canvas, and hotel lodges.

African Explorations, Afex House, Holwell, Burford, Oxon, OX18 4JS, t (01993) 822443, www.africanexplorations.com. A range of tailor-made safaris, mainly fly-in to camps and lodges with 4x4 game-drives. Any of the northern parks and Ruaha, Selous, Gombe Stream or Mahale Mountains can form an itinerary.

Bukima, 15 Bedford Road, Great Barford, Bedfordshire MK44 3JD, t 0870 757 2230, www.bukima.com. Bukima specializes in overland 4x4 expeditions across Africa in groups, lasting from 10 days to 28 weeks. Tours are on set dates and itineraries, with basic accommodation and food. A 14-day 'Gorillas and Game Parks' tour, taking in Kenya, Tanzania and Uganda, costs £350 per person (no flights included) plus local kitty.

Cazenove and Loyd, 9 Imperial Studios, 3-11 Imperial Road, SW6 2AG, t (020) 7384 2332, www.caz-loyd.com. An expensive tour operator, which specializes in tailor-made safaris.

Crusader Travel, 57 Church Street, Twickenham, Middx TW1 3NR, t (020) 8744 0474, www.crusadertravel.com. Crusader offers tailored wildlife-watching holidays, including safari game tours and 'chimp-trekking'.

Explore, 1 Frederick Street, Aldershot, Hants GU11 1LQ, t (01252) 319448, www.explore.co.uk. Focuses on sustainable eco-travel for groups averaging 16 people, who visit remoter regions, by train, ferry, light aircraft

Entry Formalities

Visas

Visas are currently required by most visitors to the country, including citizens of European countries and the UK, and of Australia, New Zealand, the United States and Canada. There is no separate visa requirement for Zanzibar, but new embarkation forms have to be filled out.

Nationals of many other countries are given a visitor's pass on arrival, which is valid for one and 'on foot safari'. A 10-day all-inclusive 'Tanzania Lodge Safari' costs around £1,500 (no flights included) plus local kitty.

Footloose Adventure Travel, 5EG3 Springs Pavement, Ilkley LS29 8HD, **t** (01943) 604030, *www.footlooseadventure.co.uk*. An independent operator offering tailored treks and safaris. Clients select a safari, a trek and a Zanzibar hotel, and Footloose plan it all.

Gane and Marshall, 7th Floor Northway House, 137–9 High Road, London N20 9LP, **t** (020) 8441 9592, *www.ganeandmarshall. co.uk*. Safaris by 4x4, boat or on foot, staying in lodges or deluxe camps, with a beach stay in Zanzibar. Also Kilimanjaro and Meru treks, the Serengeti, Ngorongoro Crater highlands, the Maasai lands, the Longido mountains and Ol Doinyo Lengai.

Guerba, Wessex House, 40 Station Road, Westbury, Wiltshire, BA13 3JN, **t** (01373) 858 956, *www.guerba.com*. Four-wheel-drive safaris in Tanzania and Kenya, with Kilimanjaro climbs and Zanzibar beach stays. A 14-day Serengeti Trail and Kilimanjaro trip costs £1,015, plus local kitty.

High Places, Globe Centre, Penistone Road, Sheffield S6 3AE, **t** (0114) 275 7500, *www. highplaces.co.uk*. Unglossy, erudite mountain travel company, which offers treks, avoiding tourist routes, around Kilimanjaro and Meru and exchanges with local people (Maasai and Chagga). Trips in the dry season in groups of up to 12 plus an expert leader. Accommodation is basic but comfortable in lodges, hotels and bunk-houses, or in 2-person mountain tents. A 16-day 'Kilimanjaro, Meru and Tanzanian Insights' trek costs £1,740 plus local kitty (no flights included).

Okavango Tours and Safaris, Marlborough House, 298 Regent's Park Road, London N3 2TJ, **t** (020) 8343 328. Okavango will create a safari holiday based on your ideas and specialist experience, basic or luxury, with high accommodation standards (luxury tents, simple cottages or tasteful hotels) and transport.

Phoenix Expeditions, College Farm, Far Street, Wymeswold, Leicestershire LE12 6TZ, **t** (01509) 881818, *www.phoenixexpeditions. co.uk*. Phoenix specializes in overland 'adventures' in purpose-built, 'comfortable but rugged' trucks, viewing wildlife in East Africa. Each person mucks in with chores and cooking; accommodation is in basic 2-person tents. The 21–26-day 'East African Wildlife' tour through Kenya, Uganda and Tanzania costs £375 (no flights included), plus local kitty.

Safari Drive, Wessex House, 127 High Street, Hungerford, Berkshire RG17 7XA, **t** (01488) 71140, *www.safaridrive.com*. Unique self-drive safaris in fully equipped Land Rovers; you travel pre-planned routes on your own daily schedule, with a discreet back-up service on hand – or you can go with a driver-guide. A 15-day self-drive safari costs around £2,750, based on 2 sharing (does not include flights).

Simply Tanzania Tour Company, 54 Cotesbach Road, London E5 9QJ, **t** (020) 8986 0615, *www.simplytanzania.co.uk*. Simply Tanzania has at its heart an ex-VSO Programme Director, which explains the unusual style of travel offered. The usual fare (safaris, beach and walking holidays) is on offer, but with an opportunity to embark upon cultural tours to see the 'real' Tanzania, visiting villages, meeting local people and finding out about their customs. Your fees go straight into the local community, and you can see the development projects they fund in action. Good accommodation. Groups number 5–10 people, usually on a 2-week tour.

Sovereign Worldwide, First Choice House, Peel Cross Road, Salford, Manchester M5 2AN, **t** 0870 3661634, *www.sovereign.com*. Personalized itineraries, which include exclusive hotels on Zanzibar, and luxury lodge accommodation on safari.

to three months and can be extended at the immigration office. Nationals of the East African Community need neither a visa nor an entry permit to visit Tanzania.

Visas should be obtained in advance, where possible, from the nearest Tanzanian embassy, high commission or consulate. In the UK, visa application forms can be downloaded from the website of the High Commission in London, *www.tanzania-online.co.uk*, and visas are issued by post within one week or in person within 24 hours. Applications must be

Tanzania Odyssey, 59 Fulham High Street, Fulham, London SW6 3JJ, t (020) 7471 8780, *www.tanzaniaodyssey.com*. Dedicated specialist operators with more than 10 years' experience creating only Tanzania and Zanzibar itineraries. Holidays and honeymoon packages are tailor-made to fit any budget, and they charge no markup on the cost of a lodge or hotel, so it costs no more to book lodges through Tanzania Odyssey than to deal with lodges directly. Presentations are held in their London offices to discuss possibilities; international clients may find the website useful, with lodge brochures to download pictures and videos.

TRIBES, the Fair Trade Travel Company, 12 The Business Centre, Earl Soham, Woodbridge, Suffolk, IP13 7SA, t (01728) 685971, *info@ tribes.co.uk, www.tribes.co.uk*. TRIBES specializes in tourism that aims not to exploit local people or compromise the environment. Tours include walking safaris with the Maasai (the proceeds go to local village projects) and trips to Chumbe Island marine sanctuary and eco-resort.

World Odyssey, 32 Sansome walk, WR1 1NA, t (01905) 731373, *www.world-odyssey.com*. Tailor-made driving, walking and horse-riding safaris.

USA

Abercrombie & Kent, t (630) 954 2944, *www. abercrombiekent.com*. With similar tours to its UK counterpart, A&K offers tailored safari holidays. Travel in a customized 4x4 vehicle, take a fly-in safari, or trek with expert guides. Accommodation is in elegant lodges or luxury walk-in tents.

Africa Tours, 217 Merrick Road, Suit 212, Amityville NY 11701-3449, t (631) 264 2800, 800 235 3692, *www.africasafaris.com*. A personalized service, with tours and accommodation to suit. This company promises to arrange 'your dream holiday'. The 11-day

Tanzanian set safari covers the northern parks, accommodation in luxury mobile tents and tented camps, and costs $4,702 (without flights).

Big Five Tours and Expeditions, t (561) 287 7995, *www.bigfive.com*. Founded by a Kenyan family 25 years ago, Big Five promise a no 'hidden charges' approach. Accommodation and food are luxurious and distinctive 'Secret Eden', a tented safari, which takes in both northern and southern parks, is an 18-day all-inclusive safari (including game-viewing by boat and at night). It costs around $11,000.

Ker and Downey, 2825 Wilcrest Drive, Suite 600, Houston TX 77042-6007, t (713) 917 0048, or t 800 423 4236, *www.kerdowney. com*. Offering a fine personal service, this top US safari operator specializes in traditional safari itineraries, which recall 'the nostalgia of yesteryear'.

Mountain Travel Sobek, 6420 Fairmount Avenue, El Cerrito, CA 94530, t 888 687 6235, t (510) 527 8100, *www.mtsobek.com*. Founded in 1969, Mountain Travel offers active adventure trips, such as a 'Hiking Safari, customized or private trips, for individuals or small groups (15 persons max), staying in comfortable camps with good food.

Travcoa, 2350 SE Bristol, Newport Beach, CA 92660, t 800 992 2003/t (949) 476 2800, *www.travcoa.com*. In its 'East Africa Explorer' safari, Travcoa offers game-viewing opportunities, hot air balloon rides, a trip to a giraffe centre and an animal orphanage, plus deluxe comfort and food in the best hotels, lodges and tented camps. The tour lasts 21 days and costs from $8,000.

United Touring Company, 1 Bala Plaza, Suite 414, Bala Cynwyd PA 19004, t 800 223 6486, *www.unitedtour.com*. A slightly more corporate operator, UTC offer both scheduled or more flexible safari itineraries.

accompanied by two passport photographs and a passport valid for at least six months.

The cost for UK and US citizens is £38 ($54), Australians $35, New Zealanders $28, Canadians $56 and other European citizens $28–50 (€33–57), apart from Irish citizens who

can get a visa at the knock-down price of £5 (€8) – in contrast to citizens of the Democratic Republic of Congo, who pay $162.

It may also be possible to obtain a visa on arrival at Dar es Salaam, Kilimanjaro or Zanzibar airports, or at the Namanga border crossing from Kenya. Standard tourist visas are issued for three months, but may be extended to six months. Visitors are advised to bring the documents submitted as part of their visa application with them, as the visa itself does not always guarantee entry.

Tanzanian Embassies Abroad

Canada: 50 Range Road, Ottawa, Ontario KIN 8J4, t (613) 232 1500, f (613) 232 5184, *tzottawa@synapse.net*.

UK: 3 Stratford Place, London, W1C 1AS, t (020) 7569 1470, *www.tanzania-online.gov.uk*.

USA: 2139 R Street NW, Washington DC 2000, t (202) 9939 6129, f (202) 797 7408, *tanz-us@clark.net*.

Customs

In theory, any video or film equipment, tape recorders, musical instruments and radios brought into the country may incur a customs bond payment, to ensure that you do not sell them. In practice, this is rarely enforced. Any journalists, TV or film producers, writers or photographers must officially seek clearance for their assignment before entering the country. Application forms can be found on Tanzanian diplomatic missions websites, or from **Tanzanian Information Services**, PO Box 9142, Dar es Salaam. Binoculars, cameras and films for personal use can be brought in freely.

Getting Around

By Air

Tanzania is well served by internal airlines. State-run **Air Tanzania** connects most regions of the country with an irregular and unreliable service. It flies to all towns once a week, larger places more often.

Coastal Travels is more reliable, flying to the northern and southern safari destinations, coast and islands.

Precision Air flies similar routes, including Mafia Island and a few less tourist-orientated destinations such as Kigoma.

Regional Air flies the northern routes between the safari parks, with a scheduled flight that includes Arusha, Lake Manyara and Serengeti.

Internal Airline Offices

Air Tanzania, PO Box 543, Ohio St, Dar, t (022) 2117500, f (022) 2113114; Boma Road, Arusha, t (027) 2503201/2; PO Box 773, Zanzibar, t (054) 2230297, *www.airtanzania.com*.

Coastal Travels Ltd, 107 Upanga Road, PO Box 3052, Dar es Salaam, t (022) 2117959/60, f (022) 2118647/2117985, *safari@coastal.cc*, *www.coastal.cc*.

Precision Air (Head Office), Ngorongoro Wing, AICC, PO Box 1636, Arusha, t (027) 2506903/2502836/2507319, f (027) 2508204/2504295, *www.precisionairtz.com*; NIC HDQ Building, Samora Av/Pamba Rd, Dar es Salaam, t (022) 2121718, f (022) 2113036.

Regional Air, PO Box 14755, Arusha, t (027) 250 2541/250 4477, *resvns@regional.co.tz*, *sales@regional.co.tz*, *www.airkenya.com*, *www.regional.co.tz*.

Zanair, P.O.Box 2113, Zanzibar, Tanzania, t (024) 2233670, *www.zanair.com*.

By Road

A fairly good central network of tarmacked roads links the main cities, from Dar es Salaam to Arusha in the north, Iringa and Mbeya in the south, and Dodoma in the heart of the country. Anywhere beyond these main routes, however, roads are frequently untarmacked, tend to be poorly maintained and are often impassable after heavy rain. This even applies to routes into the designated capital city of Dodoma from any direction other than Dar es Salaam. You will almost certainly need a four-wheel-drive vehicle to travel any distance.

Vehicles drive on the left-hand side of the road. Specific road hazards include roaming

Driving Organizations

AA, t 0870 600 0371, *www.theaa.co.uk*.
RAC, t 0800 550550, *www.rac.co.uk*.
AAA, Travel Dept, 1415 Kellum Place, Garden City, New York NY 11530-1690, t (212) 468 2600, or t (718) 279 7272; on the West Coast, 2601 South Figueroa Street, Los Angeles, CA 90007, t (213) 741 3686, *www.aaa.com*.
International Automobile Driver's Club, 8223 Bay Parkway, Suite 3A, Brooklyn NY 11214, t (718) 621 2342/3, *www.driverlicense.net*.

Car Hire

Avis, FK Motors, Pugu Road (near the airport), Dar es Salaam, **t** (022) 2861214/6, **t** (0742) 780981, **f** (022) 2861212, *avis@raha.com*.

Europcar, 2 Nelson Mandela Expressway, PO Box 40568, Dar es Salaam, **t** (0741) 786000, **f** (022) 2862569, *europcar@raha.com*.

Hertz, Sheraton Hotel, PO Box 20517, Dar es Salaam, **t** (022) 2120269/2120273, (0741) 600738 / 331662, **f** (022) 2121812, *savtour@twiga.com, hertz.tanzania@twiga.com*.

Hima Car Hire, Simu Street (behind Mavuno House), PO Box 10879, Dar es Salaam, **t** (022) 2126987, **t** (0742) 323143, *hima@raha.com*.

Serena Car Hire, India Street, PO Box 2556, Arusha, **t/f** (027) 2506593, *serenacarhire@habari.co.tz*.

wildlife, pedestrians and an assortment of vehicles travelling at random speeds. More tourists die in road accidents every year than from any of the dreaded diseases of Tanzania.

By Car

An **International Driving Licence** is required to drive and to hire a car (available in the UK from the RAC and the AA; in the USA from the AAA or the International Automobile Driver's Club). Arrange one well before you go.

These generally have to be endorsed by the police, and in areas such as Zanzibar Stone Town it is worth taking yourself down to the station before setting out, as you will certainly be stopped at a roadblock later. In Zanzibar it is more important to have the endorsement than the actual licence; the police station there will provide you with the paperwork on payment of the T.shs 6,000 fee. Self-drive **car hire** is expensive and most companies offer a car with a driver. The most reliable international operators for car hire include Hertz, Avis and Europcar; *see* box, above, and also the 'Getting Around' sections in each town.

By Bus

Buses connect just about every town, large or small, that is anywhere near a road. Bus travel is very cheap, although bus companies have different reputations for adhering to speed limits, overloading and safety, so it can be worth asking around before booking. For

bus routes and companies, *see* the 'Getting There' sections throughout this guide.

By Boat

There are many ferries plying Tanzania's three major lakes, as well as those that cross from the mainland to Zanzibar and Pemba (*see* 'Zanzibar', p.320). Keep an eye on your luggage on boat or ferry journeys, particularly if you are sitting on deck. For details of Lake Victoria ferries, *see* p.154; Lake Tanganyika, *see* pp.263; Lake Nyasa, *see* p.304.

By Rail

Tanzania has two separate railway systems, with different gauge lines. The **TAZARA** (Tanzania–Zambia Railway Authority) line links Dar es Salaam in Tanzania to Kapiri Mposhi in Zambia via Mbeya. The **Tanzanian Railways Corporation** (TRC) runs the 'Central Line' that crosses the country from Dar es Salaam in the east to Kigoma in the west, with branch lines to Mtwara on Lake Victoria in the northwest, and Mpanda in the southwest. It was built by the German colonial administration in the early years of the 20th century. The TRC lines were washed away by floods in 1997, but have been restored.

Train services are never fast in Tanzania, but are the only way of reaching some areas overland – especially the far west around Kigoma. – and are also recommended as the best means of transport to Mbeya and the southeast.

TAZARA runs reliable ordinary and express train services from Dar es Salaam. The **express** leaves on Tuesdays and Fridays at 5.30pm, and goes all the way to Kapiri Mposhi, stopping at Ifakara, Makamoko, Mbeya and Tunduma, and taking 36 hours to complete its journey. The **ordinary** service runs on Mondays, Thursdays and Saturdays at 11am and only goes as far as Tunduma on the Zambian border. It takes 24 hours to reach Mbeya, travelling at a leisurely pace through the Selous in the early morning and then wiggling through the Udzungwa Mountains and Kilombero Valley before reaching Mbeya the next morning.

Railway Offices

TAZARA, Tanzania-Zambia Railway Authority, PO Box 2834, Dar es Salaam, **t** (022) 2862191–2/2865187, **f** (022) 2862472: journeys from Dar es Salaam to Mzenga, Mwana, Fuga Halt, Kisaki, Msolwa, Katulukila, Mang'ula, Mwaya, Kisawasawa, Kiberege, Ifakara, Makambako, Chimala, Igurusi, Mbeya, Tunduma and New Kapiri Mposhi in Zambia.

Tanzanian Railways Corporation, PO Box 468, Dar es Salaam, **t** (022) 2112529/2117833: trains to Kigoma, Mwanza and Mpanda via Morogoro, Dodoma and Tabora, and marine services on Lakes Tanganyika and Victoria.

Tanzanian Railways Corporation trains run between Dar es Salaam and Kigoma via Morogoro, Dodoma, Tabora and Uvinza three times a week, leaving Dar on Tuesdays, Wednesdays, Fridays and Sundays at 5pm and Kigoma at 7pm. It takes around 40 hours to cover the interim distance of nearly 1,300km.

The train splits at Tabora, where one branch goes north to Mwanza, on the shores of Lake Victoria, and another south from Tabora to Mpanda. Another train travels from Dar to Moshi once a week.

There are three classes: **first class** is a two-berth compartment, **second class** a six-berth compartment, and **third class** a seat – if you can get one. Compartments are reserved for men or women only unless you book the whole thing. It's worth splashing out on a two-berther if you can. Fares are roughly $60 first class and $40 second class to Kapiri Mposhi, or $40 first class and $25 second class to Mbeya, on the TAZARA line, and $40 first class, $30 second class to Kigoma or Mwanza on the TRC lines. It is worth booking at least three days in advance, although you can buy a third-class ticket on the day.

All trains have dining cars, serving reasonable food and soft drinks. Security is not great on the trains, so take any valuables with you when you leave the compartment, stow your luggage away and remain vigilant.

Practical A–Z

Begging and Gifts

Begging is not a major problem in Tanzania, although there are a few beggars in the larger cities, often with afflictions such as blindness or leprosy. It is, however, becoming more common to encounter cheeky children trying their luck for gifts in rural areas. It is tourists' behaviour that determines the attitudes of Tanzanians towards them. If all Westerners dole out money, pens and sweets to children, then all visitors will be asked for them. It is better to give gifts as a sign of thanks, friendship and appreciation. If you wish to travel prepared, take items like books and coloured pens, as these are unaffordable luxuries.

Children

Tanzanians are welcoming to children and helpful to families travelling with them. Anyone travelling with young children should go prepared, as powdered milk, pre-prepared baby foods and disposable nappies are not available outside the major towns. Children are welcomed in most safari lodges, although long days of driving in the northern parks may not be suitable for all children, and it may be better to take a private safari at a slower pace, with the freedom to return to a lodge swimming pool earlier in the day! A few lodges have a policy of not encouraging parents to bring young children, so check with your tour operator or individual lodges before you go.

Climate and When to Go

Just south of the equator, Tanzania remains warm all year round, with average temperatures 25–30°C. The country is divided into three main climatic areas: the coastal area, where conditions are tropical; the hot and dry central plateau, which endures considerable daily and seasonal temperature variations; and semi-temperate highland areas, where the climate is healthy and cool.

The long rains – *masika* – fall in April and May, continuing until June on Kilimanjaro, the coast and Zanzibar. These are long monsoon showers that fall periodically throughout the day. Driving on dirt roads becomes very slow as they turn to thick black mud. There is also a period of short rains – *mvuli* – in November, which are shorter showers in the morning and evening, clearing to warm sunshine in between. The exception is the southwest of Tanzania, including Ruaha National Park, where the rains fall just once a year, between January and April. The climate from mid- to late June is dry with very low humidity, heating up until October. These months are an excellent time to visit. The weather cools down in November when the monsoon wind brings the rains. Between December and March the humidity gets higher and temperatures hotter again.

Disabled Travellers

Tanzania is not ideal for disabled travellers with limited mobility, but more adventurous people who can bear a bit of bundling in and out of light aircraft and safari vehicles can enjoy as full a safari experience as anyone else. The Sopa lodges in the north have access and facilities for disabled clients. Travellers with back problems are advised to think twice about a safari, as the roads are bumpy.

Disability Organizations

Holiday Care Service, 7th Floor, Sunley House, 4 Bedford Park, Croydon, Surrey CRO 2AP, t 0845 124 9971, *www.holidaycare.org.uk*.

RADAR (Royal Association for Disability and Rehabilitation), 12 City Forum, 250 City Road, London EC1V 8AF, t (020) 7250 3222, f (020) 7250 0212, *www.radar.org.uk*.

Tripscope, Alexandra House, Albany Road, Brentford, Middlesex TW8 0NE, t (08457) 585641, f (020) 8580 7022, *www.just mobility.co.uk/tripscope*.

Mobility International USA, 451 Broadway, Eugene, OR 97401, t (541) 343 1284, *www. miusa.org*.

Society for Accessible Travel and Hospitality (SATH), 347 5th Ave, New York, NY 10016, t (212) 447 7284, *www.sath.org*.

Electricity

Mains electricity aims for 230V, 50Hz, but is subject to strong fluctuations. Many rural tourist lodges and hotels have a back-up generator supply. You can usually find a plug somewhere to power up video cameras, laptops and mobile phones. Plugs are usually three square-pin sockets, in the British style, but occasionally you find round three-pin sockets. It's worth taking a universal adapter – and a good torch!

Embassies and Consulates

Your own country's embassy, consulate or high commission can help you in a crisis – although the US Embassy needed help itself after a terrorist bomb attack in 1998.

British High Commission, Social Security House, Azikiwe Street/Samora Machel Avenue, PO Box 9200, Dar es Salaam, t (022) 2110101/2116770–3/2117659–64, f (022) 2112951. *Open Mon–Fri 7.30–2.30.*

Canadian High Commission, 38 Mirambo/ Garden Avenue, Dar es Salaam, PO Box 1022, t (022) 2112831, f (022) 2116896. *Open Mon–Fri 7.15–3.15.*

US Embassy, 140 Msese Road, Kinondoni District, PO Box 9123, Dar es Salaam, t (022) 2668001/2666010–5, f (022) 2666701, *usembassy-dar2@cats-net.com.*

European Union Embassy, 38 Mirambo Street, PO Box 9514, Dar es Salaam, t (022) 2117473, f (022) 2113277.

Embassy of Ireland, Plot 1131, Msasani (off Haile Selassie Road), Dar es Salaam, PO Box 9612, t (022) 2602355/2722182–3/ 2724021–2, f (022) 2715966. *Open Mon–Thurs 8–1 and 2–5.*

Health and Insurance

By Dr Jane Wilson-Howarth.

When planning any journey, consider the level of fitness required for what you plan to do and try to sort out any recurrent medical problems that have been bothering you, because heat, humidity and a change of diet can make even athlete's foot intolerable.

Accidents and robberies do happen in Tanzania – as anywhere – and having travel insurance helps to prevent a bad situation from becoming worse. Most international tour operators can arrange insurance, although (especially if you are a frequent traveller) it may be cheaper to take out an annual policy. Consider buying insurance with the Flying Doctors, who use light aircraft to rescue patients from bush locations all over East Africa and transfer them to hospital, usually in Nairobi, their base for over 40 years. The service is run by the **African Medical and Research Foundation (AMREF UK)**, Kensington Charity Centre, 4th Floor, Charles House, 375 Kensington High Street, London W14 8QH, t (020) 7471 6755, f (020) 7471 6756, *www. amref.org.* Membership costs from $15 for 14 days and profits fund the foundation's excellent work for community hospitals throughout East Africa.

Immunizations

Looking after your health while visiting a tropical country like Tanzania means that you must be aware of preventative measures against all forms of sickness, before, during and after travel· immunizations are valuable but don't give total protection from all diseases.

Visit a travel clinic or your GP practice nurse at least six weeks before departure. UK travellers can get some vaccines free from their GP. Ensure that you are up to date with immunizations for polio, tetanus, typhoid and hepatitis A. The doctor should prescribe appropriate anti-malaria tablets (*see* 'Malaria', below) and may recommend one or more of the following vaccinations: yellow fever, meningitis and/or rabies. Long-term travellers should probably also be covered for hepatitis B and TB. Anyone suffering from a medical condition should consult discuss plans with their usual doctor. Some health advisors will discourage travel to Tanzania when pregnant, or with young children; malaria is especially dangerous for these people.

It is important to take meticulous precautions to avoid **insect bites**: exposed skin should be covered at dusk and repellents applied; it is best to sleep under a permethrin-impregnated mosquito net. Permethrin can also be sprayed on to clothes as an additional preventative strategy. **Malaria tablets** are also important for visitors to Tanzania. Anti-malarial tablets should be started before setting off on your trip, and continued after returning home; the timing of doses depends upon the preparation taken. Your doctor will help you choose between the three prophylactics that are effective for Africa: weekly mefloquine (Lariam), daily Malarone or daily doxycycline. Over-the-counter chloroquine and Paludrine are much less effective in the region (around 45% protection versus more than 90% for the other three), and are not usually recommended unless you have good medical reasons that prevent you taking more effective prophylactics. Homeopathic preparations are not effective at all. Consult an frequently updated, expert travel health source (see box, far right) in case of outbreaks or changes in health risks.

Heat and Sun

Most people take one to three weeks to acclimatize to hot temperatures. Try not to over-exert yourself when you first arrive, as you may risk **heat exhaustion**. Wear cotton clothes and a hat. You must also drink more water or soft drinks, and, if your appetite for salt increases, add more salt to your food.

If you must sunbathe, expose yourself gradually to the sun, beginning with 15–20 minutes a day, and avoid midday exposure between 11am and 3pm. Pack long-sleeved loose clothes and a sun cream of SPF15 or above. Being wet or in water does not protect you from the sun; water acts like a lens and will increase the likelihood of sunburn and subsequently skin ageing and cancers.

Diseases and Nasties

Some people have concerns about possible illnesses when travelling abroad. Most visitors to Tanzania, however, need only worry about the risks of diarrhoea (from contaminated food and drink) and malaria. Notes follow on health hazards.

High Risk

Bilharzia: The Rift Valley lakes of Africa are common sites for catching bilharzia, and a study at the Hospital for Tropical Diseases in London found that about one-third of the 344 cases treated acquired their disease from Lake Nyasa. Bilharzia or schistosomiasis is caused by a tiny worm which spends part of its life cycle in freshwater snails and the other part in people. The parasite causes 'swimmer's itch' as it burrows through the skin while you paddle or bathe in infected water. From the skin, the worm rides the bloodstream, traverses the lungs, where it often causes coughs 2–3 weeks

after the itch, and finally sets up home to cause an illness with fever. Untreated, this will settle (although it is best to get the infection cleared), but in locals who are constantly re-infected, the disease becomes debilitating, and can kill after 20 years or so. Travellers are mostly diagnosed and cured in a couple of months; the real sufferers are the poor, who have no access to treatment. A single dose of praziquantel cures bilharzia.

Avoidance is better than cure: avoid swimming or paddling within 200m of where water is used by locals, or where children are likely to play. It is possible to contract the disease by showering in untreated lake water. Chlorinated water, in swimming pools or showers, is safe. If you feel you have put yourself at risk, you can have a blood test at least eight weeks after leaving a bilharzia area; there may be no initial symptoms.

Diarrhoea: Travellers' diarrhoea is avoided by eating sensibly. Although there are many causes of diarrhoea, the avoidance strategies are the same for each type. Food is the main problem; ensure that yours is prepared and stored in a hygienic manner, that you always wash your hands with soap before eating anything, and that your drinking water is safe. Eating cooked-to-order hot meals in restaurants is safer than eating ready-made dishes. Be at your most cautious when you are staying in large centres of population, since the more people there are around you, the more faeces there will be. The star ratings of hotels are no guide to hygiene.

The new oral cholera vaccine Dukoral is now available in much of Europe and Canada gives quite good short term protection against travellers gastroenteritis; see www.TravellersDiarrhea.com.

Keep to the 'peel it, boil it, cook it, wash it… or forget it' rule and know about rehydration drinks. If you do contract simple diarrhoea, a light, bland diet and lots of clear fluids will settle the symptoms quickly. In the very few travellers who become especially ill, it is adequate fluid replacement that saves life, not antibiotics or anti-diarrhoeal medicines. To maintain fluid balance, an adult should drink two glassfuls of any clear fluid each time the bowels are opened, and more if you are thirsty. If you are vomiting, drink slowly, in sips. If you are passing only a scant amount of dark-coloured urine, drink more. Combinations of sugar and salt are absorbed best, so add a pinch of salt to sweet drinks or a spoonful of sugar to savoury drinks. Good drinks to take are oral rehydration salts (ORS), water, clear soups, young coconut or drinks made from Marmite, Bovril or stock cubes; weak black tea and coffee may also be taken. ORS are best for children, the frail, those with long-standing medical problems and anyone with very profuse (12 times a day) diarrhoea. If you have no appetite, eat nothing, or take light, plain, non-fatty food such as yoghurt, bananas, dry biscuits or bread. Diarrhoea that goes on for more than 3–4 days should be treated with antibiotics. Passing blood and/or mucus, and/or having a fever with diarrhoea probably means you need antibiotic treatment in addition to fluid replacement; seek medical advice.

Hepatitis: Hepatitis means inflammation of the liver. The common causes in travellers are three viruses: hepatitis A (most common, also called infective hepatitis), hepatitis B (serum hepatitis) and the newly recognized hepatitis E. Jaundice (yellowing) due to the hepatitis A or E virus is frequently acquired by travellers; it is one of the many filth-to-mouth diseases. Hepatitis B is acquired in the same ways as HIV – dirty needles, blood transfusions and sex – and will need hospital treatment.

There is a very effective vaccine for hepatitis A: two injections give at least 10 years' protection. Immunization against hepatitis B is probably not indicated for short-term travel, but its value can be discussed with your doctor or travel clinic.

Meningitis: Meningococcal infection causes fever and such an intense headache that you won't want to roll over in bed or look at light. It is a medical emergency. Immunization protects only against some types of bacterial meningitis. In Africa epidemics occur at the onset of the dry season and usually stop with the first rains in May–June.

Mosquitoes and other biters: Malaria-bearing mosquitoes come out as the sun goes down, when it is advisable to change into long trousers and shirt-sleeves and apply a repellent (containing DEET). Sleeping under an insecticide-impregnated bednet protects you from mosquitoes that otherwise will bite if you roll against the net in your sleep; tiny

Travellers' Health Advisory Services

For up-to-date health advice in the UK:

Hospital for Tropical Diseases travel clinic, Mortimer Market, Capper Street, London WC1E 6AU, t (020) 7387 4411, Health Line t (020) 7388 9600, www.thehtd.org.

Malaria Reference Laboratory, London School of Hygiene and Tropical Medicine, Keppel Street, London WC1E 7HT, premium rate line t 09065 508908.

MASTA, www.masta.org. For a personalized health brief, call t 09065 501 402 at premium rate, or call t 0870 241 6843 for the nearest MASTA clinic.

Nomad Travel Health line, t 09068 633414.

Royal Free Travel Health Centre, Pond St., London NW3 2QG, t (020) 7830 2885.

Travel Clinic, Cambridge, 48a Mill Road, CB1 2AS, t (01223) 367362.

www.fitfortravel.scot.nhs.uk for immunization requirements and travel advice.

www.fco.gov.uk/travel/countryadvice provides security information by country.

For health information in the USA contact:

Centers for Disease Control (Attention Health Information), Center for Prevention Services, Division of Quarantine, Atlanta, GA 30333, t 888 232 3228, www.cdc.gov. The central source of travel health information in North America, with a phone and fax-back service. Also publishes the invaluable Health Information for International Travel.

biters like sand-flies, which are so small that they can penetrate untreated nets, are also kept off. Once bitten, try to avoid scratching, since breaks in the skin can lead to troublesome infection. There is one excellent antihistamine spray available containing anaesthetic, sold in a pocket-sized canister, which is one answer for anyone prone to over-reaction to insect bites; otherwise use antihistamine tablets and cool compresses. A mild steroid cream such as 1% hydrocortisone is also helpful.

Sexually Transmitted Infections (STIs): HIV/AIDS and other STIs are widespread in sub-Saharan Africa. Avoid unprotected sex; do take your own condoms or femidoms, and leave unused supplies which could be life-savers for others.

Typhoid: Typhoid is rare in the region, and it is arguable that immunization against it is not necessary for travel to sub-Saharan Africa since the likelihood of contracting the disease there is small (similar to that in southern Europe). An overall figure of risk in travellers from the USA is six cases per million journeys.

Low Risk

Cholera: Even if travellers are infected, they are unlikely to suffer any symptoms from cholera. Sudden, severe and profuse watery diarrhoea, sometimes with vomiting, is more often due to E.coli food poisoning. Whatever the bug, profuse diarrhoea is treated by drinking plenty of clear, non-alcoholic fluid (see 'Diarrhoea' above). There is a new oral vaccine called Dukoral which gives two years' protection against cholera.

Dengue Fever (DF): or 'breakbone fever' is spread by day-biting Aedes mosquitoes; they breed in clean water and are common in tropical gardens. It cannot be spread person to person and the incubation period is 5–7 days. DF causes severe muscle pains (hence 'breakbone'), high fever (40°C) of abrupt onset and a measles-like rash, but the illness lasts no more than a week. There is no specific treatment, except paracetamol (Tylenol; not aspirin) for the fever and pain, and non-alcoholic fluid in plenty. The severe and life-threatening haemorrhagic form of the disease does not seem to occur in Africa.

Elephantiasis (filariasis): Those who harbour this parasite for years develop elephantine swelling of the legs, hence its name: it's also known as filariasis, because it is caused by filarial worms; they can be spread by day- and night-biting mosquitoes. It occurs in much of the tropics, but is treatable. The incubation period is from a few weeks to 15 months. The blood test for filaria is done more than six weeks after leaving a risk area.

Rabies: Rabies vaccine is an innocuous immunization and a sensible precaution for people travelling to remote places or visiting the developing world, especially regions where there are a lot of stray domestic animals. The incubation period (the amount of time you have to get treatment after a bite) depends on the severity and distance the bite is from the brain. It is important that children visiting Tanzania are immunized: young children are most likely to get bitten on the face, so there is very little time to get medical help. If dogs threaten you, stoop as if to pick up a stone to throw at them; most dogs will retreat if they think you are armed. Never handle wild animals (especially bats, jackals, foxes, mongooses, domestic and wild monkeys) that are unusually tame; they may be dying of rabies. No animal bite should be ignored; clean the wound vigorously under running water and with antiseptic or soap, then flood with antiseptic or alcohol (gin, whisky or rum) and seek medical advice promptly.

River Blindness: The unpleasant worm which causes onchocerciasis is transmitted during the day near to fast-flowing rivers where small black-fly vectors breed. Their bites cause big lumps in the skin with a bloody speck at the centre, and are itchy for days. Most commonly the disease makes the skin incredibly itchy, and is usually confined to a single limb, the arms or just the legs. Generally people need to have had heavy infestations for years before the eyes are threatened. Get any symptoms properly diagnosed and treated.

Sleeping Sickness: There is little chance of being infected by African trypanosomiasis, the sleeping sickness associated with the tsetse fly, as it does not survive in wild animals, and the swarms generally remain in one area. However, there have been some cases reported from Tanzania recently and so care should be taken. Tsetse flies are the worst blight of a safari if you hit one of their vast swarms. The best approach is to wind up the windows and drive on through. They like leafy habitats, forested lake shores and river banks or forest-savannah mosaic. They are active during daylight hours and are attracted to blue. They are about twice the size of an English house fly.

Often a small scab first appears at the site of the bite; within a few days there is usually a fever which comes and goes. There is also headache, loss of appetite and swelling of the lymph glands, especially in the neck. Eventually parasites invade the brain, causing the apathy, sleepiness and then coma that gives the disease its name. By this time treatment is difficult. Local knowledge about the disease is good, so ask before you venture into the bush. Debate continues as to whether insect repellent does deter tsetses, and any enlightening comments on this topic will be welcome.

Tetanus, Polio and Diphtheria: You will probably have been immunized against these very serious diseases as a child: all are a danger to travellers and are prevalent in Africa, although polio is nearing complete eradication. They all need boosting every 10 years.

Tuberculosis: TB is on the increase worldwide. It is a potentially serious infection that usually begins in the lungs, and is spread by infected people coughing over others. Travellers on a short trip are unlikely to risk infection. TB isn't very infectious and is only caught after a extended exposure; walking through a market puts you at no risk. It can also be contracted from infected cow's milk. Most British adults will have been immunized against TB with BCG at birth or at about age 13. Check whether this was done; it leaves a little scar on the upper arm. It never needs boosting. BCG is given in the UK and the Netherlands but is not offered in the USA or the rest of mainland Europe.

Worms: Worms are more alarming than dangerous. The most common is the roundworm (*Ascaris lumbricoides*); it looks like a large earthworm and is about 30cm long. They rarely cause problems beyond vague abdominal symptoms: most travellers will be unaware of the worms' presence until one that has died of old age emerges a year or so after it stowed away. Generally worms are avoided through good food hygiene. Thorough cooking destroys them. Hookworm, though, can be picked up by walking barefoot in damp shady places where people have defecated so are avoided by wearing shoes.

Yellow Fever: This is a very serious, untreatable mosquito-borne disease endemic in much of sub-Saharan Africa. There is a good vaccine that protects for 10 years, and become effective 10 days after the immunization. Seek up-to-date advice on whether vaccination is required or recommended before you travel to any part of Tanzania.

Small Biters

Bites from mosquitoes, sand-flies, black-flies and other blood-hungry little beasts are prevented by covering up, using DEET and Merck 3535-based repellents, and permethrin-impregnated bednets. Consider permethrin-treating your clothes too.

Bed bugs: You will only encounter these if you stay in downmarket hotels. By day these bugs lurk in cracked plaster or brick walls, bed frames and the corners of mosquito nets. Move your bed away from the wall, and keep a light on if possible. One bed bug takes 10–20 minutes to drink its fill of blood, and if interrupted will bite repeatedly until it has had enough, or you kill it. Bites are painful enough to keep you awake, and often very inflamed and itchy afterwards, otherwise there are no long-term problems.

Ticks: Ticks are widespread, and you should check your clothing and body all over after you have been out bush-walking. Once they have started feeding, the best way to remove them is to grasp the tick with finger and thumb as close to the skin as possible, and pull steadily. This often hurts. Do not jerk, twist or squeeze the tick itself. Once it has been removed, disinfect the skin with alcohol (gin, rum and whisky are fine) and wash your hands with soap and water. Tick-borne diseases are geographically localized, and local doctors know them. Symptoms tend to start with fever, aches and pains and headache. Some are treated with antibiotics. Seek medical advice.

Other Dangerous Animals

If venturing into wildlife country on foot, be sure to take a guide who understands animals. Many 'Africa hands' consider **buffalo**, **hippopotamus** and large **primates** (chimps and baboons) the most dangerous species. Buffalo are aggressive, and hippos are likely to trample you by mistake if you scare them and are between them and their river refuge.

Nile crocodiles are the other significant predator to contemplate if you are relaxing beside the river. They are merciless killers that take about 1,000 lives a year in Africa. They usually hunt victims who are drinking (or washing) at the waterside. The reptile swims at speed towards the riverbank and explodes out of the water unexpectedly. It's eyes are its only vulnerable spot. Take local advice on where it is safe to bathe.

Most **snakes** are not dangerous, and travellers are rarely unlucky enough to receive a dangerous bite. However, since the division between harmful and harmless species is far from clear, an expert should assess anyone bitten by a snake.

The bitten part should be washed with water and soap, and wiped gently with a clean cloth. This removes any venom from the skin's surface. If venom has entered the body, that part may swell, so any rings, watches and jewellery must be removed. Splinting the bitten limb slows absorption of the venom and reduces pain; application of a firm crêpe bandage is also helpful. Never cut into a snake bite; this does nothing but risk severing arteries in increasing blood loss. Tourniquets are also dangerous. Paracetamol (Tylenol) can be offered but do not give aspirin (it promotes bleeding). Prompt evacuation to a doctor or hospital is the priority, but don't panic; probably no venom has been dispensed.

Mountain Hazards

The region offers a chance to get to high altitude without experience, training or specialist equipment. Be careful, though. Mount Kilimanjaro, at 5,896m, is 500m higher than Everest base camp, which most mountaineers take two weeks to reach. Kilimanjaro presents serious risks of altitude illnesses: every year a few unlucky visitors on Mount Kilimanjaro die through ignorance and lack of preparation.

When you start your ascent, take it slowly, at a steady pace that feels comfortable for you. Don't try to keep up with macho show-offs – enjoy the scenery. If you feel yourself becoming unduly short of breath (look at your friends), slow it down even further; pace yourself to the slowest member of your party.

Altitude illnesses are dangerous because they come on quickly, and do not necessarily follow on from milder mountain sickness. Victims may be too disorientated to recognize how sick they are; they may even argue about descending – the only real treatment.

Symptoms of mild mountain sickness include: poor body performance, slight headache, fatigue, chest discomfort, insomnia, loss of appetite, nausea and vomiting. In this case, you should watch out for increasingly severe symptoms. Consider stopping for a rest day to acclimatize, or dramatically slow your ascent. Ideally descend to sleep lower down. Go no higher until the headache gets better.

Moderate to severe altitude sickness can cause rapid deterioration over a couple of hours. The symptoms include bad headache, disorientation and/or breathlessness and – most worrying - coughing up frothy or even bloodstained spit. If the victim starts to behave strangely, hallucinates or has difficulty in balancing, this is also cause for serious concern, and they should descend immediately, whatever the time of day or night. Descent is the only treatment and even going down 500-1000m will save a life.

The other hazard in the mountains is **hypothermia**, also known as exposure. It is most likely when you are cold, exhausted and/or hungry. As the body temperature falls, you feel inappropriately comfortable. Content, you lose the drive to get somewhere safe. Heat is lost more rapidly when the body is wet or chilled by wind. Don't drink alcohol since this increases heat loss. Make sure you are well equipped for your journey; be prepared for the worst possible weather. Carry a change of clothes in a plastic bag so that you can get warm and dry once you reach a safe place.

Watch the people you are walking with and be forceful if you think they are getting into trouble. Stumbling is an early warning sign. People with early exposure shiver; this ceases as they get seriously cold. Like altitude sickness, exposure clouds judgement, so it is up to the unaffected to protect sufferers. The treatment for exposure is slow, gentle rewarming. One technique is to put the victim in a sleeping bag with someone else. Insulate the body from the ground, and shelter from the wind. Hot drinks may also help.

Medical Kit

A small medical kit takes up little space and can be invaluable. Take a few painkillers, drying antiseptic such as potassium permanganate, dilute iodine, crystal (or gentian) violet or Savlon Dry spray and Band Aids or small dressings, as even small cuts may become infected if they are not covered, especially coral grazes. Oral rehydration sachets are also worth taking, and consider packing antihistamine tablets, throat pastilles and antacids. Water purification tablets or iodine drops are also very useful in those areas where water is not treated, although it is at some of the most well-established tourist hotels. Sun blocks and

About the 'Health' Author
Dr Jane Wilson-Howarth is a British GP who has worked for more than a decade in malarious regions. She is author of Cadogan's *Bugs Bites & Bowels*, a mine of useful and readable advice on travel health.

lip salves are essential for everyone, as is insect repellent, preferably containing DEET or Merck 3535.

If you wear glasses or contact lenses, you should have with you a spare pair of glasses or enough lenses and cleaning solutions to last your trip. Anyone with a medical prescription or contraception pills should also bring an ample supply and a note of the generic name and dose of the prescription, clearly written.

Media

The semi-official *Daily News* and the *Guardian*, a more independent publication, are the most widely available English-language Tanzanian daily papers. The former, extremely pro-Government and mildly simplistic, is easiest to come by. Both arrive a few days out of date in rural areas. A good, readable and informative alternative is the *East African*, a weekly publication produced in Kenya by the Aga Khan Group, on sale each Monday.

The *Business Times* and the *Express* are also produced by the IPP Media Group, publisher of the *Guardian* and the *African*, an interesting independent publication, but much harder to get hold of, as only a few issues are printed. IPP has a website, *www.ippmedia.com*.

The Government runs two radio stations, Radio Tanzania and Radio Tanzania-Zanzibar. There are also a growing number of smaller independent stations, the most established being Radio One and Capital Radio. Television channels include Independent Television (ITV), Dar es Salaam Television (DTV), and Coast Television Network (CTN).

Money

The cowrie shell was replaced as the common currency in 1896, when one rupee was exchanged for every 200 shells under the laws of British East Africa. The florin replaced the rupee, and then that in turn was replaced in 1922 by the Tanzanian Shilling (T.shs).

An official government requirement used to ensure that all tourists paid their bills in US dollars. This remains the norm for upmarket accommodation, although the rule has been relaxed and budget operators will accept either currency. Prices, where listed in the book, are in the currency you are most likely to be asked for, so US dollar prices are usually given for 'international' places, Tanzanian shilling prices for 'local' places.

Paying by **credit card** is now possible in many expensive tourist hotels and shops, but may incur an astronomical fee; check with your own bank before you go what charges it will make. Cash machines are virtually non-existent. The best option is to bring as much spending money as you will need and can keep safe in dollars, with travellers' cheques to back you up. It is best to change money in *bureaux de change* or **banks**, which pay better rates than the black market street traders, are legal, and are less likely to rip you off. There are banks in all major towns. Most banks will limit the daily transaction to $200; *bureaux de change* do not. Ask for smaller notes when changing money to Tanzanian shillings, as change can be a problem.

National Park Fees

Park fees are payable on entry to all national parks, and must be paid in dollars. Keep all documentation close at hand, as you may be required to show it on a spot check by rangers. Generally, safari driver-guides will take care of this for you, but check before you set off.

The national parks in the north have a flat fee of $50 per person per day with additional camping charges. Children under 5 are free, and under-16-year-olds pay $5 per day. Ngorongoro Crater may charge as much as $100. Katavi, Mikumi, Rubondo, Udzungwa and Ruaha national parks charge $15 a day per person, $5 for children 5–16 years old. Gombe Stream charges $40 per day, Mahale Mountains $50. Official national park guides charge $10 per day, $15 out of normal hours and $20 trekking.

A sport fishing permit is required to fish at Mahale Mountains, Rubondo Island or Gombe

Stream, costing $50 to fish between 7am and 5pm. Fishing is allowed in Selous as long as the place where you are lodged has a permit, as most do. Huts, hostels and resthouses run by TANAPA range in price from $40 for huts on Kilimanjaro to $20 for resthouses in Katavi. Camping costs $25 to $40. Filming fees are payable for any professional work. Fees are also payable for game reserves and conservation areas, generally slightly cheaper.

For further information contact **Tanzania National Parks Association (TANAPA)**, PO Box 3134, Arusha, Tanzania, t (027) 2503471/250 4082, f (027) 2508216, *info@tanzaniaparks. com, www.tanzaniaparks.com.*

Opening Hours and Public Holidays

Official office hours are generally Monday to Friday, from 8 to 12 and 2 to 4.30 or 6. Small businesses are sometimes open on Saturdays between 8 and 12.30 too.

Banks open Monday to Friday from 8.30 to 3, and sometimes on Saturdays from 8.30 to 1.

Shops are generally open from Monday to Saturday, 8.30 to 12 and 2 to 6, or later in areas around Dar es Salaam or Zanzibar Stone Town. In regions where the population is mainly Muslim, such as Zanzibar, shops may be closed on Friday afternoons, as this is considered the most important day to visit the mosque.

The combination of religious beliefs means that Tanzanians do well for **holidays**. Muslim festivals are dated according to local sightings of the phases of the moon, so their dates vary.

Packing

Anyone planning to take a safari in Tanzania is advised to pack a few lightweight items of clothing in neutral colours, as bright colours will scare the wildlife and could ruin your safari! Natural fibres are more comfortable for most months of the year in Tanzania, with something warmer for the cool evenings, especially in the highlands.

You won't need more than a few changes of clothes, as most camps, lodges and hotels have an 'in-house' washing service. You can usually find someone willing to wash your

Public Holidays
12 Jan Zanzibar Revolutionary Day
5 Feb CCM Party Day
Mar–April Easter
26 April Union Day/National Day
1 May International Labour Day
7 July Industrial Day, or Saba Saba, the 7th of the 7th; a big trade fair in Dar.
8 Aug Farmer's Day
9 Dec Independence Day/Republic Day
25 Dec Christmas Day
26 Dec Boxing Day
Eid-ul-Fitr, 2 days, celebrating end of Ramadan
Eid-ul-Adha, the end of the Mecca pilgrimage
Maulidi Day, Prophet Mohammed's Birthday

Festivals
The Zanzibar Film Festival (ZIFF), or Festival of the Dhow Countries, has run for seven years for a week in July and is well established. Films are shown and musicians from the 'dhow countries' of the Indian Ocean perform in Stone Town (*see* pp.316–17).
'Sauti Za Busara', PO Box 3635, Zanzibar, t (024) 2232423/t (0747) 428478, *busara@ zanlink.com*. The Swahili Music Festival opened in 2004 as a celebration of Swahili music culture. A roaring success to date, it is held in February, over a week.
Mwaka Koga, or Nairuz, the Zoroastrian new year, its date set according to a pre-Islamic solar calendar some time in July. Celebrated in parts of Zanzibar and Pemba (*see* p.316).

clothes in budget places too. If you plan to use these services, bring items that can withstand a pulping, as clothes are powerfully washed and wrung out by hand. Also show some sensitivity towards those who wash your clothes for a pittance. It is best to bring soap and wash your own underwear, as days without knicker elastic are awkward!

Bring long-sleeved, long-legged clothing to change into just before sundown, as this is the prime munching hour for mosquitoes. Being well covered is far more pleasant and effective than copious repellent – although this is still essential for exposed areas. These clothes will also come in handy for travel through local villages and Muslim areas; it is fine to wear shorts and swimming costumes in tourist areas, around hotels and on safari, but keep a kanga or kikoi handy to wrap around your legs if you want to stop.

Comfortable shoes with closed sides are essential if you intend to go on any walking safaris. Simple deck shoes, trainers, light lace-ups or slip-ons are adequate for a day out, but you will need proper walking shoes or sturdy boots for longer treks. If you plan to climb Mounts Kilimanjaro or Meru, pack appropriate mountain clothing (see pp.166–7).

If you are travelling on small light aircraft within Tanzania pack your clothes in a squash-able travel bag; hard Samsonite-style cases often will not fit into the hold.

Photography

It is advisable to bring all photographic equipment and film with you, especially slide or special requirement films. Colour film is available, but is expensive and may be past its sell-by date. Most safari-goers feel inspired to take many rolls of film, so bring more than you expect to need, or a large memory card if your camera is digital. For safaris, the longer the lens the better: most photographers take at least a 300mm lens, and a teleconverter is a cheap way to double the focal length of your lens. Longer lenses need more light and work better with a high-speed film: 400 ASA should be fast enough. Bring a dust-proof, knock-proof carrier for your camera and storing film in a tight-fitting airtight box or bag that will keep it cool and dark while you are travelling.

Most Tanzanians do not see themselves as a tourist attraction, and may resent being photographed. Respect the dignity and rights of people you wish to photograph by asking politely if you may take a picture. Some people may ask for money, notably Maasai around the northern parks; this is a fairly innocuous exchange that may recommend tourists to much poorer local people. Otherwise take a long lens, and be subtle!

Post Offices

There are more than 200 post offices across Tanzania and Zanzibar, but you are advised to get your mail to a central town for posting, as rural and island offices can wait days for collection. In general, post from central towns takes 3–5 days to Europe and the Middle East by airmail, and 5–7 days to the USA. Larger parcels can be prohibitively expensive, so it is better to use a shipping company if you plan to send larger items abroad.

Religion

The country is roughly divided in religious practices. No census has ever dared to ask people's religion, so all estimates are guesses. Muslims in Tanzania claim to make up around 70 per cent of the population, but a perhaps more realistic estimate is that around 35 per cent are Muslim (both Sunnite and Shia) and 35 per cent Christians, with denominations including Catholics, Lutherans, Anglicans, Presbyterians and Baptists. Many Tanzanians, however – the remaining 30 per cent – hold traditional beliefs, particularly in rural regions, often alongside Christianity or Islam.

An influx of Asian immigrants has also seen a growth in Hindu and Bohoran faiths, while many Muslims follow the Aga Khan's Isma'ili Khoja Islam. Religious beliefs are centred in certain areas: on Zanzibar Christians are about 3 per cent, while around Kilimanjaro the population is mainly Christian.

The Government of Tanzania officially adheres to a policy of strict religious equality, observing the holy days of all major groups. The best education and healthcare, however, are often still provided by missionary and mosque schools and hospitals – despite the best efforts of the socialist 'ujamaa' policy.

Visitors should be sensitive to local customs and religious practices, as a sign of respect to their hosts; it will also affect their reception. In Muslim areas it is deemed offensive to dress in clothes which reveal the shoulders and knees, for men and women alike. Women are not allowed to enter mosques, and men who do should remove their shoes and behave appropriately. **Friday**, Ijumaa, is the day set aside for visiting the mosque and praying by Muslims; opening hours may be affected. During the month of **Ramadan**, fixed annually according to the lunar calendar, when devout Muslims fast between sunrise and sunset, and feast thereafter, it is considered insensitive to eat in the streets in the daytime, and restaurants may be closed for lunch in Zanzibar.

It is seen as ill-mannered for lovers of any sexual orientation to make **public displays of affection**; holding hands is as demonstrative as it gets for most Tanzanians when in the public eye. Despite frequent hand-holding between male friends, gay relationships are not acknowledged, and kissing could incite an unwelcome reaction from onlookers.

Safety

Visitors to Tanzania are advised to take as few valuables with them as possible, and to keep large sums of money, expensive watches and jewellery out of sight as far as possible, out of sensitivity to impoverished Tanzanians and as a security precaution. Most hotels have a safe. When shopping or in a public place keep your spending money in your pockets, or a discreet shoulder bag. Keep passports, airline tickets, travellers' cheques and credit cards in a money belt that can be hidden under your clothes when on the road. Be vigilant in bus stations and markets.

Muggings have been reported recently on some tourist beaches; use your common sense, and avoid deserted areas and the back streets of main towns after dark if alone. If you feel endangered, look out for a friendly local face and ask for company. If you are unlucky enough to face an attempted mugging, shouting '*mwizi*', meaning thief, or '*mwezi*' for more than one, will bring people running to help. But use this only in emergencies, as it may incite an extreme response, with punishment meted out on the spot. All this said, most Tanzanians are trustworthy.

Shopping

Popular items for shopping in Tanzania are local **arts and crafts**, which range in style and design from region to region or the traditional skills of their originating tribe. **Stalls and co-operatives** are springing up around the country that thrive on the tourist market. They do often have a horrible tourist trap feel, but they may be the only chance you will have to find excellent pieces of art – the Makonde region, for example, may not be the best place to find better or cheaper Makonde artwork, as most artists ship their wares to Dar es Salaam and Arusha. **Craft villages** such as those run by the Maasai near the northern parks are often the most rewarding way that these dispossessed people have of making a living, and they are often impressive artisans.

When shopping in tourist centres, bargain, barter and brow-beat, walk away, pretend your dog has died and never take the first price, which is bound to be a rip-off.

Makonde ebony-wood carvings are highly sought-after (*see* pp.255 and 256). Maasai beadwork is found in the north. Elsewhere, baskets, tree barks, ceremonial drums, grass mats, pottery, paintings and batiks are found.

In Zanzibar intricately carved camphor chests and unusual painted batiks can be bought alongside a colourful range of cheap and useful kangas and kakois – worn like sarongs by Tanzanian women (*see* pp.350–51).

Sports and Activities

Football

Football is wildly popular throughout the country, and Manchester United fans have been known to profess their obsession in rural villages where there is no obvious sign of a TV. But there are plenty of local teams, which attract strong support from all.

The most popular teams in Dar es Salaam are the Simba, 'lion' in Swahili, who wear a red and white strip, and the Young Africans, who wear green and yellow. Both clubs were established in the 1920s. There is no need to look in newspapers to find out when they are playing, as their distinctive colours adorn the streets of Dar for days before any match.

Golf

A brand new all-singing, all-dancing 18-hole course has opened at the Ngurdoto Mountain Village resort on the slopes of Mount Meru in Arusha. Other golf clubs are at Dar es Salaam and Arusha Gymkhana Clubs, both of which hold tournaments on their courses. The Dar course features 18 holes, while Arusha has nine. Both accept temporary membership from visitors. There are also courses at Morogoro and Iringa.

Diving

There is good diving around the coral reefs of the offshore Indian Ocean islands Zanzibar, Pemba and Mafia, for all levels of experience. See 'Zanzibar', pp.330, 334–5, 364 and 380.

Fishing, Boating, Riding and Trekking

See 'Safaris', pp.55–70.

Telephones and Internet

Telephones

The Tanzanian telephone system is not reliable and can test even the strongest patience, with lines frequently down, cutting out mid-conversation and costing an extortionate amount even for local calls. But the situation is improving: the network has attracted a number of foreign investors and mobile phone companies to fill the void. In 1995 there were three main telephone lines per 1,000 people; now mobile lines established by Mobitel and Tritel are expanding the airwaves, although it is still unlikely that you will find service on your mobile phone far from the main towns and commercial centres.

The national network is run by Tanzania Telecommunications Company Ltd, TTCL, who will invariably greet a large proportion of your calls with a recorded message detailing code changes or telling you to call further numbers that are inaccessible too. Often the best (and sometimes only) option for making calls is by visiting a central telephone communications centre, often located near the post office. Here an operator will take down the number you wish to call and make a number of attempts to get through before connecting you.

The **international IDD code** for dialling Tanzania from any other country is t +255.

Dial t 000 as a prefix to any international number from Tanzania.

For countries within East Africa, dial t 005 for Kenya and t 006 for Uganda.

Emergencies t 112; directory enquiries t 118.

Numbers prefixed by t 0741, t 0742, t 0747 and t 0748 are mobile phone numbers.

Internet connections are becoming much more common in Tanzania, especially among tour operators, hotels, airlines and other tourist services, international organizations and businesses. You will find many Internet cafés in almost every town.

Time

Time in East Africa can be a confusing point of reference. In Western terms, Tanzania is regarded as being **GMT +3 hours**, and this is the clock used by most government services, transport timetables and in this book.

Local people, however, often run on **Swahili time**, which begins at sunrise, 6am, 'saa kumi na mbili asubuhi', which is 12 hours in the morning in Swahili time; 7am, 'saa moja asubuhi', is one hour, and so on until 'saa kumi na mbili jioni', 12 hours again, at 6pm. There is definitely room for confusion! You can work out Swahili time by adding six hours to the western equivalent, or otherwise follow the Tanzanian example, and wear your watch upside down.

Tipping

Tipping is optional, but a tip of up to 10 per cent for good service is always appreciated. Budget for a potential tip of between $10 and $15 per person per day for your safari or mountain guide if the service is good, paid at the end. Staff and guides at individual safari lodges and beach locations may be tipped individually when you are due to leave, or sometimes a box is kept for tips to be divided among all the staff (including unseen collaborators in the kitchens and laundry).

Common Exchanges

027	Arusha	023	Morogoro
022	Dar es Salaam	023	Mtwara
026	Dodoma	028	Mwanza
026	Iringa	023	Pwani
028	Kagera (Bukoba)	025	Rukwa
028	Kigoma	025	Ruvuma
027	Kilimanjaro	028	Shinyanga
	(Moshi)	026	Singida
023	Lindi	026	Tabora
027	Manyara	027	Tanga
028	Mara (Musoma)	024	Zanzibar
025	Mbeya		

Tourist Offices

Tanzania Tourist Board, 3rd Floor, IPS Building,
PO Box 2485, Dar es Salaam, **t** (022) 2111244,
f (022) 2116420, *info@tanzaniatouristboard.
com, www.tanzaniatouristboard.com,
www.tanzania-web.com.*

Tanzania Trade Centre, 80 Borough High
Street, London SE1 1LL, **t** (020) 7407 0566,
f (020) 7403 2003.

Arusha Information Centre, PO Box 2348,
Arusha, **t** (027) 2503842.

Tourist Information

The Tanzania Tourist Board in Dar es Salaam
has a range of good photocopies, maps and
information about the city, but information is
progressively more limited the further afield
you travel. The TTB internet site contains a
wealth of information about the country and
has links to many of the safari companies,
lodges and coastal or island hotels. The tourist
board is represented in the UK by the Tanzania
Trade Centre, and in the rest of the world by its
embassies and consulates (*see* p.79).

Where to Stay and Eat

Accommodation possibilities range from the
most basic bed for a night to the most
imaginative, exquisitely run, all-inclusive
'dream hideaways'. Prices range dramatically
from less than $10 to nearly $1,000 a night.

There are numerous options for 'local'
accommodation in every small town, usually
fairly basic, and varying mainly in mosquito
nets, fans, bathrooms, toilets and cleanliness,
but individual standards change very quickly

Accommodation (per person per night)

	Hotels	Safari Lodges
very expensive	$250 or more	$450 or more
expensive	$100–250	$250–450
moderate	$30–100	$100–250
cheap	Less than $30	Less than $100

Restaurants (average meal for one)

very expensive	$100 or more
expensive	$30–100
moderate	$10–30
cheap	Less than $10

and our listings cannot hope to present a true
picture of these choices a year after visiting. It
is worth checking the facilities and inspecting
the rooms before settling down for the night.

There is less choice if you are seeking something a bit more comfortable without going
into the realms of luxury provided by the
upmarket beach hotels, safari lodges and
camps, although there is somewhere decent
in almost every region of the country.

Beach accommodation ranges from exclusive islands to glitzy resort-style hotels and
backpacker-style guesthouses.

Safari accommodation is covered at length
in **Safaris and Beaches**, *see* pp.55–70.

All accommodation has been divided into
four categories. A distinction has been made
between basic hotel room rates and safari
rates, which are usually all-inclusive.
Restaurant prices tend to be very reasonable
in all but the most upmarket international
hotels and lodges.

Women Travellers

Women travelling alone in Tanzania beyond
the limits of the established tourist route will
enjoy an excellent welcome and frequently
find themselves enjoying exceptional
hospitality. They will be widely considered a
curiosity, as most Tanzanian men would not
let their wives, sisters or daughters travel so
freely. As men are generally the first point of
communication there is often a point where
they will wonder if your liberation extends to
sexual freedom too. A firm degree of rejection
is generally all that is required.

The best situation to be in is one in which
you get to meet the whole family: there is
rarely anything more amusing and fun than
spending time with Tanzanian women in the
relaxed environment of their own homes.
Sexual tension is greater on Zanzibar and in
strongly Muslim areas, where it has not been
long since a man seen talking to a woman
alone might be forced to marry her!

Arusha and its National Park

09

Arusha and its National Park

20 km
10 miles

N

KENYA

Namanga

Amboseli Game Reserve

Oldinka Legeru

A104

▲ Longido

Maasai Cultural Centre ● ● Longido
2

Ol Doinyo Lengai ▲

Kitumbeine ●

Ol Molog ●

Empakaai ☆ Crater
▲ Kerimasi

▲ Kitumbeine

Lake Empakaai

● Engaruka

Lariboro ●

Tinga Tinga ●

Kilimanjaro National Park

▲ Lolmalasin

Mkuru
2

Engare Nairobi

Ngare Nanyuki

p.160

Little Meru
▲

Ngurdoto Mtn Lodge

Sanya Juu

pp.118–99

● Kitete

Oldonyo Sambo ●

☆ Meru Crater

Momela Lodge

Liwati ●

Arusha National Park

3

Momela Lakes

Mount Meru
▲

☆ Ngurdoto Crater

Mountain Village Lodge ⌂

Moivaro Coffee Plantation Lodge

1

Ngare Sero Mountain Lodge ⌂

2
✈ Mto wa Mbo

Monduli ●

● Musa

Dik Dik Hotel ⌂

Sanya ●

Lake Manyara National Park

Kisongo ●

A104

Mserani Snake Park ●

✈ Arusha

Tengeru ●

A23

Sanya Chini

pp.118–19

Karangai Ndogo ●

✈ Kilimanjaro Airport

TANZANIA

UGANDA
KENYA
RWANDA
BURUNDI
CONGO
ZAMBIA
MALAWI
MOZAMBIQUE

Highlights

1 The ash-cone summit of Mount Meru, Africa's fifth-highest mountain

2 Cultural tourism projects around Arusha

3 The caldera of Arusha National Park

Surrounded by some of the most fascinating and varied national parks in Africa, Arusha sits snugly in the foothills of Mount Meru in a wide expanse of high, fertile volcanic land. To the northeast the impressive silhouette of Mount Kilimanjaro looms against the sky, while just a short distance northwest lie the plains of Maasailand, the mountains, rivers and lakes of Ngorongoro, Manyara and Tarangire, and the plains of the Serengeti (*see* **The Northern Safari Circuit**). Arusha even has its own national park, tucked behind the wide coffee plantations that flank the Moshi Road. The park spans a curious landscape of lakes and craters, including most of Mount Meru, providing a quiet haven a few minutes' drive from the town centre.

Arusha

An old German garrison town in the middle of Maasailand, skirted by a haphazard growth of market stalls and housing, Arusha is vibrant, colourful and thriving in its role as Tanzania's northern centre for commerce – and safaris. Most northern Tanzania safaris begin and end in Arusha (see **The Northern Safari Circuit**, pp.117–50). Equipment is assembled here for expeditions, and many people spend a night in the fertile hillsides around the town, or in upbeat Arusha itself, before taking to the road.

Arusha is an important regional centre too. The Arusha International Conference Centre is the base of the UN International Criminal Tribunal for Rwanda, which is attempting to bring the perpetrators of genocide in the 1994 Rwanda conflict to justice. A site behind the AICC is to become the permanent headquarters of the East African Community, the alliance between Tanzania, Kenya and Uganda that existed from 1967 until its collapse in 1977 over major differences in political philosophy, and was re-established in 1999 to promote regional co-operation between the same three countries. The conference centre is also the centre for business in northern Tanzania, housing major offices and tour companies; most international tour operators liaise with specialized operators here for exploration of the surrounding national parks.

As you arrive in Arusha, by air or by road, panoramic views of the surrounding countryside reveal a fertile and well-cultivated land lush with plantations of coffee, maize, beans and wheat, alongside greenhouses and fields growing fresh flowers for export. This productivity is reflected in Arusha's markets and on street corners, where huge avocados, tomatoes and maize cobs are among the produce offered for sale.

As a result of its prosperity, Arusha is very attractive to settlers, and its population has grown rapidly, from an estimated 5,300 in 1948 to 100,000 in the 1970s; today the population is probably closer to 400,000. Arusha's inhabitants are a diverse mix of nationalities and backgrounds: there is a people still known as the 'WaArusha' – the region's original inhabitants – a small group who originated from an area known as Arusha Chini. Originally thought to have been a combination of Meru and Chagga tribes, these people were later conquered by the Maasai, and subsequently assimilated many aspects of Maasai dress, language and social structures, though it is said that their accents and physical appearance remain distinct to discerning locals.

Today, African, Asian and European professionals, street traders and shanty-dwellers occupy distinct urban sectors radiating from the centre of town, the heart of which is the old German boma and clock tower, close to the conference centre and surrounded by safari operators' offices. Loud-mouthed salesmen thread through lines of Maasai women sitting shoulder to shoulder in shop doorways making traditional coloured bead jewellery. Just a few metres away the small but motley population of homeless people and beggars joins the swirling crowd. Everywhere tourists are assailed by a stream of requests to buy batiks, carvings, necklaces – or another Swahili–English dictionary. Though local poverty rubs shoulders with tourist wealth, the overall atmosphere is friendly and welcoming, and Arusha offers a cosmopolitan range of restaurants, good shopping and day trips to the singularly impressive landscapes that surround the town.

Arusha

To Moshi and Dar
Mountain Village Lodge
Dik Dik Hotel
Ngurdoto Mountain Lodge

MOSHI ROAD

Gymkhana Club

HAILE SELASSIE ROAD

Mezza Luna Hotel and Restaurant

Spices and Herbs Restaurant

Everest Chinese

Impala Hotel

Masai Camp
Colobus Club

SERENGETI ROAD

Greek Club

OLD MOSHI ROAD

The Outpost

SIMON BOULEVARD

Arusha International Conference Centre (AICC)

Mount Meru Hospital

Arusha Vision Camp

Hoopoe Adventure Tours

Museum of Natural History

BOMA ROAD

Clock Tower

Arusha Hotel

NGOLIONDOI ROAD

INDIA ROAD

The Pâtissete

SCHOOL ROAD

Naaz Hotel

Stanbic Bank

Roy Safaris

SETH BENJAMIN ROAD

Uhuru Monument

ARUSHA–MOSHI ROAD

MAKAO MAPYA ROAD

ETHIOPIA ROAD

MAKONGORO ROAD

SWAHILI STREET

Mosque

SOKOINE ROAD

AZIMIO STREET

Bookmark

KIKUVU STREET

MOSQUE STREET

MAKUA STREET

SOMALI ROAD

Kilombeto Market

STADIUM ROAD

COLONEL MIDDLETON ROAD

ZARAMA STREET

MAKUA STREET

WAARE STREET

LINDI STREET

WASANGU STREET

Bus Station

McMoody's

Shanghai

WACHAGGA ROAD

STATION ROAD

FACTORY ROAD

To Namanga

NAIROBI ROAD

MAKAO MAPYA ROAD

SOKOINE ROAD

New Market

To Dodoma
Mserani Snake Park
Elewana Coffee Lodge
Airport

N

250 metres
250 yards

Getting There

By Air

Arusha has its own **airport** 10km out of town. It is also serviced by nearby Kilimanjaro Airport, one hour's drive (48km) away on the Arusha–Moshi road. Scheduled flights include a daily service from Dar es Salaam and Zanzibar with **Coastal Travels**, 107 Upanga Road, PO Box 3052, Dar es Salaam t (022) 2117959, *aviation@coastal.cc, www.coastal.cc*.

International flights land at **Kilimanjaro Airport**, t (027) 2502223, and include the nightly **KLM** service from Amsterdam and the daily **Air Kenya** service from Nairobi. Domestic flights from Zanzibar and Dar es Salaam on **Precison Air** and **Air Tanzania** also land there.

Airline Offices in Arusha

Alliance Air, Novotel, Arusha–Moshi Road, t (0741) 335737.
Coastal Travels, Boma Rd, PO Box 3052, t (027) 2500087, f (027) 2500087.
Ethiopian Airlines, Boma Road, t (027) 2506167.
Fleet Air, Sokoine Road, t (027) 2508126.
Gulf Air, Old Moshi Road, t (027) 2502298.
KLM, Boma Road, t (027) 2506063/2508062.
Northern Air, Selina Coffee Estate, t (027) 2508059–60/t (0744) 288857, *northernair@habari.co.tz*.
Precision Air, New Safari Hotel Building, Boma Rd, PO Box 1636, t (027) 2506903/2502836/2507319, *www.precisionairtz.com*.
Regional Air, PO Box 14755, Arusha, t (027) 250 2541/2504477, *resvns@regional.co.tz, sales@regional.co.tz, www.airkenya.com, www.regional.co.tz*. Associated with Air Kenya and BA in Nairobi.

By Bus

From **Dar es Salaam**, buses follow an excellent tarmac road and take 8–9hrs. At the bus station, 'Fresh', 'Amazon' and 'Sai Baba' offer fiercely competitive rates on 'semi-luxe' and 'luxe' buses (the 'luxury' starts and ends in the availability of leg-room). The Royal Coach service (behind the Golden Rose Hotel on Colonel Middleton Rd) runs a twice-daily service of comfortable air-conditioned vehicles with toilets and free coffee, soft drinks and biscuits. It may offer better value for money than the top-end service of its closest competitors, Scandinavian Bus Lines (Kituoni Rd, just south of the bus station).

From **Nairobi**, there are a couple of shuttle services, taking roughly 6hrs each way, leaving from the Parkside Hotel ($20 one way). **Impala Shuttle**, t (027) 2507197, *impala@cybernet.co.tz*, runs a twice-daily service, leaving at 8am and 2pm, that arrives at the Impala Hotel in Arusha at 12.30pm and 6.30pm respectively. **Davanu**, Goliondoi Rd, t (027) 2504027/t (0744) 400318, *davanutz@habari.co.tz*, leaves from the Novotel, as does **EasyCoach**, a new service which claims only to use drivers who have passed safe driving courses. The shuttles also run to Kilimanjaro airport, and other transfers can be arranged.

Buses run to all major centres including Mbeya, Mwanza, and even Kampala (Scandinavian Bus Lines office). During the dry season a bus service also runs to Mwanza through the Serengeti; the price for this trip includes park fees, but it is not recommended as a cheap safari: you don't see much.

Minibus services to and from **Moshi** queue at the stand on the west side of the bus station and take up to 90 minutes. Although they are cheap (T.shs 1,500-2,000), they are often erratically driven.

Estate car taxis travel to the Kenyan border, taking 3hrs and costing T.shs 3–4,000.

By Car

Driving yourself is faster than the bus, but beware of the number of people who treat this wide 'motorway' as a pavement – every stretch of the way. Self-drive car hire in Tanzania is also invariably expensive.

Cars can be rented in Dar es Salaam (*see* pp.215–16), or in Arusha from **Hertz** through **Savannah Tours**, t (027) 2505474/t (0741) 650622, or from **Fortes Safaris**, t (027) 2506094.

History

The people of Arusha – the WaArusha – had been long established as a distinct tribe of pastoralists and farmers when the colonial powers arrived. Their social structure was influenced by Maasai ancestors, with a central warrior class and status relating

Getting Around

Arusha has a large and rambling commercial centre that radiates outwards from the clock tower at its centre. The town is navigable **on foot**, but be prepared for even the shortest walking expedition here to be frequently interrupted by the intervention of passers-by: salesmen, beggars and the just plain curious. **Bicycles** can be rented on Market Street.

Taxis around town are cheap, and especially useful when pavements become a hazardous mire during the rainy seasons. It is also advisable to travel by taxi after dark, as there has been a rise in bag-snatching in recent years. For any longer trips to outlying villages, Cultural Tourism Programmes or Arusha National Park, negotiate with a tour operator for a **car** and a **driver** who can speak English.

Tourist Information

Tanzanian Tourist Board, on Boma Road (near the clock tower), Arusha, PO Box 2348, **t** (027) 2503842, **f** (027) 2508628, *www.tanzania touristboard.com*, *www.tanzania-web.com*. The Arusha office has some good local information. It holds a list of registered safari operators and a list of 'nuisance' safari companies who have been blacklisted.

Arusha International Conference Centre, Simon Boulevard, **t** (027) 2503181, **f** (027) 2506630. Houses a large number of government offices and local businesses, airlines, hotels and some safari operations.

Tanzania National Parks (TANAPA), *tanapa@habari.co.tz*.

Courier Services

Shippers for shoppers:

DHL Worldwide Express, on Sokoine Road, next to NBC Bank, **t** (027) 2506749.

TNT Express Worldwide, also on Sokoine Road, **t** (027) 2500424/**t** (0742) 420338, *www.tnt.com/tz*.

EMS Courier Services, from the Post Office beside the clock tower, **t** (027) 2506792.

Internet

Internet connections are widely available. Expect to pay from T.shs 500 per half-hour at net cafés, up to $10 at exclusive lodges.

Hospitals and Pharmacies

AICC Hospital, Old Moshi Road, **t** (027) 2508131.

Ithna Asheri Hospital, Sokoine Road (consultations), Nairobi-Moshi Road (in-patients), **t** (027) 2506206.

Hakima Pharmacy (human and veterinary), Wapare Rd, **t** (027) 2503583; **Hoots the Chemist**, (24hrs), Azimio Street, **t** (027) 2503124; **Mak-Medics Ltd**, Seth Benjamin Road, **t** (027) 2508640; **Moona's Pharmacy**, Sokoine Road, **t** (0741) 510590.

Shopping

Arusha is an excellent town for shopping for art, crafts and curios from all over Tanzania. As the central town of the Maasai villages, it is the best place for traditional **Maasai beadwork** and **jewellery**. Buy directly from the Maasai women sitting along the pavement, or from the numerous curio shops around the town centre. Sunflower, first right off India Road walking from the clock tower, is the best **gift shop** in town; check out the sparkly flip-flops and good-quality Zanzibarian clothes. Robin's Nest and the Deco Shop on Haile Selassie Road stock **gifts** and **furniture**.

Craft shops between India Road and the clock tower stock a wide range of **Makonde carvings**, either imported from the Makonde Plateau in the south, or more frequently made by ambitious Makonde carvers who have moved north. Styles have evolved to match Western demands, so look out for new pieces as well as the traditional abstract and figurative styles. The most varied selection of all of these is at the Cultural Heritage Centre a few km west of the town centre, opposite Mserani Snake Park on the Dodoma road (takes credit cards). These are largely foreign-owned; if you prefer to support local crafts directly, *see* the Cultural Tourism section, pp.111–13.

to age. Occasionally called upon to support Rindi, the great Chagga warrior chief (*see* p.170) in his battles with other chiefs around Kilimanjaro, the WaArusha were no strangers to fighting by the time the Germans began to get caught up in these

Batiks are also commonly offered in the streets, but you can usually get a better price from the curio shops, where you will also find a range of curios made from semi-precious stones, such as malachite, tanzanite, green tourmaline and rhodolite. Tanzanita has a tanzanite lapidary and cutting workshop in the Golden Rose Arcade, Col. Middleton Rd, and a jewellery shop in Arusha Coffee Lodge.

The four main supermarkets are Kibo and Modern on Sokoine Road, Kijenge on the Moshi Road and Makwani on Swahili Street, while there is also a mammoth ShopRite – used mainly by Europeans, and pricey – on the Sokoine Road. The local markets, which have a great local atmosphere and the best prices, are Soko Kuu between Market Street and Azimio Street, and the new Kilombero on Sokoine Road – selling everything from spices to shorts and souvenirs. For books, try Kase on Boma Road, which has a good selection of local ethnic and educational literature on their well-stocked shelves. Almost directly opposite the bookshop on the other side of the road is a second-hand bookstall with a good selection of well-thumbed novels. The Bookmark, opposite the Twin Peaks Casino, is a US-style bookstore and coffee shop, recommended for its regular children's storytelling sessions.

Sports and Activities

If a round of golf appeals, temporary membership is negotiable at the Gymkhana Club, Haile Selassie Road, t (027) 2502155. Further out of town there is a full-size course at Ngurdoto Mountain Lodge.

Explore Arusha, t (0744) 69963/t (0741) 651528, conducts tours of the town, railway station, Sikh temple and nearby tanzanite mines. Walkers can also visit nearby villages; a percentage of the profits goes to a local children's charity. Local walks are organized by Tropical Trekking, near the clock tower at the heart of town, PO Box 2047, Arusha, t (027) 2502417, www.tropicaltrekking.com. Spectacular walking paths have been created

up to the rim of the Ngurdoto Crater in Arusha National Park (see p.114).

Camel rides to a nearby Maasai boma can be arranged through Mserani Snake Park (see pp.108 and 111). All excursions are accompanied. The time taken for each jaunt depends on the wishes of the rider. Rides cost less than $10 an hour for adults, even less for children.

Proficient riders can enjoy excellent horseback safaris with Equestrian Safaris, from Uto Farm just outside Arusha. The 200-hectare ranch is situated at 2,000m altitude on the northern slopes of Mount Meru, with spectacular views of the Great Rift Valley from its verandahs. The main farmhouse was built in 1937 by a South African settler and Boer trek leader, in the distinctive Cape Dutch style. Guest accommodation is now made up of basic bungalows in the gardens, with space for a maximum of 12 guests. The farm is also a livestock enterprise with dairy cattle, sheep and 32 stabled thoroughbred horses – the safari mounts. Safaris can be tailored to suit the requirements of a group, but are based around a 3- or 5-day itinerary (UK agent: Ride World Wide, 58 Fentiman Road, London SW8 1LF, t (020) 7735 1144).

Where to Stay

The most pleasant hotels at the top end of the range are all situated outside the centre, in relaxing rural and floral surroundings. These are listed below under 'Out of Town'.

Arusha Town

Expensive

Arusha Coffee Lodge Elewana Afrika, 99 Serengeti Road, Sopa Plaza, PO Box 12814, Arusha, t (027) 2500630–9, info@elewana.com, www.elewana.com. The Elewana flagship project, on the airport road 4km out of town, is a curious place: design-conscious, with leather sofas and select pan-African craftwork. The overall effect, bizarrely, is of a metropolitan lounge bar, albeit on a scale

altercations – but soon found themselves on the wrong side of both their former ally and the new colonial enemy. On 19 October 1896, a German captain, Kurt Johannes, approached the WaArusha in an attempt to secure diplomatic relations with local more akin to the generous hearth of the African farmhouse. The very good kitchen is thoroughly European, matched on the drinks front by an extensive cocktail list. Expect lavish barbecues in the mode of Carnivore, the famed Kenyan 'meaterie', where patrons select their meat cut and cooking style before handing over the ingredients to tong-wielding chefs. Rooms are available in a series of luxurious wooden bungalows throughout the grounds; once the gardens have seen a season or two they will provide a lovely retreat far from the bustle of Arusha town. Some of the rooms are close to the eating and drinking areas, so be prepared for late-night jollity.

Moderate

Impala Hotel, Old Moshi Road, PO Box 7302, Arusha t (027) 2508448, f (027) 2508220, *impala@habari.co.tz*. A good standard of accommodation in a fine garden atmosphere, the crowning glory of which is the fabulous new swimming pool. It's a huge hotel, though not overbearing, and is popular with business travellers. Of four restaurants, one provides a 24hr continental menu, and the Indian cuisine is the best in Arusha. There are plans to add a gym.

Arusha Hotel, Old Moshi Road, PO Box 88, Arusha, t (027) 2508541–3, *nah@ark.eoltz. com*. Conveniently located opposite the clock tower on the Old Moshi Road, the Arusha has reinvented itself and once again deserves its status as a central landmark. If rooms are a little lacking in imagination – muted fawns and insipid green finished with catalogue photo art – they are fitted to an international standard. Beware the rooms overlooking the street: the central location means noise from 5am. Service is professional and friendly. Beautifully maintained gardens offer respite from the dust of the town and hide a lovely pool with a toddling area. Non-residents can swim for a fee.

Mezza Luna Hotel, a few km from the town centre along the Moshi Road, PO Box 14365,

Arusha, t (027) 2504381. The 'Half Moon' provides safe and fairly basic lodging at a moderate price. Rooms centre around a small open flowerbed and lack light and views, but all are clean and quiet with ensuite bathrooms. The room price includes an inexplicable breakfast of multicoloured biscuits and highly sugared cakes, although toast and omelettes can be ordered as an extra. The adjoining restaurant has a varied menu and good reputation, especially for pizza (*see* 'Eating Out', p.109).

Klub Afriko, t (027) 2509205, *www.klubafriko. com*. An excellent option in the heart of the suburbs with spotless, airy *makuti bandas*; pool table and bar. Ironwork candelabras and elegant furniture contribute to an air of African simplicity. The restaurant offers local and western dishes. In-house safaris.

Ilboru Safari Lodge, PO Box 8012, Arusha, t (027) 2507834, *ilboru-lodge@yako.habari. co.tz, www.habari.co.tz/ilborulodge*. Situated in the well-off western suburbs of Arusha, modern with clean and comfortable accommodation for a reasonable price in prim and pristine round thatched red-brick bungalows. Gardens and rooms are spacious and immaculately respectable, the bar is well stocked and the neat dining room provides a promising menu. It is the other side of town from the airstrip, so is not recommended for overnight transfers.

Cheap

The Outpost, 37 Serengeti Road, Arusha, t (027) 2508405, *outpost@ark.eoltz.com*. A little further from the centre, in an oasis of suburban calm, but well located for restaurants such as the Ethiopian and around the corner from the Greek Club bar, this is a comfortable B&B-style lodging with a bar and nightly barbecue, set in pretty gardens. 18 en-suite timbered bungalows are tucked away in the grounds, while an upstairs room can sleep a group of 4 or 5. Excellent value.

Naaz Hotel, 2mins' walk from the clock tower, opposite Mac's Patisserie, PO Box 1060,

chiefs, but the Arusha warriors, unable to forget a German raid of the previous year, attacked and killed two missionaries. Captain Johannes returned to his base in Moshi, where he persuaded Rindi to side with him and mobilize Chagga troops to retaliate.

Arusha, **t** (027) 2502087, *naazarusha@ark.eoltz.com*. With a backpacker feel, the Naaz has good clean rooms, with or without bathroom, set around a basic but pleasant open-air seating area. During the day it becomes a focal point for clothes-washing and maintenance, but at night it is relatively peaceful. If you are early to bed or intend to sleep late, ask for a room away from the street. The adjoining self-service restaurant is reminiscent of a roadside travellers' rest canteen. Naaz sells an impressive range of doughnuts and offers a cake-baking service.

Pallson's Hotel, Market St, PO Box 14597, **t** (0744) 314732. Faces the market in a bustling street. It is nothing special, unless you happen to be charged the resident rate (T.shs 12,000), as has been reported. What looks like a dirty mark on the bed linen is on closer inspection the laundry motif!

Out of Town

The altogether more refined and pleasant options for accommodation are just outside the town, set in blooming gardens with breathtaking mountain views. They all require a taxi or private vehicle for convenient access.

Expensive

Dik Dik Hotel, PO Box 1499, Arusha, **t** (027) 2508110/**t** (0741) 510490, *dikdik@ATGE.automail.com*, *www.dikdik.ch*. Some distance from the centre, about 20mins' drive in the direction of Kilimanjaro on the Usa River, the Dik Dik is surrounded by nearly a hectare of gardens at the foot of Mount Meru. The rooms are prettily furnished double bungalows set around a central flower garden; there is also a deep pool. All rooms have minibar and TV; some come with hammocks and cots for babies and children. The living area is designed in an alpine style, and one of the best restaurants in Arusha is set on a covered verandah with fantastic views of the countryside. Barbecues and fires are lit to illuminate the night. Guided tours up Kilimanjaro can be arranged, and guides are also available for less strenuous walks to local villages. There are B&B, half-board and full-board options, with a 10 per cent discount for stays of two nights or more.

Ngurdoto Mountain Lodge, PO Box 7302, Arusha, **t** (027) 2555217, *www.thengurdotomountainlodge.com*. This grand affair is the largest hotel in East Africa, and is likely to host meetings of the newly reinvigorated East Africa Union. Set in 140 acres of grounds; the hotel encompasses the gardens of an old plantation house with burbling streams, mature trees and tidy rows of coffee bushes as well as a full size golf course. Porters in golf carts whiz up and down the lanes and cul-de-sacs that house the cottages laid out in serried ranks in the grounds. One cul-de-sac is restricted, apparently, for the use of national presidents alone. These are enormous chalets set in verdant flower gardens with cool white-washed interiors. The cottages are good value at 150 dollars per person per night, the rooms in the main hotel less so, since they have been packed in and can feel a little poky. Both have excellent facilities; a 24hr menu can be delivered to your room. Each suite – in reality a three-bedroom house – has its own guardroom and lobby. Back in the hotel there are four restaurants, with Indian and continental food.

Moivaro Coffee Plantation Lodge, PO Box 11297, Arusha, **t** (027) 2553242/3/**t** (0741) 650550, *reservations@moivaro.com*. A charismatic and unusual find, seemingly miles from anywhere, in the midst of the Moivaro Estate. In fact it is only 7km from Arusha, but it is hard to imagine life beyond this peaceful, natural setting, with its views of Mount Meru and enticing swimming pool. Guests are housed in individual chalets, all comfortably furnished. There is a great walk through the coffee plantation.

Ngare Sero Mountain Lodge, PO Box 425, Arusha, **t** (027) 2553638/**t** (0741) 512138, *Ngare-Sero-Lodge@habari.co.tz*. An old colonial farmhouse surrounded by verdant

The WaArusha were easily defeated by the punishing onslaught: their weapons and food reserves were confiscated and their houses were destroyed, until they were forced to bow to German control.

foliage on the lower slopes of Mount Meru. The house was completed in 1908, and was built by a retired German Schutztruppe officer named Augustus Leue, who chose to remain here with his family rather than return to Germany. Good quality accommodation is in a renovated farmstead building with a Zanzibarian flavour throughout and a solid 'mountain farm' charm. The most attractive aspect of Ngare Sero is the gardens that flourish on all sides; at least 200 species of bird have been spotted. A trout stream in the middle allows fishermen to cast a line for their supper, and this atmosphere is completed by troupes of colobus monkeys chattering in the trees. A stable of horses allows for saddleback exploration of local mountain trails, while early morning yoga sessions are held on a wooden lookout platform over the lake.

Moderate

Mountain Village Lodge, about 15km from the town centre, c/o Serena Hotels, PO Box 2551, Arusha, t (027) 2504058/2506304/2504159, *reservations@serena.co.tz, www.serena hotels.com*. Well-proportioned rooms set in beautifully tended gardens across a steep escarpment, with views over the vegetable gardens to the distant and often misty Lake Duluti – all designed to lighten the heart after a long journey. A network of pathways leads over tiny clear-water streams to charming semi-detached thatched bungalows, each with its own verandah and plenty of nets. Now part of the Serena hotel chain, the lodge has been renovated to an excellent standard throughout, and is everything you'd expect from a country hotel. Guests pad through richly furnished passageways to the pristine restaurant and poolside area. Unfortunately the efficiency drive succeeds at the expense of atmosphere.

Camping

Maasai Campsite, about 3km from the town centre on the Moshi Road, t (027) 2500149.

Offers camping for next to nothing, and rooms for those who are looking for a rural feel not too far from town. Its massive restaurant and bar are decked out with satellite TV, pool tables and comfortable seating. An adventure playground makes it a good choice for families. Although the bar can be lively, music finishes at midnight.

Mserani Snake Park, on Sokoine Road, some distance from the other end of town, t (027) 2538282/t (0741) 510707. There are no lodge facilities at the Snake Park, but camping and use of hot showers is free on the understanding that guests pay their way at the bar. Guests can also enter the Snake Park itself (*see* p.111) for free, and take camel rides.

Arusha Vision Campground, on Boma Road, t (027) 2503461. Another popular choice for camping at the heart of Arusha town; cheap and safe. A refurbishment is planned, but for now expect basic cooking facilities and a scruffy lawn on which to pitch your tent.

Eating Out

Arusha has a good range of international-style dining options, from Italian to Chinese.

Expensive

Dik Dik Hotel, PO Box 1499, Arusha, t (027) 2508110/t (0741) 510490, *www.dikdik.ch*. With so many independent lodges offering more personal style, there seems little reason to go for the tour operator blandness of the Dik Dik, unless you are in a bigger group or travelling as a family, when the large grounds and bigger facilities will be welcome. It's not all bad, though; individual hammocks are a thoughtful touch, and the grounds are lovely.

Moderate

Spices and Herbs Restaurant, Moshi Road, t (027) 2502279. Excellent Ethiopian cuisine: authentic spicy dishes arrive in a fine array on enormous platters to share, with plenty of choice for vegetarians and meat-eaters

In 1899 the Germans began construction of a strong fortification, a boma, which they forced the Arusha people to build. Maasai in Arusha still remember the humiliation of this task: the new colonists took pleasure in riding around on the backs of the alike. The style is tasteful minimalist. It's worth a visit for the coffee alone, which is first brought to the table as aromatic roasting beans – to awaken your senses – before it is served as a drink.

Mezza Luna Restaurant, also on Moshi Road, t (027) 2504381. A wide-ranging menu specializing in Italian food, particularly recommended for pizza and pasta. Guests choose between three outdoor covered areas for eating; as the restaurant often has a live local band playing, the set-up allows you to decide how close you sit to it.

Amar Cuisine, Sokoine Road, t (027) 2502463. Also good for Indian dishes, serving a good concoction of spices to authentic Indian musical accompaniment.

Shanghai Restaurant, Sokoine Road, t (027) 2503224. The best Chinese in town.

Everest, Old Moshi Road, t (027) 2508419. Very good dishes for a reasonable price.

L'Oasis, in the Sekei area, t (027) 2507089, (0741) 510531. Moderately priced and highly recommended Thai and Indonesian dishes.

On the Roof, on a breezy roof-top verandah on Jacaranda Street. Chunky and delicious sandwiches and salads are filling value – a good place for lunch.

Cheap

Pizzarusha, near the infamous Mashele guest-house. A charismatic pizza joint that caters for budget safari tours filling their boots on the way into or out of the bush.

Barracuda, on Boma Road, t (027) 2502823. Also for local fare at local prices; serves large, wholesome African dishes, but is gaining a reputation as a hangout for local 'bad boys', and is not recommended late at night.

Big Bite, t (0811) 650222. Tandoori and Indian.

McMoody's, on the Sokoine Road towards the outskirts of town. The most infamous fast-food joint in town. This Western-influenced enterprise is decked out with fluorescent lighting, and serves burgers, fries and ice-cream. Individual portions are inexpensive, but small. Internet booth under the stairs.

Ice Cream Parlour, also on Sokoine Road. A more limited range of burgers, ice cream and samosas can be found here.

Mac's Patisserie, near the clock tower on Sokoine Road, t (027) 2503469. An excellent range of pastries, samosas and sandwiches, home-made veggie-burgers or more meaty alternatives. A superb one-stop shop for picnics, and an enticing environment for long breakfasts over a hot cup of coffee. Mac's also doubles up as an Internet café. Newspapers, magazines and information.

The Bookmark, opposite Twin Peaks Casino, off Sokoine Road. Wide selection of African and Western novels; coffee table books; also houses Food for Thought café: smoothies, toasted sandwiches and salads.

Dolly's Patisserie, on Jacaranda Street. Good fresh breads, and freshly squeezed juices.

Entertainment and Nightlife

The Greek Club. Founded in the 1920s, for Greek expat coffee farmers, still in family hands, but reinvented as a really good bar. The emphasis is on sports, particularly soccer, but it is the site of parties and a hub of expat gossip. Bar snacks are inexpensive. US pool table. *Opens till late; closed Mon and Thurs; weekends open from 1pm.*

Colobus Club. Attracts an especially enthusiastic crowd on Fri and Sat. The music is eclectic but danceable, and the atmosphere is friendly and fun. *Open 11pm until late.*

Crystal Club. Another popular, but more rowdy, local choice with an eclectic musical menu that tends towards crooning soul classics. *Open daily from 7pm until the early hours, busier on Fridays and Saturdays.*

Maasai Club, at the Maasai campsite. A celebrated Arusha institution and felt to be the best place to meet a mixed crowd, be they overlanders; locals, expat NGO workers or even the odd miner or two. Unpretentious. *Open till midnight, sometimes later.*

Arusha and Maasai men, egging them on with whips. One Maasai recorded the growing resentment at this form of transport in his memoirs. He was particularly enraged by an unusually heavy cargo; passing the river with his charge set heavily across his back, his patience snapped and he tossed his 'master' into the water. Fearing the consequences, many Maasai went into hiding in the bush, until a Maasai chief was sent to find them. The chief explained to the mutinous group that he was acting as a mediator, and that if the group returned to work all would be forgiven. The runaways marched back into the new town in a column of about 400 men; as they strode down Boma Road, the entire troop was gunned down in the street – one of history's many warnings never to trust a 'safe conduct' pass. It is said that the 'mediator' was promptly promoted. The bloodstained fort was completed in 1900 and became a barracks for 150 Nubian soldiers, later being made the regional government offices until 1934, when it was turned into the Arusha Museum of Natural History.

A steady influx of traders and farmers into Arusha in the 19th century, notably Indian traders, private German farmers and immigrant Africans, stimulated economic growth, prompting the German administration to conceive an 'idealistic' vision of a vast white settlement of their own construction. The Germans came up with several schemes to import settlers – from bizarre backgrounds. The first of these plans back-fired when the Boer farmers of German origin who had taken up the offer of free farmland proved too uncouth for the ideal community; they were mainly squeezed out into Kenya. The grand scheme was revised: now 10,000 German peasants from settlements around the Volga Basin and Caucasus in southern Russia were to be imported. The four families who arrived as a test project were painfully disappointed to discover that Arusha did not have four harvests a year, as they had been led to believe, and soon made their way to Tanga begging to be sent back to Russia.

The first school was constructed in 1914, and called Boma School. It is now the site of the Arusha Lutheran Church. The railway to Moshi was completed in the 1920s, boosting Arusha's position as the centre for trade and development at the heart of northern Tanzania's coffee-growing regions. The population continued to grow, and eventually the town gained enough status to give its name to the most influential political dictates of President Nyerere: his 1967 Arusha Declaration – made in the town – outlined his policies for a 'Model of African Socialism', ideals and policies that influenced the livelihood and outlook of the nation for the following 20 years .

Arusha Town

The most famous old colonial building is at the heart of the town: the original German fort, or boma, built to suppress the discontented Arusha, now houses the **Museum of Natural History** on Boma Road, near the post office. It used to exhibit a collection of dusty stuffed animals, but is being renovated; for the time being the exhibits have been dusted, pending further work (*open Mon–Fri 8.30–5, weekends 10–5; adm, children half price; guided tours available; t (027) 2507540*). Just behind the natural history museum, the most famous new building in Tanzania is the shockingly ugly but well-used **Arusha International Conference Centre** (AICC), a mass of offices, which houses the UN International Criminal Tribunal for Rwanda. It is constantly teeming with high-security cars with flashing lights. The tribunal staff contribute to

Arusha's economy like nothing else; it is they who are primarily responsible for the recent boom enjoyed in the town. Most safari operators in Arusha have offices in the AICC, too. The **Arusha Declaration Museum** on Makongoro Road (*open daily 9.30–6; adm, children half price; tours available; t (027) 2507800*) is dedicated to the post-Independence history of Tanzania. Although it is small and by no means exhaustive, it does provide some food for thought. The central **Kilombero Market** (*open daily*) is currently being rehoused in a grandly renovated covered market building. The colourful throng of stalls displays a staggering range of odds and ends from coconut-grating stools to flip-flops – often more fun to study than buy.

Mserani Snake Park, opposite the Cultural Tourism Centre about 15 minutes out of town heading towards the Serengeti on the Dodoma Road (*open Mon–Sun 7.30–midnight; adm, children half price; PO Box 13669, Arusha, t (027) 2538282/t (0741) 510707*), has a variety of snakes behind glass representing a range of local and national species, with some labels, and a number of small crocodiles, monitor lizards and other reptilian delights in dismal-looking pools.

Cultural Tourism Programmes

Developed to give tourists a chance to gain deeper insights into the country that they are visiting, the Cultural Tourism Programmes introduce interested travellers to local people who have been trained as guides to provide information about their area. These local schemes are low-key, all different and each developing in line with the specific needs and possibilities of an area and its community, but their shared aim is to bring tourist cash within reach of local people and development projects.

Executed with advice from the Netherlands Development Organization (SNV), the programmes aim to fund major local requirements, such as irrigation, education or ecological work; visitors pay a pre-arranged fee to these funds. The arrangement gives foreigners and local people the chance to meet and to explore cultural differences and interests, so that the tourist experience is often immeasurably enhanced as well as contributing to development. Programmes near Arusha include those at Mkuru, Longido and Mto wa Mbo. The Mkuru and Longido projects have been set up with local Maasai tribes, and are both a couple of hours' drive from the town.

Mkuru

Mkuru is north of Mount Meru, not far beyond the Momela Gate of Arusha National Park. Its Maasai people have developed a **camel camp**, assisted by Heifer Project International. Here you can arrange a camel safari guided by Maasai warriors. Camels are ideally suited to survival on the semi-arid plains between Mount Kilimanjaro and Lake Natron, and there are now about 100 of these long-legged dehydration-resistant beasts in Mkuru. Camel-hump safaris can last a couple of hours or a number of days, bumping as far as Lake Natron or Ol Doinyo Lengai, the 'Mountain of God' (*see* pp.136–7). Any trek through this landscape will encounter plenty of wildlife and birds along the way, and the views of Kilimanjaro, Meru and the Longido Mountains provide a stunning backdrop. The Mkuru Maasai can also take you on bird walks, or on a rather more strenuous climb up the pyramid cone of Ol Doinyo Landaree, a 2hr hike.

There are three 'luxury' cottages for visitors to the camel camp to stay in, each with beds for two. There is a tap inside each; the toilet is outdoors (also with an excellent view of Kilimanjaro). No food or drink is available at the camp, other than tea or coffee with camel milk; visitors are encouraged use the kitchen's energy-saving stoves to prepare their own food. The project at Mkuru aims to build and run a school in the village with the proceeds, greatly improving local education.

Longido

Longido, 100km north of Arusha on the Nairobi River, runs an interesting local project in a rural area that still shows visible traces of its unusual colonial history. Heavy fighting broke out between the Germans and the British during the First World War in this region. Local stories tell how a single German soldier hid behind a rock, sniping at the British soldiers, until a Maasai warrior was bribed to creep up behind the attacker and spear him. The remains of an ancient graveyard commemorating the soliders who died here has disappeared into the encroaching bush, but a walk passes a tree covered with 'European drawings' – crude graffiti – and continues through dramatic landscape, past huts used by boys awaiting ritual cleansing ceremonies.

The walks around Longido merit a full day trip, but the village can also be visited as a half-day or two-day tour. The cattle market takes place on Wednesdays, attracting colourfully decorated Maasai from the landscape in every direction. The Longido land-scape is fascinating to explore with the knowledge of a local Maasai guide. Unusual wildlife not commonly seen in the national parks, such as gerenuk, lesser kudu and klipspringer antelope, are common in its bush and mountains, as are animals such as giraffe, zebra and gazelle. Your guide can point out birds like masked weavers, barbets and secretary birds, demonstrate medicines collected by Maasai from the bush, and take you to a boma to experience the tribal way of life, including food prepared by the women's group. Proceeds from the project are being put towards cattle dip to protect the herds against ailments that kill around 1,000 of the tribe's cows each year.

One of the most fascinating people to look out for in Longido is the coordinator of the tourism programme, Mzee Mollel, a local Maasai who has studied sociology in Zambia and Australia. He is a fount of information, and a delight to converse with. On the whole, however, the Maasai guides at Mkuru and Longido are experienced at leading but their English is limited – although they are proficient in hand signals – so it is advisable to take a translator with you. Most tour operators can provide a guide to accompany you and arrange camping equipment. Before visiting either of these villages, ensure that you are adequately prepared, with enough drinking water (three litres a day is recommended if walking in the sun) and food, sun protection, a hat, walking shoes and thorn-resistant clothes.

Mto wa Mbo

At the town of Mto wa Mbo, on the road south into Lake Manyara National Park, the local population is made up of an extraordinary spectrum of Tanzanian tribes. This unusual mixture has been attracted by the fertility of the land here, transformed from an arid land unattractive for habitation by an extensive irrigation system established in the 1950s. As news of this 'new' land spread, people came from all areas and settled here to farm and work the land according to their own experience. Fruit and vegetable seeds have been brought from all over the country, and people of different tribal backgrounds produce food according to traditional methods.

A visit to the tourism project at Mto wa Mbo can introduce you to local Chagga farmers who brew their own banana beer, and a farmer from Kigoma, Mzee Filipo, who cultivates palm trees to make palm oil. Alternatively you can head to a waterfall 5km north of town, and see the papyrus lake where local Rangi people collect papyrus for mats and baskets, and the Sandawe families make bows and arrows for hunting. There are a number of places to buy provisions in Mto wa Mbo, and a couple of very basic guest houses offering accommodation (*see* p.127).

The project is based in an office behind the Red Banana café in Mto wa Mbo. Unfortunately, the building, and many others along the high road of the town, may soon be demolished owing to a trenchant government policy determining correct road width. If it disappears, the Twiga campsite will direct you to the guides. For more information visit the tourist information office on Boma Road (*see* p.104).

Arusha National Park

A 30-minute drive from Arusha, Arusha National Park is excellent for birdlife and butterflies. Its forested woodlands are alive with excitable primates, including chattering blue and colobus monkeys and large families of baboons. The park is an idyllic spot for a day's peace and quiet in scenic surroundings. There is also decent accommodation if you wish to spend a night or two, and the slopes of Mount Meru, within the park, are a good place to acclimatize for a Kilimanjaro climb – as well as being a decent climb in their own right.

History

The first European to discover the strange landscape around the foothills of Mount Meru that is now Arusha National Park was a Hungarian, Count Samuel Teleki, in 1876, who two years later made the first recorded climb above the snowline on Mount Kenya, reaching 4,680m. He recorded seeing a large number of hippos and rhinos in the Arusha area, but you are unlikely to come across a rhinoceros here today.

By 1907 much of what is now the park had been settled by a German family called Trappe, who turned it into a cattle ranch. The elder Mrs Trappe was one of the first female professional game-hunters in East Africa; at her behest a large part of the family's Momela Estate was set aside as a game reserve. When the area became a national park in 1960, the estate and farm were incorporated into it. Many of the place names are from the Maa language, a reminder of the previous inhabitants of this land – the park boundaries also absorbed several Maasai settlements. As this small park has grown since its 1960s' conception, its name has mirrored the landscape of its three distinct areas of crater, lake and mountain. It started off as

Getting There

Most Arusha tour operators can arrange a **car** and **driver** to take you to the national park, or you can **hire a car** in Arusha.

Tourist Information

National park entrance fees are $25 per day plus $5 for a vehicle permit, payable to the **Park Warden**, t (027) 2503471/2504082, or at the park gate.

Many tour operators can also arrange for you to **climb Mount Meru**, and will ensure that you have suitable food, equipment and porters if you need them. A fully equipped climb costs upwards of $200 per person per day, including the park requirements for an armed ranger ($20 per day), hut fees ($20 per day), park fees ($25 per day), rescue insurance ($20 overall) and the cost of a guide, food, transport to the park and porters. The price is lower if you climb in a larger group. Factor in tips at around $10 per person per day for your guide (*see* pp.122–4 for tour operators).

New **walking trails** accessible to all abilities follow the crater rim of the Ngurdoto Crater (the mini Ngorongoro). There are a number of impressive viewpoints along the route. **Canoeing** on Momela Lakes is organized by Green Footprint, who have an office with Serena Active, Manyara Serena Lodge, t (0748) 445171, or go to *www.greenfootprint.co.tz*.

Where to Stay

Momela Wildlife Lodge, PO Box 999, Arusha, t (027) 2506423 (*moderate*). For an idyllic getaway, the Wildlife Lodge sits between the dark peaks of Mount Meru and the silvery snows of Kilimanjaro. Acclimatize here if you plan to conquer Africa's highest mountain. The lodge is a collection of whitewashed round bungalows with *makuti*-thatched roofs, set in well-kept colourful floral gardens. The rooms are not luxurious, but the fireplaces still blaze when the mountain air is chill and the little houses are clean and charming. The lodge is also proud to uphold its connections with Hollywood: the John Wayne film *Hatari* was filmed around the farmhouse, and the film is a favourite form of evening entertainment. The dining area is named after the Hollywood hero, and entirely adorned with a mural in his honour. Full board.

The Dik Dik Hotel, Ngare Sero, Moivaro Coffee Plantation Lodge and Mountain Village Lodge all provide smart, comfortable accommodation close to Arusha National Park (*see* 'Arusha' pp.107–108).

Camping

There are four **campsites** in the park, all in scenic surroundings with water and loos, and firewood provided. Contact the park warden (*see* above) to book a spot to pitch your tent.

Ngurdoto National Park, made up of Ngurdoto Crater and the Momela Lakes. In 1967, Mount Meru was incorporated, and the park was renamed Meru Crater Park. More recently it has become Arusha National Park and now covers 137 square kilometres.

Ngurdoto Crater

Ngurdoto Crater, formed over 15 million years ago, is the combined remains of two neighbouring volcanoes that have collapsed to form one pear-shaped caldera, stretching up to 3km across. The steep sides of the bowl sides are richly forested; the base is swamp and plains and riverine forest. You cannot descend into the crater; instead follow the newly created walking trail, an easy climb along the rim, or drive through the forest around the rim and walk or climb the short distance to a lookout point to see baboons trekking across the crater floor, alongside the odd lumbering elephant and wide-winged birds. The prehistoric features of a silvery-cheeked hornbill or a huge, solitary hamerkop are a common sight, as are magnificent raptors soaring upwards on the warm air currents. Verreaux's eagle, identifiable by its wide wingspan, or peregrine falcons with their small pointy features, both circle upwards over the crater floor, scanning the ground for prey.

There are numerous hides, viewpoints and picnic areas and one campsite on the crater rim from which to watch the birds and other wildlife, but for even wider and clearer views continue on to the Momela Lakes, where there are further sites above the watering holes.

Momela Lakes

The Momela Lakes were formed from the muddy depressions caused by volcanic activity. Slightly differing mineral components and algae growth in the alkaline waters of the lakes make each shimmer a slightly different colour in the sun, and all attract a wide variety of colourful birdlife such as Egyptian geese, pink-backed pelicans and greater and lesser flamingos (the flamingos are migratory and most commonly seen in October and February). The greater crested and little grebe are both common, as is the black-winged stilt. The driving route around these striking pools might take you past pods of ponderous hippopotami, or you might glimpse bushbuck, reedbuck, waterbuck and buffalo, encounter the occasional elephant or witness the galloping gait of giraffes. Guided canoeing trips across the waters of the smaller lake are an excellent way to see the wildlife up close (see box, left).

Mount Meru

Mount Meru is Africa's fifth-highest peak. The rugged ash cone of this dormant volcano has not seen any lava action for a century, and is not predicted to do so in the near future, so those wishing to climb its 4,566m height can eliminate one concern. A hike up and down Meru is usually a three- or four-day round trip, if you take it at a relaxed pace and explore the plains, forests, moorlands and volcanic lava desert that make up its landscape. If time, funds and stamina permit, it is a good idea to climb Meru as a means of acclimatizing before attempting the summit of Kilimanjaro. Meru also has the advantage of being far less visited than its grand neighbour, so the lower slopes are more densely populated with wildlife and there is a good chance of encountering larger animals such as giraffe and antelope. Although Meru is smaller than Kilimanjaro, with no snow-covered peaks, the climb up it can be extremely cold and requires proper mountain gear for overnight camping. Meru is also very steep in parts, and climbers will need stout walking shoes. To plan a Meru climb, you may require the services of a tour operator in Arusha (see pp.122–4).

Shorter Walks on Mount Meru

For those less energetic or adventurous, or pushed for time, there is an hour-long walk from the open plain of Kitoto through the forest to Jekukumia river and a short

A Typical Mount Meru Itinerary
Devised with assistance from Tropical Trekking (see p.105).

Treks generally begin and end at **Momela Gate**. A path leads up from here to dense mountain rainforest where huge moss-covered cedar trees grow, and there is always a chance of encounters with buffalo, giraffe and colobus monkeys. Many climbers stop for a picnic along the way, perhaps at **Mayo Falls** (1,900m), to rest and breathe the fresh forest air and maybe bathe in the cold, clear mountain stream. The walk continues in the afternoon through the beautiful upper rainforest to **Meru Crater** and then **Miriakamba Hut** at 2,700m for supper and the first night on the mountain.

After breakfast on day two, trekkers traverse the lower alpine regions on the northern crater rim in order to reach the Saddle Hut at 3,500m. This walk is quite steep and requires a major effort from even the fittest of climbers. As you approach the Saddle Hut the vegetation dwindles to low moss-covered bushes and shrubs that can survive such high altitude. You will usually reach the hut by mid-afternoon, and can rest or summon more energy to explore the rocky summit of **'Small Meru'**, from where the views are superb in all directions, and the sharp **Crater Rim** leading to the **Meru Summit** is revealed.

Trekkers spend the night at **Saddle Hut**, with breathtaking views of the night sky above the cloud line. You can start the ascent to the summit in the early morning, as early as 2am, aiming to reach the summit at sunrise. It's best to do this climb at full moon, but take torches in case it is not bright enough. Between the Saddle Hut and the summit the reduced oxygen of high altitudes cuts climbers' breath short and the pace is slow. When you reach the summit you can enjoy the first morning light while recovering from the night's exertions. The views are spectacular as the orange-red sky fades behind Kilimanjaro and the morning sun rises over the African plains.

The descent continues back along the **Crater Rim** to the **Saddle Hut** for a picnic stop, and on in the afternoon to reach **Miriakamba Hut**, for the final night. The next day brings climbers back down to **Momela Gate** along a trail that wends through open glades where buffalo and bushbuck can be observed in the morning light, and there are often fabulous views of the Momela Lakes and Mount Kilimanjaro.

distance on up the mountain to either **Meru Crater** or **Njeku**. The forest ends abruptly on the rim of Meru Crater, with views of the sheer cliff face rising 1,500m to the ash cone summit. The walk to Njeku is longer, and leads to an ancient sacrificial site once used by the people of Meru in times of drought. *Njeku* literally means an old woman who commands great respect, but here it refers to the site of an old juniper tree, which is the source of a legend about an old woman who had the power to make rain. Continuing further on from Njeku brings you to a viewpoint overlooking a waterfall gushing through a gorge of the Ngare River. A new trail leads up to the Ngurdoto Crater: walk along the rim to the first viewing point at Leitong, and ascend until the final vista at Vikindu. Information is available at the gate and all walks through the park must be arranged with park officials there. Walkers must take an armed ranger for protection in case of encounters with irritable buffalo.

The Northern Safari Circuit

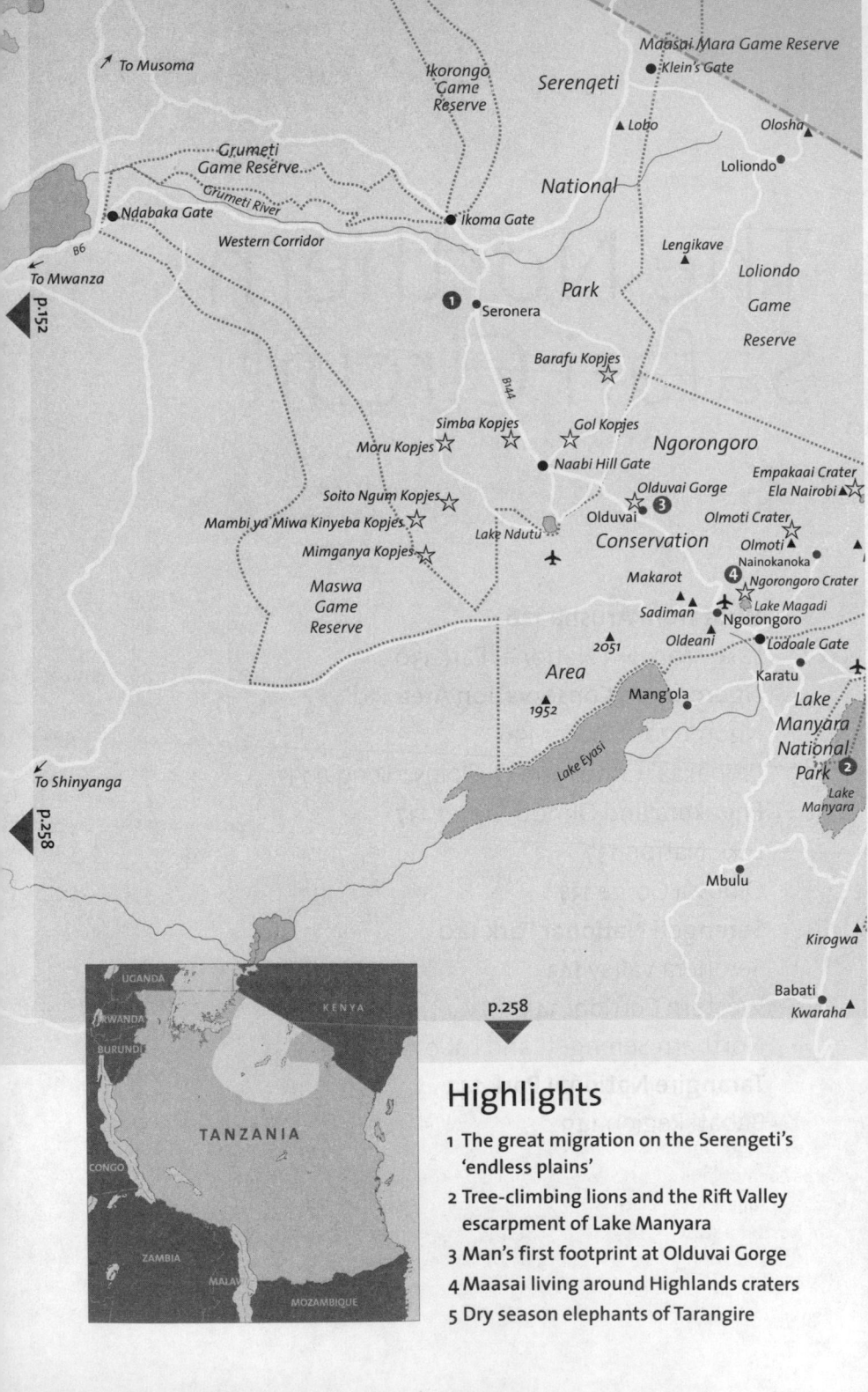

To Musoma

Ikorongo
Game
Reserve

Maasai Mara Game Reserve

Klein's Gate

Serengeti

Lobo

Olosha

Loliondo

Grumeti
Game Reserve

Grumeti River

Ndabaka Gate

Ikoma Gate

National

B6

Western Corridor

To Mwanza

p.152

Lengikave

Loliondo
Game
Reserve

Park

1 Seronera

Barafu Kopjes

Ngorongoro

Simba Kopjes

Gol Kopjes

B144

Moru Kopjes

Naabi Hill Gate

Empakaai Crater
Ela Nairobi

Soito Ngum Kopjes

Olduvai Gorge **3**

Olmoti Crater

Mambi ya Miwa Kinyeba Kopjes

Olduvai

Olmoti

Mimganya Kopjes

Lake Ndutu

Conservation

Nainokanoka

Makarot

4 Ngorongoro Crater

Maswa
Game
Reserve

Sadiman

Lake Magadi

Oldeani

Ngorongoro

Lodoale Gate

2051

Area

Karatu

Lake
Manyara
National
Park **2**

1952

Mang'ola

Lake Eyasi

Lake
Manyara

To Shinyanga

Mbulu

p.258

Kirogwa

Babati

p.258

Kwaraha

TANZANIA

UGANDA

KENYA

RWANDA

BURUNDI

CONGO

ZAMBIA

MALAWI

MOZAMBIQUE

Highlights

1 The great migration on the Serengeti's 'endless plains'

2 Tree-climbing lions and the Rift Valley escarpment of Lake Manyara

3 Man's first footprint at Olduvai Gorge

4 Maasai living around Highlands craters

5 Dry season elephants of Tarangire

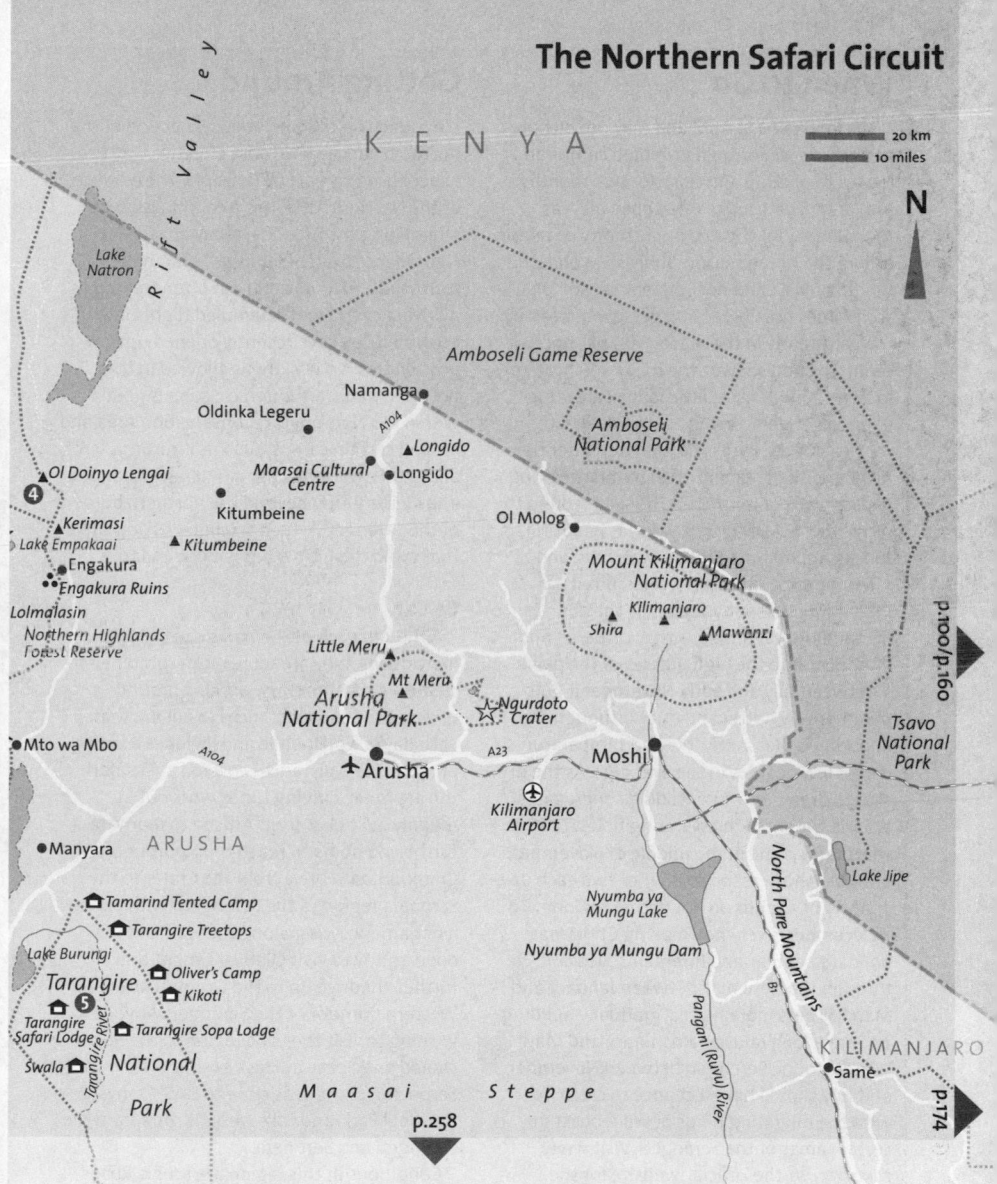

The Northern Safari Circuit

KENYA

20 km
10 miles

N

Lake Natron

Rift Valley

Amboseli Game Reserve

Namanga

Oldinka Legeru

Amboseli National Park

▲ Longido

A104

Ol Doinyo Lengai

Maasai Cultural Centre

● Longido

④

▲ Kerimasi

Kitumbeine

Ol Molog

Lake Empakaai

▲ Kitumbeine

Mount Kilimanjaro National Park

Engakura

Engakura Ruins

Kilimanjaro

Lolmalasin

Shira ▲

▲ Mawenzi

Northern Highlands Forest Reserve

Little Meru ▲

Mt Meru ▲

Tsavo National Park

Arusha National Park

☆ Ngurdoto Crater

p.100/p.160

● Mto wa Mbo

A104

A23

Moshi

✈ Arusha

Kilimanjaro Airport ✈

Manyara

ARUSHA

North Pare Mountains

Lake Jipe

🏠 Tamarind Tented Camp

Nyumba ya Mungu Lake

🏠 Tarangire Treetops

Lake Burungi

Nyumba ya Mungu Dam

🏠 Oliver's Camp

Tarangire

⑤

🏠 Kikoti

Tarangire Safari Lodge 🏠

🏠 Tarangire Sopa Lodge

KILIMANJARO

Swala ●

National Park

● Same

p.174

Pangani (Ruvu) River

B1

M a a s a i   S t e p p e

p.258

Tanzania's Northern Safari Circuit is renowned for some of the finest game viewing in all of Africa. Its natural abundance of wildlife, together with the annual migration of millions of animals across these northern reaches, makes up a flourishing ecosystem that is now benefiting from hard-fought conservation measures. Nearly 25,000 square kilometres of these superb rolling landscapes have been preserved in their natural state. As little as 20 years ago wide tracts of this land were inhabited only by rural nomadic tribes, many of which have now been turfed off it to make way for wildlife preservation. The challenge that faces this region now is to balance tourist exploitation with the rights of indigenous people, the environment and its wildlife.

When to Go

The **long rains** in **April and May** provide the perfect excuse for smaller tented camps and lodges to pack up and close for two months, but larger chain lodges stay open all year round and offer the rare opportunity of safaris during the 'green season'. **June** is a wonderful month to visit, and not yet peak season, so it's sometimes possible to still get lower rates. By travelling early in the season you risk encountering the odd shower, the roads are invariably in a dire condition and the lodges are struggling to get going again as they deal with repairs, but the land is rejuvenated after the rains, and the greenery and abundance bring widespread contentment. The land around the fertile reaches of the Rift Valley is beautiful. June is a good time for bird-watching and offers a profusion of butterflies, but it is a little harder to spot animals, as the abundance of standing water means they disperse, and disappear into the high grasses of the plains.

Between **July** and **early November** it gets progressively hotter and drier, although the humidity is pleasantly low and temperatures drop a few degrees in the evenings. As the dry season draws on, more wildlife congregates around the shrinking watering holes. The **short rains** come in the middle of **November**, bringing showers for an hour or two each day, or at night. Clouds do not gather for long.

December is very hot, making Christmas holidays popular, and it remains pleasant through the New Year. Between **January** and **March** it gets more humid, gradually building up to the long rains again in April and May. Visitors to the Serengeti between **November** and **July** should have a chance to catch up with the migrating herds of wildebeest in certain areas of the Serengeti. Visit *www.tanapa.com*, the 'official' website for the Serengeti, a well designed 'infotainment' site with lots of pretty pictures.

Getting There

Most safaris in the north begin and end in Arusha. It is possible to **fly in** directly to Arusha or Kilimanjaro Airport, or to arrive by **bus**, **car** or **taxi** from Dar es Salaam or Nairobi (see 'Arusha', p.103, for details).

Getting Around

A round trip that includes a selection of the northern parks is the most effective way to experience this part of Tanzania. The essence of the Northern Circuit is a combination of stops along the Arusha–Lake Manyara–Ngorongoro Crater–Serengeti– Tarangire–Arusha route. Tours are most often treated as a **driving** circuit, but scheduled **flights** into bush airstrips have recently opened up new possibilities. No **walking** is allowed in the northern parks, although trekking is good within the Ngorongoro Conservation Area and around certain camps, such as Kirurumu above Lake Manyara, Tamarind near Tarangire and Klein's Camp beyond the northern borders of the Serengeti, which arrange walking trips that avoid the unmarked park boundaries.

By Car

Although each of the parks can be visited individually, they are more often combined to create a safari itinerary, working around driving times and distances to ensure that each day is worthwhile and includes a variety of terrain. The distances covered on a safari trip are great. Driving times work out at roughly 2½ hours from Arusha to Manyara, a further 1½ hours to reach the Ngorongoro Crater, 4 hours' drive from the Crater to the Seronera region of the Serengeti (with excellent game-viewing along the way, and the opportunity to visit Olduvai Gorge), and a further 3hr drive up to the Grumeti River and Western Corridor of the Serengeti. Anyone wishing to visit the Lobo region to the north should anticipate at least 4–5hrs' drive from Seronera. Tarangire is close to Lake Manyara National Park, and takes around 3hrs from the Serengeti and Seronera.

Conditions in this region are tough. Roads have improved dramatically in recent years, especially around Arusha, and those leading to the game parks. A splendid new road snakes through the Ngorongoro highlands as far as the crater gate, making the drive from Arusha much less arduous than in the bad old days. Even so, once in the parks the roads are rough, and anyone who has not travelled on African roads may not be impressed; be prepared for a bumpy and dusty ride.

For a safari in the north of Tanzania it is generally advisable to take a sturdy four-wheel-drive Land Rover or Land Cruiser that will cushion you from some of the bumps, or a minibus. It is just about possible to get around most places without a 4x4 in the dry season, but you will spend most of your safari inside your vehicle. Rules in the northern parks dictate that all vehicles have closed sides to protect people and animals, although most have open pop-tops. The best pop-top vehicles have a roof that raises up as a sunshade; others flip open, leaving passengers exposed. While they may afford enviable photo opportunities of the underbelly of a leopard, they remove a vital element of protection. Discuss your needs with your tour operator.

You can explore the parks alone in your own vehicle: around 1 per cent of visitors to the Serengeti enjoy a self-sufficient safari. It is only really advisable if you own or at least know the vehicle, which should be fully equipped with plenty of spare tyres in good condition, surplus petrol, a decent jack and tow ropes. Never rely on the petrol signs on maps, as these stations quite often run dry and it can be days before the next delivery. It is well nigh impossible to lay your hands on a good map of the Serengeti; a compass or GPS device is about the most reliable navigation tool if you do not know the routes. Self-drive cars can be hired from Arusha (*see* p.103), but even the most independent drivers would be well advised to take a local guide on board.

In fact it is often just as economical and far less hassle to use a local tour operator and informed driver-guide. In this way you have someone who will keep his eyes on the road while you appreciate the views, and who can provide expert wildlife and local knowledge, often with a selection of reference books to fill any gaps. Driver-guides are usually practised at spotting animals, and familiar with the idiosyncrasies of the habitat and animal behaviour, as well as knowing roads, park maps and emergency procedures, such as what to do when both of the petrol points in the Serengeti have run out of fuel. All good tour operators travel with radio back-up – essential in an emergency, but also useful for tracking wildlife with the assistance of other guides in the region.

By Air

There are **bush airstrips** at Lake Manyara, Tarangire and the Ngorongoro Conservation Area, and three in the Serengeti, at Seronera, the Western Corridor for Kirawira and Grumeti, and the north for Lobo, Migration Camp and Klein's Camp. There is a **scheduled daily circuit** between all of these airstrips (except Ngorongoro) with **Regional Air**, CMC Building, PO Box 14755, Arusha, **t** (027) 2502541, *www.airkenya.com/docs/regair3.htm*. It is also possible to **charter flights**. Ngorongoro is a charter airstrip only. There are frequently difficulties landing there due to low cloud and fog, and it is crucial to pre-arrange transport to meet you on arrival as there are plenty of lions waiting to greet you! Kilimanjaro to Arusha is $45, Arusha to Manyara $65, Arusha to Seronera $165 and Arusha to Grumeti $190.

Coastal Travels, **t** (022) 2117959/60, *aviation@coastal.cc, www.coastal.cc*, links the Serengeti with northwest Tanzania: from Grumeti and Seronera to Mwanza and Rubondo (for Lake Victoria and Rubondo National Park).

Although it is a shame to miss the drives into the parks, consider flying if long hours of driving will be a problem. Fly-in safaris are increasingly possible: Conservation Corporation and Elewana offer them as a matter of course; expect smaller outfits to follow suit. Guides and vehicles are provided on arrival. For many, the ideal choice is to drive the circuit one way and fly out, although this requires a healthy budget.

Where to Stay

There are now five main hotel groups specializing in lodges in the northern parks, and a number of smaller, independent lodges and permanent and mobile camps. These are easily characterized and fall into distinct price brackets, although tour operators often have special deals that can result in minimal price differences over a seven-day itinerary.

Conservation Corporation, CC Africa, Private Bag X27, Benmore, Johannesburg, South Africa, **t** (027) 11 8094300, **f** (027) 11 809440, *information@ccafrica.com, www.ccafrica.com*. A selection of individual and well-appointed camps in the Serengeti (Grumeti and Klein's Camp), Lake Manyara (Manyara

Tree Lodge) and Ngorongoro Crater (Ngorongoro Crater Lodge), designed for the utmost in safari comfort and created with a sense of humour and architectural flair. This luxury does not come cheap: all of these camps, which aim to be eco-friendly, are at the top of the price range, with rates of around $550 per person per night full board, including all game-viewing activities.

Elewana Afrika, 99 Serengeti Road, Sopa Plaza, PO Box 12814, Arusha, **t** (027) 2500630–9, *info@elewana.com, www.elewana.com*. The Elwana lodges are Sopa Lodges' new élite property clutch, and include the triumphant Tarangire Treetops and Migration Camp in Serengeti. Top marks to Sopa: these lodges guarantee a safari of distinction. By 2006 there will be 14 lodges around the country including on Zanzibar.

Serena Hotels, PO Box 2551, Arusha, **t** (027) 2504058/2506304/2504159, *reservations@serena.co.tz, www.serenahotels.com*. Serena lodges uphold high standards of eco-friendliness, use indigenous design and employ Tanzanian craftsmen. The hotels are large and provide reliable service and good restaurant cuisine. They are slightly more affordable, with double rooms around $340 per night full board – but game-viewing costs are extra. Kirawira, a luxury tented camp on the Grumeti River in the Western Corridor, is an exception, closer both in calibre and size to its more upmarket rivals.

Sopa Lodges, PO Box 1823, Arusha, **t** (027) 2500630/9, *info@sopalodges.com, www.sopalodges.com*. A notch down in safari chic, often ambitiously designed with glass walls, indoor waterfalls and curious colour schemes. The chain was mainly built in the 1980s in 1970s style; recent renovations have incorporated ornate new décor that adds an opulent gloss. Double rooms $280 full board.

The formerly state run **Wildlife Lodges** at Seronera, Lobo, Lake Manyara and Ngorogoro have been taken over by **Hotels and Lodges**, PO Box 2633, Arusha, **t** (027) 2544595/2544795/6, *res@hotelsandlodges-tanzania.com, www.hotelsandlodges-tanzania.com*. Hotels and Lodges are doing their best to rehabilitate the lodges, but at the end of the day they are vast glass enclosures that mar the safari landscape. Invariably in superb locations, the accommodation is decent, if mildly boxy and unimaginative.

There are also a handful of extremely good, small **independent lodges** dotted around the circuit, which can provide a welcome alternative to the larger hotels, and often have a more secluded atmosphere. They are all individual in character and design. A couple of tour operators also run their own **private camps**, of a very good standard and value. There are also plenty of opportunities to avoid them all and enjoy a **private mobile camping safari**. For independent lodges, private camps and mobile safaris, *see* listings for each park, and tour operators, below.

Camping

It is illegal to camp anywhere in the national parks other than in designated camping grounds. These are divided into public and private campsites. **Public campsites** generally have rudimentary and often fairly grotty facilities, and you share the site with whoever else has pitched up that night – most likely an overland truck. **Private campsites** are hard to distinguish from the surrounding area. You have to bring in everything you need, including water, and take everything away again, including rubbish. All campsites must be pre-booked and get full in advance during the busy seasons, especially the private ones. There is an additional charge for camping on top of the daily park fees, $25 per night for the public sites, and $50 for the private sites.

Safari Tour Operators

Despite taking place in some of the poorest regions of the developing world, African wildlife safaris are an expensive luxury targeted at relatively wealthy Westerners. There are, however, safari tour operators in northern Tanzania to suit almost every budget, of which most have very high standards, employing well-informed and sometimes multilingual guides. Sadly there are also a number of opportunist fly-by-night operators with extremely bad reputations, who bundle clients into poor vehicles that are liable to break down, and fail to provide an adequate service. The **Tanzanian Tourist Board** on Boma Road in Arusha, **t** (027) 2503842, *www.tanzaniatouristboard.com*, holds a list of all registered, reliable operators, and a blacklist of notoriously unreliable companies. It is really worthwhile checking these lists before you hand over any money. The operators listed below are all well established and provide a high-quality service appropriate to their price.

Expensive

Hoopoe Adventure Tours, India Street, PO Box 2047, Arusha, **t** (027) 2507011, *information@ Hoopoe.com, www. hoopoe.com*. Hoopoe has a reputation as one of the best safari operators in Arusha. It maintains consistently high standards for a price that reflects its reputation, without being excessive. Hoopoe specializes in mobile luxury tented camping trips that can also be combined with nights in luxury lodges. All safaris use private Land Rovers, with interesting, knowledgeable and resourceful driver-guides. Excellent local knowledge, an eye for detail and good cooking make their camping trips a resounding cut above the average. A partnership with Tropical Trekking (*see* p.124) means that Hoopoe benefits from the expertise of the trekking company in planning walks. Hoopoe also runs Kirurumu tented camp on Lake Manyara, manages Tamarind, a luxury camp just north of Tarangire, and can arrange a variety of bespoke expeditions.

Nomad Tanzania Ltd, PO Box 681, Usa River, Arusha, **t/f** (027) 2553819/20/29/30, *bookings @nomad.co.tz, info@nomad.co.tz, www. nomad-tanzania.com*. An exclusive operation specializing in private tented camps and walking safaris. The standard of guiding is excellent, whether you choose to pay a premium for one of the 'named' guides or not. All safaris aim to steer well off the beaten track to avoid crowds and facilitate a more private safari experience. Nomad runs a variety of safaris combining light mobile walking safaris with luxury tented camping at private camps. To make this option more affordable for those travelling in pairs, the company has devised 'Serengeti Safari Camps', mobile or static camps for up to eight people, who arrive and depart with their own driver guides. The safaris aim to include plenty of walking – often with a

Maasai armed only with a spear – picnics and cook-out bush breakfasts. Attention is paid to the mix of a fine gin and tonic.

Flycatcher Safaris, 172 Serengeti Road, PO Box 591, Arusha, **t** (027) 2544109/2544979/ 2506963, **f** (027) 2508261, *flycat@habari.co. tz, www.flycat.com*. A small but experienced operation offering expert guides and Land Rovers modified to ensure that all window seats have equally good views. Flycatcher runs tailor-made camping and luxury lodge-based trips with a high standard of service. Expertise in devising unusual safari routes through the Western Corridor and to its own tented camp on Ruhondo Island makes it the best choice for visiting either of these destinations. They have a seasonal camp for chimp-tracking at Mahale, one of only three operations in the park.

Amazing Tanzania, PO BOX 2, Karatu, **t** (027) 253 4308, *sales@amazingtanzania.com, www.amazingtanzania.com*. A small but experienced operation (run out of Gibb's Farm, p.128) specializing in mobile camping safaris geared to suit the requirements of a group, and extended camping expeditions. The guides' knowledge of the bush keeps clients returning year after year, so new safaris are constantly being devised. At the moment Gibb's is working on a combination of Northern Circuit safaris with Ruaha and Katavi National Parks down south.

Moderate

Roy Safaris Ltd, Haile Selassie Road, off the Old Moshi Road, 1km from the clock tower, PO Box 50, Arusha, **t** (027) 2508010/2507057/ 2507940/2502115, **f** (027) 2508892, *roysafaris @intafrica.com, www.roysafaris.com*. An excellent choice, representing great value for money and attentive service. Roy run luxury lodge safaris to all the major Northern Circuit hotels in pop-top Land Rovers, Land Cruisers and one extended car that takes seven people. It also excels in budget camping safaris, which can be upgraded to 'semi-luxury' with the addition of bigger dome tents and mattresses and better furniture. All the guides speak English and a couple also speak French; all are equipped with good first aid and cultural knowledge. Roy Safaris can organize off-the-beaten-track camping trips to Lake Eyasi, home of the Hadzabe hunter-gatherers and Datoga people, and treks to Empakaai and Olmoti Craters (each 3 days from Ngorongoro), and to Lake Natron via Engakura during the dry season. The company is also an experienced and reliable operator for climbs of Mounts Kilimanjaro and Meru at reasonable prices.

Tropical Trekking, t (027) 2502417, **f** (027) 2508907, *www.tropicaltrekking.com*. It is hard to find anyone more experienced or better informed than Tropical Trekking for all walking, trekking and mountain climbing trips around Arusha. As a partner of Hoopoe Adventure Tours (*see* p.123), its walks are an accessible addition to any Northern Circuit safari. Trekking options include North Maasailand, the Ngorongoro Highlands, climbs of Ol Doinyo Lengai, and walks from Makarot Mountain to Little Olduvai or Lake Eyasi. The company also specializes in walks through a private concession of 200 square kilometres of conservation area in Loliondo, and dry season walks through Monduli Rain Forest. The company has a reputation for extremely well equipped and catered climbs up Mounts Meru and Kilimanjaro, on the less well-trodden routes. There is scope for all, even those with limited time or energy.

Bushbuck Safaris Ltd, PO Box 1700, Arusha, **t** (027) 2507779/2544186/2544308, **f** (027) 2544860, *bushbuck@bushbuckltd.com*, *www.bushbuckltd.com*. A family-run business keen to promote quality and service as a top priority. Bushbuck operates a large fleet of reliable 4x4 vehicles modified for a comfortable safari experience, all fitted with two-way radios and maintained to a high degree of repair, and ensures all driver guides are knowledgeable and well-versed in the idiosyncrasies of the Northern Circuit as well as their vehicles. Bushbuck Safaris has links with the Serena hotel chain, for those who wish to fly between locations.

Cheap

Kearsley Travel and Tours, PO Box 142, Arusha, **t** (027) 2508043, **f** (027) 2508044, *kearsley@ark.eoltz.com*, *www.kearsley.net*. Dar office, PO Box 801, **t** (022) 2115026–9, *kearsley@raha.com*. Among the longest-running safari operators in Arusha – established in 1948 –

specializing in lodge-based tailor-made Northern Circuit safaris in four-wheel-drive Land Rovers or minibuses. Also organizes Mount Kilimanjaro climbs.

Sunny Safaris, PO Box 7267, Arusha, **t** (027) 2507145, **t** (0744) 268475, *info@sunnysafaris.com*, *sunny@arusha.com*, *www.sunnysafaris.com*. An alternative budget option since 1984. Safari-prepared vehicles fitted with pop-top roof for game-viewing and two-way radios. Budget camping safaris and lodge-based safaris are possible, with cheaper rates for groups. Walks on the foothills of Mount Meru and longer 5–6-day walks in the Ngorongoro Highlands can be arranged. A typical itinerary for such a walk might be starting from the ranger post at Nainokanoka, walking to Olmoti Crater, then on up to Empakaai Crater, with subsequent nights at Nayobi, Ngarasero and Lake Natron. Five-day walks around Monduli Highlands are another option, offering a chance to see the landscapes for less, even if gourmet comfort levels are not quite up to those of the top luxury operators.

Leopard Tours Ltd, PO Box 1638, Arusha, **t** (027) 2508441-3, **f** (027) 2504131, *leopard@yako.habari.co.tz*. Long-standing reputation as decent budget operators with drivers who are largely well-informed and friendly. Leopard runs a extensive number of cars and is familiar with all the main regions of the parks, so providing a good safari service for anyone happy with an itinerary that does not stray too far from the beaten track.

Wildersun Safaris, Joel Maeda Road, PO Box 2587, Arusha, **t** (027) 2548847–9, **f** (027) 2548223, *wildersun@cybernet.co.tz*, *www.wildersun.com*. A large operator specializing in upmarket lodge-based accommodation, but keeping overall costs lower by filling spaces for regular fixed date departure safaris in minibuses and Land Cruisers.

Tourist Information

Tanzania National Parks, TANAPA, PO Box 3134, Arusha, **t** (027) 2503471/2501930–1, *info@tanzaniaparks.com*, *www.tanzaniaparks.com*, manages all areas designated as national parks and aims to maintain a balance between preservation and use.

The National Parks and Game Reserves

Today the Serengeti-Mara ecosystem is made up of a vast mosaic of adjoining game reserves and national parks crossing the border of northern Tanzania and southern Kenya and covering more than 24,900 square kilometres of grassland and forest. The immense size of the **Serengeti National Park** alone, which at 14,504 square kilometres exceeds the size of Belgium, Wales or Ohio, guarantees each tourist vehicle at least one blissful moment of apparently absolute isolation.

The neighbouring **Ngorongoro Conservation Area (NCA)** is a markedly different environment, visibly shaped by volcanoes and the tectonic plate action of the Great Rift. The land is pockmarked with giant craters, the most famous of which, the **Ngorongoro Crater**, has attracted an unusually rich variety of resident and migratory East African wildlife. Nowadays these highlands are also home to a large population of the Maasai tribe, many of whom were displaced from the surrounding National Parks. The NCA aims to preserve the traditional Maasai tribal lifestyle while conserving the environment for wildlife and serving the tourist market.

A large tract of land at Tarangire, and a swath between the escarpment of the Great Rift Valley and Lake Manyara, became national parks during the 1970s. These smaller parks in the north are also worth exploring. **Lake Manyara National Park** is an easy and enjoyable two hours' drive from Ngorongoro, and a completely contrasting environment. Lush green forests, palm trees and clouds of butterflies surround visitors at the gate, tempting you into a magical maze of driving routes through woods and glades. Lake Manyara, like its neighbour on the southern side of the plains of Maasailand, **Tarangire National Park**, is a haven for bird-watchers. Tarangire has a more open, hilly landscape studded with ancient baobab trees, stretching along both banks of the Tarangire River, with superb views along the length of the valley. This is the central water source for all resident and passing wildlife.

These northern parks support a vast ecosystem as herds of wildlife travel according to the season across the boundaries of each park and between the borders of Kenya and Tanzania; the **Northern Safari Circuit** has evolved into a sequence of conservation and game-controlled areas, which include all land required by migrating animals in the course of the year. This area relies on the preservation and protection of outlying areas: the 'circuit' is far more than simply a pleasure park for tourists. Widespread international interest in the unusual balance of such a wide-ranging ecosystem has meant that the region has benefited from extensive research and foreign investment – it is said that since 1966 the Serengeti has been one of the most studied areas in the world. Its infrastructure and experience with tourism and conservation are far ahead of the rest of the country, setting precedents for other parks to follow or avoid.

Poaching, however, continues to be a real problem for all the conservation areas, especially given the serious and widespread rural poverty. Villages on the outskirts of parks and game reserves tend to rely on wild animals for food, and kill when crops or livestock are threatened by ranging wild creatures. Animals such as antelope, buffalo and zebra are sold from the hunting reserves at far lower prices than farmed meat, but free still prevails over cheap when life is so hard won. **Tanzania National Parks Association (TANAPA)** and a number of foreign investors have worked to combat this situation by education and improved living standards. They have been undermined by an unforeseen but with hindsight predictable response: once they have built schools and encouraged new business, the population fast increases as outsiders move in to share the benefits, and problems of demand outstripping supply arise once more.

West from Arusha

The road from Arusha runs west towards Lake Manyara, Tarangire National Park, Ngorongoro Crater and the Serengeti across the wide, open plains of Maasailand. It is straight and clear, with views across the plains to an arc of craggy mountains, part of the Great Rift Valley escarpment, on the horizon. This is the land of the Maasai, a wild and mainly uncultivated stretch across which the tribe roams, grazing its cattle. Often the unaccustomed eye can make out nothing but wilderness in each direction, a greenish sea under the shimmering sun. Then, in the distance a dart of red picks out a lone Maasai walking from one far-distant region to another, often on a journey of a day or more. The Maasai people have sought to remain true to the traditions of their tribal lifestyle, and fought to resist the encroaching changes of the modern world. But on this route to the northern parks it is common to see Maasai who have made one proud concession to modernity and now make the journey along the tarmac highway on shiny Chinese frame bicycles, yet still wearing their traditional dress of red shuka robes, and pedalling armed with a well-honed stick to ward off snakes.

Most safaris and many mountain-climbing expeditions in northern Tanzania begin and end in Arusha (*see* pp.99–116 and 120–24). All driving safaris from Arusha require a two-hour minimum drive to the nearest park gate, taking a route from the centre of Arusha into the magnificent spread of countryside beyond.

History

The land covered by the conservation areas of northern Tanzania is characterized by geographical extremes. Africa's highest mountains are here, alongside alkaline lakes and hot mineral springs. All the elements are shaped by volcanic action and make up a landscape extraordinary due to its precarious position in the realm of the Great Rift Valley, poised over the meeting point of tectonic plates beneath the earth's crust.

The Great Rift, approximately 6,400m long, 50km wide and 100–1,000m deep, has created a vast fertile spread, without which this large expanse of East Africa might be as arid as the wide Sahara. Its landscape undulates dramatically, thrown upwards in rifts, faults and the craters of volcanoes that have covered the land in rich minerals, making it green and prolific and in turn creating rivers, lakes and clouds. The most famous of these wild northern plains is the Serengeti, formed of layers of ash puffed across the land by the volcanic eruptions of Ngorongoro and the three cones that make up Kilimanjaro. Its name comes from the Maa phrase 'Siringet', meaning 'endless plains', as the Maasai people who have made their lives on its broad expanse called this region when they emigrated here 200 years ago.

The first European to glimpse these plains was probably a German explorer, Oscar Beaumann, in 1892, but the Serengeti really captured the imagination of the Western

Photography

The Maasai people throughout this region are impressive-looking, and their photogenic harmony with the surroundings is inspiring for photographers. But many Maasai – especially those living close to the parks – will be reluctant to let you photograph them without paying a small fee for the privilege. Ask around for the going rate.

Sports and Activities

The Manyara Serena Lodge is the base for **Serena Active**, otherwise known as **Green Footprint**, Manyara Serena Lodge, t (0748) 445171, *www.greenfootprint.co.tz*. Offers mountain biking, hiking and abseiling in the Lake Manyara area; also canoeing all year round in Arusha National Park.

Where to Stay

Around Mto wa Mbo

The **Holiday Fig Resort** (*cheap*) has rooms or camping, with a small pool. The **Twiga Campsite and Lodge** (*cheap*) offers rooms with bathroom or camping. Both are signposted as you enter the town.

Lake Manyara National Park

Very Expensive

Manyara Tree Lodge, CC Africa, Private Bag X27, Benmore, Johannesburg, South Africa, t (027) 11 8094300, f (027) 11 809440, *information@ ccafrica.com*, *www.ccafrica. com*. This exclusive lodge tucked in the embrace of a mahogany forest on the shores of the lake would be fit even for the resident royalty –

the renowned tree-climbing lions of the nearby Maji Moto pride. You could be relaxing in any one of the world's luxury boutique hotels, yet the lodge is a remote hideaway in a far-flung corner of the national park. The compound teems with wildlife; it is the bush, the real deal. Ten tree-house suites lie around an opening in the forest canopy that houses a boma-style enclosure and discreet swimming pool. The communal area, in the form of a ripe pod, opens artfully from the forest floor to reveal a cavernous eating and drinking area over two levels. Chefs attend to all manner of delicacies in the open kitchen. A shop sells the latest in bush chic. The service is faultless, though the experience could feel a little formulaic. Following the El Niño floods, the camp has retreated further away from the lakeshore, and it is no longer possible to view the lake from here.

Expensive

Kirurumu Tented Lodge, PO Box 2047, Arusha, t (027) 2507011, *information@hoopoe.com*, *www.kirurumu.com*. Kirurumu takes its name from a Bantu word meaning 'echoing waters', describing the sound of the river running nearby. It is owner-run, and the most atmospheric choice here, with permanent tented rooms built on stilted wooden platforms, designed to give each tent a private bush enclosure with its own un-disturbed view, and hot, powerful showers with solar-heated spring water in every tent. The open-sided dining room and wood and rock-enclosed bar also make the most of the location; food and service are excellent. Meals rely heavily on fresh fruit, vegetables and herbs from Kirurumu's own organic garden, and are enhanced by a selection of

world in the 1920s, when reports of the unusually large number of lions here began to circulate among those with guns and a taste for the hunt. By 1950 so many animals had been killed that changing attitudes deemed it necessary to make the endless plains a game reserve; they became a fully protected national park in 1951.

In the 1960s, the work of Professor Bernhard Grzimek, then president of the Frankfurt Zoological Society and author with his son Michael of *Serengeti Shall Not Die* (1959), highlighted the importance of protecting the land required by millions of wildebeest, zebra and antelope in their annual migration across the plains. The two Grzimeks believed in preserving the region as a 'primordial wilderness', and that no fine wines from the bar. If all this is not enough, there is a romantic 'honeymoon tent', not exclusively reserved for honeymooners. The camp's position outside the park means that Kirurumu is free from park rules – such as walking restrictions – and the lodge specializes in botanical walks through the surrounding bush with Maasai guides who can describe the medicinal uses of plants. The many resident bird species will delight bird-watchers. Full board.

Manyara Serena Lodge, PO Box 2551, Arusha, t (027) 2504058/2506304/2504159, *www. serenahotels.com*. Another good option, also in an elevated position on the escarpment ridge, the Manyara Serena is constructed on an intriguing design with barely a straight line to be seen. The whole resembles a rambling village centred around a bar and pool that perches above the landscape with a stunning 'drop-off' effect. The views from the poolside bar are far-reaching, and with a large telescope to play with it almost rivals the Ngorongoro Crater Lodge for the full-on sundowner safari experience. Rooms have all amenities and immaculate, individualized decoration. The restaurant serves delicious food too.

Lake Manyara Hotel, Hotels and Lodges, PO Box 2633, Arusha, t (027) 2544595/2544795, f (027) 2548633, *www.hotelsandlodges-tanzania.com*. The only other choice above Manyara, in a fantastic location with wide views over the park. One of the formerly state-run Wildlife Lodges, and, like the others around the Northern Circuit, not the place for dreaming, as the layout is based on concrete blocks and basic purpose-built rooms. It is, however, well equipped for wheelchair access. Prices include free transfers to and from the Manyara airstrip, and it

is cheaper than its posher neighbours. The savings hardly justify the style difference, but the swimming pool and location are pleasant enough if you don't make comparisons. All accommodation above Lake Manyara is situated high on the escarpment, off the main road that leads into the Ngorongoro Conservation Area and the Serengeti. This road continues from the Lake Manyara region through a fertile, cultivated region of the Rift Valley, which has been inhabited and farmed by the Iraqw people for 2,000 years. There are excellent alternatives for accommodation here among the coffee plantations and red earth furrows of this wide valley, just 3hrs' drive from Arusha.

Moderate

Gibb's Farm, t (027) 2534040 or Arusha booking office, PO Box 6084, t (027) 2508930, f (027) 2534418, *reservations@gibbsfarm.net*, *www.gibbsfarm.net*. The most charismatic of these rural options, a 1930s coffee plantation with terraced gardens on the outer slopes of the Ngorongoro Highlands and Rift Valley escarpment. Gibb's Farm is a remarkable hideaway between the national parks and conservation areas, a surprisingly English country garden high on a wide African hillside tucked between fields of maize, beans and coffee. Built in the early 20th century by German settlers, Gibb's became property of the British Custodian of Enemy Property after the Second World War. In 1948 it was sold to British war veteran James Gibb, who settled here with his wife Margaret. He restored the neglected coffee farm and she planted a small vegetable and flower garden. The farm became a lodge in 1972, 12 years after Ngorongoro Conservation Area was established around it. The coffee

people – not even native tribes – should live within the nature reserves. As a result of their efforts and subsequent studies into the annual path of the migration, the boundaries of the Serengeti were extended and the Ngorongoro Conservation Area emerged as a separate entity. Many Maasai were moved to other regions; debate continues today as to the fairest future for those who were displaced from the land.

From 'River of the Mosquito' to Lake Manyara

Before reaching the national park you pass through a colourful and rapidly growing small town called Mto wa Mbo, which translates enticingly as 'River of the Mosquito'.

plantation was sold after Gibb died in 1977, leaving enough land for flower and vegetable gardens and a dairy, which supply the lodge with armfuls of organic vegetables such as strawberries, tree tomatoes and squash. The lodge itself is a series of bungalow rooms set around the old colonial farmhouse, under trailing flower-laden eaves. The gardens are pristine, brimming with flowers – especially between October and January. The septuagenarian Margaret Gibb still lives on the estate and needed improvements to the estate will take place under her custodianship; expect the level of comfort to rise a notch, with baths and imported mattresses. A new dining room is planned to take advantage of the glorious views, but the character of a private farmhouse will remain. Gibb's Farm is also a good spot to stop for a wholesome buffet lunch of savoury pies and salads, which must be booked in advance and costs around $20 per head. Otherwise its views and gardens make it an elegant spot for morning or afternoon tea, en route from Lake Manyara to Ngorongoro. The lodge has a bird list of 165 local species spotted to date, and various alternatives for afternoon or day trips, including a walk through the Ngorongoro Montane Forest to the 'elephant caves' where elephants forage for salt, walks to the Rift edge for sundowners with a view, or to the small town of Karatu 4km from the farm, to see local women preparing 'fast food' for travellers and selling a range of goods from their roadside stalls. Closer to home, guests can grind and prepare coffee beans from the estate or visit the farm to milk the cows.

Plantation Lodge, t (027) 2534364–5, *plantation @les-raisitng.de, www.plantation-lodge.de.*

16 expansive bungalows with comfortable space for 35 or so. Renate is a self-proclaimed 'bush mama', who previously managed nearly 4,000 workers on nearby coffee estate. Renate and her husband designed and built the lodge and gardens from scratch, with truly impressive results; the rooms are well proportioned and beautifully decorated. There is a happy contentment in the air. The lodge is perfect for small groups of friends or families who want to share peaceful times exploring the local area. There is a pool and lots of hidey-holes throughout the grounds. The hosts have a long and heartfelt love for the African bush, and can provide an excellent soft safari experience for those turned off by the crowds and dust of the circuit. A good place to stop for lunch on the way to the crater.

Kifaru Lodge, t (0744) 999387, *kifarulodge@ hotmail.com, www.kifarulodge.com.* Set atop the Shangri-La coffee estate grounds, the lodge looks down across the red rolling hills of the Rift Valley. It is in the care of a German-Austrian couple, a musician and actress, who settled in the area following an epic horseback journey across the continent. They are clearly ecstatic with their new-found roles as hosts for the lodge. Flowers tumble over the well kept lawns and scent the air. A red-brick pool echoes the landscape and a pair of hammocks swing in the tall Grerelia trees. For those seeking more strenuous pastimes, there is a tennis court. A new stable awaits the arrival of the intrepid Bureperd horses which carried the couple on their adventures: the lodge will run 3–4-day horse safaris across the Rift valley down to Lake Eyasi or over to Lake Natron. German and English spoken.

Here is the Milton Keynes of the Northern Circuit, a new town that has developed since the irrigation of this previously dry and barren stretch of land during the 1950s. The project has successfully transformed hundreds of hectares of land into profitable ground for farming, and attracted newcomers from all over the country – nowhere else in Tanzania have so many different tribes gathered together in such a small area, and with each practising traditional methods of production there is a fascinating spread of activity. Banana beer is brewed, palm oil is pressed, papyrus baskets are woven, bows are strung and arrows are sharpened for hunting, and cattle are herded across the surrounding plains (*see* 'Cultural Tourism Programmes', pp.111–13). There is a number of budget hostels and campsites here, and several bars and *dukas* for last-minute provisions, a picnic lunch or evening meal.

Lake Manyara National Park is about three hours' drive from Arusha through Maasailand, following the direction of Tarangire for most of the way until the cross-roads. The final right-hand stretch of the road to Manyara has a troubled life as a result of harsh rains causing potholes, and it can be a long and bumpy ride.

Lake Manyara National Park

Lake Manyara National Park is a small but scenic park, excellent for bird-watching, a good area to find elephants, and offering the chance to spot a tree-climbing lion. It is a good soft introduction to the safari experience, a pretty park through which a mainly forested driving route wends its way between the banks of the soda water Lake Manyara and the impressive rise of the Great Rift escarpment. Manyara is often visited for half a day at the start or end of a safari, as it lies en route to Ngorongoro and the Serengeti. On reaching the park you first encounter a small **museum**, or rather a room packed with an ageing collection of badly stuffed birds and animals. It is probably better to continue into the park and take a chance with whatever might come your way in its full bodied and living form. The park swarms with butterflies just after the long rains, from May to June. Elephants, giraffes, buffalo and wildebeest can be found grazing in unexpected clearings or heading towards the water to drink or wash and the rivers provide scenic vistas for animal-spotting. Warthogs thrive here, fat and tuskered, and it is a natural playground for baboons and monkeys. The **tree-climbing lions**, although rarely seen, have inspired extensive theorizing about the wonders of evolution. Lions have also reportedly been seen up trees in the Serengeti, although these are even more rarely spotted than those around Lake Manyara, where the low branches of the acacia provide a fine frame for apprentice climbers.

Ngorongoro Conservation Area

On the western edge of the Great Rift Valley, halfway between the grand expanse of Lake Victoria and the reaches of Mount Kilimanjaro, the Ngorongoro Conservation Area covers 8,300 square kilometres of geologically bizarre landscape. It is largely made up of a range of volcanic peaks known as the Crater Highlands, which encompass a variety of different habitats, from Olduvai Gorge, where in the 1950s evidence of human existence that pre-dated all known human traces was excavated, to Ngorongoro Crater, famous as a microcosm of East African wildlife. Not only is the area unique for its concentration of natural wildlife and its geological and archaeological phenomena, but it also provides the Maasai tribe with an area where its people can maintain their pastoral lifestyle in a semblance of traditional ways.

The route into the highlands climbs steeply through a rich growth of spectral moss-draped trees, rising out of the mists that often linger around them. The land is high and green at the topmost altitude and summons a daily blanket of cloud to smother its wide expanse on most mornings. These rolling heights sweep towards the sky, their furthest reaches revealing a richness of life that forms a hazy pattern into the distance. The hillsides are speckled with zebras, the grass marked by the dark circles of the round Maasai family homesteads known as bomas. Here and there the distinctive red of the *shuka* cloths worn by the Maasai might catch your eye beside a herd of tawny cattle. It is always a place of unusual beauty, especially after the long rains .

The southwest boundary of the conservation area borders Lake Eyasi in the area where the Hadzabe people live. The Hadzabe, or Hadzapi, are thought to be the last remaining enclave of the most ancient Tanzanian cultures. Their language is similar to the click language used by southern African bushmen, and they continue to follow a traditional hunter-gatherer lifestyle across the savannah around the lake. Yet it is becoming increasingly hard for these people to cling to their ancestral traditions, as the increasing population of neighbouring tribes, swollen by displaced people, and the extended boundaries of the national parks, have decreased their hunting grounds and depleted their water sources.

History

The strange landscape of the Ngorongoro Conservation Area has a history that extends into prehistoric times. It begins more than three and a half million years ago, when Ngorongoro was a vast volcano, probably greater than Kilimanjaro: its intensely violent eruptions blew its top inwards and filled the cone with ash, leaving the formation standing today as the largest unbroken volcanic caldera in the world. The ash preserved an extraordinary catalogue of prehistoric human life in distinct layers at Olduvai Gorge nearby, where Professor Louis Leakey was to discover the earliest remains of hominoid man, a sequence of perfectly preserved footprints.

The ancient remains of cattle bones, hammered stone bowls and tools found on the crater floor suggest that a later culture of pastoralists lived in the Serengeti and Ngorongoro Crater up to 10,000 years ago, digging wells and water channels. They left stone circles – probably used to pen their cattle – on the plains. The Iraqw people also settled in Ngorongoro 2,000 years ago and constructed the advanced irrigation systems at Engakura. They now farm the fertile reaches between Lake Manyara and the Ngorongoro Highlands on the high Rift Valley plateau; their cultivation skills are evident over wonderfully fertile hillsides richly patterned with crops.

Around 1700 the Datoga peoples arrived, including a warrior-like group known as the Barbaig, Nilo-hamitic pastoralists similar to the Maasai, who in turn arrived in Ngorongoro in the early 1800s. Organized by war, the Maasai were well known to the 19th-century explorers and caravan trains for their ferocity. Battles between the Barbaig – whose warrior class controlled the highlands by force – and the Maasai were hard-fought. The Maasai emerged victorious and forced the rival cattle-herders out to Lake Eyasi, but both tribes remember the wars with reverence. The Maasai refer to the Barbaig as 'Mang'ati', meaning 'respected enemy'; Barbaig elders make pilgrimages to honour the graves of their ancestors in the lerai forest on the crater floor.

The first Europeans settled in the crater under the rule of German East Africa. Two brothers divided the crater floor between them, and each built a farm and kept a herd of cows – despite the Maasai reclaiming them. Distraught at losing cattle to warriors and lions, they invited a colonial hunter, named Hunter, to rid their crater home of predators. Hunter did such a masterful job that he was offered half the crater for a guinea on the death of its owner. The farm remains can still be seen, a set of ruins to the north of the Munge stream, and a ranger post beneath the Wildlife Lodge.

The NCA was the base for the research carried out by Professor Bernard Grzimek and his son Michael that highlighted the need to preserve the area's unique wildlife.

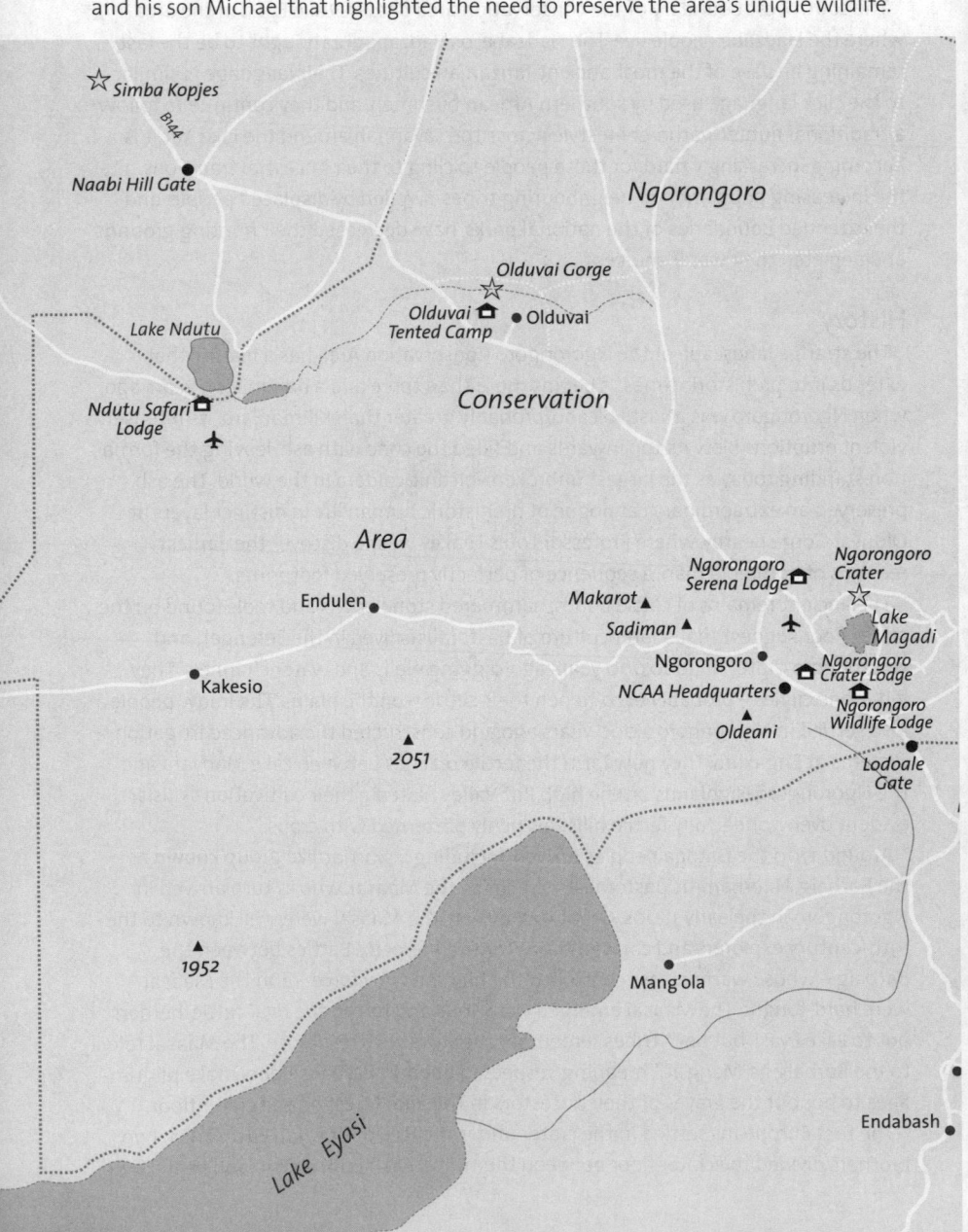

Michael died in a plane crash here; he and the work he did to safeguard this place of natural beauty are commemorated on a plaque inscribed with the words, 'It is better to light a candle than to curse the darkness.' The Ngorongoro Conservation Area Authority now manages the crater and a vast swath of the surrounding highlands. It is a model for native community and conservation projects and an important experiment in multiple land use: it aims to strike a balance between protecting wildlife, safeguarding the interests of the Maasai tribe and providing for tourists.

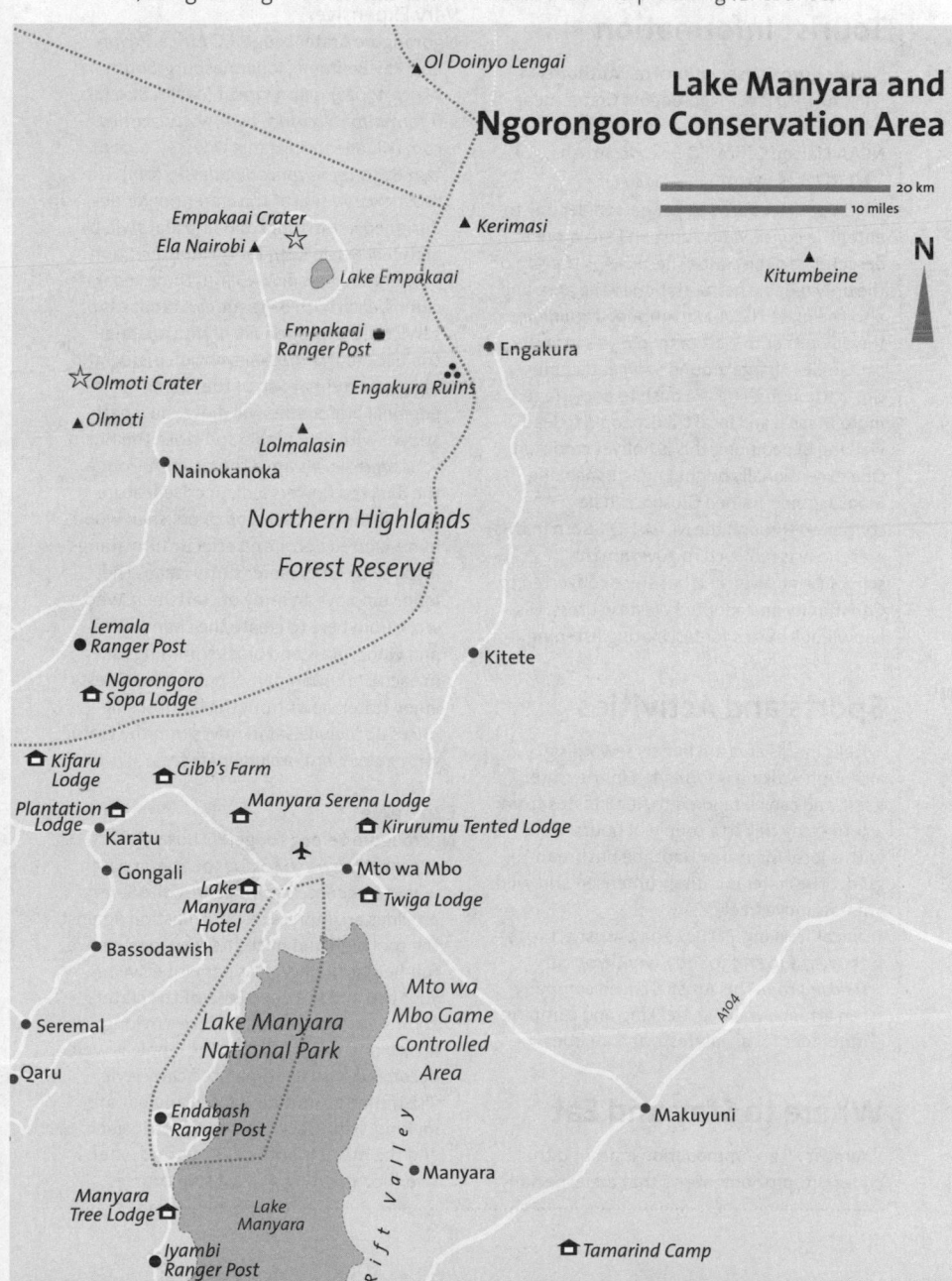

Lake Manyara and Ngorongoro Conservation Area

Getting There

The Ngorongoro Crater is a 5hr **drive** from Arusha. There is an Ngorongoro **airstrip**, used for private charters but subject to extreme weather conditions, especially fog, so it is not always viable for landing.

Tourist Information

Ngorongoro Conservation Area Authority (NCAA), PO Box 1, Ngorongoro Crater (near the Serena Lodge on the crater rim).
NCAA Liaison Office, PO Box 776, Arusha, **t/f** (027) 2503339.

NCA park fees are $30 per person per day to enter the conservation area and $10 more to descend into the crater. The NCAA is the site of the only reliable petrol station in the area and also the place to come to arrange a guide for the day, either to walk or to join you in your car. Guides charge around $20 per day, plus tips. Although there is a push to encourage more Maasai and local tribespeople to lead walking expeditions, this is not yet common. One exceptionally bright English-speaking Maasai guide, named Gibson, can be contacted through the NCAA HQs. Born in this area, he was removed to government schooling at seven and has since converted to Christianity and adopted Western dress. His knowledge makes for fascinating listening.

Sports and Activities

Treks in this area are hugely rewarding, although walking is forbidden in the crater itself, and can be tailored to fit all tastes from a 3- to 5-day trek to a couple of hours' walk with a local Maasai or Hadzabe bushman guide. The crater is entirely unfenced and wild animals move freely.
Tropical Trekking, PO Box 2047, Arusha, **t** (027) 2502417, **f** (027) 2508907, *www.tropical trekking.com*. This Arusha-based company can arrange walking, trekking and camping itineraries for all interests and abilities.

Where to Stay and Eat

Almost all accommodation is around the crater rim, providing views that are especially fantastic at night. The Ngorongoro Crater's rim touches cloud for most days of the year; the highlands wake up to a misty fog in most months other than the high dry season of December and January, but it generally lifts during the day, and all the hotels and lodges are open year-round.

Very Expensive
Ngorongoro Crater Lodge, CC Africa, Private Bag X27, Benmore, Johannesburg, South Africa, **t** (027) 11 8094300, **f** (027) 11 809440, *information@ccafrica.com, www.ccafrica. com* (UK agent: Tanzania Odyssey, **t** (020) 7471 8780, *info@tanzaniaodyssey.com*). The most exceptional of the crater rim lodges, designed in a distinct and unusual style by architect Sylvio Rech for the Conservation Corporation. It is divided into three separate camps, each with 6–12 suites. Standards of service are exceptionally high, a nostalgic trip back to the 1920s heyday of aristocratic big-game hunts: each of the rooms has a personal butler, who will draw you a bath strewn with rose petals and stoke the fire in your room. Roses are a theme in the lodge, the dark red flowers a distinctive feature against the rich backdrop of polished wood, hand-crafted décor, and eclectic furnishings inspired by an 'explorer's trousseau'. The lodge employs an army of craftsmen, who work from here to create the chandeliers and wood, glass and brass trimmings seen in each of the company's properties. Guests enjoy crater views from the bathtub. Big prices do include safari drives into the crater with guides, but exclude park fees.

Expensive
Ngorongoro Serena Lodge, PO Box 2551, Arusha, **t** (027) 2504058/2506304/2504159, *www.serenahotels.com*. Nearby, the Serena provides an impressive rocky bastion against the cool highland mists. Its cosy rooms have full-height sliding-glass panels between your bed and the open jaws of the crater. Rooms are laid out on two levels in long lines along the crater rim. The whole is well decorated with hand-painted cave-style illustrations. The dining room and bar are inviting, with crackling wood fires in each, and the menu is both delicious and extensive, incorporating at least four courses.

Ngorongoro Sopa Lodge, Sopa Lodges, PO Box 1823, Arusha, t (027) 2500630–9, f (027) 2508245, *www.sopalodges.com*. A lavishly decorated, slightly older establishment on the eastern aspect of the crater. The Sopa is popular with larger groups and Asian families on safari. The lodge is based around an impressive glass-fronted central atrium that overlooks a pool. Rooms are well presented, spacious and warm; each has its own glass-fronted verandah from which to enjoy crater views, with the added attraction of both bathtubs and showers. The restaurant has a good reputation and excellent atmosphere when the central open fires are burning; guests make the most of having to retire early from safari when the crater closes by enjoying long, leisurely meals.

Ngorongoro Wildlife Lodge, Hotels and Lodges, PO Box 2633, Arusha, t (027) 2544595 /2544795–6, f (027) 2548633, *www.hotels andlodges-tanzania.com*. The only other walled and roofed choice on the escarpment. Although it occupies a fantastic location, the architecture is heavy concrete and glass, and the box-like bedrooms are strung along in a row. This is another formerly state-run hotel, that needs a lot of love to get it up to scratch; it simply doesn't compare with the competition.

Moderate

Ndutu Safari Lodge, Room 235, 2nd Floor, Ngorongoro Wing, AICC, PO Box 6084, Arusha, t (027) 2506702/2502829, f (027) 2508310, *bookings@ndutu.com, www.ndutu. com*. The only smaller, more personal lodge-based alternative in Ngorongoro, on the boundary of the Serengeti, south of the Naabi Hill Gate. This low-key lodge, quietly situated on the warmer banks of Lake Ndutu, is a small and charming choice with simpler but good-quality accommodation. The area is excellent for bird-watching, with an astounding 400 species of birds listed on the camp records. It is excellently placed in the path of the great migration from December until early March. The lodge was built for an eccentric safari-loving colonial named George Dove, whose portrait hangs in the hallway. While searching in a nearby valley for building rocks for his camp, Dove was intrigued to discover a large number of fossils. He mentioned this to Mary Leakey, leading her to instigate archaeological digs in the area, and discover the ancient, world-famous footprints at Olduvai (*see* pp.137–9). One of the features of the camp is a cast of a staggeringly large pair of horns of the now extinct herbivore *Palarovis*. Dove opened the camp in 1967 as a basic safari-goers' bolthole intended to last for just a few years. Its small thatched stone rooms are designed in a utilitarian block style, but are well placed in a wild location with wildlife close at hand and the chance to sit back and enjoy silent, uninterrupted sunsets. Ndutu is closely linked with Gibb's Farm (*see* p 128), which supplies masses of fresh home-grown produce to its dining tables each day. The central areas are comfortable and well designed. The bar and dining room are open-sided to make the most of fresh air and views beneath makuti thatch. Each night a campfire is lit beneath the stars, and serval cats scuttle across the rafters for snacks. Room prices double in the high season, and you have to book early to have a chance of getting space.

Olduvai Tented Camp, t (027) 2502460, *peter@tanganyika.com, www.tanganyika. com*. This tented camp is 3km from the road, precisely in the middle of nowhere, sheltering in the stone-clad skirts of a towering obelisk that rears up from the vast Olduvai plain; 4x4s roar past the hidden road to this camp on their long journey to the Serengeti. Once the dust settles, a sense of emptiness returns. Life at the camp exists in an inhospitable tangle of wild sisal and thorny acacias. Echoing barks ring out from the rock hyrax, the local rodent. Camp life is extremely low-key: showers sprinkle from a bag-like contraption, and tents and food are basic; the camp would best be avoided if it weren't for the fantastic game-viewing opportunities at certain times of the year. After the rains, the sweet grasses entice animals migrating from the Serengeti; the Olduvai plain is the farthest point in their journey before they return north. The trained eye of the local Maasai helps visitors pick out the approaching game. Hardy walkers can tackle the peak of Mount Le Magurut, a steady 6–8hr climb. Evenings can be spent star-gazing at the Serengeti constellations from a seat in the bar.

Ngorongoro Crater

The famous Ngorongoro Crater, the world's largest intact volcanic caldera, is In an exceptional geographical position, forming a spectacular bowl of about 265 square kilometres with sides up to 600m deep. This is the stalking ground of around 20,000–30,000 wild animals at any one time, the most densely packed concentration of wildlife in Africa. The crater floor's environments include grassland, swamps, lerai forest (small patches of forest made up of yellow-barked acacia or 'yellow fever tree'), and Lake Makat, a central soda lake filled by the Munge stream. These habitats attract all kinds of wildlife to drink, wallow, graze or hide, and, although the animals are free to roam in and out of this contained environment, the rich volcanic soil, lush forests and spring-fed lakes on the crater floor incline both grazers and predators to remain. The crater thus holds an astonishing microcosm of East African wildlife within its boundaries and has achieved renown as the 'eighth wonder of the world'. Ngorongoro Crater is where you are most likely to see the endangered black rhino in Tanzania: a small population thrives in this idyllic and protected environment – one of the very few areas where they continue to breed in the wild. When viewed from above the crater looks vast, with herds of buffalo or elephant reduced to the size of ants. It is an amazing feeling to gaze down from any of the lookouts or strategically placed lodges and campsites on the crater rim; the sensation is one of elemental elevation, a godly perspective that warps all sense of size. But an *Alice in Wonderland* effect takes place as you enter: the famous crater feels surprisingly small once inside, and one day is quite sufficient to drive around it. Unfortunately its size and fame mean that you are unlikely to be alone in the crater, and the strict opening hours of the descent road, from 7am to 4pm, mean that all tourists pack in at those times, which can give a safari here a somewhat constricted feel. Ngorongoro still offers, however, the most rewarding safari if time is limited. Plans to raise the entrance fee and limit the length of safari times are all in an effort to preserve both environment and experience

Empakaai Crater and Ol Doinyo Lengai

Possibilities for walking and exploring in the stunning highlands and smaller craters also included in the conservation area provide a chance for more isolated exploration. The less visited **Empakaai Crater** encompasses beautiful forests and a deep lake. At 6km across it is a fraction of the size of the Ngorongoro Crater, but it is well worth a visit for the scenery alone. To get there is a hard slog, four to five hours' drive each way on a rough and rugged track. From the end of the driving track, accompanied by an armed ranger to ward off angry buffalo, you can take a couple of hours' or a half-day walk into the crater, which is densely forested and inhabited only by the buffalo and the odd Maasai, although the latter tend to stay around the top. The rim offers excellent views of Ol Doinyo Lengai, the Great Rift Valley and Lake Natron from the northern and eastern side, and distant peaks of Mount Kilimanjaro on a clear day – although it can be misty and cloudy up here.

Just beyond the NCA boundaries, **Ol Doinyo Lengai** is an impressive volcanic crater cone, now the only remaining active volcano in this region. Its continuous rumbling, bubbling and steaming earned it its Maasai name, 'Mountain of God', and the strange dark peak is held in great regard in Maasai legends and traditions. Many Maasai have climbed its slopes accompanied by a village elder to make sacrifices or prayers: women for fertility, boys seeking to learn the wisdom of men. Dust and ash from its eruptions, blown northwest, created the fertile Serengeti Plains, with the help of its now dormant neighbours. Visitors can arrange to climb its steep, sulphurous sides to peer into the tumultuous crater, but you may be content with a more distant view, particularly good from the rim of Empakaai, and from the peaks of Makarot (Lemagrut).

Engakura and Olmoti Crater

To the east side of Empakaai Crater, just beyond the boundaries of the NCA, lies an important archaeological site whose story is shrouded in mystery. This is the ruined 'city' of **Engakura**, a highly advanced web of ancient stone dwellings based on a complex irrigation system. At close quarters it is hard to gain much enlightenment from the stone rubble that remains, but aerial photographs reveal an intricate network of lines that show a distinct picture of a developed civilization. It is not known who built Engakura, which dates from around 500 years ago. Elders of the Iraqw tribe claim that they inhabited that area before 'marauding warriors' forced them to move on. But although the Iraqw are cultivators they have no history of irrigation or building in stone. Others believe that Engakura might have been the work of a Bantu people called the Sonjo who now inhabit an area further north and west of Lake Natron and have traditions of irrigation, although they do not build in stone either. Engakura is a long drive from the Ngorongoro Crater, and probably only worth including on an itinerary if you have a special interest in the archaeology of the area and are prepared to camp overnight in the northern reaches of the conservation area.

Another fine spot off the beaten track for walking and scenery is **Olmoti Crater**, west of the track between Empakaai and Ngorongoro craters, where the spring source of the Munge River breaks through a notch in the crater rim to create a fine waterfall. If you call at the ranger post at Nainokanoka and negotiate to take an armed ranger with you, you can walk through the forest up to the top of the falls.

Lake Natron

A stunning soda lake under the craggy brow of Ol Doinyo Lengai, the Masaai's 'Mountain of God', the lake and its environs has been overlooked by safari companies because of its remoteness. A new camp will be opened here by the same team that runs the Moivaro Coffee Estate (*www.moivaro.com, see* p.107) on the outskirts of Arusha. In recent years the bleak solitude afforded by an imposing landscape has attracted more visitors; go now while it's still quiet. The lake is home to a plethora of game and birds, and is a notable breeding ground for the lesser flamingo: their numbers swell into the millions. Sadly, in 2004 bird flu swept through the population and it was decimated, though conservationists are hopeful the numbers will revive.

Olduvai Gorge

To the west of Ngorongoro Crater is Olduvai Gorge, the site of Professor Louis and his wife Mary Leakey's discovery of 3.5-million-year-old hominoid footprints – until

The Maasai

Of the 129 recognized tribes in Tanzania, the distinctive features and reputation of the Maasai are perhaps the most familiar to tourists, especially those visiting the northern parks and the Maasai Steppe. These people have lived and grazed their cattle on this land for over 200 years. Today they maintain a tribal lifestyle in the face of the modern world, even as it impinges ever more on their pastureland and on the traditional beliefs and practices that are the essence of their existence. Under the rule of colonial and post-Independence governments over the last century, however, the Maasai have become more peaceable, no longer raiding for cattle and wives and inspiring the overwhelming terror of which their ancestors were so proud.

The Maasai are pastoral nomads, thought to have migrated to northern Tanzania southwards from Sudan along the course of the Nile. History and legend tell that the tribe aimed to reach South Africa, but was thwarted by tsetse-fly-borne sickness and combat with the Hehe near Dodoma. Now Maasai clans are settled across northern Tanzania, an area of settlement extending north into Kenya's Maasai Mara.

The tribe is organized into a rigid class and age system that grooms all boys to become warriors. Traditionally the Maasai survive on a strict diet of the blood, meat and milk of their cattle and increase their numbers for combat through polygamous marriage. Their most problematic belief is this: that god first created the Maasai and then he created cattle to keep the Maasai alive, making all the cattle of the world the Maasai's by divine right. Their cattle-rustling skills have brought generations of strife with their neighbours; the Datoga, Hadzabe, Chagga, Pare, Shambaa and Sandawe peoples have all come into conflict with the Maasai, building fortresses for defence. The law has, however, now effectively curbed the Maasai's more ruthless practices.

The Maasai remain a distinctive people but have had to make concessions. The preservation of their livelihood is contentious, especially since they have been moved out of the national parks of the Serengeti, Lake Manyara, Tarangire and Arusha that they formerly inhabited. The Ngorongoro Conservation Area has made special allowances for their cyclical nomadic lifestyle, to which the fertile grazing pasture and permanent water of the Ngorongoro Crater floor are crucial – the same regions that are so attractive to wildlife. Only the Maasai are permitted by park rules to bring cattle to graze here, as their lifestyle has traditionally been compatible with the wildlife and the land: they would never kill a wild animal for food. A Maasai who kills

recently the earliest ever excavated evidence of human existence (the most recent contender for 'earliest human ancestor so far' is a 5.8-million-year-old hominid creature, *Ardipithecus ramidus kadabba*, whose remains have been found in the Middle Awash region of Ethiopia).

It was the fossicking of eccentric safari-loving colonel George Dove in the 1960s that led to the discovery of most-ancient man. While looking for building materials for his safari camp at nearby Ndutu, Dove stumbled on large numbers of fossils, which he mentioned to his archaeologist friend Mary Leakey. She and husband Louis began excavations, and found that volcanic ash from Ngorongoro had preserved an extraordinary catalogue of prehistoric human life in distinct layers.

a lion, however, is fêted for his bravery, and will be given cattle and even wives. The Maasai claim the Ngorongoro lions are afraid of them, and traditional songs that boys sing to girls during dancing ceremonies include such boasts as, 'I am strong/ I killed a lion/I stole a cow/and ate it all!' The Maasai tribes have been allowed to live in the Ngorongoro highlands but not to settle inside the crater, venturing there on foot only to graze and water their cattle. While the very cold highlands are not ideal for Maasai clothing and life, the population has increased from eight families in the 1970s to a number of extended villages and family bomas housing hundreds of people. The distinctive red cloth used by Maasai tribes, called *shuka*, is rubbed with natural dye to create its striking colour, and with fat to make it waterproof and warm, helping the Ngorongoro Maasai to withstand severe changes of temperature.

Traditional Tribal Structures

Maasai tribal life is strictly structured into seven age groups, each with a role in ensuring the well-being of the tribe. Once out of the cradle, the *Engayok* phase, boys spend their *Layooni* years herding cattle in open pasture. From the ages of seven to 16 they move further afield searching for water, accompanied by warriors who teach the younger boys about bush survival and war. The boys practise with slingshots, spears and arrows and learn from the elders about natural medicines and tribal stories. Before they become warriors, the boys must be circumcised, a major ceremony carried out every seven years to include all boys in the 11 to 17 age group. After circumcision boys are known as *Sikoliyo* as they prepare for a cleansing ceremony to become *Murran*, warriors. They are sent into the bush for around three months, painting their faces with white dyes, living in wood shelters and catching their own food. They use ostrich and guinea-fowl feathers from birds they have caught to decorate themselves. Other preparations include eating more than usual quantities of cattle's blood, meat and milk – with the aid of a concoction of boiled acacia bark called *kiloriti*, which enables the digestive system to assimilate this intense dose of protein. *Kiloriti* is also used for strength or to overcome illness; it is said that after drinking the brew one man is able to eat an entire cow. It can take from three months to a year before the boys are proclaimed part of the warrior class. They grow their hair longer, paint their faces ochre, and take on a spear and a role defending the tribe. Once married, a boy is called *Orpaiyan* until 'middle age', about

Four different hominoids were discovered in the rock strata of the river canyon, showing gradual stages of development over 2,000 years. The famous footprints can be seen at the **Olduvai Gorge Museum**, which also charts the findings.

Olduvai can be visited easily as a detour while travelling between Ngorongoro Crater and the Serengeti. The gorge is named after *Oldupai*, the Maasai word for the wild sisal plant that grows vigorously in this area. It is said that German translators misinterpreted the name, and it is now commonly pronounced and spelt Olduvai.

To the north of the gorge is a curious black sand dune known as the **Shifting Sands**, in reference to its steady progress across the plains. A small black heap of volcanic ash, it moves about 17m a year, retaining its pure windblown form. To get there is a

10 years later, brings the ceremony that makes him a respected elder, *Ilmoruak,* with the ritual of 'stick and tail'. At this a mother shaves her son's head and he is allowed to drink alcohol for the first time, brewed from fermented aloe roots and honey. No longer a boy, he becomes part of the tribal government, deciding on punishments and interaction with other tribes, advising children and telling tales. *Olaibon* is the highest rank, an intermediary between the people and their ancestral spirits.

Maasai women, distinguished by ornate beadwork necklaces, long earrings and headdresses, do not have such an exciting life. They marry very young, often being promised to a future husband as soon as they are born. Maasai women collect all food, feed all children, collect firewood, build fires and cook – as well as counting the cattle in at night. Maasai women's life expectancy is less than half that of Western women. Women build family huts too, cementing a shell of sticks with cow dung. The huts usually have a curving passage to reach a central chamber, where the fire is a central feature. One small hole acts as a chimney, so the hut becomes a warm, dark, smoky warren, divided in two to allow young cows to live alongside the family for warmth and safety. The huts of one family are arranged in a circle, called the 'boma', showing the number and order of wives in the family, with the first wife on the right hand of the man, the second on the left, the third on the other side of the first, the fourth beyond the second, and so on. The husband tends to move in with the youngest wife and to pay regular visits to the others. The tribe held polygamous marriages as the ideal to maintain numbers when the warrior class suffered heavy losses and the survival rate of children was low. But the speed of population increase in conjunction with diminishing freedom to roam the land has forced the Maasai to re-evaluate their traditional marriage customs. Many Maasai clans are now imitating other tribes, turning to cultivation, keeping fewer cows and expanding their diet.

Yet Maasai tend to remain fiercely true to their cultural roots: even after spending many years in higher education, members often return to the tribe and reassume its culture. A number of those who have remained in broader society, however, have had prominent careers, with several in parliament. Most notably, Prime Minister Edward Sokoine, second to President Nyerere, was of Maasai origin. Billed to succeed Nyerere, he suffered a fatal car accident at the height of his career. He is remembered in almost every Tanzanian town and city, where there is invariably a street named in his honour, and the university at Morogoro bears his name.

very slow and bumpy drive from Olduvai, followed by a long and slow drive back to the main road – so it's more than just a quick detour. The views are lovely, but it might mean sacrificing precious hours in the Serengeti if your time is limited.

Serengeti National Park

The Serengeti National Park is broadly divided into three distinct areas, the **Seronera Valley** and Seronera River, the **Western Corridor** and the northern **Lobo** area that extends northwards to join the Maasai Mara. There is always plenty of resident and migratory wildlife action. It is hard to imagine a name more appropriate than

Serengeti, from the Maasai word *seringit*, meaning 'endless plains'. Russet and green grasses and trees spread like a sea beyond each distant horizon. Although this is the most famous and well-visited of all the Tanzanian national parks, it remains a land of surprises. Its vast expanses often appear to be havens of peace and quiet from a distance, but when scrutinized reveal themselves to be alive with predatory energy.

The Serengeti is one of the most celebrated wildlife reserves in the world. Some credit for its acclaim must go to the Kenyans for so diligently promoting their own tiny corner of it, but the recognition it receives from wildlife filmmakers, tourists, researchers – and Tanzanians – has ensured a conscientious approach to conserving this stunning tract of land in its natural state. The Serengeti covers nearly 15,000 square kilometres of magnificent Tanzanian land, and its seeming infinity of short grass plains provides an exceptional landscape for wildlife viewing. It is justifiably famous for its dense concentration of wildlife – especially the big cats – as well as for being the stomping ground of the great migration, a massive accumulation of 1.6 million wildebeest, 200,000 zebras and 350,000 gazelles, stretching their legs over 2,000 kilometres in an annual race to find water and green grass for their survival.

History

A sign hangs over the entrance to the Serengeti proclaiming 'This is the world as it was in the beginning'. While it is hard not to romanticize this claim when alone among vast ancient boulders strewn between land and sky, this expanse has had its

Getting There and Around

The most effective and enjoyable way to see the Serengeti is from the comfort and safety of a large **4x4 vehicle**. You can save money by opting for a **minibus** safari, gathering a handful of like-minded friends and family to share the experience (and thus the expense), or by joining a set-date-departure itinerary with a group. This last option is the best for single travellers, who otherwise bear the brunt of heavy single supplement charges. Some **overland truck** companies include the Serengeti on their route, and it is even possible to take a **bus** through the park from Arusha to Mwanza – not recommended except as a last resort.

The ideal way to experience the life of the Serengeti is with a **driver-guide**, standing with your head protruding from a pop-top vehicle and enjoying a clear 360° view while your driver negotiates the potholes. A good guide should be able to regale you with fascinating facts about wildlife and know when and where it might be seen – especially as he may be able to swap information with other guides around the park. He will take responsibility for the hardships the vehicle invariably endures, change a tyre while a lion paces hungrily behind, and have radio contact should you disappear into the infamous Hidden Valley. With luck he can help you follow up your interests, try to satisfy any idiosyncratic passions or whims and even inspire new ones. If time is limited, as it invariably is, the most effective way to make the most of it is by asking someone who knows the ins and outs of the Serengeti to lead you to the action.

If you can afford it, it is worth angling for your own private vehicle and thus the liberty to go at your own pace unhindered by the conflicting interests of fellow travellers: big-cat fanatics may want to remain near a discovered pride and watch every twitch and yawn, while bird-watchers might prefer to speed behind the flash of every coloured wing.

Tourist Information

Entrance fees to the Serengeti are $30 per person per day, which should be included in the price of your trip if you travel with a tour operator. **Guide and camping fees** are extra, with a $30 fee for foreign-registered vehicles.

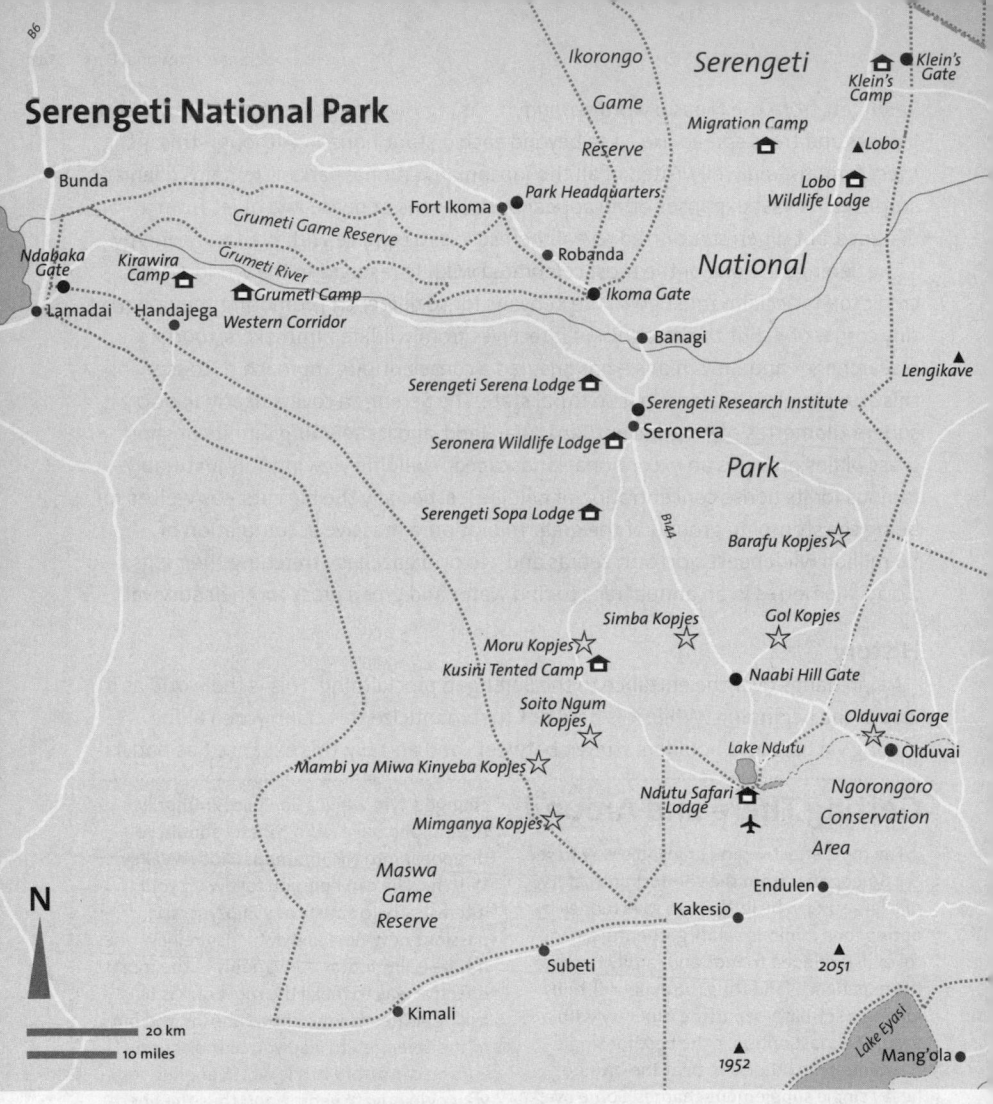

Serengeti National Park

Bunda

Ndabaka Gate

Kirawira Camp

Grumeti Game Reserve

Grumeti River

Grumeti Camp

Lamadai   Handajega   Western Corridor

Fort Ikoma   Park Headquarters

Robanda

Ikoma Gate

Banagi

Ikorongo Game Reserve

Serengeti

Migration Camp

Klein's Camp   Klein's Gate

Lobo

Lobo Wildlife Lodge

National

Lengikave

Serengeti Serena Lodge

Serengeti Research Institute

Seronera Wildlife Lodge   Seronera

Park

Serengeti Sopa Lodge

B144

Barafu Kopjes

Simba Kopjes   Gol Kopjes

Moru Kopjes

Kusini Tented Camp

Naabi Hill Gate

Soito Ngum Kopjes

Mambi ya Miwa Kinyeba Kopjes

Olduvai Gorge   Olduvai

Lake Ndutu

Ndutu Safari Lodge

Ngorongoro Conservation Area

Mimganya Kopjes

Maswa Game Reserve

Endulen

Kakesio

2051

Subeti

Kimali

N

20 km
10 miles

1952

Lake Eyasi

Mang'ola

fair share of history. Around 200 years ago these wide plains, the realm of nomadic pastoral tribes, were named 'Seringit' as the Maasai swept southwards. The Maasai lived at one with the natural order; armed with a spear, they killed only the odd lion for self-protection. The natural balance changed when the first organized safaris began here in the 1920s, as Western big-game hunters began to think of the 'endless plains' in terms of rich game pickings, and forged routes in with their arsenals. Rumours about the lion population made the area world-famous. In 1929 the Seronera Valley became a game reserve and in 1950 the Serengeti a closed game reserve, in which certain species were fully protected; a national park was established a year later, initially including Ngorongoro. In 1959 the highlands and crater were sectioned off as a conservation area and used to re-house any Maasai remaining within the Serengeti. Its boundaries were extended north and south to include the full migratory path.

The Great Migration

During the months of the great migration, all that can be seen from horizon to distant horizon is wildebeest after wildebeest, joined by herds of gazelle and zebra, who share a curious symbiotic relationship with the wildebeest: zebras have a natural sense for the presence of danger, and seek safety in a crowd of grazers slower and more stupid than themselves – who benefit from the alert. You are likely to come across bloody death scenes during the migration, as all predators from big cats to crocodiles make the most of the easy pickings. A common indication of a kill is rapid hyena action, or vultures circling like dark specks of ash in a single area of the sky, then swooping to land. The migrating herds follow a broad pattern of movement and behaviour through the months of the year, but the exact speed and location of the migration is as unpredictable as the weather; they move in accordance with the rainfall, or promise of it. Wild animals cannot be relied upon to be in any one place at a set time, so holiday plans cannot be tailored to coincide with the migrating hordes, but mobile camping safaris are often altered to fit the pace of that year, and driving safaris can generally find the action.

Between January and February the migrating herds are based across the plains on the borders of the Serengeti and Ngorongoro Conservation Area, west of Olduvai Gorge. These months are the calving season, with most zebra foals born in January, and the majority of wildebeest calves born in February. In March the herds spread out across the short grass plains of the Serengeti, crossing the boundaries around the Naabi Hill Gate and spreading outwards as offspring increase the numbers. Through April and May they remain in the southwest, slowly shifting into the central plains on the western Serengeti side of Naabi Hill Gate. In June to early July the herds move westwards through the Seronera region and on up into the Western Corridor. Through August they continue northwards, until they reach the Maasai Mara in Kenya and remain there for the duration of September and October. During November the herds spill back down the northeastern strip, until they return to the plains area just outside the Naabi Hill Gate again in December.

Seronera Valley

The most popular entrance to the Serengeti is the southeastern Naabi Hill Gate from Ngorongoro, which opens on the Seronera Valley, a vibrant wildlife area at the heart of the Serengeti. The Seronera is characterized by wide open grassy plains patched together within a network of rivers that ensure year-round water supplies and keep this region incredibly rich in wildlife. This region in particular is studded with distinctive rock **kopjes** (pronounced 'copies', from the Dutch 'kop' meaning 'little head'), clusters of huge granite rocks, weathered through the ages to form distinctive shapes rising out of the plains – a haven of shade and water for all animals in the dry season. The kopjes also make excellent navigational features: Simba, Gol, Barafu, Maasai, Loliondo and Moro Kopjes are the most prominent. Maasai rock paintings up to a couple of hundred years old are still visible at Moro Kopjes, just about accessible through the surrounding bush during the dry season (the path gets wildly overgrown

Where to Stay and Eat

The **Seronera Valley** is the best region to be based if you have limited time to spend in the Serengeti. Its lodge and camp accommodation is excellent, and offers feasible driving trips into the northern and western regions.

Very Expensive

Kusini 'Sanctuary Lodges', PO Box 427, Arusha, **t** (027) 2509816, **f** (027) 250 8273, *www.sanctuarylodges.com*. Kusini is a luxury tented camp in the southern Serengeti. The lodge has nine en suite tents with private showers and terraces that have elevated views of the surrounding plains. Candlelit meals in the dining tent or banquets on a nearby kopje are very much the scene, and the Kusini watering hole offers a tranquil siesta/safari during the middle of the day! The overall experience is fantastic if not a touch expensive. Kusini plan to open an even smaller tented camp, Little Kusini, in January 2006.

Expensive

Serengeti Serena Lodge, PO Box 2551, Arusha, **t** (027) 2504058/2506304/2504159, **f** (027) 4155/1885, *www.serenahotels.com*. An excellent choice, on a hillside at the very heart of the Seronera Valley, this is a fantastically designed hotel, constructed in an East African-style design from local rock, wood and thatch. Makonde carvers have shaped and polished and carved every door handle and rail, and rooms are in unusual but superbly comfortable 'pixie' houses that resemble mushrooms. They feel very private, with just three spacious and comfortable rooms in each. Most have good, uninterrupted views across the surrounding Serengeti Plains. Views are good from the central dining room and the cosy bar too, both of which are slightly higher up the hill beneath *makuti* thatch, a stone's throw from the Serena Lodge's crowning feature, a magnificently situated pool. The restaurant is notable, with much of the food cooked before your eyes in the open-air kitchen, and nightly buffets. The management and staff are friendly and attentive, and can arrange for numerous extras, such as flowers, fruit and champagne to greet guests on arrival. The Serena group have recently opened **Mbuze Mawe Tented Camp** at the heart of the Serengeti, providing 16 couples with voluminous tented accommodation and bedside safari action. Each tent houses two double four-posters, and a double sun bed on the veranda – and the pre-opening blurb promises a wealth of good tented safari pleasures such as bush breakfasts, lantern-lit suppers and bush walks as well as Ikoma dance displays.

Serengeti Sopa, Sopa Lodges, PO Box 1823, Arusha, **t** (027) 2500630–9, **f** (027) 2508245, *info@sopalodges.com*, *www. sopalodges.com*. Some distance from the Serena, in a fantastic position high on a westerly escarpment near Moro Kopjes. This is an older but recently renovated hotel, dating from the late 1970s, with its two-storey buildings spreading out to either side of the central communal areas, designed so that all rooms enjoy the views. The rooms are decorated in an intriguing, charming style, with an impressive rocky water feature at the centre of the reception area, and a wooden giraffe to greet guests in the dining room. The atmosphere is one of colourful comfort over homogenized style, the service is good, and the restaurant (which has stunning views) provides a fine buffet range and a selection on its *à la carte* menu. The Sopa has a swimming pool overlooking the plains, which teem with migrating wildebeest in early June and November. Full board.

Seronera Wildlife Lodge, Hotels and Lodges, PO Box 2633, Arusha, **t** (027) 2544595/2544795–6, **f** (027) 2548633, *res@hotelsandlodges-tanzania.com*, *www.hotelsandlodges-tanzania.com*. Snugly situated in the middle of the Seronera Valley, it could be fantastic. The lodge is built into a rock kopje that forms an architectural feature, creating a roof over part of the dining room. Rooms are designed in a somewhat institutional style and are slightly old and worn, but decent and clean. The formerly state-owned Wildlife Lodge has recently been taken over by Hotels and Lodges, though to date the company has spent little on updating it. Expect food and drink to be adequate if not startlingly original.

Balloon Safaris

Serengeti park rules and regulations are very strict, as they have to be in order to preserve this magnificent wilderness, but they do limit opportunities for taking much exercise. Zooming around in the bush searching for wildlife is adrenaline-inducing in itself, but for that real heart-stopping edge of excitement the only answer is a balloon safari. These are operated in the Seronera region by Serengeti Balloon Safaris, The Adventure Centre, PO Box 12116, Arusha, t (027) 2508578, f (027) 2508997, *www.balloonsafaris.com*. The company has a desk at all major hotels in the Seronera area, or your tour operator should be able to arrange a booking for you.

Balloon safaris take place in the early morning; hotels and operators will ensure that you are picked up and transported to the launch pad at some dark hour before daybreak. Take a warm sweater. The balloon is assembled in the gathering dawn, and passengers embark into a horizontal basket that is then gently puffed vertical as the vast bubble overhead inflates. This is a fantastic way to get an entirely different perspective on the plains below, giving you a true sense of the vast spaces below and providing fabulous photographic opportunities. A balloon trip is especially good if the migration is in the Seronera region, as otherwise the actual game-viewing potential is slim. The trip is followed by a sumptuous champagne breakfast in the shade of a spreading acacia with great views all around. The breakfast is a lavish and jolly affair, spread along a long table with much merriment and warmth as the sun finds its heat. The lure of floating over the Serengeti in a hot air balloon is certainly great; when you consider the price it's definitely a treat: costs vary marginally with the seasons, but allow around $400 per person for the whole trip.

after the rains) and only ever to be attempted after a thorough search for lions. The Seronera Valley has resident herds of buffalo, topi, hartebeest and impala, waterbuck, reedbuck and dikdik, numerous giraffes, warthogs, and a rich pageant of bird life of all colours and sizes. It was the large prides of lions in this valley that enticed the first safari game-hunting expeditions here nearly a century ago, and these rolling southern plains down to the Naabi Hill Gate are the area in Tanzania in which you are most likely to encounter cheetahs. The lines of sausage trees along the Seronera riverbanks provide the perfect environment for languid leopards to camouflage themselves on sun-dappled branches, and the famous lions roam at large.

Western Corridor

To the west of the Seronera the Serengeti branches out along the westerly reaches of the Grumeti River into an area known as the Western Corridor. This area is more wooded than the Seronera, and, although it has a good population of resident game, it is harder to spot the beasts in the bush. The best time to visit is June and July, when the migration moves north from the Seronera and faces the often fatal challenge of crossing the crocodile-infested river. The crocodiles rely entirely on this annual spring feast, and spend the rest of the year in an idle, yellow-toothed, mud-covered wait.

Where to Stay and Eat

Western Corridor

Very Expensive

Kirawira Camp, PO Box 2551, Arusha, t (027) 2504058/2506304/2504159, f (027) 2504155, www.serenahotels.com. The Western Corridor has some luxurious options; this beats them all. A permanent tented camp, elegantly furnished in 1920s safari style, with Victorian reproductions including studded leather folding wardrobes and polished brass taps and trimmings. The lavishly tented dining area is laid out across dark polished teak floorboards covered with rich woven rugs and furnished with writing desks and safari memorabilia. The camp's hilltop position gives fabulous views across the Serengeti bush. Kirawira has captured a nostalgic atmosphere, most enjoyable as the sun sets and its many lamps twinkle to life in the African night. The camp is landscaped to provide easy paths between the tents, even in the dark, and has an inviting pool. Guests enjoy à la carte meals served on fine china and silver. This ultimate in Serengeti safari luxury comes at an astonishing price.

Grumeti River Camp, CC Africa, Private Bag X27, Benmore, Johannesburg, South Africa, t (027) 11 8094300, f (027) 11 809440, www.ccafrica.com. A fabulous Conservation Corporation camp, its features crafted in wood, stone, canvas and steel. The double tents have been designed to create a light and airy atmosphere, complemented by wooden floorboards, dinky wooden bathrooms and hand-built beds. The décor is in a contemporary 'artisan' style dotted with antiques. Each tent is set in private surroundings in the bush, a short walk along paths lit by flares to the wood and stone dining room, which includes a central open fire and outdoor pizza oven to stimulate a healthy appetite. It also boasts a cool, clear swimming pool – everything for your comfort. It costs slightly less than Kirawira, but is still far from cheap.

Lobo

Expensive

Migration Camp, t (027) 2500630–9, www.elewana.com. It is a joy to arrive at Migration Camp and find its clear swimming pool shining like a mirage after the 93km drive over rough roads from the Seronera. This attractive permanent tented camp is set in absolute isolation among wide flat rocks and spreading acacia, by a northern branch of the Grumeti River; footprints in the mud in front of the tents indicate the nightly grass-mowing activities of local hippopotami. The camp has recently been

Northern Serengeti and Lobo Area

The landscape changes yet again as you head north from Seronera. Beyond the Orangi River the land opens out into the wide Togoro Plains, clear and sunbaked. The route continues through this landscape for about three hours, until you reach the hills and huge worn-smooth rock kopjes of the Lobo area, haunt of at least two known extended lion prides. Further north is the Mara River, which marks the border between the Serengeti and the Maasai Mara in Kenya. Although a passable road leads across, the border crossing is closed to tourists.

Loliondo Community Conservation Project

The northern region of the Serengeti is bordered to its east by the Loliondo Game Controlled Area. The landscape in this region is stunning, distinguished by coloured granite rock formations and extended views across rolling grasslands, wooded hills and water courses – barely visited by tourists. Those who do travel this far are richly rewarded. At the Community Conservation Project at Loliondo visitors meet and walk with local tribespeople and camp on their lands in return for supporting the Maasai upgraded and reduced in size, and is now regarded as one of the best tented lodges in the Serengeti. Chunky wooden furniture and wrought iron fittings kit out the two-storey library and bar, and a long, low-level dining area with wonderfully gnarled wooden posts supporting a fine *makuti* thatch over-looks the rugged landscape surrounding the camp. The 20 sleeping tents have a very private feel and are linked by soft paths lit by gas lamps as darkness falls. Excellent food is served either in the dining area or under the stars, with options to arrange for a supper in the bush around a camp fire.

Moderate

Lobo Wildlife Lodge, Hotels and Lodges, PO Box 2633, Arusha, t (027) 2544595/2544795 6, f (027) 2548633, *www.hotelsandlodges-tanzania.com*. Built into the surrounding kopjes of these remote northern reaches and attracting a good number of rock hyraxes, which sun themselves and scuttle back and forth across the central rock gardens, the accommodation is fairly dusty and utilitarian, but the situation is good and the terraced square rooms decent enough. The restaurant does not have a reputation for its culinary skills, but it can manage sandwiches for lunch, and guests look considerably more well-fed than the notably slim local lion population. Full board.

Beyond the Northern Boundaries

Very Expensive

Klein's Camp, CC Africa, Private Bag X27, Benmore, Johannesburg, South Africa, t (027) 11 8094300, f (027) 11 809440, *www.ccafrica. com*. Secluded luxury high on the Kuka Hills, beyond the boundaries of the Serengeti but commanding superb views back over it. Klein's is not bound by park rules, so the maximum of 16 guests at the camp can enjoy night drives and safaris in open-sided vehicles, and walk in the bush. A camp tradition is for all guests to climb the small hill behind the camp at sunset to sip sun-downers at the top, but the views from the central dining and bar area are equally impressive. The entire camp is decorated with solid furniture. It inspires peace, with the knowledge that it is a great distance from civilization. Guests sleep in eight cosy round cottages built from local stone and thatch, each done out in classic 'safari' style with polished wooden floors and pale nets and linens for a good night's sleep after a post-safari dip in the small pool. The area around the camp is good for birds and elephants, and particularly worth visiting during the months of the migration in late July and October; at other times of year there may be few animals. Prices are full board and include game-viewing.

village of **Oloipiri**. Beyond the park boundaries, guests are freer – night drives and walking safaris are possible, combining wildlife viewing with village visits. With the income generated from tourism, the village has developed clean water supplies, medical and educational facilities. The project was highly commended by the British Guild of Travel Writers for a 'Silver Otter' global award for eco-tourism in 2000.

Tarangire National Park

To the south of the open grass plains of southern Maasailand, Tarangire National Park covers 2,600 square kilometres of grass and flood plains, acacia woodland and regions of dense bush with giant baobab trees quite unlike the green forests of Manyara. Unspoiled, with wide views to distant purple volcanic mountains, the hilly land is dominated by the Tarangire River valley, which attracts migrating animals in the dry months. Recently the woodland habitat of fever trees and umbrella acacias along the river has been opened out by fire and heavy use of the area by elephants. Between July and September the concentration of animals around the river is almost

Where to Stay and Eat

Very Expensive

Tarangire Treetops Camp, Elewana Afrika, 99 Serengeti Road, Sopa Plaza, PO Box 12814, Arusha, t (027) 2500630–9, f (027) 2508245, *elewana@africa-reps.com, www.elewana. com*. A grove of giant baobabs hide this most quirky of camps, with splendid treehouses dotted over a generous plot. The camp has a good aspect atop a kopje and benefits from passing breezes, although the landscape is unstintingly spartan. The communal area boasts a cathedral-like dome and is built around yet another ancient baobab, with a sunken lounge area around a central fireplace. A small swimming pool is overlooked by a shady rest area stuffed with armchairs. The camp has been completely remodelled with a clever use of recycled materials throughout. As the camp is sited within a Maasai conservation area, $20 per person per night is given to the nearby village. The camp is quite far from the park – a 45min drive – but game is frequently seen in the area, and well-guided walking safaris leave camp every day.

Swala Tented Camp, Sanctuary, t (027) 250 9816, *tanzania@sanctuarylodges.com, www. sanctuarylodges.com*. Swala is the perfect *Out of Africa* tented camp. Set in a remote southwest corner of Tarangire, the camp's nine private tents spread over the slopes of a marsh; a tactical coup for a bush camp since its ready access to water is enticing to elephants – even lions and leopards during the dry season. Shaded by a fine acacia canopy, the fabric of the tents and the timbre of the service exude the opulence of traditional safari. The fine detail makes sleeping under canvas a luxurious experience. A teak deck leads to the interior, where Moroccan thick-weave rugs lie around a vast bed and fine writing desk; there is even a hunter's trousseau. *Swala* means antelope in Kiswahili; and an endearing troupe of pretty impalas skips through the camp. The rare lesser kudu can also often be seen here. The current hosts, a Finnish and English couple, have impressive expertise.

Oliver's Camp, PO Box 425, Arusha, t (027) 2502799, *oliverscamp@aislialodges.com, www.asilialodge.com*. A small tented camp just outside the park, in its own wilderness, well suited to solitary types. It's a tough drive down to the park's western reaches, but it has a real bush appeal. The dining, kitchen and laundry tent are spread out among the rocks and trees. Ancient boulders nearby provide a good vantage point for sunset-watchers, and attract admirably agile rock-climbing klipspringer antelopes.

Kikoti Camp, Arusha, t (027) 2508790. Kikoti is lovely, well run and a bush camp delight. It

as diverse as in the Ngorongoro Crater. The area's ecosystem is balanced by a local migration pattern followed by most animals other than lions, who don't abandon their territory. Easier to spot when the migration arrives and they stalk their prey, the resident lions slip easily between the grasses, mean and lean. Other animals disperse in April and May, when widespread greenery and standing water encourages the grazers to roam further afield. In June the eland and oryx begin to return, followed by elephants. Tarangire is renowned for its elephant 'pow-wows', when herds congregate in one area at the end of the rainy season to mate. The 22-month gestation period is timed so that the birth coincides with the rainy season two years later. Zebras and wildebeest return through July, and by mid-August all the animals are congregating again around the only reliable water source, the Tarangire River. The calving season for wildebeest and other beasts falls from January to March, to make the most of the fresh grass during the rainy season. In every season colourful birds swoop and strut as you pass; you are likely to spot the paradise whyder and yellow-collared lovebirds. Less attractive flying beasts are one of the park's drawbacks: the resident tsetse fly, a pest with an irritating stinging bite (*see* pp.90–91).

sits on a ridge with distant smoky blue views of the Rift Mountains. Roupel starlings chatter away, bringing life to the bush. It has 16 double tents and offers night drives and walking safaris, though at 2km from the boundary it is practically inside the park. Sundowners take place from the vantage point of Kikoti Rock, the local megalith, in a truly airy bar with proper leather armchairs. Avert your eyes from the occasional curio excess and you will be in heaven. Has good hot showers and 24hr electricity.

Moderate

Tamarind Tented Camp, PO Box 2047, Arusha, t (027) 2507011, *information@houpoe.com*, *www.kirurumu.com*. For a more traditional safari under canvas, Tamarind provides a high standard of camping in the bush just beyond the park. It is approached through fertile fields and sits in a clearing in dense bush. The position allows for night drives and excursions to nearby villages, which are participating in conservation schemes in exchange for aid with clean water and healthcare. Good for couples who can't stretch to private luxury camping – it's absolutely authentic, as these tents are often dismantled and carted off to the Serengeti. Each 'Larsen' tent has its own shower and toilet, and comfortable wooden beds, with one 'honeymoon' suite. Sleeping

tents face a bar tent. The dining tent contains a communal table that is arrayed each night with culinary delights prepared by the camp chefs. Alternatively, guests can request starlit meals around the open fire. **Tarangire Sopa Lodge**, Sopa Lodges, PO Box 1823, Arusha, t (027) 2500630–9, f (027) 2508245, *www.sopalodges.com*. A certain freshness of style, with sliding glass doors, a *makuti*-style thatched roof and new paint in the heart of bush burned to a bronze by the sun. Well positioned at the centre of Tarangire. The restaurant food is good, and guests are encouraged to consume countless courses – easily done while enjoying fine views of the park.

Cheap

Tarangire Safari Lodge, PO Box 2703, Arusha, t (027) 2507182, f (027) 2507182. A permanent camp high on an escarpment with clear views up the Tarangire River. The double tents are arranged in perfect serried ranks, side by side to face the sunrise over the river, while the stone dining area and bar are well designed to enjoy sundowners, and the cooking is good. It has recently been renovated to a good standard throughout. It has a clear blue pool, and solar-powered hot-water showers in each tent. The double tents are excellent value; meals are extra, with packed lunches on offer.

Babati Region

The western reaches of Tarangire extend south to Babati, a fine area of countryside occupied by the Barbaig and Datoga tribes, inaccessible and rarely visited. The main reasons to travel the appallingly rough Arusha–Dodoma road are to scale the heights of **Mount Hanang** or to view the ancient **rock paintings at Kolo**, near Kondoa. Both are about halfway along the dreadful road, best visited as a round trip out of Arusha.

The Babati region is a place of great natural beauty and interest, much of it provided by its mix of resident peoples: three tribal groups live on the hills and plains in the shadow of Mount Hanang. This is the land of the Barbaig, reputed rainmakers, who were pushed south by the Maasai in the 1880s (*see* p.131). It is also home to the Datoga people, renowned for their agricultural skills, especially terrace farming. Neither tribe admits to giving the region its old name, Man'gati Plains: the name translates as 'cattle-stealer and trouble-maker', although bets are on the nomadic cow-herding tribe (the Barbaig) rather than the pastoral agriculturists (the Datoga). The area also extends into the territories of the Iraqw tribe and it is thought that the

Getting There

There is a **weekly bus** to Babati from Arusha, which continues south to Dodoma in the dry season. Otherwise arrange a trip through an Arusha tour operator. One of **Hoopoe Tours'** drivers hails from this district (*see* p.123).

Where to Stay and Eat

The scarcity of accommodation makes it worth taking a **tent**, although there are basic local **guesthouses** in Babati, 80km north of Kolo, and in Kondoa, 25km south of Kolo. There is also a guesthouse in the village of Katesh.

Hadzabe people, now largely settled around the Lake Eyasi region, and Sandawe bushmen ranged freely around this region before the advent of the Bantu tribes 2,000 years ago. Nowadays they stay further north, but these descendants of early San-bushmanoid groups are the most likely creators of Kolo rock paintings.

Kolo Rock Paintings

The extremely rare collection of rock paintings at Kolo near Kondoa is a mystery. It seems likely that the images were originally the work of the hunter-gatherer bushmanoid tribes, who have an ancestral history of rock art, and some Sandawe clans claim that their ancestors were responsible for the paintings. But, as the collection varies so greatly in age and style, it might be that later Bantu-speaking peoples added their own handiwork to the older images. It is estimated that they are somewhere between 200 and 4,000 years old; research carried out by Mary Leakey in the 1960s identified nine different styles that may relate to different eras and artists. Some of the work is black and white, some in coloured earth and ochre tones. Many of the older images have faded, while others have been painted over by successive generations. Those remaining range from stick-man paintings to oddly moving scenes, such as a group of two masked men abducting a woman from two other men who cling on to her. Others show animals and hunting scenes, images of people playing musical instruments, and paintings that anticipate abstract expressionism.

The paintings are quite easily accessible, following a quarter-mile walk across fields, although the most interesting are the most difficult to reach, requiring a rocky climb. There is a very helpful guide working for the Antiquities Department in Kolo who can lead you to each of the sites, but apart from his invaluable presence little is being done to preserve this ancient artwork. The paintings are described in detail and recreated in *Vanishing African Art*, which includes Mary Leakey's research.

Mount Hanang

This little-climbed mountain is the ninth highest in East Africa, and is known as 'the forgotten mountain'. Mount Hanang is an extinct volcano, rising to a height of 3,417m above the surrounding plains, and can be climbed in a long day, estimating around six hours for the ascent and the same coming down.

It is worth employing a local guide from Babati or the foothill village of Katesh to accompany you on the climb. Contact **Kahembe's Enterprises**, via JM Tours, Arusha, **t** (027) 2506773, **f** (027) 2508801, or Mr Kahembe directly by post, PO Box 366, Babati, to arrange longer hikes and walks in the area. He can also organize extended walks that include longer visits and stays with different local people.

Lake Victoria

11

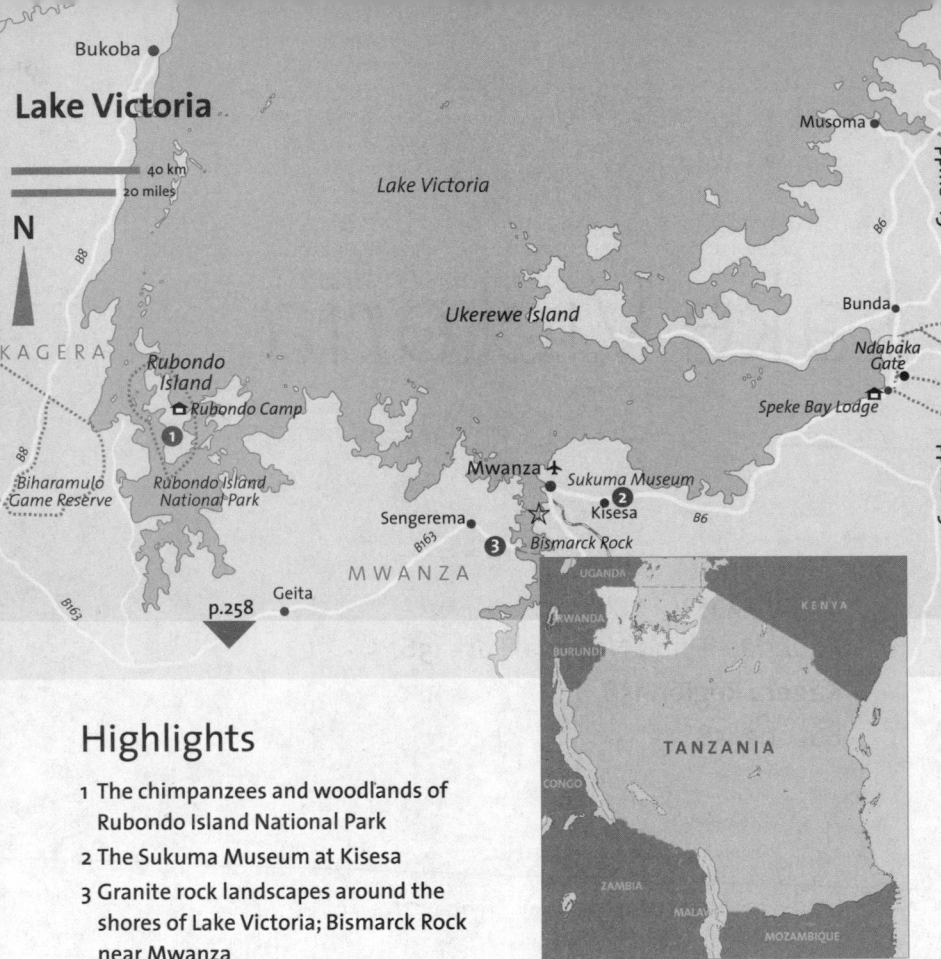

Highlights

1 The chimpanzees and woodlands of Rubondo Island National Park
2 The Sukuma Museum at Kisesa
3 Granite rock landscapes around the shores of Lake Victoria; Bismarck Rock near Mwanza

The largest lake in Africa, and at 68,800 square kilometres second in size globally only to Canada's Lake Superior, Lake Victoria first gained its mystique as the legendary source of the Nile so keenly sought by 19th-century explorers. Unlike Tanzania's other major lakes, Lake Nyasa and Lake Tanganyika, which lie in the Great Rift Valley that cuts a deep scar across Africa, Lake Victoria is high up on a plateau and only 70 metres deep. The boundaries of Kenya, Uganda and Tanzania meet in the lake, with most of its waters actually in Tanzania. These waters are the source of life for thousands of villages around its shore, and for the region's economy: fishing, cotton production and tanning. The lake itself has become a tourist attraction.

Mwanza

A three-hour drive west from Ndabaka Gate, the westernmost point of entry to the Serengeti National Park, on the shore of Lake Victoria, brings you to the district of Mwanza. The road from the Serengeti to Mwanza, skirting the southern shore of the lake, is initially well tarmacked and smooth, continuing in this way for kilometres past the small farms, homesteads and cotton gins that characterize the region. This good start is deceptive, as the road quite suddenly, about two-thirds of the way along, dissolves into one of the worst apologies for a highway imaginable, a heavily potholed assault course all the more appalling as a result of a botched attempt to tarmac it some years ago. Thick dust clouds envelop the final stretch of road into Tanzania's second largest town and next busiest commercial centre – the road here boasts a disturbingly high incidence of bus accidents. **Mwanza** is the central trading port for Lake Victoria, including international trade and travel to and from Uganda and the coast. Its proximity to gold- and diamond-mining towns around **Geita**, a little further west, makes Mwanza port a focal point for all mining concerns and shipment. It is also a stopover for many travellers en route to and from Rwanda and Uganda. Mwanza is a good point of departure to visit Rubondo Island, and in the dry season a starting point for safaris through the Northern Circuit to Arusha.

It is not certain from which exact point the English explorer John Hanning Speke first caught sight of the vast lake, like a sea, that was proven in 1858 to be the so sought-after source of the Nile, but it is likely that it was not far from Mwanza. Speke was brought here by a tribesman who suggested that this expanse of water 'probably extended to the end of the world', and Speke felt instinctively that he had discovered the 'fountainhead of that mighty stream...the Nile'. No sooner had he stumbled on this awesome water source than he is reported to have taken out his shotgun and made an end of some red geese, so making two records at once: the first European to see the lake, and the first man to shoot something on it.

The views of Lake Victoria are the most spectacular aspect of Mwanza, particularly its distinctive rounded granite rock landscape. Striking rock kopjes rise up out of the lake waters, the most impressive, **Bismarck Rock**, with a strange pointy rock hat. It is on land around such rocks that Sukuma people's houses are built. Just before reaching Mwanza, the route wends through a sprawl of picturesque rural Sukuma homesteads ranging up steep green hillsides to either side, piled precariously above one another and linked by a network of footpaths that scramble up the hillsides.

Sukuma Museum

Fifteen kilometres back east along the bumpy road – an hour's bus journey, so it's worth finding a car – is an interesting museum of the history of the Sukuma people at Kisesa, in Bujora Parish. The Sukuma Museum celebrates the traditions and history of the Sukuma people, the most numerous of all Tanzania's 129 tribal groups. Traditionally this people was grouped into 52 distinct chiefdoms around the shores of Lake Victoria, and only classed together in the colonial era. Legend tells how the old kings would extend their territories in a leisurely manner, gambling their borders over games of *bao*. Now, Sukuma clans extend south and west through the Kagera, Mwanza and Shinyanga regions, and other Sukuma have moved to distant regions of Tanzania. The museum includes a series of 'pavilions', each exhibiting different aspects of traditional Sukuma life. At its heart stands an impressive circular two-storey construction, containing vast drums that were collected from each chief following Independence. The drum was the central means of communication within

Getting There and Around

By Air

This is the most reliable way to reach the shores of Lake Victoria. **Coastal**, Mwanza Airport, t (028) 2560441/t (0748) 520949, connects the northern safari circuit with the lake and with Rubondo National Park. It operates a daily service from Arusha, Grumeti and Seronera to Mwanza ($200). A Coastal flight also connects Grumeti with Rubondo twice a week ($110), from where it is also possible to return to Mwanza twice a week. They also have a fleet of charter planes based at Mwanza and Geita, the centre of gold-mining.

Air Tanzania, PO Box 592, Mwanza, t (028) 2401059, f (028) 240529, *www.airtanzania. com*, flies daily between Dar es Salaam and Mwanza. **Precision Air**, New Mwanza Hotel, PO Box 11208, Mwanza, t/f (028) 2560027, *pwmwz@africaonline.co.tz*, also flies to Mwanza daily from Kilimanjaro Airport.

By Bus or Car

It is also possible to reach Mwanza and the shores of Lake Victoria by **bus**, but this is not really recommended: the roads are only occasionally tarmacked, pot-holed throughout and deteriorate further in the rains. However, it is rumoured that the road is to be upgraded in the near future. Bus services operate from **Arusha** to Mwanza, through the Serengeti, taking about 36hrs, and from **Kigoma** and **Dodoma**. Buses from **Dar** to Mwanza take a good 3 days. From Mwanza to **Bukoba**, on good roads after Mwanza, takes 6hrs. **Musoma** is around 18hrs from Arusha through the Serengeti. Buses to eastern destinations leave from the new Buzuruga terminal about 5km from Mwanza town centre.

Driving is not recommended either; petrol can be hard to come by and you will need spare tyres, a tool kit, a basic knowledge of car maintenance, food and, crucially, water.

By Train

The train is an option if you are travelling to Mwanza from Kigoma, Tabora, Dodoma or Dar.

There are three services a week from Dar, via Morogoro, Dodoma and Tabora. To come from Kigoma you must change at Tabora. These routes are operated by the TRC, PO Box 468, Dar es Salaam, t (022) 2110599 ext 2607, direct line t (022) 2117833/t (0744) 262659, *ccm_atu@ trctz.com*, *www.trctz.com*, and form an important cargo corridor from Uganda to the coast via Lake Victoria and Mwanza.

By Boat

Ferries run from **Mwanza** to **Bukoba**, on the northwestern shore of the lake, and **Musoma**, on the northeastern shore, and to Bell Port in Uganda. There are also smaller ferries and motorboats from Mwanza to **Ukerewe Island**, **Rubondo Island** (about 300km away), **Saa Nane Island**, **Kome Island** and **Maisome Island** – the last two returning the next day. Ask at the port about ferries or cargo boats that ship goods around the lake. Safety has improved since the MV *Bukoba* sank in 1996, with as many as 1,000 people on board (its official capacity was 430) including a family of 20 returning from a funeral and a church choir; 3 days' mourning were declared and President Mwinyi led a funeral attended by 5,000. All the same, you may choose to avoid the older steamers plying these routes.

Ukerewe Island is easily accessible from Mwanza on a new **daily ferry service** which departs Mwanza daily at 2.30pm and leaves Nansio Port for the reverse journey at 8am daily. The crossing takes around 3hrs.

Tourist Information

The website *www.mwanza.com* is dedicated to the town and its goings-on, but is regularly being updated or often simply does not work. Note that the lake is not safe for swimming owing to the risk of contracting bilharzia.

Sports and Activities

To arrange a safari, or for assistance with flights to Rubondo Island National Park or car

this rural culture, and was used to summon people with news, perhaps announcing the birth, death or enthroning of a king, or for feasting, dancing or welcoming a new moon. Other pavilions include a typical Sukuma house, filled with all the implements hire, contact **Dolphin Tours and Safaris Ltd**, Kenyatta and Post Road, PO Box 336, Mwanza, **t** (028) 2500096, *dolphin@mbio.net*. They have competitive rates and helpful staff, who can arrange a Northern Circuit safari from Mwanza, accommodation at Serena lodges. **Fourways Travel** on Station Road is also widely recommended, **t** (028) 2502273/2502630, *fourways.mza@ruha.com*.

Where to Stay and Eat

Mwanza Town
Hotel Tilapia, PO Box 82, Mwanza, **t** (028) 2500517/2500617, **f** (028) 2500141, *tilapia@mwanza.com* (*expensive*). There is not much choice for accommodation in Mwanza, but this is the nicest option, a short distance out of town on Station Road. It is the only good hotel on the waterfront, and has a pleasant two-storey wooden deck housing its restaurant and bar, and a swimming pool. The food is reputedly good. Rooms are in individual whitewashed bandas with air-conditioning.
New Mwanza Hotel, PO Box 25, Mwanza, **t** (028) 2501070, **f** (028) 2503202, *nmh@newmwanzahotel.com* (*expensive*). Recently refurbished, the New rivals the Tilapia, though retains its characterlessness. It's the top-of-the-range business hotel in town and is more centrally located. It is the only other hotel with air-conditioning, efficient service and clean rooms.
Iko Hotel, **t** (028) 240900 (*moderate*). Situated in the same area as the Tilapia Hotel, the Iko is a good option for a middle-of-the-range stay in Mwanza. Although some of the rooms show signs of wear and tear, all rooms have air-conditioning and larger suites have TVs and baths.

The nicest budget rooms are just outside the town centre, and both of these choices provide excellent value for money and a good friendly atmosphere.
New Park Hotel, PO Box 11614, Mwanza, **t** (028) 2500265 , **f** (028) 2500265 (*cheap*). Not far from the centre, the New Park provides decent rooms with TV for a good price. Corridors run along open balconies with clustered seating areas and wooden furniture that give it appeal.
Aspen Hotel, Uhuru Street, PO Box 11567, **t** (028) 2500988 (*cheap*). Just next door, the Aspen is clean and modern with large en suite rooms that come with fridges, similar to the New Park, and single beds that could sleep two. The restaurant boasts singular arrangements of imitation flowers but has a comfortable atmosphere, as does the curiously named **Dispence-Bar**.

Mwanza Region
Speke Bay Lodge, PO Box 953, Mwanza, **t** (028) 2621237, *spekebay@africaonline.co.tz, www.spekebay.com* (*moderate*). Close to the Ndabaka Gate of the Serengeti National Park, a welcoming and pleasant place to relax on the shores of Lake Victoria. Rooms are designed in the style of traditional whitewashed Sukuma houses, arranged around a bar with good views of the lake. Bungalows, permanent tents, double, triple or family rooms are available. The lodge can arrange transfers to Mwanza Airport, Grumeti or Kirawira airstrip.
Sukuma Mission at Kisesa, Bujora Parish, PO Box 76, Mwanza, slightly closer to Mwanza town, in the middle of the bad stretch of road (*cheap*). Good budget accommodation can be enjoyed here, with basic bungalow rooms available, full board an option. Painted terraced wooden huts are sociably arranged, with a relaxed, sandy barefoot atmosphere. Campsites are also available for next to nothing.

Musoma
Tembo Beach Hotel, on the waterfront 1.5km from the town centre, PO Box 736, **t** (028) 2622887 (*moderate*). The Tembo has its own private beach at Old Musoma Pier, and boasts a restaurant and bar overlooking the lake with very comfortable accommodation. Room prices depend on lakeside views and luxuries.

of daily life, including charms and snake skins for spiritual harmony. Nearby, the spirit doctors' pavilion houses more charms and skins, in a unique display of the paraphernalia once brandished by the most renowned Sukuma medicine men, whose photos and images adorn the walls. The pavilion closest to the heart of most residents houses the costumes and instruments of the different Sukuma dance and music troupes, packed with poison horns and charms against charms – the serious competition of dancing has frequently incited foul play. Music and dancing is one element of the Sukuma culture that remains alive here, not simply as a shrine to the past, but as a living centre for future development. Founded in 1950 by Canadian missionaries led by Father David Clement 'Klementi' and inaugurated by President Nyerere, at the heart of this museum is a thriving **church and school** dedicated to St Cecilia, patron saint of music. Painted images, especially in the church, show close integration between traditional Sukuma beliefs and those brought in by the missionaries, who evidently spent a great deal of time establishing links between the tales told by local faiths and Bible stories. The church and museum organize an annual festival following the feast of Corpus Christi, beginning on 6 June and continuing for two weeks. Sukuma people gather here for daily dancing and singing competitions among the different troupes, and prizes are awarded amid feasting and celebrations. Museum charges range from T.shs 1,000 for simple admission to T.shs 40,000 to watch snake-dancing.

Mwanza's Islands

The tiny island of **Saa Nane** is a wildlife sanctuary with the atmosphere of a slightly run-down and depressing zoo. Most animals are caged and sad – particularly leopards and chimpanzees; lions and rather disorientated wildebeest and hippos roam free. It can easily be reached as a day trip from Mwanza and there are some nice places to picnic, but you're better off saving your time and energy for Rubondo Island National Park. Boats to the sanctuary depart from the jetty near the Tilapia Hotel in Mwanza five times a day and take five minutes; entrance is T.shs 1,000 including the boat trip.

Ukerewe Island, Kome Island and **Maisome Island** can also be reached by ferry from Mwanza. There is not much to see on the islands, but it can make a pleasant trip, with lunch, dinner or a night at one of the small local restaurants or guesthouses.

Rubondo Island National Park

Rubondo Island is a far cry from the popular tourist trail and remains an undiscovered haven for nature-lovers to spend a few nights of relaxation while continuing their safari experience in rather a curious way. On this island hideaway off the shores of Lake Victoria, an unusual combination of indigenous and introduced wildlife is free to roam the dry tropical forests and glades. The original island inhabitants – crocodiles, hippos, lizards, sitatunga antelope and countless species of birds – were joined in the 1960s and 1970s by a whole range of other animals, including suni and roan antelope, giraffes, elephants and rhinos, porcupines, black and white colobus monkeys and chimpanzees. All of these are flourishing within the 240 square kilometres of protected island, except the rhino, which has not been seen for years.

The island is free of cars and has no human population other than its rangers, making it a haven for the wildlife and peaceful, safe and easy to explore. There is an

Getting There

Airline schedules have incorporated Rubondo within the northern safari flying circuit. Several services fly direct from Serengeti airstrips: Coastal operates a twice weekly service out of Grumeti, Arusha, Mwanza and Seronera, while in peak season Precision Air runs a scheduled flight from Seronera or Kirawira airstrips.

You can hire a **boat** from Mwanza all the way to the island – a long boat trip – or **drive** to the nearest land base at Nungwe near Nyamirembe, about 300km from Mwanza, which takes 6–7hrs, from where the boat trip takes about half an hour. The boat can be pre-arranged with the park warden.

Where to Stay and Eat

Rubondo Island Camp, c/o Flycatcher Safaris, 172 Serengeti Road, PO Box 591, Arusha, t (027) 2506963, f (027) 2508261, *flycat@ habari.co.tz, www.flycat.com (moderate)*. There is only one lodge on the island for tourists, thoughtfully designed to provide a private and calm environment for visitors, and well situated at the midst of a network of walking paths for daily exploration. The restaurant and bar are built into a rocky outcrop overlooking the water's edge, and accommodation is a curious combination of tent and permanent structure, with a stone bathroom attached at the back and wooden frames with working hinged doors built into the front. These are set back away from the lake, in a spacious green clearing – complete with swimming pool – and surrounded by naturally growing palm trees. While life on this little island is well protected from the rigours and intrusions of life beyond its shores, there is a chance that an excitable tribe of chimpanzees might carouse through the camp. Staff and rangers are always close at hand to administer assistance. The bar is well stocked, the kitchen loads tables with superbly prepared dishes, and an atmosphere of fine living pervades.

Camping is possible at the national park campsite, and can be booked through the Park Warden, Rubondo Island National Park, PO Box 11, Geita, or through the headquarters of the Tanzania National Parks Authority, t (027) 2503471. Campers need to bring all equipment and food, though it is possible to eat at the Island Camp with a few hours' notice.

Fishing is allowed on the lake beyond the park boundaries, if you get a permit, which costs $50, from the park warden. Boats and equipment can be arranged in Mwanza.

unusual abundance of red coral trees and forest flowers; ground and tree orchids and fireball lilies bloom between October and December. Visitors are sure to be rewarded by an inspirational and unusual wildlife experience, with a chance of having the island entirely to themselves. The lakeside island beaches are the domain of a number of hippopotami and crocodiles – exciting viewing for boating safaris. The waters are also frequented by a multitude of diverse birdlife: fish eagles and kestrels ride the coastal wind currents, and sacred ibises, cormorants, little egrets, herons and storks all perch like statues before swiftly demonstrating their skill at diving and fishing.

Rubondo's inland forests are threaded with atmospheric woodland paths better known to local wildlife than human footfall, and home to a host of creatures, including those genetically closest to humans – **chimpanzees**. The chimp populations here are less habituated to human contact than the more famous ones at Gombe Stream or Mahale Mountains. In accordance with research methods at Mahale, Rubondo's chimps are being habituated by a team from the Frankfurt Geological Society using a slower method: direct contact, such as feeding, is no longer condoned. Successes have been made and tracking is now on offer to tourists, though there is much less chance of encountering the chimps than in the parks of Mahale and

Gombe, partly because they are few, and the island area large. The day-long treks start from the ranger posts at Kamea and Irumu.

Kagera Region

The Kagera region extends over the tip of land on the western shore of Lake Victoria and the Virunga Mountains, bordering Uganda, Rwanda and Burundi. This is traditionally the land of the Haya people, but also of the Ha and the Nyambo, the Sumbwa, and a new group that has evolved from the joining of the Baganda and the Haya, known as the Gandakyaka. The Karagwe Kingdom, one of several former kingdoms in this region of northwestern Tanzania, was recorded in the journals and diaries of explorers John Hanning Speke and a fellow officer, James Augustus Grant. When the two men arrived in this remote region, they were greeted by 'a most delightful king', called Ruwanika, whom they described as having 'a mild, open expression' and an 'ever-smiling countenance'. Apparently Ruwanika liked his women fat, and encouraged them to drink so much milk that they could hardly move their hands and knees. The kingdom was established in the 15th century by the chief of the Hima, Ruhinda. Legend tells how one Hima king, Ndagara, forged a special hammer on his anvil which he threw across the Kagera Valley, killing his arch-enemy, King Gahindiro of Rwanda.

Today, the Kagera Region is a major area for growing robusta coffee, which is exported to Dar es Salaam on boats via Mwanza. In the last decades the Kagera region has endured almost incessant bad luck. It suffered the worst aftermath of Tanzania's incursion into Uganda to overthrow dictator Idi Amin in the late 1970s, although close neighbourly relations between the two countries have since been resumed. Since 1994, however, the region has suffered from another regional catastrophe: Kagera has housed vast numbers of refugees from Rwanda, Burundi and the Democratic Republic of Congo (formerly Zaire). The refugee camp on Benaco Hill, Ngara, was said to be the largest in the world.

Bukoba

The second largest port on Lake Victoria, Bukoba is the last town on the lake's shores before Uganda. The port town has taken over from old Karagwe as the main town centre in this region, and is a major port with a large population in a beautiful, though little visited, region. The countryside here is at high altitude and cool, green and fertile. It is still in the region of the WaSukuma and Haya people, renowned for their tall stature and good looks. The Haya people compare with the Chagga of Kilimanjaro in terms of academic success and achievement in Tanzat Reserve.

Bukoba is the base for trips to **Minzaro Forest Reserve**, a 250km square groundwater forest on the border with Uganda, with excellent birding.

Mount Kilimanjaro

12

Mount Kilimanjaro

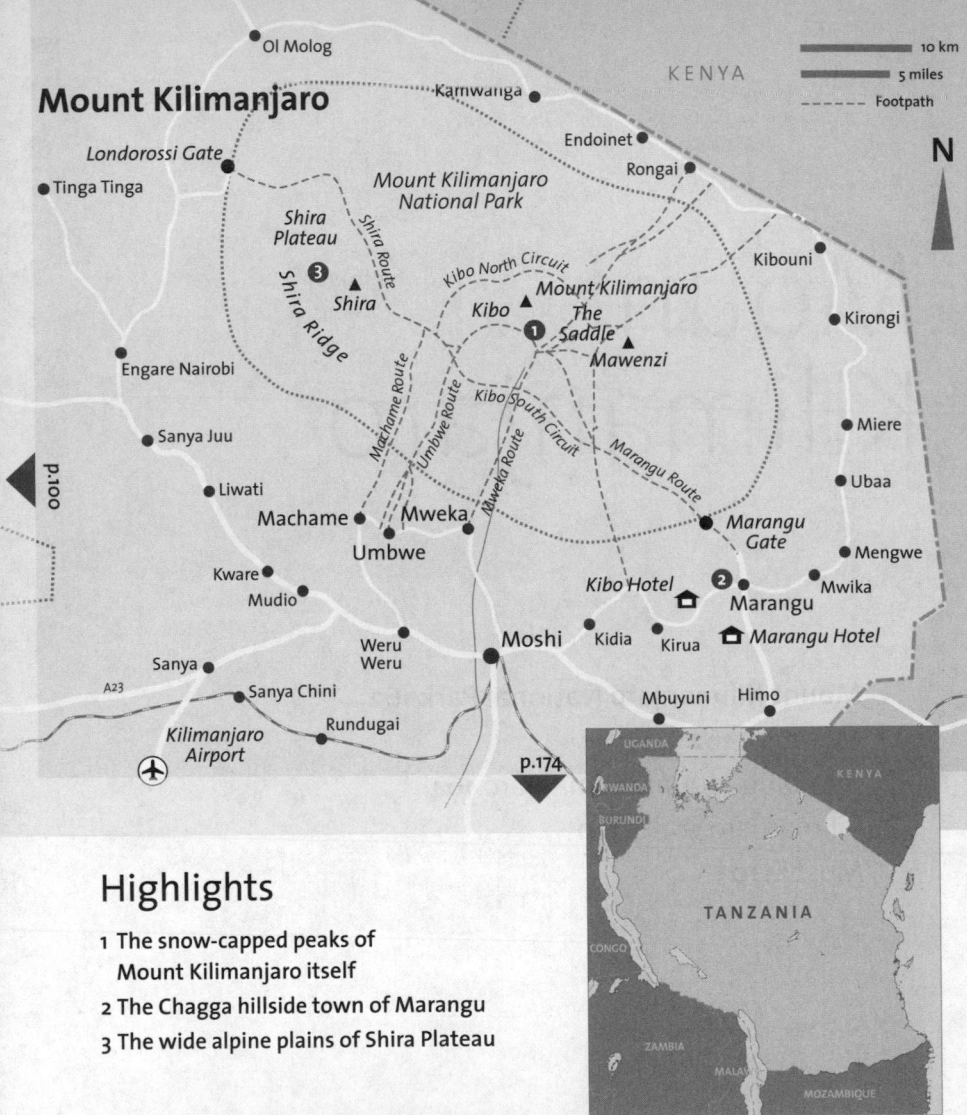

Ol Molog

Kamwanga

KENYA

10 km
5 miles
- - - - Footpath

N

Londorossi Gate

Tinga Tinga

Endoinet

Rongai

Mount Kilimanjaro
National Park

Shira
Plateau

Shira Route

Kibouni

3

Shira

Kibo North Circuit

Shira Ridge

Mount Kilimanjaro

Kibo

The
Saddle

Kirongi

Engare Nairobi

Machame Route

Umbwe Route

Kibo South Circuit

Mawenzi

Sanya Juu

Mweka Route

Miere

Liwati

Marangu Route

Ubaa

Machame

Mweka

Umbwe

Marangu
Gate

Mengwe

Kware

Mudio

Kibo Hotel

2

Mwika

Marangu

Weru
Weru

Moshi

Kidia

Kirua

Marangu Hotel

Sanya

A23

Sanya Chini

Rundugai

Mbuyuni

Himo

Kilimanjaro
Airport

p.100

p.174

KENYA

UGANDA

RWANDA

BURUNDI

CONGO

TANZANIA

ZAMBIA

MALAWI

MOZAMBIQUE

Highlights

1 The snow-capped peaks of
  Mount Kilimanjaro itself
2 The Chagga hillside town of Marangu
3 The wide alpine plains of Shira Plateau

Dismissed by 19th-century Europeans as an impossible myth, the snow-topped equatorial mountain of Kilimanjaro has now long since been charted and climbed, stories of its resident man-eating spirits relegated to the realms of folklore. The mountain continues, however, to preserve a mystique that defies all recent knowledge of its slopes, representing a powerful life force for the local Chagga people and all those who have built their lives around it. Mount Kilimanjaro provides rich volcanic soils for agriculture and an endless source of pure spring water. Images of its snowy peaks rising majestically from fertile green foothills have become a powerful motif for this land of extremes. Few could deny a very distinct sense of awe when the cloud clears to reveal a glimpse of the towering cone, shining bright in the tropical sun. Yet one of the most amazing aspects of the mountain now is the accessibility of its peak to climbers with no mountain-climbing equipment or real experience of scaling such heights. The number of climbers has escalated to more than 1,000 a year during the last century, quite a development since Hans Meyer made history as the first European to scale the highest point of Kilimanjaro in 1889.

History

Mount Kilimanjaro is one of the largest volcanoes ever to erupt through the earth's crust, rising to 5,895m above sea level, just 330km south of the equator. The massif is made up of three adjoining volcanoes that ascend in height from the extinct peak of Shira (3,962m) and dormant cones of Mawenzi (5,149m) to the dormant, snow-capped cone of Kibo (5,895m). The highest point of Kibo, known as Kaiser Wilhelm Spitze by the colonial Germans, has been named Uhuru Peak since Tanzanian Independence. The highest point of the eroded shards of Mawenzi Crater has retained its German name; it is called Hans Meyer Peak, in commemoration of the mountaineer's ground-breaking climb to the topmost peak.

One million years ago the land where the massif stands today was a gently undulating plain. Lava rumblings beneath the plates of the Great Rift Valley began a series of volcanic eruptions through the earth's surface, and these early fractures were followed by the emergence of Shira, Mawenzi and Kibo roughly 750,000 years ago. Together the three peaks grew up to 5,000m before Shira collapsed inwards and

'Kilima-njaro'

As with many Swahili names, there is much unresolved speculation about the origins of the name Kilimanjaro. *Kilima* could have come from the Swahili word *mlima*, meaning mountain, curiously adorned with the diminutive prefix *ki-* to make it 'little mountain' – most likely employed as an amusing or affectionate term – in addition to the suffix *-njaro* meaning 'greatness'. *Jaro*, however, is also similar to the Chagga term for caravan, and as the mountain was a landmark for caravans of traders, where water and supplies could be replenished, it might well have been referred to as the '(little) mountain of caravans'. Yet another possible explanation for the meaning of *njaro* is that it was the name of the evil spirit who resided on the icy summit, referred to by the first Europeans as 'Njaro, guardian of the mountain'. Other explanations include a mistranslation from the Maasai word for spring source water, *njore*, so that 'Kilima-ngare' would have meant 'hill of springs', but became 'Kilima-njare' or 'Kilima-njaro' in translation.

The problem with all these hypotheses is the combination of originating languages to make up the two parts of the name. The most likely name would have evolved first from the Chagga people who live around the volcano, and they claim that the term evolved from their term *kilelema*, meaning 'which has defeated' in conjunction with their word for caravan, *jyaro*, or birds, *njaare*. The final name of 'Kilimanjaro' could have evolved as a combination of all these, reflecting the interpretations of all the different people who have regarded the mountain from their own perspective. It is interesting to note that the thriving settlement on the southeast side of the mountain is named 'Marangu' in the Chagga language, translating as 'full of water'.

Mawenzi became extinct and began to erode. Kibo continued growing to the formidable height of 5,400m and the thick black lava that erupted through its cone 360,000 years ago created most of the dramatic scenery that makes up Kilimanjaro's distinctive mountainscape. Since then the action of the years has been harsh, and the face of the mountain has changed as a result of glaciers melting and re-forming, landslides and erosion. Streams have carved distinct routes through the mountain rock, and vegetation has taken hold at every altitude that it can survive.

Kilimanjaro's human history is much more recent. Ancient artefacts have been unearthed on the lower mountain slopes, such as lava stone bowls and an axe, that could indicate the existence of African cultures here more than 2,000 years ago – the mountain's earliest human traces. Around 500 years ago a Bantu-speaking people called the Chagga arrived on the mountain, and still live on its slopes today. As for the future, the snowline is receding and it is predicted that Kibo will lose its ice cap.

Mount Kilimanjaro National Park

A massive 756 square kilometres above the 2,700m contour of Mount Kilimanjaro was made into a national park in 1973, and is surrounded by a wide band of rich wet tropical forest with six established national park access routes through it. The stunning forests around the mountain were originally established as a game reserve in 1921 and are now preserved under the conditions of a forest reserve.

Marangu

The ideal base for climbing Kilimanjaro is the scenic mountain village of **Marangu** at the main national park gate. Perched high in the foothills beneath the lowest line of tropical forest, Marangu is a traditional old village inhabited by the Chagga people for many centuries. The majority of mountain springs and rivers run down the south and eastern side of the mountain, creating a fertile cultivated enclave.

The cool climate around the mountain has attracted European missionaries and settlers since the Germans first came here and realized its charm in the mid-1800s. The colonial influence is still much in evidence, with schools and churches of every denomination nestling in the rolling hills behind each winding turn of the tarmac road. The indigenous Chagga people were receptive to the missionaries, welcoming the influx of European education systems. Chagga chiefs Rindi of Moshi and Sina of Kibosho, of warlike tendencies, had risen to prominence in a battle for supremacy among the numerous Chagga states in the late 19th century, but both were thwarted by the German colonists – who decided the matter by assuming power themselves.

British colonists later saw that the Chagga people prospered from a healthy climate and fertile land but were prone to destructive in-fighting, and resolved to unite the tribe under one chief to represent its interests. They chose a leader from the Marealle clan of chiefs which had dominated the region for generations, Thomas Marealle, who had a degree in Social Welfare from the London School of Economics. On 17 January 1952 Governor Sir Edward Twining installed him as Chagga Chief Marealle II. Photos from the ceremony show Marealle swearing allegiance to HM King George VI

When to Go

Mount Kilimanjaro National Park follows a broadly similar climatic pattern to the rest of northern Tanzania. The altitude, however, affects mountain conditions throughout the year. The **short rainy season** is in November and the **long rainy season** from April until early June, with cloud cover on the mountain usually persisting a couple of weeks beyond the end of the rainy seasons. The **dry seasons** run from January to March and July to October; the first is usually warmer, while the second tends to be clear and dry during the day but colder at night.

The seasons clearly affect climbing conditions: the park is open all year, and climbers continue to ascend to the peak in all seasons, but it is both safer and more pleasant in the dry seasons. It may, however, **rain** on the mountain at any time of year. **Temperatures** on the mountain drop about one degree centigrade with every 200m gained in height.

Getting There and Around

By Air

Marangu is 48km from Moshi and 90km from **Kilimanjaro Airport**, t (027) 2502223, served by international flights including the daily **Air Kenya** service from Nairobi, t (+254) 2605745, *www.airkenya. com*, and **domestic flights** daily from Dar es Salaam and Zanzibar on **Precision Air**, NIC HDQ Building, Samora Av/Pamba Rd, Dar es Salaam, t (022) 2121718, *pwdar@africaonline.co.tz, www.precisionairtz.*

com or **Air Tanzania**, Ohio St, PO Box 543, Dar es Salaam, t (022) 2110245, *commercial@ airtanzania.com, www.airtanzania.com.*

By Car or Bus

All the **main roads** in this area are well surfaced. There is a regular **minibus shuttle** between Moshi and Marangu (small charge), which departs from either end when it is full. The bus stops at the junction at the bottom of the hill, from where you can catch a lift with one of the vehicles running up to the national park gate, just above Marangu. If you pre-book a climb with a tour operator, transport between Moshi and Marangu or the airport, your hotel and the park gate will be arranged.

Where to Stay and Eat

Most hotels in Marangu also organize Kilimanjaro climbs. Accommodation on the mountain is in wooden huts or tents.

Expensive

Protea Aishi, PO Box 534, Moshi, t (027) 275 6948, f (027) 2756821, *proteaaishireservations @satconet.net, www.proteahotels.com/aishi.* Hidden in a gully on the side of a ravine, the hotel is a Hansel and Gretel confection of mountain kitsch. Close to the trail head at Machame, it is without question the finest-quality place to stay for climbers. Its rooms are immaculate, in the international style with minibar and widescreen TV while its swimming pool has views of the peak and is solar-heated. Service is what you would expect from Protea, a major South African

dressed in leopard and monkey skins, and being presented with a ring of gold. He had the vision to see his people united as a progressive African community.

The area around the village is scenic and worth exploring at leisure. Walks can be made among local farms with banana, coffee, maize and yam plantations, to visit the seven waterfalls cascading from the Una, Moonjo and Kongwe rivers, or to caves dug by the Chagga tribe during the incessant Maasai wars – up to a kilometre long to hide women, children and livestock from the marauding foe, their depth ensuring that smoke from cooking fires would not give them away. You may pass antique straw and grass Chagga homesteads, varying in size and shape according to the sex and status of the inhabitants. Visits can be made to the blacksmiths of Mamba, who make farming tools and Maasai weaponry, or the Chagga softwood carvers. The Kibo Art Gallery (originally Nyumba ya Sanaa), run by the Tanzanian artist Elimo Njau, hotel chain. Local walks and cultural tourism tours are available, as is a programme of activities in nearby Arusha National Park.

Capricorn Hotel, PO Box 938, Marangu, t (027) 2751309, f (027) 2752442, *capricorn@africaonline.co.tz, www.africaonline.co.tz/capricorn hotel*. The closest hotel to the park gate, in fact so far up the mountain that it is necessary to travel a distance away from the hotel to enjoy any views of the peak. It is an old-fashioned hotel, and is the only place to go in Marangu if you are looking for formal service. It provides a stylish and comfortable haven from which to enjoy magnificent south-facing views of the Pare Mountains and Taita Taveta plains. Rooms are furnished with large sprung beds, bedside lamps, and baths that fill with plenty of hot water. Ask for one of the rooms in the new wing; made entirely from pinewood, these are lighter and sit higher on the hillside. Service is good in the circular central restaurant and bar. It's a good-sized, stylish development with a freshwater stream running through the garden, and the sounds of bird calls all around. Full board.

Moderate

Marangu Hotel, PO Box 40, Moshi, t (027) 2756591, f (027) 2756594, *marangu@africaonline.co.ke*. Easily the most charismatic choice in the village, it embodies the colonial-style appeal of Kilimanjaro over the past century. The hotel continues to operate under the same family management that has lived in the farmhouse for generations. It is set in immense gardens, a magnificent well-tended spread of flowering shrubs and trees from which the peaks of Kilimanjaro and Mawenzi can be an encouraging sight on a clear morning before a climb. The gardens also conceal a clean swimming pool in a secret hedged garden, and a croquet lawn. Accommodation is in endearingly dog-eared but comfortable little bungalows around the gardens, each with a private bath or shower. There is a well-stocked bar and lounge. Don't expect too much style from the kitchen; the restaurant reminded of an under-used school canteen, though vegetables are freshly picked from the garden.

Nakara Hotel, PO Box 105, Marangu, t (027) 2756571/t (0744) 277300, *nakara-hotels@iwayafrica.com, www.nakara-hotels.com*. Gaily painted elands and other fauna hide away in the garden of this neat hotel. Rooms are small but brightly furnished to a good standard. With laidback service, it is the best choice for larger groups of younger climbers. The restaurant doubles up as a TV room, and offers filling meaty stews and cold beer.

Cheap

Kahawa Shamba, *www.kahawa shamba.com*. An award-winning initiative that offers visitors an opportunity to spend time within a community of coffee-farmers on the slope of Kili. Guests stay in one of four Chagga huts and are looked after by a host family, who housekeep and prepare local food to a high standard. The huts have en suite bathrooms and are no ordinary affair. Its visionary potential was recognized at the Responsible Tourism Awards 2004.

displays a number of religious paintings by Njau, and sculptures by others. There is a colourful weekly market in the town, selling mounds of seasonal vegetables, second-hand clothes and a mesmerizing array of kangas in a jovial atmosphere.

Climbing Mount Kilimanjaro

Mount Kilimanjaro is one of the highest mountains in the world that tourists with no mountain experience can climb with relative ease, although it remains a considerable feat of human endurance to reach the summit: climbers cover at least 80km on foot over the five days it takes to ascend and descend again, and the breathable oxygen at the top is less than half the amount at sea level.

There are six main routes to the summit of Kibo from the Tanzanian side of the mountain. The easterly routes – **Marangu** and **Mweka** – converge with routes from

Kenya west of the Saddle, which links the peaks of Mawenzi and Kibo, for the final ascent to Uhuru Peak. The Rongai route ascends Kili from the north by the Kenyan border, with views of the Amboseli plains. The park has opened up a driving route (three hours and bumpy) from Londorossi Gate to the Shira Plateau (3,350m) west of Kibo, the start of the **Shira** route, which joins up with the **Machame** and **Umbwe** routes for the final stretch. The most commonly climbed are the Marangu route – the easiest and least expensive (five or six nights staying in huts on the mountain) – and the more scenic Machame route (five nights camping). An especially good one is the Machame route via Karanga Valley, staying overnight in the High Camp.

The **Marangu route** is the most popular, and considerably easier than any of the other ascents to the summit: it is commonly known as the 'tourist' or 'Coca-Cola' route owing to the relative ease of the climb and soft drinks sales along the way. Climbers cover the 34km each way over at least four or five nights on the mountain, making use of three stages of wooden huts for overnight accommodation en route. This accommodation is shared by a number of climbers in rather close quarters, but is dry and warm. The first two of these huts are manned by permanent staff.

The first day's climb follows excellent gravel pathways recently laid out through the forest reserve to Mandara Huts at 2,700m. The second day continues through heather to the edge of short cropped moorland plains, finishing up for the night at Horombo Huts at 3,720m. At this level the climbing incline remains gentle, but thinning oxygen can dramatically slow the pace of walking. Many climbers spend an extra night at Horombo to acclimatize before the final push to the summit. From here, Moshi

The Kilimanjaro Landscape

With most of the old lowland forest now cultivated and settled, the first experience of the native mountain environment begins with the dense vegetation of **tropical montane forest** that surrounds the mountain between 1,850m and around 2,800m. Cloud condensation mainly gathers around the forest, so this area is damp or often drenched with rainfall, creating an intriguing mass of plant life and running rivers between endemic tree species such as the formidably tall *Olea kilimandsharo*, that grows up to 30m high. The area of **heath** just beyond the treeline also enjoys a relatively misty and damp environment as cloud hovers above the density of trees. This is covered with heather and shrubs such as *Erica arborea* and *Stoebe kilimandsharica*, and a number of dramatic-looking proteas. From around 3,200m a wide expanse of **moorland** extends beyond the heath and above the cloud line, so that here the skies are generally clear, making the sunshine intense during the days and the nights cool and clear. Hardy endemic species of giant groundsels (*Senecio*) and lobelia (*Deckenii*) towering up to 4m high thrive in this moorland zone and give the landscape a strangely primeval atmosphere. Even higher, beyond 4,000m, this sensation intensifies as the landscape develops into a more bizarre **alpine desert**, with sandy loose earth and intense weather conditions and temperature fluctuations so dramatic that barely any plant species survive other than everlasting flowers, mosses and lichens. Only the odd lichen survives beyond 5,000m, where the landscape is predominantly **rock and ice fields**, as climbers experience the final steep push to the summit.

Organizing a Trek

Tour Operators, Guides and Porters

By far the most satisfactory way to plan a trek up Kilimanjaro and to ensure you get the most out of the experience is to organize it through a reputable tour operator. It is possible to do this before you arrive in Tanzania, or, once there, through companies in Moshi, Marangu or Arusha. As with safaris, it is worth choosing an established company with an office. All guides should be registered, and have documentation to prove it. The **International Mountain Explorers' Connection** has an office in Moshi, next door to the Da Costa Hotel, Mawenzi Rd, **t** (0744) 817615, *karen@mountainexplorers.org*, from where the Kilimanjaro Porters' Assistant Project operates. Ask here for up-to-date information. The accredited guides and porters who accompany tourists on their Kilimanjaro climbs are of inspirational experience and strength of spirit. The **KINAPA office** at the Marangu Gate has a list of official guides, which it is well worth checking. Each guide has his own stories to tell, of such feats as carrying altitude-affected climbers from Arrow Glacier over the height of the window buttress to the tree line in the middle of the night.

The increasing number of climbers each year has made it necessary for the Mount Kilimanjaro National Park to insist that all climbs are pre-booked. Access is with a **pass** only, and these are no longer available at the park gate. Climbers are in fact required to follow one of the established walking routes, and to be accompanied by an official guide. Most walkers choose to climb with porters too, who carry at least some of the supplies needed to get up the mountain; if you are planning to camp, porters will be essential. If you intend to stay in the mountain huts you or your operator should book places in the huts before you set off, as they are limited.

Owing to the over-use of wood, the park authorities have had to stop climbers having open fires on the mountain.

Costs

The ascent of Kilimanjaro is an expensive undertaking. The minimum cost for a 5-day climb is around $800. This price, however, includes park fees – around $375 including hut fees on the Machame route or $470 including hut fees on the Marangu route – a compulsory rescue fee ($20 per person per climb), plus the rescue fee for your guide ($20), and a daily entrance fee for your guide ($10). Once these basic fees have been added up, you are not paying an extortionate amount for guides' and porters' salaries, transport, food and fuel. However, do make sure that all these fees are included in the price when you book your trek. Rescue fees must be paid for anyone intending to ascend above 3,000m. It is also usual to tip your guides and porters when you return safely at the end: budget on giving $10 per day to a guide, $8 to his assistant, $7 to the cook and $5 to a porter. Make sure you tip your porters directly, don't rely on the guide doling tips out fairly; porters invariably receive a very small wage for their labours, and actually survive on tips. When working out how many porters and guides you might need to employ to assist your climb, consider that a porter can carry 15kg, of which 3kg will be his own equipment and clothing. No porter should be expected to carry more than this – if he does, it may lead to injury. For a comfortable climb it is often necessary to take about three porters per climber (on wages of around $9 per day each), and a climber guide for the group (around $10 day). At least one porter should be employed as 'assistant guide' to accompany you to the top of the mountain. All park fees must be paid in cash or travellers' cheques.

It is generally cheaper to go in a larger group, with the obvious drawback that it may be more difficult to pace the ascent to meet everyone's needs. Prices also tend to increase with the difficulty of the route chosen.

Equipment

Tour operators equip their groups with food and cooking utensils. They can generally provide camping gear and bedding materials, but many prefer their own sleeping bags.

Temperatures on the mountain drop severely with height, around five degrees centigrade with every 1,000m climbed. At night it may be 8–10°C at Machame Hut, –5°C to –8°C at Shira Hut, –11° at Barafu Hut, and the summit could be as cold as –20°C. It is therefore necessary to ensure that you are properly equipped with warm clothing and trekking gear, including a water- and windproof jacket and trousers, a woollen hat or balaclava, gloves and a scarf. Also pack boots and light trainers, several pairs of socks, fleeces and thermal underwear and a small wash kit and towel. Waterproof clothing is essential to protect against damp that might otherwise lead to hypothermia. Sunglasses or snow-goggles are also required, plus sun protection, first aid kit and insect repellent, whistle, water bottles and a torch.

Fitness and Health

Although it is possible to trek a route to the pinnacle of Kibo without climbing equipment, it remains a serious endeavour that requires a good level of physical fitness and stamina, and a realistic awareness of the potentially serious effects of high altitudes – in 2004 four people died as a result of altitude sickness. Many tour operators request that clients have a physical check-up before attempting to scale the mountain. It is recommended that climbers should be able to run for half an hour without feeling out of breath. It is of vital importance that anyone ascending above 3,000m be aware of the symptoms and remedies for altitude sickness (see pp.92–3).

Recommended Tour Operators

Hoopoe Adventure Tours, India St, PO Box 2047, Arusha, **t** (027) 2507011, **f** (027) 2508226, www.hoopoe.com. Excellent guides and provisions. Can organize equipment hire.
Zara Tours, PO Box 1990, Moshi, **t** (027) 2750011/2754240/**t** (0744) 451000, **f** (027) 2753105, zara@kilinet.co.tz, www.kilimanjaro.co.tz. Excellent local knowledge.
Roy Safaris Limited, Sokoine Road, PO Box 50, Arusha, **t** (027) 2502115, **f** (027) 2508892, roysafaris@intafrica.com, www.roysafaris.com. A reliable tour operator based in Arusha, with years of experience organizing Kilimanjaro climbs. Provides a good service and fine camp cooking for reasonable rates.
Dik Dik Safari, PO Box 1499, Arusha, **t** (027) 2508110/**t** (0741) 510490, **f** (027) 2508110, dikdik@ATGE.automail.com, www.dikdik.ch. The Swiss management proudly sends its

guides to the Alps for good old-fashioned mountain training.
Shah Tours and Travels, PO Box 1821, Moshi, **t** (027) 2752370, **f** (027) 2751449, kilimanjaro@eoltz.com. Well recommended.
Trans Kibo, PO Box 558, Moshi, **t/f** (027) 2750096/**t** (0741) 511334. Responsible tour operators who can arrange all forms of mountain climbing excursions, and car hire.
Mauly Tours. Mrs Mauly operates out of Moshi and charges half what anyone outside of Moshi does. Very highly recommended. She will arrange porters, extra clothing, permits.
The best **hotels** in Marangu are also reliable and experienced in organizing climbs with excellent guides, especially the Marangu Hotel and the Capricorn Hotel (see pp.163–4).
Marangu Hotel. Arranges fully equipped climbs. Hotel staff supervise packing of equipment, bedding and catering with special prices for those staying at the hotel before and after their climb. A cheaper option is the so-called 'hard way': climbers arrange their own equipment and catering and the hotel organizes porters. All climbers are given a full briefing before they climb. The guides at Marangu have up to 40 years' experience. One of their older guides, Emanuel, still climbs, although he is now more than 65 years old, and all four of his sons have followed in his footsteps.
Capricorn Hotel. Arranges more expensive Kili climbs along the Shira route over 8 days. The Machame route (6 days), Umbwe route (5 days), and Marangu route (5 days) can be arranged for slightly less. For those wishing to experience ice-climbing on the Heim Glacier, a serious and expensive undertaking, the trip takes 8 days.
Kibo Hotel, PO Box 102, Marangu, **t** (027) 2751308. Arranges all-inclusive climbs of Kilimanjaro, with 5- or 6-day treks along the Marangu route, and rates increasing along all other routes. Can also arrange minibus transportation from Kilimanjaro Airport, and the Namanga border post with Kenya.
Kiliman Horse Safaris (Allan), **t** (0744) 263170, www.kiliman.com. During shooting for the 2001 IMAX film on the mountain, Allan took care of logistics, organizing the ascent of a 140-strong crew. His horse-riding safaris are well recommended and can last from one to several days.

township and the Pare ranges can be seen on a clear night. On day three or four, walkers press on across a cloudless expanse of moorland for three hours, until the landscape changes again beyond the Last Water Point at 4,200m. The walk continues across a barren stretch of alpine desert to Kibo Huts at 4,700m. The final ascent from Kibo on the fourth or fifth day is the most arduous, including a hard climb of about 6km with little oxygen. Most climbers attempt to reach the summit (Uhuru Peak) for dawn, which means setting off from Kibo Huts at midnight. From the top it's a quick descent to Horombo Huts for the night, then a morning's descent to the Marangu Gate.

The beautiful **Machame route** is highly rated as the most scenic route up Kilimanjaro, with diverse vegetation and wide views. The route can take either five or six days, depending on the fitness of the climbers; the final ascent is steep in each case. The route sets off from Machame village, and reaches the first hut, Machame Huts, at 3,000m where the forest meets the heather. The track continues across moorland to Shira Hut on the western side of Kibo, with excellent views over the Shira Plateau. From here it is usual to follow the Shira route to the Lava Tower Hut at 4,630m and then join with the Umbwe route down to Barranco Camp for an overnight at 3,950m. Beyond the Lava Tower there are a number of possible route choices. Very fit climbers may continue to ascend the much steeper route via Arrow Glacier, although the hut here is no longer in use. Otherwise from Barranco Camp climbers ascend to Barafu Hut by the Mweka route, and continue on this trail on the final ascent to the summit. This route usually descends by the Mweka route.

The **Rongai route** is wonderfully scenic. Like Machame, it can be completed in five days, though a sixth is recommended for acclimatization. Starting from Nale Moru (2,000m), the first campsite is reached after a 700m climb. The second day is spent climbing through moorland to the Third Cave campsite. Four or five hours the next day takes you to the base of Kibo. From here the ascent follows the Marangu route.

The **Mweka route** is the most direct path to the summit – short but extremely painful. It is the steepest and most demanding, taking four days in all and including a very hard climb on the third day. The Mweka Hut and Barafu Hut en route are both basic, unfurnished and with no toilets. The route is often followed on the descent.

The **Shira route** is popular with those who have accomplished it, but is a long climb taking up to seven nights and eight days. To join this route, climbers access the park through the Londorossi Gate on the western side of the mountain. From here it is possible to take a 4x4 vehicle as far as the Morum Barrier in the dry season, and walk the final stretch to the Shira Plateau, rejoining the Machame route at Shira Hut. It's a scenic route, with superb views even from the car park. Climbers are advised to spend a couple of nights at Shira Hut to acclimatize before continuing via the Lava Tower.

The last major route followed is the **Umbwe route**, which takes at least five days to complete in all. Umbwe is a short route and recommended as a scenic ascent trail only, although the climb is almost continually hard and steep and often requires an ice axe between the Breach and Arrow Glaciers. This is a very demanding and potentially dangerous climb, which should only be approached by experienced climbers.

Kibo's crater is a worthwhile detour: it's roughly circular with an inner cone extending to 5,800m (100m lower than the summit at Uhuru Peak). At the centre

European Explorers' Quest for Mount Kilimanjaro

The mystery of Mount Kilimanjaro puzzled 19th-century European explorers. Arab trade routes relied on the mountain spring waters, yet references to it are scarce in Arabic texts. It is mentioned by a 12th-century Chinese trader and a 16th-century Spanish geographer. Explorers knew of the mountain's existence, however, mainly from Ptolemy's *Geography*, an account of the classical world written in AD 145. His description of the coast of Azania includes reference to 'great snow mountains' inland that are surely the volcanic peaks of Kilimanjaro. Ptolemy's texts, however, did little to help the extended debate – even fracas – in geographical societies of mid-19th-century Europe over the reality of a snow-capped equatorial mountain. The inaccessibility of the African interior at this time, just 150 years ago – so fraught with hazards and fatal diseases that many explorers were beset with ills before their journeys had even begun – heightened the mystery surrounding Kilimanjaro.

In fact the first Europeans to reach the mountain were driven by a greater purpose: they were commissioned by the Church Missionary Society in London to teach the word of God to the 'heathens'. Swiss missionary Johannes Rebmann, following in the footsteps of fellow missionary Johann Ludwig Krapf, first published reports in the *Church Missionary Intelligencer* in 1849 describing the snowy peak south of the equator. Learned geographers greeted Rebmann's report of a tropical area of 'everlasting winter' with scorn, and dismissed his account as 'visions of his imagination'. For Rebmann, however, certainty that the peak was topped with snow explained the extraordinary legends that had dogged him on his journey to the land of the 'Jagga' or 'Dshagga'. When planning the mission with Krapf in 1847, the Governor of Mombasa warned that Mount 'Kilimansharo' was inhabited by 'djinns'. The Europeans were already familiar with tales of evil spirits that could stiffen the legs of men so they died and stop gunpowder in the barrel of the gun, and that protected the silver powder at the top of the mountain from the reach of men. The missionaries, more familiar with the magical substance, were able to recognize it as snow.

One of the most dismissive geographers was William Desborough Cooley, convinced by Arab traders' tales that a mountain existed strewn with red pebbles of fine carnelian and determined to perpetuate this myth against all evidence. Nonetheless, in 1857 the president of the Royal Geographical Society sent 'clever and adventurous traveller Captain Burton' to ascertain 'if there really be lofty snow-covered mountains under the equator, as descried in the distance by our missionaries'. Burton was not fated to solve the conundrum: he failed to reach the legendary mountain. It was not until 14 July 1861 that explorers Richard Thornton and Baron von der Decken made it to the mountain slopes. Despite their difficulties in persuading porters to climb higher than the forest cover, the two collected enough data to finally supply the RGS with an accurate estimate of its proportions.

an inner crater with walls between 12m and 20m high contains another concentric minor cone, the centre of which falls away into the 360m span of the ash pit. This is the 120m-deep central core of the volcano, and casts sulphurous boiling smoke from its depths despite the frozen, snowy outskirts.

Kilimanjaro Walks

Most visitors to Kilimanjaro are inspired by an ambition to conquer its peak, but the whole national park provides a haven for trekking in startlingly different scenic areas that range from forests through wide open moorland to the stark frozen reaches of the high plateau. The contrasts on these slopes make for varied treks for anyone without a burning desire to plant a flag on the summit. One alternative is to take the road in to **Shira Plateau** (*see* p.168), where walkers can enjoy a day, or a couple of days with overnight camping, exploring the wide alpine plain and stunning views above the cloud line. The plateau was formed from a collapsed, lava-filled caldera, the ancient crater walls still discernible like a faint circle of broken battlements; its flat expanse is crisscrossed with mountain streams. It's an especially superb walk in the dry months when there is less chance of mist. When the clouds lift to reveal the western breach of Kibo and the edge of the Shira Ridge it is possible to see two sides of the volcano, with the ash cone rising in the middle. The **forest reserve** around the lower slopes is good for walking too, with tracks leading though a mystical world of trees entwined with creepers and alive with bursts of birdsong and colobus monkeys chattering.

Moshi

Moshi is a small town in the shadow of a monumental mountain. In fact a hefty 890m above sea level, the town feels as though it has settled on lower ground, surrounded as it is by craggy volcanic peaks. The views from its potholed streets are a magnificent panorama of distant volcanic outcrops and the crowning peaks of Kilimanjaro, 48km away. The surrounding volcanic soil is watered by mountain streams, ideal for arabica coffee crops. It's a good alternative base to Marangu for climbing Kilimanjaro, with many more options for budget accommodation and tour operators, but it remains an African market town at heart. Darkening but elaborately carved stonework from colonial times, incorporating Arabic influences, is surrounded by post-Independence architecture from the 1970s. Moshi is a Chagga word meaning 'smoke', which could be a reference to volcanic eruptions, the clouds that gather around the mountains, or the impressive steam train that puffed between here and Tanga and Dar es Salaam. Moshi first gained prominence under the rule of Rindi, the great 19th-century Chagga warrior. Rindi of Moshi and his rival Sina of Kibosho had both built impressive fortresses, but Rindi convinced colonial German troops to unite with him against his adversary, signing away his territories rather than succumb to an undignified defeat. Both these powerful chiefs were hanged a few years later. Moshi emerged as an important colonial centre of administration following the success of German colonization in the area. The construction of a railway in the early 20th century linking the coastal ports to Moshi and the boma town of Arusha ensured the growth of the northern region. Though the railway is today sadly neglected, the town has continued to sprawl across the plains, its economy some-what enlivened by the proceeds of the lucrative industries of 'Kili climbing' and cut-flower cultivation. Economically the town is tied to the rising star of Arusha, but clearly remains its poorer relative, much to the chagrin of local entrepreneurs.

Getting There and Around

By Air

International and domestic flights land at Kilimanjaro Airport (*see* p.163).

By Bus

The bus service from **Dar es Salaam** to Moshi is very good, with buses running daily along the smooth tarmac road that links these major towns. The journey takes about 8hrs. Passengers can opt for varying degrees of comfort, which equate to being more or less squashed and getting there faster. Scandinavian Bus Lines and the Dar Express both run a reliable and quick service.

From **Tanga** the bus takes 4–6hrs, depending on stops along the way that in turn depend upon crops, which make going slow after a harvest, when it is loaded and unloaded at every stop along the way!

By Train

Moshi is at the end of the old railway line that once formed an important connection between Arusha, Tanga and Dar es Salaam. This line is now only utilized between Dar and Moshi, for freight only. It looks unlikely that passenger services will resume.

Sports and Activities

Ameg and Impala hotel **swimming pools** are open to non-residents for a fee of T.shs 3,000. The Ameg pool has a lovely sun deck, and more room for cavorting, though the Impala has its fans too, and is more secluded.

Where to Stay

Moderate

Kilemakyaro Mountain Lodge, PO Box 661, **t** (027) 2754925/**t** (0744) 651583, *kyaro@habari.co.tz, www.kilimanjarosafari.com*. High above Moshi town, halfway between the plains and the stars. Though it feels a little fusty and forgotten, the views make it worth a look-in, especially for those who don't plan to climb the mountain. The fittings in the 10 bandas were clearly once of the best quality and the soft Egyptian cotton sheets guarantee a good night's sleep. Moshi folk make the trip to enjoy the rural location and for the simple buffet food served from Thursday to Saturday. A large hole in the ground augurs well for the construction of a swimming pool in the near future. It is expensive for the facilities.

Ameg Lodge, PO Box 247, **t** (027) 2750175/**t** (0744) 058268, *rishishah@ameglodge.com, www.ameglodge.com*. The Kenyan owners bring a new standard to the region, with an emphasis on providing for the business traveller. There is a high-speed Internet connection, with connectivity in some rooms, and a well-serviced business centre. The restaurant is elegant if lacking in intimacy, while the food, especially the Italian dishes, are delicious. With a very good swimming pool and sunken poolside eating area, the lodge is consistently popular with expats. It also boasts the first gym in Moshi.

Impala Hotel, PO Box 7613, Lema Rd, Moshi, **t** (027) 2753443, **f** (027) 2753440, *impala@kilinet.co.tz, www.kilimanjaroimpalahotel.com*. This townhouse hotel, set in landscaped gardens, bustles with efficiency. Polished until they gleam, parquet floors are adorned with embroidered rugs. The house has tasteful Art Deco touches. The 11 double rooms are a mixed bag; some are excellent – airy and well appointed, with mahogany furniture pieces. The poolside suites are the best, though more costly. The food is tasty and the Indian cuisine a speciality, though service is achingly slow.

Bristol Cottages, 98 A Rindi Lane, PO Box 104, Moshi, **t** (027) 2755083, *briscot@kilionline.com*. The cottages are set around a quiet courtyard in the heart of the town, right by the bus station. Neutral décor and rooms in understated African good taste contribute to the serenity of the place. Depending on your perspective, the service might be pleasantly low-key or verging on the neglectful! The food is basic: burgers, chicken and chips and sandwiches.

Uhuru Lutheran Hostel, PO Box 933, Moshi, **t** (027) 2754084. Good-value accommodation, set in quiet grounds just over 1km out of town on the Kilimanjaro Road (take the northern turn at the roundabout opposite the YMCA). Rooms are comfortable and spacious, all self-contained with hot running water and private balconies. The pleasant restaurant serves excellent food, including a decent buffet breakfast. A taxi to and from the town centre is cheap.

New Kinderoko Hotel, Double Road, PO Box 8682, Moshi, **t** (027) 2754054, **f** (027) 2754062, *kinderoko@kilionline.com*, *www.kinderoko.com*. Has a pleasant open court-yard just behind the front door with enough fresh air and foliage to create a relaxed bar and sitting area. The hotel provides old and creaky but well-appointed doubles, with the possibility of splashing out on a 'double deluxe', thus earning yourself a disconcert-ing boardroom-sized formica desk and sofa section. The restaurant has a good vege-tarian choice. It is well loved by volunteers, who pack the late bar.

Avoid the **Hotel Newcastle**, next door, unless you wish to have a peek at a living monument to Alcatraz. The cell-like quarters and high steel corridors are not recommended for anyone with a hint of vertiginous tendencies.

Cheap

Coffee Tree Hotel, PO Box 484, Moshi, **t** (027) 2755040. A vast, purpose-built multi-storey edifice at the centre of the top end of town, built from the coffers of the Coffee Corporation. It's a good choice for budget accommodation, with rooms arranged around wide, open-sided corridors with palms and pot plants regularly placed along them in a genuine and effective attempt to lessen its 1970s austerity style. Its top floor restaurant and bar is all windows and parquet floor, with simple food served in a bright and relaxed atmosphere. A range of rooms from self-contained singles to 'executive doubles', all including breakfast.

YMCA, PO Box 85, **t** (027) 2752362. A central position as good as that of the Coffee Tree, with hundreds of very clean and neat little box rooms arranged on each floor. The sheets are clean and the security is good, so the place has developed a good reputation. The building is ranged around a large, well-tended swimming pool, free to all hostel residents as long as they adhere to the

notices requesting decent dress outside the pool area. All rooms share bathrooms. B&B.

Lutheran Church Hostel, to the south of the town centre. Very spartan little boxrooms at a very reasonable price, with the added advantage of church singing and sermons booming through the tiny netted window to brighten your day. Simple but decent, with shared bathrooms. A wholesome breakfast of bread and jam and bananas with chai is held in sociable surroundings. The only disadvantage of the hostel is the location, which is quite a long way out.

Hotel Buffalo, on Chagga Street, behind the main road, to the southwest of the bus station. Also clean and new, with hot running water in communal showers and good-value rooms. The bar and restaurant are pleasant, and the food is good.

Rombo Cottage Hotel. Signposted up a muddy track leading off the Marangu road, a short distance from the town centre. A small comfortable home-grown establishment with seven clean, simple self-contained doubles and a popular local restaurant.

Eating Out

Cheap

Golden Shower, about 2km out of town on the Marangu road, **t** (027) 2757990. An excellent choice for hearty, well-prepared international dining.

China Garden, past the YMCA in the CCM building. A good Chinese restaurant, it has been unanimously recommended by all who have tried it, and serves welcome dishes of rice and noodles.

Kitchen de Genève Rose Garden and Children's Paradise, near the Rombo Cottage, sign-posted up an extremely muddy track off the Marangu road. A very unusual atmosphere. The restaurant has a lovely garden, with roses, stone chessboard tables and a remarkable coloured 2m-high Kilimanjaro at the end of the 'Children's Paradise'. The menu has a mix of popular 'Western-style' dishes, such as chicken and chips and omelettes, enlivened with local dishes with beans, curries and rice.

Usambara and Pare Mountains

13

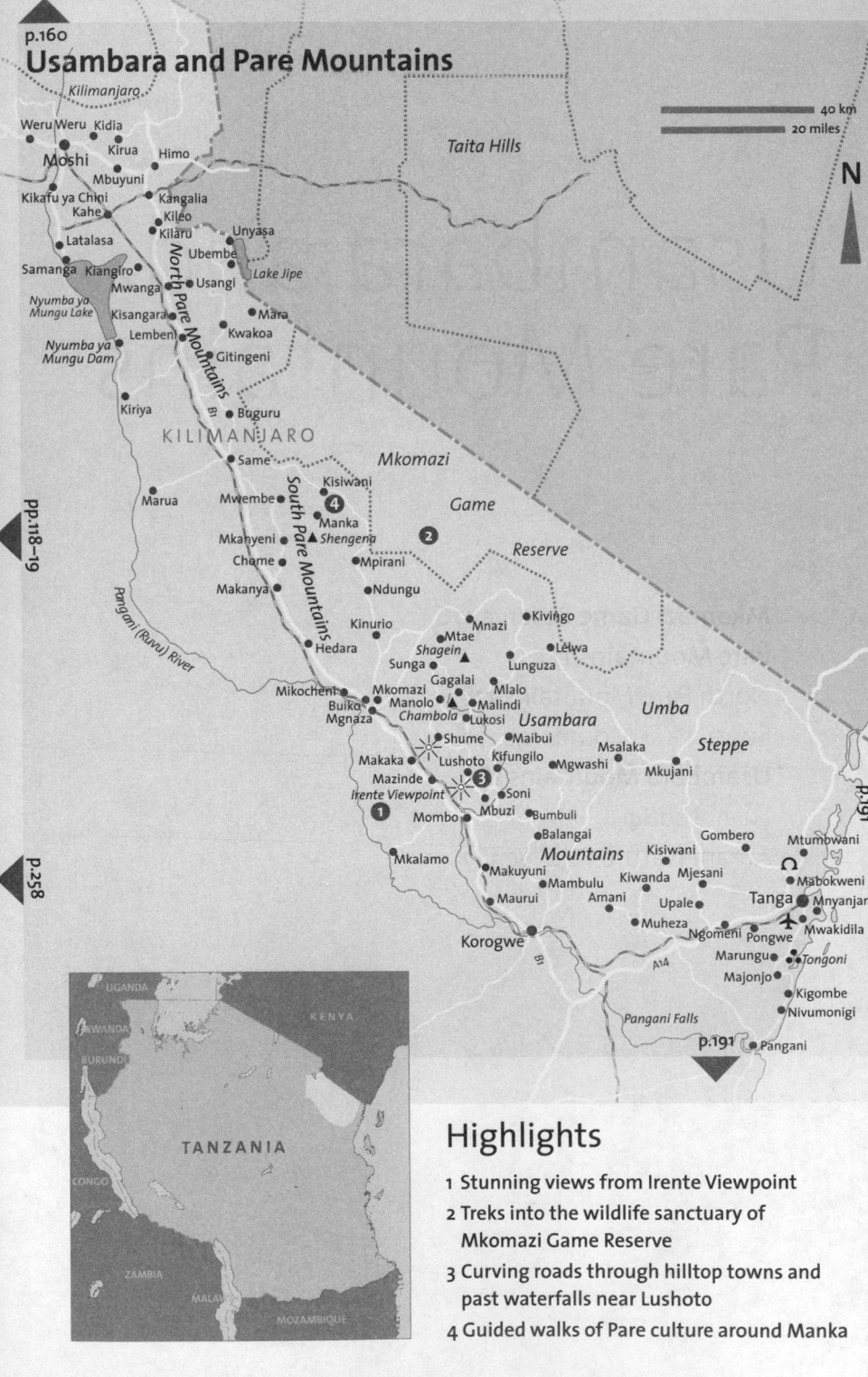

Usambara and Pare Mountains

Kilimanjaro

Weru Weru   Kidia
Moshi   Kirua   Himo
    Mbuyuni
Kikafu ya Chini   Kangalia
Kahe   Kileo
Latalasa   Kilaru
Samanga   Kiangiro   Ubembe   Unyasa
Nyumba ya   Mwanga   Usangi   *Lake Jipe*
Mungu Lake   Kisangara   Mara
Nyumba ya   Lembeni   Kwakoa
Mungu Dam   Gitingeni
Kiriya   Buguru

Taita Hills

40 km
20 miles

N

North Pare Mountains

KILIMANJARO

Same   *Mkomazi*
Marua   Mwembe   Kisiwani   4
    South Pare Mountains   Manka   *Game*
    Mkanyeni   *Shengena*   2
    Chome   Mpirani   *Reserve*
    Makanya   Ndungu

Pangani (Ruvu) River

Kinurio   Mnazi   Kivingo
    Mtae   Lelwa
Hedara   *Shagein*   Lunguza
    Sunga   Gagalai
Mikocheni   Mkomazi   Mlalo   *Umba*
Buiko   Manolo   Malindi
Mgnaza   *Chambola*   Lukosi   *Usambara*   *Steppe*
    Shume   Maibui   Msalaka
Makaka   Lushoto   Kifungilo   Mgwashi   Mkujani
Mazinde   3
Irente Viewpoint   Soni
1   Mombo   Mbuzi   Bumbuli   Gombero   Mtumbowani
        Balangai   Kisiwani
Mkalamo   *Mountains*   Mjesani   Mabokweni
    Makuyuni   Kiwanda   Tanga   Mnyanjani
    Maurui   Mambulu   Amani   Upale   Mwakidila
        Muheza   Ngomeni   Pongwe
Korogwe   Marungu   *Tongoni*
            Majonjo   Kigombe
    Pangani Falls   Nivumonigi
        p.191   Pangani

UGANDA   KENYA
RWANDA
BURUNDI
TANZANIA
CONGO
ZAMBIA   MALAWI   MOZAMBIQUE

Highlights

1 **Stunning views from Irente Viewpoint**

2 **Treks into the wildlife sanctuary of Mkomazi Game Reserve**

3 **Curving roads through hilltop towns and past waterfalls near Lushoto**

4 **Guided walks of Pare culture around Manka**

The North and South Pare and the Usambara Mountains form the northern strand of Tanzania's Eastern Arc Mountains, a 'necklace' of ranges that loops through northeast and southeast Tanzania. This arc really begins in the Taita Hills in Kenya and sweeps through the Pares and Usambaras before curving into the Nguu, Nguru, Ukaguru and Rubeho mountains further south. The crescent cuts a southern swath through the Uluguru Mountains that tower over Morogoro and links up with the stunning Udzungwa Range east of Iringa before finally coming to a stop in the Mahenge Hills that extend south of the Kilombero Valley.

The history of the Eastern Arc extends back to a shady stage of prehistory in the Oligocene epoch of the Tertiary era, when Africa broke away from the Gondwanaland supercontinent and drifted to its present position. It is suggested that the chain was formed around 25 million years ago, at which point layers of rock were forced upwards to form an island of plant life that has since become a haven of climatic stability. A multitude of species were rescued from the intensive heat of the plains, so that the elevated thickets of tropical rainforest you see here are far more ancient than anything on the relatively youthful Mounts Kilimanjaro and Meru.

These mountains provide excellent and varied opportunities for trekking among a wealth of wildlife that comprises 30–40 per cent of Tanzania's plant and mammal species despite only covering around 2 per cent of its national landmass. The range is a natural haven for bird-watchers too, with the second highest diversity of bird species in Africa after the Ituri forest in the Congo.

From Moshi south to Tanga, the B1 is a smooth tarmac road, with consistently great views and interesting people along the way. Mountain ranges loom upwards above the impressive expanse of Nyumba ya Mungu, the 'House of God' dam, south of Moshi, beyond which the impressive peaks of the North and South Pare Mountains can be glimpsed to the east of the road, a rising stretch of the scenic Usambaras behind. This journey follows the path of an old railway track and a number of sisal plantations – legacies of the colonial era – and presents open views to the west over the Lalatema Mountains and on across the rolling plains of the Maasai Steppe. The countryside offers walking opportunities in rare natural environments.

This route provides several options to turn off the beaten track and explore the scenic mountains that rise up along the eastern side of the road. Throughout these ranges, Cultural Tourism Programmes provide tourists with an opportunity to explore scenic rural areas of subsistence farming and to mingle with local communities. The programmes make it possible for visitors to explore the landscape and discover the region's local history, see arts and crafts, experience traditional dances or share home-cooked dishes with local people – or simply make a scenic overnight stop between Moshi and Tanga or Dar es Salaam.

As you go south, accommodation options are progressively more developed: only very simple places to stay are available in the North Pare Mountains, becoming more organized in the South Pares, while further south in the breathtaking valleys and rocky heights of Lushoto in the Usambaras an excellent tourist centre provides numerous choices and good local information on the area. All of these provide a rewarding – and less expensive – diversion from the popular tourist route.

Mkomazi Game Reserve

Squeezed between the Tanzania–Kenya border and the eastern aspect of the Pare range, the 3,500 square kilometres of Mkomazi Game Reserve rank among the most inaccessible reserves in Tanzania – and that's quite a claim. The landscape is wild and ancient, with isolated rocky hills and baobabs rising up above a sea of green-grey nyika bush or open savannah shaded by umbrella acacias. The wildlife of neighbouring Tsavo National Park in Kenya clearly pays no heed to country boundaries, and during the wet season herds of **elephant**, **zebra** and **oryx** migrate to this lonely expanse of African bush, joining a resident population of **giraffe**, **elephant**, **gerenuk** and **hartebeest**, a host of other **antelope** species and predators such as **lion**, **leopard** and **cheetah**. In past years 78 species of mammal have been recorded in the park, and more than 400 species of bird. All of these are now receiving desperately needed nurture and protection from a National Priority Project to restore the park to its full potential from a state of acute dilapidation and degradation. The project, masterminded by the Tony Fitzjohn/George Adamson African Wildlife Preservation Trusts, goes further than simply restoring the land: it has created a sanctuary for the intensive protection of endangered species and threatened animals.

The reserve was established in 1951, when it held one of the densest populations of rhino in East Africa, but its remote situation and lack of funding allowed poaching,

Getting There and Around

Roads around Mkomazi are **not good**; mainly dirt, they are particularly bad during the rainy seasons. If you have your own vehicle it is possible to **drive in** via the turn-off at Same. Otherwise the owner of the Sasa Kazi Hotel near the bus station at Same can organize car hire. As most of the reserve is inaccessible by car it is best explored on foot. **Trekking** into Mkomazi can be arranged through Hilltop Tona Lodge (*see* p.178) in the South Pare Mountains. The terrain is wild and hilly, and it is necessary to hire an armed ranger to accompany any walking party from the Zange Gate towards the north of the reserve. Entrance to the reserve costs $20 per day.

Where to Stay

Ibaya Camp offers the only place to stay within the boundary of the park, a *banda* with just two bedrooms, assuring visitors of an exclusive if not luxurious experience. Booking can be arranged via the Sasa Kazi Hotel.

Nomad Safaris, Nomad Safaris, PO Box 681, Usa River, Arusha, **t/f** (027) 2553819/20/29/30, *bookings@nomad.co.tz, info@nomad.co.tz, www.nomadguides.com*, organize camping trips into Mkomazi and should be able to advise if you want to arrange an upmarket expedition. Otherwise there are the following options on the margins of the park.

Cheap

Lutheran Hostel, Same. Probably the best place here, clean, near the market, with en suite rooms.

Elephant Motel, Same. Has good, comfortable rooms and decent food in the restaurant. Breakfast included.

Savannah Hotel, Same. More simple rooms.

The **Hilltop Tona Lodge**, Mbaga (*see* p.178), is another good option for visiting Mkomazi. The mission at **Dannholz Cottage** (*see* p.177) has four guest rooms too. **Camping** is possible at one of three campsites: Ibaya, Kisima and Njiro. Bring all equipment and supplies.

The **Sasa Kuzi Hotel** does not have its own rooms, but it is the source of all good tourist information and can provide local meals.

overgrazing, fires and trophy-hunting to debilitate this natural resource until it was in desperate condition. The rhino population was wiped out, and only a tiny number of elephants survived on its vast expanse. The reserve has undergone a renaissance under the field direction of Tony Fitzjohn, formerly right-hand man to George Adamson on the famous Kenyan Born Free project. With the support of the Wildlife Preservation Trusts, endangered species such as the African black rhino and African hunting dog have been reintroduced into the reserve. One programme aims to encourage the hunting dogs to breed in captivity prior to release, while the rhino sanctuary has been constructed and stocked with rhinos imported from South Africa. There are many plans in progress to relocate rhinos here from South African, US, UK and Kenyan zoos: four have arrived already and are faring well in the wild. The release of others is being negotiated, but the preparations are complex: not only do the logistics of flying these enormous beasts have to be worked out, but efforts have to be made to get over the zoo animals' fear of open spaces, and to maximize the breeding potential of newcomers without offending resident males.

After nearly two decades of dedication to regenerating the reserve, roads and airstrips have been cleared, water sources pumped and dams built so that there is enough water to share between local people and animals, and rangers have been recruited to finalize an intensive security system for vulnerable animals. The trust has also implemented an outreach programme to provide education for villages around the reserve on environmental and conservation issues, and to create a forum for discussion of the issues to do with living on the outskirts of a protected area.

Most importantly, the elephant population has increased dramatically from 11 at its lowest ebb to more than 1,000 now, including many breeding females and their young. The latest recruits are an adopted elephant named Nina – who is doing so well she has two males in tow – and an orphaned lioness called Jipe. For further information on the **Wildlife Preservation Trusts** contact 301 North A Street, PO Box 5352, Oxnard, CA 93031-5352, USA, *info@mkomazi.com, www.mkomazi.com*.

Pare Mountains

The Pare Mountains are the northernmost link in Tanzania's chain of ancient Eastern Arc Mountains and a great place to explore local culture.

The Pare people who give their name to these mountain ranges are known to have had an extensive fortified capital near Same (pronounced Sah-mey) in the late 18th century, built by Chief Ghendewa, who formed a conscript army and unified the tribe in a sophisticated social system before being killed fighting the Chagga people. Reverend Jacob Jenson Dannholz, a Lutheran missionary from Leipzig in Germany, founded one of the first missions in the Tanzanian interior up in the mountains at Mbanga and lived there from 1908 until 1917, trying to convert the Pare from their warrior-like ways. He built a church and farmhouse on Tona Moorland, now known locally as the White Man's House, but officially called 'Dannholz Cottage' in honour of the man who built it. The cottage has been used by missionaries, who have made four

Getting There and Around

The best way to visit these mountain ranges is to make arrangements with a tour operator in Arusha or Dar es Salaam for a **car and driver** for the required number of days, giving you the added benefit of the guide's knowledge of Swahili and the area. Alternatively **hire a car**, but ensure that you take a 4x4.

For those with more time and an adventurous spirit, it is possible to take a **bus** along the main road and then take local transport from the relevant junction town. Buses run frequently between Tanga and Dar es Salaam to Moshi and Arusha, stopping at all major towns and junctions along the way. Public transport for Hilltop Tona Lodge (*see* below) in the tiny village of Manka in the Mbaga Hills departs from Same. The last bus from Same to Mbaga leaves at 2pm, but enquire at the Sasa Kazi Hotel near the Same bus station. The hotel can also arrange for private cars to ferry visitors to the reserves.

Tourist Information

For details of the North and South Pare Cultural Tourism Programmes, contact the **Tanzanian Tourist Board**, 3rd Floor, IPS Building, PO Box 2485, Dar es Salaam, **t** (022) 2111244, *www.tanzania-web.com*, *www.tanzaniatouristboard.com*, or **Cultural Tourism Programme**, Coordination Office, Ngorongoro Wing, AICC, PO Box 1045, Arusha, *www.infojep.com/culturaltours*, *info@tourismtanzania.org*.

Where to Stay

Hilltop Tona Lodge, PO Box 32, Mbaga-Manka, **t** (022) 2600158 (*cheap*). The best options to stay in this area are either in or arranged through the lively and strangely painted haven of the Hilltop Tona Lodge. The centre is run by Mr Elly Kimbwereza, whose enthusiasm for this superbly rural area is infectious, his knowledge inspiring. Mr Kimbwereza has built a number of cottages high on the hillside, each a breathtaking climb to reach, but all affording superb views across the steep valley to the plains. They are fairly well equipped, with a promise of hot as well as cold running water; any signs of slight dilapidation are liberally concealed with crocheted doilies. There is also an impressive stilted 'conference room' with circular 'portholes' from which to enjoy the view in absolute peace. It's an ideal place to stay for backpackers or for anyone glad of a decent, clean bed and fresh water to wash in. The wealth of assistance provided by Mr Kimbwereza and his team to ensure that visitors discover whatever aspects of the local area interest them most make Hilltop Tona Lodge much more than an overnight stopover. The lodge has a 'tentative price list', for guiding services and activities around the area: payments per group per day, with additional half-day fees, overnight fees, village development fees and porter fees – all well under $10. Accommodation is similarly reasonable, with lunch and dinner available if ordered in advance for next to nothing. Camping around Hilltop Tona Lodge or on Mzee Mrutu's farm at the Duma Viewpoint is possible for a negligible fee. To visit one of the renowned local healers will set you back less than the price of a packet of aspirin, while traditional local dancers may be persuaded to display their skills for a minimum of T.shs 5,000.

bedrooms available for visitors ever since. Ironically, Dannholz is better remembered for writing a guide to Pare oral traditions – which has helped to keep them alive – than for the success of his evangelical pacifism.

North Pare Mountains

The North Pare range stretches for about 60km north–south from the town of Mwanga, about 50km south of Moshi. The route to **Usangi**, at the heart of the mountains, leads uphill from **Mwanga**, where huge palm trees thrive in the abundance of water that flows off the escarpment. A small, secluded central town surrounded by 11 peaks, Usangi is also the heart of a bustling economic community that operates a number of local factories producing bricks, stoves, pottery and clothes. Usangi is fun to visit when the local market enlivens the streets on Mondays or Thursdays, as people from the surrounding villages congregate to buy and sell the fruits of their hard cultivation of the fertile mountain terraces.

Views from the top of these mountains are impressive, revealing the glittering expanse of lakes such as **Lake Jipe** and **Nyumba ya Mungu**, the 'House of God' lake, looking north towards Mount Kilimanjaro. The only problem is getting there: the best way is to contact teachers at **Lomwe Secondary School**, the centre for a development project, and take a guide. Most of the guides on loan from the centre work full-time as farmers, craftsmen or teachers. With the help of the scheme they have worked out a number of walks for visitors, which they guide in their 'spare' time. These may take a half- or full day, exploring the Pare clan-forests, traditional site of all tribal ceremonies and magic rites, or going via farms and homesteads to find caves dug in **Goma Hill** to conceal the Pare tribe from rival tribes, slave traders and colonial powers. A nearby hut treasures a cache of the skulls of Pare chiefs who died in tribal and colonial wars.

The walks can be extended, continuing as nature walks from Goma Hill through forest reserves to the flat table top of **Kindoroko Mountain**, or exploring villages and viewing stone terraces and irrigation systems, old churches and the graves of early missionaries – reminders of the early colonial German influence. Another option is to climb **Kamwala Mountain**, passing the Chegho Moorland where an old farmer called Mzee Kiya can tell you stories about the miracles that have taken place here, before the steep final ascent through forest to the peak. Longer walks can also be arranged, with overnight stays at the Banduka family house in the village of **Kisangara Chini**. Accommodation is available at the school's small guesthouse and, through the cultural tourism programme, with villagers in Lomwe.

If you can't walk or don't like walking, a guide can show you around in your car, stopping off to visit progressive farmers and relics of tribal wars and colonial rule. The short distance to Usangi from Moshi or Marangu makes it an easy day trip. Proceeds from the project aim to develop energy-efficient wood-burning stoves, in an effort to conserve the forests and reduce the workload of local women who gather the wood.

South Pare Mountains

The rural spread of the South Pare mountains is another magical, forested expanse of hidden villages, valleys and homesteads clinging to steep hand-built terraces, with plenty to inspire curiosity. Just after the turn-off from the main road at Same a signpost is inscribed with the words 'South Pare Mountains Cultural Tourism Programme' – the only indication for many mountainous miles around that there is anything in this area orientated towards outside visitors to the area.

Mbaga Hills

The project here is located high in the Mbaga Hills, in an area with an extraordinary local and colonial history. There are two routes up to Mbaga from Same on the main road: the best route is **via Kisiwani** and passes alongside the boundary of Mkomazi Game Reserve; the other route follows a precipitous mountain path through rich forest **via Mwembe**, passing through the tiny hamlets of **Mhezi**, **Kwizu** and **Marindi**. The mountain route frequently threatens to deteriorate beyond a driveable state, and you are well advised to attempt these mountain tracks only in a 4x4 vehicle. Watch out for the local children, who seem to be magnetically attracted to passing cars, in a state of excitement at the arrival of motorized newcomers, though asking directions may incur a bewildering multitude of answers. A few daylight driving hours to spare and dedication in persevering with the precipitous mountain road bring you to the **Hilltop Tona Lodge** at **Manka** (*see* p.178), centre for a Cultural Tourism Programme set up by the Netherlands Development Organization (SNV) and the Tanzanian Tourist Board (TTB). Here the project aims to improve traditional irrigation systems and replant deforested areas to prevent soil erosion and conserve water supplies.

The traditional Pare culture is still much in evidence, inspired by the memory of legendary leader Mashombo of Mshewa, who had a reputation for his army of sorcerers and witches. Witch doctors from here are so renowned that people travel long distances to seek the benefits of their powers; even urban dwellers from Arusha venture south to decipher unusual problems. **Malameni Rock**, where according to local legend children were sacrificed to appease evil spirits until the 1930s, can now be climbed after receiving special spiritual instruction from the hut below. It is not far from here to the **Mghimbi Caves**, which furnished a natural hideaway for local tribes during 19th-century slave raids. Both rock and caves can be visited as a half-day walk.

Ikongwe Village

More spiritualism can be found among the tropical fruit trees and banana palms in Ikongwe village. Reached as a full day's excursion from Mbaga, it is a beautiful and fruitful place that is believed to be a gift from the heavens, and where a very distinct religious community has now developed. Also viewed with great respect by local communities is Mpepera Viewpoint atop **Mpepera Hill**, where a cross has been erected to represent the peace between resident Catholic and Protestant communities. The viewpoint is used by locals as a peaceful area for prayers; for the less religious it offers awe-inspiring views of Mount Kilimanjaro, the Mbaga Hills and Mkomazi Game Reserve when the skies are clear. Full-day walks can also be arranged into local villages to visit families brewing beer by traditional methods, or you can take a longer hike through unspoiled woodland such as **Shengena Forest**. Here it is possible to camp under the stars, waking up for a sunrise hike up **Shengena Peak** – at 2,463m above sea level the highest point in the Pare and Usambara Mountains – to discover fresh springs and troops of colobus monkeys and enjoy magnificent views over Same and Lushoto. All or any of these can be visited in the company of local Pare guides contacted via Hilltop Tona Lodge (*see* p.178), who are keen to explain their cultural and natural environment with an ever-improving command of English.

Usambara Mountains

There is only one tarmac road into the Usambara Mountains, and this is the one that wends from Mombo to the small waterfall town of Soni, and along a lush and picturesque river valley to Lushoto, the centre of regional administration. This extraordinary region is tucked high in the hills, with a surprising local and colonial history. Again the region has an aura of sublime natural beauty, with deep valleys and rushing mountain streams at the foot of steep terraced hillsides that rise up to meet the misty morning. An abundance of plant species in their dense thicket has earned this often overlooked, hidden corner of Tanzania a name as 'the Galapagos of the plant world'. The Usambara range is divided into east and west by the 4km wide Lwengera Valley that lies in between.

History

While the mountain range itself is 25 million years old, the earliest human traces here are a mere 3,500 years old. The rock was forced upwards into its present shape, forming an island of plant life that has since been a haven of climatic stability, preserving species from the intensive heat of the plains. But, while the indigenous African violet thrived in its quiet, natural state, subsequent populations of man in these mountains endured a far less stable existence. There is evidence of early iron-working Neolithic settlements here between 3,000 and 3,500 years ago, followed by an influx of Bantu peoples who migrated here from the central African Congo region around 2,000 years ago. From the mingling of the newcomers with the original tribes came the Shambaa, or Sambaa, people of the Usambaras today.

The Shambaa clans traditionally welcomed refugees to their mountainous realm and were supposed to have lived harmoniously with their neighbours, although little is known of them until the early 18th century and the arrival of the first king of the Usambaras, Mbega, father of the Kilindi Dynasty. Family members of this ruling class are remembered with reverence and awe, and rumours abound of their pale-coloured eyes and distinctive pale skin coloration, and of how their magical powers were strong enough to make rain. King Mbega was also reputedly a professional bushpig-hunter from the Nguru Mountains, who considerately took a wife from each clan and provided each with a son to rule it.

From the middle of the 1800s the Usambaras were fraught with violent struggles as the Shambaa tribes were subject to attacks from neighbouring tribes plundering livestock and food, and later from slave-traders. When the infamous Maasai tribe assembled on the westward plains and began to threaten the Shambaa livelihood in a determined and warlike quest for grazing land and cattle, the mountain tribe developed greater political and military structures under the leadership of Mbega's grandson, Kinyashi. Thanks to its elevated position and respected cultural hierarchy the kingdom survived.

On Kinyashi's death his son Kimweri (of the Kilindi dynasty) was proclaimed 'Simba Mwene', the Lion King, and he became a powerful military leader, eventually controlling much of the South Pare Mountains from his base at Vuga, near Soni. But, as the

When to Go

Although the rainy season follows the pattern of northern Tanzania with **long rains** between April and May and **short rains** in November, the altitude in the Usambaras means the climate is much cooler than the lowlands and plains.

It is recommended to take long-sleeved shirts and jumpers even through the **'dry'** months between June and October, as the nights are still quite cold, and a cloudy day might merit it.

Getting There

By Car

Turn off the B1 at Mombo between the Caltex and BP fuel stations. The road from here makes determined progress over the 33km to Lushoto, following the route of the original **cobblestone road** built more than a century ago by German administrators, but allow a good hour and half to cover this short distance with all its hair-raising mountain bends. Rural colonial homesteads and lodges are signposted around 15km beyond Lushoto in the villages of Mkuzi and Migambo, and again it is recommended to leave plenty of time to reach these before nightfall, as the windy and potholed road is badly lit.

By Bus

Bus services run from Dar es Salaam, Tanga and Arusha. Direct services from all three should be in operation; if not, take a bus to Mombo, and change there. Local minibuses regularly ply the route, and may be a better alternative for snaking up the mountain road.

Where to Stay

Lushoto Town

Accommodation in Lushoto Town is much more basic than 'Out of Town' options.

Cheap

Lawn's Hotel, PO Box 33, Lushoto, t (027) 2640005, f (027) 2642311. The best choice in the centre, quirky and atmospheric, with good views from the rooms. Lawn's is one of the oldest hotels in Tanzania with almost a century of history behind it, emanating a warm, aged atmosphere most evident in the dark wooden reception and restaurant with cavernous smoky fireplaces all illuminated by dusty shafts of sunlight. Accommodation is in detached round bungalow-style rooms, with well-worn en-suite bedrooms and bathrooms looking out over a sloping lawn. An imaginatively conceived 'honeymoon house' commands unblemished views of the hillside beyond, and the promise of a hand-built super-double bed with artistic trimmings. The hotel has the benefit of a 'games room', providing table tennis, badminton and darts, and a satellite TV in the cosy bar, videos and a small library for guests' use. Mountain bikes are available for hire. Horse riding can be arranged, as can mountain walks and bird-watching. The Greek owners' enthusiasm for food and wine is evident in the cooking, which relies on fresh produce from the garden. Breakfast is included and personal fires lit on request. Rooms with shared bathroom are cheaper. Camping is possible on the lawn with use of hot showers and toilet facilities.

Mandarin Hotel, high above the town about 1km along the road to Irente Viewpoint. This budget hotel has a friendly atmosphere and promises to provide decent budget accommodation with good views, although it is said to pick up a bit of noise from the town at night. The Mandarin has been recommended for its excellent local cooking. B&B.

Lushoto Sun, opposite the Catholic church near the park in the town centre, t (027) 2640083. Self-contained budget accommodation in the town centre, with good, clean rooms and hot running water.

Kilimani Guesthouse, a short walk from the town centre. For about the same price, the Kilimani is clean, well kept, and has also been recommended.

Out of Town

The best and most atmospheric places to stay are outside Lushoto in the villages of **Migambo** and **Mkuzi**. During the 1930s these were the smart colonial suburbs of Lushoto, realm of colonial officers and retirees. Despite its relative inaccessibility, this quietly high-profile enclave was the first rural district to receive electricity in Tanzania in the 1930s. The grand old stone farmhouses have retained an old-world charm, transporting the visitor back to a world of 19th-century European colonial values. Hand-crafted wooden dressers are laden with painted china, fires burn brightly in wide hearths, armchairs and sofas are soft and worn, on thick rugs and parquet floors, looking out over colourfully tended flower gardens. All this is tucked away in these high mountains of sub-equatorial Africa, quiet and timeless, and close to the start of forest trails.

Moderate

Grants Lodge, Maigambo, Lushoto, PO Box 859, Tanga, t/f (027) 2642491, *www.grantslodge. com, tanga4@tanga.net*. Boasts all the above qualities and provides a homely atmosphere to return to after the exertion of brisk walks in the mountains. Friendly staff encourage and assist in planning walks with the aid of a comprehensive house book that provides details and directions, and they may also be persuaded to escort you as a guide. The climate is ideal for families with children or older visitors. Run in the style of a family house, with rooms named 'Cosy', 'Tibetan' and so on. Drinks are available on a help-yourself honesty-book basis from the fridge and cabinet at the bottom of the stairs. The house feels as if it has been spirited from a different time and place, particularly the comfortable old sitting room and heavy wooden furniture in the parlour-style dining room where guests enjoy a full breakfast and tuck into hot plates of home-made cooking in the evenings. Full board.

Müller's Mountain Lodge, PO Box 34, t (027) 2640204, f (027) 2640205, *mullersmountain lodge@yahoo.com*. Swiss-run and slightly larger, slightly older and also slightly cheaper. Lawns and gardens surround this romantic old stone house at the top of a small hill, and extensive woodwork within gives a snug impression of a ship's hold. The hotel will help you find guides for walks in the luscious scenery round about.

Viewpoint and Bellavista Campsite. An old campsite at Irente Viewpoint – its name

determined to make the most of its setting – it has been renovated and improved by Louis, the charismatic proprietor. He has exciting plans for it and the cooking he will do, although so far guacamole is the only recommendation. Usefully, there are a couple of bandas available for those without camping gear.

Soni

Cheap

Soni Falls View, PO Box 20, Soni, t Soni 45 or 27 (call the operator on 900 and ask for Soni 45 or 27). Overlooking the river and with some good views of the waterfall, the Soni Falls was opened in 1939 and has obviously seen better days. The communal dining areas and verandahs provide a pleasant environment for relaxation, while rooms vary in standard from slightly to very dilapidated. But the atmosphere is peaceful and quiet, the accommodation good value.

Maweni, on the right-hand side up the hill, looking out of town. A little further out of the centre, another ex-colonial construction revived with local nurture. Known as 'the place of many rocks', this very inexpensive place sits high on a hillside with a forest of fir trees extending beyond. It has a peculiar atmosphere, with ghostly echoes of an abandoned institution, its cool flagstone floors and basic furniture lavishly patched up with fluorescent knitted doilies. This rural hideaway is billed as having its own pool, which seems to be simply wishful thinking – there's no sign of one! Hardy types on a strict budget might be lured by the very low prices for self-contained doubles, even lower with a shared bathroom.

Hotel Kimalube, first turning on the right as you approach Soni from Mombo. A more atmospheric reception in the budget range, the Kimalube is lively and popular with a motley crew of truck drivers and girls. Masterfully managed by a large, charismatic 'mama', who is said to have persuaded her German lover to buy the property. A wholesome local-style supper is well worth its very low price. Washing facilities are communal, with cold running showers and buckets of hot water delivered on request.

local clan chiefs, Kimweri's sons, became more adept at raiding the slave caravans for arms to retaliate invasions, they also began fighting among themselves for greater power, so decentralizing and weakening the dynasty. Vuga was retained as the Shambaa capital, and the background of military organization enabled the Shambaa tribes to support the 1888–9 Bushiri Uprising, but the weakening power base allowed the German administration to walk in, having quashed the rebellion. Arriving at a time of chaos and disarray enabled the Europeans to persuade individual chiefs to sign away their territories for small reward.

The cool, pleasant climate of the Usambaras attracted a number of settlers to its wide green valleys and so charmed the German administration that they originally wanted to make it their colonial capital, and called the town Wilhelmstal after Kaiser Wilhelm. The land is wild and steep, but the newcomers implemented building and engineering that still reflect their attitudes. They constructed a solid cobblestone road to climb the 33km between Mombo and Lushoto which remains mainly unchanged to this day (although resurfaced), and it is still possible to see their original brickwork in the many mountain stream bridges along the way. This rises on a gentle incline, to allow oxcarts to pass back and forth with heavy loads, and is shaded by an imposing avenue of wide trunk plane trees. Settler farming flourished, encouraging the building of a number of stone homes designed in the colonial style, still much in evidence today. The area was cultivated, albeit with some shaky starts: the Germans set out with grand plans to develop coffee plantations here, but after they had cleared the forest and planted crops it became evident that the new plots did not provide enough shelter. Fruit trees, however, flourished, especially pears and plums, and the area continues to export fresh produce around the country. Success was also found with plantations of sisal, which made certain planters wealthy men with the freedom to set up country retreats in areas such as Lushoto, where crops also extended to rubber, cotton, tobacco, sugar, wheat and maize.

When Tanganyika was made a Mandate Territory under the League of Nations and then awarded to Great Britain for administration after the Versailles Treaty of 1919, the British discouraged settlers. There were still, however, many civil servants who did need and build their own houses. Many of these good-looking buildings can still be found around the Lushoto area, adding to the bizarre combination of old colonial German and British alongside African homesteads all situated in a distinct natural and yet well-cultivated landscape.

Lushoto

Lushoto is a neat and friendly town with charm, which rambles up two sides of a valley to cultivated hillsides. The high-altitude location gives this surprisingly large town the clean-aired feel of a mountain village. There is something rather surreal about its efficient bank, churches and government offices, still operating with a quaint old-worldliness. A sleepy colonial air still clings with the mist around well-preserved stone buildings from another generation. There is much to explore around

Lushoto itself and places to stay good for walks and days out with families (*see* Grant's Lodge, Irente Viewpoint and other places, below), and it is also an excellent point of departure for treks to other towns and villages in the Usambara Mountains.

The excellent tourist office in Lushoto (signposted left past the bank) is extremely helpful in organizing guides for driving, walking or trekking around the area. It provides numerous options for camping, overnight stays with local families or days out; guides charge about $15 per day per person, on top of a $10 charge paid to the tourism project. Tipping should be discretionary according to the service provided, but if you take an official guide there should be no cause for complaint.

Irente Viewpoint

One of the easiest and most impressive natural areas to reach on an enjoyable walk from the town centre is Irente Viewpoint. This is a wild rocky outcrop, approached along a narrow, flower-fringed walkway and emerging at a giddy windblown height above the Maasai steppe. Views are superb, and nearby scenery is impressively dramatic. The round trip takes between three and four hours on foot from the town, although if you have your own vehicle you can drive a large portion of the way if desired. Any guide from the tourist office can show you the way to the viewpoint, but the route is clear from Irente Farm. The farm has developed as a worthwhile stopover for buying picnic goods, since it has been established as a reliable producer of whole-meal breads, jams and fresh dairy products (and any traveller to Tanzania for any length of time will appreciate the joy of a delicious cheese supplier). The farm has also received attention from the legendary local home-maker, known as Comrade 'Kipepe', meaning 'butterfly', who has sculpted his family home entirely from mud, including the table, benches, shelves and water system. Kipepe has now built a mud shop, '*duka*' in Swahili, at Irente, artistically topped by the wide head of a horned cow.

Ubiri and Vuli

More home-made goods can be found in production at the landscaped and lovingly tended Catholic Mission of the Montessori Sisters in Ubiri, where wines, cheeses and jams can also be inspected, tasted and bought. The mission can be visited on a three- to four-hour walking round trip from town. A slightly longer walking trip of between four and five hours leads up to the farmlands of Jaegertal, through an impressive fruit tree nursery and on up to the village of Vuli which has benefited from irrigation, conservation and farming projects. This walk can also include a return trip via the Lushoto Arboretum or Herbarium, an impressive collection of pressed plants and leaves that were collected from all around Tanzania during the German era. To see the collection, ask for Mr Msangi or Mr Mabula.

Mgamba

Guides can take you on a walk to the Mgamba Rain Forest, inhabited by troops of dashingly collared colobus monkeys and numerous species of forest bird, including the Usambara akalat and Usambara weaver, making this a particularly rewarding destination for anyone with a special interest in bird-watching. It is possible to camp at the quiet site equipped with a toilet and running water, near a disused sawmill at the centre of the forest, or to make your way to the comfortable and welcoming lodges at Mkuzi and Migambo, mentioned below. The walk to Mgamba from town also goes via the royal mountaintop village of Kwembago, the ancient centre of the Daffa family, a sub-clan of the traditionally revered ruling class the Kilindi Dynasty. This trip takes between five and six hours on foot, and returns through the village of Mgamba, from where it is also possible to catch a bus back to Lushoto or on to Mlalo.

Mtae

Longer trips can be made over a period of days, either camping or staying in guest-houses on route. An excellent longer trek leads through the forests, mountains, valleys and villages between Lushoto and the quaint and historic village of Mtae, an important elevated boundary post on top of a mountain with incredible views between the Maasai plains and the lands of the Shambaa high on the westernmost rim of the West Usambara escarpment. The first German European missionaries were allowed to build their church in Mtae (sometimes written Mtii), having survived the ordeal of being led to an ancestral burial site by the local chief and amazing him when they were not destroyed or distracted by the potentially fatal '*mizumu*', the spirits of the dead. The panoramic views from here are worth the climb, with mile upon mile of extraordinary landscape stretching to the far horizon to reveal the South Pare Mountain Ranges and Mkomazi Game Reserve, Nyumba ya Mungu reservoir and sometimes even the peaks of Mount Kilimanjaro some 250km away.

The first road down the western face is presently being constructed to Mtae with donations from the descendants of the first European visitors, so forging a historic link between these mountains and the Maasai plains below. A couple of simple but welcoming guesthouses in Mtae provide very cheap rooms (the Mwivano II is slightly more costly than the Kuna Maneno). A local café near the bus station provides wholesome plates of local food and home-made breads, and a nearby bar sells beer – although not necessarily cold. Between the villages of Mtae and **Sunga** lies the new **Limbe Travellers Rest Camp**. With a few rooms and camping available, it is recom-mended since it is affiliated with the tourist office in Lushoto, and owned by the vice-chair of the Friends of the Usambara Society. The camp is on the bus route between Mtae and Lushoto. The journey between the towns takes around three hours; buses leave Lushoto in mid-afternoon and Mtae at 5am the following day.

Mlalo

New tours have recently been added to the range organized by the Cultural Tourism Programme, one of which heads even further into the Usambara range, to discover the isolated and idiosyncratic town of Mlalo, clinging high in the hills 30km from Lushoto. Surrounded by a dramatic backdrop of wild mountain peaks, Mlalo is a rambling sprawl of extraordinary homes designed with two storeys and prettily carved wooden balconies in a neatly cultivated and terraced valley irrigated by the Umba River. The town produces a number of hand-crafted pots in the tradition of the Shambaa, who once believed that the creator god Sheuta formed people from the earth as a potter works her earthen vessels. Ancient beliefs hold that pot-making is the work of women, with techniques passed down from mother to daughter. Their pottery, and pots made in the nearby village of Kileti, are then transported to the Lushoto market for sale. Buses run daily between Lushoto and Mlalo, via **Mgamba**, and take around two hours. The **Afilex Hotel** is generally recommended as the best guesthouse, although be prepared for reading by gas lamp, as there is no electricity this far into the mountains.

Soni

The nearby village of Soni, about 25 minutes south of Lushoto by car or the regular *matatu* minibus service, is famous for its waterfalls. The route between Soni and Lushoto is inspiring, and Soni itself is a pleasant little market town on the banks of the rocky waterfall. Although not as impressive as many to be found on walks deeper into the mountains, it is of a decent enough height and volume to justify the steep walk down to the lower banks, or a coffee in the bar at the **Hotel Falls View**.

Amani Nature Reserve

The German colonial government soon realized the rich potential of this mountain region for cash crops. While early coffee plantations in this region were not terribly successful, settlers reaped the rewards of sisal, tobacco and spice farms. Coffee is one of Tanzania's principal cash crops today, but remains a volatile commodity on the world market. Tanzanian coffee-farmers' profits are frequently hit by plunging global prices as even their finest Arabica beans still do not guarantee a stable income. In the late 19th century an arboretum was established at Lushoto to study the local environment. Its researchers soon became aware of an unusual density of diverse wildlife in the Usambaras. As a result, 13 forest reserves were surveyed and gazetted in the area, including 8,380 hectares at the Amani Nature Reserve north of Muheza.

The original 1902 reserve now incorporates 1,065 hectares, owned by private tea companies and managed by the East Usambara Tea Company and Amani Botanical Gardens – one of the largest botanical gardens of its kind in Africa. A large number of indigenous species were left rooted, and more than 1,000 species of exotic trees were imported from foreign climes. Many of these can still be identified by their ancient metal nameplates, still legible if a little dusty, but the reserve and gardens are now extremely overgrown and large areas impenetrable. Walking paths that have been cleared enough to enjoy run from the top of the hill to a **resthouse** and the reserve's **research centre**, a steep climb by all accounts, even in a tough 4x4 vehicle: if you go up the hill in a car you will be besieged by tea plantation workers desperate for a lift.

The research centre was officially closed during the Second World War, although it made a contribution to the war effort by extracting quinine from the local cinchona tree. When the British were able to invest in the area after the war they planted 2,200 hectares of tea in regions that were already cultivated and built a hydroelectric power station, the remnants of which can still be seen. The research centre reopened in 1953,

When to Go

The high-altitude landscape creates a **cooler climate** in the mountainous nature reserve with a tendency to misty mornings and fresh breezes in most months of the year other than the high dry season.

Getting There

The route to Amani leads through Muheza, a small but lively market town that is also a popular stop for **buses** between Tanga and Dar es Salaam. From there arrange a lift with the Forest Project (*see* right).

Where to Stay and Eat

Good accommodation is on offer near the grassy enclosure opposite the Information Centre in the foothills of the forest reserve.

Moderate

The **Malaria Medical Research Centre Resthouse**, located in the village, is open to tourists if its rooms are not already occupied by researchers.

Cheap

Zigi Guesthouse, PO Box 1449, Tanga, **t** (053) 2646907, *usambara@twiga.com*. Rooms are small but clean and self-contained.

Amani Nature Reserve Rest House, East Usambara Catchment Forest Project, PO Box 1494, Tanga, **t** (053) 2646907, **f** (053) 2643820, *usambara@twiga.com*. A range of accommodation in wooden huts reminiscent of Cub Scout adventure holidays. The newly renovated cabins are, however, very clean and pleasant. Four rooms share one bathroom and each room has enough small wooden beds and mosquito nets for seven people – with numerous instructive notices pinned to the walls with tin tacks. The stripped wood interiors create a cosy mountain refuge feel. Each little house has a balcony overlooking the forest. Full board, plus a reservation fee. A negligible fee is charged for camping.

with an emphasis on agriculture. It is now a centre for malaria research. Concerted efforts to regenerate the reserve and gardens for tourists have led to restoration of the old German stationmaster's house, dating from 1905–10, which has been converted into a fine information centre. Plans are afoot to develop maps and a guidebook for visitors. Maybe the next step will be to clear and tend the land itself!

The nature reserve is signposted from just beyond **Muheza** town. From there the road passes through a magical, abundant region of rural homesteads surrounded by a mesmerizing array of fruit trees and vegetables neatly planted in rows. There is enough seasonal variety to produce a crop of something desirable most months of the year. The orange harvest in mid-June sees the sandy roads piled high with citrus fruits, often stacked so high that only the head of the vendor can be seen behind the display. Women sashay along the roadside with buckets of oranges balanced on their heads, the buckets so tall that their arms are only just able to reach and grasp the rim. The mango harvest in December is perhaps even more plentiful and at other times of year the stalls are piled with copious coconuts, peppers, maize and more.

The local people here are said to be very cautious with their money. Outsiders believe that anyone producing crops around this market town so widely renowned for its fresh produce must be relatively rich. To the unknowing eye, however, this is a typical Swahili village with perhaps a slightly higher than average proportion of brick houses, well kept but not out of the ordinary. The reason for this is held to be that the locals claim everyone else would come and steal their wealth away if they visibly improved their living standards!

The Coast North of Dar

14

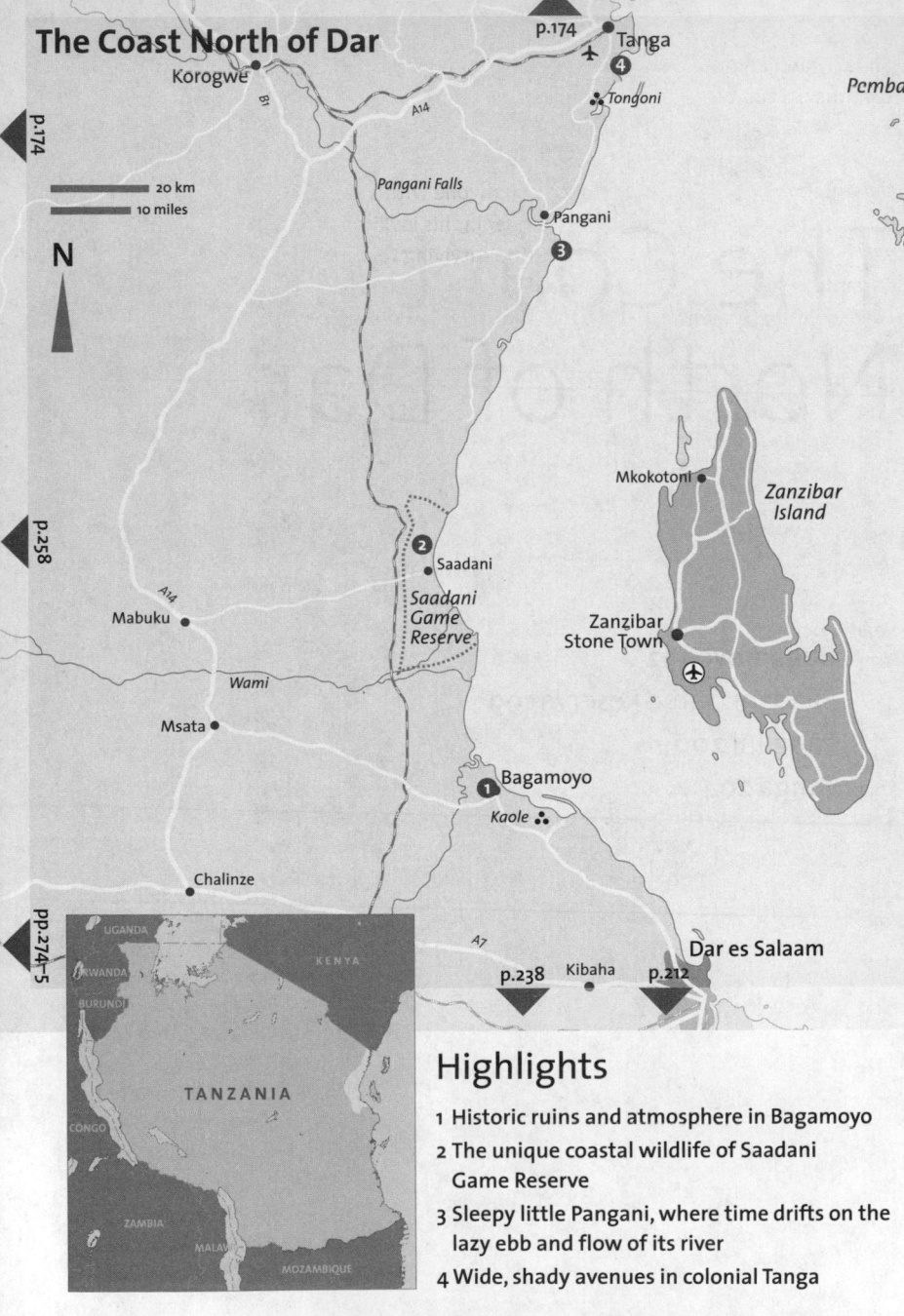

The Coast North of Dar

Highlights labels on map:
p.174, Tanga, Tongoni, Pemba, Korogwe, Pangani Falls, Pangani, Mkokotoni, Zanzibar Island, Saadani, Saadani Game Reserve, Mabuku, Zanzibar Stone Town, Msata, Wami, Bagamoyo, Kaole, Chalinze, Dar es Salaam, Kibaha, p.238, p.212, A7

Highlights

1 Historic ruins and atmosphere in Bagamoyo
2 The unique coastal wildlife of Saadani Game Reserve
3 Sleepy little Pangani, where time drifts on the lazy ebb and flow of its river
4 Wide, shady avenues in colonial Tanga

The Indian Ocean coast of Tanzania has seen an extraordinary pattern of visitors arriving, departing and settling on its shores over several thousand years. While the entire East African coast has attracted successive waves of sailors and merchants, adventurers and explorers from over the sea and migrating tribes from the interior,

Shirazi, Arabic, Portuguese and European settlers have built and abandoned commercial capitals along the Tanzanian stretch. For travellers today, the nature of the land itself is often treasure enough – a coastline of clean coral sand beaches as white and soft as rice flour shaded by palm trees and lapped by the shimmering blue-green waves of the ocean – but, for anyone with a shred of curiosity, a string of historic towns from different eras slumber in this idyllic setting, curious, crumbling reminders of a more prosperous past. The surviving towns of Tanga, Pangani and Bagamoyo, north of Dar, bustle today with the bright pace of contemporary Swahili coastal life, in unusual and often magnificent surroundings. From them you can also explore coastal game reserves, make underwater explorations into the world of coral reefs, or visit natural lagoons, islets and sandbanks on the deck of a traditional dhow.

History

The history of the Indian Ocean coast is one of many centuries of sea-trading, with links to great civilizations from the ancient Egyptians, Sumerians, Phoenicians and Romans to later Arab dynasties and Europeans from the Portuguese Vasco da Gama on – all coming to these shores in search of raw materials and luxury items. This East African coast has in fact played a part in international trade networks for nearly 5,000 years since the Egyptians sailed down the Red Sea and round the Horn of Africa, recording their travels in stone carvings at Karnak in 2050 BC. Trading connections were well established by the 1st or 2nd century AD, as recorded in the *Periplus of the Erythraean Sea*, a guide to the ports of Arabia, East Africa and India and their links with China, written at the end of the 1st century by a Greek merchant based in Egypt.

From the earliest days, a few merchants settled along the coast, intermingling with local Bantu people, but these settlers barely affected African culture. The greatest immigration to this coast followed the growth of Islam between the 8th and 10th centuries; as a result of religious and political upheavals after the death of the Prophet Mohammed, refugee families emigrated from the Arabian Peninsula to settle along the Azanian coast, which they called the 'Land of Zanj'. They founded settlements that developed into thriving centres of Islamic culture. One sailor and Arab writer, Abu'l Hasan 'Ali al-Mas'udi, recorded an account of his travels to Zanj at the end of the 10th century AD: he describes the 'villages of Zanj' stretching for '700 parsangs'– equivalent to 4,000km, the distance from the Red Sea to a point on the mainland level with southern Madagascar.

In the era of Arab settlement, the coast remained a focal point for Indian Ocean trade. Monsoon winds blew wooden dhows across the ocean from Arabia and India in the east, laden with textiles, hatchets, daggers, awls and glass, as well as wine and sometimes wheat. The dhows set sail again when the winds changed direction, laden with cargoes of gold, tortoiseshell and ambergris. This land of plenty earned a reputation all around the Arabian Sea.

Legend tells how many of the settlements along the Tanzanian coast grew from one spectacular emigration led by Ali bin Sultan Hasan of Shiraz, the capital of Fars in Persia. Stories tell how in AD 975 he had a dream that a rat with iron jaws was gnawing though the foundations of his palace; he interpreted the dream to be a threat to the very foundations of his family and rule, and resolved to move them all away to somewhere safer. The timing would have coincided with the Islamic upheavals. The sultan organized himself, his six sons and their entourage into seven separate boats, and they all set sail for Zanj on the monsoon winds. Somewhere in the middle of the Indian Ocean they were separated by a storm which caused each dhow to land at different points along the coast and islands, including Mafia, Kilwa, Pemba, Tongoni (Tanga) and the Comoros. Ali bin Sultan Hasan's story was intended to ensure the newcomers' welcome as descendants of a valiant and wise Shirazi king – many people along the coast still claim Shirazi descent. Similar tales of the Shirazi Sultan of Kilwa relate how he bought Kilwa Kisiwani for a length of cloth, sending his son Bashat to the Mafia archipelago to govern his sultanate there. More realistic accounts tell how, from the 8th to 11th centuries, émigrés from the Persian Gulf first settled further north on the Azanian coast and gradually moved south to settle along the coast of present-day Tanzania between the 12th and 14th centuries. Many of these settlements achieved great prosperity from Indian Ocean trade, but suffered a close-to-devastating decline following the arrival of the Portuguese in the 17th century.

Bagamoyo

Bagamoyo has a pervasive atmosphere of past glory that is strangely coloured by the knowledge that its reputation was built on the cruelty, hardship and suffering that were the bedrock of the slave trade. It is now a curiously calm town, its white coral sand beaches deserted but for a few fishermen, with huge plantations of palm trees dating from the industrious days of the Zanzibari Sultans, left to grow old in peace. The shores of Bagamoyo are pounded by the frisking waves of the Indian Ocean, and at its centre is a fascinating – although dilapidating – collection of buildings from the days of Arab and German settlement. Many of these are now empty, but remain hauntingly powerful images, subjected to the continual weathering of a ruinous sea breeze. Bagamoyo is the site of the first Christian church on this stretch of coast; Kaole down the road is also the site of one of the first mosques. This now-charming ancient town may have lost its old supremacy as a dubious trading port, but remains a superb beach location with good natural areas nearby, such as the Ruvu River Delta and offshore coral reefs, that make worthwhile trips in themselves. It's an easy journey from Dar es Salaam, which is 65km south and about 1½–2hrs' drive, with good roads at least half the way.

History

The known history of Bagamoyo dates back to the 9th century, when trade was first established with the interior: the local population collected salt and dried fish to trade for ivory, rhino horn and leopard skins; later trade expanded to include tortoiseshell – and slaves. Islamic traders and settlers from overseas brought new wealth to earlier Bantu-speaking settlers from the west of Africa, and the interaction between them developed a new language of the coast that became Swahili (*see* p.23).

'Be Still My Heart'

Discussions of the name's etymology continue to fascinate. The most common explanation given is 'Bwaga-moyo', translated as 'be still my heart', or 'lay down the burden of my heart', most often interpreted to have been the lament of slaves reaching the last step of African soil before hopes of staying were stripped away and they were shipped to foreign lands, leaving their hearts forever in their homeland. Another interpretation is that the name arose from the caravan porters and traders who considered the port a final release from their journeying, and for whom the sentiment to 'lay down the burden of the heart' was the relief of work being done.

Song of the Caravan Porters

Be happy, my soul, let go all worries,/Soon the place of your yearnings is reached
The town of palms, Bagamoyo./Far away, how was my heart aching
When I was thinking of you, you pearl/You place of happiness, Bagamoyo.
There the women wear their hair plaited/You can drink palm wine all year round
In the garden of love, Bagamoyo./The dhows arrive with streaming sails
And take aboard the treasures of Uleias/In the harbour of Bagamoyo.
Oh, what delight to see the ngomas (dances)/Where the girls are swaying in dance
At night in Bagamoyo./Be quiet my heart, all worries are gone
The drum beats and with rejoicing/We are reaching Bagamoyo.

Until the early 18th century the port was a couple of kilometres south, at Kaole. As a result of encroaching mangrove swamps or lack of good water, the settlement at Kaole was moved to Bagamoyo. Kaole, however, was not abandoned: it was selected as an administrative base by Sultan Said of Zanzibar, who appointed *liwalis* there to gather taxes. Sultan Barghash later resettled the area with Baluchi troops. It remains a place of great historic and spiritual importance, one of the first sites for formal Muslim worship in East Africa and the site of the earliest mosques.

Bagamoyo, on the other hand, is surrounded by fertile soil, and its proximity to the rice-producing areas of the Kindgani or Ruvu River Delta meant it was able to support a larger population than the port at Kaole. It became a major coastal port settled by Omani Arabs, their families and slaves during the 18th century. The settlers formed a formal financial alliance with the resident Zaramo and Doe tribes at the turn of the 19th century, when their new town came under threat from marauding Kamba tribes; the allies shared a desire to protect their trade.

The importance of Bagamoyo came from its position at the beginning and end of important caravan routes into the interior, which led to its development as a flourishing centre for commerce and culture. In 1880, the residents were estimated to be around 1,000, but the town continued to sustain a substantial population of travellers and traders, returning from and preparing to embark upon their caravan journeys. Bagamoyo achieved great prosperity, with a bustling marketplace that became a centre for the most expensive of all commodities – slaves and ivory – as well as continuing to trade less controversial goods such as dried fish and salt, copra and gum copal. The local boat-building centre continued to grow in size and

Getting There and Around

The **road** from Dar es Salaam is good for a while, following the New Bagamoyo road smoothly until it meets the Old Bagamoyo road – at least an hour of sandy potholes before you bump and jerk your way past the site of Kaole Ruins and into Bagamoyo town.

Buses and **minibuses** run regularly from Dar es Salaam, leaving the city from the Ubungu terminus. The journey takes at least 3hrs and tickets cost T.shs 1,000–3,000. Kaole is just off the Dar–Bagamoyo road, so you can get a ride on any of the buses plying this route to visit the ruins.

Bagamoyo itelf is small enough to explore **on foot**, though it is fun to hitch a ride with the cycle-taxis: for T.shs 500, you are swept off your feet and plonked on a surprisingly comfy seat over the rear wheel.

Tourist Information

The best place to hire the services of a guide is the **Mission Museum**. You may be offered a trip in a fishing dhow, but for safety's sake it is better to organize a boat trip through one of the resorts' more stable trip boats.

A Note on Security

There have been several reports of muggings in recent years, though locals say the establishment of a new district police authority in the town has done much to outlaw petty crime. Regardless, be aware when carrying valuables, and avoid the beach at night.

Where to Stay and Eat

Expensive

Lazy Lagoon Island, just south of Bagamoyo, 70km north of Dar (Foxes of Africa, PO Box 10270, Dar es Salaam, **t/f** (0741) 327706/ **t** (0744) 237422/**t** (0748) 237422, *fox@safari camps.info, fox@twiga.com, fox@bushlink. co.tz*. An excellent mid-priced beach lodge alternative for travellers seeking seclusion and peace off the mainland. This tiny private island is 8km long, forming a long-limbed spit that curves out into the sea, creating a lagoon in its wake. The resulting landscape offers a satisfyingly authentic beach idyll. The bandas are dhow-wood and arch into the bush like dhow sails. Decorated with a driftwood feel and softened with pleasing chintz, they are inspired ocean lookouts. At low tide the sea falls below the reef; water-babies need to be alert to the fact that activities are subject to the whims of the tides. Swimming is possible in the lagoon at all times, and there is a seawater swimming pool on the terrace. Guests cross the 2km to the island by motor boat. Trips and picnics can be arranged to nearby islands and sandbanks. Diving can be arranged, and the lodge has Lasers; sailing and fishing are enthusiastically punted by the lovely Kenyan couple living there as managers. The food is excellent. The Foxes can offer fly/drive packages to the island combining a safari at one of their numerous bush camps in the south.

Livingstone Club, Pink Shark Ltd, PO Box 105, Bagamoyo, **t** (023) 2440059/80, **f** (023) 2440104 , *info@livingstone.ws, www.living*

reputation, no doubt doing a tidy business in repairs too; the customs house was constantly busy and the town revelled in good food, clothes and conversation, as vivid tales of the caravan trails were endlessly recounted.

Bagamoyo also became a centre for religion. The French Catholic Fathers of the Holy Ghost negotiated with the resident Shomvi Arabs and Zaramo tribe for the right to land and establish a mission, a right that was granted by the *diwans* in 1868, after the intervention of the French Consul for Zanzibar and the Sultan. The first church was built, featuring in the lives and accounts of later great travellers passing through to pit their wits against the harsh realities of these northern caravan routes.

The Arabs, Zaramo and Doe worked out an understanding based on the premise that they were inhabiting land under the sultanate, governed and managed by a stone.ws. The smart and luxurious expanse of the Livingstone Club comes as quite a surprise in the low-key atmosphere of the town, but the central communal area, called 'the Club House', is spacious, opulent two-storey affair, well designed for relaxation, with a focus on the swimming pool and beach. Ten brick bungalows house 40 individual rooms with hand-crafted wooden beds equipped with mosquito nets and fans, air-conditioning and mini-bar. Activities at the resort include tennis, archery, mountain-biking and table football. The Pink Shark dive centre is well recommended, and also offers canoeing and windsurfing. You can also arrange a guide around Bagamoyo town at the club. The resort is particularly keen to attract the Italian charter market that has recently swamped Zanzibar in the summer months, and has an airstrip to transport passengers from the island, or from Dar. Full board an option.

Moderate

Badeco Beach Hotel, Bagamoyo Development Corperation, PO Box 261, Bagamoyo, **t** (023) 2440018, **f** (023) 2440075. Good lodgings in 12 thatched double rooms with a relaxed and friendly atmosphere. The restaurant produces simple but good lunches and the bar has a sound system; a good choice to eat with a sea view, fresh and good food. The central area is open thatch, overlooking the shoreline, with the sea pounding very close below at high tide. Air-conditioning extra.

Bagamoyo Beach Resort, PO Box 250, Bagamoyo, **t** (023) 2440083, **f** (023) 2440154. A quiet, charismatic and low-key place run by a French couple with a taste for good cooking and a passion for the local area. They have 18 well-worn air-conditioned bungalows with balconies and good-sized beds with mosquito nets, or a cheaper option of traditional open-air huts on the beach. The hotel can arrange a crèche on the beach under the supervision of the hotel babysitter, and will organize windsurfing, snorkelling, diving and excursions to Zanzibar or surrounding islets and reefs. Table tennis, volleyball and *pétanque* are among the entertainment. Trips can organized from here to the Ruvu River Delta or Bagamoyo town. Double bungalows with en-suite bathrooms and breakfast, or huts without breakfast on offer.

Cheap

Traveller's Lodge, PO Box 275, Bagamoyo, **t** (023) 2440077, **f** (023) 2440154. Excellent value for spacious semi-detached rooms with verandahs overlooking a palm-fringed beach. All have good nets and fans and are set in sweeping gardens. A small bar and shady restaurant ensure that guests have plenty of good food and drink; staff are friendly and the atmosphere is tranquil, although occasionally the bar is swamped by pert children from the International School. Self-contained doubles or camping.

Alpha Motel, on Rumumba Road, PO Box 85, Bagamoyo, **t** Bagamoyo 56 (call the operator on 900 and ask for Bagamoyo 56). The best choice for budget accommodation, near the market and the bus station, with a good outdoor area and clean rooms.

system of the sultans' government officials, the *diwan*, *liwali* and *akida*. This worked smoothly until 1888, when Sultan Said signed a treaty with the German East Africa Company, allowing it to collect customs duties on his behalf. Where the sultan's officials had always collected a few duties slightly haphazardly when a large fish was caught or a cow was slaughtered, the Germans devised a much grander system of taxation. When the German officials showed their allegiance to the sultan by cutting down his flagpole, the townspeople began to unite on an undercurrent of unrest. A crowd gathered to complain at the German East Africa Trading Company House at the end of 1888, troops were dispatched from the SS *Moewe*, and at least a hundred protesters died. The events were a precursor to a greater, organized rebellion, the Bushiri Uprising (*see* p.203).

As a result of Bushiri, a Major Herman von Wissman was posted to the northern coastal region as German Commissioner for East Africa, accompanied by a sizeable force of Zulu and Sudanese infantrymen. On his arrival von Wissman transformed the face of Old Bagamoyo, building a number of fortified houses from which to quell the rabble. A party of European travellers reached Bagamoyo in 1889 to find it renovated as a 'neat German colonial town', a succession of two-storey houses with tin roofs.

This rather fractious and exhausted caravan party included Henry Morton Stanley, his aide Jephson, and the eminent Jewish, German-born, Turkish-Egyptian-blooded, international intellectual – Emin Pasha. The Pasha had been 'rescued' by Stanley from a fine life of carousing and fun defending the British Empire as governor of Equatoria, now southern Sudan. Stanley's extremely arduous mission, beset with suffering in the jungles of Zaire, had been to 'bring back the Pasha' from Sudan on behalf of the British Government and Belgian King Leopold, but it took 11 months to persuade the Pasha to gather up his men, his families and his possessions and leave. Von Wissman greeted the group cordially, and arranged a triumphal salute and banquet, which took place in the new two-storey officers' mess. The welcome greatly cheered Emin Pasha, especially when it was compounded with a cable of congratulations from the new German Emperor, Kaiser Wilhelm II. His spirits rose amid an abundance of speeches and drinking, until the awful news was brought that Emin had toppled off the balcony and fallen through the palm-covered roof below, to land with concussion. When Emin awoke, he decided to rejoin his fellow countrymen, the Germans.

Bagamoyo Town

Bagamoyo is fun to explore on foot, searching for clues and relics to its unusual past. Plenty still remains to be seen, and there is an excellent **Mission Museum** in the Sisters' building at the centre of town to help fill in the gaps.

Remnants of the earliest days of Bagamoyo can be found just beyond the town centre on the road from Kaole Ruins. The **Old Fort** and **Provision House** (near the turning to Badeco Beach Hotel) were the first stone buildings built in the area, in 1860 during the Arab era, although they were later taken over by the Germans and became a police post until 1992. The Old Fort was originally used to hold slaves before they were shipped to Zanzibar, and rumours tell of an underground passage to the shore once used to herd the slaves to waiting boats. Further along the path, on the right-hand side, is a small **German Cemetery** contained within a neat coral wall enclosure. This is the site of about 20 graves of Germans killed during the Bushiri Uprising, the first serious uprising of Arabs and locals against the colonials, which took place in 1889–90 (*see* p.203). A German deed of freedom for a slave is reproduced on a tree that is rather oddly referred to as the German Hanging Place.

Carrying on down this route into town along India Street you pass **Liku House**, an old two-storey building on your left, its shady awning supported on slim iron columns around the central front door. This was the first colonial administrative centre, used for about a decade while the Boma was under construction between 1888 and 1897. The **Boma** is a short distance closer to the town centre, also on your left as you continue along India Street. It is an elaborate U-shaped two-storey construction

Bagamoyo Art School

Bagamoyo Art School, 'Nyumba ya sanaa', was built on its present site, south of the Old Fort towards the ruins at Kaole in 1981, but it has an important history dating back to 1962 and the early days of Independent government. The school was originally established at the behest of the Ministry of National Culture and Youth following a decision to form a national dance troupe that would make the nation proud and aware of its numerous cultural dances. In 1969, 20 young Tanzanian students completed a challenging four-year stint training as acrobats in the People's Republic of China, and ten musicians joined them to form the new National Acrobatics Group. In 1974 the National Drama Troupe was formed to encourage, develop and perform Swahili plays (or translations) around the country. The financial constraints were so great, however, that the dream never became reality: in 1979 the national troupes disbanded, and in 1981 the Bagamoyo Art School was developed at Bagamoyo as a more viable use of funds. The college now specializes in training students in performing arts, dance, drama, technical theatre, music and fine art. Each year 400 potential students who have passed their school exams at 16 undergo a week of auditions, from which 100 are shortlisted; 15 students are ultimately selected. The school is government-funded, but students must also work or find funds to pay an additional T.shs 75,000 each year.

Until 1991 the Government employed all graduates, but funding was stopped when the World Bank and IMF insisted on the retrenchment of the civil service – the Ministry of Culture was the first to suffer. Nevertheless a handful of excellent theatre companies established by former students continue to survive, such as the theatrical Lighters Art Group, the musical Amani Ensemble, and the CTG, community theatre group. The Art School provides excellent weekend entertainment with fortnightly shows and performances. These are usually advertised through the traditional Tanzanian method of advising the Primary Schools, but as a visitor you will probably do better to walk down to the Art School and enquire. The **Bagamoyo Arts Festival** runs through the last week of September, during which performances, exhibitions and workshops run from Wednesday to Sunday, with a $10 entrance fee charged. Contact Mr Juma Bakari, PO Box 32, Bagamoyo, **t** (023) 2440032, **f** (023) 2440154.

A well-funded media school is due to open near the Kaole ruins, with a mission to train a new generation of journalists schooled in the ways of the free press. Whether this will impact on the tourist's experience of the town remains to be seen; though it seems a possibility that passing travellers may find their day enlivened by the activities of junior hacks eagerly nosing their way to a story or two of the Wazungu!

crowned with crenellations, showing pointed arches on the first floor and a tunnel of curved arches below. This became the grand centre for administration after it was completed in 1897, and now continues to function as the headquarters for the district commissioner of Bagamoyo, in front of the Uhuru monument and bandstand.

Crossing Bomani Road and continuing north brings you to Customs Road, past the grand elevation of the **post office** at the intersection, with its beautifully carved door and smart painted verandah on the first floor. Next door, heading east down Customs

Road towards the coast, the old **fish market** has a number of heavy stone tables shaded from the heat of the sun. These are still used to sell and gut the day's catch, but, until the boats come in, the market provides a cool respite for locals – who while away the hottest hours playing games on the table tops.

Continuing eastwards brings you to the **Customs House**, on the right at the end of Customs Road. This was rented to the Germans by the eminent Sewa Hadji, who had it built in 1895. Sewa Hadji was the son of a merchant trader from the Hindu Kush, present-day Pakistan, and his family established successful trade posts in Zanzibar and Bagamoyo. He went on to prove himself as a philanthropist, donating the rather grand three-storey first **school** with filigree ironwork balustrades in the centre of town to be used for mixed-race education, and establishing the first **hospital**, which still stands as part of the present hospital building today. When he died in 1894, his will requested that posthumous earnings from his property be used to support the hospitals and help lepers. The **caravanserai** on Caravan Street would have once been the focal point for all activities at the centre of old Bagamoyo town, as it was here that all equipment and supplies for long excursions into the interior were prepared. The central building is two storeys high, the ground level flanked by wide verandahs to assemble supplies. These are then surrounded by a broad courtyard and a front row of single-storey outbuildings.

Christian Bagamoyo

The **First Church** was built in 1872 by Father Antoine Horner of the French Fathers of the Holy Ghost, after permission was granted by the Sultan of Zanzibar and French Consul in response to a growing outcry against the slave trade here. On the 24th of February two years later the body of Dr David Livingstone, who had journeyed to the interior fighting slavery, was brought here from Ujiji, more than 1,500km away, by his loyal assistants, Sisi and Chuma, before it was shipped home to its final resting place in Westminster Abbey. A small cemetery marks the graves of early missionaries, and a shrine erected by freed slaves in 1876 has the words *Saluminus Maria* picked out in flowers. Many of the famous explorers and missionaries who made their names travelling this land visited the First Church, including Burton, Speke and Grant. It is also near where a rather less admirable character, the German colonist Carl Peters, was rescued: he fell exhausted, starved and half-dead into the arms of a German mission here in 1884, following his preliminary madcap rush around the interior, raising his national flag and securing numerous 'treaties' on behalf of Bismarck.

The **Livingstone Memorial Church** was built in the late 20th century to commemorate the missionary and explorer who had played such a pivotal role in publicizing and so putting an end to the misery of slavery in this part of the world. The memorial church has a simple corrugated iron roof with arched windows and wooden benches within. A small path leads from the church to the sea shore, where a **green marble cross** commemorates the spot at which Father Antoine Horner first stepped ashore from Zanzibar in 1860, before building the first Christian church on the mainland.

Father Horner lived at the **Holy Ghost Mission**, shrouded in trees at the shady end of Mango Tree Drive. The mission was established in 1871, a statue of the Sacred Heart erected later in 1887. The mission museum in the Sisters' building shows a collection of exhibits that recount the unusual history of Bagamoyo. The mission was used to buy slaves their freedom; few attempted to return to their homes, often thousands of kilometres away, many settling instead in **Freedom Village**, close to the mission.

Wissman, the German Commissioner, constructed the **Dunka Block House** on Bunda Road at the end of the old caravan route in 1889 as a means of defence during the Bushiri Uprising. The flat mango and coral stone roof has an outdoor ladder up to it, from where troops could fire on rebels below. This marked the end or the beginning of the caravan route from Bagamoyo to Ujiji, 1,500km away on Lake Tanganyika.

Kaole Ruins

Five kilometres south of Bagamoyo are the ruins of the 13th- and 14th-century settlement of Kaole, the original town that was abandoned to make way for the new port. The ruins of two mosques and a series of about 30 tombs are on a sandy site occasionally shaded by an ancient palm; they are widely considered an especially sacred site, and the larger of the mosques is thought to date from the 3rd and 4th centuries, making it one of the earliest examples of Islam in Africa. The other mosque and tombs probably date from the later settlement, around 1300; similarities have been noted between this mosque and the Great Mosque at Kilwa, with which Kaole would have had strong trading connections. Kaole remains an important sacred site for Muslim prayers, and offerings are frequently left inside the tombs. A guide can sometimes be found on the site and will show you around, for a tip.

Ruvu River Delta

If you're suffering from nature withdrawal symptoms, natural interest can be found north of Bagamoyo on a boat trip into the Ruvu River Delta, where hippos wallow merrily and numerous resident birds including kingfishers, herons, ibises and bee-eaters, weavers, shrikes, migratory pelicans, flamingos and more can be spotted.

Saadani Game Reserve

Saadani Game Reserve is a curious little nature reserve stretching for 30km along the coast north of Bagamoyo, covering a small but unusual natural area within its 500 square kilometres. The wildlife population is varied, and includes small numbers of elephant, lion, leopard, buffalo, reedbuck, hartebeest, wildebeest and eland, as well as rare red duiker and an unusual subspecies of 'Roosevelt' sable antelope. Animals are not always in evidence, however, and it is worth considering Saadani simply as a good coastal region in which to get away from the hubbub of the city and enjoy some fresh air, with the potential of spotting some very wild wildlife. It is also possible to take a river safari along the crocodile- and hippo-infested Wami River, or just to enjoy the beaches, which are quite deserted but for the odd local fisherman lugging or selling his catch. There are good places to swim, although the shelving is shallow and the water may be murky on account of the nearby river swirling up sand sediment.

Getting There

Saadani Game Reserve is 4–5hrs' drive from Dar. Zanair, PO Box 2113, Zanzibar, t (024) 2233670, *www.zanair.com*, fly from Zanzibar and Dar to Saadani four times a week.

Where to Stay

A Tent With a View Safaris, PO Box 40525, Dar es Salaam, t (0741) 323318, f (022) 2151106, *tentview@intafrica.com, www.saadani.com*. Organizes safari stays at its Saadani Safari Lodge, 1km north of Saadani village, in bandas on the beach, full board for $95. Park fees $20 a day. Day-long boat safaris $35 per person, game drives $30, walking safaris $15. Solar-powered showers, a bar/library, 'rustic' restaurant and treehouse.

Otherwise, one **public campsite** is available, which can be booked through the **Saadani Game Post** in the village. Bring your supplies.

The southern boundaries of the park border on the river; to the north the shady canopies of Zaraninge Forest make for a cool region to explore on foot and discover a wealth of endemic plant and animal species. You can also visit a small turtle sanctuary here, established to save the green turtles that lay their eggs along this sandy shoreline, and see young rescued turtles swimming blissfully protected in their pond before they come of age and are released back into the perils of the sea.

The village of **Saadani** in the reserve is interesting to look around, searching for signs of its historic past: Saadani was once a fairly important trading port, yet another point at which slaves brought along the caravan routes were sold and shipped overseas; it developed into a fully fledged coastal town in the German era, resplendent with a colonial fortress. There is little tourism in the reserve, and few places to stay, but it but makes an easy overnight or weekend excursion from Dar es Salaam.

Pangani

Pangani is a sleepy little town on the banks of the Pangani (Ruvu) river, 66km south of Tanga. A ferry service shuttles to and fro between the ancient old town of **Bwemi**, with its crumbling mosques and Arabic houses on the south bank, and the quietly dilapidating **'new' town** where a number of grand ruins from all eras of rule act as reminders of a once more glorious past. The slow wooden motor boats wait at each shore until they are filled, and a loud general banter bubbles up between the gradually increasing cargo of colourfully swathed passengers. No one is hurrying, and time seems to drift as if on the lazy ebb and flow of the river and sea beyond. But there are signs of quiet industry at the old warehouses and factory sites along the river, where groups of men congregate to work on mending nets or gathering baskets of coconuts or husks. Beyond, clusters of single-storey Swahili houses are variously painted and coloured with signs, and women sit under shady verandahs in their coloured kangas selling bundles of delicious honeyed rice cake.

History

Little Pangani town may once have featured more impressively in the realms of history as the site of the ancient market town of Rhapta, described in the *Periplus of the Erythraean Sea*, the 1st-century Greek merchant's famous guide to the trade ports of the Indian Ocean. This book describes the trading port of Rhapta situated at a great river mouth, south of the 'Mountains of the Moon.' Although it is generally agreed that Rhapta must have been in what is now Tanzania, no remains have been identified; the likelihood is that the great river mouth has finally swallowed up the old town in silt deposits either here at Pangani, or further south near the great Rufiji River Delta. The old mosques on the southern banks of the Pangani river suggest that there was an early Muslim settlement here. Local stories tell of the ruins of a great palace that has since succumbed to the forces of nature, entwined in the roots of fig trees and crumbled to dust by the erosion of the cliff. Yet none of the graves and ruins of ancient Muslim settlements in villages around Pangani has been found to date from earlier than the 14th century.

It is known that Pangani was occupied by the Portuguese for a time, and that thereafter more Arab traders settled in the area throughout the 18th century. They traded with the local Zigua tribe, selling belts and beads in exchange for food. The Arabs and

Getting There and Around

By Air

Zanair, PO Box 2113, Zanzibar, t (024) 2233670, www.zanair.com, fly from Zanzibar and Dar to Pangani four times a week.

By Car

There are two **driving routes** to Pangani, both in fairly dismal condition. The best of these runs south from the junction at **Muheza** on the road from Dar es Salaam to Tanga, and the other heads directly south from **Tanga**. Amazingly, the route from Tanga can take up to 1½hrs, although it's only 66km.

The driving time from Arusha should be estimated at 6–8hrs; to cover the 377km from Dar es Salaam takes 5–6hrs.

By Bus

Minibuses shuttle regularly between Pangani and Muheza and cost c. T.shs 500. From here it is then possible to catch **buses** east into Tanga, northwest up to Mombo for Lushoto or south to Dar. The **bus** from Tanga to Pangani goes once a day and takes 2–4hrs, on account of the horrible state of the sand road that connects the two. The route is bumpy and the bus often extremely overcrowded, although if you can negotiate a window seat it is possible to appreciate the interesting scenic diversions along the way. It's worth preparing to spend at least a night in Pangani if you are relying on local transport.

Where to Stay and Eat

Since the arrival of very good choices of lodge, Pangani is on the up and up: an excellent destination away from the tourist hordes.

Expensive

The Tides, t (0741) 325812, thetides@habari. co.uk. Renowned as an immaculately run, friendly, family-owned lodge with great cooking and excellent hospitality. The lodge is on the quiet length of beach at Ushongo outside Pangani Town. The German owner is a highly experienced game fisherman, and offers thrilling sea-fishing trips. Guest stay along the beach in bandas cooled by whitewash and stone-flagged floors.

Emayani Beach Lodge, 'Kwa Joni', just over 10km south of Pangani town centre, on the opposite side of the river, PO Box 111, Pangani, t (027) 2501714/t (0742) 401199, emayani@habari.co.tz, www.emayanilodge. com. A curious and pleasant little lodge outside Pangani town, with 12 thatched bungalows on a stretch of sandy beach near the ocean. Fishing is available on the shore, or beyond the reef on small fishing boats, and picnics can be arranged for days out on the boats. The lodge also has 12 catamarans, windsurfers, and snorkelling equipment.

Travel to both lodges by boat can be arranged through David Pinkerton at Tinga Tinga Resort, on the Tanga–Pangani road.

the resident Zigua apparently developed a good mutual understanding and reliance on each other, and the town remained a quiet dhow port until the mid-1800s. The writings of explorer Richard Burton shed light on the town's economy in 1857, when he visited: he recorded with precision that the annual export trade was 35,000lbs (1,600kg) of ivory, 1,750lbs (800kg) of rhino horn and 160lbs (70kg) of hippo teeth, alongside a more mundane daily trade in mangrove poles and maize.

Around the time of Burton's visit, life in Pangani began to alter dramatically, as Shirazi settlers began to increase trade links along the Pangani river until the port developed into a major terminus for trade in ivory and slaves, the last stop for the overland caravan route from Lake Tanganyika. The Arab population developed a smart whitewashed town beneath the minaret of a central mosque, and the town was surrounded by successful tobacco and sugar plantations.

But, as with so many of Tanzania's coastal settlements, the major social upheaval came when the German colonists shouldered their way into command of the sultan's

Mashado Pangani River Lodge. Across the river from Pangani Town you will see this fabulously grand-looking palace on a steep cliff. The lodge is closed awaiting renovation.

Cheap
Tinga Tinga Resort, PO Box 13, **t** Pangani 22 (call the operator on 900 and ask for Pangani 22). A pleasant and friendly beach resort just north of Pangani, with unusually large and spacious hexagonal rooms with *makuti*-thatched roofs and windows on four sides creating an open and airy atmosphere. The helpful management can arrange excellent historical walking tours of Pangani for a very reasonable price, or otherwise make the most of their seafaring equipment. Snorkelling, fishing and exploring trips to Mziwe Island 8km away can be made in local *ngalawa* outriggers (T.shs 25,000 return trip for two) or by motorboat (around T.shs 66,000 for a 5hr charter for 10 passengers). River cruises up the Pangani river depart at around 4.30pm and return at about 6.30pm as the sun sets. Guests reach the confluence of the fresh river and sea, and watch pied kingfishers deftly darting for fish. It is a good resort for families, with a short flight of steps wending down to a private, wild beach. The hotel specializes in cooking local seafood, but the lack of a central dining area means that guests are encouraged to eat in the privacy of their own verandahs.

Pangani Beach Resort, also 3km from Pangani Town, PO Box 13, Pangani, **t** (027) 269031–3. A decent and relaxing spot on Mkoma Bay with a good sea view and swimming beach. Although there are just 10 self-contained rooms there is also a conference hall, and a good outdoor barbecue. The resort also runs 'safari' trips to Mziwe Island and local coconut plantations.

Pangadeco Hotel, Pangani, PO Box 76. The slightly wild and windy Pangadeco is a charismatic budget option, set among coconut palms beside a breezy stretch of beach with a vast bank of coconut husks to negotiate between the two. Rooms are very simple but quiet and clean, and equipped with mosquito nets and fans, but all eight share a couple of rather grim and ancient bathrooms. There is no restaurant as such, but staff will arrange for plates of good cooking to be brought to you in the bar area if required. The new **Stopover Bar** nearby has a little more atmosphere after sunset, when the music system is cranked into action.

River View Hotel, conveniently positioned even closer to the town centre on the harbour road. Cleaner, smarter and newer. The restaurant and bar area is pleasantly designed so that guests may enjoy their *nyama choma* (meat barbecues) and river views simultaneously. This little hotel has designed quaint stone-based beds, with three spacious doubles and seven little singles; all share bathrooms.

The Bushiri Uprising

In 1888 Pangani became the centre of Sheikh Bushiri ibn Salim al-Harthi's famous rebellion against German colonial rule. It all started when a young German official named Emil von Zewlewsky – known as 'Nyundo', the hammer, in Swahili – heavy-handedly threatened the sultan's officer, insulted the Muslim religion and 'sneered at the sultan'. To complete his insult, and make sure there was no dissension, Zewlewsky ordered 100 marines onto the beach to smash property and pull down the sultan's flag. Bushiri was incensed. He was a proud, aristocratic Arab, immaculately and expensively dressed, who vehemently held his own al-Harthi community to have every bit as much right to the land as the sultan, let alone his German lackeys. The sheikh organized a group of militant dissidents to battle the German occupiers, digging trenches and fortifying their houses, and blockading Zewlewsky in his headquarters. He raised a rampant army of about 20,000 wild tribesmen, Arabs, Muslims, non-Muslims, slave-traders and slaves.

There was evidently some confusion over the exact purpose of the army. While some thought they were defending the lands of the sultan, Bushiri himself had plans to prove himself as an independent warlord. The only unifying theme was an uncontrollable anger against the German colonists. His army was successful in keeping the foe from their beaches for a time, but the supremacy of Bismarck the Iron Chancellor was not to be mocked, and before long greater forces were dispatched from Europe.

The unrest was quelled by May 1889, when a new imperial commissioner, Major Herman von Wissman (he of Bagamoyo fame) was appointed in Pangani to placate the already slightly cooling rabble with the force of seven warships, extensive modern weaponry and numerous Sudanese and Zulu troops. By June Wissman had recaptured Saadani and then Pangani, and in December Bushiri too was captured as a result of the huge reward on his head; he and his collaborators were publicly executed. The German powers were victorious, and continued to stake their claim on Tanganyika territory with warfare and village-burning. Not all the Germans survived the attacks, however: young Zewlewsky 'the hammer' met his fate at the hands of Chief Mkwawa's Hehe warriors near Iringa.

domain on the mainland immediately after the death of Sultan Barghash in 1888, signing an agreement with his brother Khalifa. The Germans offered Arab residents positions in government in exchange for the fine stone houses that they had built in the area, and demanded that the Sultan's officials, the *akida*, levy a mass of European-style taxes on everything from burial and inheritance to property. Anyone who failed to comply was liable to have property confiscated; German occupiers and Arab residents were soon at loggerheads. Locals still recount that the early colonial methods of discipline relied heavily upon beatings and relate how one colonial administrator developed such a talent with his stick that he was even able to defend himself from the jaws of a man-eating lion – coming out the victor from a potentially fatal combat.

When the new British administration arrived after the First World War, the Pangani residents were still reeling from the violence of the German methods, and welcomed the relatively less draconian British regime. But, although the British did attempt to communicate more with the local people and were to a certain degree more under-standing, they continued to rely on the local officials created by the Germans, and enforced tax payments just as strictly – with a penalty of imprisonment on those who did not pay. The British era did, however, also see continued growth in schools and education, free to all who wished to attend, with the crucial caveat that those who took advantage of it should follow the Christian religion. The divide between Muslims and Christians is quite even in this region – more so than elsewhere – as a result of the families' and tribes' receptive attitude to education in exchange for religion.

The old people of Pangani remember the latter years of the colonial era with fond-ness as a time good for business, with wealth created by the *mkonge* (sisal) plantations. Four large estates around Pangani – at Sakura, Kibinda, Mwera and Bushiri – thrived at this time, and continued to do so for a while after Independence. As the price for sisal began to drop on the world market and salaries were reduced, some people began despondently wishing for a return of the old protectorate. Coconut plantations were planted as the sisal harvests lost their value. They were profitable for a while, but the trees have aged and no one had the foresight to replace them in time, so the crops decreased considerably. There is now little work for Pangani locals beyond a basic subsistence on coconut, fish and small-scale seasonal crops. Employment levels have officially dropped to 10 per cent, compared with nearly 100 per cent under British rule – at least as the nostalgics remember it. Many young people from Pangani are forced to move away to Arusha or Dar es Salaam for work.

Sightseeing in Pangani Town

Pangani is a quiet but pleasant town to explore on foot, with the remnants of old Arabic and colonial buildings still in evidence on the northern bank and considerably older, very early mosques on the southern bank, in the old town. The old **German Boma** still stands north of a very battered and sadly dishevelled **Uhuru Monument**, situated near the ferry port; the old **Customs House** is becoming dilapidated just a few paces further west.

Guided walking tours of Pangani can be arranged with the Pangani District Cultural Office. The tours take about two hours, and cost very little for groups of one to six people, payable to the guide. Boats can also be hired for trips up and down the river or out to Mziwe Island; ask for Mr Ramadan Msada, a fisherman who speaks good English, at the Tinga Tinga Resort, the River View Hotel or the Pangadeco Hotel.

Tanga

The wide and shady avenues of Tanga are the first clue to its past. It is evident within minutes of arrival that Tanga was once a thriving colonial and industrial centre, complete with strict town-planning, immaculate roads, a fine-looking hospital, police posts and an imposing gaol. But the huge steel hulks of old ships have now turned to rust in the old harbour, and the paving stones are loose and sporadi-cally sprouting weeds. These are signs of the misfortune that has befallen the once fine town that thrived here, but which has since suffered harsh economic decline.

Getting There

By Air

Coastal Travels, 107 Upanga Road, PO Box 3052, Dar es Salaam, t (022) 2117959–60, *aviation@coastal.cc*, *www.coastal.cc*, fly from Dar to Tanga daily at 2pm arriving 3.35pm, at a cost of $100 per person each way.

By Bus

Tanga is well served by regular buses from **Dar es Salaam**, which take 4–6hrs, on good roads all the way, and cost T.shs 3,500. Buses also run to **Lushoto**, taking 3hrs, for T.shs 2,500, and to **Moshi**, which is a 5hr trip.

The bus to **Pangani** takes almost as long, 4–5hrs, for T.shs 800, although it is only 60km away, as the road is so bad, so it's not really viable to visit Pangani from Tanga as a day trip.

Routes to **Arusha** and on can be planned via **Chalinze**, 245km west of Tanga at the junction of the Tanga–Dar/Dar–Arusha road, through which buses run regularly – but it is not recommended to get stuck there overnight.

By Train

Although the station at Tanga is still in good working order, there are **no passenger trains**.

By Boat

Sepideh ferries stop at Tanga en route to and from Mombasa, Pemba, Zanzibar and Dar es Salaam. Contact **Mega-Speed liners** or their Tanga agents, **Coco Travel and Tours**, t (027) 244131/244332, *cocotravel@cats-net.com*.

Getting Around

Tanga is largely navigable on **foot**, although this can mean covering a fair old distance if you are keen to explore the town centre, the Ras Kazone peninsula and beyond. It is worth hiring a **bicycle**, especially if you are energetic enough to cover the distance to Amboni Caves. Bikes can be rented for T.shs 100–200 per hour from the roundabout between the bus stand and the train station on Taifa Road.

Tourist Information

There is a handy **Communications Building** that remains open for telephone calls and fax services long after the **post office** has closed, tucked away in a quiet back street towards the harbour along Usambara Street, on the left-hand side past the post office.

Where to Stay

Moderate

Mkonge Hotel, on Bomba Road, PO Box 1544, t (027) 2643440, *bushtrek@tanzanet.com*. The smarter places to stay in Tanga have always been around Ras Kazone peninsula, which is still the site of the nicest old colonial place, the Mkonge Hotel. It is now fairly ancient but remains a solidly built structure, with wide gardens and breezy terraces perfectly designed for the enjoyment of sundowners overlooking the ocean. Most of the old leather armchairs and original décor have been left intact, but the new management also pays attention to food and service. Rooms are along long corridors; it is worth requesting one with views of the gardens and sea. There is a good restaurant with a decent *à la carte* menu to suit all tastes. Prices include breakfast, air-conditioning and telephone, with upgrades to deluxe 'double special' (including a fridge, flowers and a fruit basket) possible for an extra $5.

Cheap

Ocean View Breeze, PO Box 2344, t (027) 2643441. The best-value, best-quality option, in a great location at the town centre, is the Ocean View Breeze, which still has an atmosphere of fresh newness despite opening more than two years ago. Rooms

Tanga hardly feels large enough to classify as Tanzania's third-largest city, or its second most important port, but it is extensive enough to have developed several distinct areas. Row upon row of small Swahili houses and shops extend southwards behind the railway line, reminiscent of purpose-built workers' accommodation dating have balconies overlooking the streets to the sea and all have smart furnishings, clean self-contained bathrooms with working hot showers, and security on every floor. Staff are friendly and the hotel has a surprisingly warm atmosphere for its size. Popular but quite tiny restaurant. Excellent value.

Marina Hotel, PO Box 1028, Tanga t (027) 2644362. Marina Hotel has all the character of age and old stone, and a pleasantly relaxed and sunny atmosphere in its central whitewashed courtyard, which also acts as the dining room and bar. Thirty rooms range around the two storeys, all clean although quite dark, with fine sheets and comfortable-looking beds. Doubles with a fan are very good value; you pay more for air-conditioning or a suite.

Hotel Kola, Indian Street, Tanga, t (027) 2644206. Another fairly good and reasonably priced choice at the centre of town, with an atmosphere a little more clinical and business-like than either of those above. The restaurant is endearingly pink but short on window space. The menu is reliable and decent. Doubles with private bathroom, air-conditioning or a fan.

Raskazone Hotel, PO Box 5101, Tanga, t (027) 2643897. Back out at the eastern end of town is a small and unusually charming establishment tucked away on a quiet residential backstreet, with very friendly Chagga owners who keep it immaculately neat. The gardens are weirdly reminiscent of a crazy golf course, and the external décor owes much to the proliferation of bright enamel house paints, while the hotel itself has the feel of a rambling private house, all covered in creepers. Individual *makuti* thatch umbrellas cover the private seating areas set aside for guests at the restaurant or bar. The private car park at the back of the hotel provides safe parking. There are 10 rooms, each different and priced accordingly, from simple doubles with a fan to doubles with air-conditioning, or an executive suite,

which is rather a cosy old sitting room with sofas and TV, complete with exercise bike!

Panori Hotel, PO Box 672, Tanga, t (027) 264 6044, f (027) 2647425. Similar but in a more European style, welcoming, comfortable and safe, particularly suitable for families with children. Its location some distance from the town centre on the Ras Kazone peninsula makes this a good choice if you have some form of private transport, be it motor- or pedal-powered, or you can resign yourself to taxi rides. All rooms have air-conditioning and en-suite bathrooms, but some are nicer than others, depending on whether they are in the new wing or the old wing. Some of the older rooms have a better situation, but are damp and due for renovation. The restaurant has an extremely good reputation, and is said to provide the best food in Tanga. Rooms in the new wing cost more.

Inn by the Sea, next door to the Mkonge Hotel and closer to town, t (053) 2644613. A far simpler affair, which feels more like a beach resort, with rows of wooden self-contained bungalows with air-conditioning, lined up beneath a long verandah. There is a basic but pleasant open-air restaurant, where all food must be ordered in advance. Doubles with or without air-conditioning. B&B.

New Era Guesthouse, to the east of Tanga town centre, just beyond Hospital Road, PO Box 1430, t (027) 2643466, f (027) 2647523. A curious, shambling old house, it certainly has character, and an effusive management with a flair for artistic expression. The proprietress is an enthusiastic artist, and many of her paintings feature in the numerous very differently proportioned and variously comfortable rooms. There is space to relax outside, although the whole is pervaded by a sense of better days gone by. A range of rooms from self-contained with air-conditioning or fan to just a bed.

Hotel Bandorini, close to the town centre on the harbour front. An old favourite with backpackers which has no doubt seen better

from the Industrial Revolution, and the thousands of people who live here are a mix of the numerous main regional tribes, with many others besides. Exploring the town a little further brings you to the looping coastal road around the peninsula of Ras days since it was built during the German era more than 100 years ago. The extremely affable proprietor, Mr Tushar Patel, born in Tanga in 1936, extends a good hand of hospitality and can provide welcome support and advice on transport problems. This makes up for an unusual atmosphere at the hotel, which is better described as the old boys' house. Nevertheless it is worth a visit, even if only for the great buffet suppers served at the outdoor terrace restaurant, which is spacious and comfortable and very good value for healthy appetites. Rooms share bathrooms. Breakfast included.

Planters Inn, right in the centre of town on Sokoine Street, **t** (027) 2647819. This other old backpackers' favourite feels as though it's really had its day: it's an ancient haunt with creaking old wooden verandahs that feel as though they might give way beneath you at any moment, and the rooms, although cheap, are dark, dirty and entirely unappealing. There is supposedly cold water available, but it's not always in evidence. Nevertheless, the bar is definitely worth a visit, like a trip back in time. A corner cupboard in the bar contains an impressive collection of miniature tipples that look as if they've been there for ever, surprisingly preserved considering the wild history of the place, which came into its own just after the First World War as the favourite gambling haunt of the Greek sisal planters.

Asad Hotel, Barabarakumi Street, PO Box 2004, Tanga. The bus station is set back behind the town in the mainly Swahili quarters, and if you arrive late at night it may not be worth negotiating the distance to the town centre unless you are with a reliable guide. Basic but passable and fairly inexpensive rooms can be found very close at hand here at the Asad. There is an adjoining restaurant with a limited menu (not much choice for vegetarians) and dubious satellite TV channels to entertain you. Self-contained doubles with fan.

Eating Out

Cheap
Patwas, opposite the BP station. Sells glasses of the best mango lassi in the world in a cool, spacious and leafy restaurant. They also serve up fantastic samosas and mouth-watering curries at affordable prices.

Food Palace, on Sokoine (Market) Street, near Hotel Kola Prieto. Well worth seeking out, especially if you have worked up an appetite with your excursions. Portions are huge, but all fine and fresh. Extremely good Indian cuisine with plenty of welcome choice for vegetarians. There is a barbecue outside on some nights. *Open all day; closed Mon eves and throughout Ramadan.*

Kingfish Restaurant, in the centre of town on Independence Avenue. Serves decent good-value meals, especially fish, all day.

Hotel Bandorini. Mr Tushar Patel can also arrange for a delicious feast to be prepared and served on the terrace outside, over-looking the sea, for a reasonable price.

Tawakal Café, on Taifa Road. An excellent spot at any time of day, with good fresh juices, cornbreads and coffee.

Entertainment and Nightlife

There are a number of popular live music bands or disco nights in Tanga.

Casa Chica Club (sometimes written 'Lakasachika'), on Independence Avenue is the most regular and reliable venue. There is a disco or live session on Wednesdays, Fridays, Saturdays and Sundays, with sounds ranging from Congolese taped music to the popular band 'Black Star' or 'Nyuta Nyeusi' *taarab* music. Entrance around T.shs 2,000.

Mkonge Hotel, (*see* p.205). Holds a disco at weekends.

Kazone. Here a number of large, detached residential houses sit sleepily in the sunshine, soaking up a salty air of bygone beachside elegance that the waterfront with its sailing and swimming clubs and grand old colonial-era hotels once nurtured.

History

When the British explorer Richard Burton visited the settlement of Tanga in 1857 he described a collection of 'thatch pent-roofed huts, built upon a bank overlooking the sea'. He estimated the local population to be 4–5,000 people, including 15 Baluchis and 20 Indian merchants, all held in check by the sultan's troops under his appointed *wali*, or governor. When the German East Africa Company came here in 1888, after persuading the sultan to lease it a 16km-wide strip along the coast of Tanzania, Tanga was a small fishing village that sustained a certain amount of trade with Bagamoyo. The town also sent annual caravans inland to the Usambara and Pare Mountains, to Kilimanjaro and into the Maasai regions to return laden with ivory for sale. A handful of Omani residents chose a quieter life here, but in essence this was a rural region occupied by a number of distinct tribes, including the Digo people and the Bondei, whose name means 'of the valley' – squeezed south from Kenya by their neighbours – and the Shambaa and Pare people from nearby. Another migrant group was the Segeju, who are less in evidence today as a result of intermarriage, but who built a number of protective walled enclosures around the Tanga region during the 19th century as a defence against the Maasai. Some of these have angled spy-holes similar to those at the Gereza at Kilwa and Fort Jesus in Mombasa, which may indicate Arab influences in design and construction. The Zigua people, perhaps the original people of the Tanga region, stuck to their turf just south of Tanga and developed a fearsome reputation. A large tribe, they took many wives and remained resistant to mission- aries bartering education for the Christian faith.

All these tribes were adept at the commercial exchange of the caravan routes, but none was prepared for the German port that sprang up at the end of the 19th century. The colonial power began developing Tanga's small harbour to accommodate steamers after the port of Bagamoyo proved too shallow, and in 1893 completed a Moshi–Tanga railway line. In the same year the first school in Tanzania was built and run, initially by the German Colonial Society, later by the German administration, who gained a reputation for rigorous discipline – brutally meted out with canes and chains – but were evidently successful in their mission to organize a structure of education that focused on learning the German language, reading, writing and craft skills.

The fertile lands around Tanga and up into the Usambara Mountains were soon profitably cultivated. Extensive sisal plantations were laid out, but progress was thwarted by the First World War, in which Tanga was the site of one of the most infamous military blunders in East Africa. Thousands of Allied troops were dispatched from boats for a surprise attack on the Germans along the Tanga coastline, but the surprise was theirs when they arrived to find the dense mangroves along the beaches impenetrable, and German troops fully prepared for their arrival. They were repulsed further by an aggressive swarm of disturbed bees and were forced to abandon crucial supplies and weapons in retreat. An estimated 800 men died, with almost as many injured in various ways. This episode and other events of the war on Tanzanian soil are excellently if imaginatively recounted in William Boyd's novel, *An Ice-Cream War*.

In the years following the war, the population of Tanga was altered as the German settlers moved away and the sisal plantations were taken over by a contingent of feisty Greek farmers. The Greeks developed a wild reputation for popular gambling sessions during which entire estates might change hands, and for a while Tanga was renowned throughout Tanzania as a party town. The planters enjoyed halcyon days, garnering enormous prosperity from their sisal crops until the mid-1950s, when sisal prices crashed. The crop has never really recovered as a result of the proliferation of manufactured fibres, although it is still a worthwhile business for many of the smaller, recently privatized farms. In quieter times today, the population of Tanga is largely dependent on local dhow trade with the Tanzanian and Kenyan coast, and the cement and brick factories that are situated just west of the town.

Sightseeing in Tanga Town

The **Tanga Ropeworks** near the post office at the centre of town has examples of the various ropes made from sisal, once the lifeline for the town's prosperity. The ropeworks is opposite the old German-built court house, which remains an imposing structure that still administers law and order.

A walk along Independence Avenue, parallel to the sea front, leads past the clock tower erected in 1961, towards the **library**, a substantial building in front of a pleasant arched courtyard, which was opened by the British Governor Sir Edward Twining in the mid-1950s. Just west of the library you come to the old **boma** – a large, heavy and imposing structure situated in a prime position overlooking the old harbour. A more curious and attractive legacy of this colonial era can be found a couple of blocks directly south, where the quaint and seemingly entirely unchanged **railway station** seems to have been lifted straight from a picturebook of European country stations a century ago. Sadly this rail route is no longer functioning for passengers. To get here, walk through **Uhuru Park** and follow Station Road south. **Tanga School** is situated on the eastern aspect of the park.

Amboni Caves

Just 8km north of Tanga, Amboni Caves are an exciting diversion if you have a little time to spend in Tanga; they are a protected portion of more than 207km of limestone caves dating from the Jurassic age, which have inspired a number of mystic legends. Local people have traditionally regarded the formation as being supernatural, and call them *Mzimu wa Mabavu*, the 'dwelling of a powerful deity'. People come from all the surrounding areas to offer prayers and sacrifices, seeking cures from sickness, suffering or lack of fertility, and in certain areas of the caves you will find dusty bottles of oil, perfumes and charred incense. The caves proved a formidable sanctuary for

Getting There

The simplest way to reach the caves is to take a **taxi** from the town centre and ask the driver to wait. A return trip from town should cost around $5.

There are occasional **dala-dalas** running this rural coastal road from the Uhuru Park terminus, which are considerably cheaper but only advisable if you can spare most of your day to wait. Most run to Amboni Village, but some might be persuaded to go all the way to Kiomoni Village, which is closest to the caves.

Alternatively, it might be worth negotiating for a **bicycle** to rent from the roundabout in Tanga (*see* p.205) or around the market.

individuals during the Mau Mau rebellion in Kenya, particularly the now-legendary Elias Samuel Oselloetango, who continually thwarted British attempts to capture him. This evasive hero – or anti-hero, depending on your point of view – used the caves to hide with Paulo Hamisi between 1952 and 1956, and during those years managed to spread all manner of tales about his exploits vanishing from prison cells and living in this underground maze. An unappealing description of his scarred, dark, heavy complexion and lock of curly hair hanging low on his forehead brings the Wild-West-style legend to life on yellowing 'wanted' posters hanging in the guide's hut.

It is possible to take a guided tour through many of the caves at Amboni, now under the protection of the Antiquities Act of 1964. The exceptional natural rock formations are impressive, but do not expect more elucidation from the 'guided tour' than a man with a torch leading you through the maze and pointing out odd stalactite formations that seem to have the appearance of the Virgin Mary, a roaring lion, or finally 'Kilimanjaro', while you are standing at the bottom of a very steep pile of rocks, from the top of which the path continues. Nevertheless, it is absolutely imperative to take a guide, as there have been fatalities when individuals have gone in alone. The tour is great fun, but not recommended for claustrophobes, vertigo-sufferers, or anyone nervous about climbing, squeezing and scrambling through often quite small dark spaces. The honeycomb cave maze is liberally inhabited by bats and absolutely unlit.

The caves are around 4km south of **Galamos Sulphur Springs**, a naturally warm spring that was discovered by a Greek sisal plantation owner called Galamos. These are said to be curative, especially for skin complaints and arthritis, but bathing possibilities are not very attractive since the old bathing house has fallen into disrepair.

Tongoni Ruins

Near the village of Tongoni, 20km south of Tanga off the Tanga–Pangani road, are the ruins of a much older settlement of the same name that date from the 13th to 16th centuries, as well as mosques, tombs and defensive walls from the 18th and 19th centuries; many of these older sites are now thickly overgrown, and access to many is difficult or impossible. *Tongoni* is a Swahili term meaning 'place of ruins', or more literally 'forsaken place', although it is said that earlier inhabitants called the place *Sitahabu*, meaning 'better here than there'. These were ancestors of some present-day inhabitants of Tongoni, remembered as Shirazi migrants from Kilwa who found the deserted ruins and occupied the houses. Perhaps a few generations passed before the earlier alternative was forgotten and their home was renamed Tongoni.

Remains of the most ancient settlement at Tongoni are mainly found to the north and east of the ruined large central mosque and tombs, which notably include a number of 14th- to 15th-century pillar tombs. The pillars have scalloped indentations that would have once been decorated with glazed porcelain saucers, as seen at the domed mosque at Kilwa, but none of these pieces remain intact. Many have extensive frieze work carved around. A plain, double walled tomb near a fallen pillar tomb that rests on the east wall is considered significantly spiritual, as local tradition tells how this is the tomb of a Sharif, a descendant of Prophet Mohammed. People still bring offerings here, especially women hoping for children.

Dar es Salaam

15

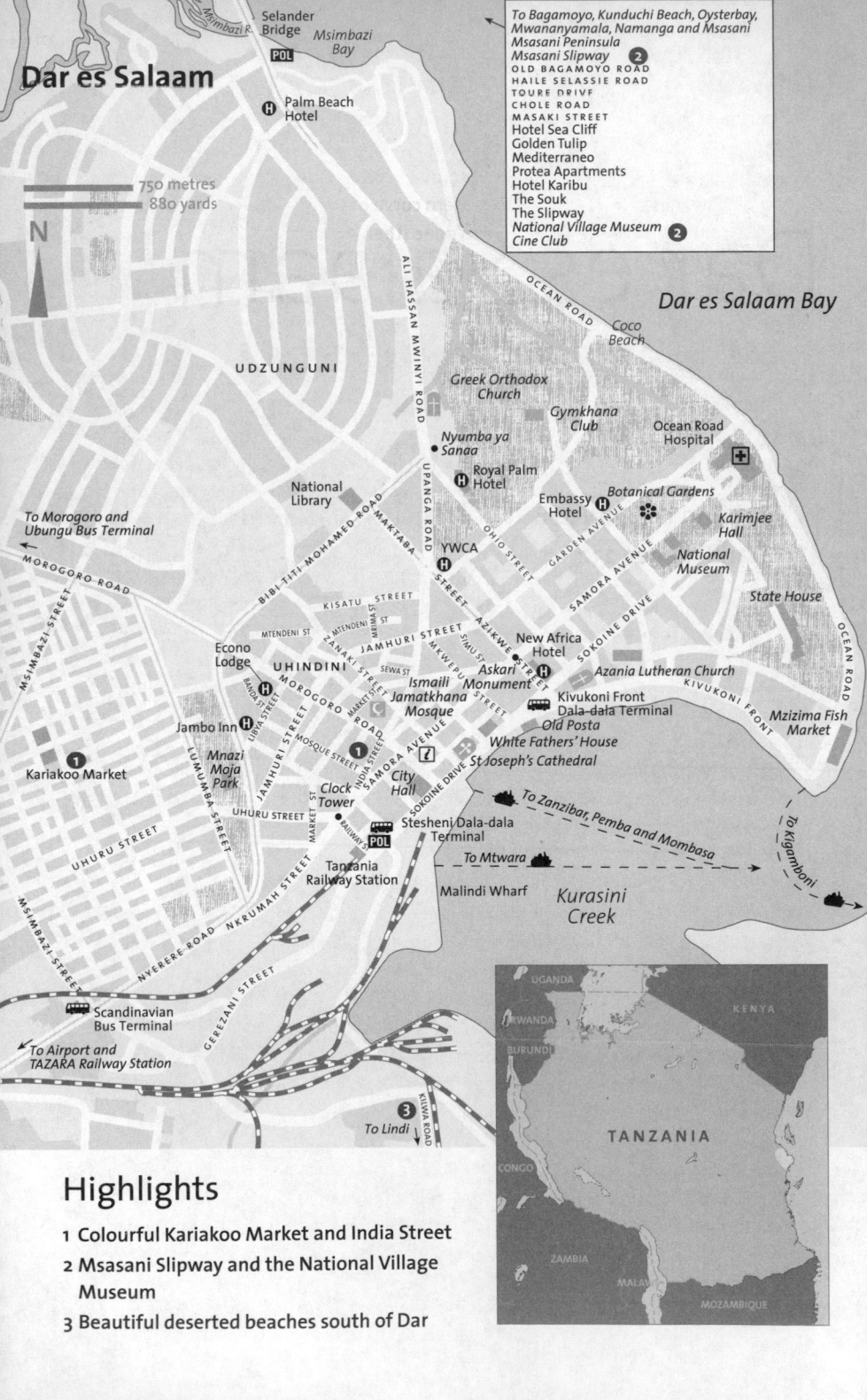

Dar es Salaam

Selander Bridge
POL
Msimbazi Bay
Msimbazi R.

To Bagamoyo, Kunduchi Beach, Oysterbay,
Mwananyamala, Namanga and Msasani
Msasani Peninsula
Msasani Slipway ②
OLD BAGAMOYO ROAD
HAILE SELASSIE ROAD
TOURE DRIVE
CHOLE ROAD
MASAKI STREET
Hotel Sea Cliff
Golden Tulip
Mediterraneo
Protea Apartments
Hotel Karibu
The Souk
The Slipway
National Village Museum ②
Cine Club

Palm Beach Hotel

750 metres
880 yards

N

UDZUNGUNI

OCEAN ROAD

Dar es Salaam Bay

Coco Beach

Greek Orthodox Church

Gymkhana Club

Ocean Road Hospital

Nyumba ya Sanaa

Royal Palm Hotel

Embassy Hotel

Botanical Gardens

Karimjee Hall

National Library

To Morogoro and
Ubungu Bus Terminal

MOROGORO ROAD

ALI HASSAN MWINYI ROAD

UPANGA ROAD

OHIO STREET

GARDEN AVENUE

YWCA

SAMORA AVENUE

National Museum

State House

BIBI TITI MOHAMED ROAD

MAKTABA

KISATU STREET

MTENDENI ST

MTENDENI ST

MIRAMBO ST

JAMHURI STREET

ZANAKI STREET

SEWA ST

MARKET STREET

SINU ST

MKWEPU STREET

AZIKWE STREET

New Africa Hotel

Askari Monument

SOKOINE DRIVE

Azania Lutheran Church

KIVUKONI FRONT

MSIMBAZI STREET

Econo Lodge

UHINDINI

MOROGORO ROAD

MOSQUE STREET

BANDA ST

LIBYA ST

Ismaili Jamatkhana Mosque

Kivukoni Front
Dala-dala Terminal

Old Posta

White Fathers' House

St Joseph's Cathedral

Mzizima Fish Market

Jambo Inn

Mnazi Moja Park

LUMUMBA STREET

JAMHURI STREET

INDIA STREET

SAMORA AVENUE

①

City Hall

Clock Tower

SOKOINE DRIVE

To Zanzibar, Pemba and Mombasa

Kariakoo Market ①

UHURU STREET

UHURU STREET

MARKET ST

RAILWAY ST

POL

Stesheni Dala-dala Terminal

To Mtwara

To Kigamboni

Tanzania Railway Station

Malindi Wharf

Kurasini Creek

MSIMBAZI STREET

NYERERE ROAD

NKRUMAH STREET

GEREZANI STREET

KILWA ROAD

Scandinavian Bus Terminal

To Airport and
TAZARA Railway Station

To Lindi ③

TANZANIA

UGANDA
RWANDA
BURUNDI
CONGO
ZAMBIA
KENYA
MALAWI
MOZAMBIQUE

Highlights

1 Colourful Kariakoo Market and India Street

2 Msasani Slipway and the National Village Museum

3 Beautiful deserted beaches south of Dar

Orientation

The centre of Dar es Salaam is essentially contained within a semi-circular area around the old harbour to the southeast. The two main roads in the city centre are the roughly northeast–southwest axis **Samora Avenue**, and **Sokoine Drive**, which runs parallel to it, branching off at the eastern curve of the harbour into **Kivukoni Front**. During the colonial years Samora Avenue (then Acacia Avenue) was the most fashionable shopping street; it remains a popular retail area, and a brief walk or drive along It shows plenty of the charismatic architectural features of its past. The area around it, Sokoine Drive (formerly City Drive) and Kivukoni Front (once known as Azania Front) is today the most reliable area of town for currency transactions, tourist information and communication centres, such as phones and Internet cafés.

Bibi Titi Mohamed Road, which leads into **Ali Hassan Mwinyi Road**, effectively bypasses the city centre from the airport to the west and the **TAZARA train station** in the south to the **Msasani Peninsula** across **Selander Bridge** to the north. **Ocean Road** follows the coast, from where Kivukoni Front reaches the eastern end of the harbour, north along the coast to where It joins up with Ali Hassan Mwinyi Road again just before the bridge.

Dar es Salaam is reinventing itself. This coastal capital is emerging as a city that is cosmopolitan and even enjoyable to explore. It remains at heart a bustling Swahili market town, yet is a centre of trade and commerce attracting ambitious Africans from all of Tanzania and its neighbouring countries, and international communities who come to this port for all manner of business. Here is the hub of communication in Tanzania, a far cry from the lifestyle and experiences of the rural majority. Residents of the metropolis are known as *mbongo* – 'person with brains' – brains being a requisite for survival amid the populous chaos at the heart of this town. But for city-lovers Dar has plenty of quirks, and a reasonably loping East African pace anywhere beyond its hectic centre. Its Indian Ocean location offers realms of respite: a wild coastline and sea breeze, easy excursions and seaside accommodation.

The city physically reflects the paradox of Indian Ocean calm and enterprise. High-rise residential buildings and gleaming office blocks have grown up around the city centre and certain suburban areas, and yet the old character of its periodically Arabic, German and British colonial and African past is still much in evidence in the low-rise red-tiled roofs on the main streets and the *makuti*-thatched suburbs. Laden ocean-going tankers cruise across the horizon, and in their wake Arab dhows skim the waves and dock on shores green with mangroves and palms.

Despite confusion over the role of Dar es Salaam – officially demoted from capital city in 1973, but still awaiting the actual transfer of government to Dodoma – it remains the most urbanized centre of Tanzania and its commercial capital, so acts as a good mirror of the country's economic state. The range of new businesses, cafés, restaurants and products now available reflects the success of the market reforms urgently introduced in 1986. Compare Dar today with the dilapidated streets and empty shops that reflected the demoralizing poverty of Nyerere's well-intentioned socialism and its disastrous economic policies until well into the early 1990s;

Getting There

By Air

Dar es Salaam is Tanzania's most popular point of entry and departure. The airport, PO Box 543, Dar es Salaam, t (022) 2242111, is the country's busiest, and operates a number of scheduled flights to and from Europe and other African countries. As there are no direct flights from the United States, travellers from there will have to connect in Europe or fly down to Johannesburg and then fly north again – SAA flies to Dar es Salaam daily.

The domestic terminal is Terminal One and the international terminal less than 1km away Terminal Two. Be aware that some internal flights (notably Precision Air) leave from the international terminal. Taxis are always available to shuttle passengers between the two.

International Airline Offices

Emirates, Haidery Plaza, A.H. Mwinyi Road, t (022) 2116100–3/2116095/2116792. Flies daily to and from Dubai.

British Airways, based at the Royal Palm Hotel, Ohio Street, PO Box 2439, Dar es Salaam, t (022) 2113820–2, f (022) 2112629, www.ba. com. London to Dar es Salaam on Mon, Thurs and Sat nights, arriving next morning and returning the following day in the morning.

Ethiopian Airlines, TDFL Building, between Ohio Street and A.H. Mwinyi Road, PO Box 3187, Dar es Salaam, t (022) 2117063–5. Flies every day, except Friday, from Addis.

KLM, Peugeot House, intersection of Bibi Titi Mohamed Road and A.H. Mwinyi Road, PO Box 3804, Dar es Salaam, t (022) 2113336–7, f (022) 2116492, klmdaressalaam@intafrica. com. Nightly direct from Amsterdam, via Kilimanjaro International Airport.

Kenya Airways, Peugeot House, intersection of Bibi Titi Mohamed Road and A.H. Mwinyi Road, t (022) 2119376–7. Flies twice daily from Nairobi to Dar es Salaam and Zanzibar.

Swiss, Luther House, Sokoine Drive, PO Box 2109, Dar es Salaam, t (022) 2118870. Three flights a week from Zurich.

Air France, Peugeot House, at the intersection of Bibi Titi Mohamed Road and A.H. Mwinyi Road, t (022) 2116443/2118779.

Air India, Bibi Titi Mohamed Road, opposite Peugeot House, t (022) 2152642–4.

Air Zimbabwe, Avalon House, 1st Floor, Zanaki Street, t (022) 2123526/2121747.

South African Airways (SAA), Raha Towers Building, PO Box 5182, Dar es Salaam, t (022) 2220058, f (022) 2244031, www.flysaa.com.

Domestic Airline Offices

Coastal Travels, 107 Upanga Road, PO Box 3052, Dar es Salaam, t (022) 2117959–60, f (022) 2118647/2117985, aviation@coastal.cc, www. coastal.cc. Also has an information desk at Domestic Terminal One, t (022) 2843293/ t (0741) 325673, f (022) 2843033. The premier national carrier. Operates a scheduled and charter service to most tourist destinations, especially national parks, and can assist with last-minute safari itineraries.

Air Tanzania, ATC House, corner of Ohio Street and Garden Avenue, PO Box 543, Dar es Salaam, t (022) 2110245–8, f (022) 2113114. ATC has improved immeasurably, and is now a reliable choice for direct flights to less obvious destinations. It cannot compare with the diversity and reliability of Coastal.

Precision Air, NIC HDQ Building, Samora Av/Pamba Rd, Dar es Salaam, t (022) 212 1718, pwdar@africaonline.co.tz, www.precision airtz.com. Scheduled flights to most destinations between central and northern Tanzania, and to Mafia Island; also planes available for charter.

A number of companies run charter flights and have offices in the domestic terminal.

Skytours, Domestic Terminal, Dar Airport, PO Box 2161, Dar es Salaam, t (022) 2117730/ t (0742) 770800/770888.

Tanzanair, Domestic Terminal, Dar Airport, t (022) 2843131–3, (0741) 406409, info@ tanzanair.com. Also has a sales office at the Royal Palm Hotel, PO Box 364, Dar es Salaam, t (022) 2113151, reservations@tanzanair.com. The company also hires out the Tanzanian government equivalent of Air Force 1, the US presidential plane; a tiny, perfect jet.

Zanair, Domestic Terminal, Dar Airport. Also has an office at Malindi Street, PO Box 2113, Dar es Salaam, t (022) 2232993, f (022) 2233670, zanair@zitec.org.

By Bus

Catching a bus in Dar es Salaam has always been a complicated affair: in the past there were five terminals and countless operators to choose from; now at least nearly all long-distance buses depart from one central terminus, about 20mins from the town centre on the Morogoro Road. The new **Ubungu terminus** is a reliable one-stop shop for buses to all destinations; all enquiries, reservations and ticket purchases can be made here. The Ubungu terminus is accessible by dala-dala from the Kivukoni Front terminus or any of the dala-dala stops en route. Ubungu is a notorious hangout for pickpockets and petty thieves, so hold on to your bags.

One alternative – convenient if you are based on the other side of the town centre – is the excellent private service operated by **Scandinavian Bus Lines**, t (hotline) (0748) 218484–5, t (022) 2184833, Head Office, PO Box 2414, Dar es Salaam, t (022) 2861947, *info@scandinaviagroup.com*, who have their own terminus on the road out of town towards the airport, on the junction of Nyerere Road and Msimbazi St. They run buses to Iringa, Mbeya, Songea, Dodoma, Moshi, Arusha and Nairobi. You may board the bus at the terminus, or pick up their service at the Ubungu terminus, through which all services pass.

As a very broad guideline, estimate the following journey times: 6hrs to Tanga, 8hrs to Moshi, 10hrs to Arusha, 12hrs to Mombasa, 36hrs to Mwanza, 8hrs to Iringa, 20hrs to Mbeya.

By Boat

Ferries run to and from Zanzibar and Pemba islands, Mombasa in Kenya and Mtwara down south from the ferry port near St Joseph's Cathedral on the harbour front at the centre of Sokoine Drive. For Zanzibar ferries contact the universal hotline number, t (0744) 491609. Fares for non-residents are $35 for economy and $40 first class.

Sea Express, t (022) 2114026/2116732; Zanzibar t (024) 2234690/t (0744) 278692.

Azam Marine, t (022) 2133024/t (0741) 334347.

Flying Horse, t (022) 2124507.

Sea Star Services, t (0748) 789393/781500 or Zanzibar, t (0744) 310953/t (0747) 411505.

For Zanzibar and Pemba, contact **Mega Speed Liners**, t (022) 2110807/t (0741) 326414.

For Mtwara, Zanzibar or Pemba contact **Zanzibar Shipping Corp.**, t (022) 2152870.

By Train

The **TAZARA** railway station is an impressive station building on the corner of the Nelson Mandela Expressway and Nyerere Road, t (022) 2860340–7/t (0741) 615370/t (0744) 600084 (customer services); station manager t (0744) 609985. The TAZARA railway operates services south from Dar es Salaam to New Kapiri Mposhi in Zambia via the Udzungwa Mountains and Mbeya, with trains departing Dar on Mon at 10am (ordinary), Tues and Fri at 3.15pm (express).

The Tanzania Railways Corporation trains, departing from the **Tanzania Railway Station**, PO Box 468, Dar es Salaam, t (022) 2110599 ext 2607/t (0744) 262659, direct line t (022) 2117833, *ccm_atu@trctz.com*, *www.trctz.com*, head west to **Kigoma** via **Morogoro**, **Dodoma**, **Tabora** and **Uvinza**, on Tues, Fri and Sun, departing at 5pm, and to 'up-country' destinations such as **Mwanza** on the same days (it's the same train, which splits at Tabora). The journeys can be very long – especially cross-country to Kigoma, 1,254km away, which takes up to 40hrs. For a modicum of comfort and safety, take a first-class compartment with only two beds. A first-class single ticket is around T.shs 45,000 per person, and a second-class ticket in a six-bed berth around T.shs 35,000 (note that fares are paid in T.shs). Men and women are separated unless the whole compartment is taken. First- and second-class tickets should be booked in advance, but third-class tickets can be bought on the day of travel. Take care of your property.

Getting Around

By Car

For reliable car hire contact the following:

Hertz Cars c/o Savannah Tours, PO Box 20517, Dar es Salaam, t (022) 22112967/t (0741) 600738/331662, *savtour@twiga.com*, *hertz.tanzania@twiga.com*, *www.savannahsafaris.com*. Offices at the Royal Palm Hotel. Provide good, reliable hire cars and drivers for long-haul trips and safaris. They have a wide choice of vehicles, each priced according to size and the distance you intend to travel. Prices vary, but the cost of a 4x4 with driver for a day starts at $130.

Business Rent a Car, 16 Kisutu Street, **t** (022) 2122852/**t** (0744) 604958, **f** (022) 2122852. Recommended: good value and reliable day and longer-term hire.

Evergreen Car Hire, PO Box 1476, Dar es Salaam, **t** (022) 2182107/2183345/2182107/ **t** (0741) 324538, *evergreen@raha.com*. A range of vehicles. Estimate around $40 per day for a self-drive Toyota, to $90 per day for a Land Cruiser. If you take a driver, there will be an additional cost of around $15 per day for his overnight allowance.

Green Car Rentals, Nkrumah St, opposite the Railway Clinic, **t** (022) 2183718/2182022/ **t** (0744) 780055, *greencars@raha.com*, *rdhanji@cats-net.com*, *www.greencars.co.tz*. Short or long-term rentals, chauffeur- and self-driven cars. Also camping safaris, tour packages and hotel and lodge bookings.

If you need a car for a single day, it might be worth negotiating with a taxi driver for a full-day price. This could cost around $50–100, depending on how far you wish to travel.

Taxis

There are plenty of taxis available in Dar es Salaam. They range from velveteen-interior boy-racer dream-mobiles with black-tinted windows and scarlet trimmings to stock-car material that seems scarcely likely to deliver you to your destination. Always negotiate the fare before you set off, and stick to it once it has been agreed. If your destination is out of town the driver will often wait, assured of a return fee later.

By Bus and Dala-dala

Dala-dala is the transport of the majority in Dar es Salaam and these minibuses frequently set new world records for the maximum number of people in a small, four-wheeled vehicle. For much less than a 'dollar-dollar' you can cover most of the city at a reasonable speed. The dala-dala is a relatively new addition to the city transport system, having emerged over the last decade as a popular private initiative in line with laws liberalizing trade. It is best to catch dala-dalas at the terminus if possible, as it can be well-nigh impossible to squeeze in at subsequent stops. In the town centre, catch dala-dalas outside the old post office (Posta) on Kivukoni Front, or at the main terminal, Minazi Mirefu ('Tall Coconut Palms'). There is a terminus at the Tanzania Railway Station, known as Stesheni, and one at Kariakoo Market. The destination of each dala-dala is yelled repeatedly by the *Mgiga debe*, whose name literally translates as 'he who crams things into a can'. He doubles up as a diligent conductor.

One common destination is Mwenge, the site of the handicraft and sculpture market, some distance up the Bagamoyo road to the north of town. This dala-dala passes the Village Museum and the Palm Beach Hotel. Another goes to the airport, known as 'ndege' (short for Uwanja wa Ndege, literally 'Stadium of Birds'). The Ilala bus goes via Kariakoo and Ilala markets to the TAZARA Railway Station, and Temeke goes south to Mtoni and Mbagala on the Kilwa Road. Ubungu goes to the new bus terminus on Morogoro Road.

Tourist Information

Tanzania Tourist Board, 3rd Floor of the IPS Building, **t** (022) 2111244, **f** (022) 2116420, *www.tanzaniatouristboard.com*, *www.tanzania-web.com*. A helpful office, which supplies a wide selection of maps and contact details. Most information is on Dar es Salaam and the coastal towns, but it also holds dusty files with nationwide contacts.

Emergency Services, **t** 112/**t** (0741) 322112.

Central Police Station, **t** (022) 2115507.

Salander Bridge Police Station, **t** (022) 2120818.

Oysterbay Police Station, **t** (022) 2667322–3. There are also police stations at Bugurumi and Chang'ombe.

Nordic Clinic (Scandianvian doctors on 24hr call), **t** (022) 2601650/2600274, emergency **t** (0741) 325569, **f** (022) 260214, *nordic@ intafrica.com*, *www.nordic.co.tz*.

Oysterbay Medical Clinic, Oysterbay Shopping Complex, **t** (022) 2667932.

The Flying Doctors: in emergencies contact the Nairobi Office on **t** (+254) 2 501301–3.

Shopping

Arts and Crafts

Just beside the Royal Palm Hotel, the **Nyumba ya Sanaa** ('House of Art') encourages young artists, some disabled, to sell their unusual paintings, carvings, weaving, batiks and pottery. The prices are high, but so are the standards of work for sale. There are also some unusual and very original figurative clay sculptures for sale at the small stall inside the **Village Museum** car park. There is always a selection of crafts for sale from stalls along **Ali Hassan Mwinyi Road** near the junction with Haile Selassie, but prices are often high for the quality, and bargaining is required.

The **Tinga Tinga Arts Cooperative** market at Morogoro Stores, Haile Selassie Road, Msasani, t (022) 2668075 (*open 7–6*), has an incredible range of goods painted in the bright, colourful style called Tinga Tinga after its originator, Edward Saidi Tingatinga. Tingatinga was said to be inspired by the new manufactured paints used by Europeans for house-painting (the centuries-old house-painting traditions in Africa had always relied on natural dyes). Tinga Tinga art is created with bright quick-drying enamels. The images tend to be flamboyant representations of native animals and birds, fruit and vegetables or, recently, exceptionally complex town and village scenes. There are a number of stalls along the dusty road outside the centre. Inside, the display of vast canvases, painted wooden fish, plates and tea trays is truly staggering. Other good examples of Tinga Tinga art can also be found at **Mwenge**, **Nyumba ya Sanaa** and the **Msasani Slipway**.

Often a slightly cheaper deal can be negotiated a few kilometres out of town along Bagamoyo Road at the **Mwenge Handicraft Village**. Here, a huge community of Makonde carvers and craftspeople create a wide range of wooden sculptures and household items. The quality is variable, but prices are reasonable and open to negotiation. Many of the carvers at Mwenge are Makonde, and employ traditional carving techniques. The Makonde people originated in Mozambique, but have steadily spread throughout Tanzania, bringing the mastery of their art and their dancing with them. Their work is traditionally carved in ebony, but conservation measures now protect this endangered and extremely slow-growing tree. Many Makonde in southern Tanzania, around the Makonde Plateau, plant a seedling ebony tree each time they cut one down, but these will still take around a hundred years to reach maturity. Carvers often use an alternative hard wood from the *Pterocarpus angolensis* tree, but as this is considerably lighter in colour than ebony it is often blackened with boot polish.

Art N Frame, t (022) 2602700/t (0741) 323300, sells curios, supplies artist's materials and has a lovely framing service, as well as a gallery. It is centrally based in Msasani.

Markets

Everything under the sun (except Tinga Tinga) is sold at **Kariakoo Market** (*open 6am–6.30pm*). This is an exceptional and thriving centre for all local goods, and a focal point for all forms of commercial enterprise. Outside, all manner of cheap foreign goods are laid out for sale, surrounding the vast double-storey building that was originally erected in the early 1920s as a military depot for stores and supplies. The building was then surrounded by forest with just a few 'squatter' Swahili houses around. Goods are also offered for sale by the touts who roam among the traffic with a mind-boggling selection of items – known collectively by the now rather passé Swahili slang for anything cheap, plasticky and of poor quality, 'Taiwan'.

Also outside the main doors is a noisy **fresh goods market**, with a selection of impromptu stalls selling herbs and fruit, vegetables and fish and even aromatic, freshly cooked food. Inside, a magical mass of goods is piled high to the ceiling, including every household item a Swahili family could need: coconut-scrapers and giant pestles and mortars, bowls, plates, candle-holders, terracotta pots and coloured umbrellas dominate the centre of the ground floor. These are surrounded by stalls selling flours and spices, seeds and gardening implements. On the upper level is much more of the same, supplemented by textile shops selling *kanga* and *kitenge* cloths, and shiny new sewing machines. On all levels, negotiate the best possible price.

Also popular as a local market for fresh goods, **Ilala Market** is on the same dala-dala route as Kariakoo.

Imported Goods

There are ever-increasing opportunities to spend lots of money on imported Western goods in Dar, as the development of shopping malls grows to cater to the sizeable expat population. These have mushroomed along the Old Bagamoyo Road, and in the vicinity of the US embassy. The best include **Royal Plaza**, next to the US embassy in Mikocheni, **Mayfair Plaza**, **Shoppers' Plaza** on the Old Bagamoyo Road, or the **Arcade** nearby. The **Oysterbay Shopping Centre** beside the defunct Oysterbay Hotel is also smart, with a mass of small boutiques and a range of goods and services. The **Slipway** at Msasani Peninsula has a bookshop and some clothes shops tucked among its restaurants and bars.

For more prosaic supermarket shopping, there is a cavernous **Shoprite**, t (022) 2181272, on the airport road, as well as a smaller branch at the Slipway. Other, smaller supermarkets specializing in imported goods continue to spring up around the town centre; a good selection may be found on Samora Avenue.

Where to Stay

There's a wide range of accommodation in Dar, although it's on the expensive side and often noisy. Business and pleasure travellers alike may well be advised to consider staying a short distance north of the city centre on the northern beaches. These tend to offer better value for money in terms of comfort, service and location, and are only 15–30mins from the town centre (*see* pp.233–5). The list below shows hotels within Dar itself.

Very Expensive
Kilimanjaro Kempinski Hotel, USA reservations t 1 800 426 3135, *www.kempinski-daressalaam.com*. Will this truly be the first international five-star hotel in Dar? The jury is out until the opening. To give an idea of the scale, an entire floor will be dedicated to a 'wellness suite'. In former days the hotel was a Dar landmark, and the new management have consciously revived the 'Kili' name; though the waterfront area which it used to crown hasn't maintained its appeal, and the other international hotels are mostly clustered around the botanical gardens on the other side of town. The old hotel has been replaced by an undistinguished block with mirrored windows that provide more than a touch of bling. Plans are afoot to use the beach to develop an enticing leisure area. However, a busy

harbour road separates the beach from the hotel. The hotel will have 180 guest rooms and suites; 2 executive floors and an executive lounge, 3 international restaurants, 3 bars, spa, outdoor pool, and casino. Rooms will have satellite TV, broadband, 24hr room service, and butler service for the suites.

Expensive
Hotel Sea Cliff, Toure Drive, Msasani Peninsula, PO Box 3030, t (022) 2600380–7, f (022) 2600476/419/451, *seacliff@tztechno.com*. A smart, upmarket option with a good feel and a superb situation overlooking the sea. A good 15mins' drive from the airport, it generally requires a taxi or private transport to reach the heart of town. Snacks and drinks are available from bars and good restaurants in the vicinity: the **Fisherman** nearby is the only dedicated seafood restaurant in town. Rooms are comfortable and appealing, especially if you can secure a sea view (more expensive). It has a swimming pool and excellent e-mail and office facilities are available in the business centre.
Royal Palm Hotel, Ohio St, PO Box 791, t (022) 2112416, *www.moevenpick-hotels.com*. A good option for an upmarket stay in the town centre. As well as plush public spaces, the hotel has a great outside pool, spa and several very good restaurants (especially **Tradewinds**) as well as easy access to the local golf course. The hotel also has a travel agency for organizing safaris, a BA shop and even an in-house dentist. Rooms are fairly simple but do have all mod cons.
Golden Tulip, Toure Drive, Msasani Peninsula, PO Box 6300, t (022) 2600288, f (022) 2601443, *enquiries@goldentuliptanzania.com*, *www.goldentuliptanzania.com*. The hotel, with its vast and lofty reception area, could be a fine example of modernist African civic architecture. Luxurious fabrics and restrained fittings give it an opulent and calm atmosphere. The open design makes the most of its prime oceanfront location, allowing a heady breeze to course through the public areas, where a cosmopolitan élite lounge on easy chairs, reading and chatting. The terrace area is popular for intimate meetings and leads up to a wide and deep royal blue infinity pool. There is an ATM and bank in the hotel, an *à la carte* restaurant

and grill. All rooms have Internet access, a balcony and a marble bath.

Holiday Inn, Garden Avenue, PO Box 80022, **t** (022) 2137575, **f** (022) 2139070, *www. holiday-inn.com/daressalaam*. Unashamedly geared to the business traveller, the Dar Holiday Inn succeeds at replicating the neat reliability of the international chain. Borders the botanical gardens. Sunday brunch is popular. The curio shop has a wide range of quality gifts and stocks the delectable OneWay T-shirts.

Anyone facing an extended stay in Dar es Salaam might like to consider taking an apartment, although these are only available at the top end of the market.

Protea Apartments, just out of the centre on Theatre Square, at the corner of Haile Selassie and Ali Hassan Mwinyi Road, PO Box 2158, **t** (022) 2666160/2666665, *proteadar@ cats-net.com*. Protea provide fully serviced air-conditioned apartments on a daily or monthly basis. These are around a central pool and restaurant, and include satellite TV, telephone and e-mail connections and use of the business centre, breakfast room, laundry, barbecue area and gym. Studios, or 2–3-bedroom suites available for a monthly rate. The ambience is uninspiring, but the apartments offer good value for money over longer periods. The impressive security provision stops at the gate: as a result guests should be alert on leaving or entering the area and are advised to travel by car.

New Africa Hotel, on the corner of Sokoine Drive and Azikwe Street, PO Box 9314, Dar es Salaam, **t** (022) 2117050, **f** (022) 2116731, *newafricahotel@raha.com*. The new New Africa is a fun old hotel in the town centre. It stands on the location of the old Kaiserhof Hotel, one of the first hotels to grace Dar city centre, but it bears little resemblance to the original German colonial haunt. The rooftop Thai restaurant makes a pleasant, if expensive, choice for a good night out, as does the popular New Africa Casino (open to the public) on the second floor. The casino boasts the most up-to-date slot machines and smart roulette, blackjack, poker and pontoon tables, with bingo on Wednesdays at 9pm and on Sundays at 4.30pm.

Courtyard Hotel, Ocean Road, PO Box 542, Dar es Salaam, **t** (022) 2130130/2130560, **f** (022) 2130100, *courtyard@raha.com*. Among the nicest choices in the mid-range, recently refurbished, just beyond the town centre. Rooms are arranged around a central court-yard in three storeys of carved wooden balconies, all twined with trailing bougain-villaea. At the centre, shady tables are arranged in a garden with a clear pool in the middle. Smart, clean rooms are fully equipped with all the comforts of satellite TV, safe, mini-bar, ISDN phone lines, kettles, marble bathrooms and fine upholstery. The hotel also provides a library, business centre and car rentals. Its Indian restaurant has a good reputation in its own right. Alternatively there is a café and snack bar for faster food. Genuinely good value. Superior or standard doubles available.

Moderate

Mediterraneo, off Kawe Rd, PO Box 36110, Dar es Salaam, **t** (022) 2618359/**t** (0744) 812567, *info@mediterraneo-tz.com*. Seven km out of town along the Old Bagamoyo Rd, the Mediterraneo is the creation of a renowned Dar restaurateur. The terrace of rooms feels like an afterthought; the main event is undoubtedly the restaurant overlooking the bay. Luckily the food, and the peaceful location, is good enough to warrant staying a night or two. Décor is distinctively Italian/African. Wrought-iron bed frames and simple fabrics are easy on the eye if not providing much comfort, but at the price it is a treat. Quiet location (no access to beach). The pool is large but not well cared for.

Peacock Hotel, on Bibi Titi Mohamed Road, near Mnazi Moja Park, PO Box 70270, Dar es Salaam, **t** (022) 2120334, (0741) 327457, *www.peacock-hotel.co.tz, reservation@ peacockhotel.co.tz*. At the centre of town, the Peacock is clean and provides a friendly service for its idiosyncratically furnished rooms. Despite the strangely ornate and frilly décor, all accommodation is air-condi-tioned and complete with satellite TV. In a good location for travelling, close to the airport and TAZARA railway station. There is also a passable rooftop restaurant.

Hotel Karibu, Haile Selassie Road, Oysterbay, PO Box 3152, **t** (022) 2602946, **f** (022) 260 1426, *karibu@afsat.com*. To the north of town, close to the ocean, with a welcoming air of efficiency and air-conditioned rooms. The air is a little fresher in this part of town, and the small but clean swimming pool provides refreshing respite. Karibu's restaurant specializes in Indian cuisine. Comfortable doubles. A fashionable nightclub has opened downstairs, showcasing music from Kenya, and the local scene.

The Souk, Msasani Slipway, PO Box 250, **t** (022) 2600893/**t** (0741) 300097, **f** (022) 2600908, *slipway@coastal.cc*. The Souk rooms are hidden away in the upper reaches of the Slipway shopping plaza. The rooms are newly decorated and clean but characterless and quite poky. Good value compared to Protea's apartments, though best used as a day room or for an overnight stop only. Its overriding advantage is its easy access to restaurants and the bar scene while remaining in the security of the Slipway.

Cheap

Palm Beach Hotel, PO Box 1520, Dar es Salaam, **t** (022) 2132938, **f** (022) 2119272, *palmbeach@cctz.com*. The best choice for a fairly central, reasonably priced and atmospheric hideaway in town. The Palm Beach claims to be the oldest hotel in Dar es Salaam, and was certainly an elegant 'deco'-style choice in its heyday. These days the interior has a musty well-worn atmosphere, with just-perceptible echoes of its past grandeur. Towels and linen might be a little threadbare, taps might drip and doors creak, but the hotel is friendly, comfortable and safe, and a light breakfast can be enjoyed in sunny comfort in the open-sided morning room. The outdoor restaurant is a popular spot for relaxed dining or drinking in a shady garden, complete with vocal-frog-filled fishponds and *makuti*-thatch sunshades. The menu is fairly simple but good, especially for light snacks and lunches, with vegetarian choices. For later evening entertainment **Sugar Ray's Sports Bar** at the back of the hotel is a popular spot for chi-chi *mbongos* and Dar residents. The city shuttle bus and dala-dalas stop just beside the hotel (heading in the direction of Mwenge). En-suite doubles or cheaper rooms with shared bathroom available. Children under 12 half price.

A variety of budget accommodation clusters just north of the Mnazi Moja park between Morogoro, Jamhuri and Libya Streets.

Jambo Inn, Libya Street, PO Box 5588, **t** (022) 2114293. Popular with backpackers and frequently full. Rooms are decently priced and clean, although their popularity has taken a toll on the décor. The adjoining Indian-style restaurant and sweet shop both dish up welcome treats at quite reasonable prices.

Econo Lodge, corner of Libya and Banda Street, **t** (022) 2116048-50, **f** (022) 2116053, *econo lodge@raha.com*. Signposted off Libya Street just a short walk from the Jambo, than which it has less character but is more peaceful, with large-scale neon-lit interiors. It is the other end of the scale from the friendly atmosphere of the smaller lodges, but the rooms are clean with private bathrooms, the breakfast is decent and sleeplovers can find quiet rooms on upper floors.

Traffic Light Motel, Maragwo Road, **t** (022) 2223438. Much cheaper. Its profits support a primary school for disabled children. Staff are welcoming and efficient.

YWCA on Upanga Road, **t** (022) 2122439. Staff at the ever-popular YWCA are neither as welcoming nor as efficient as those at the Traffic Light, although it remains a popular choice for good central rooms for women and couples alike. The adjoining restaurant is remarkably cheap and good. Breakfast included, family rooms available.

YMCA, Ali Hassan Mwinyi Road, PO Box 767, **t** (022) 2110833 , **f** (022) 2135457. Not as good as the YWCA, which allows men too; 70 rooms, most with twin beds.

Lutheran House Hostel, on Sokoine Drive, PO Box 389, **t** (022) 2121735. A vast block structure situated beside the church. Rooms are spacious, dark and cool. The adjoining restaurant has been converted to a cheerful Chinese. It's best to book.

Salvation Army Mission, Mgulani Hostel, **t** (022) 2851467, *bamartin@maf.org*. The best-value accommodation in this range is a good way from the town centre in pleasant surroundings on the Kilwa Road. Rooms are set around gardens with a swimming pool and the atmosphere is more Kilwa than Dar. Singles, doubles and triples available.

Sukuma Push. Anyone stopping over between flights will find decent enough budget accommodation near the airport at this oddly comfortable budget hideaway. Staff are friendly (but the service is eccentric) and the rooms are centred around a garden bar with super-loud satellite TV. Inspect rooms before checking in, as standards vary.

Eating Out

There is a great deal of choice in Dar es Salaam, covering almost all international cooking styles and almost any budget. The Slipway, on the western front of Msasani Peninsula, north of the town centre, houses most of the best restaurants – Japanese, Italian and French – and a number of other eateries aimed at the foreign market.

Expensive

Royal Palm Hotel, Ohio Street, PO Box 791, t (022) 2112416. Fine dining is available here at the **Serengeti**, a smart restaurant which serves a continental menu, the **Kibo** restaurant which also offers continental food at slightly lower prices, or the Indian restaurant, the **Raj. Tradewinds** is the newly opened steak house.

Sawasdee at the **Africa House Hotel**, t (022) 2117050. An excellent choice for dining is the fine, ornate **Thai** rooftop restaurant, where the food is enhanced by excellent views. It often does a weekend brunch accompanied by a live band. The **Bandari Restaurant**, t (022) 2117050, downstairs provides simple but reliable international-style cooking in pleasant but characterless surroundings.

Hotel Sea Cliff on Toure Drive, Msasani Peninsula, PO Box 3030, t (022) 2600380, f (022) 2600476. Towards the north of town, comfortable, good-quality fine dining is on offer at this hotel's **Dhow Restaurant** where the chefs make the most of fresh local produce, especially with their seafood and spicy Indian-inspired dishes. For something a little unusual and relaxed, but with a good atmosphere and memorable spice and colour, try the **Karambezi Café** (also in the hotel), an 'Afro-Mediterranean-styled restaurant and bar'. The fun atmosphere is brightened yet further with live music on

Tues, Thurs and Sun nights. The Karambezi's greatest pull is its 24hr opening and its situation, by the ocean. Prices are not cheap anywhere in this hotel or the shopping centre, and nor is transport there and back.

Chui Bar, next to Smokies, up from the Slipway, t (0745) 660660. Serves lunch on its elegant terrace bar, overlooking the harbour. The menu has an imaginative range of African and Mediterranean dishes. It also has a feisty drinks menu, a consequence of its role as Dar's premier nightclub.

Moderate

Mediterraneo Hotel, Kawe Beach, 20mins' drive up the Old Bagamoyo Rd, t (0744) 812567. Delicious Italian and Spanish home cooking. Squid ink pastas; gnocchi and fabulous lobster. Italian naughty puddings. Eating takes place on a quiet terrace overlooking the cresting waves of the bay. A swimming pool is open to non-residents for a pre-food dip, but there is no access to the beach here. There is a new branch at the Alliance Française, at the Las Vegas Complex.

EuroPub, Kawe Beach, Old Bagamoyo Rd. Also in the Kawe Beach area, and equally good. Popular with more wealthy expats as a quiet out-of-town hangout, this area is more difficult for tourists without their own vehicles. However, if you can arrange transport for the 20min drive, then this is a recommended destination. Good continental menu.

Holiday Inn, t (022) 2137575, f (022) 2139070, *www.holiday-inn.com/daressalaam*, has two restaurants, the **Baraza Grill, Café and Bar**, and the **Kivulini** restaurant, which are fast establishing themselves in the Dar food scene. Kivulini has the best breakfast in Dar, an expansive buffet with flaky butter croissants and endless coffee refills. From 6am every day, on the mezzanine floor.

Addis in Dar, 35 Ursino Street, off Mgombani Street on the way to Shoppers' Plaza, PO Box 23212, t (0741) 266299. A fun choice, cited by many as the best food in Dar, offering Ethiopian-style cooking. The restaurant is well furnished and comfortable, just a short trip from the town centre. *Closed Sun.*

Turquoise, Sea Cliff Village, t (022) 2600979/ t (0741) 239729. Turkish cuisine in a breezy Mediterranean setting; cakes and *pâtisserie*.

The Fisherman, Sea Cliff Village, dishing up sizzling fish steaks at the only seafood restaurant in town.

Rickshaw, off Chole Road at the tip of Msasani peninsula, t (022) 2601611. Excellent Chinese food in a pleasant atmosphere.

Q Bar, Haile Selassie Road, Oysterbay, t (0744) 282474. Continental food. The current chef was formerly at the more expensive EuroPub on Kawe Beach, and he is fêted for providing very good cuts of meat at a decent price. Cocktails and shooters lubricate this lively pool bar and restaurant.

Garden Bistro, Haile Selassie Road, opp the Indian High Commission, Oysterbay, t (022) 2600800/t (0748) 741741. Four restaurants offering Indian and continental menus, and a lovely spot with gardens and wooden seating. If you are not a party animal, avoid on weekend evenings – this is currently the hottest ticket in town with a heaving disco floor right next to the dining areas.

Slipway, Msasani Slipway. European-style cooking is on offer here, adding a French touch to the range of international cuisine. The menu is good, with some decent wines, served in a smart, dusky atmosphere.

Alcove, Samora Avenue, t (022) 2133042/2137444/t (0741) 324319. In the city centre, has a popular reputation for its delicious Indian and Chinese food.

Open House, t (022) 2131342. Dar-dwellers favour this, the Alcove's more authentic sister restaurant, tucked in beside the Ngazija Mosque on Sewa Street, just off India Street.

Hong Kong, at the junction of Zanaki and Bibi Titi Mohamed Road, near the city centre, t (022) 2136622. Good for lunch.

Sichuan Restaurant, by the National Library on Bibi Titi Mohamed Road, t (022) 2150548. Highly recommended. Secure parking.

Jan's Pizzeria, on the Kimweri Road, Namanga, t (0744) 282969. The ever popular and expanding pizzeria has good Italian food with a fantastic cheese and cold-cuts counter that is definitely worth knowing about if you plan any self-catering; friendly and enthusiastic management and atmosphere, with takeaway an option.

Azuma Restaurant, at the Slipway, t (022) 2600893. Intriguing, good and authentic Japanese and Indonesian food in congenial, breezy surroundings. Some tables on a quiet upstairs wooden balcony with views of the sea, and the quality of food and service is far higher than the price range would suggest.

The Terrace Italian Restaurant, Msasani Slipway, north of the town centre, t (022) 2600893. On a wooden deck overlooking the sea, a worthwhile choice for a relaxed night out when the weather is hot, enjoying good pizzas and cold drinks.

Cheap

Barbecue Village, Nkomo Street, opposite Las Vegas Casino, t (022) 2667927. Continental and Indian *à la carte* and buffets. *Closed lunch and Mon.*

Arca-Di Noe, Msasani Namanga, PO Box 206, t (022) 2667215. Very good for pizza and pasta; Wednesdays is their 'Pasta Festival': eat as much pasta as you can. The owners also run a well-stocked deli in Msasani.

La Taverna, on Old Bagamoyo Road, t (022) 2667146. Cooks up reliable Indo-Chinese cuisine, Italian pizzas and barbecue. *Open for lunch and dinner.*

Hard Rock Café, Mkwepu Street. Worth visiting more for the air-conditioned interior and collectable T-shirt than the 'American and French' menu, but it remains a popular meeting place with a pool table and bar.

Forodhani's, at the Hotel Tourism and Training Institute beside the Kilimanjaro Hotel on Kivukoni Front. An unusual but well recommended venue, especially good for lunch. This is also the location of the old British **Dar es Salaam Club**, and provides good-quality, unusual food in interestingly nostalgic surroundings. Groups can hire the long dining hall and enjoy a conscientiously prepared and presented three-course meal. If this seems a bit much, a wholesome and regular meal of fish and *ugali* is served on the outside terrace 1–2pm.

The Oysterbay Grill, Oysterbay Hotel Shopping Complex, t (022) 2600131–3/t (0744) 604926. Buffet lunch and *à la carte* dinner menu. Friday is 'eat all you can' fondue night; Thursday is steak night.

Debonair's Pizza, Steers Complex, Ohio Street/Samora Avenue, t (022) 2122855. Pizza restaurant and delivery service.

Palm Beach Restaurant at the Palm Beach Hotel on Ali Hassan Mwinyi Road, t (022) 2132938/2130985. A range of small snacks such as kebabs in pitta bread, salads, chips and toasted sandwiches for lunch or supper.

Jambo Inn, Libya Street, PO Box 5588, t (022) 2114293. A relaxed backpacker atmosphere, and a vast book-like menu of excellent, delicious Indian dishes (although ostensibly including Indian, Pakistani, Chinese and English) alongside giant chapatis and good chips. Squeeze into the close-packed tables and benches outside, or go for smarter, air-conditioned indoor dining. The tiny shop also sells chocolates, cakes and sweets.

The Retreat, on the junction of Mrima and Mtendeni Street in Jamhuri, t (022) 2128048. Good southern Indian cooking, well worth tasting, albeit in somewhat shabbier surroundings. This vegetarian choice is especially popular with the Hindu minority; strictly non-smoking, serves no alcohol.

Ally's, Msasani Slipway, t (022) 2600893. Fine frothy cappuccino, home-made hash browns and eggs done any which way make Ally's a good breakfast destination. This place is also known as 'the Pub'. Energetic air-conditioning and a constant stream of CNN.

Cafés, Snacks and Barbecues

Epidor, Samora Avenue, t (022) 2136006–7. A newly opened café with croissants, light lunches, salads and sandwiches.

Amadeus Café in the Oysterbay shopping centre. More casual European treats are on offer in this mini café on the other side of the peninsula, where George and Pauline serve crêpes and home-made milkshakes, English breakfasts and Italian coffee. *Open 10am–midnight, closes 4pm Mon.*

Cine Club, on the beach just off the Old Bagamoyo Road. A popular spot for children, especially at weekends, and serves good-quality local food in a pleasant atmosphere.

Fairy Delights Cafés. Enjoy this café with its fey name at two new locations: they serve a good range of cold sodas and snacks, ice-cream and milkshakes. The Shoppers' Plaza branch is more of an all-round dining experience, with a daily buffet, pizzas,

burgers and rolls. It also has a bakery. Find Fairy Delights at Shoppers' Plaza on the Old Bagamoyo Road, t (022) 2700998, (*open daily 8am–8.30pm*), and the ice-cream parlour at Msasani Slipway, t (022) 2601122 (*open till midnight weekends, Mon–Fri 10pm*).

Salamander Café, on the corner of Mkwepu Street, one block west of the Askari Monument on Samora Avenue, t (0744) 465758. Has a ghostly atmosphere of a once much grander past. It was built during the German era, and features a fine red-tiled roof and first-floor verandah. Although a little shabby and old these days, it remains a shady place to enjoy sodas and samosas and watch the world go by. *Daytime only.*

Some say the very best food to be had in the city is at simple kebab stalls. Unpretentious, well-cooked meat cuts, but blink and you'll miss the teeny-tiny salads served alongside.

Barbecue House, Nkomo Street, opp. Las Vegas Casino, t (022) 2123663. Indian-style BBQ.

Chuchu's, Shoprite Complex, Nyerere Road, t (022) 2183329. Barbecued steaks, 'bitings' such as samosa, *kachoris*.

Bali's, Aly Khan Rd, Upanga, t (0748) 609800, Indian and continental barbecue.

Entertainment

The **British Council**, t (022) 2116574–7, shows films in English on Wednesday evenings at its premises on Samora Avenue. There are English-language film nights at the Slipway in Msasani, t (022) 2600893 on Tuesday evenings, beginning at 7pm and 9pm.

Alliance Française, Upanga Road and Ufukoni Road, at the Las Vegas casino complex, Msasani, t (022) 2111331/2131406, *afdar@africaonline.co.tz*. Cultural events and gigs.

New World Cinema, Old Bagamoyo Road, t (022) 2772178/2771409/t (0748) 610875 (*booking office opens at 1pm*), *www.tanzaniadirectory.com*. Tanzania's first cinema complex, with four movies showing daily. Has special screenings of Bollywood and Western classics on Sunday afternoons, and an eating place with decent Indian food.

Avalon Cinema, Zanaki Street. Indian and Western movies.

Nightlife

Anyone with a yen to party the night away will find plenty of choice on the streets of Dar. There are a handful of bars with an upbeat atmosphere and the added entertainment of pool tables, music or films. On Friday and Saturday nights the city is buzzing with live bands. Anyone serious about their music and seeking a full line-up of the night's entertainment should get hold of a copy of the free *Dar es Salaam Guide*, or *What's Happening in Dar*, available in hotel foyers.

Bongo Flava is a Swahili-inspired version of hiphop. Its name derives from the name given to city residents: '*mbongo*', meaning brain. It is said that, to live the life of Dar, young urbanites must keep their head, or brains, about them. Bongo Flava is an incredibly high-energy musical style. Songs tend to tell silly stories of boys and girls, rather than the harsher reality bites common to the more hardcore US hiphop. Artists include 'Hakuna Kalala': Never Sleep. Tanzanian music has traditionally been outshadowed by the harder-edged sounds of Kenyan dance music; when Kenyan DJs vist Dar, it is perceived to be a major event. The music is darker and sexier. However, Bongo Flava is maturing.

Club Bilicanas, Simu Street, near the Hard Rock Café on Mkwepu Street. Claims to be 'one of the best discos in East Africa'. It's big, it's got lots of flashing lights. It's not the only place in Dar that gets worked over by smart-looking prostitutes, but men should be aware that it might not just be their irresistible charm that leads the local women to chat them up. It also has a casino.

Garden Bistro, opposite the Indian High Commission at the end of Haile Selassie Road, Msasani, on the right, t (022) 2600800. Mixed and lively dancing bar opens till late, currently the most happening bar in town, and a touch cliquey. Disco lights in the *makuti* dance area give way to a darkened *shisha* lounge. The cocktails are good. Three restaurants; *upstairs open till 12pm*.

Msasani, Chole Road. Currently the most happening club in town, live music on Friday nights, a *shisha* smoking lounge.

Chui Bar, next to Smokies up from the Slipway, t (0745) 660660. This members' bar tries to maintain its exclusivity by charging a T.shs 10,000 entrance fee. The club is all zebra-print fabrics, marble floors and smoked glass. The air-conditioned disco is good fun, though the outside terrace bar makes the place. If you stay up very late you can watch the first dhows sail out in the morning. It also has an expensive but very good lunch menu. *Evenings opens at 10pm*.

Blue Palm, Mikocheni B area. A more jazz, blues and rock'n'roll swing, with live music. The InAfrika band have a regular Thursday night slot. Saturday night is disco flavour.

Q Bar, next to Karibu Hotel on Haile Selassie Road, t (0744) 282474. A good evening pub with pool tables and a fun atmosphere, with lots of happy hour offers 4–7pm. Often has a band on Fri and Wed. Food is good value – steaks and ribs, etc. *Open from 4pm*.

Sugar Ray's Sports Bar, behind Palm Beach Hotel. Has a screen that comes into its own during big sporting events but is also sometimes used to show fairly recent movies.

Bahama Mama, in Kimara on Morogoro Road. Good local and world music and popular local food and drinks with a good feel.

Sweet Eazy Lounge at the Sweet Eazy Restaurant at Oysterbay Shopping Complex, t (0745) 754074. A sophisticated but relaxed lounge bar with Western dance music. Recommended. InAfrika Band play Thursdays for a buffet dinner and dance. *Opens late at weekends only*.

Much More Music Bar, Bilicanas Complex. *Opens till 7am at weekends*.

Sugar Mamas, Bilicanas Complex. Sister bar to Much More. Ladies' nights on Friday.

California Dreamers, next to Las Vegas Casino, Upanga Road and Ufukoni Road. Late-night dancing bar with an enthusiastic expat crowd and lots of prostitutes.

Casinos and Other Entertainments

Las Vegas Casino, Upanga Road and Ufukoni Road. Admission charge plus whatever you lose at *vingt-et-un* and roulette.

New Africa Casino, New Africa Hotel, t (022) 2119752.

Sea Cliff Casino, at the Hotel Sea Cliff, t (022) 2600380, ext 3080.

Cosmic Bowling Alley, Sea Cliff Village. *Open 5pm–2am; closed Mon*.

then the city earned a sorry reputation for being dirty, crime-infested and sadly down at heel, to be avoided for all but the most necessary stopover, despite being the country's main port of entry and departure and the base for refugees and exiled political groups from the apartheid regime in South Africa.

Now numerous hotels welcome international travellers, while the old architecture of the city centre still colours the topsy-turvy character of these Swahili streets. Dar es Salaam has emerged again as a vibrant multicultural centre, supporting a thriving street culture around new shopping and office complexes, museums, galleries, eateries and markets. Travellers with a couple of days to spend in this East African metropolis now have more than half a chance of enjoying them.

Despite its renaissance, however, or perhaps because of the new inequalities it has brought, it is not entirely safe to go out alone after dark. Avoid walking in poorly lit back-street areas of the city or on deserted beaches alone. Muggings are the most common form of crime, and tourists are clearly a conspicuous target. Keep your cash and valuables hidden and take a taxi if you want to wear your posh jewellery out for the evening at a smart restaurant or function.

History

Dar es Salaam was a late developer, born of visionary ideals that conceived It as a thriving centre for all trade and communications along the East African coast, a plan that took more than a century to come to fruition. Until the late 19th century there was nothing here but two small rural villages on either side of a river, but by the turn of the 20th century the population had grown into a hotchpotch of diverse cultures and religions. The city's present-day inhabitants still include a large proportion of the original Zaramo tribe and coastal Swahili people mixed with other tribal groups, and the city has European, Hindu and Muslim, Indian and Asian areas.

In common with all the main coastal regions this central port has been subject to constant wrangling for control. Since it was originally founded by Sayyid Majid bin Said, the Sultan of Zanzibar (1865–1870), it has been taken over first by German and then British colonists, and finally achieved Independent home rule almost a century later. Much of its history of occupation can be charted in the city's architecture, astonishingly preserved after years of devastating poverty. The desperate lack of funds has resulted in little rebuilding or renovation until the last few years, and the result is an intriguing collection of buildings from every era and colonial context.

The Sultanate: 1862–1886

Dar es Salaam has been through many changes since its founder, Sultan Majid of Zanzibar, gave it the Arabic name Bandar-ul-Salaam, meaning 'Haven of Peace', which transmuted into the Swahili name Dari Salama, meaning 'House of Peace'. Although no one is absolutely certain which name came first, it seems that hopes were high for the new settlement that he developed in this natural harbour, which he imagined would become the focal trade centre for the entire mainland coast.

Before the advent of the sultan, the land was occupied by two small villages separated by a stretch of water that forms the present-day harbour. On the southern side was the village of Magogoni, and to the north was Mzizima, 'the healthy town'. Mzizima was soon swallowed up by the sultan's new development, and became the central portion of Dar es Salaam today, with only the Mzizima Fish Market on Banda Beach still preserving the name. The sultan began his grand plan to create a mainland caravan terminus and port that would be a centre for commercial trade along the East African coast as early as 1862, but it was the end of 1865 before he laid the plan for the roads that were to circumnavigate the harbour, along the lines of present-day Sokoine Drive. When the town and port areas were defined, he began to build himself a grand two-storey crenellated stone palace on the southwestern end of the front, near the present-day railway station, east of the clock tower.

After the first flurry of activity the new port town experienced a serious setback. In 1870, at the age of 36, Sultan Majid had a sudden accident in his palace and died – he was prone to epilepsy, and may have suffered a fit. He was swiftly succeeded by Sultan Barghash, who had little regard for his half-brother's plans for mainland expansion and instead concentrated his own interests on the islands of Zanzibar. Control of the coastal region returned to the more robust settlements at Bagamoyo and Kilwa Kivinje. The new development at Dar es Salaam fell quickly into ruin and disrepair. Wild reptiles, birds and beasts of the bush took up residence in the sultan's palace and state buildings. Yet, though the next 17 years saw Sultan Majid's dream town fall into neglect and decline, they also allowed a more realistic community to establish itself, as the diverse commercial farming and trading community integrated with the resident Zaramo tribes. Local trade and production increased steadily, as did the population, which by now mainly consisted of the original Zaramo people, Swahili Muslim and Hindu traders, and Arab ship-owners, merchants, planters, soldiers and officials. The foreign consulates and dignitaries that Majid had wooed at his grand opening kept an eye on the business potential of the area.

Although Sultan Barghash professed disinterest, the sultanate continued to collect revenue from Dar's now extensive mainland coconut plantations, and duty from the use of the new harbour where coconut, rice , rubber and fish were traded for cloth and beads. Barghash retained his own representatives in the city, appointing a governor, called first an *akida* then a *wali*, and an army of Arab and Baluchi troops to ensure that his fees were collected.

The German Era

In 1887 the German East Africa Company moved into the house of the sultan's governor and persuaded the sultan to let them take over the job of collecting custom revenues. They paid the Zaramo for land concessions and took administrative control of the city from the sultan in a very short time. The sudden threat that they posed to the established economic alliance, and their widely enforced new taxes (on such items as the people's huts), pushed the Zaramo, Swahili and Arabs into joint action. After less than a year of European administration, the people revolted. This uprising is often misleadingly referred to as the Arab Revolt on account of its belligerent Arab instigator, a coastal sugar-plantation owner called Bushiri ibn Salim al-Harthi (*see* p.203), but in reality the majority was united against the newcomers.

The people held out for long enough for the Germans to take the matter seriously. After a few buildings were destroyed and a certain amount of damage done, the East Africa Company was stripped of its power in order to make way for the German Government's colonial authorities – backed by the army – to overcome the revolution and take control of the city in 1891. The German colonists transferred their seat of government from Bagamoyo, whose port was unsuitable for their steamships, to Dar es Salaam, which became the new central seat of administration for German East Africa. The harbour's coastal connection with Zanzibar was broken; ties between the island and mainland were severed for the next 20 years.

Race, religion and wealth quickly defined the city's residential areas. Although these divisions have eased somewhat since Independence and subsequent conscious attempts at integration, it remains very apparent that the city's districts are based on social divisions. Although Dar es Salaam hardly existed before the late 1800s, there was a spate of construction during the latter years of the 19th century that has been sporadically continued by each successive government.

The Twentieth Century and Beyond

Dar es Salaam remained in the control of German East Africa until British Occupation in 1916. In 1919 it came under the full jurisdiction of the British-administered Tanganyika Territory and remained a part of it until 1961, when the country gained independence. In the early years of the century Dar es Salaam grew, with new developments of smart housing to accommodate colonial residents and government officials. The German officials had built fine villa residences behind the principal administration buildings on the Azania (now Kivukoni) front, along wide streets and surrounded by a botanical garden. These were set on pillars with thick whitewashed walls and airy rooms; most had two storeys and covered verandahs, and were built so solidly that many still exist to the east and north of the centre. With such smart foundations to build on, the British made Dar es Salaam the capital in 1920.

Selander Bridge was also completed at the end of the late 1920s, helping further growth north towards the Msasani peninsula, through Kinondoni, Regent Estate and Oysterbay. The colonial residential area continued to expand, and during the 1930s the region north of the golf course at Ras Upanga was developed along the sea front. The boom slowed during the Second World War, and only continued at a much more cautious pace after 1945.

Of the two colonial powers, the Germans were notably more effective in creating elegant and permanent structures than the British, who suffered intense economic upheaval after the wars and were perhaps more aware of the transient nature of their occupation. The British generally favoured rebuilding and redesign over the construction of expensive new buildings, although they did establish the golf course, Gymkhana Club and King George V Memorial Museum, now the National Museum.

Meanwhile, the less grand parts of the town, the residential areas for the working class majority, were developing with great speed. The growing Swahili population, catering for the needs of the new upmarket suburbs of Kinondoni and Oysterbay, expanded north and southwest of Msasani. The working class grew in response to the developing commercial centre. Dar es Salaam remained a township until 1949, when it became the first municipality of Tanganyika governed by the British protectorate. In December 1961, at Independence, it was elevated to city status, and the clock tower at the southern end of Samora Avenue was erected to celebrate the event.

Locals relate how clean and peaceful the old town was before Independence, and comment on the increased mess since. But this does not quite tie up with parallel tales of extreme famine and misery after the Second World War, when things were so bad that the Zaramo reputedly sold themselves as slaves. The population chart of Dar es Salaam shows an estimated 900 inhabitants in 1867, 10,000 in 1894, 140,000 in 1952 and 272,515 in 1967. The city now has a population of about two million.

Around the City

Dar es Salaam does not have much to offer in the way of glamour, and neither does it boast a mass of exceptional sights: the charm of the city is its surprisingly relaxed pace, against a curious background of mixed cultures and architectural styles. The National Museum, however, houses an excellent collection of relics from the country's extraordinary past, and a number of interesting, motley old buildings around the city centre paint the picture of its eclectic history. If the heat or exertions of the day in the town's bustling centre send you in search of relaxation, you can head for luxurious Western-style surroundings at Msasani Slipway, catch the breeze at the more relaxed Coco Beach at Oysterbay, or otherwise take time out closer to town in the pleasantly shaded garden bar at the Palm Beach Hotel.

Askari Monument and Clock Tower

One of the best landmarks for orientation in the city centre is the **Askari Monument** at the junction of Samora Avenue where Maktaba Street bisects it – about halfway along it between Bibi Titi Mohamed and Ocean Road: from it the town radiates in a predominantly grid-like fashion – allowing for fairly reliable navigation.

Th monument itself is a superb memorial to those who fought in the First World War, particularly the African troops and porters on whom the war under the equatorial sun so relied. The pillar was not originally intended to hold an Askari – the Swahili name by which Tanzanian soldiers in the British Army were known – at all, but instead a rather pompous statue of the first German Commissioner, Herman von Wissman, who was billeted here in 1888 to put an end to the Bushiri Uprising. The British removed or destroyed all such monuments to the previous colonial power, and swiftly took Wissman down on their arrival. The Askari statue and relief work on its plinth were sculpted by an Englishman, James Alexander Stevenson; it was set into its present position in 1927. The inscription, in English and Swahili, is by Rudyard Kipling.

The **clock tower** at the western end of Samora Avenue is another good point for orientation, although distinctly less artistic and certainly less imaginative. It was erected in 1961 to celebrate Tanzanian Independence. Most of the oldest buildings in Dar are found between these two points, especially facing the sea on Kivukoni Front and Sokoine Drive, and to the northeast of the monument by the Botanical Gardens.

Colonial-era Dar

Anyone interested in seeing the remnants of the colonial era should not find it hard, especially on the eastern peninsula where the characteristic whitewashed stone edifices date mainly from the days of the German administration. Its offices were purpose-built from scratch at the eastern end of the harbour, the opposite corner from that focused on by Sultan Majid's original town plan, leaving his developments on the western corner for the port and warehouses. The heart of the new city lies around these colonial buildings and offices, dating from the 1890s, that curl along the peninsula of Kivukoni Front and Sokoine Drive. You can still see the old **High Court**, now the **Magistrate's Court**, and the **Secretariat**, two-storey buildings painted white, with impressive wooden shutters and upper balconies overlooking the waterfront.

The German colonials also built a number of residential dwellings in this corner of town to suit their favoured stone design, with two storeys supported on pillars, and often a verandah at first-floor level. There are also a number of bungaloid residences here, typical work of the British administration, and a fine museum (see below).

These are surrounded by the old **Botanical Gardens**, started in 1893 by the first director of agriculture, Professor Stuhlmann, who went on to direct the Research Centre at Amani in the Usambara Mountains (see pp.187–8). Parts of the gardens have been restored recently and new labels added, and some are now enclosed within the grounds of the National Museum. The remainder is always open to the public.

The impressive Ocean Road Hospital to the east of the gardens between Samora Avenue and Ocean Road was also built during this era, in 1897, and is still widely referred to as the **German Hospital** although it has been officially renamed the Government Hospital. The thick whitewashed walls belie its colonial roots although the architectural influences are distinctly Arabic, with a grand two-storey verandah opened with elegantly pointed arches, and unusually ostentatious adornments of octagonal domed towers topped with spiky iron stars. The hospital still receives aid from its original German benefactors, and was the home of the team who identified the tuberculosis bacillus. To this day, it has a very highly regarded cancer ward.

The National Museum

Shaaban Robert Street, t (022) 2122030; open 9.30–5.30; adm, students half-price.

The original single-storey construction with its red-tiled roof was built in 1940 and called the King George V Memorial Museum until 1963, when its name was changed. The building acts as the museum offices and a striking new block houses archaeological and historic exhibits from all over Tanzania. It has prehistoric relics from Olduvai Gorge, and remains found in Kilwa and Mafia, dating from the 14th-century gold trade. There are also interesting colonial-era photographs on display.

Government Buildings and Mzizima Fish Market

Nearby **Karimjee Hall** also dates from the British era, and was the home of the pre-Independence Legislative Council, built by and named after a family of sisal traders who remain pre-eminent today. This was the seat of the government before the capital was transferred to Dodoma, and it remains in use for political functions and committee meetings. Its impressively fine exterior is set off by surrounding gardens, filled with screeching peacocks. Directly south of Karimjee Hall, the grand new **State House** does a good impersonation of the White House in Washington DC, this one set in state within a high-walled enclosure on Kivukoni Front, close to the High Court.

This eastern peninsula is the place to visit the bustling **Mzizima Fish Market** at its tip (*open daily, and best visited in the early morning*). Also catch the ferry from here to **Kigamboni**, where there are some quiet beaches and the direct coastal road to the southern beaches (*see* pp.232–6).

New Africa Hotel and Harbourside

Heading directly southeast from the Askari Monument along Azikwe Street brings you past the site of the first colonial hotel, once the infamous Kaiserhof Hotel and then the **New Africa Hotel** after the British took it over. This is now the *new* New Africa Hotel: it has recently undergone drastic rebuilding and does not bear much likeness to the old low-rise original.

Further along, on the sea front, is the prettily red-tiled, somewhat Hansel and Gretel-style **Azania Lutheran Church**, which dates back to 1898; it has been excellently renovated and is now in good repair. Following the harbour road in a westerly direction leads you on to Sokoine Drive and past the **Old Posta** on the corner of Mkwepu Street. This old post office dates from the German era, and still has a distinct grandeur in its stature and red-tiled roof that has not been entirely lost since its post-Independence facelift. Directly in front is the central **dala-dala terminal**. Just a few paces further west is a seaside **market** and the **ferry port** for boats to Zanzibar island, Lindi and Mtwara down the coast. Almost directly opposite the ferry port, facing the harbour, is **St Joseph's Catholic Cathedral**, which was begun almost as soon as the Lutheran Church was completed, and finished in the early 1900s. It was designed in a grand Gothic style, and is a powerful building with its carved single spire, measured arched and buttressed finish.

While most of Sultan Majid's buildings and dockside warehouses have not survived, the grand two-storey **guest residence** that was used to welcome foreign consuls to the new city in 1867 still stands just beyond the cathedral, on the corner of Sokoine Drive and Morogoro Road. This later became the **Old Boma** after the arrival of the Germans, but remains one of the oldest features of Dar es Salaam .

The oldest non-administrative building sits back on the corner opposite the old post office, just about propped up between the Ministry of Water, Energy and Minerals and a secondary school. This is the **White Fathers' House**, originally built by Sultan Majid in 1865 as a town palace to house his many wives. The sultan sold it to the White Fathers' Mission in 1922; they renamed it Atiman House after Adrian Atiman, a dedicated doctor whom the White Fathers had saved from slavery in his early years.

Uhindini – the Asian District

The **Asian district**, known widely although unofficially as Uhindini, developed in a very centralized way, starting from a central area northwest of Samora Avenue. The

Indian market area along India Street has now expanded into the maze of roads beyond Jamhuri Street. This area is a jumble of shop fronts beneath family residences, offering a diverse combination of often quite inspired architectural styles where families have built on extra storeys, balconies and carved verandahs as their wealth has increased. The area is also divided internally into different Indian communities, with individual **mosques** and **temples** at the heart of each.

The fine **Ismaili Jamatkhana mosque** on Upanga Road was the site of an impressive act of fund-raising by the Aga Khan (grandfather to the present Karim Khan), when he recognized the need for donations to enhance the living and education standards of the local community. He encouraged all who attended the mosque to donate money and wealth in excess of his own body weight, and succeeded in amassing enough gold, diamonds and money to tip the scales. This sort of behaviour caught the eye of the beautiful actress Rita Hayworth, who later married the sultan.

Kariakoo Market

The continually growing residential suburbs offer plenty of opportunities to see traditional local **Swahili houses**. Some of the oldest African houses are clustered in the colourful and busy dirt roads around Kariakoo Market (beware of pickpockets in the crowds outside the market). This grid-like formation of streets west of the centre was devised in the German era in a bid to counteract the ill effects of overcrowding and slum-dwelling that resulted from the always dangerously high population levels. Most of the houses are of a regular single-storey, rectangular design, although the internal layout varies dramatically according to the resources available to each land-lord or family. Many now have a tap connected to the mains water supply, whereas they all used to rely on a public standpipe in the street. Such suburbs have developed small commercial centres, with numerous local *dukas* for all kinds of groceries and supplies, and charcoal-vendors, millers, shoe-cleaners and others opening up a room of their property to trade. Further town planning continues to the north around Ilala; in the decades since Independence the National Housing Corporation has built blocks of flats, which are now rented at premium rates.

Udzunguni – the 'Place of the Europeans'

Following the Upanga Road north leads on past the old **Gymkhana Club**, and into the region historically known as Udzunguni, the 'place of the Wazungu', or Europeans. The population ultimately expanded from Upanga through Oysterbay to Msasani, but changing times have seen this area develop into the domain of the rich and famous; big house spotting in this area is an art. Every taxi driver knows who lives where, and can point out the sheer magnitude of some of the **government houses** – notably that of the president – the various **embassies** located here, and the British Petroleum residence where Roald Dahl lived in his early career working for the oil company. These grand properties, now home exclusively to the expatriate community, were originally built by wealthy plantation owners as a city retreat. The biggest money-spinner was sisal, used in rope manufacture and supplied to navies and industries worldwide. In 1961 nylon was invented and the bottom fell out of the sisal market. Later that year, independence brought dozens of ambassadors to the new state, all looking for suitably elegant accommodation. The shrewd planters sold out to the new embassies which keep residencies there to this day. If you go as far as Oysterbay you will find **Rita Hayworth House**, the temporary home of the legendary Hollywood star, out on a secluded limb on the cliffside.

Palm Beach

Just beyond the city centre en route to the coast, the **Palm Beach Hotel**, close to the Ocean Road on Ali Hassan Mwinyi Road, is a good place to take a break. Relax in the shady garden bar, and appreciate the heady Art Deco aspirations of the new colonists in the early 20th century. The Palm Beach has hardly been remodelled at all over the last hundred years, and is therefore quite justified in its claim to be the oldest hotel in Dar es Salaam: the British, who generally rejected new building in favour of cheaper remodelling, transformed old Kaiserhof Hotel into the New Africa, and remodelled the old governor's residence to become the present-day State House.

National Village Museum

Bagamoyo Road, t (022) 2700437; open 9–6; adm, charge for photos.

The National Village Museum has full-scale examples of traditional buildings from all over Tanzania, showing the wide range of styles. At the time of writing exhibits show distinct signs of neglect, but plans are afoot to redevelop the museum in the near future; all exhibits are at least well signed. The museum frequently invites dance troupes – especially Makonde Sindimba dancers – from all over Tanzania for weekend sessions from 6 to 8pm, a popular choice for parents with children. Watch for the unusual sculptor's stall to the left-hand side as you enter: he sometimes has an interesting and unusual display of superbly crafted clay figurines to exhibit or sell.

Msasani Peninsula and Mwananyamala

Beyond the museum lies the **Msasani Peninsula**, thought to have been one of the first Arabic settlements on the coast, with the ruins of an ancient graveyard and an old fishing village nearby. Nowadays it is an airy new residential area. Inland from Msasani is an area known as **Mwananyamala**. Before its development in the early 1900s this was a swamp frequented by wild animals. Mothers crossing the area at dusk or in the dark had to tell their children *Mwanyanyamala* – 'Baby, don't cry' – so they would not attract the attention of wild animals and could get safely to the other side. Mwananyamala is best avoided these days, since wild things of a human disposition inhabit the streets at night, and the area is known as a haven for drug-dealers.

Dar Beaches

Although there are sandy, wave-pounded beaches close to the city centre, such as **Coco Beach** on the Ocean Road, swimming is not recommended here as the current is strong and lives have been lost. Even paddling is perilous due to the ubiquitous spiny

Getting There and Around

By Air

Visitors to Ras Kutani or Amani can take a 10min flight from Dar es Salaam to the airstrips which serve each individual hotel. **Coastal Travels**, 107 Upanga Road, PO Box 3052, **t** (022) 2117959–60, **f** (022) 2118647/2117985, *aviation@coastal.cc, www.coastal.cc*, regularly charter back and forth, and charge about $180 each way for a three-seater plane.

By Bus or Car

A **shuttle bus** service runs from outside the New Africa Hotel in Dar es Salaam city centre to the **northern beaches** stopping at Jangwani Sea Breeze, White Sands and the Beachcomber Hotel. The trip costs T.shs 8,000/$13 per vehicle, so the individual cost depends on the number of fellow passengers. A **taxi** from the centre costs around T.shs 15,000, from the airport around T.shs 25,000. All of these beach hotels are accessible by **car** along Jangwani Road from the junction off the Old Bagamoyo Road. Bahari Beach and Silver Sands are further north along this road towards Bagamoyo, and are both signposted.

There are two **driving routes** to the best **southern beaches**: one is a longer inland route taking around 1½hrs from the city centre, the other is a coastal route, reached via the car ferry at Mzizima Fish Market south of Dar's centre, which takes 1hr when the road is in good condition, 3hrs if it's bad.

To follow the coastal route, take the crowded 15min ferry ride to the rural ferry port at **Kigamboni**. The nearby beaches at Kigamboni are a welcome respite if you're seeking a day's refuge from the city. While away time in one of the simple beach bars, or take a picnic and enjoy the peace and quiet. This area is experiencing quite fast-paced development; hotels and lodges are being built to meet the demands of the backpacker market. To reach the more secluded beaches, continue by car from the port, following the tarmac road southwards until it bears sharp right. Continue straight on here (not to the right), and after about 28km Ras Kutani and Amani Beach Club are signposted. A new tarmac road runs along the coast; allowing for a clear run from Dar to take only 45mins. To hire a car to get here from Dar es Salaam (*see* pp.215–16) will cost in the region of $150, including taxes.

Sports and Activities

Just next door to the White Sands Hotel on Mbezi Beach is **Water World**, the first water slide park in Tanzania and the biggest in Central and East Africa, with five pools and an airborne maze of blue tubes. It bears a striking resemblance to every water slide park in the Western world, but at only T.shs 2,000 entry it may be the cheapest anywhere. The Silver Sands Hotel has PADI diving, windsurfing, waterskiing, snorkelling and parasailing facilities. An 18-seat pleasure cruiser and glass-bottomed kayaks offer boaties a chance to indulge. Kite-surfing will soon be available.

Where to Stay

Northern Beaches

Expensive

White Sands Hotel, Jagwani Beach, PO Box 3030, **t** (022) 2647620–6, **f** (022) 2647875, *fom@hotelwhitesands.com, www.hotel whitesands.com*. Only 15mins' drive from the centre of Dar, on Mbezi Beach, a grand business hotel with smart, well presented rooms, all sea-facing and reasonably priced. An atmosphere of ordered cleanliness pervades, even around the fair-sized swimming pool and surrounding sandy areas studded with sunshades. The beach is very tidal, so it's not a sure-fire choice for a dream beach holiday, but it offers a peaceful place to relax and escape the pressures of town. The restaurant has a varied *à la carte* menu, with seafood, vegetarian or Indian choices all moderately priced; wine is expensive.

sea urchins embedded in the rocks and pools. For a really good beach it is worth heading out of town to escape the crowds. There are plenty of beaches to the north of town where you can stay without being too far from the bustling centre, but the

Families with children may prefer the **Pool Bar**, with its good selection of pizzas, burgers, salads and chips. Each Saturday night the hotel arranges a poolside barbecue and disco entertainment. Sunday is family day, with lamb roasted on a spit. B&B or half-board possible. Long-term rates and timeshares available.

Beachcomber Hotel Resort, Jagwani Beach, PO Box 4868, **t** (022) 2647772, *beachcomber @afsat.co.tz, www.beachcomber.co.tz*. This new hotel has recently been completed at Jangwani, the closest beach to the city centre. It's a smart and colourful upmarket choice, offering immaculate and comfortable accommodation, a health club, and an open-air Jacuzzi. There are regular shuttle services to town and the airport. B&B.

Bahari Beach Hotel, Kunduchi Kondo, PO Box 9312, **t** (022) 2650352, *bbhbuz@intafrica.com*. A surprisingly pleasant large beach hotel set between a pleasant open stretch of parkland and a good sandy beach decked with well-spaced sunshades, and just half an hour from Dar es Salaam city centre. The hotel has 100 spacious rooms built into round two-storey pink coral rock bandas. Every room faces the beach and has a balcony sitting area. There's a vast central bar. Wide flights of steps lead to the beach.

Silver Sands Hotel, Kunduchi Beach, PO Box 60097, **t** (022) 2650231/2650567, **f** (022) 2650428, *silversands@africaonline.co.tz*. A short distance south of Bahari Beach Hotel, with a very different atmosphere: soft sandy pathways and a Zen-patterned sand floor in the outdoor dining room, which has good sea views. The hotel is small and friendly, with simple but surprisingly comfortable, pleasantly decorated accommodation in recently converted immaculate terraced bungalows. The rooms surround a rather utilitarian courtyard, but work continues on the garden at its centre. The **Hangover Clinic** or the **Castle Corner Bar** are good spots for afternoon or late-night drinking. The beach is clean and good, with stone groynes to contain the sand and a number of palm trees for shade. The Silver Sands is popular with overland truck parties, and has separate facilities for camping with vehicle for a minimal fee. The hotel has a scuba club and is developing plans to allow scuba-divers freer access to the Marine Park on Mbudya Island, alongside eco-friendly watersports.

Moderate

Jangwani Sea Breeze Hotel, PO Box 934, **t** (022) 2647067/**t** (0741) 325908/320875, **f** (0741) 320714, *jangwani@afsat.com*. Among the choices closer to the city centre, Jangwani is a small and curious beach hotel with plenty of atmosphere and cosy character only 20 minutes' drive from Dar. The hotel is a favourite with German tourists, and the dining room and indoor bar accommodate Continental tastes with an aromatic selection of home-baked seed and rye breads and lavish buffet breakfasts. The hotel is rather oddly arranged on either side of a quiet coastal road, with a swimming pool at each side. Bedrooms are very well appointed with satellite TV, telephone, fridge, safe and sitting area, and all have a choice of fan or air-conditioning. The beach bar and open restaurant at the water's edge have good views; a live band entertains on Saturday nights. The Sunday buffet is a popular excursion from town. The **dive centre** can take you through PADI and SSI courses or organize scuba trips on the reefs beyond the islands.

Southern Beaches

The two good options for staying on the coast south of Dar es Salaam are both 'luxury hideaways' on a delectable and unspoilt stretch of coral sand that extends for mile upon mile. A new moderately priced lodge was due to open in 2005 in the grounds of the Horse Club – one to watch, managed by a rising star of Dar's restaurateurs.

Expensive

Ras Kutani, PO Box 1192, Dar es Salaam, **t** (022) 2134802/2113220/**t** (0741) 334234, **f** (022) 2112794, *www.selous.com*. An elegant, well

much smarter, more idyllic beaches are about an hour's drive south of Dar. There is less choice here, with just two choices for luxury accommodation; both of these have a 'hideaway' appeal, with a sensation of being a long way from anywhere, reinforced established beach hideaway designed in a simple style to suit the surroundings. It sits in a cushion of tropical forest on the banks of a wide freshwater lagoon. Access is via a short walk through wooded paths and a row across the natural pool to a welcoming woodern jetty. The lodge has just 12 private and well spaced *bandas* extending through a fragrant hillside of tropical forest to the powder-soft beach below. The open-plan bar and dining area are liberally furnished with colourful cushions to create a refreshing atmosphere in which to enjoy the extremely high-quality cooking and friendly, attentive service. Ras Kutani provides an escape from the outside world in airy natural woodland, a dreamy environment for visitors to relax in hammocks on their private bamboo banda verandah, in the bar or on the beach (where you are furnished with a small flag to wave or plant in the sand when drinks or snacks are desired). *Boules* and volleyball, boogie boards, kayaks and a laser sailboat are available, plus cards, chess and backgammon for mental stimulation. A new game-fishing boat allows guests to make the most of the abundantly fruitful waters that lap the edge of the broad reef that protects the bay (available subject to tide and weather).

Amani Beach Club, PO Box 1736, Dar es Salaam, **t** (0744) 410033, **f** (022) 2667760, *protea amani@amanibeach.com*, *reservations@ amanibeach.com*, *www.amanibeach.com*. Quite a different style of exclusive accommodation is on offer here at the Amani Beach Club, tucked about 10 minutes away at the other end of the beach with opulent and grand gardens. Also with only 12 rooms, those at Amani are grandly designed in heavy coral rock in the Arabic style. Each of these is a vast and spacious marble-floored 'cottage' with opulent bathroom, air-conditioning, satellite television and built-in options for radio and music. Rooms are packed with Arab-style antiques around a large four-poster bed swathed with nets and chintzy cushions. The hotel is set in colourful gardens where vibrant bougainvillaeas bloom around a huge and ancient old baobab tree. The Beach Club also has a large, clean swimming pool at its centre, and a choice of two restaurants for dining on the beach or in the main building. The club has recently hooked up with Adventure Camps to provide combined fly-in beach and safari holidays; watch out for these holidays, they may be good value (contact **Coastal Travels**, *see* p.214).

Moderate

The Horse Club Lodge (contact Josephine, proprietor of the Horse Club, **t** (0744) 000235), will be known by another name when it is launched in 2005. The enthusiasts at the Horse Club aim at nothing less than a renaissance of equestrianism in East Africa. The endeavour began after Josephine rescued horses from a government farm, where they were badly treated with little to no regard for the future quality of the stock. The breeding and training programme continues to gather pace. Individually tailored programmes of lessons and hacks are available; there are plans to provide preparatory training for riders about to embark on riding safaris. **Camping** at the stunning location is possible, if campers bring all their own food and water supplies. Otherwise, guests will stay at the new **lodge**, which promises to be well conceived, and far cheaper than the other two options in the bay. The lodge will be built in the grounds of the club, yet with separate management. Guests will stay in one of ten beachside stone bandas, with a seawater pool and a large *makuti* chilling area. Expect food and drinking to be excellent; it comes from the team behind Chui Bar and the Mediterraneo hotel in Dar. Either the bar and restaurant will not open to non-residents, or a hefty day charge will be levied, to ensure that Dar hordes do not descend. Horse-riding packages will be offered. Guests will be able to eat at Ras Kutani.

by the forests and gardens that surround them. Both are highly recommended for the outstanding quality of their cuisine too. The coastal regions to the north of the city are more built up, but a string of suburbs here offer beach stays for all budgets.

The beaches and 'resort locations' just north of the city centre are 15–30 minutes away by car, and also served by bus. Many of these **northern beaches** are only accessible through the hotels that cluster along this coastline, and most of these sandy stretches have a more worn palm-cluttered look than their more remote and wild counterparts to the south of the city. However, offshore islands provide pretty good dive sites to explore and there are dive centres here with the facilities to kit you out and show you around. Be aware that many of the larger hotels, such as White Sands and Bahari Beach, charge an access fee to their beaches if you are not staying at the hotel. As a safety tip, you are not advised to walk along the beach between hotels alone, especially at dusk, as muggings have been reported.

A popular location for day-trippers is the generally uninhabited **Bongoyo Island**, which has a beautiful beach accessible by scheduled boats from Msasani Slipway. The boats leave at 9.30, 11.30, 1.30 and 3.30pm; the last boat to return leaves at 4.30pm. The beaches are less crowded on weekdays, when the clutch of tiny palm-leaf shelters are available free of charge. At weekends it is an idea to catch an earlier boat to ensure bagging a banda. A roguish fisherman cooks up deliciously simple fish and chips. Legend has it that he used to lay in wait for tourists and rob them, before he discovered he could feed them and make more money. Snorkelling trips to the reef are fun, and there are a number of nature trails through the impenetrable interior of the island. Coastal Travels plans to build a small lodge on the other side of the island at some point.

Mbudya Island, beyond Bongoyo Island, 4km south of the Silver Sands Hotel beach, is a protected natural area attracting at least 50 species of birds. It is surrounded by healthy coral reefs with good diving. It currently belongs to the Marine Park Board, although the Silver Sands Hotel has set up an information centre about the island and reefs, run by a resident marine biologist. This, and the promise of a day's tranquillity near to the city, has encouraged a growing trickle of tourists to travel to the island with local fishermen, raising the funds to replant coral. Mbudya Island is most easily accessible from the beach locations further north, especially the White Sands, Bahari Beach and Jangwani Sea Breeze. Boat trips to the island take ten minutes.

Anyone dreaming of true seclusion far from the madding crowds should consider heading instead to the **southern beaches** around Ras Kutani, where the sea has a frisky wave and the sand is fine and pristine. This stretch of coast is far from any built-up town or community, with just a couple of farming and fishing villages beyond the forest, so visitors should be prepared to leave the outside world behind them. The mainland coast does not experience such dramatic tidal extremes as the islands, but the sea is a little more lively, so offers fun options for surfing. Nearby reefs and natural lagoons provide perfect snorkelling options, but there is no dive school here. Explore the wild coastline on horseback, riding over sand, through waves and along shaded bush trails, with the local riding centre. Watch out also for the work of the turtle protection scheme (contact the Horse Club for details) which is doing well in the region. Locals are paid to conserve the nests and eggs as they are hatching. The success of the scheme means it will be extended to other endangered animals in the fragile coastal forest ecosystem.

The Coast South of Dar

16

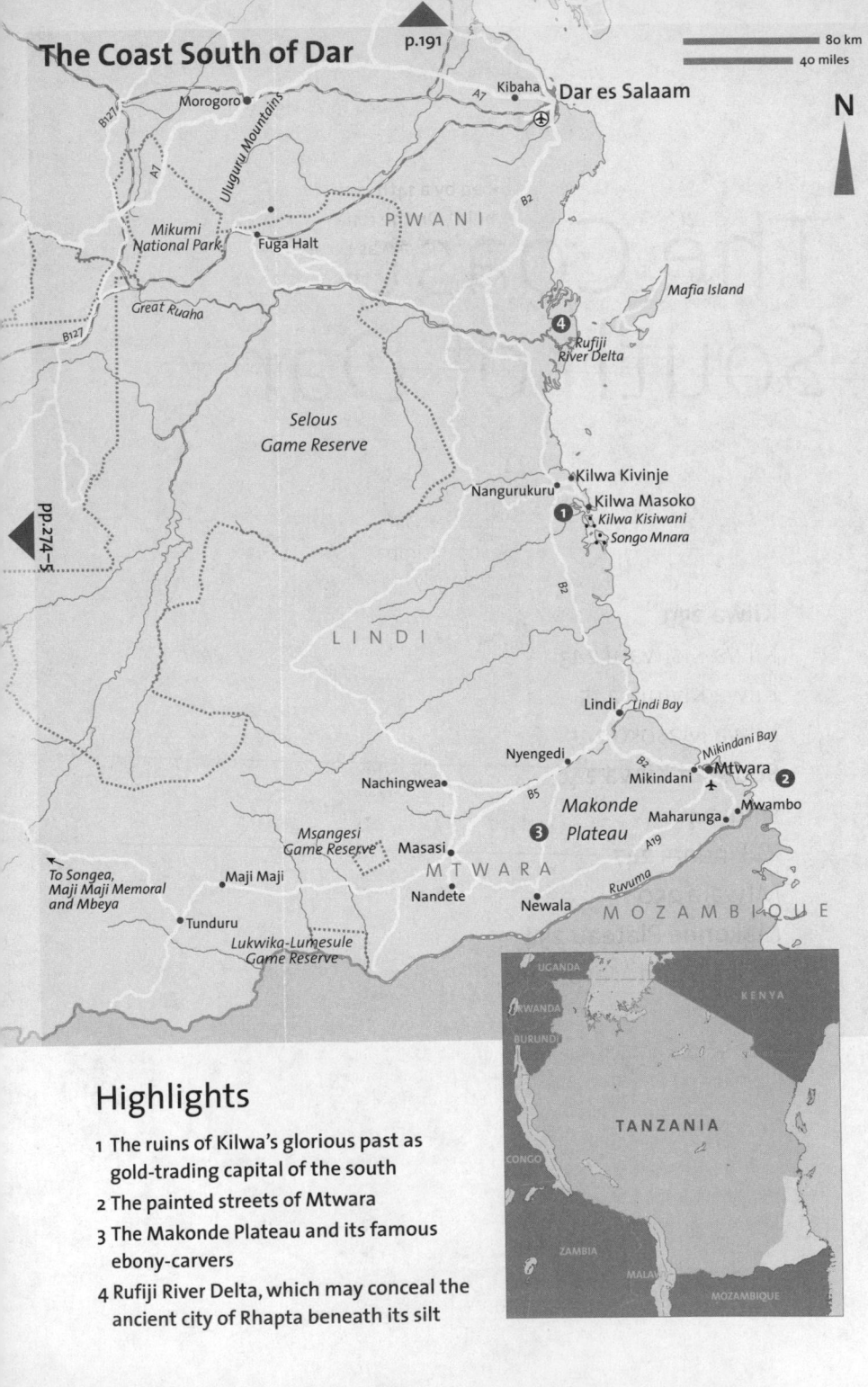

The Coast South of Dar

p.191

80 km
40 miles

N

pp.274–5

Morogoro

Kibaha   **Dar es Salaam**

A7

B27

Uluguru Mountains

A1

Mikumi National Park

Fuga Halt

B2

PWANI

Great Ruaha

B127

Mafia Island

4 *Rufiji River Delta*

Selous Game Reserve

Nangurukuru   Kilwa Kivinje
1   Kilwa Masoko
Kilwa Kisiwani
Songo Mnara

LINDI

B2

Lindi   *Lindi Bay*

Nyengedi   *Mikindani Bay*
B2
Nachingwea   Mikindani **Mtwara**
B5   **2**   Mwambo
Makonde Plateau   Maharunga
Msangesi Game Reserve   Masasi   **3**   A19
M T W A R A
To Songea,   Nandete   Ruvuma
Maji Maji Memoral and Mbeya   Maji Maji   Newala   **M O Z A M B I Q U E**
Tunduru
Lukwika-Lumesule Game Reserve

UGANDA   KENYA
RWANDA
BURUNDI
TANZANIA
CONGO
ZAMBIA
MALAWI
MOZAMBIQUE

Highlights

1 The ruins of Kilwa's glorious past as gold-trading capital of the south

2 The painted streets of Mtwara

3 The Makonde Plateau and its famous ebony-carvers

4 Rufiji River Delta, which may conceal the ancient city of Rhapta beneath its silt

The Indian Ocean coast south of Dar es Salaam shares its past with the stretch north of Dar and the Zanzibar archipelago – a history of trade and settlement, the mingling of African, Shirazi and Arabic civilizations to form an early Swahili culture (*see* pp.191–2). This southern Pwani ('Coast') region boasts the hidden ruins of the once-grand settlement of Kilwa, described by a 14th-century traveller as 'among the most beautiful of cities, and elegantly built'. On the route south to the gold-trading port at Sofala, in present-day Mozambique, Kilwa was the key port for the southern ivory- and slave-trading routes to the interior. Today, attempts are being made to open a new commercial corridor to Malawi and Zambia via the more modern southerly port of Mtwara. Until this happens, the Makonde Plateau inland remains a remote area of Tanzania, most famed for the ebony carvings of its Makonde people.

Kilwa

Just 300km south of Dar es Salaam and 105km north of Lindi, Kilwa sits almost halfway along the Indian Ocean coast between Dar es Salaam and the border of Mozambique, on some of the worst, seasonally impassable roads imaginable. As a result, the historic town has become notoriously hard to visit: it has the reputation of a sleeping beauty in her castle surrounded by a forest of thorns. Yet it is a region of extraordinary historical interest with abundant archaeological remains that chart coastal Swahili culture over 1,000 years, listed as a UNESCO World Heritage Site.

History

Kilwa has a strange history that has led to it evolving into three distinct areas: the ancient island settlement of Kilwa Kisiwani – 'Kilwa of the island'; the old colonial town of Kilwa Kivinje – 'Kilwa of the casuarina trees' and the central, modern port town known as Kilwa Masoko – 'Kilwa of the market', which functions as the present-day district headquarters. Although lacking intrinsic historical interest, its central position and proximity to the airport make Kilwa Masoko the best base for accommodation while visiting the surrounding area; it's also within easy reach of good beaches.

The most ancient and historically important of the Kilwas is Kilwa Kisiwani. This was the original Kilwa settlement, dating from as early as AD 800. The remains of some original structures, particularly mosques, predate the first Arab settlement and indicate an earlier Muslim Swahili culture existing as a result of trade links. An excellent exhibition of the discoveries unearthed at Kilwa by archaeologist Neil Chittick in the 1960s is on display at the National Museum in Dar es Salaam (*see* p.229); it's well worth visiting before you see the ruins to understand and imagine the lavish cosmopolitan luxuries that were once prevalent among these ancient stones.

Kilwa means 'fishing place', and the island settlement grew from a small fishing village into a flourishing world-renowned port town, perfectly situated to handle a boom in Indian Ocean trade. Just north of Sofala and south of Zanzibar, Kilwa became a key port for the import of textiles and china shipped through the Persian Gulf, and for the export of African slaves and gold. The resultant prosperity inspired some of the grandest buildings in pre-colonial equatorial Africa, and sparked a wrangle for

Getting There

The road to Kilwa is appalling, losing its tarmacked surface about 100km out of Dar and becoming impassable in the rainy season. The journey (about 300km) takes a minimum of 12 hours. It is, however, possible to get a **bus** from the main Ubungu terminus in Dar, departing at 6am; the return bus also departs Kilwa at dawn. Book in advance, especially for the return journey. Another option is to take one of the buses travelling to Mtwara and Lindi, get off at Nangurukuru, the intersection for Kilwa, and continue on a local minibus – these are frequent, and travel on a good tarmac road for the last few kilometres. This route is less reliable in reverse, as buses may be full once they reach Nangurukuru from the south. **Coastal Travels** (*www.coastal.cc*) now have scheduled flights from Dar daily.

Getting Around and Tourist Information

Kilwa Masoko is the port for sailing to Kilwa Kisiwani and the island of Songo Mnara. Anyone wishing to make a trip to either of these should first visit the **Department of Antiquities** on the main road just before the port and report to the District Cultural Officer, currently Mr Mohamed Mtule. The learned Mr Senyagwa, District Executive Director, may be able to assist in any areas of study that are not covered elsewhere. Having shown your passport, signed the visitors' book and paid a minimal fee of T.shs 1,500 towards the upkeep of the ruins, it is also possible to negotiate for a boatman or a guide to accompany you.

The combined trip to Kilwa Kisiwani and Songo Mnara is a full day's outing, and it is worth making arrangements the day before if you wish to visit both; sailing on to Songo Mnara can be arduously slow if you are at the whim of tide and wind direction, but there is at least one motorboat for hire if you persist in asking for it! Kilwa Kisiwani is a 15min boat ride from Masoko. A sailboat to Kisiwani will cost around T.shs 4,000, and a further T.shs 6,000 to Songo Mnara. There is a last-minute harbour charge payable to a man in a box at the port entrance. Visiting the ruins at Kisiwani merits at least a 2–3hr visit, as it is necessary to walk some distance between the ruins. It's at least a 45min walk between palace and mosque.

Where to Stay

Kilwa Masoko

Kilwa Ruins, t (023) 2202876 (*moderate*). The newest and best place to stay. Situated on the beach, it has about the best restaurant in the area and can arrange trips to the ruins and Songa Mnara island.

New Mjaka Guesthouse, on the main road (*cheap*). Although there are no upmarket choices, the New Majka provides decent enough rooms in detached bungalow *bandas* with en-suite bathrooms and even a sitting room. The rooms are blessed with running water, fans, nets and electricity, and are kept clean and hospitable. It's a family-run establishment and meals tend to be limited to whatever is available that night. There is little English spoken in Kilwa, so it's worth keeping a phrase-book handy for negotiations; if you have communication problems at Mjaka try asking if Dula is around. The **Masoko by Night Bar** next door, or the **Memory Bar** across the street both have a pleasant atmosphere.

Masoko Hilton Hotel, closer to the beach near Masoko Primary School (*cheap*). This friendly little guesthouse is also good, with clean and well-kept rooms. The restaurant next door is also immaculately kept and a good choice for wholesome and inexpensive plates of local cooking.

Kilwa Kivinje

The atmosphere of this now sleepy small town makes it a pleasant place to explore for a day – which can be done easily from Kilwa Masoko; accommodation in Kilwa Kivinje is limited to some very basic guesthouses.

New Sudi's Guest House (*cheap*). Very much a local place, with basic rooms and no water, but a good seaside atmosphere.

Fourways Guest House (*cheap*). Very basic indeed, and not very clean-looking, either.

The Legend of Kilwa's Sultan

Legend tells that in the late 12th century the island was bought for a length of cloth by the self-proclaimed Shirazi Sultan Ali bin al-Hasan. Four hundred years later it was recorded that he provided enough material to stretch all around the island – nearly 25km of cloth. During his reign, this hugely wealthy sultan issued a vast number of copper coins in his name, which continue to be unearthed by grubby-handed children clutching well-worn handfuls or slivers of these relics, with a precocious eye for their exchange value against tourist dollars. Sultan Ali bin al-Hasan's family ruled for three generations, but had the power wrested from them in 1300 by the established and powerful Mahdali family.

power and control that eventually proved the downfall of a now-legendary civilization. The ruins at Kilwa show a recurring pattern of rising and falling fortunes typical of coastal trading networks dependent on global demands for gold, but eventually the ancient city lost prominence and fell into disrepair. These days a population of around 600 inhabits Kilwa Kisiwani; the ruins are skirted by neat rural East African villages surrounded by copious small stick fences to keep rampaging warthogs from the vegetable gardens. You may still come across one or two extraordinary-looking families with pale skin and strangely pale eyes whose names and features indicate descent from the original Shirazi settlers.

Kilwa's Gold Trade

Kilwa's importance developed as a port midway between Zanzibar and the gold and slave-trading port of Sofala at the mouth of the Zambezi in Mozambique. The town was a key trading point for timber and ivory, gold and slaves brought along well-worn caravan routes from the interior and exchanged for goods from Arabia, Persia and India. The wealthy merchant inhabitants lived in a grand style, with opulent lifestyles reflecting their worldly connections. Descriptions of the island in its heyday, while the Arabs were controlling the gold trade from Sofala, give an evocative impression of its charms. Ibn Battuta, a devout, wealthy and educated Muslim with a reputation for travelling that earned him the title of 'traveller of the age', described Kilwa when he saw it first in 1331 as being 'among the most beautiful of cities, and elegantly built…'. Ibn Battuta held the status of a *qadi*, judge of Islamic *sharia* law, and was invited to visit Kilwa by Sultan al-Hasan ibn Sulayman, who had himself spent two years in Mecca. At this time, the Sultan would also have held dominion over the grand developments on the nearby island of Songo Mnara.

Kilwa experienced a surge in wealth and prominence from trade when gold demands were at their peak in the early 14th century, reflected in the stone buildings that were built at this time. In 1320 the Great Mosque was enlarged to four times its size, and domes were added to it and the historic Husuni Kubwa Palace. A profusion of town houses were built in the town centre from quarried coral and lime, designed in a regular, measured, less grand style with flat roofs on wooden rafters supported by pillars. Stone houses remained the preserve of the wealthy; clay, wood and thatch homes continued to be constructed around the outskirts. There is now little evidence of these original buildings on Kisiwani, since older domestic buildings were plundered for stone during a successive phase of affluence during the 18th century. The ruins on the nearby island of Songo Mnara are the best remaining example of this early style. The mosques escaped this demise, as even their stones are considered sacred.

Portuguese Control

This beautifully organized settlement at the centre of the gold route so impressed the Portuguese that more than 150 years later they wrested control of it by force. When the first Portuguese fleet, commanded by Pedro Alvares Cabral, arrived in the early 1500s it was greeted with such suspicion by Sultan Ibrahim of Kilwa that there was a stand-off at sea for two days. Ultimately the fleet gave up and sailed away from Kilwa, which had refused to accept demands for a Portuguese trading port under Christian dominion. Before setting sail, however, the Portuguese sailors had not failed to note the elegance of the island port, with its vast palace and courtyards, fountains, orchards and mosques. One, Gaspar Correa, wrote, 'The city comes down to the shore, and is entirely surrounded by a wall and towers, within which there are maybe 12,000 inhabitants... The streets of the city are very narrow, as the houses are very high, of three and four storeys, and one can run along the tops of them upon terraces.'

The infamous Vasco da Gama returned in 1502 to take a strong line with the sultan, proposing to bombard the town to smithereens unless the sultan bowed to the Portuguese occupation and paid an annual tribute in gold. The Portuguese desire to overthrow this irritatingly resistant stronghold and control the flow of gold should not be underestimated. They attacked, looting and plundering the town, which the sultan had deserted in the night. Finally the Portuguese flag was raised in Kilwa. The new rulers were even more eloquent about the stronghold. In 1503 Dom Francisco d'Almeida wrote, 'Kilwa, of all the places I know in the world, has the best port and the fairest land that can be... In it are lions, deer, antelopes, partridges, quail and nightingales and many kinds of birds and sweet oranges and pomegranates, lemons, green vegetables, figs of the land, coconuts and yams and marvellous meats and fishes and very good water from the wells.' Unfortunately, the Portuguese were responsible for the devastating decline of this 'fairest land', as the dispossessed Arabs had no fortune to maintain the town and it fell into disrepair. Just ten years after Dom Francisco's proclamation, the Portuguese abandoned their blissful island home and centred their power on islands further north. Kilwa's luck was not set to improve, as shortly after, in the late 1500s, the island was subjected to a surprise attack by the Zimba tribe from Zimbabwe, who are reported to have eaten a large proportion of Kilwa's inhabitants.

Omani Arabs took control of Kilwa at the beginning of the 1700s, but Kilwa regained its independence in 1770. Trade saw a brief revival in the 18th century, as international commercial trends dictated an increase in demand for ivory and slaves, and Kilwa experienced a building boom. Mosques were renovated and a new fortified palace constructed, so impressive that it was known as Makutani, 'the place of the great walls'. This phase of prosperity was short-lived: in 1784 Omani Arabs returned and once again wrested political control, with true conquering verve claiming jurisdiction by building over the Portuguese foundations. This was the start of Kilwa's long decline.

Kilwa Kisiwani

Visitors to Kisiwani tend to arrive on the shore beneath an impressive ancient fort generally called the **Gereza**. This monumental stone edifice is a typical coastal fortress, added to by successive generations of rulers. The Portuguese constructed the original fort in less than three weeks. They were evidently satisfied by their efforts, judging from the proud report from Francisco d'Almeida to the King of Portugal in 1505, offering 'years of [my] life for the King to see ... it is so strong that the King of France could be awaited there, and has lodgings in very fine houses for twice as many people as are left there now'. The structure as it is today is mainly the handiwork of the Omani Arabs who built over the old Portuguese remains when they took over Kilwa in the 18th century. When explorer John Hanning Speke visited in 1857 he noted that the inscription above the door of the fortress was still legible, recording that the gate was built in 1807, some time after the Arabs had regained control. Today the rooms in the northeast corner are in the best condition, although the entrance hall with its stone benches and arrow slits maintains an eerie sense of the building's original function. Musket bullets and beads have been found in the preserved rooms, and two German cannons remain rusting in the central courtyard. Now the only battle the Gereza faces is the continual encroachment of natural forces. Wind and sea have eaten into its once-powerful stone, its courtyards are turning to grass, and high on its tower a baobab has taken root.

Kilwa's Mosques

A short walk brings you to the monumental and remarkably well-preserved remains of the **Friday** or **Great Mosque**. When the Great Mosque was built in the 11th century it would have been a small typical Swahili coastal design with a flat roof, supported on nine 16-sided wooden columns in rows of three. This is now the open-air northern portion of the standing mosque, and the remains of the original open-air washing area are evident on the western side, with a small sunken courtyard and sandstone blocks for rubbing the feet dry after washing. The growing demand for gold in India and Europe and resultant prosperity of the port three centuries later in 1320 saw the mosque dramatically enlarged to reflect the increased status of the town, and crowned with its charismatic domes. These would have been influenced by the growing awareness of international architectural styles practised on the opposite shores of the Indian Ocean, and the finished design became the glory of the coast. Unfortunately the elegant eight-sided pillars were not strong enough to support an ambitiously large dome on the southeast corner, and after the roof began to crumble these were reconstructed with slightly less refined coral limestone blocks. Chittick's excavations in the 1960s revealed the foundations of the **Great House**, a palace behind the mosque. An interesting link between all of the important buildings on Kilwa is the intricate underground passage system that was used to carry water between the Gereza, mosque and palace. The passages extend to 12m deep in places.

Nearby is the **Small Domed Mosque**, a miniature reproduction of the Great Mosque. This tiny ruin has a fascinating and unusual charm, with a neat symmetrical nine-domed square flanked by a tiny washing room. The ceiling inside is carved with small roundels that were once filled with colourful Oriental ceramics, still evident in some areas, and the roof is crowned with an impressive stone obelisk, missing its top portion, which has broken off. The Small Mosque was based on the remains of a much older building, and would have originally been elevated on a platform above the level of the street. To the south and southeast of the central mosques are three **cemetery** areas, one of which is said to contain the tombs of the Kilwa sultans; another is known as the 'graves of the 40 sheikhs' – apparently the result of a protracted argument that resulted in all 40 of them dying on the same day.

Makutani, the 'Place of the Great Walls', and the Husuni Kubwa

Beyond the mosque, at the western end of town, are the remains of a lofty construction known as **Makutani** or 'Place of the Great Walls', a palace for the sultans in the late 17th and 18th centuries. The western aspect is designed as a network of grand reception rooms, courtyards and kitchens, with long stone tunnels from floor to floor that would have served as an early and elaborate form of indoor pit latrine – they cause great consternation among most of the guides who show you around.

A mile from the centre of town stands lasting evidence of a far more opulent and elaborate culture of sultan rule that predates the Makutani settlement by at least 300 years. At the height of Kilwa Kisiwani's wealth and prestige an exceptionally grand and fascinating palace, the **Husuni Kubwa**, was built away from the town centre on the island coast. The palace is a fine architectural spread of open and arched courtyards, three-storey elevations of rooms and an elaborate octagonal bathing pool that shows a style and expertise quite unlike anything else on the Zanj coast at this time. This fantastic stronghold was positioned to command views over Kilwa harbour, and benefit from the coastal breeze. Visitors enter the palace through the **Domestic Court**, climbing a series of worn stone steps that reach a high platform at the end of a long courtyard with open porticoes to either side. The next room on the west side is the **Pavilion**, where the sultan performed his public duties, commanding views of the coast from a pleasant cool and shady arena. To the west again is the **Audience Court**, where the sultan would also have received his visitors. The lower half of the coral wall is carved with small square niches, which are thought to have contained flickering gas lamps. This area is likely to have been used for entertainment such as dance performances, with audiences seated on the steep flight of steps at the eastern end. A **foot tank** is built into the stairs at the entrance to the Pavilion, so that all visitors attending the sultan could be certain to arrive with fragrant, freshly washed feet.

Husuni Kubwa was only occupied for three generations, at most. The exceptional opulence of a palace so grand simply could not sustain its own momentum. Even filling the pretty little octagonal swimming pool would have required scores of slaves hand-carrying water – enough buckets to fill its 80-cubic-metre capacity. The sheer enormity of the manpower and the logistics required to run the beautiful palace on the clifftop were incompatible with any change of fortune, and now the ruins represent the mesmerizing peak of power, grasped and then lost for ever.

Kilwa Kivinje

Kilwa Kivinje developed as a prosperous mainland port town during the reign of Sultan Sayyid Said bin Sultan (1806–1856), and continued to feature as an important trading post for the German colonialists. The Arab building boom was in the early to mid-19th century; the Germans carried on building in the late 19th century. The stone buildings along the waterfront are from the German colonial period – the boma, customs post and two large houses in Mjengera Road. Just off it is an old Islamic building complex – a walled open space containing a house, small mosque, *bikira* (washing facilities) and a cemetery. It has been noted that there are surprisingly few mosques in the old quarter of town: one story tells that the German District Officer complained bitterly about the noise of the daily *azan*, the Muslim call to prayers, close to his residence. A new Friday Mosque was swiftly constructed outside the old town centre, and the old one abandoned. Time has had its own revenge: a German monument of 1888, flanked by four up-ended cannons, is now mostly submerged by drifting sand piles. Kivinje continued to operate as a clandestine slave-trading port until 1884, when a British initiative placed vice-consuls at three major ports along the coast to quash the last vestiges of the trade. In a sign of Kivinje's continuing decline, the district headquarters were transferred in 1956 from Kivinje to Masoko, which has a deeper harbour and was closer to the airstrip.

Kilwa Masoko

The new main town of Kilwa Masoko sits astride the main coastal road with an air of sun-baked Wild West sleepiness pervading its daylight hours. It comes alive when night falls: a large market gathers in the sandy streets parallel to the beach and the streets are illuminated with small fires cooking fish and maize; crackling sound systems crank into action from the surrounding collection of small bars and restaurants. During the day, the beach is pleasant to walk along, with some more secluded areas for swimming. Keep your valuables safe while bathing.

A new aid and tourism initiative has been launched recently to make the most of Kilwa's tourist potential in collaboration with aid projects. The Swiss-run scheme intends to promote the region around Kilwa and the Rufiji River Delta to the north. Still in its early stages, it focuses on marine safaris devised and led by local fishermen, such as 'walkabout' tours of coral reefs for children, or coastal walks with local guides, overnighting on wooden platforms in treetops. Diving with hippos is also on offer, as are night-time croc-catching trips in pirogues: in this bizarre sport, crocodiles dozing on the banks of the Rufiji River are dazzled by torchlight before being locked in an embrace by the thrill-seeking 'hunters', who re-release the beasts into the river – none the worse for wear, they swear. The reciprocal aid project aims to improve schools, hospitals and airstrip safety, and to involve local people in preserving flora and fauna. The scheme is run by **Cape Ltd**, which can be found at PO Box 1, Kilwa Masoko, where Thomas Jansson is in charge, or in Dar es Salaam, **t** (022) 2213203/2214675–7/2213200/ **t** (0742) 7852000, *cape.ltd@african-sky.com*, *www.african-sky.com*.

South of Kilwa

South of Kilwa the road improves again before reaching the relatively prosperous southerly ports of Mtwara, Lindi and Mikindani, and heading inland to the Makonde Plateau, home of the famous ebony-carvers. This region borders Mozambique, easily reached across the Ruvuma River on foot at low tide or by river ferry at high tide.

Lindi

The small town of Lindi is an uneventful, quietly dusty port town that makes a welcome stop if you approach it travelling south on the long hot road from Kilwa. There is little immediately to indicate its more glorious past, now barely discernible from the scattering of unusual and diverse ruins among the grid of dusty low-level housing and shop fronts. The town preserves, however, an atmosphere of self-sufficiency and quiet industry that gives it a curiously dignified feel despite its declining fortunes during the 20th century. It has two large mosques and a fine Hindu temple at its centre, and a distinctly Asian and Arabic character, with many Indian merchants still based here for their port of trade. The surrounding natural areas include clear beaches to the north of town and areas of rainforest nearby at the Litipo Forest Reserve near Rutamba village; both are worthwhile excursions.

Lindi Town

Omani Arabs settled in Lindi during the 18th century, leaving a legacy of carved door lintels and an old stone tower on the harbour front that stand as witness to their era

Getting There

Buses depart the Ubungu terminal in **Dar es Salaam** for Lindi most days, with an overnight stop on the way. It's an excruciatingly long journey on roads that are impassable after rain; it's worth booking a seat in advance. There is a good tarmacked road on to **Mtwara** and **Masasi**, with frequent buses to Mtwara.

Where to Stay and Eat

There are a few restaurants in Lindi's main street for good food and a handful of decent budget rooms. It's also possible to find good, cheap rooms in the village across the bay.

Nankolowa Guesthouse, Rutamba Street, just south of the clock tower and market. The best all-round choice for accommodation, which is not only central, clean, well-furnished and pleasant, but has a decent dining room and a good menu to boot; it's advisable to order in advance. The staff are helpful and welcoming. Choose between self-contained rooms with fan or cheaper 'standard' rooms.

Coastal Guest House, beside the fruit and vegetable market on the coast to the north of the harbour. Sadly the choices for beach-side accommodation in town are generally fairly grotty, although they are on the whole cheaper as a result. The Coastal is the best, although there are no mosquito nets and no restaurant.

Malaika Restaurant, on the main road east of the market heading for the coast. Clean and cool, with superb air-conditioning, serving wholesome plates of home cooking to delight the heart. It does not provide an enormous amount of choice, but the 'thali'-style mix of dishes is a good choice.

Maji Maji Restaurant, south of the bus station. A worthwhile spot for decent local dishes at a local price.

of power. The port became an important centre on the slave-trading caravan route between Lake Nyasa and Kilwa Kivinje in the 19th century when it fell under the jurisdiction of the Sultan of Zanzibar; it was at this time that the **clock tower** now standing at the town centre near the **market** was built. Later Lindi became the main seaport for Lake Nyasa and, during the German era, was made the administrative centre for the entire Southern Province. Its coast was developed to include a customs house and store house for the German East Africa Company. The dilapidated and overgrown **boma** north of the Arab tower overlooking the sea and immaculate parallel-line town planning are reminders of the German period. Seafront benches and ancient old hotels suggest that Lindi was a popular resort for expatriate farmers to spend time at the coast in a degree of comfort, but the town was abandoned during the years of the British protectorate in favour of the town of Mtwara with its deep natural port. The surrounding area was severely damaged by the disastrous British scheme to make a fortune from groundnut crops, on completely the wrong type of soil. Injury was added to dismal fortune when the town suffered cyclone damage in the 1950s. A walk up the seafront and into the market is a pleasant diversion and will reveal most of the landmarks mentioned above.

Beaches and Trips

The best beach is **Mtema Beach**, about 5km north of the town centre. It's possible to take a ferry from the port at the end of Amani Street to the village across the bay, where it's also possible to stay. Another good excursion that is worth taking as an overnight trip is to **Litipo Forest Reserve**, some distance out of town, near the village of Rutamba. This last remaining patch of rainforest is a peaceful natural area, with a couple of small lakes to either side. The forested region at the centre is alive with hundreds of birds. Buses leave twice each morning from Lindi town centre, and take around three hours, travelling at an average speed of just over 10km per hour.

Mikindani

It is an extraordinary experience to arrive at Mikindani at the end of a long, bumpy and extremely dusty drive from Dar es Salaam – or even just from Kilwa. After mile upon mile of rural distances with often no sign of human habitation, with the exception of the rows of shops and restaurants in the efficient but slightly character-less town of Lindi, the final bend in the road that reveals Mikindani town can seem to be a fairytale encounter. Nestling between mountains and sea on a large circular natural lagoon, this tiny town has the historic atmosphere of quiet quaintness that attracts visitors to tiny villages in the English Cotswolds or Italian hilltop villages in Umbria. The winding streets are flanked by a hotchpotch of thatch and mud, stonework with balconies, and carved wooden doors from the Arabic and colonial days. It is not as ancient as Kilwa Kisiwani, was never as important as Bagamoyo, and has experienced a similar downturn in its fortunes, changing from a thriving port town to a quiet backwater almost overnight. But over the years Mikindani has received small doses of nurture that have kept the character of the town distinct.

History

As with most of the port towns along the coast, Mikindani suffered a succession of rising and falling fortunes with the turning tides of trade. Its perfectly protected bay provided naturally sheltered anchorage and it was the closest seaport for trade caravans from Lake Nyasa, and from the territories that are now Zimbabwe, Zambia and the Democratic Republic of Congo. Arab trade and settlement at Mikindani is thought to extend from the 9th to the mid-19th centuries, as seen in the remains of ruined mosques and graves. Prior to the Arabs' arrival there was a settlement of Makonde from Mozambique at Mvita, to the northwest of the lagoon, where some interesting tombs with carved plaster decorations inset with porcelain bowls can still be seen. By the late 15th century trade routes stretched from Mikindani through Zambia and Malawi as far as Zaire and Angola. Ivory, tortoiseshell, copper and animal

Getting There

Mikindani town is just under 10km from Mtwara along a busy and pleasant **tarmac road**. A regular **dala-dala** service runs from Mtwara market to Mikindani until mid-afternoon, charging passengers T.shs 200 each. There are a number of **taxis** in town, usually found either near the market at the top of town or around the petrol station. Anyone providing accommodation in Mikindani town should be able to arrange transfers to the airport at Mtwara, but if a taxi is required it is worth arranging it in advance.

Where to Stay

The Old Boma at Mikindani, Mikindani, PO Box 993, Mtwara, t (0748) 360110, *oldboma@ mikindani.com*, *www.mikindani.com*; in the UK: Trade Aid, Burgate Court, Burgate, Fordingbridge, Hants, SP6 ILX, t (01425) 657774 (*moderate*). Lovingly restored to reveal its original grandeur and accommodate guests in style, with a pool surrounded by flowering trees and a poolside bar, excellent views down the hillside over the town and bay. All rooms have grand, hand-carved wooden beds and clean white linen, with balconies facing the sea or coconut groves. This is definitely the place to stay in Mikindani.

Ten Degrees South, *tendegreessouth@twiga. com* (*cheap*). A small and homely establishment on the seafront. The hotel is based in an old two-storey colonial stone building

with tiny wooden shutters and doors, all of its rooms named after great explorers (complete with the odd wooden arrow shaft sunk into the door frame). Whitewashed walls throughout create a clean and fresh atmosphere. Beds are large and comfortable with hand-crafted wooden bases, good mattresses and mosquito nets. Guests share a bathroom and toilet that face a small, peaceful central courtyard. An innovative menu is available at the bar, with plenty of fresh seafood, and a pizza oven is promised. All food is served under *makuti* umbrellas with views across the bay – or cable TV, depending on your preference. The friendly Europeans who run the place are refreshingly relaxed and can provide a wealth of local and diving information from years of experience living in the area and analysing underwater life on the reefs. They can also arrange trips to visit talented local Makonde carvers such as the nephews and sons of Mzee Hendrick (*see* p.256).

Eating Out and Activities

The **Mikindani Yacht Club** is a new venture offering great food and of course various boating activities. Otherwise, both the Old Boma at Mikindani and Ten Degrees South have good restaurants.

Diving can be arranged from both the Old Boma and Ten Degrees South – see *www.eco2.com* and *www.mikindani.com* for further details. Diving is centred in the newly gazetted Mnazi Bay Marine Park.

The Story of Babu Banda and the German Treasure

The hillside behind the town is pleasantly wooded. A not-too-steep track from behind the old boma leads up through sunlit glades to a superb viewpoint and the site of rather unusual industry. This is the domain of Babu Banda, an obsessive local witch doctor who has been subjected to a number of instructive dreams by ancestral and Arab spirits, the essence of which were to tell him of German treasures buried at the summit behind the boma. Since the dreams he has dogmatically undertaken the task of unearthing the riches. As he works, his figure casts a long shadow against the carefully dug wall of a crater-like hole about six metres deep, centimetres away from another abandoned crater just beyond. He tells how seven treasure-seekers were here before him, but were plagued by dreams of an Arab instructing them to leave and finally frightened off or killed by a huge snake. Babu Banda also has dreams of the Arab, who told him to dig seven paces from the biggest baobab tree, but he employs powerful magic to keep the snake away. His treasure so far includes an immaculate bronze 1kg weight, and he claims to have discovered a cache of guns, but has decided not to dig deeper around that site in case he disturbs unexploded arms. His dedication to unearthing the wealth of his dreams is revealed impressively when his simple spade is set down against the cavernous depths he has carved into this red earth hillside. Meanwhile his family perch against the skyline, cooking *ugali* and sheltering under the snaking branches of the precariously rooted trees with the family rooster happily ensconced on Babu Banda's wife's head. They have vowed that when they find the treasure the rooster will meet the cooking pot.

skins were exported, and manufactured weaponry and clothes imported. Demand for exports lapsed in the early 16th century with the disruptive activities of the Portuguese along the coast, but picked up again in the middle of that century when the whole coastal region came under the jurisdiction of the Sultan of Zanzibar, and slave-trading became big business. Trade continued to fluctuate until the next boom, around the 1850s, when Arab trading peaked once more and the little southern town became a major trading centre. If you had arrived in Mikindani at this time you would have encountered a busy port town settlement above a spectacular ocean lagoon.

Mikindani Town

Most of Mikindani town as it stands today dates from the mid-19th to early 20th centuries, after it regained prominence as a trading centre for Arab dhows purchasing ivory and slaves. Many of the ruins in the old town were the homes or trading posts of the first foreign traders, distinguished by their carved doorways and flat roofs, while wealthier merchants built themselves two-storey houses with intricate balconies above shop fronts.

Mikindani came to the attention of the Europeans towards the end of the 19th century when Dr David Livingstone recorded his stay here early in 1866, before embarking on his final expedition inland. **Livingstone's two-storey house** with superbly carved wooden doorways was renovated by the Ministry of Antiquities in 1981, when an unprepossessing corrugated iron roof and a commemorative plaque were added. A couple of decades after Livingstone's stay the town became subject to German colonial rule: the Germans made Mikindani their district headquarters, and constructed a number of impressive two-storey coral rag houses with fretwork balconies on the upper level. Some of their more elaborate constructions have recently been subject to extensive restoration work. The old **German boma** sits high on the hillside overlooking the town and bay with 1895, the date of its completion, inscribed over the door. It was designed as a fortress, but included an administration office and an officers' residence and mess with the luxury of a tennis court on the eastern side. It later became a police station, but was abandoned during the 1960s and fell into disrepair, before undergoing a stunning and extensive restoration by the charity Trade Aid, which is working to develop eco-tourism in Mikindani.

The German colonial administration renovated and rebuilt the old 19th-century slave market with heavy, classically styled coral columns and looping open arches, converting it into a public **market** close to the waterfront to keep it functioning as a commercial centre and commemorate the slaves who were shipped from here. The market too has recently undergone a colourful restoration masterminded by Trade Aid, who have filled in the open arches and painted the exterior; sadly the building now sits empty and purposeless. Nearby, the old **prison** on the waterfront (near the main bus stop) has been in a very poor state of repair since being bombarded in the First World War. It could do with similar attention.

Inland, the first colonists implemented large-scale farming schemes for sisal, rubber, coconut and oilseed crops; as business boomed and the trade ships grew larger it became necessary to build a new deep water port, but the administration opted for a cheaper alternative, moving the port 10km south to Mtwara, where there was already a naturally deep channel to support the trade. The British colonial government moved the district headquarters from Mikindani to Mtwara after the First World War, sealing the economic fate of Mikindani.

Nowadays the families of Mikindani rely mainly on fishing and traditional dugout boats, their dhows bringing home a subsistence catch. However the tiny town still harbours a few surprises: a walk around its historic centre reveals a smart, well-maintained **Hindu temple** at the heart of its otherwise Muslim population, and a number of interestingly carved wooden doors and frames similar to the Zanzibari style.

Mtwara

Mtwara is a delightful and unusual town that emanates charisma and charm. The colonial influence in its conception is evident at a glance along its wide main street, Tanu Road, where an orderly avenue of flame trees cast shade on the pavements and neatly frame a whitewashed church tower at the far end. Wide streets and vibrantly painted buildings, now known as the *maduka makubwa* or 'big shops', off Uhuru Road, date from the days of the British protectorate and form part of a pleasant environment well maintained by the regional government. Schoolchildren were brought here during the 1940s and 1950s to show them the effects of 'modernity', and

Getting There

Mtwara is not the most accessible region of Tanzania, with **road links** so poor that local inhabitants are prone to give a joyous welcome to any visitors who make it to their remote corner. This may all change soon: plans to develop the 'Mtwara Corridor' trade route between Malawi, Zambia and Zimbabwe have been discussed for many years, but recent developments have suggested that it might actually happen. One of the proposals is to construct a link road between Mtwara and Malawi via Masasi, Tunduru, Songea and Mbamba Bay, where it would connect with ferries between the Tanzanian shore of Lake Nyasa and Nkhata Bay in Malawi.

By Air

For the time being the Air Tanzania flight schedule makes it possible to reach Mtwara. **Air Tanzania**, on Tanu Road (*www.airtanzania. com*), the main road through the centre of Mtwara, t (023) 2333147, flies direct to Mtwara from **Dar es Salaam** daily. Flights take around 45mins, return to Dar on the same day, and cost about T.shs 80,000.

By Car or Bus

The road from Dar es Salaam to Mtwara and Mikindani is an arduous 400km of bumpy dirt track and dilapidated tarmac, which is often rendered impassable between Nangurukuru (the junction for Kilwa) and Lindi during the rainy season. In a **private vehicle** – a 4x4 is essential – it takes around 18hrs. An overnight stopover at Kilwa Masoko is recommended as the most manageable means of covering the distance on this route.

By **bus** the journey from Dar takes between 24 and 30hrs altogether, and may include at least one long – and very welcome – break on the way. In the dry season buses leave daily from Dar es Salaam at around 8am and from Mtwara any time after 9am, with tickets costing between T.shs 5,000 and T.shs 10,000 ($8 and $16). Buses also travel regularly along the southern route via Masasi (about 200km and a 3-hour trip) and then on terrible roads to Songea and Mbamba Bay or Makambako.

By Boat

It's a couple of hours' drive from Mtwara to the Ruvuma River and the border with Mozambique where, at low tide, it is possible to cross the wide river bed on foot with only an ankle-deep stretch to paddle through. But beware that the river rises fast when the tide comes in, and it is a long and hot trek across to the immigration office in Mozambique. Locals make this trip, but some advise tourists against crossing in this way to avoid the danger of crocodiles and hippopotami. A launch makes the trip when the waters are high, and charges passengers around $2 per person. A new **car ferry** service has been established, crossing every day at high tide for $7.50 per vehicle. The vehicle transit has been set up to facilitate a coastal driving link between Tanzania and Mozambique – a community project undertaken by a dynamic Benedictine community guided by the impressive figure of Father Ildefons Weigand (*see* p.254).

By sea, the **MV *Safari*** ferry plies a weekly course from Dar es Salaam to Mtwara, leaving every Wednesday and returning every Friday; it takes about 24 hours each way. Seasickness sufferers report having been horribly afflicted on this journey. A first-class ticket will set you back T.shs 10,000. Enquire at the port for times and reservations.

Getting Around

Mtwara town covers a large area, and is ideally explored by the favoured form of local

Mtwara retains a sense of independence and pride despite the dire state of the surrounding infrastructure. The lack of tourists visiting this southern corner means there are pristine stretches of glorious beach and a fantastic number of coral reefs that have not previously been explored by anyone other than scientists. The region also has a number of historical sites nearby, and its proximity to the Makonde Plateau provides opportunities to meet and watch Makonde carvers at work.

transport, a **bicycle**. These can be rented from any of the bike stores crowded around the market or arranged through your hotel. **Taxis** are most likely to be found around the bus stop in the market area.

Tourist Information

The central **telephone office** is next door to the **post office** off Tanu Road, and is busy and efficient whenever the lines are up.

The **Tanzanian Chamber of Commerce** (TCCIA), **t** (023) 2333807, *tcciamor@ud.co.tz*, provides business services including e-mail and Internet access. It loans computers and business directories, but unfortunately it is not exempt from the horrendous phone connections that prevail in Mtwara. It is also working to increase the productivity of the local farming and fishing trades and to promote cross-border trading and the expansion of Mtwara port.

Where to Stay and Eat

Basic budget accommodation and guest houses are generally situated at the centre and to the south of town, with more substantial, mid-range choices on the Shangani Peninsula, overlooking the sea to the north.

Moderate
Southern Cross Hotel, **t** (023) 2333206. The best bet for reasonable accommodation in Mtwara has recently reopened.

Cheap
Tinga Tinga Inn, in the Shangani area. A dusty, fusty, German-run place with decent rooms that provide a cool respite from the beating equatorial sun. It seems quite popular and the rates are reasonable.

Finn Club, on the Shangani Peninsula, has good, clean, expensive-looking accommodation nearby (ask at the bar or in the restaurant), in a smart house.

CATA Club, run by the Cashew Authority of Tanzania, also has rooms to let.

Makonde Beach Resort (formerly Litingi's), out of town. Decent accommodation on a beach just out of town between Mtwara and Mikindani.

Mtwara Deluxe Restaurant. Provides a diverse 'deluxe' menu in an immaculate air-conditioned building opposite the Tanzanian Chamber of Commerce near the *maduka makubwa*, with a choice of African, European or Indian-style food accompanied by *ugali*, rice, chips or mash. All their variety and spice comes at a fair price for a huge main course, more if you have starters and puddings. Mtwara Deluxe also provides a selection of good-looking quiches, samosas and other perfect snacks or picnic fare.

There are a number of bars and restaurants around Mtwara that provide pleasant places to catch the breeze and enjoy a drink. Only a couple are actually worth visiting for the merits of their menus: these include the **Finn Club** in Shangani, which provides decent and satisfying dishes of good, filling grub, and the bar at **Kwa Limo**, following the track off Tanu Road opposite the post office.

Fun daytime drinking spots are abundant, specializing in sodas, milkshakes, chocolates and other delicious snacks and goodies. An excellent choice is the **Container**, to the east of the *maduka makubwa*, behind the Henflora Indian shop that sells numerous imported goods at vastly inflated prices. Alternatively take a break at the unnamed café and milkshake bar almost opposite the Uhuru monument, with tables and chairs arranged beneath a canvas roof and enclosed by a very smart black and white picket fence.

History
When the British administration developed Mtwara Port after the First World War it did so to accommodate the vast new trade ships it envisaged would be required for the infamous 'groundnut project', not having yet discovered that its lack of planning would soon cause grand-scale embarrassment. The scheme was meant to replenish post-war stocks of edible oils, and was implemented on a large scale near Mtwara in Nachingwea as well as around Kongwa, north of Morogoro, and Urambo near Tabora.

Generous financial backing and modern farm equipment were thrown at the project, but without proper pilot schemes to establish the suitability of the soil and climate. The crops were planted over thousands of hectares but the expensive machinery imported to bring the benefits of modern farming methods proved totally inefficient on hot African soil – and the soil was totally wrong for groundnuts. Much of the work was finally done by hand and a total of £36.5 million was written off as a farming error of epic proportions.

But perhaps the folly of the scheme will have proved worthwhile in the long run if the deep-water port at Mtwara is developed to sustain trade from Malawi, Zambia and Zimbabwe. Mtwara port can handle a capacity of 70,000 tonnes of cargo; this is now sorely under-utilized, but could be more than doubled to 150,000 tonnes if the 'Mtwara Corridor' – a proposed overland trade route – is ever in fact developed. The local fishing trade, presently small-scale, could also be increased to industrial levels. The most popular export from Mtwara now is cashew nuts, a cash crop whose fluctuating value on the world market makes for a fraught harvest in late October. Recently oilseed crops such as castor, which proved successful in this area when the groundnuts failed, have been reintroduced.

Mtwara Town and Beaches

Mtwara is a pleasant town to hang out in. Some of the best diversion here can be found by simply exploring the **market**, a maze of shops and stalls around the bus station, or the area outside the main covered market, where local medicine men sell a wealth of lotions and potions to cure anything from impotence to unrequited love; the latter comes with a warning to be certain that the love harnessed is truly desired, as it is said to be so powerful that the recipient may fall into abject despair if their affection is not reciprocated. A selection of **Makonde carvings** can be found for sale at a small hut on the side of Tanu Road, near the Catholic Church; a much larger selection is exhibited for sale every Wednesday at the Benedictine **St Paul's Church** east of the market in the Majengo area. This church is also well worth visiting on its own merit to see its walls, painted with an excellent collection of narrative paintings by Father Polycarp Uehlein. His vibrant biblical representations have a whimsical, dreamlike quality and form part of a larger collection in Tanzanian churches, including one in Dar es Salaam and many in the south.

The **Shangani** area has a relaxed sandy atmosphere, with a decent enough beach beyond the **Finn Club** for swimming after a hot day in town. The club is equipped with a table-tennis table and small swimming pool in addition to a well stocked bar and covered restaurant. It has changing rooms with showers if you are heading to the beach, and may be persuaded to keep an eye on your bicycles. A man-powered ferry runs between Msangamkuu Peninsula and the dock in Mtwara Bay where fish is bought and sold, cooked or freshly caught, at a bustling shanty-style market on the beach. The sunsets from here are superb. The whole peninsula is rural and sandy; sheltered areas can be found along its northern beaches for walking or swimming, while the view facing back south to Mtwara port is frequently adorned with the bulky mass of vast cargo ships.

The town makes a good central location for exploring the surrounding area, with frequent local transport back and forth from Mikindani, and possible excursions to Msimbati, the Makonde Plateau (*see* below) and Mozambique.

The Mtwara region has attracted healthy attention from missions and aid groups over the years. The most long-term and successful of these is the **German Benedictine Mission**, headed by Father Ildefons Weigand, based in the Majengo Quarter. The most evident, **Rural Integrated Project Support (RIPS)**, *finnagro@finnagro.com*, works with local government to support health, education, rural trade and transport projects. The volunteer-based ecological research group, **Frontier**, *frontier@twiga.com*, has spent nearly three years in the area researching marine life along the coast. Its work has led to the introduction of a national ban on dynamite-fishing – on the basis of video material showing the destruction of coral reefs. Frontier has also created ecological education programmes for fishermen and children. It next hopes to put an end to the destructive practice of mining coral for building: rows of pyres where coral is burned to make lime concrete for building can still be clearly seen on the road between Mtwara town and Mikindani. Its research data is revealing a richness of natural marine life around Mtwara which may lead to the creation of a new marine park.

Makonde Plateau

Mtwara is the best base for excursions into the region around the Makonde Plateau, which rises up to 900m above sea level and is the Tanzanian base of the Makonde tribe. The plateau remains an essentially rural area, made more difficult to explore as a result of extremely poor road connections. The best form of communication and local knowledge is through the local Anglican and Catholic Church organizations, which have developed a popular parish network here since the early 19th century. Each of the towns here somehow manages to thrive despite all being so cut off; again, there is hope that the 'Mtwara Corridor' will improve the infrastructure here and provide opportunities for these self-sufficient communities.

Newala and Masasi

The first major town directly west of Mtwara is **Newala**, a remarkably upbeat town considering its remote location on the southern border, linked to the outside world only by diabolical untarmacked roads in each direction. The town is on a hillside over-looking the Ruvuma Valley, with impressive views south all the way to Mozambique. The road from Mtwara wends its way up to it through wild woodlands. The altitude and woods create a cool and breezy climate, with mists. Building in the town is concrete and stone, with fireplaces to ward off the cold. It is worth making the trip out to the Shimu ya Munga – 'Hole of God' – a steep drop off the Ruvuma Valley with views of the wild mountains beyond. Views are good from the old German boma too.

Continuing west from Newala brings you to the the town of **Masasi**, the district capital and another feisty southern centre. Masasi sits at the end of the tarmac road

The Makonde

The Makonde are one of Tanzania's most populous tribes, famous in East Africa for their distinctive ebony carvings. The tribe originated in Mozambique, where many members still live, although as the people have migrated and scattered the tribe has devolved into a multitude of separate villages governed by hereditary chiefs and elders. Specific collective names have developed to refer to the situation of different Makonde, such as Makonde 'by the sea', 'of the plateau' or, when referring to the Makonde remaining in Mozambique, 'of the tattoos' – the tribe traditionally made small scarring cuts on the faces of women at different stages of life and implanted an ebony plug through their top lip. Although some suggest that this was to dissuade other tribes from stealing their women to sell as slaves, it is likely that the tradition went back further. The Makonde of Tanzania are now eliminating it altogether; quite apart from forcing the top two front teeth out of kilter, the practice is generally considered to hinder the Makonde girls from seeking education and work in the new republic. It is also widely held that the Makonde who have moved northwards into Tanzania are more progressive in the development of their carving styles; many have continued to move north from the Makonde Plateau to sell their carvings and work throughout the country.

Carving is fundamental to the history of the Makonde tribe. A tale is told of how, originally, there was one being, who was half-man and half-animal but remained neither. One day he took a piece of wood and carved a tall and wonderful sculpture, then set it outside his house that night as he slept. The next morning the sculpture had grown into a woman, and she was the first Makonde.

The tribe is traditionally matrilineal, meaning that Makonde women own any inheritances and children, and men often move to a new wife's family after marriage. All the tribal women are afforded great respect, whether they are old or young, alive or dead, and have a wide reputation throughout Tanzania for their sexual expertise. The family is a central structural unit, with housing built up in two concentric circles as it expands. The carvings reflect the tribe's most important values, mainly following themes of *ujamaa*, in this context meaning family, or ancestors, spirits and dreams. It is also common to find Christian religious imagery now, especially around the Mtwara region, where many Makonde have converted. Most Makonde Christians have chosen Roman Catholicism. Only a tiny number of Makonde have converted to Islam. The largest proportion remain true to their traditional beliefs.

Family sculptures are often represented by groups of abstract figures joined in a circular design, and ancestors may take a literal shape or otherwise be translated into very abstract spirit forms, which then move into the popular realm of the dream carvings. These are carvings inspired by powerful dreams, or sometimes cloud patterns and structures that suggest images. These will often evoke quite disturbing images of spirits called *shetani*, representing ancestors or evil spirits. Makonde boys learn to carve properly around the age of ten, although they may have played with tools and wood before this time; later they decide whether their talent will lead them into figurative carving or to create domestic utilities such as bowls and plates.

Getting There and Around

Buses from Mtwara to Newala take 6–10hrs and cost T.shs 2,000. Between Masasi and Newala the bus route takes 3hrs and costs T.shs 1,500. Buses also run regularly from Mtwara to Masasi, taking 6–7hrs.

Shopping

Anyone who dreams of arriving in the Makonde Plateau to find a huge selection of undiscovered original carved artworks to buy at a cut rate is very likely to be disappointed. The reality is that carvings are created in the privacy of each artist's or family's home. Owing to the lack of infrastructure and paucity of visitors to the southern regions, the carvings are taken to Dar es Salaam, Arusha and other tourist centres by either family members or dedicated buyers. A few are taken to local towns, such as Mtwara. So, sadly, you are more likely to find quality work in tourist centres than by cruising the maze of dirt tracks around the plateau. It is worthwhile trying to buy direct, however, if you can find someone to take you into the countryside and introduce you to a carver or family of carvers, such as **Mzee Hendrick**, the highly regarded subject of a BBC documentary about the Makonde called *Ipingo* – Swahili for ebony. The family champions new ecological measures to preserve the future of the ebony tree, which takes hundreds of years to mature: each time one is cut for their work they replant saplings. Budding sculptors can also arrange to spend a period of time with the carvers, who are happy to teach their techniques to those interested in learning. Introductions to the Hendrick family can be arranged by Ten Degrees South

in Mikindani (*see* p.248). For other contacts to buy or commission work direct, try asking Father Ildefons Weigand in Mtwara (*see* p.254).

Where to Stay and Eat

Newala

Cheap

Plateau Lodge, on the road up to the old German boma. Has decent rooms with bathrooms; 'standard' rooms cheaper.

Country Lodge, a short distance from the town centre on the Masasi Road. Also good, with rooms in a similar style to the Plateau; the same price range.

Sollo's Guesthouse, a short distance beyond the Country Lodge. The best bet for even cheaper, cleaner accommodation. The restaurant here is also refreshingly good.

There are a number of basic local places to stay in the town centre.

Masasi

Cheap

Saidi Guesthouse, near the town centre. The smartest and best-value accommodation in Masasi. Fine rooms with en-suite bathrooms and possibly a working TV.

Chilumba Guest House, on the main road near the petrol station. Good rooms with nets and fans.

Masasi Hotel, on the opposite side of the road. Also good value, with large, clean rooms with nets and fans. It also has a restaurant.

Top Spot Restaurant, opposite the petrol station in Masasi. A pleasant garden area in which to enjoy cold beers and decent plates of local cooking.

from Lindi and Mtwara to Songea, at the junction of the circular route to the towns of the Makonde Plateau. It sits snugly surrounded by the Masasi Hills, with easy walking tracks to rocky outcrops of the granite kopjes and caves, one with rock paintings. The town developed from the Anglican Universities Mission to Central Africa settlement for freed slaves in the late 19th century and continues to thrive as a missionary centre. The foreign influence has given the town a reputation for being *kama Ulaya* – like Europe – more an indication of the quantity of Western goods imported by the missionaries than a real lifestyle comparison. Tanzania's President Benjamin Mkapa grew up in Masasi, and still has a house in town.

Dodoma to Lake Tanganyika

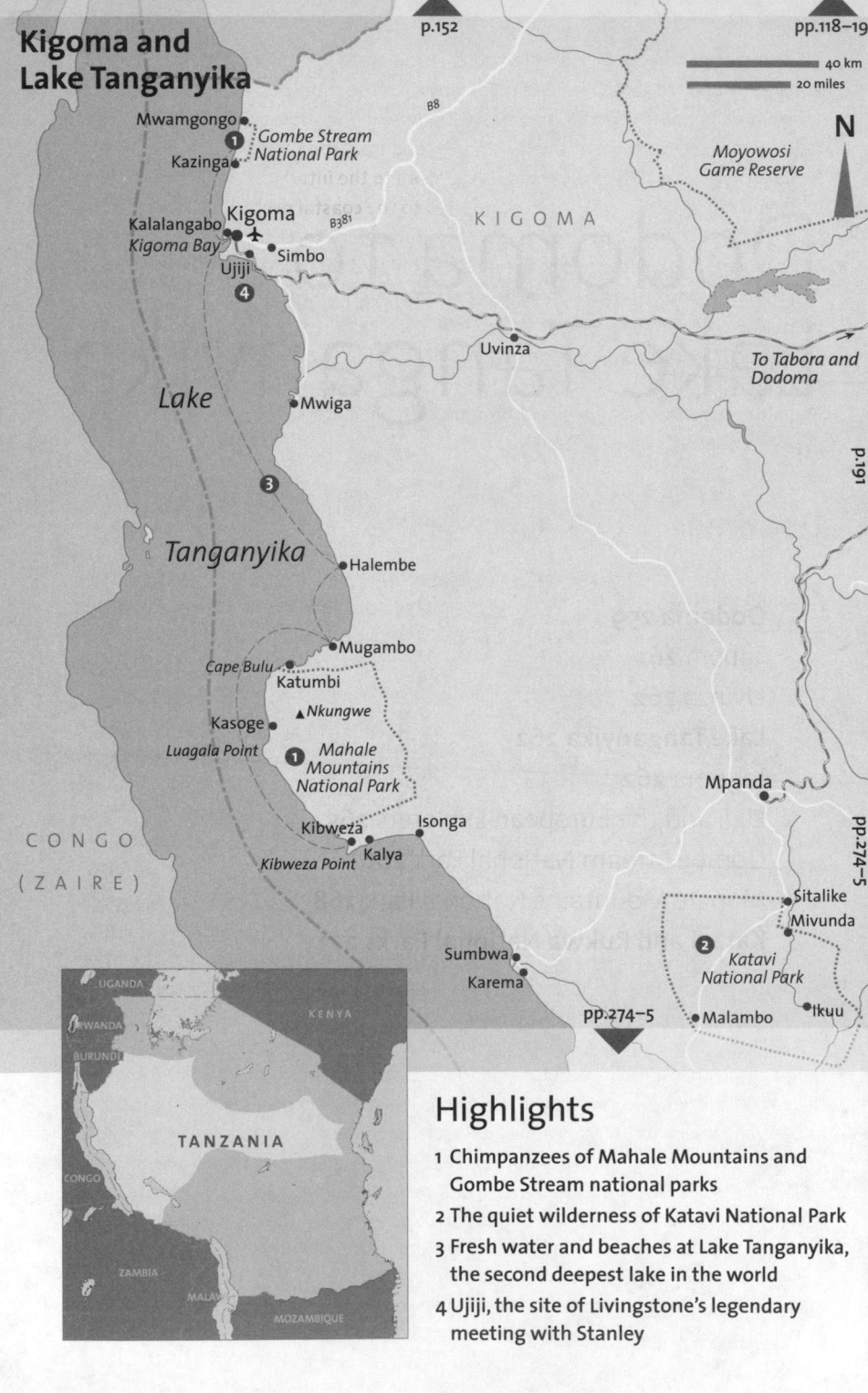

Kigoma and Lake Tanganyika

p.152
pp.118–19

40 km
20 miles

N

Mwamgongo
❶ Gombe Stream National Park
Kazinga

KIGOMA

Moyowosi Game Reserve

B8

Kalalangabo
Kigoma Bay
Kigoma ✈
Simbo
Ujiji
❹

B381

p.191

Uvinza

To Tabora and Dodoma

Lake

Mwiga

❸

Tanganyika

Halembe

Mugambo

Cape Bulu
Katumbi
▲ *Nkungwe*
Kasoge
Luagala Point
❶ *Mahale Mountains National Park*

Mpanda

pp.274–5

CONGO
(ZAIRE)

Kibweza
Kibweza Point Kalya
Isonga

Sitalike
Mivunda
❷ *Katavi National Park*

Sumbwa
Karema
pp.274–5
Malambo
Ikuu

UGANDA
RWANDA
BURUNDI
KENYA
CONGO
TANZANIA
ZAMBIA
MALAWI
MOZAMBIQUE

Highlights

1 Chimpanzees of Mahale Mountains and Gombe Stream national parks
2 The quiet wilderness of Katavi National Park
3 Fresh water and beaches at Lake Tanganyika, the second deepest lake in the world
4 Ujiji, the site of Livingstone's legendary meeting with Stanley

A railway line traverses central Tanzania from east to west, from the commercial and to most intents and purposes political hub of the country, Dar es Salaam, via the officially designated capital, Dodoma, to Kigoma on the shores of Lake Tanganyika. Built by the colonial Germans between 1905 and 1914, the 1,238km-long railway follows the principal Arab caravan trading route to the interior, along which salt, ivory and ultimately slaves were transported to the coastal ports. It's the same route that was later followed by English explorers Burton, Speke, Livingstone and Stanley on their various quests, and by the mad Frenchman Debaize. Now it's a long, dusty and frankly uninspiring corridor across barren drought-prone plains past painfully poor villages. To any traveller on this route it's a relief when the scenery begins to change on the approach to Kigoma, gradually turning to indigenous forest, swamp and miombo – the first indication of the treasures ahead at Gombe Stream and Mahale Mountains national parks, famous for their chimpanzee populations, and of the deep waters of Lake Tanganyika.

Dodoma

Pinpointed at the very centre of Tanzania, the region of Dodoma is an arid agricultural one that has acquired an unusual prominence since the decision was taken in 1973 to make **Dodoma city** the capital of the United Republic of Tanzania. While the location was chosen for its centrality, to ensure that no part of the country or section of its racially mixed population felt excluded from the heart of power, it remains exceptionally remote for anyone at all to visit – despite the completion of a tarmac road from Dar es Salaam via Morogoro. It remains today the 'designated national capital', pending complete transfer of official functions from Dar; the transfer was scheduled for completion in 1990, but lack of funds have seen it rescheduled. The State House, President's Office and nearly all ministries are still in Dar es Salaam, although the Tanzanian Parliament does meet for sessions here at the Bunge, for which government officials make their way from Dar es Salaam, and disappear again when the debates are over. It's interesting to note that the German administration considered making Dodoma its capital but decided against it. Founded in 1907 under German colonial rule, during the construction of the railway across Tanzania, Dodoma became the British provincial HQs between the First World War and Independence.

Dodoma's official status has breathed a gentle breath of fresh life into the regional home of the once almost-forgotten Gogo people and given them a chance to bend the ears of flurries of passing politicians. The Gogo developed a fearsome reputation as caravan raiders during the earliest days of trade, when this dusty centre existed as an important transit point. They now share the region with the Sandawe people, descendants of early hunter-gatherer tribes, and the Rangi and Burungi peoples. Accomplished farmers, the Gogo succeed in cultivating a number of productive crops despite the distinct lack of rain in the region – between the two world wars famine killed 30,000 people here. The sandy soil here has proven ideal for cultivating groundnuts, which proliferate alongside maize, millet and beans, but the region is mainly distinguished by its most recently introduced cash crop, a somewhat unusual one for

Getting There and Around

By Air

Coastal Travels, 107 Upanga Road, PO Box 3052, Dar es Salaam, t (022) 2117959/60, aviation@coastal.cc, www.coastal.cc, flies from Arusha to Dodoma on Tues, Fri and Sun, making the return trip to Arusha on Mon, Thurs and Sat for $150 each way. Coastal Travels also fly from Dar to Dodoma on Mon, Thurs and Sat, returning the following day, for $240 each way.

By Train

Trains run between Dar es Salaam and Kigoma via Morogoro, Dodoma, Tabora and Uvinza three times a week, leaving Dar es Salaam on Tues, Fri and Sun at around 5pm and Kigoma at 7pm. It takes anywhere between 24 (rarely) and 36 (frequently) to 42 (unfortunately) hours to cover the interim distance of nearly 1,300km. The train splits at Tabora, where a separate branch goes north to Mwanza, on Lake Victoria (see pp.152–6), and another line goes south to Mpanda.

It can be an arduous trip to cross the country in this way, but it is possible to buy a degree of comfort and safety if there are at least a couple of you travelling and you take a first-class compartment with only two beds. A first class single ticket for the whole cross-country trip costs T.shs 45,000 per person (payable in local currency), and a second class ticket in a six-bed berth T.shs 35,000. Men and women will be separated unless the whole compartment is taken. First- and second-class tickets should be booked in advance, but third class 'seats' can be bought on the day of travel and are cheaper; there's no guarantee that you'll find a seat. Trains depart Dodoma westwards between 8am and 10am, after an overnight journey from Dar. A separate branch line travels from Dodoma to Singida via Manyoni, though there is little reason for travellers to follow this route. Trains leave Dodoma at 8am on Wed, Fri and Sun. For 'Central Line' information contact Tanzania Railways Corporation, TRC Building (corner of Sokoine Drive and Railway St), PO Box 468, Dar es Salaam, t (022) 2110599 ext 2607, direct line t (022) 2117833/ t (0744) 262659, www.trctz.com.

By Bus or Car

There is a good tarmac road all the way from Dar es Salaam. Roads from other directions – Iringa to the south and Arusha to the north – look straight and direct on the maps, but are in fact best avoided as they are in very poor condition. Buses run regularly from Dar's Ubungu terminus via Morogoro, a journey taking 7–9hrs, depending on the bus and the state of the roads. There are buses on the north–south routes too if you're desperate or determined. If you plan to continue west from Dodoma, your only realistic option is the train.

The centre of Dodoma is small enough to walk around; most accommodation is within walking distance of the train station.

Where to Stay and Eat

Dodoma Hotel, at the centre of town, PO Box 239, t (026) 2322991 (moderate). If you have to overnight here this is your best bet – the closest you'll get to a tourist-class hotel here. It provides a reliable standard of rooms in an old colonial hotel, but no hot water. The new management has recently refurbished it. It is also the home of a popular weekend disco. Book in advance in case there's a parliamentary session in progress.

Nam Hotel, PO Box 1868, t (026) 2352255 (moderate). A big old three-storey place with a good atmosphere. Large, safe, clean and quiet rooms. It also has a decent restaurant serving a range of Western dishes, although both restaurant and bar gather a rowdy crowd at weekends.

National Vocational Training Centre, next to the parliament building, 10mins' walk from the station, t (026) 2322181 (moderate). A good alternative if food is a priority: the staff are all training to be chefs and waiters, and judging by standards here most of them will have successful catering careers. The rooms are modern and clean, with hot water.

Horombo Malazi Guesthouse, opposite the Town Hall on Madiwani Road (cheap). Basic accommodation in a central location.

The Climax Club on the edge of town is recommended as a good place for a frolic in the swimming pool and a beer.

East African agriculture – grape vines. The vineyards were introduced by Italian missionaries with a balanced set of priorities in 1957, and are said to produce a very potent port, not widely available at present.

Tabora

Halfway between Dodoma and Kigoma, at the junction of the railway from Mwanza in the north, Tabora is a useful intersection, but offers few reasons to linger. The Tabora region is the traditional centre of the Nyamwezi tribe, and was originally referred to as Unyamwezi after the tribe, whose name means 'People of the Moon' in Swahili; it is thought that the name was earned in response to the people's startling emergence from this stark region of the interior. The first Arab caravan arrived in around 1800, and just 30 years later the town had become a central staging post in the early 19th-century trade boom. In its heyday in the 1800s the town of Tabora was called Unyanyembe, and Chief Fundikira of Unyanyembe capitalized on the reputation of the Nyamwezi people as long-distance traders in partnership with Arab traders, trading slaves and ivory as well as more traditional goods such as salt, beeswax and copper. Connections with the coast grew very close – a strategic marriage even took place

Getting There and Around

By Air

Precision Air, NIC HDQ Building, Samora Av/Pamba Rd, Dar es Salaam, **t** (022) 2121718, *pwdar@africaonline.co.tz, www.precisionairtz.com*, runs a daily (except Thurs) airbus flight from Dar es Salaam to Kigoma via Tabora.

By Train

Tabora is a **central junction** for trains from **Dar es Salaam** (24hrs), via Morogoro and Dodoma, to **Kigoma** (12hrs), via Uvinza, and the connecting lines for all stations north to **Mwanza** (12hrs), and to **Mpanda** in the south (14hrs). Services on the Mpanda branch line leave Mon, Wed and Fri at 9pm. Trains run each way three times a week; changing may require a night in Tabora. Those arriving by train will find a mass of **taxi** drivers willing to take you into town for around $2. Taxis can also be picked up in town, by the market.

By Car or Bus

Roads into Tabora are notoriously **poor**, with long stretches disintegrating to nothing after rain. **Four-wheel-drive** is essential for any driving excursion to Tabora. Travel prepared.

There are **buses** daily to **Dodoma** and **Shinyanga** from Tabora, and twice weekly to **Mbeya**, taking 24hrs.

Where to Stay and Eat

Cheap

Tabora Hotel, close to the station on Boma Road, **t** (027) 6670 ext 2378. The best bet for comfortable, atmospheric and good-value accommodation and top of the range in Tabora. It is also the only hotel likely to be open and willing to admit guests arriving on the train in the middle of the night. The hotel was originally built as a hunting lodge by a German baron, and later became the Railway Hotel. The imprint of colonial style echoes along its cool, shady verandah and garden, and rooms are all up-to-date with en-suite bathrooms. The hotel restaurant is a welcome treat, with a varied menu.

Hotel Wilca, just north of the Tabora Hotel on the junction of Boma Road and Lumbaba Street, **t** (027) 5397. Clean rooms with nets and fans for less than the Tabora. Limited menu but good food in its restaurant.

Fama Hotel, **t** (026) 2604657. A sweet, clean and friendly little hotel with a great restaurant, though some rooms look a little tired.

Moravian Hostel, beyond the market on Lumumba Street. The cheapest lodging in town with a friendly atmosphere, and simple doubles with mosquito nets for a pittance; quite a distance from the train station and does not have a restaurant.

between the daughter of Fundikira and the father of the most renowned of all the Afro-Arab traders, Tippu Tip (*see* p.354). Chief Mirambo, a subsequent head of the Nyamwezi and one of the greatest of all the clan chiefs, came close to uniting the morass of tribes in the interior before his death in 1884. Nyamwezi chief Isike defended Tabora against the onslaught of German colonial rule in 1891, but when his defeat seemed inevitable he blew himself up inside the tribal arms house, hoping to take some Germans with him. Today, the Nyamwezi grow cotton and tobacco as cash crops, and keep livestock for subsistence. The regional honey is greatly sought after and still follows the same trading route to the coast, although it is now transported along the railway line that follows the old caravan route from Kigoma to Dar es Salaam.

Tabora town is mainly focused around the station, the only tangible, reliable connection with life beyond the town, which is extremely laborious to reach by road, even at the height of the dry season. The **Kwahira Museum**, 10km out of Tabora, is dedicated to David Livingstone, who presumably passed through here on his travels.

Uvinza

Two-thirds of the way from Tabora to the shores of Lake Tanganyika, Uvinza means 'place of salt'. Local excavations have revealed that it has been just that for more than a thousand years. It remains an effective producer of this invaluable mineral today, although it is no longer such a profitable commodity. Uvinza continues to export along the same trade routes to the Indian Ocean coast and across Lake Tanganyika as were used by the salt kings of Uvinza between the 5th and 19th centuries.

Lake Tanganyika

Lake Tanganyika is not only the longest freshwater lake in the world, at 675km long, but this exceptional inland ocean is also thought to be 1,440m deep, the second deepest anywhere after Lake Baikal in Siberia, and 70km wide; its waters fill the deep crevasse of the Great Rift Valley, and it is said to hold a fifth of the world's fresh water. Thought to be over nine million years old, the lake is still largely unpolluted by industry or habitation. The waters are clear and a joy to swim in, notably the bilharzia-free areas that are well away from human habitation, such as the shores of Mahale Mountains National Park. Snorkelling reveals an abundance of colourful fish living in healthy equilibrium, around 220 species, most of which are endemic, around two-thirds of them cichlids. The entire aquatic population lives in the top 200m of oxygen-rich water, and numbers have remained healthy despite their popularity with lake-dwellers as a tasty supper, and the bustling trade in exporting them for Western aquaria.

Kigoma

Kigoma is the northernmost town on the Tanzanian shores of Lake Tanganyika, bordering both Burundi and the Democratic Republic of Congo (formerly Zaire); the lake itself constitutes the Congo border, but has officially been declared a free trade zone. Kigoma's situation has historically made it a port for trade, exporting local goods, foodstuffs and palm oils, and salt from Uvinza for more than a thousand years.

Getting There and Around

By Air

Precision Air, Maarifa House, Ohio Street, PO Box 70770, Dar es Salaam, t (022) 2121718, f (022) 2113036, *pwdar@africaonline.co.tz*, *www.precisionairtz.com*, flies daily except Thurs to Kigoma from **Dar es Salaam**. The flights leave Dar at 1.35pm and arrive in Kigoma at 4.45, returning at 5.10pm to touch down in Dar at 7.50pm. A return costs $460.

By Train

Trains run between **Dar es Salaam** and Kigoma via **Morogoro**, **Dodoma**, **Tabora** and **Uvinza** three times each week (*see* p.260).

By Boat

Kigoma is the mainland spot from which to arrange transportation to **Mahale Mountains** and **Gombe Stream** national parks. It is often necessary to spend a night in Kigoma after arriving by air or train, before setting off for the national parks, as boat trips (especially to Mahale) can only run in the early mornings when the lake is calm. Water taxis ply the lake shores, or speedboats to the parks can be arranged by the Aqua Lodge or the Kigoma Hilltop Lodge (*see* p.264).

Boats also travel further afield, in peacetime, from Kigoma to the Democratic Republic of Congo, Burundi and Zambia. A UN 'superfast' boat runs to Kiloni in Congo. Steamers, ferries and cargo boats travel to places in southern Tanzania such as Kasanga in **Rukwa**, or to Mpulungu in **Zambia**, or Bujumbura on the shores of **Burundi**. The ancient **MV Liemba** still creaks between each of these destinations, as it has for nearly a century, First World War bomb damage and mid-1970s repairs notwithstanding. The Germans brought the MV *Liemba* to Kigoma by rail during the war, and assembled it there for use as a military expedition ship against the British in Zambia down the lake. It still runs twice weekly, leaving Kigoma on Wed at 4pm – 'war and weather permitting' – arriving at Mpulungu on Fri (10am), departing Mpulungu again on the same day (4pm) and arriving back in Kigoma on Sun (10am). It leaves Kigoma again on Sun (4pm) to arrive in Bujumbura on Mon (10am), leaving Bujumbura again on the same day (4pm) to arrive back in Kigoma on Tues (10am). The *Liemba* frequently runs behind schedule, so travellers relying on the service should allow up to 2 days' leeway. The 2-day journey to Zambia is a colourful way to experience life on the lake and is worth the effort for those with relaxed itineraries. Though it's ancient, the first-class cabins are OK. The ship holds a stately course a short distance from the shore to be met by flotillas of boats ferrying passengers and hawking supplies. Its extraordinary career and a starring role in *The African Queen* mean the *Liemba* is much loved in the region, and its fame is set to spread following the release of a recent documentary, filmed with local musicians (*www.liemba.com*). In acknowledgement of its age, the *Liemba* is sometimes supplemented by MV *Mwongoza*.

A ticket in a **first-class cabin** with two bunks costs $55, in a **second-class cabin** with four bunks and poor ventilation $45, and a **third-class seat** $40 – try to get a place on deck. Times can be confirmed and tickets can be booked through the **Tanzania Railways Corporation**, PO Box 468, Dar, t (022) 2117833.

The port remains the central focus of the town: colourful boats clustered along the sands of Kibirizi Beach ply a mellow trade between villages and towns on the lake shores. The town is bumbling, laid-back – and businesslike; the business of the town is carried out in the shade of its mango trees. The most prominent people in the region are the Ha, said to have been considered so loyal and hardworking by the first colonial settlers that they were much sought-after to work on the new colonial plantations, and in the 1940s were the third most numerous tribe. When the settlers left, the Ha struggled to build their own economy, having never developed cash crops or industries of their own.

In the late 19th century Kigoma became the first landing stage for Europeans on Lake Tanganyika. Sir Richard Francis Burton and John Hanning Speke arrived on its

By Car and Bus

Kigoma is a very, very long way from anywhere by **road**; the only route even worth contemplating is to **Mwanza** but it's not much fun – the journey takes at least 36hrs and is only possible in the dry season. The Saratoga line does it on Tues, Lake Transport on Fri. The only recommended road trip from Kigoma is to **Ujiji** for the Livingstone Memorial, which takes about half an hour by car.

Where to Stay and Eat

Moderate

Kigoma Hilltop Lodge, PO Box 1160, **t** (028) 2804435–7, **f** (028) 2804434, *kht@raha.com*, *www.kigoma.com* (or Dar es Salaam, PO Box 19746, **t** (022) 2137181/2130501). The lodge takes pole position on the headland of Kigoma bay, a couple of km from the town centre. It boasts a glitzy list of facilities – two restaurants, a swimming pool and gym – although there is no alcohol available and it is often deserted. Non-residents can use the pool – which enjoys a fine view – for a $3 fee. Smart air-conditioned rooms in self-contained bungalows have all mod cons, including satellite TV. The restaurant is recommended to be good but pricey. Internet access. The hotel sends guests to its camp at Mahale, and on excursions to Gombe. Fishing and water sports available.

Aqua Lodge, near the lakeshore, **t** (028) 2802586. Recently reopened to tourists – periodically used to billet mining workers – good mid-range accommodation. The lodge has the only sandy beachfront in town and keeps tanks of bright aquarium fish. Sunset Tours is based here – the cheapest option for excursions to Ujiji, Gombe and Mahale.

Tanganyika Beach Hotel, even closer to the lake shore than the Aqua Lodge, **t** (028) 2802694. Much older than its rivals, well worn but atmospheric, with gardens that sweep down to the lake. It has become a popular evening spot for sundowners, and for its rowdy Saturday night disco, but generally has a quiet and pleasant atmosphere. Major refurbishment in 2005 hopes to create a rival for the Hilltop with a pool, new VIP suites and prices to match. The hotel will stay open through building work.

Diplomatic Villa, a quiet three-bedroom guesthouse on the hillside a little way from the lake. The little fenced garden is drenched in bougainvillaea and perfect for repose. The house is simple but clean with a kitsch lounge with satellite television, and large rooms. Secure parking.

Cheap

Away from the lake, **Zanzibar Lodge**, on Lumumba Road, is recommended, as is the **Catholic Mission**.

Kigoma has enjoyed an upsurge in nightlife since the arrival of the UN. All the hotels do food, but you could try **Ally's**, a local restaurant on the Lumumba Road, the wide, tree-lined main street to the port and station, or the **New Stanley**, which also offers all-day BBQ beach trips. **Website Bar**, Mjamwema Rd, is the newest and best bar in town, offering simple BBQ food. **Sandra's**, on Stanley Av, is similar in style. According to locals the nature of its business is questionable, and there are certainly a large number of girls hovering around its tables. Despite this, it is relaxed.

shores in 1856 (*see* p.265). In 1886, journalist Henry Morton Stanley came here in search of the missing missionary, explorer and scientist Dr David Livingstone, although the two men actually met a few kilometres south in Ujiji. The house where Dr Livingstone stayed in Kigoma still stands. It still remains a serious undertaking to reach Kigoma overland by road; the railway from Dar es Salaam is the most reliable route, although for several months in 1997 it was entirely out of action owing to the severe 'El Niño' floods that devastated East and Central Africa. The railway culminates in an elegant three-storey station, built by the Germans in 1915 and linked to their other impressive construction here, the Kaiser House, by a long underground tunnel.

Kigoma is 24km, as the crow flies, from Gombe Stream National Park and 120km from Mahale Mountains National Park.

Ujiji and the European Explorers

The town of Ujiji, just 10km south of Kigoma, is a curious place, not immediately suggestive of its antiquity and roots as one of the oldest market towns in East Africa. The first Europeans to discover the town were in barely any state to appreciate its ancient charms, when, on 13 February 1858, they climbed a hill so steep that it killed one of their donkeys. From the top, they saw Ujiji for the first time below, and the waters of Lake Tanganyika beyond. Sir Richard Francis Burton, the brilliant linguist and explorer, and his companion, John Hanning Speke, were exhausted and dangerously ill after an expedition from Zanzibar that had taken them more than a year. They had come on the proceeds of the Royal Geographical Society to find the 'Coy fountains of the Nile', still searching for the source that they believed might emanate from the 'Sea of Ujiji'. Perhaps travellers today can still identify with the sentiments expressed by Burton when his impaired vision cleared and the waters of Lake Tanganyika lay before him, '...in the lap of the mountains, basking in the tropical sunshine... Truly a revel for sight and soul!' But disappointment lay in store for the explorers, who had to accept the sad truth that the waters of Lake Tanganyika flowed south, so the Nile's 'Coy fountains' remained elusive as ever – until 1858, when Speke found that Lake Victoria was its true source (*see* p.153).

Some years later Ujiji once again proved the salvation of another brave explorer, the missionary Dr David Livingstone, whose life work to end the slave trade in Africa ironically led to him having his life saved at Ujiji by the traders whose profession he so despised. The town probably bears a little resemblance today to the small, dusty but established centre that once bore witness to a historic meeting of two very dedicated and distant European travellers in 1851. When journalist Henry Morton Stanley greeted Livingstone with the now-legendary words 'Dr Livingstone, I presume...' he was said to be standing in the shade of a mango tree in this sunbaked town of Ujiji, close to the shore of Lake Tanganyika. Stanley's opportune arrival came when Livingstone had reached his lowest ebb, and, despite their extreme differences in character and purpose, the two men amicably explored Lake Tanganyika together.

A slab of concrete was erected to commemorate their meeting beneath the original mango tree, but the effect was to wither the tree to dust. Some bright spark took a graft from the dying plant before it faded away altogether, and now the Royal Geographical Society has graced one of these healthy, younger trees with a smart new bronze plaque. A vast, weird concrete breeze block monument also commemorates the meeting, with another brass plaque and a map of Africa, divided by a carved cross. The small museum is more endearing than informative, containing a number of odd local paintings and papier-mâché figures representing the historic reunion. Its curator, Bingo, is a font of knowledge and will happily regale the visitor with tales of colonial adventure. Still more extraordinary Europeans continued to arrive at this distant East African town in the wake of Burton, Speke, Livingstone and Stanley, including, in 1878, the eccentric French clergyman Alexandre Debaize, who arrived in town with an eclectic assortment of luggage including 24 umbrellas, two suits of armour and a portable organ. Remains of the old slave market and the avenue of mango trees that marks the slave caravan route on the road between Kigoma and Bagamoyo can also be seen. Since the advent of conflict in Congo, the town has become an important base for UN operations. An impressive old Wellington plane dominates the airstrip and can be heard rumbling over the town on its way to deliver supplies across the lake. The UN presence is mostly imperceptible to the casual visitor, but has contributed a new prosperity to the town.

Gombe Stream National Park

The tiny national park at Gombe Stream is just 52 square kilometres – Tanzania's smallest – a small strip of densely forested land world-famous for its **chimpanzees**: it offers visitors a rare chance to see chimps in their natural environment.

When to Go

Chimps are easier to find in the **wet season**, when they do not wander so far, but offer better photo opportunities during the **dry months** of July–Oct and Nov–Dec.

Getting There and Around

Gombe Stream National Park is 24km north of Kigoma as the widowbird flies and borders on Lake Tanganyika, separated only by a path between the park and the lake to give access to fishermen and local villagers.

The only way to reach Gombe Stream is **by boat** from Kigoma. The cheapest way to do this is to fight your way aboard one of the crowded tin-roofed **water taxis** that collect passengers from Ujiji or Kalalangabo village just north of Kigoma Bay – best reached from Kigoma by land taxi. These leave frequently. The boats make several stops along the way and take roughly 4hrs. Otherwise, for a fee of around $100, you can charter one of these boats for your group. The Aqua Lodge and Kigoma Hilltop Lodge (see p.264) can also arrange speedboat trips for $165 one way, reducing the journey to 25mins. They usually do this as part of a package including camping or *banda* fees, park fees, guide fees, meals, Kigoma accommodation, airport transfers, etc.

The **lake steamers** MV *Liemba* and MV *Mwongoza* stop at Mwamgongo (see p.263 for days and times), just north of the park, from where you can walk back along the beach to the park or hire a small boat to take you to its

visitor centre. Once in the park, you have no choice but to walk.

Tourist Information

The national park headquarters are at **Kasakela**, on the beach towards the north of the park (the water taxi drop-off point). The price to visit this tiny haven is high: each tourist has to pay **park fees** of $100 per person per day (note, this is for time spent in the forest, rather than at the research station), $20 for children aged 5–16, under-5s free, plus a fee of $20 for a **mandatory guide**.

Where to Stay

There is a hostel, resthouse and campsite at **Kasakela**, the site of the research station. The resthouse has two rooms with nets but no fan. The hostel can accommodate 10 people, with small sleeping rooms, a communal verandah and an eating area.

Camping is permitted at a designated site on the beach. Visitors should bring all equipment and supplies, although it may be possible to buy fish from local fishermen on the beach. Ask at the village and someone may even prepare simple meals for you, for a good tip. Nonetheless it is better to be prepared. A tin trunk is recommended to protect food from marauding baboons. Strangely, Resthouse hostel and camping fees are the same price; around $20 per person for camping, while the hostel is $10.

The Gombe Stream Chimpanzees

Chimpanzees are our closest relations, sharing more than 95 per cent of our genes. One of the genes that most of us do not share ensures they are covered in long black hair all over except for their faces, ears, fingers and toes. Baby chimps are born with light pink skin and a white tail-tuft of hair. As the chimp matures its skin darkens to deep brown or black, and the tuft disappears at the age of 8–9 years. Young adults have sleek, glossy black coats. At 20–25 years old, males go brown or grey on the lower back and legs, and both sexes start to go grey and bald. Many chimps live into their 30s; the oldest known chimp at Gombe reached the ripe old age of 45.

Chimps live in communities of about 20–100 individuals. They do not stay together all the time, but share a common home range (around 30 sq km), which they roam around in smaller groups of five or so, keeping in touch through calls. All members of a community may assemble at a spot where food is plentiful for days at a time.

Adult males form the stable core of the community. Usually supportive of each other, they spend their lives in the group they are born into, patrolling and protecting their range against neighbouring communities, when necessary chasing and occasionally even killing hostile strangers. Adult females mate promiscuously with several different males, sometimes even from different groups, but as they grow older mature females tend to settle into regular consortships, sometimes going off with one partner for several days or weeks to mate exclusively. Family ties are close. Infants are born after an 8-month gestation period, well formed, and able to cling on to their mother's belly. They are not weaned until the age of four or five, and even after reaching adulthood at 11 or 12 stay close to their mother for the rest of her life.

Chimpanzees communicate through loud calls. The most common call is the 'pant-hoot', a crescendo of hoots often by all the chimps in chorus. The hoot may be accompanied by drumming on trees and is intended to let the other chimps know where the group is. Male groups often hoot when travelling, all chimps give irregular excited barks when they find food, and loud, tense screams if under attack. Playing infants make a sound similar to laughter. Chimps travel on the ground, walking on the soles of their feet and the knuckles of their hands at a fast pace in single file. When chimps from one group meet up their behaviour can appear confrontational until relationships within the group have been re-established; at this point grooming may start. Males mostly groom other males, females any chimp in the family unit.

Some of the most interesting observations at Mahale Mountains and Gombe Stream involve chimpanzees' use of tools. Chimps have been observed to use flexible vine stems to 'fish' termites out of holes to eat. They are fastidiously clean, and use bunches of leaves to wipe dirt from their bodies. The leaves are also chewed to make absorbent 'sponges' to draw water from a hollow. While the chimps' diet is mainly vegetarian – fruit, nuts, seeds and bark topped off by termites – they also hunt at times, catching anything from small red colobus monkeys to bushpigs and bushbuck.

It has acquired its impressive reputation as a result of long years of study of the chimpanzee population here by Dr Jane Goodall. She and her team have been observing and recording the chimpanzee population at Gombe for more than

40 years, since the research station was established here in 1960 (the area had already been gazetted as a game reserve in 1943, and became a national park in 1968). Interestingly, Goodall was not a scientist: she was sponsored by anthropologist Louis Leakey to watch the chimps as a non-scientist, supposedly without preconceptions about chimp behaviour. This idea has paid off, as many of her observations have not tallied with established scientific theory: she has witnessed unexpected meat-eating habits and seen the chimps using tools for eating and cleaning. The team devotes its time to studying both individual chimps and their social patterns (*see* box, p.267).

The park's 200 or so chimps are habituated to human presence, and there is a good chance of seeing them around the feeding station, a 10–15-minute walk up the forested Kakombe valley from the research station at Kasakela. Researchers are constantly on duty at the feeding area, recording details of chimps who come to get free bananas. The researchers will be able to point you in the direction of any chimps in the area. Some visitors find it disappointing to see the primates in an environment that is not wholly natural, but there aren't many other places where you're likely to get within five metres of a chimp. To maximize your chances of seeing a chimp, allow at least two days; tame as they are, they do not always appear on demand.

As well as a population of around 200 chimpanzees, the forests are also home to red colobus, red-tail and blue monkeys. The high-altitude evergreen forests and wood-lands do not provide a suitable habitat for feline predators or opther carnivores,, and the park is quite safe for walking safaris – there are several good trails to follow, to Kakombe Waterfall or up Mitumba Valley. It is also a haven for birds and bird-watchers and the lakeshore attracts hundreds of butterfly species. To the delight of visitors, mosquitoes do not breed here.

Mahale Mountains National Park

The vast stretch of tropical forested national park at Mahale Mountains meets the lapping fresh waters of Lake Tanganyika along a pale sandy shore. Here visitors can combine a powerfully intense safari experience with a 'beach' holiday on the banks of the lake, combining snorkelling and fishing with forest walks on the trail of our primeval ancestors, chimpanzees. At dawn the sun glints across a steep mountain range, rising to 2,462m at Nkungwe Peak, and, as there are no roads in the park, all the pretty trails that lead through its glades and distances are only open to those who walk them. Numerous pathways and tracks allow visitors to enjoy truly beautiful forest walks and the chance of encountering some of the many different inhabitants of the lowland forests and higher brachystesia woodlands and savannahs.

Hundreds of coloured butterflies (more than 30 species) and forest birds dart across the sunlit paths, and the odd otter may be met near the lake. These paths are also foraged by warthogs and bushpigs, and, while elephants, buffalo, yellow baboons and monkeys favour the cover of the northern regions, the lower, southern reaches are the terrain of rare roan and sable antelope, kudu and eland in the shadow of leopards. Hippos can be found where river waters swirl into the lake, and on closer inspection it may be possible to see river cobra; these are very shy and pose no threat to humans but ribbon through the waters close to the shore. The trees are the merry domain of giant and red-legged squirrels and excitable troops of vervet, red colobus and white spot nose monkeys, as well as a new subspecies of Angolan black and white colobus monkey found on Mount Nkungwe. But most who travel the hard distances to be here come for the chimpanzees of the habituated M group. Their trails are deftly tracked through the forest by father and son guides from the local Tangwe tribe. The trackers' clear delight in the chimps shows the easy familiarity between man and ape. The Tengwe are generous initiators into the lives of the wild chimpanzee, their

When to Go

The park is ideally visited during the **dry season**. The heavy **rains** are in November, with lighter showers through February, March and April, drying out in May, when the forest is especially verdant.

Getting There and Around

By Air

All flights direct to Mahale are **charter flights**, and its extremely rural location many miles from any other likely destination demands an exorbitant price for such flights. **Nomad Tanzania Ltd**, PO Box 681, Usa River, Arusha, **t/f** (027) 2553819/20/29/30, *bookings@nomad.co.tz*, *info@nomad.co.tz*, *www.nomad-tanzania.com*, run charter flights to their Greystoke Mahale camp from Kigoma daily on request at a cost of $385 per person and to/from Arusha on Mon and Thurs for $450. It is essential to travel light; 15kg is the maximum per person allowance including hand luggage.

By Boat

Boats to Mahale leave **Kigoma** in the early morning when the lake is calm. Anyone arriving in Kigoma after this time, on a scheduled flight or the train from Dar, will have to spend the first night in Kigoma. High-speed boats can be arranged through **Aqua Lodge** or **Kigoma Hilltop Lodge** (*see* p.264) and take around 6hrs, or 1½hrs by fast boat.

The MV *Liemba* takes around 10hrs to reach the village of Mugambo, 15km north of the park, from where you can hire a local motorboat or arrange a pick-up from the Mahale park headquarters. There are also local boats to Mugambo, which take for ever. Once at Mahale, the only ways to see the park are by boat and on foot. Boating safaris generally cost around $25 for a long day trip.

By Car

It is possible to drive close to Mahale Mountains National Park, but this requires serious road hours and an adventurous spirit. It takes a full day of driving from the closest town, the friendly rural town of **Mpanda**, to the waters of Lake Tanganyika, from where a boat is still required to get to the park.

Tourist Information

The **Mahale Mountains Wildlife Research Centre**, PO Box 1053, Kigoma, **t** (028) 2802072, is near the Aqua Lodge in Kigoma. The **park fees** are $50 per person per day, $20 for children aged 5–16, and under-fives free. Guide fees are $20 per day. The centre can assist in finding transport to and from the park. Otherwise tour operators can arrange transport, guiding, camping equipment and food supplies. Contact the **Kigoma Hilltop Hotel**, the Aqua Lodge (*see* p.264) or, for UK bookings, **Hoopoe Adventure Tours**, **t** (020) 8428 8221, *hoopoeuk@aol.com*.

Where to Stay

Mahale Mountains camps are open from the third week in May to early November and again from December to mid-April. **Greystoke Mahale**, PO Box 150, Usa River, **t** (0741) 512312/**t** (0741) 324341 (c/o Nomad Tanzania, *see* above) (*very expensive*). The only elegant place to stay in the chimp park, beautifully designed and positioned on long-held traditional knowledge augmented by a rigorous scientific understanding gained from 40 years of working with primatologists.

On 23 March 1874, V.L. Cameron docked at Ras Kungwe, the bay just on the northern peak of Mahale Mountains National Park, on a journey from Bagamoyo that was to make him the first European to cross present-day Tanzania from east to west. Two years later Henry Morton Stanley reached the same spot, having come comparatively close some years before when he finally caught up with Dr David Livingstone in Ujiji, a short distance from Kigoma, on 10 November 1871. The park was gazetted in 1985 as the first Tanzanian national park intended for walking safaris.

Kangwena Bay beach, between forest and lake. A fairy queen retreat in the shadow of forested mountains by the bleached shores of Lake Tanganyika. A night spent here is the stuff of castaways' dreams: thoroughly cocooned in luxurious comfort while gazing out at the dazzling night sky and listening to the gentle rhythm of the lakeshore waves. The huts snake artfully back into the jungle to reveal a generous living space fashioned from antique dhow wood. A little further back steps lead up to a room, hardly a bathroom but a bathing suite, with copper-piped gushing showers and fresh laundered towels. Skip up a ladder to a place of quiet reflection on the hideaway deck. The camp was designed by a couple, one of whom designed the outlandish exterior structure, reminiscent of something out of *Star Wars*, the other the carefully considered interiors. The good design is brought to life by a quiet army that attends to every need before melting into the palm tree shadows. Meals are served to the sound of friendly banter, all under the careful eyes of a pair of dotty pied wagtails. The food created is astonishingly good and adds to the impression that a little magic is at hand in the workings of the camp. At first light every person in the camp has an ear cocked for chimp calls, for this is the main event. On looking across the sun-dappled forest floor the first glimpse is caught of the troupe. Witness the ongoing soap opera that is M group, lovingly chronicled by the Tengwe guides. Back at the water's edge, afternoons are spent snorkelling after iridescent cichlids from a dhow that glides silently through the azure waters; this lake is plentiful and often fresh tilapia are served for supper. Good relations evidently prevail between the camp and the local Tengwe tribe; the Tengwe Trust devises imaginative development projects to help the villagers. Go here if you can. Stay here for ever if you can.

Nkungwe Camp, c/o Kigoma Hilltop Lodge, PO Box 1160, t (028) 2804435–7, f (028) 2804434, *kht@raha.com*, *www.kigoma.com*, or contact the Dar es Salaam office, t (022) 2137181/2130501 (*very expensive*). A little way north from Greystoke Mahale is Nkungwe, the first affordable tented camp in Mahale. Built on the beach where the river Sisimba meets the lake, the camp has seven en suite canvas tents and plans to build three more. Though it cannot hold a candle to the magic of its neighbour, the camp has all the loveliness of the lakeside and amply meets visitors' needs; it cooks up lots of barbecues on the beach, and the bar is well stocked. Sadly, the camp is powered by a generator and there is a faint but audible whirring. Perhaps as the camp grows up teething troubles such as this will subside. The camp has excellent guiding and is within the territory of M group, the habituated and best known chimp troupe.

Flycatcher Safaris, 172 Serengeti Road, PO Box 591, Arusha, t (027) 2544109/2544979, f (027) 2508261, *flycat@habari.co.tz*, *www.flycat. com* (*expensive*). A seasonal luxury tented camp on the public campsite, on a beautiful beach a little further north than the permanent camps. Flycatcher excels at mobile safaris and this camp is well recommended.

The park also houses a cheap resthouse, providing spartan accommodation, or permits camping in designated areas. Contact the Mahale Mountains Wildlife Research Centre for information.

Bird-watching at Mahale

Although the very diverse species birds of Mahale are still in the process of documentation, the local researchers and scientists have made extensive progress, to which they invite all other enthusiasts to add their findings. Spectacular fish eagles are a common sight, flashing their piebald wingspan as they wheel and dive in the shoreline waters of Lake Tanganyika. Where the park meets the shore a number of grassland species have been noted, such as **red-collared widowbirds** (*Euplectes ardens*) making nests in the reeds. **Speckled mousebirds** (*Colius striatus*) favour the stands of oil palm around the former site of Kasiha village, and **bee-eaters** and **rollers** can often be seen around the slopes of Mount Nkungwe, where you might also glimpse an impressive **crowned eagle** (*Stephanoetus coronatus*). In the forests along the Kansyana Valley the brightly plumaged **Ross's Turaco** (*Mussophaga rossae*) makes its nest in the high treetops, from where its raucous song is often mistaken for chimp calls. **Crested guinea fowl** scratch through the elephant grass, their inky black bodies topped proudly by a royal blue crest. **African snipe**, **green sandpipers** and **crested larks** can often be seen slightly closer to the ground.

Tourism is growing in the park, with two new luxury outfits setting up camp since 2002. While high fees can ensure the sustainability of the park, there are fears that unscrupulous operators may exploit the popularity of chimp safaris. Celebrity visits from Robbie Williams and a booking from Madonna are proof that the word is spreading, an inevitable consequence of improved access to the area. In response, the rangers have drawn up a strict code of conduct. Visitors are asked to help ensure that these are observed. In every way possible, the chimps must remain undisturbed: no loud noises or sudden movements, while visitors should try to keep to a distance of five metres or more. No one who feels unwell may enter chimp territory.

The Mahale Chimps

Mahale Mountains covers 1,613 square kilometres, and the Japanese primatologists who have been observing the chimpanzees at Mahale for more than 20 years estimate that there are 700 chimps in its forests, perhaps half of the world's population of wild chimpanzees. The population at Mahale has demonstrated a number of different characteristics from those at Gombe; they eat and use tools differently. Mahale chimps have a charming grooming routine: they grip each other by the hand, thrusting their arms in the air while the free hand explores the exposed hairy armpit. Mahale experts insist they are better-looking than Gombe chimps. The Mahale troupes have been the subject of extensive research by the Primate Research Institute of Kyoto University, Japan, who have been studying at Mahale since 1965. In the company of these researchers Professor Michael Huffman has recorded extensive evidence of the chimps in the wild using certain plants for medicines. Younger chimps observe their elders to learn which plants are good; local tribes claim to have established their own traditional remedies for illness by watching and following sick animals, who guide them towards roots and leaves with medicinal properties.

Katavi and Rukwa National Parks

Katavi National Park is sometimes deceptively described as 'near' Mahale. This is a purely relative term with reference to Tanzanian distances. On maps it appears accessible, but the 'main' road through western Tanzania that runs merrily through the middle of Katavi is by no means a smooth ride. Despite its great size, 4,471 square kilometres, and its inherent variety of animal and birdlife, it is perhaps one of the most underestimated of all the Tanzanian national parks – due largely to its remoteness. Those who do set up camp on its plains are quite content to leave it that way.

The landscape of Katavi, together with Rukwa National Park 'nearby', was created as a result of a minor fault in the western Albertine Rift which formed a wide alluvial plain. The park has a central, very flat valley floor which forms spectacular flood plains after the rains, and attracts huge herds to its bounty from the surrounding hills. The broad bleached plain becomes a mass of tall flowing grasses at the height of the dry season, extending to distant mountains beyond. These grassy plains attract enormous herds of **buffalo**, especially during July, and herds of **elephants** gather here around February each year. People familiar with the park joke that the animals in Katavi haven't read any of the behavioural rule books for their species, explaining why huge herds of **hippos** – up to 300 can be seen at one time – uncharacteristically gather here to spend hours sunbathing during the heat of the day. There are more than 400 species of birds here, including commonly seen **pelicans**, the **Angolan pita**, the **black-faced barbet** and the **blue swallow**.

When to Go

Katavi comes into its own during the **dry season** between May and October, when the plains animals gather into herds and assemble at the remaining waterholes. But the park becomes a bird-watcher's paradise around **Christmas**, after the November rains, although the animal life is more widely dispersed at this time.

Getting There and Around

It is possible to take a **charter flight** between Mahale and Katavi – with Nomad Tanzania (see p.269) for $205, daily on request. Nomad also fly from Kigoma daily on request, $385 per person and to/from Arusha on Mon and Thurs, $450.

The **roads** into Katavi are notoriously **bad**, requiring a full day of driving from either **Uvinza** to the north or **Mbeya** to the southeast via **Sambawanga** and **Mpanda**. It is also possible to take the train to Mpanda via Tabora and drive from there.

Where to Stay and Eat

Mutterings among old safari hands suggest that the authorities will give the go-ahead to open Katavi up to tourism. Four luxury camps should open within the next couple of years. A visit to this park is highly recommended. Meanwhile, Foxes have recently opened a seasonal tented camp, which joins that belonging to Nomad, the masters of bush chic and the team behind Greystoke Mahale, see pp.269–70.

Nomad Tanzania, see p.269.

Foxes of Africa, PO Box 10270, Dar es Salaam, t (0741) 327706/t (0744) 237422/t (0748) 237422, fox@safaricamps.info, fox@twiga.com, fox@bushlink.co.tz, UK contact t (01452) 862288, www.tanzaniasafaris.info.

A couple of **basic hotels** and **guesthouses** are found in Mpanda, 40km south of Kigoma, where there is an airstrip and a train station. Try the **City Guest House**, recently recommended. **Camping** is possible for a couple of dollars at **Chief Nsalambo's campsite**, but for all camping go fully prepared.

The Southern Highlands

18

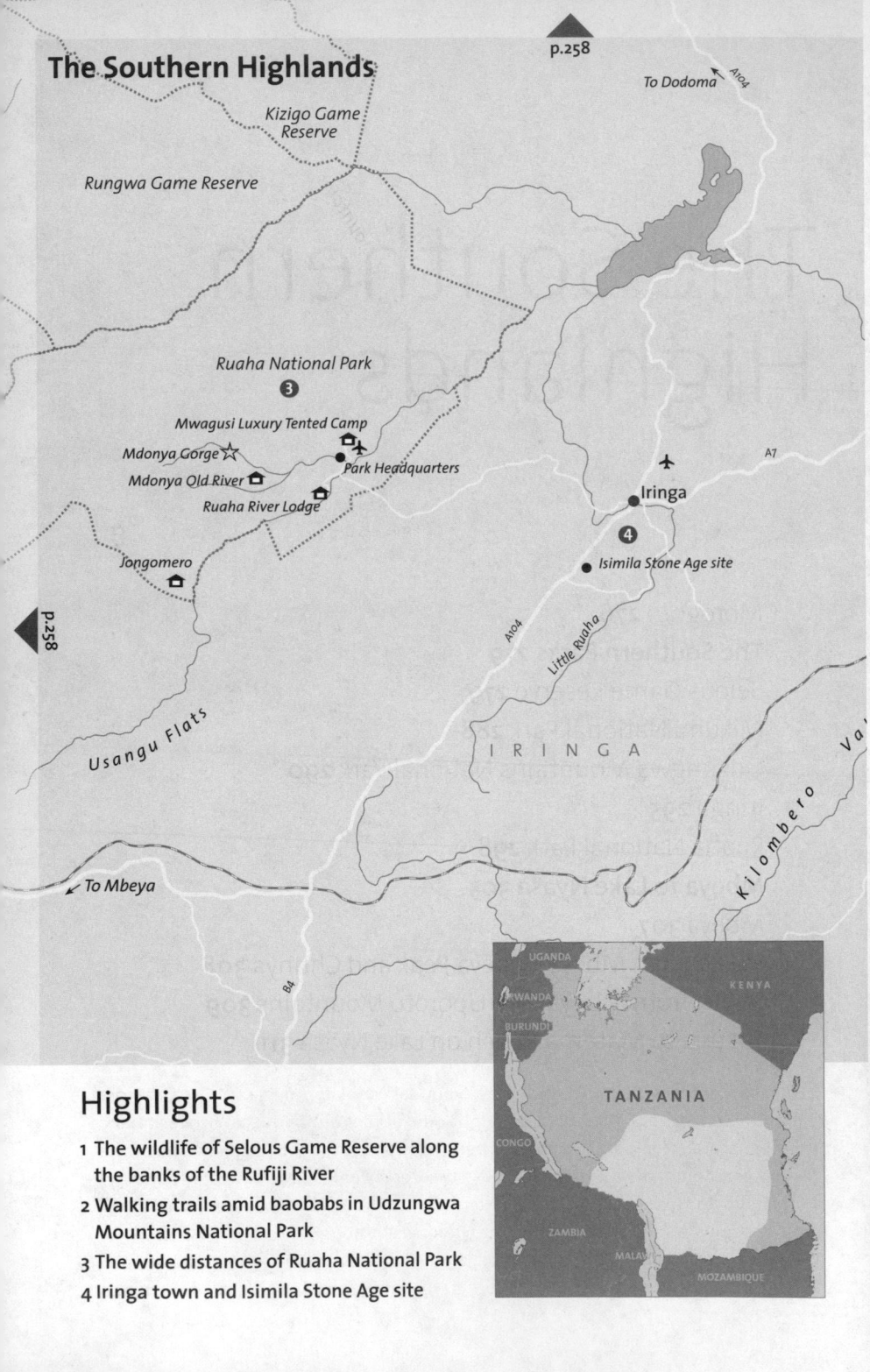

p.258

The Southern Highlands

To Dodoma

A104

Kizigo Game Reserve

Rungwa Game Reserve

Ruaha National Park

3

Mwagusi Luxury Tented Camp

Mdonya Gorge ☆

Mdonya Old River

Park Headquarters

Ruaha River Lodge

Iringa

A7

Jongomero

4

Isimila Stone Age site

p.258

A104

Little Ruaha

Usangu Flats

I R I N G A

To Mbeya

Kilombero Va

B4

Highlights

1 The wildlife of Selous Game Reserve along the banks of the Rufiji River
2 Walking trails amid baobabs in Udzungwa Mountains National Park
3 The wide distances of Ruaha National Park
4 Iringa town and Isimila Stone Age site

UGANDA

RWANDA

KENYA

BURUNDI

CONGO

TANZANIA

ZAMBIA

MALAWI

MOZAMBIQUE

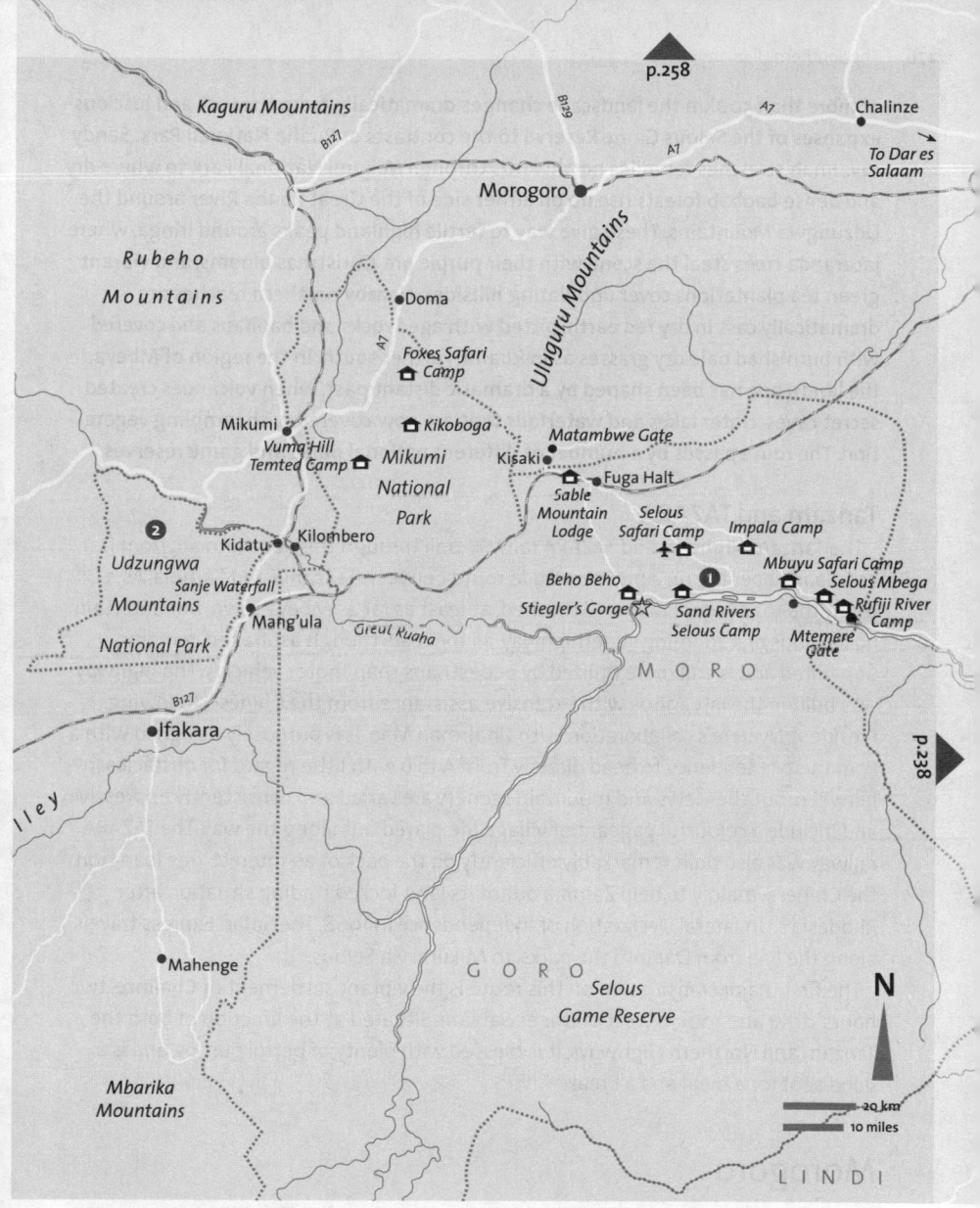

p.258

Kaguru Mountains

Chalinze

To Dar es
Salaam

Morogoro

Rubeho

Mountains

Doma

Uluguru Mountains

Foxes Safari
Camp

Mikumi

Kikoboga

Matambwe Gate

Vuma Hill
Temted Camp

Mikumi

Kisaki

National

Fuga Halt

Park

Sable
Mountain
Lodge

Selous
Safari Camp

Impala Camp

2

Kidatu

Kilombero

Mbuyu Safari Camp

Udzungwa

Beho Beho

Selous Mbega

Sanje Waterfall

Stiegler's Gorge

1

Rufiji River
Camp

Mountains

Mang'ula

Great Ruaha

Sand Rivers
Selous Camp

Mtemere
Gate

National Park

M O R O

lley

p.238

Ifakara

G O R O

Mahenge

Selous

Game Reserve

N

Mbarika

Mountains

20 km

10 miles

L I N D I

This chapter follows a route southwest from Dar es Salaam, cutting a swath across the southern reaches of Tanzania, through some of the country's least appreciated areas of natural, scenic and historical interest. These are the southern reaches of the Eastern Arc Mountains, which originate in the North Pare range south of Mount Kilimanjaro and extend through the Usambaras to the Morogoro region, where this chapter begins. It follows the range south and west through the Uluguru and Udzungwa mountains to Mbeya, then on to the Uporoto and Livingstone Mountains, which extend to Lake Nyasa and the borders of Zambia and Malawi. Over a distance of more than 500km the landscape changes dramatically, from the vast and luscious expanses of the Selous Game Reserve to the contrasts of Ruaha National Park. Sandy savannah stretches for miles northwards through Mikumi National Park to where dry and dense baobab forests rise up on either side of the Great Ruaha River around the Udzungwa Mountains. These give way to fertile highland peaks around Iringa, where jacaranda trees steal the scene with their purple pre-Christmas blooms, and vibrant green tea plantations cover undulating hillsides. Nearby northern reaches are dramatically cast in dry red earth, pitted with aged rocks and baobabs and covered with burnished pale dry grasses as in Ruaha. Further south, in the region of Mbeya, the landscape has been shaped by a dramatic distant past, when volcanoes created secret caves, crater lakes and waterfalls that are now covered with rambling vegetation. The route passes by a number of different national parks and game reserves.

Tanzam and TAZARA

The Tanzam Highway and TAZARA railway trail through this southern arc from Dar es Salaam, opening up a precious trade route between Tanzania and Zambia. As a result the road is generally well finished, at least as far as Mbeya town, but entertain no illusions of a zooming superhighway, as the road, though asphalted, remains unpainted and is still more utilized by pedestrians than motor vehicles. The highway was built in the late 1960s with extensive assistance from the Chinese, following President Nyerere's collaboration with Chairman Mao. It is purposely designed with a Roman-style tendency to head directly from A to B with little regard for obstacles in between, but the views and mountain scenery are varied and consistently impressive, and include a colourful pageant of village life played out along the way. The TAZARA railway was also built remarkably efficiently on the back of an interest-free loan from the Chinese, mainly to help Zambia out of its land-locked trading situation after Rhodesia's Unilateral Declaration of Independence in 1968. The Safari Express travels along the line from Dar into the parks, to Mikumi via Selous.

The first major transit town on this route is the vibrant settlement of **Chalinze**, two hours' drive and 100km west of Dar es Salaam. Situated at the junction of both the Tanzam and Northern Highways, it is blessed with plenty of petrol pumps, and is a good spot for a meal and a break.

Morogoro

Morogoro town is a small, green and industrious agricultural market town in the shadow of the Uluguru Mountains, with fresh mountain air and an abundance of fruit and vegetables, and a relaxing, laid-back atmosphere. Its situation halfway between north and south, coast and interior, mid-way between Dar es Salaam and Dodoma and en route to any westerly destination, makes it a bustling transit point; while there is little of specific interest to merit a special journey, anyone exploring this route at an unhurried pace will find invigorating rural scenery and a decent choice of accommodation. Others may wish to make the most of a chance to play golf on the old colonial 9-hole course.

Getting There

By Car or Bus

From Dar es Salaam the road trip takes around 3hrs by **car**, or 3½–4hrs if you travel by **bus**. There are buses every hour daily between Dar and Morogoro (buses Islam and Saddiq have good reputations) and daily services from Arusha (10hrs) and Dodoma (6–7hrs). The bus station is in the centre of Morogoro.

By Train

The train from Dar es Salaam is agonizingly slow, at least 4hrs. Morogoro station is on the central line linking Dar with Kigoma in the west, Mwanza in the northwest and Mpanda in the southwest; travellers from the west are well advised to take the train as far as Morogoro and then take to the road for the last leg to Dar and the coast. Contact Tanzania Railways Corp, PO Box 468, Dar es Salaam, **t** (022) 2110599 ext 2607, direct line **t** (0220) 2117833/**t** (0744) 262659, *ccm_atu@trctz.com*.

Sports and Activities

Those wishing to play on the **golf course** must pay a non-members' fee of $10, with an extra charge for a caddy over nine holes.

Where to Stay

Moderate

Hotel Oasis Ltd, PO Box 624, **t** (023) 2604178/ 2603535/2602930/2604743, **f** (023) 2604178. A smart, comfortable new hotel just out of the centre on Station Road, greatly favoured by the numerous business travellers to the town. The hotel provides an excellent standard of clean accommodation around a central garden courtyard, and while the price for such luxury is steep for this part of the country, it does include a decent buffet breakfast and satellite TV. Single, double or twin rooms and mini-suites.

Morogoro Hotel, PO Box 1144, Morogoro, **t** (023) 2603270–2, **f** (023) 2604001. Built opposite the Golf and Gymkhana Club in 1975, and with typical government efficiency opened 10 years later. The hotel has accommodation in 1970s-style circular cabins with corrugated iron roofs, dotted around the grounds, surrounding a neon-lit bar and dark restaurant. Musty and dull. Staff from here can arrange guides up to 'Morningside', or other walks in the Ulugurus.

Cheap

Hilux Hotel, **t** (023) 2603946, **f** (023) 2603956, near the Catholic Church on the old Dar es Salaam road. Slightly cheaper, and also good, the Hilux remains a popular spot for a drink in its garden bar. Smart, clean double rooms.

Kola Hill Hotel, a short distance from the town centre past the Morogoro Hotel, on the road to the Rock Garden, PO Box 1755, **t** (023) 2603707. An appealing new, cheap and atmospheric choice. The central sitting area is pleasant and friendly with stunning views of the hills, and the in-house cooking is superb and well priced. The choice of fine rooms includes self-contained doubles with satellite TV and air-conditioning.

Economically, Morogoro struggled to find its feet in the late 20th century, after suffering the devastating effects of nationalization on its factories during the 1970s. Although a familiar sense of dog-eared disintegration still clings around many of the old colonial stone buildings and crossroads, today its tree-lined streets are shady and cool. The town now thrives on its popular reputation as a central agricultural market, and the old soap, oil and canvas factories that closed in the 1970s have recently reopened under new privatization schemes. Morogoro supplies most of its wares to vendors in Dar es Salaam, its dusty roads are probably known to every lorry.

Typical indications of colonial occupation can be seen in an old boma and numerous churches, as well as wide streets lined with avenues of trees – and a rather smart golf course in the scenic foothills of the mountains. The town was the site of an evasion by German commander Paul von Lettow Vorbeck when he was pursued by Jan

Masuka Village Hotel, a short distance from the town centre along the old Boma Road, PO Box 930, t (0744) 280223. A charismatic option, also with unusual circular cabins, but this time built from stone and tiles and with flower beds around the edges of each and at the centre of it all. There are approximately five rooms to each roundel, and although a little dark they are equipped with mosquito nets and bathrooms. The Masuka Village benefits from a more rural atmosphere and hilly backdrop, and has a pleasant central restaurant from which to enjoy the location. The food is good, but relatively highly priced.

Mama Pierina's, next door to Hotel Oasis on Station Road, t (023) 2604640. Used to be a popular haunt for mid-range rooms, with a decent enough restaurant at its heart, but these days it is rather downbeat: the mosquito nets are holey and the rooms are pretty uninviting, with beds only suitable for short guests. The restaurant does an impressive line in frozen pizzas, and rather more heart-warming rice and curry dishes. Nevertheless, it is just a short walk from the station, the staff are friendly, the bar is stocked, and the atmosphere is OK.

New Tegetero Hotel, on the main Madaraka Street. Cheaper, and more conveniently situated close to the bus station and market at the town centre, good, clean rooms with good nets, fans and bathrooms. The restaurant is equally good value.

There is a wealth of choice for budget stays in the centre of town around the market and bus station, making the most of the location by charging a high price for a shoddy service.

Lukanda Family Lodging, at the top of Lumumba Street. The most popular; basic, decent double rooms with shared baths or singles with bathrooms.

Eating Out

Cheap

New Acropol Hotel, on the old Dar es Salaam Road. An eaterie popular with expats and those doing business in town; good food.

New Green Restaurant, at the town end of Station Road. A pleasant enough place to relax and watch the world go by. Prices are decent for a good range of Indian-style curries and rice dishes.

Two particularly delectable food shops, located alongside the cathedral just off the old Dar es Salaam road, are well worth a visit, especially for those in need of delicious picnic items for further journeying. One sells a range of home-made ice creams, pastries and cakes; the other, next door, has a fantastic selection of cheeses and cooked meats. A welcome discovery! Both are closed Sun and Mon, open until midday on Sat and closed for 2hrs, from 12 to 2, on Tues to Fri.

Nightlife

Evening entertainment centres around Saturday nights at the **Morogoro Hotel Disco**, which occasionally has a live band or a sound system. The **Garden Bar** of the Hilux Hotel and the **New Acropol Hotel Bar** are popular throughout the week.

Christiaan Smuts in 1916, then commander of the British East African army, during the East African events of the First World War. Smuts, entirely unaware of the distances over which von Lettow would elude him, was smug in the opinion that his adversary would find himself trapped in Morogoro, because the Uluguru Mountains would inhibit southerly progress. The British troops were dumbfounded to discover the music that they had heard on approach was a mechanical piano playing in the Bahnhof Hotel (now the rather dishevelled Savoy Hotel, near the railway station); inside they found the *Schutztruppe* barracks, defecated on and abandoned.

Around Morogoro

Beyond the town, the Morogoro region is a wild, rural expanse, with local cash crops of coffee and sisal. The sisal is exported to Europe, the United States and China, and used in Tanzania to make rope, string, stuffing for mattresses and bags for coffee export. The **Kilombero Valley**, just south of the **Udzungwa Mountains** and Udzungwa National Park, is rich in natural wildlife, and grows plentiful staples such as rice, maize, millet, fruit, vegetables and sugar cane, which supplies two sugar factories in the valley. The southerly town of **Ifakara**, off the beaten track, is home to a number of talented women who weave fabulous thick, colourful lengths of cloth on their looms, and give intrepid visitors a far better price than they would get in Dar es Salaam.

One of the main joys of Morogoro is its proximity to the **Uluguru Mountains**, which rise up around its southern reaches and provide excellent ground for easy forays into unspoilt countryside. There is also an unusual botanical garden known as the **Rock Garden Resort** (*open 9am–late; adm*), a lasting gift from thoughtful Japanese bene-factors. A few paved stone paths lead to a bubbling river dancing among rock boulders where parties of mothers and children wash and play beneath the shade of palms and natural woodlands. It also has clean, picturesque camping sites, and a café just inside the entrance gate. To get there, follow Kingalu Road south past the post office, just over 1km beyond the Morogoro Hotel (the old golf course on your right); the resort is signposted on the right. Visiting the rock gardens may inspire higher climbs to waterfalls beyond. One popular destination for walks is an old German villa called '**Morningside**' in a scenic forest clearing a couple of hours' walk from the town. It's an interesting route from the town, following Boma Road southwards for about 10km past the old German boma, and meandering along the hill path past trees and streams. The Rock Garden Resort and Morogoro or Oasis Hotels can arrange guides.

The Southern Parks

Although more central than strictly southern, these parks and reserves have earned their name as an alternative to the more renowned Northern Circuit. The popularity of the northern parks has had a dramatic effect in overshadowing the attractions of southern Tanzania. These are the less-explored gems of the Tanzanian wildlife reserves, often overlooked despite their vast size and ecological diversity and the high standards of guiding available. There are also a great range of alternatives for fine-quality accommodation in small, individual camps and lodges.

Unlike the night-by-night mobile circuits available in the north, the south is better suited to a lodge-based safari that relies on the guiding expertise of each camp. It is possible to develop an itinerary that combines different aspects of the southern parks with a small number of lodges linked by internal flights or possibly driving.

Selous Game Reserve

The Rufiji River, with its lagoons, sandbanks and lakes, and the surrounding forests and woodlands that make up the northern, accessible part of the Selous Game Reserve, creates a very unusual safari environment. The spectrum of wildlife is diverse, and distinct in that this southern location attracts a unique combination

Getting to the Southern Parks

By Air

The parks have a growing network of **flights** that provide options for combining a selection of lodges. **Coastal Travels**, 107 Upanga Road, PO Box 3052, Dar es Salaam, t (022) 2117959/60, f (022) 2118647, *www.coastal.cc*, runs a daily scheduled flight service to each of the six airstrips in the Selous from Zanzibar, Arusha and Dar es Salaam for $130 one way, continuing into Ruaha and then on to Arusha from Selous on Mon, Thurs and Sat for an additional $270. The direct route into Ruaha from Dar or Zanzibar on the same days costs $300. **Precision Air**, NIC HDQ Building, Samora Av/Pamba Rd, Dar es Salaam, t (022) 2121718, *pwdar@africaonline.co.tz, www.precisionairtz.com*, flies thrice weekly between Dar, Iringa and Mbeya, on Tues, Thurs and Sun.

By Road

The main road from Dar es Salaam to Iringa and Mbeya leads through Morogoro and Mikumi, past the Udzungwa National Park and into Ruaha just past Iringa, via Kalenga. Although the road has an excellent tarmac surface with rewarding views and constantly changing scenery along the way, it is a long drive, and worth considering as a one-way trip combined with a flight in or out.

By Train

The **Foxes' Safari Express** travels along the TAZARA line into the parks, from Dar es Salaam to Mikumi via Selous. Contact Foxes of Africa, PO Box 10270, Dar es Salaam, t/f (0741) 327706/t (0744) 237422/t (0748) 237422, *fox@safaricamps.info, fox@bushlink.co.tz, fox@twiga.com*. The train – two carriages decked out with easy chairs and a bar – couldn't be less like the Orient Express, but is well worth checking out for the sheer novelty of it, and for excellent game viewing. The train leaves Dar's TAZARA station in the morning; arrival time in Mikumi will be some 6–8hrs later, Selous 4–6hrs. However, prepare for the journey to take several hours longer: any problem on the track takes considerable time to resolve. The Foxes plan to improve reliability. The train is scheduled to correspond with BA and Swiss

arrivals; and will leave Dar es Salaam 3 times a week, Sun at 9am, and Tues and Fri at 10am. A one-way trip to Selous or Mikumi costs $120.

The **Tanzania-Zambia Railway Authority**, **(TAZARA)**, PO Box 2834, Dar es Salaam, customer services t (022) 2860340/7/t (0741) 615370, station master t (0744) 609985, runs ordinary and express train services from Dar es Salaam through Fuga Halt (for Selous), Mang'ula (Mikumi), Ifakara (Udzungwa Mountains), Iringa (Ruaha) and Mbeya. The ordinary train service runs on Mon at 10am, and the express on Tues and Fri at 3.15pm. Make sure you ring customer services to check that the express service is stopping at the destination you need, as this varies. The stations are all a reasonable distance from the park gates, so it is necessary to pre-arrange a transport connection with your destination first. The lodges are geared up to do this, but will need plenty of notice, and may charge.

Getting Around

By Air

The parks comprise a vast expanse of southern Tanzania, and the distances often motivate fly-in safaris that rely on lodge transport. As most of the lodges operate all-inclusive packages for game-viewing, it is generally worth joining their resident guides. Apart from benefiting from their local knowledge, you will also have the opportunity to explore on foot with armed rangers in the Udzungwas, Selous and Ruaha, by boat along the waterways of the Selous and by open-sided vehicle everywhere but the Udzungwas, where walking is the only option.

By Car

Mikumi and **Ruaha National Parks** are accessible by road and have options for self-drive safaris. There is also a good driving route to the Udzungwa Mountains. It is still possible to visit the **Selous** in your own vehicle but the route from Dar es Salaam is an arduous 7–10hr haul, and the driving routes and restrictions inside the park are not easy. There are plans afoot to improve the very rough road between Mikumi and the Selous , which is presently hardly passable during the high dry season but remains marked on maps.

of eastern and southern African wildlife, both resident and migratory – notably a curious and colourful assortment of more than 440 known species of birds and a healthy population of African hunting dogs. Covering almost 50,000 square km, an area greater than Switzerland, the Selous Game Reserve is one of the largest areas set aside for wildlife preservation anywhere in the world, although only a small northern portion is allocated for photographic tourism – access to the southern region is strictly prohibited. The waterways and plains reflect all the changing colours of the sun and attract numerous well-feathered water birds, raptors and predators.

The Selous was declared a World Heritage Site by the UN in 1982, but the number of visitors is still fewer than 5,000 a year. The vast area contained within the boundaries of the Selous Game Reserve accounts for 5 per cent of the landmass of Tanzania, yet there are just a few options for tourist accommodation, all high-quality, low-impact lodges that maintain high standards. The freedom to take walking and boating safaris within the reserve means that guiding standards are also especially good and can extend to include excellent options to fly-camp overnight in the bush. The tourist sector north of the Rufiji River extends to Stiegler's Gorge in the west and the TAZARA railway in the north, and contains all the various forms of vegetation to be found in this ecosystem. The combination of the river – its meandering streams, ox-bow lakes and swamplands – with open woodlands, plains and dense thicket forests, makes the Selous an interesting ecological environment and an ideal safari location.

Selous Landscape

The scenery of Selous Game Reserve is varied, with unusually green grasses and tangles of vegetation, and provides a string of photo opportunities with each turn in the path. The river routes are characterized by legions of **borassus palms** along the banks that grow up to 25m tall, and leave a tall headless totem when the water courses change direction and they become too thirsty to survive. The same demise is thought to explain the spooky silhouettes of ancient **leadwood trees** (*Combetum imberbe*) that remain intact, preserved when they die after up to two millennia of life, leaving a skeletal perch for songbirds and raptors that retains a perfectly still photogenic pose. The Selous conserves a surprisingly colourful African landscape, and the white forms of the leadwoods are in stark contrast to the surrounding vibrancy of well-watered greens and a ranging palette of sandy terracottas.

The eastern area of the reserve around Selous Safari Camp, Rufiji River Camp and Impala Camp is a grassy woodland, with a mass of **terminalia** trees and sweet-scented **African mahogany** trees providing fragrant shady areas through which to enjoy walking safaris. Further north, and westwards towards the rise of the Beho Beho Mountains and Camp, the land is mainly covered by low **miombo woodland**. It takes a full day trip to travel between these two areas from the respective camps.

The western reaches of the reserve are the least developed, with magnificent views across the woodlands and plains of the southerly hills. Here the Rufiji River forms a narrow 8km creek through a chasm in the hard rock. This scenic region is now called Stiegler's Gorge, after a Swiss fellow who came to a sorry end when he met an elephant here.

History

An ancient stone-age people left tools and bowls in the region, after which there are no records of human activity until the northern boundary village of Kisaki became the junction for two important caravan routes that connected with Kilwa on the coast for ivory- and slave-trading from the 13th century on. The town remained a centre for generations, but early explorers – Burton, Speke and Thompson – described the area in the mid-19th century as being sparsely populated by people or game.

The Maji Maji Rebellion of 1905

In the early 20th century this region became famous for igniting the most historic and violent uprising against German domination, despite the colonial schemes to introduce cash crops, railways and roads here. It was their methods that were the problem: these included forced labour at a pittance and harsh new taxes enforced by *akidas*, literate Swahili government agents who governed by cracking their whips. Resentment and bitterness were, unsurprisingly, widespread among local villagers, but it took an unusual turn of events to give them the confidence to retaliate.

The most famous rebellion began at Ngarambe, northwest of Kilwa. This was the home of Kinjikitile Ngwale, a widely renowned spirit medium whose possession of the snake spirit Hongo and affiliation with the greater spirit of Bokero attracted thousands of pilgrims. While anti-German fervour was growing, as demonstrated by the uprooting of introduced cotton crops, Kinjikitile spread the word that he had spiritual water – *maji* in Swahili – that would protect local warriors from German bullets. Word spread that this 'war medicine' was available, and the time had come to unite and fight. Clan leaders came from more than 300km away to north and south, and warriors were assembled with arrows and spears, a few cap guns and plenty of the special *maji*, mixed with castor oil and millet seeds, to defend themselves.

German troops were aware of rumours about unrest, but did not imagine there was much to worry about. They were taken by surprise when, in the summer of 1905, clan leaders destroyed a thatched boma in Liwale with flaming arrows, and speared a party of missionaries on safari. The headquarters of the colonial administration in this southern enclave were burned. Although most colonial farmers were safely out of the firing range in the more pleasant climate around Kilimanjaro, the German governor in Dar es Salaam sent a message to Berlin: 'Fear bordering on panic'.

The rebels put up a spirited fight as the Germans mustered their forces to retaliate, but the magic spirit water was not powerful enough to deflect machine gun bullets. Nearly 8,000 Mbungo and Pogoro warriors died trying to storm Mahenge Boma before Captain Hassel climbed down from his boma tower and opened a bottle of champagne to celebrate victory. An estimated 120,000 Africans died as a result of fighting or starvation before they were defeated, and perhaps three times that number suffered starvation as a result of the vicious famine that ensued from Governor von Gotzen's scorched earth policy: he dispatched troops to steal or burn all grain and crops. The Maji Maji Rebellion swept through the entire southern region in 1905–6 and, despite its certain failure, the uprising is widely considered the first instance of unity among the disparate tribes of Tanzania.

Getting There

By Air

The Selous has **airstrips** at Mtemere (Rufiji River Camp, Impala Camp), Beho Beho, Kibambawe (Sand Rivers Selous), Siwandu (Selous Safari Camp) and Stiegler's Gorge, all of which are accessible by **charter flight** from Dar es Salaam or on **scheduled daily flights** with **Coastal Travels** from Arusha, Zanzibar and Dar es Salaam (*see* p.280).

By Car

Access via **Mtemere Gate** on the eastern side of the park is 240km and 7–8hrs' drive from Dar es Salaam, via Kibiti. An alternative, longer route is 350km and 7–9hrs from Dar es Salaam, depending on the condition of the road that leads to **Matambwe Gate** in the north through the Uluguru Mountains. The Selous Conservation Programme has produced a guide to the Selous that recommends a short cut turning left just before the AGIP filling station 15km before Morogoro, and emerges 20km south of the town on the main road to Kisaki.

By Train

Both **Foxes' Safari Express** and the **TAZARA** railway run from Dar es Salaam, *see* p.280. Riding into the Selous by luxury or ordinary train is only for the brave-hearted!

Getting Around

Four-wheel-drive vehicles are essential inside the reserve; most of the lodges operate vast open-sided Land Cruisers or Land Rovers. For those who have been on safari in the north, the use of vehicles open to the elements will come as a real treat. **Walking** is also an option, but all walking safaris must be accompanied by an armed game scout or ranger and in groups of no more than six.

One of the best ways to see the waterways of the Selous is by **boat** on the Rufiji River, although private boats are not allowed; all lodges use aluminium boats with outboard engines and a canvas shade. Some are flat-bottomed and have been known to skim over a lurking crocodile, with no harm to the croc. During high dry season the river becomes a concealed maze of shallows, around which the boatmen must skilfully navigate.

The Selous Management Plan has laid down specific restrictions to protect areas of the reserve from excessive use, and this includes only permitting vehicles registered to lodges to take safaris to the region around the lakes in the Mtemere–Matambwe area. The lodges with permits are Selous Safari Camp, Impala Camp, Rufiji River Lodge and Beho Beho Camp. Only Sand Rivers Selous Camp is allowed to take visitors further than the Hot Springs.

Sports and Activities

Walking and boating safaris are generally a morning or afternoon excursion, but can be extended if arranged with your guides. Both are exciting and always varied, according to the unpredictable nature of the bush and the swirling waters; all walking safaris must be accompanied by an armed ranger for your own safety. Selous Safari Camp and Sand Rivers Selous can organize **fly-camping** expeditions into the bush, walking with a guide and setting up camp each night. These

The game reserve was named in 1922 after an English explorer, Captain Frederick Courtney Selous (pronounced 'Seloo'), who met his fate beneath Sugar Mountain in Beho Beho, in combat with the Germans during the First World War. Selous was the son of a chairman of the London Stock Exchange, who finished his public school education with a passion for Africa inspired by the writings of Livingstone. In 1871, rebelling against his family's desires for him to enter the medical profession, he travelled to South Africa and embarked on a now legendary expatriate lifestyle. A friendship with King Lonbengula in Bulaweyo allowed him to travel freely through Matabeleland, one of the last areas of wild big-game herds that had survived exter-mination by the first Europeans. Selous earned himself a reputation as the 'greatest expeditions require a great deal of organization and personal service, and are often more expensive than the usual daily rate for a lodge.

Fishing with a line is permitted in the reserve, with the potential to catch either a cat-fish or the prized tiger-fish, on the condition that your lodge can supply a permit.

All the camps have good **swimming pools** for a post-safari dip.

Where to Stay and Eat

Very Expensive
Sand Rivers Selous, run by Nomad Safaris, PO Box 1344, Dar es Salaam, **t** (0741) 333335/ **t** (022) 2865156, **f** (022) 2865731/2617060, *sand-rivers@twiga.com, www.sand-rivers-selous.com*. A smart, permanent camp stylishly designed in chunky dark wood with stone flagstones. It has views over a wide and dramatically rocky stretch of the Rufiji River, eight spacious *bandas* on stilts with a shaggy overhanging thatch, each with one side open to the river, giving clear views of the water and sandbanks from lavish net-covered beds. The lodge has a congenial British colonial atmosphere and a taste for safari chic – including gin and tonics on a scenic hilltop to complete a long walk through the bush, tea in the afternoon and candlelit dinners. Sand Rivers is very serious about safaris and provides a very high standard of food, service and guiding.

Beho Beho, UK contact Africa-Reps Ltd, **t** (020) 8750 5655, *www.africa-reps.com, www.beho beho.com*. This place has been fabulously redesigned and renovated from its previous incarnation as the first hunting lodge in what was then a very remote wilderness. Beautifully situated, this hunting lodge was the playground of a coterie of big-game hunters, until Christopher Bailey, a Welsh millionaire shipping merchant, bought the property in the 1970s on a promise to encourage tourism; instead, he kept the house as his private bush playground. The lodge is now in the hands of the old man's son Charlie: good news for game but also for the photographic tourist. Beho Beho, or 'wind' in Swahili, is fabulous; a luxurious stone built retreat with entrancing views across the plains. The eight cottages are truly enormous; with king-sized beds, cobblestoned bathrooms and outdoor showers. A real highlight of Beho Beho are the open fronts to each room that have fantastic views across the bush below and the bonus of having telescopes on each airy verandah. The hosts are very talented cooks and raconteurs, specializing in seafood served by candlelight under African skies. The guiding is top-notch – passionate and well-informed. Fascinating insights into animal societies abound; enquire after the welfare of the termites – you won't be disappointed! The camp will offer smart bush-camping options in the future.

Expensive
Selous Safari Camp, EPO Box 1192, Dar es Salaam, **t** (022) 2134802, **f** (022) 2112794, *info@selous.com, www.selous.com*. An authentic and elegant permanent tented camp tucked among the palm trees on the banks of the Rufiji River. The camp is spacious and stylishly designed, with a shady swimming pool. A richly furnished

of the white hunters', distinguishing himself from other trigger-happy expats by his keen interest in nature, and propounding early theories on conservation and natural history – which did not entirely curtail his career as an animal-killer. Selous's skills as a tracker and hunter, as recorded in his bestselling accounts *A Hunter's Wanderings in Africa*, sold to an enthralled audience in Victorian England. Widely celebrated, he began leading safaris through the bush; he organized an extravagant hunting safari for Roosevelt and entourage in 1909 (*see* pp.56–7).

Retired in Surrey by the outbreak of the First World War, Captain F.C. Selous felt that he could contribute to the war effort in East Africa. He joined the 25th Royal Fusiliers in Nairobi and pursued retreating German *Schutztruppe* through southern Tanzania, dining room and bar are raised high on stilts. The camp has 12 permanent tents that have their own private verandahs and outdoor showers and are colourfully bright and airy. The atmosphere is relaxed and comfortable; an inspired gourmet menu belies the rural bush location, even on intrepid fly-camping expeditions. Standards of guiding and wildlife expertise are hard to beat. Prices when compared to those of competitors offer exceptional value.

Impala Camp, Adventure Camps, PO Box 3052, Dar es Salaam, t (022) 452005–6, f (022) 2452004, www.adventurecamps.co.tz. A well-built, traditional tented camp on the banks of the Rufiji. A touch of luxury is provided by a clear blue swimming pool. The tented rooms are of a good standard (they should be for the price!), set along the riverbank and hidden amid borassa palms and tamarind trees, though each has a secret river view from the verandahs. Bright kikoti fabrics enliven the canvas and period-style furniture gives comfort. The food is fairly good, mostly idiosyncratic African interpretations of classic Italian and English dishes. A real bush family atmosphere prevails; Impala is a new camp and still fine-tuning its operation; the signs are promising.

Rufiji River Camp, c/o Hippo Tours and Safaris Ltd, PO Box 13824, Dar es Salaam, t (022) 2775164/2771610/t (0741) 320849, f (022) 2775165, info@hippotours.com, www.hippotours.com. A short boat trip further up, the River Camp was one of the first tented camps in the area and so claims a superb location overlooking a wide curve in the river. The dining area and bar are well positioned for the sunsets; accommodation is in 20 permanent ground-level tents. Its Italian management has made it very popular with Italian tourists, who have a tendency to travel in large and rowdy groups and require pasta for supper every night. The camp is also popular with an equally large and rowdy population of vervet monkeys.

Mbuyu Safari Camp. Mbuyu is currently closed due to an interminable legal dispute between the management and government agencies. It may reopen in the near future.

Moderate

Selous Mbega Camp, t (022) 2650250, f (022) 2650251, zapaco@afsat.com, www.selous-mbega-camp.com. Mbega translates as monkey in Swahili, and accounts for the camp's location in the middle of a forest. It vies with the Mountain Lodge for the backpacker dollar, and offers good deals for those arriving by road. Accommodation is in permanent tents with a treehouse living area overlooking a waterhole. Well located for access to the lakes of the Rufiji river.

Sable Mountain Lodge, t (022) 2701497/t (0741) 323318, safariscene@intafrica.com. Near Kisaki, outside the Game Reserve boundary. On a wooded hillside, with eight simple stone cottages and four luxury tented bandas. Offers fly-camping. Inclusive or exclusive rates are available, so it is an ideal option for those on a tight budget. The lodge is a half-hour drive from Matambwe airstrip; and about the same to the Fuga Halt station; the lodge will do transfers free of charge from the latter. The camp is well established and pleasant, though it is quite a drive from the river system.

an arduous pursuit in which he refused to ride on horseback, insisting on marching alongside his depleted column of men. Each night when his men retired to their tents, Selous disappeared into the bush with his butterfly net to collect specimens. The captain was 64 when he was killed by a German sniper at Beho Beho. Trenches remain in the Selous, a legacy of the German campaign, led by commander Paul von Lettow Vorbeck, who resisted more numerous Allied troops here for four years.

More recently, another expat Englishman, Constantine Ionides, has developed a reputation as a hunter with a bent for conservation, playing a key role in controlling elephant poaching with the support of Tanzanian game officer Mzee Madogo in the 1990s. Now the reserve is divided between photographic tourism and hunting, the

Selous Wildlife and Birds

The many intricate waterways and tributaries of the ever-meandering Rufiji River Delta attract a healthy population of **elephants**, and are packed full of grunting **hippos** and yawning **crocodiles**. The banks attract different-sized herds of plains game depending on the season. Herds disperse after the rains and later regroup when the water sources concentrate. A mass of water birds can be seen along the sandbanks, lagoons and riverine channels, where colourful-legged **terns** and long-legged yellow-billed **storks** make up a comical feeding trio with huge-beaked **pelicans** in the shallows; twitchers might watch out for the **Madagascar squocco** or a white-backed **night heron**. The swift and elegant flight of African **skimmers** is a delight to see, as is the feisty interaction between birds – the statuesque **Goliath heron** vying for territory with a broad-chested **African fish eagle**. Boat trips along the river are coloured with glimpses of at least eight different species of **kingfisher**, and up to nine different **bee-eaters** can be found in the woodland areas, including the **bohm** and **swallowtail bee-eaters** and, in the height of summer, the northern species of **carmine bee-eater** can be seen. The lucky bird-watcher may also catch an evening glimpse of **Pel's fishing owl**, a small nocturnal fellow.

Safaris throughout the Selous, away from the river too, provide a rare opportunity to spot an uncommon range of animals. The woodlands and savannah support a wide diversity of wildlife, particularly **antelope** and **wildebeest** and a famously large population of **elephants**, but the terrain makes chances of seeing them much harder than on flat, short grass plains such as those of the Serengeti. A number of **lion prides** reside in the Selous, and there is always the possibility of a chance encounter in the bush. More often their roars can be heard from your lodge beds at morning and night. The river and bush habitat also suits the reclusive nature of the **leopard**, which has a reputation for being frustratingly hard to find although they are also prolific here, and again it is possible to catch a tantalising glimpse of scratches and signs of their activity in trees; there remains, however, a fair chance of spotting them.

African hunting dogs, a rare and protected species throughout Africa, are currently thriving in the Selous where they are less plagued by hyenas than elsewhere in Tanzania, although **hyenas** are also common here. Research has indicated that there are 800 dogs roaming this area, three times the concentration of anywhere else in Africa. **Giraffes** seem to extend their necks above bushes around every turn in the road, and are often surprised into cinematically slow-motion but surprisingly graceful flight. Skittering **zebras** are an impressive sight against the burnished grasses. You might encounter either of the two resident species of wildebeest, the black-bearded **gnu** and the southern species of **Nyasa wildebeest**, or come across a herd of grumpy **buffalo**.

There is a possibility of a chance sighting of a less moody but more beautiful rare **sable antelope** around Matambwe and up to Stiegler's Gorge, and sometimes the

latter being the major source of income required to police the area against poaching and thus support the entire conservation area. Around 210 foreign hunters pay a vast sum of money to shoot up to 2,000 designated animals, the reserve's quota, between impressive figure of a **greater kudu** is seen standing proudly with its long spiralled horns aloft. The Selous is home to large herds of **eland**, the largest antelope of all, and the Selous eland are reputed to grow the longest horns of any in East Africa. These huge record-breaking antelope with astonishing agility for their size are a fairly common sight. You may also come across an **eastern bohor reedbuck**, smaller than an impala, or the hefty features of the **Lichtenstein's hartebeest**, a breed unique to the Selous. Maybe you will see a shy white-banded **bushbuck** or more common **waterbuck**, with its target-like round ring characterizing its rump.

Poaching

The number of **elephants** in the Selous accounts for almost half of all elephants in Tanzania, but their population has suffered dramatically, and dropped by almost two-thirds at the hands of poachers. Poaching has been a huge problem here since oil prospectors cut swaths into the bush in the early 1980s, and inadvertently allowed poachers easy access, even by vehicle, to previously remote parts.

The **black rhino** has almost been poached to extinction. The population has dropped dramatically from an estimated 3,000 in the early 1980s to fewer than 50 today, purely as a result of demand for their horns, more often to make Yemeni dagger handles than the infamous Chinese love potions. The remaining Selous rhinos remain hidden in the dense thickets and are rarely seen, but conservation efforts in the 1990s have increased the population, and it is requested that any sightings are reported and identification photos taken if possible.

Poaching became a way of life for many local people who became reliant on wild game for food during the 1980s when Tanzania experienced an economic food crisis that resorted to national rationing. For local people who had traditionally hunted wild animals for food, the money to be made from selling elephant ivory to the *bwana mkubwa* (the big men), often Arab or Somali middlemen, gave the *jangili*, as the hunters were known, wealth, pride and status. The game wardens were struggling, as the growing number of *jangili* earned more money, had better vehicles, guns and even shoes. But the tide turned when the army combined efforts to end the ivory trade. Weapons were seized by the military from entire villages, and hunters were arrested, imprisoned or whipped to leave lifetime scars. The result has been a remarkable preservation of threatened species, but consideration has had to be given to the rural villagers who have had their livelihood banned, and are prohibited from harming animals that stray into their crops to enjoy a rare feast, while people starve. With statistics still standing at around 200–300 lives lost to wild animals in Tanzania annually, especially to lions, crocodiles, hippos and elephants, it is no surprise that villagers on the outskirts of the reserve are less keen to preserve the lives of these fellow residents. A plan is now being enforced to allow a controlled cull of the largest population of buffalo in Africa.

July and November. The aim is to restrict human impact. Plans are under way to expand the area for photographic tourism on the south side of the Rufiji River.

Mikumi National Park

Back on the Tanzam Highway, 150km south of Morogoro, north of the Selous Reserve, lies Mikumi, the most accessible of all Tanzania's national parks. Mikumi has the attraction of being within easy driving distance from Dar es Salaam with a couple of good options for accommodation, which makes it a fairly inexpensive option for a self-drive weekend safari in scenic wide open savannah. The park actually straddles the highway near the Uluguru Mountains south of Morogoro, and offers the chance of a brief safari thrill for anyone travelling through by bus or truck. In the past vehicles used to thunder through the 50km stretch heedless of speed restrictions, and road kill has been a major problem, but the introduction of a number of brightly painted speed bumps might increase the chance of seeing something still alive.

Despite its small-time reputation, Mikumi is the third-largest national park in Tanzania, enclosed to the south and east by a semicircle of the **Uluguru Mountains**, rising to 2,743m, and the **Vuma Hills**. These look down across the wide, flat expanse of

Getting There and Around

Light **planes** can land at Mikumi airstrip during the dry season. Foxes of Africa (*see* p.280) operate a daily service.

The **Tanzam Highway** runs through the middle of Mikumi National Park, making it the easiest park to reach by **car**. There is a good vehicle repairs garage at the park head-quarters. Petrol is sometimes available there too, or from petrol pumps in Mikumi town.

The Safari Express, run by Foxes of Africa (*see* p.280) is a thrice-weekly luxury **train** service travelling from TAZARA station in Dar. The journey to Mikumi takes 7–8hrs, and costs $120 one way; prepare for delays.

Tourist Information

Park fees into Mikumi are $15 per person for a 24hr stay; park guides join you on safari for $10 per vehicle per day, or $20 walking. The park's accessibility makes it worth a day trip, with fine sunset views from the restaurants of Vuma Hill Camp and Kikoboga. Wildlife action is most in evidence during the **dry season**, between June and February, when even the rarest species brave the open plains to reach the remaining waterholes.

The park backs a number of initiatives to support local communities: it has set up schools and clinics around the boundaries. A small medical dispensary runs from the park

HQ, useful for first-aid assistance. Avoid this small park during holiday weekends, when it is awash with Dar-ites escaping the city.

Where to Stay and Eat

Mikumi National Park

Moderate

Vuma Hill Tented Camp, Foxes of Africa, PO Box 10270, Dar es Salaam, **t/f** (0741) 327706/ **t** (0744) 237422/**t** (0748) 237422, *fox@safari camps.info, fox@twiga.com, fox@bushlink. co.tz*, UK contact **t** (01452) 862288, *www. tanzaniasafaris.info*. A beautifully appointed tented camp high in the Vuma Hills. Furnished throughout with teak hand-crafted furniture, the camp is a testament to classic safari camp design. The restaurant and bar are at lofty heights on a circular platform with superb views over the Mkata Plains, and the menu promises hearty continental cuisine. A deep swimming pool is tucked into the rock plateau below. Each of the tented rooms is airy, private and peaceful. A stay here up in the hills complements perfectly a few days at the Foxes' other Mikumi camp, the Foxes' Safari Camp on the plains.

Foxes Safari Camp, Foxes of Africa, *see* above. The Foxes Safari Camp has a theatrical sense of place on a kopje overlooking the over the red earth plains of Mkata. The open-sided the **Mkata Flood Plains**, which provide a good spotting ground for a variety of larger animals. Lions, leopards, elephants and buffalo range among the numerous baobabs and palms around the edge, while herds of up to 100 impala range across the plains. Towards the centre of the park, water collects into water courses and swamps, attracting hippopotami, as well as the odd monitor lizard and various water birds. Proximity to the northern border of the Selous means that a number of animals migrate between the two areas, including the Lichtenstein's hartebeest and African hunting dog. The miombo woodlands in the southeast are also a stalking ground for sable antelope and families of shaggy white-collared colobus monkeys; herds of eland and family groups of greater kudu may also be seen between these two areas.

Just before entering the park you reach the roadside village of **Doma**, clearly distinguished by the rows of 'basket' trees that line either side of the road. These are trees strung with all manner of locally woven baskets and bags, with a few rugs thrown in for good measure, an innovative sales method that ensures that every passing vehicle can appreciate the range of crafts available.

living area enjoys surveillance worthy of a hilltop fort. A playful light shapes distant mountain ranges that encircle the plains and give a sense of enclosure, underscoring its faraway feel. The animals pass their days wandering by the local borehole. Sunsets are spectacular; if you happen to go during rainy times you can watch the clouds amass and charge across vast skies. Twelve tents are comfortable, if not luxurious, and the camp has a wild and rustic atmosphere. If you prefer an informal atmosphere then this will please you. The food is home-cooked English cuisine; the camp is emphatically not a place for committed 'foodies'. A lovely deep pool with sheltering *banda* gives succour to tired safari makers and from time to time thirsty elephants too. Hiking is permitted in some areas, and it is possible to foray into the Udzungwas, a green mountain park a 2hr drive to the south.

Kikoboga, c/o Oysterbay Hotels, PO Box 2261, Dar es Salaam, **t** (022) 2668062–4, **f** (022) 2668631, *Oysterbay-hotel@twiga.com*. Good solid accommodation just beyond the park gates at the long-established Kikoboga, previously known as the Mikumi Wildlife Camp. It is a rustic stone camp that sits on the edge of the plains, so that every private verandah and communal seating area offers close-up views of any wildlife action. A small waterhole just beyond the restaurant is popular with elephants and a troupe of

rambunctious yellow baboons, and there's always something to spot in the distance. The restaurant provides good basic fare in generous portions. A particularly good camp for families with children, as each *banda* has a double room and separate, snug children's room. Tiny pool.

Cheap

A **student hostel** in the park headquarters provides basic accommodation for 62, with shared bathrooms and kitchen. Prior booking necessary. Contact Park Warden in Charge, Mikumi National Park, PO Box 62, Mikumi.

There are two **public campsites**, with tap water, sunshades, long-drop toilets and fireplaces with wood supplies, and one **private camp site** with no facilities on the northwestern loop road.

Mikumi Town

At the southern boundary of the national park you come to the small town of Mikumi. **Genesis Motel and Snake Park**, PO Box 18, **t** (023) 4385 (*cheap*). Decent budget rooms at this charismatic little hotel, which provides small, self-contained chalet rooms, and runs a pleasant bar and unusual little restaurant (sister of the Udzungwa Mountain View Hotel at Mang'ula), which specializes in seasonal game meats with a full four-course menu. There is an adjoining snake park (*open 9–6; adm*).

Udzungwa Mountains National Park

The Udzungwa Mountains National Park is a sumptuous forested reserve that has recently been declared the sacred preserve of walkers. The land is ancient, a portion of the Eastern Arc Mountains pushed upwards by faulting in the earth's crust millions of years ago, and its steep slopes preserve a rare tropical forest that is home to a realm of unique plants, birds and animals. It is also the only area in Tanzania where the forest cover remains unbroken from the lowlands to the high mountain forests.

These forests are remarkably unspoilt, a wilderness of extremely beautiful woodland routes – with no driving tracks at all. Of the five official trails, two bring walkers to the spectacular 170m drop of Sanje Falls, with colourful and long-ranging views from the top up to 100km across the Kilombero sugar plantations and a mosaic of grasslands. The areas around the falls become an incredible blur of butterfly colour after the rains in December, April, May and June, when flowers and air alike are often filled with hundreds of swallowtails and blue salamis (*Salamis temora*). Another trail leads up to Mwanihana's peak, a demanding but rewarding hike that demands a good level of fitness from climbers. The highest peak of all is Luhomero, 2,576m above sea level – requiring two nights and three days to climb there and back. A number of rivers, streams and waterfalls make their way down these slopes into the Great Ruaha River, accumulating enough velocity to power the majority of the country's electricity from the hydroelectric turbines at Kidatu, and to irrigate the crops to the south.

History

Udzungwa Mountains National Park is the most recently gazetted of Tanzania's national parks, although it has been a forest reserve since the British created the Mwanihana and West Kilombero Scarp reserves in the early 1950s. The park covers 1,990 square kilometres, almost one-fifth of the 10,000 square kilometres that comprise the Udzungwa mountain range; it is bordered by the Great Ruaha River to the north and Kilombero Valley to the southeast. The present park – the first national park to be declared on the merits of its forests – was created in 1992.

The history of the land, however, is an ancient one: the base of these mountains dates from 650 million years ago, and the dense tropical forest that covers the mountain is thought to be a pocket of vegetation preserved from the time of the Gondwanaland supercontinent that existed 30 million years ago. Leaping forward in time, archaeologists around this area and Isimila have unearthed **Stone Age** hand axes and tools carefully crafted by these early hunter-gatherers. The archaeological study that has been carried out here also provides evidence of a major migration through this area during the 1st and 2nd centuries AD, during which iron-working Bantu-speaking tribes progressed eastwards and displaced native hunter-gatherers.

Later, the **Dzungwa** people, one of the six sub-groups of Hehe peoples who resisted German colonization for seven years before the Maji Maji Rebellion (*see* p.282), were pushed out of the Iringa area by their fellow tribesmen and resisted on the mountainside. From the position of weakness that saw them succumbing to the pressure to move, the Dzungwa found themselves in a stronger position around a richly fertile

Getting There

The Udzungwa Mountains National Park is a 6hr drive from Dar es Salaam, following the Tanzam Highway to Mikumi town and then taking a left turn to Kidatu (hydroelectric power station). After Kidatu the road crosses the river and becomes a slow and bumpy dirt road for the last 24km.

Tourist Information

Park fees are $15 for 24hrs, payable at the park gate, where it is also possible to arrange local trained guides for $10 per day – all are advised to make use of their knowledge and expertise. It is also possible to negotiate porters to assist your climb. The park office provides toilets and guide books, pamphlets and souvenirs. **Fuel** is available from Kidatu, but better **vehicle repair** is available at Mikumi and Morogoro garages. Items such as fruit, vegetables and bottled water can be bought locally, but bring in other supplies.

There are good local **medical facilities,** with a small emergency district hospital in Ifakara and a mission hospital in Kilombero. Visitors covered by the Flying Doctors can be picked up from the Kilombero Sugar Company airstrip.

Where to Stay and Eat

There is not much choice in Mang'ula, with only a couple of options, both within easy distance of the park gate. The route from Mikumi takes just over 2hrs, which makes it feasible to explore the Udzungwa Mountains National Park in a day trip from Mikumi, while staying at Vuma Hill or Kikoboga (*see* pp.288–9).

Cheap

Udzungwa Mountain View, PO Box 99, **t/f** (025) 3357 (*cheap*). Top choice of the two Mang'ula options, run by the same management as the charming older Genesis Motel in Mikumi. The hotel is well located for excursions into the mountains and national park; guides can be arranged for you here. It has eight good, clean rooms containing both a double and a single bed with en-suite bathrooms. Camping is available in the grounds. Meals in the **Carnivore Club** restaurant are well prepared and proudly presented, with a menu including buffalo, hartebeest and impala, as well as the more usual chicken, beef, goat and fish, and cooked breakfast.

Twiga Resort, close to Mang'ula village, just outside the park gate, PO Box 30, **t** Mang'ula 39 (call the the operator on 900 and ask for Mang'ula 39). Spacious, clean, rather characterless doubles, some with bath or shower. The rooms are set around a courtyard garden, a little bit gloomy, although weary climbers or those anticipating the trek can usually get a cold beer. The restaurant serves simple wholesome dishes for a decent price, but the best aspect of Twiga is its superb situation, with great mountain views.

Baobab Valley Campsite. Continuing along the highway between Mikumi and Iringa, the road follows a winding route through a sparsely populated region known as Baobab Valley. In the middle, the campsite is a relaxed and inspired hideaway, where travellers can find a patch of rural Tanzania prepared for them to pitch a tent, and enjoy a friendly ecological welcome. The young proprietors have created a stylish thatched setting around which the project grows. It feels like the product of a hippie dream. A rescued monkey called Casper shrieks from the sofa and a Staffordshire bull terrier keeps watch over it all. The campsite sits in a clearing perched on the sandy banks of a crocodile-friendly tributary of the Great Ruaha River. Twelve thatched sites with gas- and wood-burning stoves are set around a central restaurant, with plans for a bar and deck over the river. A swimming pool was among the first priorities of the campsite pioneers. Every area is intended to run eventually on environmentally sound power

mountain, watered with abundant rain and spring source rivers. Their name means 'People Who Live on the Side of the Mountain', and the name Udzungwa has probably evolved as a result of linguistic corruption by German interpreters.

Udzungwa Mountains Wildlife

Among all the species of wildlife in the Udzungwa forests, several have been found that are unique to this area. The endangered **Iringa** or **uhehe red colobus** monkey (*Colobus badius gondonorum*) is found here, and a much rarer and shyer **Sanje crested mangabey** (*Cercocebus galeritus sanjei*), discovered in 1979 as a result of an unusual encounter by two wildlife ecology researchers from Dar es Salaam University: while collecting plants in the forest, they heard a strange sound that seemed to resemble a mangabey monkey call, but, as the nearest populations of mangabey were thought to be in southern Kenya, the researchers imagined that they were suffering hallucinations. However, their Tanzanian guide described the animal that they had heard, although he only knew it as *n'golaga*, the Swahili name for the species. When he took them to find some *n'golaga* in the forest canopy the next day, the researchers glimpsed the first sight of this unique species of mangabey in the early morning mist. Unlike the Kenyan species, the Sanje mangabey has a pale face and light grey body, and stands about 75cm tall, excluding its long tail. But the researchers wanted to get a better look, and were delighted when their guide took them to see a tame *n'golaga* which had been adopted by local children after their father accidentally shot her mother, which he had mistaken for a yellow baboon. The researchers knew that this species was unique, and were even more excited to see its unusual tufty fringe – until it became clear that the children had styled her mangabey crest in an extreme haircut, to keep the hair out of her eyes.

The other extremely rare species unique to the Udzungwas is a bird, the 'globally threatened' **Udzungwa forest partridge**, which was first recognized as a significant, unusual species of partridge in July 1991. Legend tells how a researcher living in the forest had just devoured his partridge supper when, on closer inspection, he realized

Such a naturally attractive area has not been overlooked by other peoples from different areas, and has attracted a migration of tribes including the **Pogoro** (farmers and hunters), the **Bena** from the Upper Kilombero valley and some **Chagga** from the region around Kilimanjaro. The people on the eastern side of the mountain believe in a mountain god they call Bokela; they use certain regions of the park for sacrifice and worship, especially during hard times such as disease, drought and famine. There was great unease when TANAPA, the Tanzanian National Parks Agency, started to assess the mountains, as it was thought that Bokela would be offended if the area was farmed or logged. It is now widely believed that Bokela is content with the present situation, and supports conservation of his mountain.

Community and Conservation Projects

The late development of the national park means that it has benefited from recent TANAPA and Community Conservation Services (CCS) policies that take account of the local people who will be affected by conservation measures. So the communities of Udzungwa have not suffered as drastically as people around earlier national parks (such as the Maasai in the Serengeti) and have been consulted about any potential restrictions on their lifestyle. Local people have traditionally relied on the forests for that the bird was unfamiliar, and for a time became concerned that he might have eaten the last one. Fortunately, although still rare in the Udzungwa forests, the partridge has since been spotted more frequently in the west of the national park, and recently also near Luhomero Mountain; it appears less often on menus too.

The Udzungwa partridge is just one of many extremely rare bird species in this region. The Udzungwas are home to many unusual species, such as the **Iringa akalat** (*Sheppardia montana*), mainly spotted between 1,600m and 2,400m in regions around the outskirts of the national park, and the **white-winged apalis** (*Apalis chariessa*), which may be seen feeding among other birds on the forest floor. The recently discovered **rufous red-winged sunbird** (*Nectarinia rufipennis*) was identified here in 1981, and is more common in the forests between 600m and 1,700m. It joins two other very rare species of sunbird in the Udzungwa forests, the **amani** (*Anthreptes pallidigaster*) and the **banded-green sunbird** (*Anthreptes rubritorques*).

Other rare species exist in the Udzungwas in denser populations than found elsewhere, such as the **dappled mountain robin** (*Arcanator orostruthus*), the olive-flanked **ground robin** (*Cossypha anomala*), the **black-backed cisticola** (*Cisticola eximus*) and the **red-capped forest warbler** (*Othotomus metopias*). Another pretty bird common to the area is the red-brown-headed **Mrs Moreau's warbler** (*Bathmocercus winifredi*), named by the renowned Africa ornithologist R.E. Moreau after his wife, Winifred. The Moreaus were also responsible for naming another warbler after a family member, when they called a small tail-wagging warbler after their daughter, Prinnia.

Five amphibian and reptile species have also been discovered to be unique to the area – a species of **toad**, a **tree frog**, a **chameleon**, a **forest gecko** (*Cnemaspis uzungwae*) and a skink – a type of **lizard**. The tiny **Udzungwa puddle frog**, with a distinctive band across its eyes, was distinguished and recorded in 1983.

centuries, using the wood for building, fuel, medicines, household utensils and weaving materials, honey gathering and utensils. Bamboo and reeds are used to make baskets for carrying fruit and vegetables, and animals such as the bush pig, tree hyrax and forest antelope have been hunted for meat. The Hehe people traditionally use black and white colobus monkey furs as a part of their ceremonial dress.

Since the national park has been established, local people are only allowed into the forests on Fridays and Sundays to collect dead wood for cooking fuel and grass for thatching, but any form of axe or knife is prohibited within the boundaries. If you are between **Kidatu** and **Mang'ula** on either of these days you will see scores of women of all ages emerging from the forests with vast bundles of wood balanced on their heads. Frequently the load is so great that it exceeds a woman's own height and requires the help of someone else to lift it into position, but once it's arranged she will often carry it a number of kilometres home. The WWF are supporting an extensive reforestation programme, to educate and encourage the community to plant trees and seedlings, for both fruit and wood, around their land. Those with practical knowledge of traditional medicines are allowed a three-month pass to gather the ingredients from the forest. This enclave is pleasantly reminiscent of the mountain-dwelling communities around Lushoto in the Usambaras. The mountains obviously once attracted missionary zeal: there are several schools and various denominations of churches dotting the steep sloping hillsides. Yards are well kept, fruit is grown in gardens, and flowers for decoration. Fat chickens and brightly coloured kangas generate an air of contentment and wellbeing here and the road passes lime stacks for burning limestone, showing a growth in the construction of hand-built housing.

Walking Trails

Prince Bernhard Waterfall Trail: starting from behind the park headquarters, this flat 1km loop trail, although not very inspiring, is one of the best opportunities for seeing monkeys and rare birds owing to the type of trees and openness of the path. At the end of the trail are the falls, which are often surrounded by a range of colourful butterflies; from here you can follow the loop back or follow the stream of water down – a route only for the adventurous, as the trail disappears and the river becomes your guide. After about an hour of clambering over and under fallen trees and wading through water you reach the main road and are 5mins from the park headquarters.

The **Mwanihana Trail** is a 38km circuit and can only be done as a 3-day, 2-night trek. Although it is still in its infancy in regards to the other trails in the park, the government have plans to open this up, dependent on funding. In its current state the trail is still well worth the time and effort; it incorporates all of the region's biospheres, from closed canopy, grassland, cloud forest and mountain forest to the second highest peak in the range, Mwanihana Peak (2,156m). There is also the opportunity to see elephants, leopards, buffalo, the rare Abbott's duiker and a range of birdlife, and the best chance to spot the endemic Sanje crested mangabey. Restrictions on walking the trail apply, so enquire at the park gate. You will need to be accompanied by an armed ranger for the duration and have your own camping equipment for the trek, including food and water.

Although the entire trek is three days, you may also walk the first part of the trail on its own. Beginning from a gate opposite the Mountain View hotel, the path winds through a small local plantation before ascending a small ridge, which offers fine views across the valley. Owing to the openness of the vegetation, it has excellent opportunities for spotting both birds and mammals. The best time to walk this one-way trail is first thing in the morning, before returning for breakfast at your hotel.

The highlight of the Udzungwa Mountains is the **Sanje Waterfall Trail**. The walk lasts for approximately four hours, with the first three being the toughest. Once you break the forest canopy you are rewarded with superb views across the plains. The trail also offers the best chance for spotting both black and white colobus monkeys as well the endemic red colobus. At the top, cross the river and continue up for a further 10 minutes to the Sanje Falls where the first of a series of three waterfalls plunges into a refreshing pool ideal for swimming in. Your return route takes you down the east face of the mountain giving excellent views of the third and largest waterfall from below.

Alternatively, there is a shorter and slightly easier walk across the base of the mountains. The **Sonjo Trail** passes two smaller waterfalls, suitable for swimming in, and lasts approximately three hours.

Iringa

The town of Iringa nestles on a 1,600m-high plateau at the heart of the Southern Highlands, almost entirely hidden from view until you come upon it. It is an unusually attractive town, with wide streets lavishly lined with flowering jacarandas – a legacy

Getting There and Around

At present there are no **flights** into Iringa. It's an 8hr **bus** trip to Iringa from Dar es Salaam, via Morogoro, costing around $10. Buses travel along this route daily, continuing to Mbeya. The most reliable company running between these points is Scandinavian Bus Lines, PO Box 1269, Iringa, **t** (026) 2702308.

Dala-dalas operate from the central bus station, where the central **taxi** rank is also found. The town is big enough to make a **bicycle** a welcome friend, and multi-speed mountain bikes and good old-fashioned one-speed bicycles (the all-popular Chinese model), can be rented near the main market. If you wish to visit Kisolanza Farm or the Mufindi Highland Lodge, they can arrange transport to and from Iringa.

Where to Stay

Iringa Town

Moderate

MR Hotel, Mkwawa Road, Iringa, PO Box 431, **t** (026) 2702006, **f** (026) 2702661. The large and rather unprepossessing MR Hotel is the best and smartest option for a decent, clean room with en-suite bathroom and air-conditioning. The staff are good-willed and friendly. The adjoining restaurant provides a decent breakfast, and is small, popular and well recommended for lunch and dinner. A pleasant balcony area in front of reception is a good spot for fine views over town. Staff can arrange for guides to lead you on local walks. Breakfast included.

Cheap

Isimila Hotel, PO Box 216, **t** (026) 2702605. Built in an unusual 'modern' style which could almost have been smart, but instead is rather dingy and remains a monument to poor design. The rooms are mediocre and

the restaurant looks unappetizing, but the bar forms a pleasant and well-lit focus for the establishment, and seems to attract a regular clientele. Breakfast included.

Huruma Baptist Centre, just behind the Danish School on Mwembe Togwa Street, which runs directly north of the bus station, **t** (026) 2700184. An altogether better, cheaper choice, the Baptist Centre is a couple of kilometres from the town centre, but regular dala-dalas shuttle back and forth and it is a safe spot to park private vehicles. The rooms are well presented and good value. The restaurant is reliably good; it is often necessary to book in advance. Fine breakfasts.

Lutheran Centre, to the north of town at the end of Kawawa Road, **t** (026) 2701990. There are numerous budget options around town, with a range of inexpensive rooms available: the Lutheran Centre is the most popular. Rooms here are simple but clean. En-suite singles or doubles sharing bathroom less.

Out of Town

Moderate

Kisolanza Farm, PO Box 113, Iringa, *kisolanza@bushlink.co.tz*. A civilized oasis of colour and fresh floral charm 51km south of Iringa and 21km northeast of Mafinga. Kisolanza is a colonial farmhouse, built in sturdy stone and set in fabulous gardens with a view. It is managed and run by Nicky Cox, who has reclaimed and restored this Ghaui family homestead with indomitable enthusiasm. Although Nicky despairs at ever keeping the grass green, her breathtaking gardens are vivid with colour and make the most of unusual features provided by vast worn rocks, mature jacaranda trees and wide reaching views across savannah grasslands to the distant hills. The farm offers three comfortable self-contained cottages for guests, who gather in the main farmhouse for meals at candlelit tables. Visitors can of its colonial origins. The overall impression created by the town is one of organization and investment – all its major roads were immaculately resurfaced In 1999 – and the central market is vibrant, busy and amply piled with fresh, colourful goods. The high-altitude climate has attracted a healthy population of expatriates, many of whom have returned to the area as a result of the extensive tea plantations further

also explore the farm, which raises cattle and grows cereals and coffee, or swim and fish in the lake. Those with a sporting desire for a game of golf can organize trips to the tournament-level course at Mufindi. Plans are afoot to add horse-riding, as well as a tennis court and croquet lawn. Kisolanza can arrange for guests to be collected from Iringa Airport and continue into Ruaha National Park, which is 3–4hrs' drive. Cottages half-board, or camping.

Mufindi Highland Lodge, Foxes of Africa, *see* p.288. Another excellent alternative for anyone keen to experience an unusually cool and beautiful mosquito-free region of the Southern Highlands. It too is a family farm, superbly situated 150km south of Iringa in a stunning region that is popular with tea-plantation enthusiasts, yet hardly visited by tourists. These steep, hilly reaches demand no park fees, rules or regulations for walkers. They provide a fresh climate for anyone with a love of wide open spaces and woodlands. Narrow maze-like roads wind across these vibrant green hillsides to the distant reaches of the lodge. The central restaurant and bar rise like a quirky Celtic castle in this surprisingly Scottish-looking – although distinctly sun-drenched – landscape. Its solid form is constructed from rough-hewn blocks of stone and homely timbers. The restaurant boasts wide views from its solid second-storey balcony, although the roomy fireplaces upstairs and down are a testament to the cooler climes of these highland nights. In the same vein, each of the log cabins is fitted with a bath tub and sub-terranean log-burning water heating system, and is complete with thick duvets. A recent addition is a more secluded log cabin overlooking the lake; two vast rooms can house up to five people in each. Guests can join the sociable meals in the main dining area, or can entirely do their own thing, since the cabin has a dining and lounge

area. A grassy lawn tennis court has recently been laid, and wending garden paths lead to a secret croquet lawn. Guests can explore the surrounding woodlands and hills on foot or by vehicle, or ride one of the many horses that range freely around the farm. Mountain bikes are also available for those energetic enough to brave the slope, and streams are stocked with rainbow trout for fly-fishermen to try their hand. A golf course suits all abilities. A number of forest walks can be followed to the edge of a nearby escarpment, where the land drops a dramatic 600m into the Kilombero Valley below. At night the clear air is filled with the song of frogs and cicadas, and a magical landscape is illuminated at full moon. Mufindi makes a good setting to spend a few days relaxing and exploring an unspoilt environment, made more welcoming by the enthusiasm and creative verve of the Fox family. For a slightly higher price, horse-riding, mountain biking, guided walks and drives, and a visit to a tea factory are all thrown in.

Eating Out

Staff Restaurant, just off Store Street near the market. One of the best little corners to enjoy a good, local-style, local-priced meal.

Hasty Tasty Too, just past the clock tower on Uhuru Street. The expatriate population ensures a good choice for more Western tastes. This popular little café opens early to do a roaring trade in breakfasts. It continues through the day with a range of Indian dishes; it is most often packed at every meal.

Lulu's Bakery, nearby, tucked away in a parallel back street (left off Benbella Road). The fabulous picnic-preparing haven of Lulu's Bakery, a Greek-run corner of Iringa with an old-world café feel, serves up a fine selection of home-made pastries (sausage rolls!), sandwiches, ice-creams, chocolates, toffees and so on. *Open Mon–Sat 8.30–3 and 6.30–8.*

Chief Mkwawa's Skull

Iringa town developed following the eventual victory of the German colonists over the Hehe tribe and its supporting tribes after their valiant resistance to European rule in the 1890s. This resistance was spearheaded by the infamous Hehe Chief Mkwawa, whose formidable war cry is thought to have inspired the naming of the tribe. Mkwawa had established a formidable **fortress** at Kalenga, a few kilometres outside Iringa, now on the road into Ruaha National Park, with outer walls measuring 13km end to end; the walls are said to have been 'four metres high and as wide as a road', and enclosed a smaller, also fortified, inner courtyard. Mkwawa's tribe practised archery with poisoned arrows, which became a deterrent for groups of slave-raiding Arabs, until he secured an alliance with them in exchange for supplies of ivory and leopardskin. But no such alliance was made with the European colonists, who remained irreconcilably at odds with the warrior-like Hehe and their supporting tribes. Mkwawa's men made a lasting impression on the German troops in 1891 when they carried out an ambush at Lugalo and trounced the colonial forces.

Humiliated and furious, the Germans retreated in order to regroup and to plan their retaliation. Three years later, in 1894, they returned for a rematch, and destroyed Mkwawa's fort. Now the remnants of this ancient rock and clay-moulded stronghold have been whittled down to a rather large mound in the middle of Kalenga village. It is still possible to cast an imaginative eye over the sandy remains of the fortress; the vague outline of the fort walls can just be made out around the edges of a sun-scorched football pitch, but the final onslaught of bullets and grenades launched by German troops from the top of a nearby hill effectively obliterated it. On 19 June 1899, after seven years of resistance, Chief Mkwawa shot himself through the skull rather than surrender to his German foe. Somewhat ungraciously, the thwarted colonists chopped his head off and sent it back to Germany, where it came to rest in the Bremen Anthropological Museum (of all places) for more than 50 years, gathering dust. But the Hehe did not forget, and continued to demand its return until, on 19 June 1954, it was finally returned to Mkwawa's grandson, Chief Adam Sapi. That day is now a holiday for the Hehe, on which everyone drinks a brew of fermented millet and maize and contributes a cow or money for the celebrations. Although the original dictate of the 1967 Arusha Declaration concerning distinct tribal practices forbade the memorial, it has been reinstated since the centenary of Chief Mkwawa's death in 1999. Chief Mkwawa's skull is now on display in the small **memorial museum** on the outskirts of Kalenga village. The caretaker, Francis Kalenga, will let you into the museum and provide a detailed, amusing account in return for a small donation. If you find the place locked, despatch a local child to find him.

To the right of the museum you can see the impressive '**palace**' built by the Hehe people to honour their chief and his family, even though their rule became only nominal after Independence and the devolution of tribal powers. The palace looks surprisingly like an English country house, and was built on donations from each member of the tribe. Mkwawa's grandson, Adam Sapi, was speaker of Tanzania's first parliament and a highly regarded politician. He died in June 1999, and his son, Mfuimi, takes on the nominal role as head of the Hehe.

south at **Mufindi** and continue to nurture business interests in the town. There are a number of pleasant hotels and restaurants. There is also a thriving Christian community, whose grand **cathedral** with its brick façade and whitewashed nave and aisles beneath a neat tile roof is raised high on the hill at the entrance of town.

Iringa is small and friendly enough to explore on foot or on a bicycle in the course of a day, with a few interesting old colonial buildings such as the **old boma**, **town hall** and **hospital**. Outside the police station a **monument** commemorates the native warriors who died in the Maji Maji Rebellion.

Around Iringa

The surrounding area provides good walking country. A good destination to the north of the town is Chief Mkwawa's favourite spot for meditating, known as **Gangilonga Rock**, the 'Talking Stone' in the language of the Hehe. It takes a few minutes to climb to the top, with good views of the town once there.

Just outside Iringa, **Isimila Stone Age site** is considered one of the most exciting areas for Stone Age archaeological finds in East Africa. The site is a dry lake-bed, and was discovered in 1951 by a schoolboy who came across an axe head. It is thought, from the number of tools found in the area and a number of blocks and boulders that were probably used to shape the granite and quartzite rock, that Stone Age man camped on the shores of the lake and shaped and worked his tools here. A number of fossilized bones have also been found showing the prehistoric forms of species of elephant, hippopotamus and giraffe. The site is signposted from the main road 20km south of Iringa. The **site office** and small **museum** (*open 9–6; adm*) is about one kilometre further from this turning; it houses an exhibition of some of the tools, bones and fossils found in the area that are thought to date from around 60,000 years ago. A guide can also take you around the site, a walk that takes about an hour. A short walk along the valley brings you to the **Isimila Gully**, a scenic red earth area that has been naturally sculpted and eroded into impressive sandstone pillars and eerie formations that loom overhead on each side of the valley – a good spot for a picnic! A taxi from Iringa to Isimila costs around $20, or take a dala-dala in the direction of Tosamaganga and get out at the Isimila turn-off.

Continuing southwards past Kalenga, the fortress base of Chief Mkwawa (*see* box, p.297), along the road to Mbeya, the landscape continues to reflect the hot and dry climate with bleached grasses and baobabs reminiscent of Ruaha National Park.

Ruaha National Park

The wide distances of Ruaha National Park have a drama quite unlike any other Tanzanian park. Here the land has its own kind of remoteness. It is an ancient place in the Great Rift Valley, where mile upon mile of age-old sandy red earth has been worn and bleached by the sun, and the hilly distances are punctuated with the distended elephant-battered girths of countless massive baobabs (*see* p.302), as many as a thousand years old. The combination of ochre-red earth, pale russet grasses and the parched paths of wide sand rivers appeal to images of an archetypal African land.

When to Go

The climate in Ruaha is similar to the rest of Tanzania, moving slightly towards a more southern African pattern of **single season rains**, with the short rains in November being less distinct and the long rains of late March and May varying in intensity. The **dry season** between May and November is best for general wildlife viewing, as animals are centred around fewer water resources. However, butterfly enthusiasts and bird-watchers will find more to excite them in the months around the rains, between January and May; some say the two-week break from rain in February is unparalleled for scenery, though the break is notoriously difficult to predict, and during this time many of the outer routes become impassable; drivers should get detailed advice from park wardens regarding safe driving routes. During the hot months of October and November the valleys of Ruaha are prone to dramatic thunder and lightning storms.

Getting There

By Air

Scheduled flights with **Coastal Travels** (*see* p.280) from Dar and Selous on Mon, Thurs and Sat take around 2hrs and cost $300. Coastal flights return from Ruaha to Dar and Zanzibar on Tues, Fri and Sat. Coastal have a new scheduled flight from Arusha to Ruaha on Tues, Fri and Sat returning Mon, Thurs and Sat.

By Car

The road from **Dar es Salaam** via Mikumi is 650km and takes around 10hrs, including a 3hr stretch from Iringa. Most drivers reach the park via the historic village of Kalenga, and from this point to the park entrance the road is disconcertingly straight, passing through small populous villages, which begin to thin out closer to the park boundaries. The road is sandy, and drivers unfamiliar with this terrain should take it more slowly than the open distances tempt, as there is a real likelihood of 'fishtail planing', which has been the cause of accidents in the past.

Getting Around

Ruaha offers game viewing **on foot** or from open-sided **4x4 vehicles**, both of which can be arranged by your camp or lodge; you can also do a self-drive safari if you have your own vehicle. All walking safaris must be accompanied by an armed ranger, who can be contacted from the park gates.

Tourist Information

Contact the **Park Warden**, Ruaha National Park, PO Box 369, Iringa, for park fees, armed rangers and camping information.

Where to Stay and Eat

There are currently four camps in Ruaha plus possibilities for camping, or joining mobile tented camps with upmarket tour operators.

Expensive

Mwagusi Luxury Tented Camp, bookings c/o TropicAfrica, 14 Castelnau, London SW13 9RU, t (020) 8846 9363, *tropicafrica.uk@virgin. net*). A rare gem on the safari circuit, Mwagusi is a family-run lodge tucked away in the far northeast corner of the park, on the banks of a curve in the Mwagusi Sand River. It is an area where all manner of local wildlife dig holes in the sand to drink the clear waters that flow beneath, and the camp brims with a rare passion for the place that is infectious. Mwagusi is owned and run by Chris Fox, whose knowledge of this area extends back to long holidays spent camping in this area before it even became a national park, and whose family helped to ensure that the land was gazetted and fully protected in 1964. He developed the camp as an offshoot from the Ruaha River Lodge, originally managing that camp and using the Mwagusi location for extended fly-camping safaris. It is not unusual to wake in the early hours of morning with the magnetic lure of a sublime sunrise over the sand river, to pad out onto your sandy private balcony to see Chris taking a bare-foot morning stroll in the company of a very large and ancient tuskered elephant. Chris trains and encourages all his camp guides to feel as at home as he does in this wild and golden land and their knowledge is compounded by a unanimous enthusiasm and sensitivity. Morning and afternoon driving safaris are by open-sided Land Cruiser, with a maximum of six people in the viewing seats; there is a pervasive sense of anticipation that encourages all to hold their breath as tracks are studied and followed by driver, spotter and guide. Mwagusi also excels in inspiring walking safaris into the bush, which impart an even deeper sense of the greatness of the place, and amplify the sensation of the smallness of your own little life in a much bigger picture. The camp is an all-natural, elegant construction that can accommodate eight couples in style. Clothes are washed and folded, tea is left on the balcony with the dawn, and supper is laid on a long white table under a host of twinkling stars by a quiet team of magical, invisible camp elves. Meals are shared at long communal tables laden with a fantastic gourmet spread. This place is a world apart.

Ruaha River Lodge, c/o Foxes of Africa, *see* p.288. Also built and run by the intriguing Fox family, who have nearly 40 years of experience of Ruaha. It was the first camp built in the area, and must take credit for choosing one of the most spectacular locations imaginable. The situation is naturally dramatic, as the lodge extends along the rocky shores of the Great Ruaha River in an area where there is rarely a view without a dash of wildlife to colour it, especially during the dry months from June to November. The lodge seems to grow from every rocky outcrop and crevice in winding paths, linking clusters of stone and thatch bandas. It has been divided into three distinct areas and guests may require safari vehicle transfers to one of the vast central dining *bandas*. Food is simple and wholesome, some imported from the Fox family's farm in the wonderful highlands around Iringa.

Jongomero Permanent Tented Camp, c/o Selous Safari Company, PO Box 1192, Dar es Salaam, **t** (022) 2134802/2113220, *info@ selous.com, www.selous.com*. Those who have had the fortune to visit this camp rarely keep it quiet: it has an excellent word-of-mouth reputation. Established by the successful owners of the Selous Safari Camp, Jongomero exudes simple bushlife charm, with imaginative décor, and huge tents decorated with hand-crafted dhow wood. With only eight tents, the camp is relaxed and intimate, but always maintains the special touch and provides the added detail. It is run by a dedicated team who endlessly and apparently easily produce tables that are groaning with food; crackling open camp fires and starlit meals contribute to a sense of bush adventure. In daytime, after the exertions of the safari, an appealing swimming pool offers the chance to cool off. As with all Selous Safari Camp properties, guiding is very good, led from open-sided vehicles or on leisurely walking safaris.

Mdonya Old River, Adventure Camps, PO Box 3052, Dar es Salaam, **t** (022) 452005/6, **f** (022) 2452004, *www.adventurecamps.co.tz*. Mdonya Old River is one of the newest camps in Tanzania. With only 10 tents, the aim of Mdonya is to experience the wildness of the bush and not revel in luxury while being there. The tents are perfectly adequate but not over-the-top, and the level of service and general standards are not what you will receive at either Jongomero or Mwagusi. However, this camp really is special, as its atmosphere is very different from most camps throughout Tanzania. Currently run by an ex-lion researcher, Malcolm Ryan, Mdonya would prefer to be described as a permanent fly-camp. Game regularly walks straight into and through the camp, and it is very rare to see anyone else during your stay there. There really are not many places like this camp left in the entire country.

Camping

There is a **campsite** at Msembe, near the airstrip, on the banks of the Ruaha River, which has long-drop toilets, but no running water. Water is available nearby at the huts of the **park hostel**, which sleeps 32. All visitors must have their own transport. Bookings for the campsite or *bandas* should be made through the park warden (*see* p.299).

Ruaha Wildlife

The joy of Ruaha is that there are hardly any people, but a huge variety of wildlife lay claim to its hilly savannah and bush. Ruaha has one of the largest **elephant** populations of any African park. The dry, open hillsides encourage **antelope** and **buffalo** to gather into large herds, seeking safety in numbers. The terrain is good for seeing predators, especially **lions** and potentially **leopards**, as well as packs of **African hunting dogs**. The many rivers and swamps around the Great Ruaha River are alive with **hippopotami**, **crocodiles** and **fish**, and the many **giraffes** and **zebras** that roam the plains make their way to the shores of the water to drink. Ruaha is the only East African park with both **greater** and **lesser kudu** and **sable** and **roan antelopes**; like the Selous, it has an unusual combination of east and southern African wildlife and birds. The **red-billed wood hoopoe**, **violet-crested turaco** and **racquet-tailed roller** are among the many coloured migrants, and just a small selection of the 480 species of bird that have been sighted within the park. The wetter months during the first third of the year are the best months for bird-watching, when the beauty of the park is enhanced by the blooming miombo woodland flowers. The miombo woodlands are dominated by 15 species of **brachystegia trees**, while the rolling grass plains are covered with various different **acacias**, spiny **commiphora** and plenty of **baobab trees**. Around 1,650 plant species have been identified in the park, most of which bloom.

Poaching

In recent decades poaching has been a serious problem in Ruaha, decreasing the population of 22,000 elephants recorded in 1967 to only 4,000 in 1987 – which still represents one of the largest numbers in any African national park. It is heartening to know that numbers have recovered by up to 12,000 since 1987 as a result of the park's very successful anti-poaching action, which has made exemplary efforts to fully involve and understand local communities and their needs.

One result of the serious dent in the elephant population is that there are fewer mature animals that have grown to full size (usually around 60 years of age), and it is rare to see any elephant with a fully developed pair of tusks. These days it is more common to come across tuskless and small-tusked elephants, once an anomaly and yet now a far higher proportion, the survivors of the brutal massacres of ivory-hunters. The high proportion of tuskless elephants has inspired research into natural selection, but it still remains to be seen whether future generations will breed more small-tusked and tuskless elephants, or whether the large-tusk gene that produced the 3m-long tusks plundered by the ivory traders will prove dominant once again. It is encouraging that the elephants in Ruaha are still breeding enthusiastically; large numbers of female elephants around the park can be seen with babies. The intimate social structure of elephant herds is complex: they have been proven to be highly intelligent animals that show collective grief over death within their groups, often gathering around the dead elephant, and trying to carry the body away. All the same, it remains surprising that the Ruaha elephant populations do not show great signs of nervousness around people, considering the brutality they have suffered.

Part of the present-day attraction of Ruaha is its distant location, which demands a long drive or an expensive flight, and means that the park is hardly visited by tourists. Covering 10,300 square kilometres, Ruaha is the second-largest national park in Tanzania after the Serengeti. It begins on the high plateau around Njombe River in the northwest and slopes across a wide valley to the Great Ruaha River in the south-east. Such a vast and fascinating landscape makes it an ideal location for a longer safari, not less than four–seven nights – not least to make the cost of flying in worth-while. There are currently four options for permanent accommodation within the national park, two of which are run by brothers who explored and fell in love with this land as children. Trips to Ruaha are often combined with the Selous Game Reserve, as the two locations are complementary in their landscapes and wildlife, yet part of the same scheduled flight route.

The park was part of Rungwa Game Reserve until it was made into a fully protected national park in its own right in 1964. It now forms an important component of the 30,000 square kilometres of protected ecosystem that covers Rungwa, Kisigo and Ruaha. It is named after the Great Ruaha River – 'Ruaha' is the Hehe word for 'Great' –

Baobab Trees

The vast and bizarre features of the baobab tree are a striking feature of the African bush. Of all the eight species of baobab worldwide, the African variety, *Adansonia digitata*, is the largest, and the most impressive. While these trees may inspire a certain awe in most passers-by, they represent a deep-rooted significance in the lives of the people and animals who live around them. The baobab is brimming with life-giving properties that are nutritional, medicinal and practical, earning it a popular reputation for being a spiritual tree. Every part of the tree can be put to use: the fibrous, stringy bark can be largely stripped without killing the tree, and used to make rope, string, fabric and netting. Various parts of the tree are used for medicines, to reduce malarial fever and relieve eye infections, gum diseases, boils, burns and dysentery to name but a few, and the fruit has such a high vitamin C content that it is popularly used to combat symptoms of scurvy. A drink made from the bark is said to make a person strong, and one made from the soaked baobab seed is believed to protect the drinker from crocodiles. The trunks and cavities store water that enables the trees to survive in dry areas through the hot summer months, and thirsty elephants often batter the trunks to plunder the water supply. The baobab can sustain an amazing amount of abuse, and will continue to flower and function even when elephants – assisted by zebras and giraffes – have chewed a hole right through the middle. The trees live for generation after generation of human life: the baobab is known to grow for at least 800 years, some say even as long as 2,000 years. Individual trees become the focus of rural village life, as their broad branches and tangled roots provide a naturally comfortable and shady communal area and their longevity ensures a historical place in the community. The massive trunk can grow a circumference of up to 25m and often becomes hollow; this area has been used across southern Africa to provide a spiritual tomb for chiefs, as well as being home to many unknown spirits that are widely believed to inhabit the peculiar gnarly forms.

and in the 1970s–80s dams were built at Kidatu and Mtera to exploit the river's great-ness for electricity. Yet visitors to Ruaha in the dry season today may be disappointed to find that the great river is just a meandering trickle – even if it does concentrate the wildlife around the remaining pools. Until recently the Ruaha never ran dry, but in the last decade it has been entirely drained during the dry season. Its power and might as a perennial water reserve have been depleted by agricultural practices and rice-growing initiatives upstream, which have reduced the quantity of water and created a situation that is ecologically near-disastrous. The river fish population has already suffered, and now crocs and hippos are being forced to squeeze into ever more rarefied patches of water between the rains, in a sort of wildlife musical chairs. The Ruaha's population of rare freshwater oysters is vastly diminished, and there are fewer places for the rare plover to nest. The effects on biodiversity are incredible. The park had, however, already been made accessible year-round by a bridge built across the Great Ruaha River nine years ago. Fortunately, in recent years, science has proven the devastating effect of mismanaged agricultural practices. More cogently, since the river's water system directly powers 50 per cent of the country's electricity, its demise has affected the workings of the air-conditioning systems of the rich and powerful in the cities. Consequently, the political will is growing to work out a lasting solution.

The Fox family, whose lives after settling in the region are inexorably entwined with the fortunes of the water system, have established a trust to highlight sustainable solutions. The 'Foxes Wildlife and Community Conservation Trust' can be contacted via *www.tanzaniasafari.com*. The prime minister declared in 2001 that a long-term sensible solution would be found. While concrete steps have not yet been taken, those concerned are hopeful that change will happen, and that the river will once again flow all year round.

Mbeya to Lake Nyasa

Continuing south from Ruaha, beyond Makambako the region becomes green and mountainous until you reach the landscape all around Mbeya, rucked and pitted with a staggering range of fabulous formations. Here the Eastern Arc of the Great Rift Valley almost meets the Mbeya Range, which rises up in a northwesterly arc beyond Mbeya town, crowned by the glittering quartz-crystalline silhouette of Mbeya Peak. South of the town, the Uporoto Mountains form a dense and fertile region punctuated with volcano-top villages, waterfalls and the blue circles of crater lakes scattered all the way down to the shores of Lake Nyasa (Lake Malawi on the other side of the border). To the east is Mbeya Plain, stretching out to the Safwa Scarp and the great flat-topped - mountain of Ishinga, shaped by time from a vast expanse of sandstone layers.

The most recent serious volcanic activity to shape the Mbeya–Iringa region occurred between 20 and four million years ago as a result of the rift action between underlying tectonic plates. As a result, this region presents a wide spread of mountains, crater lakes and lava or ash plains, with a mass of natural interest throughout. The open plain between the Eastern Arc Mountains and the Mbeya

Getting There and Around

By Road

Regular bus services connect with **Dar es Salaam** (almost 900km or 20hrs driving), **Iringa, Morogoro** and **Dodoma**. Travellers are advised to take safety precautions on night buses along this route, as thefts have been reported. It may be preferable to break the trip in Iringa, if you cannot keep an eye on your luggage from your seat all the way.

There are also regular buses on to **Tukuyu** and **Kyela** to connect with the lake steamer from **Itungi Port** or **Matema** to Mbamba Bay (with connections to Songea) and other villages in southern Tanzania, or Nkhata Bay in Malawi. A daily bus leaves Mbeya at 5am and arrives in Matema after sunset. Buses also run direct from Kyela to Matema, or via Ipinda, where there may be a long wait for a connection. However, the best way to reach **Matema** from Mbeya is by **car**. The road that leads to the lake is windy, bumpy, frequently muddy, and difficult even in a four-wheel-drive – but very picturesque on the way.

There is another bus from Mbeya to **Njombe**, one of the highest and coldest parts of Tanzania, and on to **Songea**, **Tunduru** and **Masasi** for the **Makonde Plateau**.

By Train

Mbeya is a main stop on the **TAZARA** railway route, which passes through here three times a week. Mbeya railway station is about 5km out of town, but you can arrange to be met.

By Boat

The best way to see the northern part of **Lake Nyasa**, with the Livingstone Mountains looming above it to the east, is to take the **lake ferry**. It's very much a local affair, with crowds of people at every tiny village port along the eastern shore watching its painfully slow docking, unloading and loading. If you adapt to its pace, however, it's a colourful trip. At each stop floating vendors paddle out and gather around the ferry selling fruit.

It's worth checking with bus drivers in Mbeya before you set out from there whether and when lake ferries are running – of all Tanzania's unreliable transport, the ferries are perhaps the most unreliable. Two Tanzanian ferries and one Malawian ferry chug up and down from **Port Itungi** to **Lupingu, Manda, Lundu, Nindai, Liuli** and **Mbamba Bay**, some continuing to **Nkhata Bay** and in Malawi.

The **MV** *Iringa* leaves Itungi on Thursday mornings, arriving at Mbamba around midday on Fridays, and in Nkhata on Friday afternoons. It departs Nkhata again late on Fridays, reaches Mbamba 4–5hrs later, and arrives back in Itungi on Sunday mornings. It leaves Itungi again on Mondays, repeating the rcuit to arrive back again in time for the Thursday departure.

The **MV** *Songea* also sails between Itungi and Mbamba Bay, and the **MV** *Ilala* – the Malawian vessel – sails up and down the western, Malawian, side of the lake, crossing to Mbamba Bay once a week on Tuesday nights, arriving in Mbamba on Wednesday mornings and returning to Nkhata late on Wednesdays. It is often 6–12hrs behind schedule, and when it lags too far the service is cancelled to allow it to catch up with itself.

Tickets on all the ferries are cheap; it's well worth paying an extra $16 for a cabin. Tickets be bought at Port Itungi or on the boats.

Tourist Information

While it is possible to arrange **guides** for walks and days out in this region with the more upmarket hotels in the region (Utengule Country Hotel is probably the best), there is an extremely well recommended and worthwhile organization in town, which can provide reliable, informative and friendly guides. **Sisi Kwa Sisi**, Tourism Office, **t** (0741) 463471, *sisikwasisi tours@hotmail.com*, is a locally run initiative managed by Nico Ntinda and Felix Amndo, who have a joint reputation for being 'lovely'. They will meet travellers from the train or bus station, and arrange accompanied walks and excursions around Mbeya for a very reasonable price plus their own travel expenses. Nico and Felix speak good English themselves and are training other local guides as their enterprise expands. You can find their offices at the bottom of the hill near the bus station, beside the roundabout with the rhino sculpture. Even if you feel a guide might be superfluous, it is worth having Nico and Felix around for the benefit of translating Swahili exchanges as you explore, or to arrange for you to visit local traditional healers or visit rural villages. There have also been security concerns for tourists wandering the outskirts of Mbeya unaccompanied, which will be less of a concern if you are guided. There are endless combinations of walks in all these surrounding mountains, with landscapes and unusual attractions to suit all time schedules and energy levels.

Where to Stay

Mbeya Town

Moderate
Mount Livingstone Hotel, off Jamatikhana Road, **t** (025) 2503331, *www.twiga.ch/TZ/ mtlivingstone.htm*. The smartest and most distinctly hotel-like of all the options in Mbeya. There is a choice of very comfortable B&B accommodation that includes armchairs for a relaxed 'sitting-room' style. A garden bar presents a pleasant new area and gives guests even more choice. The *à la carte* restaurant has been highly recommended. Dishes are moderately priced. Breakfast included.

Cheap
Rift Valley Hotel, PO Box 1631, **t** (025) 2504429. Designed around some sort of a garden, but has a dark and musty old atmosphere despite the fact that it has just been built. The restaurant offers a varied menu with a range of decent-looking dishes: plenty of avocados and prawns. B&B.
Mbeya Peak, on Acacia Street, PO Box 822, **t** (025) 2503473. Both cheaper and nicer, with grand old corridors and a real sense of age and history. The atmosphere is somehow lively and helpful, and all of its 17 rooms are characterful, even if they are not in pristine condition. Located near the ice-cream parlour on Lupu Street and a popular-looking nightclub next door. The restaurant is good, with a cheap menu.
Holiday Lodge, just behind the Rift Valley Hotel on Lumumba Street, **t** (025) 2502821.

A good choice. Small, with clean rooms and a pleasant atmosphere. A decent restaurant flickers in the shadows of a perpetual TV.

Around Mbeya
Utengule Country Hotel, PO Box 139, Mbeya, **t** (025) 2560100, *www.utengule.com, utengule@twiga.com (moderate)*. The most comfortable and welcoming choice for accommodation is out of Mbeya town, set in the coffee plantations around it. The lodge is part of the Utengule Coffee Estate, which produces excellent arabica coffee. Guests can enjoy walks through the plantations, complete with explanations about harvesting and production, and also enjoy exceptional freshly grown, ground and lovingly brewed coffee whenever required. The site was chosen by the original farmer because it was his favourite spot to climb to with his wife after a long day to admire the view or to watch the sunset. He gradually set about building a lodge to which he could invite his friends for parties, and his original quirky little round rooms are still prominent with fantastic views from an elevated hillside position. These have now been joined by a run of stylish new rooms, stunningly designed almost entirely in wood, with separate rooms in a spacious, detached private bungalow with views across the southern hillsides. The lodge applies its 'country club' appeal by providing a number of sports and games facilities to appeal to all tastes: in-house amusements include a swimming pool, tennis, badminton and beach volleyball courts, and a bar complete with pool tables and a dartboard. There is a mini-golf garden and a giant chessboard, for fun-sized competitions, and motorcycles and mountain bikes for rent. Guests can be kept amused for days just by remaining at the hotel, although the management also have expertise in arranging and advising on itineraries for walking and excursions in the surrounding area. All guests return in the evenings to a superb restaurant, where tables are prepared under an elevated curving verandah to ensure that all diners enjoy the cuisine with a fabulous view over the Southern Highlands. The hotel will arrange free transfers to and from Mbeya

station or airport, if arranged in advance. Rates include breakfast.

Tukuyu

Langiboss Hotel, a short distance from the town centre on the Masoko Road, not far from the German boma, t (025) 2562080 (*cheap*). The best choice in Tukuyu, among a range of random guesthouses, is the old Langiboss Hotel, a basic but welcoming establishment. Rooms are simple and inexpensive. The adjoining restaurant and bar ensure that you will not go hungry or thirst for a beer. Order meals in advance, where possible, and hope that your visit does not coincide with a spirit-calling session. Doubles with en-suite showers or cheaper rooms with shared baths available. Buckets of hot water can be provided if there is none on tap at the time.

Kyela

There are a couple of guesthouses in Kyela.
Pattaya Central Guest House, on the main road between the Upete and Jafina bus stands (*cheap*). The best value, with beautifully presented double rooms.
Bikututa Guest House, a little further from the town centre (*cheap*). Also good for those on a tighter budget. None of the rooms is self-contained, but all are clean and the shared bathrooms are fine.

Matema Beach

Lutheran Guest House, on Matema Beach (*cheap*). Provides a range of accommodation for travellers, with some excellent, basic but charming and spacious cabin-like rooms facing on to the beach. It is worth checking the rooms first, as all they boast differing degrees of character, dilapidation and cleanliness. Some larger rooms are suitable for families travelling with a handful of children, or available at a reasonable price for a group of four or five. Self-contained double rooms or cheaper bungalow huts with shared bathrooms are on offer. A tiny **beach bar** serves Africafé, tea and snacks all day, and provides a wholesome breakfast for guests. A fairly basic cheap fish and chips or rice lunch and supper is also available. The atmosphere around the

guesthouse is friendly and relaxed, and it is easy to while away hours in a gentle ebb and flow of conversation in the shade of the trees that grow along the edge of the beach here. Snorkelling along the eastern and western shores of the beach is good too, although there are no tourist facilities as such here, and you will need to supply your own equipment.

Eating Out

Mbeya and Around

Utengule Country Hotel (*moderate*); *see p.305*. The most enjoyable spot to enjoy some really good cooking is high in the hills west of Mbeya town at the Utengule Country Hotel. A fine situation and excellent home-grown coffee make the short drive out of town worthwhile for either lunch or dinner, but limited space makes it advisable to book in advance.

Mount Livingstone Hotel (*moderate*); *see p.305*. This is the best place to eat in town. The restaurant has a bright and airy aspect, complete with plastic flower decorations. The food is good.

Sombrero Restaurant, Post Street (parallel to Sisimba Street) (*cheap*). Snacks and light meals are available all around town; the Sombrero has some of the best. It's a very clean and fresh new eating house with a surprisingly modern and airy 'diner' feel, constructed like a large railway carriage with an open kitchen at one end. It serves an excellent menu for all meals of the day, including great samosas to eat as snacks.

Eddy's Restaurant, at the far western end of Sisimba Street (*cheap*). A pleasant place to rest awhile, housed in a very pretty flower-covered bungalow with a colourful vine-entangled verandah. The bar inside is spacious and clean, and equipped with a large television that attracts an eager crowd. The airy verandah is a good place to watch the world go by.

Holiday Lodge (*cheap*); *see p.305*. Another reliable spot for wholesome dishes of the day, providing good food served with rice or chips, without great choice.

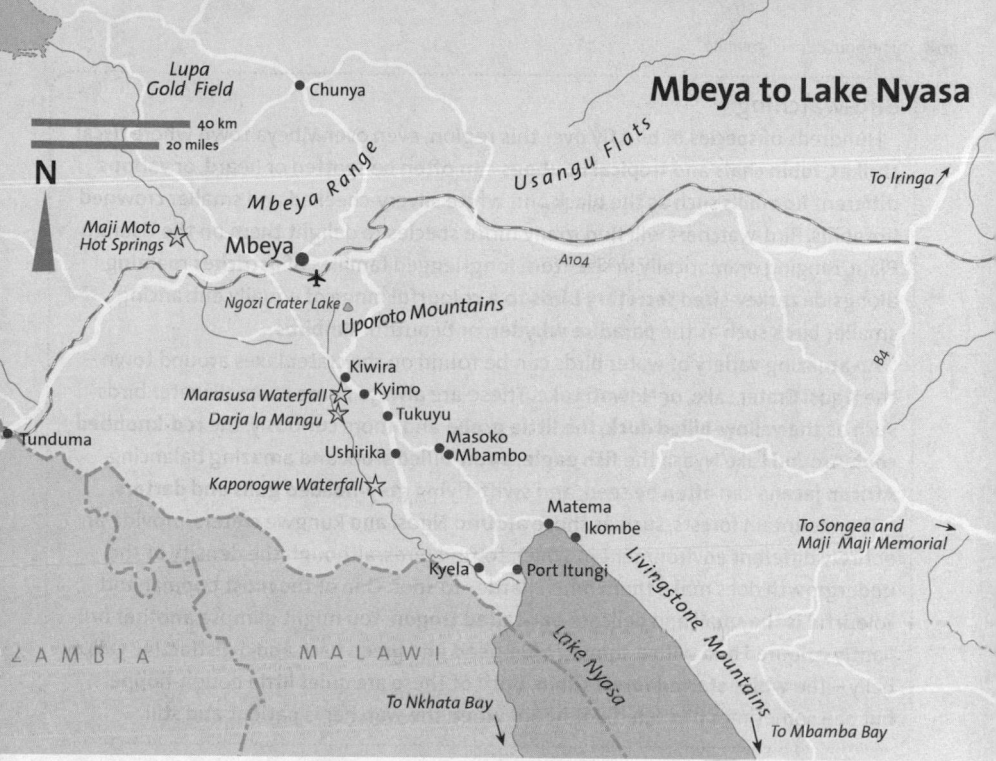

Range was converted into a research station in 1927 to assess the potential for gold-mining in the area. The rifting faults of the surrounding mountains certainly appear to contain a wealth of riches, but what glitters here is most often not gold, as most of the exposed strata of these mountains are composed of quartz crystals sparkling in sunlight. The Lupa goldfields witnessed a gold rush in the 1930s, but were closed a couple of decades later. Panning continues here today on a very small scale, in the form of local backyard industry, and is occasionally rewarded by a small granule of gold. A continual growth of other small industries has supported the expansion of Mbeya since, especially commissioned work on the road and railways.

This section has been researched with the help of an excellent old publication called *Welcome to Mbeya*, a collection of detailed walks and excursions recorded around the Mbeya region, compiled mainly by Father Phillip Leedal of the White Fathers.

Mbeya

Mbeya itself, Tanzania's third-largest town after Dar and Tanga, is a sleepy but thriving metropolis that has grown from a now-abandoned gold-mining station established in 1927. The town has developed industry, and although it's not the prettiest place, the surrounding area is very peaceful, with exciting natural landscapes and interesting homesteads and coffee farms to discover by car or on foot.

A couple of spare hours can be well spent on the outskirts of town, enjoying a good circular walking route that leads into the forests to the north of the town and

Bird-watching

Hundreds of species of bird fly over this region, even over Mbeya town where **fiscal shrikes**, **robin chats** and **tropical boubous** can often be spotted or heard, or various different **hornbills** such as the black and white silvery-cheeked and smaller crowned hornbills. Bird-watchers will find many more species to delight them on the Usangu Plain, ranging dramatically in size from long-legged families of **ostriches** roaming alongside turkey-sized **secretary birds** to a colourful range of equally entrancing smaller birds such as the **paradise whyder**, or beautiful **sunbirds**.

An amazing variety of water birds can be found on the crater lakes around town – the Ngosi Crater Lake, or Ndwati Lake. These are always home to small water birds such as the **yellow-billed duck**, the **little grebe** and, more curiously, the **red-knobbed coot**. Around Lake Nyasa the **fish eagle**, **open-billed stork** and amazing balancing **African jacana** can often be seen, and swift-flying **grey-headed gulls** and **darters**.

The mountain forests, such as those around Ngosi and Rungwe craters, provide an entirely different environment in which to find birds, although the density of the undergrowth does make them much harder to spot. One of the most popular and colourful is the small and delicate **bar-tailed trogon**. You might glimpse another brilliantly coloured bird with a shining blue head and green back and a distinctive yellow belly – the **white-starred forest robin**. Both of these are quiet little bough-hoppers, but can sometimes be seen if not heard when the watcher is patient and still.

provides panoramic views back over Mbeya along the way. Head northwards all the way to the top of Lupa Way until it crosses over Kaunda Avenue, turn right and almost immediately left into a cul-de-sac and follow the pathway at the end to the top of the hill. This leads through a forest of eucalyptus and wends its way along a ridge at the base of Loleza Peak, which stands 2,656m high above. Halfway along the side of the ridge, fork right and head for a mature pine forest, crossing the stream as you go. Continue through pine trees to the track, turn right and right again when the path divides. This will lead you back on to Kaunda Avenue and Lupa Way via Nzowa Road.

North from Mbeya: Mbeya Peak and Chunya

The magnificent peak that towers above the peaks clustered around the town to the north is **Mbeya Peak**, standing 2,826m high. There is more than one way to climb this mountain, and the easiest begins with a scenic drive along the road towards the old, now near-desolate gold-rush town of **Chunya**. A 3,000g carat of gold is said to have been found here at the height of its fame as centre of the last gold rush, in the 1920s and '30s. Remains of the old gold mines can still be seen, and occasionally gold-panners' interest in this dusty old town is revived.

To reach the mountain, follow the Chunya road for about 13km out of Mbeya, until you reach the sign to **Kawetire Farm**, after which a left turn heads west through the forest plantations. Follow this road under **Loleza Peak** past two villages until you reach the end of the driving road in a mature pine plantation. Lock your vehicle and follow the track on foot to the ridge, where you turn right and cross the saddle to the peak. Low-grade garnets can be found along the way, and the views from the top are fantastic if the weather is good. Back on the Chunya road, continuing northwards brings you to excellent hidden picnic spots: the **World's End Viewpoint** at the end of the track leading to Chunya Forest has stunning views overlooking the Usanga Plain beyond Mbeya; follow the track to the right and all the way to the end.

The second route to Mbeya Peak goes via the coffee-growing stronghold of **Lunji Farm** near Mbalizi, around 10km west of Mbeya and 7km from Utengule Country Hotel, which can arrange walks to the peak and through the surrounding area. From here there are four possible paths to follow up to the summit. Although the route up is said to be steeper than the ascent of Kilimanjaro, it is nothing like as high, and presents excellent views across the wide African savannah on one side and a patchwork of fields on the other – especially photogenic at dawn. The walk takes around three hours up and two hours down, by the steepest route. The Utengule will often combine a trip to Lunji Farm and the peak with a visit to the **Songwe Bat Caves** en route, and **Malonde Hot Springs** nearby. The area is incredibly scenic, but conceals hidden crevices and unusual rock formations, and it is recommended that walkers take a guide, for both safety and interest.

South from Mbeya: The Uporoto Mountains

The driving route south from Mbeya is green and fertile and packed with interesting off-road diversions. The tarmac route connecting with the **Malawi** and **Mbamba Bay** ferry service is smooth and well finished, oddly reminiscent of the Riviera scenery in *The Italian Job* as the road curves neatly around the mountain edge with occasional impressive drops to either side. It's an enjoyable drive through constantly changing and impressive scenery – past volcanic mountains, crater lakes and waterfalls flowing over basalt rock, wending though bouncy tea plantations coloured a striking newborn green, and on down to the perennially lush and bountiful forests of the Livingstone Mountains – land of the Nyakusa people.

Ngosi Crater and Lake, just a short distance south of Mbeya, is the remains of an extinct volcano that has now collapsed to form a wide caldera filled with shining alkaline 'soda' waters. Locally the crater lake is said to possess powers of ancestral spirits: the waters change colour from time to time; the colour change is said to be caused by a huge snake that resides at its centre, and witch doctors climb down to the water's edge to collect ingredients for medicine and sacrifices. Ngosi means 'the big one' – it stands at 2,621m – and dedicated climbers are well rewarded with excellent views from the top of the sharp crater rim, from where the lake gleams below with a tranquil air; beyond, the land is pocked with smaller volcanic peaks. The walk to the rim takes about an hour ascending, through upland grasslands and tropical forests where families of colobus monkeys chatter, and flocks of birds take refuge. To reach Ngosi Crater, take a right turn about 2km past the village of **Isongole** (Idweli), which lies about 33km from Mbeya on the Tukuyu Road. After 2km take the right-hand fork, and after another 1km it will be necessary to leave the car and walk. You are well advised to leave someone with the car to guard against break ins, a real risk here. The path leads into the forest for about 2.5km and then, opposite a large single tree, begins the climb to the top of the crater. Just before it, the path branches in two: the right-hand path leads swiftly to the peak; the left-hand one leads down to the lake's edge, taking about half an hour to descend.

Unlike Ngosi, the volcanic cone of **Mount Rungwe** still stands, dominating the landscape to a height of 2,960m. The forests around Rungwe are still wild and unkempt, and almost entirely uninhabited by people, although there is a healthy population of colobus monkeys and other forest creatures. It can be climbed from the Kagera Estates timber camp – turn left at Isongole on to the Kiwira Forest Station Road, and then right after 11km, just before the forest station – but this is only recommended during the dry months between June and November, or during a clear spell in February. Follow the old road up on foot, and veer right at the foot of the volcano – even though this path slopes downwards initially. An alternative climb is possible from the Rungwe Moravian Mission, from where it is worth taking a guide to follow the complicated route to the top. Rungwe volcano remains active in parts, and you pass hard basalt lava flow along the way. The rock over which the lava flows dates from the Pre-Cambrian era, some 1,800 million years ago. Estimate a full day to climb.

The market town of **Kiwira** (also called Mwankenja) is 50km from Mbeya on the Tukuyu road, lying close to the Kiwira River. The undulating land around this valley has formed a number of waterfalls and scenic watery rock formations close to the town. The most accessible waterfall is 4.3km from the main road: leave Kiwira on the road signposted to Igogwe Hospital, and follow the road over a bridge over the river; turn left and cross the Igogwe Stream, park and ask directions to the **Marasusa Falls**, following a narrow path along a line of trees between the cassava plantations. The falls are an impressive basalt drop, with a number of consecutive pools. They are popular for family washing sessions, and provide a scenic rural setting for a picnic.

To reach the **Ndulilo Falls** demands a less complicated driving route, but a more adventurous walking route, through a dark, bat-filled cave. To get there, park at the Igogwe Hospital and walk for 10 minutes to the river, where there is a sink hole on the south bank, through which the river used to flow before it changed its path. If you follow the sink hole down you are liable to disturb a few sleepy bats, but will reach the base of the falls.

Unfortunately the most impressive of the water and rock phenomena in this region has evolved rather too close to a prickly military-run prison college for complete comfort. The wonderfully named **Daraja ya Mungu** (Bridge of God) is an inspiring stretch of rock arching over the rushing river, which has etched its pathway beneath. The view is especially pretty as the sun sets, and the land is picturesque until you reach the college. The proximity of this institution means that the road closest to the bridge has been iron-fenced and covered in signs prohibiting photography: beware the wrath of officials who find you bending the rules! To get to the bridge, turn right at a tiny village just before Tukuyu, on a corner 7km from Kiwira. The road is fairly good; follow it around until the bridge can be seen, then park and walk down the incline from there. There are other interesting features around the region, but it is now harder to access the hole where the river falls into a rock 'cauldron', known as **Kijungu** (Cooking Pot) because the college insists you acquire a permit.

Tukuyu to Matema Beach on Lake Nyasa

The small town of Tukuyu perches on top of **Ntukuyu Volcano**, almost halfway between Mbeya and Lake Nyasa at an altitude of 1,600m. Its elegant vantage point makes it worth visiting for the views that it affords of the surrounding countryside; if you are planning a leisurely foray through the mountains it is probably a good idea to fix up some accommodation (*see* pp.305–306), either at Tukuyu or on the shores of Matema Beach on Lake Nyasa, as a round trip including diversions will take at least two days. Accommodation in both places is basic, although slightly nicer on Matema Beach.

The town flourished for a while during the German era, and earned the name Neu-Langenberg for a short period after 1901, when it became the centre for German administration in the region, following the demise of the previous headquarters on the lake, Alt-Langenberg, after the doctor died of malaria there. The colonists left an old **German boma**, now in a fairly poor state of repair but worth a visit if you are in town. You can see lines of basalt lava flowing down the hillsides nearby.

The great range of the **Livingstone Mountains** southeast of Tukuyu is the result of extreme rift action that would have occurred prior to the volcanic eruptions in the region; Lake Nyasa lies in the rift floor. As a result, there are a number of good alternatives for trekking in this region, both north of Tukuyu and south, around **Masoko Crater Lake**. This extinct volcanic crater, 19km south of Tukuyu, is an impressive lava formation, now covered in lush vegetation. A short walk through the trees takes you to the water's edge, where it is possible to swim. A number of old coins from the German era have been found (and sold) along the way. The crater lake is just off the eastern road from Tukuyu, which also passes **Kalambo Hot Springs** en route to Ipinda (not to be confused with Kilambo Hot Springs near Kyela, *see* p.312). This is a far more dusty and less smooth route towards the lake than the western road, which has a smooth tarmac surface almost all the way through Kyela to the port at Itungi.

About 8km down this fine westerly road you come to the village of **Ushirika** (also known as Mpuguso). Good walking and swimming possibilities are found a 2km walk from here at **Kaporogwe Falls**. To find them, turn right at Ushirika following signposts to Kaporogwe, follow signs to the leprosarium – where you can get permission to park your vehicle – walk past the buildings and head down the hill beyond, continuing straight on for about 2km. This brings you to the top of the falls, where a precarious bridge crosses behind a pretty gardenia tree to a good picnic area and vantage point over the falls, sheltered beneath an impressive overhanging slab of basalt. It is possible to climb down the falls, with care, and find routes into caves behind the curtain of water plummeting down, and to swim in the pool beneath.

Continuing south, 44km from Tukuyu and just before Kyela, a signpost points left to **Kilambo Hot Springs**. These are definitely springs and not pools – entertain no illusions of therapeutic bathing – but the track leads right to them, at the base of the hillside, and the surrounding woodlands are a haven for orchids. **Kyela** itself is a small town 56km south of Tukuyu with little to recommend it to visitors, unless for reasons of commercial trade or to seek a bus to Itungi Port for the lake steamer to Mbamba Bay on the southern border of Tanzania, or Nkhata Bay in Malawi.

Matema Beach

For relaxation, peace and quiet it is better to abandon Kyela for **Matema Beach**, where there is fine accommodation almost at the water's edge, plenty of fresh fish and wide open views. The thick, golden, granular sand of the bay of Matema is lapped by the fresh waters of Lake Nyasa, and provides a refreshing point for quiet contemplation in the shadow of the Livingstone Mountains, which run down to the eastern shore of the lake. It is a rural region where the focus of activity is fishing and the chores of daily life – mending fishing nets, repairing local dug-out canoes, preparing for night-time excursions – yet it seems that most people along the beach have time for a chat. The land here is hot, a strong contrast from the volcanic Livingstone Mountains behind you and to the east and west, and much life on Matema is spent seeking shade after midday. Sunburn is a regional hazard for pale skins.

Matema provides a good central base for exploring the local countryside and mountains. The beach is approached through stunning forested regions, where dense greenery and thickets conceal clusters of **Nyakusa houses**, many of which demonstrate inspired building methods involving complex palm weaves and raised platform storage huts for pots, chickens, water and grain. A number of these have also been painted and decorated with unique designs and images, apparently drawn with local dyes. There are also plenty of fine earthenware pots in evidence in every household and fireplace, generally the product of the Kisi people who live in this area and are famed throughout Tanzania for their clay-working skills. These pots are sold wholesale from **Ikombe**, south of Matema, where you may also have the chance to see them being made, and in Matema itself at the Saturday morning **market**, for which they are shipped from Ikombe by canoe. The are also often found sold for extremely good prices at morning roadside stalls between Matema and Mbeya. From here they are exported to Arusha, Iringa and Dar es Salaam, increasing in price with distance travelled. Beware linguistic confusion here: it can be extremely disconcerting when you catch a lift with a driver to find a pot, and are proudly driven dusty kilometres to reach the port.

The Zanzibar Archipelago

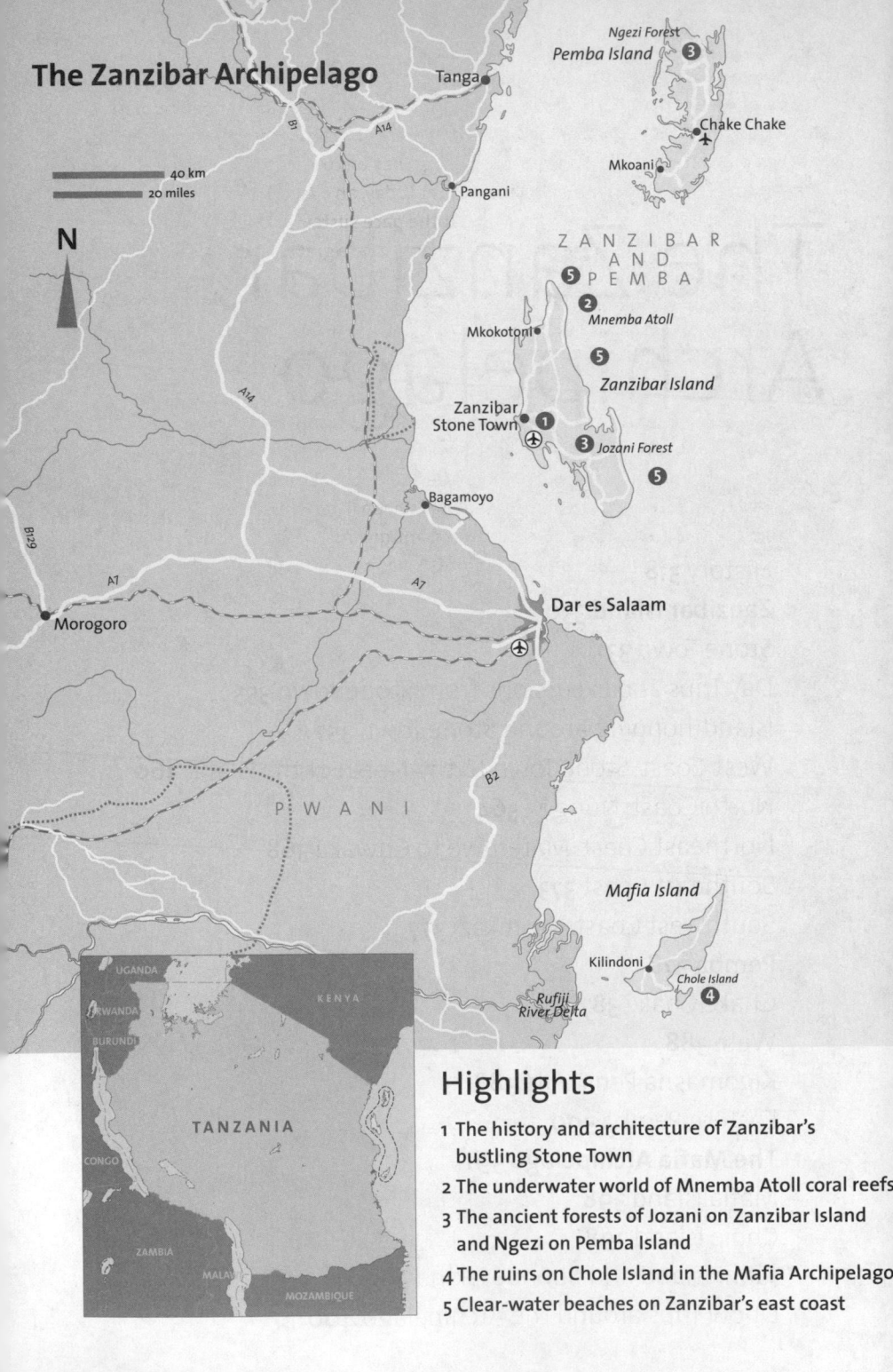

The Zanzibar Archipelago

Tanga

Pangani

40 km
20 miles

N

Ngezi Forest
Pemba Island ③
Chake Chake
Mkoani

Z A N Z I B A R
A N D
P E M B A

⑤
②
Mnemba Atoll

Mkokotoni
⑤
Zanzibar Island

Zanzibar
Stone Town ①
③ *Jozani Forest*
⑤

Bagamoyo

B129

A7
A7

Morogoro

Dar es Salaam

P W A N I
B2

Mafia Island

Kilindoni
Chole Island
④

*Rufiji
River Delta*

UGANDA
KENYA
RWANDA
BURUNDI
CONGO
TANZANIA
ZAMBIA
MALAWI
MOZAMBIQUE

Highlights

1 The history and architecture of Zanzibar's
bustling Stone Town

2 The underwater world of Mnemba Atoll coral reefs

3 The ancient forests of Jozani on Zanzibar Island
and Ngezi on Pemba Island

4 The ruins on Chole Island in the Mafia Archipelago

5 Clear-water beaches on Zanzibar's east coast

An image of Zanzibar floats into the mind's eye as a fairytale island, evoking dreams of Arabian nights, of romance and of spirits dwelling among the ruins of its elusive history. It is said that sailors scented its spices on the wind before their dhows beached on white coral sand shores; on arriving they discovered a land quite distinct from any other – and so it remains in most part today, an oasis of green in a turquoise sea, its rural centre now drifting at the pace sustained on foot or bicycle.

On a map, the Zanzibar archipelago is a few dots in the great Indian Ocean, off the coast of mainland Tanzania. For such a tiny portion of the Republic, Zanzibar has a history and reputation that far exceeds its size. The islands are a world of paradox, a plentiful island paradise that has witnessed a harsh history of domination and slavery. It has emerged in the 21st century with a heady brew of mixed African and Arabic cultures poised between tradition and the imperatives of the modern world: you might look out across the translucent, shimmering channels of the ocean and see a wooden dhow skimming the waves beneath a billowing sail, built to a design unchanged for centuries, and watch it moor beside a shiny new hydrofoil; you might walk through streets of private houses that have been lived in by generations since 1800, and then return to an elaborately carved antique Arabic four-poster bed in a hotel, to switch on cable television by remote. Times are constantly changing in these Indian Ocean islands, which in the past five years have embraced technological advances that took the Western world a century to reach.

The Zanzibar Archipelago

The Zanzibar archipelago is made up of Zanzibar Island – also called Unguja – the island of Pemba, Tumbatu Island, and smaller satellite islands, including Chapwani, Bawe, Chumbe, Chunguu and Mnemba, most of which can be visited on boat trips from Unguja. Zanzibar Island is 86km long and 39km wide, separated from the mainland by 35km of Indian Ocean over a shallow coral shelf. Pemba lies 41km northeast of Unguja, is much smaller – about 64km long and 22.5km wide – and is separated from the mainland by the narrow but extremely deep and often dangerous Pemba Channel, which drops to a depth of more than 1,000m. The larger creatures of the sea – whales, sharks and barracudas – swim here, and huge manta rays navigate the clear, salty depths on the outskirts of the reefs.

The coral rock outcrops that make up the islands were once mainly forested, but have now been almost entirely turned over to agriculture, with spice and coconut plantations dating from the days of the first sultan. The last remaining areas of natural forest are protected, at Jozani on Zanzibar Island, Ngezi and Msitu Mkuu on Pemba. Baobabs have self-seeded and rooted wherever there is enough earth to sustain them. Villages cluster in the shade of these great life-giving trees, while beyond them stretch wide, open areas of low bush. Fertile soil allows for a fantastic range of fruit and vegetable plantations that flower and crop throughout the year. Mango trees have been planted all over the islands, especially on Pemba. Rice, too, has been grown on Zanzibar since the Persians first planted it; it's now a staple dish.

The exposed coral rock of Zanzibar's eastern side has a thin covering of vegetation and few crops. Many of the coastal villages are dependent on fishing and the

Festivals

Zanzibaris do quite well in terms of public holidays and festivals, as they observe **Muslim** celebrations, **Christian** and **Hindu** holy days, **national** holidays and **traditional** festivals. Perhaps the most unusual annual festival held in Zanzibar is the **Mwaka Kogwa Festival**, held in villages across Zanzibar but most famously at Makunduchi, in the southeast of the island around the third week of July. This traditional festival is a New Year celebration held according to the old Shirazi solar year – so it is unlikely that you will meet anyone who can tell you the exact date, unless you visit the village elders of Makunduchi who spend much of the rest of the year working it out. The celebration originated in Persia (it coincides with the Persian new year festival of Nairuz), and the extent to which it relies on fire, flames and burning suggests Zoroastrian roots, although the festival today has become entirely detached from religious beliefs. The festivities continue over four days, beginning with a widely renowned event in which a number of people, supposedly including a traditional medicine man, enter a *makuti*-thatched hut, which has been built for the occasion. The hut is set on fire, and the inhabitants must wait until the blaze has caught before making their escape with a good sense of ritualistic drama. This popular event is followed by an even stranger ritual, in which all inhabitants from the north and south of the village gather into their respective groups, and while the men from each area fight each other with sticks (more often banana palms these days) the women join in by shouting abuse. The outcome is supposed to clear the air for the new year ahead. This show of strength is followed by communal feasting, along with singing and dancing for the following days. The Muslim community here is very strong, and, while they appreciate the absurdity of upholding such an ancient ritual that has little to do with their religious beliefs, they also remain deeply superstitious about abandoning the practice which ensures that crops and participants will be purified and endowed with good luck for the year ahead. Outsiders are welcomed to the festivities, as it's believed auspicious for villagers to have a guest.

Also in mid-July, the recently introduced **Cultural Festival of the Dhow Countries**, or **Zanzibar International Film Festival** (ZIFF) has now run over two weeks for eight consecutive years, and is an established fixture in the Zanzibari and film-world calendars. Each year it has been better organized and better attended by film-makers and musicians from throughout the 'Dhow Countries' – a term used to describe all nations bordering the Indian Ocean and also the whole of the African continent, despite the lack of seafaring borders. Increasingly, it is visited by industry professionals from the West, with the growing concern, in the aftermath of the 9/11 attacks, to screen films made from a Muslim perspective. The festival is is run from an office in Stone Town, with most of the film screenings and bands playing in the Old Arab Fort, although a number of other venues are also secured around the town. Tourists pay a small fee, or can buy a pass for the entire festival, and locals are encouraged to attend free of charge. The majority of the films are cartoons or documentaries, often dubbed or subtitled, which are then taken to rural regions of Zanzibar and shown in public screenings. The musical side of the festival has also developed a worthwhile and diverse play list of performers; the atmosphere in Stone Town during this time is heightened by the influx of talented musicians of all nationalities spilling out of every guesthouse and bar. The film festival has been joined by a rising star in the cultural lexicon: the 'Sauti Za Busara', the annual Swahili Music Festival, PO Box 3635, Zanzibar, t (024) 2232423/t (0747) 428478, *busara@zanlink.com*. It takes place over three days in the Forodhani Gardens on the seafront.

Dates observed in the Muslim calendar are determined by the observance of the moon, and so do not synchronize with the calendar year. The Muslim festival of **Ramadhan** is strictly observed towards the end of the year or beginning of the New Year, as a mark of respect for the month in which Mohammed received the first of the Koran's revelations. He was said to have received the first revelation on the 20th day of the month, on a night known as the Night of Determination: this is said to be the night on which God determines the course of the world for the following year. It is a devout month set aside for prayers and purity, and those following the Muslim faith fast between the hours of sunrise and sunset, and refrain from any act that may be considered a physical indulgence, such as eating, drinking of any kind, smoking or sexual activity. Families and friends gather together after the sun sets to break their fast. Christians and visitors to Zanzibar during this time are expected to respect the restraint of their fellow men, and not to eat, drink or smoke in public areas during the day. Most local restaurants will remain closed during the day, and, while those catering to the international market remain open as usual, they often screen any open sides from the street. Tourists are also advised to be cautious in exploring the streets of Stone Town between the hours of 6pm and 8pm.

Towards the end of the lunar cycle, everywhere Muslims wait with anticipation for the new moon to break into the night sky. At this moment Ramadhan is deemed to be over. At this time of year, the new moon is a glorious sight; its spectral dark side can clearly be seen behind a glinting crescent of light. The festivities of **Eid-ul-Fitr** follow the rigours of Ramadhan with celebrations marked by prayers and feasting and the exchange of gifts and giving of alms. Huge and lively street festivals take place late into the night. Everyone dresses up in their finery; boys are given pop guns that resound thorugh the alleyways of Stone Town. Children stay up late playing lucky dip for bright Tupperware plates and bowls. Music and friendly gambling games and card trickery entertain the adults. Eid, or Eidi as it is popularly known, is also often referred to as Sikukuu, which literally translates as 'days of celebration', or 'holiday', and lasts for four days. Two months later comes **Eid-ul-Adha**, the traditional date for the *haj*, the annual pilgrimage to Mecca. Three months later is the date of **Maulid**, and celebrations in honour of the Prophet's birthday. Christian occasions such as **Christmas** and **Easter** are also celebrated and held as public holidays, as is the colourful Hindu festival of **Diwali**. Hindu festivals in particular are noisily celebrated.

For sport fans, there is the **International Triathlon and Marathon**, held in November. Both events are over Olympic distances and are hosted in fantastic scenery. The participants have come from East Africa, Asia and Europe.

The month of January is highlighted by a traditional secular festival of **dhow races**. Hordes of Zanzibari fishermen compete to complete a route from Forodhani Gardens around Prison Island. Most of the races are played out in small *ngalawa* outriggers.

development of seaweed as an export crop to Asia. Seaweed is processed into carrageenan, bizarrely the basis of ice-cream, Spam and toothpaste. The fishermen operate at small-scale subsistence level, using nets, lines, hand-held spears and sticks. Women ply the shallows with nets and poke sticks for octopus at low tide. Seaweed-farming provides an important income for local women, who are responsible for the plantations. They cultivate their crop by attaching small sprigs of seaweed to strings, which are pegged out in rows just beneath the tide line. These plots require a great deal of work and attendance, but the crop can increase tenfold in a couple of weeks.

The island bedrock of coral rag is the basis for the roads, on which many tyres are burst, and is used to build rugged homesteads, in which the coral is mixed with a limestone 'cement' that you can frequently see being made on the sides of the road – an environmentally unfriendly use of coral that is now being discouraged. As on the mainland, it is common to see houses that seem to have been abandoned halfway through the building process, although actually the vast expense and effort involved in building a house results in a long-term 'layer by layer' approach, additions made in accordance with erratic income flow. The trees growing through the centre will be felled just before the roof is added.

History

The very name of the main island of Zanzibar reflects a core element of its history: 'Unguja' means 'transition', and from the earliest dates of its known history this little island has attracted a remarkable number of visitors to its shores and seen an exceptional exchange of goods.

The **early history** of Zanzibar has been reconstructed from stories, early writings and intelligent supposition, making it often almost impossible to disentangle the truth from the web of myths and legends. It is likely, however, that the first inhabitants of the islands were descendants of early hominoid man – from Olduvai Gorge on mainland Tanzania – who journeyed to the Zanzibar archipelago in dugout canoes during the Neolithic period of the late Stone Age, around 4000 BC. It is known that travellers from the ancient kingdoms of Sumeria (6000–3000 BC), Assyria (2000–612 BC), Mesopotamia and Egypt travelled and traded with the East African coast, and it is probable that Zanzibar was known to at least some of these early trading civilizations. It is thought that the Phoenicians visited Zanzibar on their journey to Sofala (in present day Mozambique) in around 1000 BC. In subsequent centuries trade routes passing through Zanzibar developed into a powerful commercial network that extended to include the Silk Route trade from China to India.

Shirazi Settlers and Arab Traders

In the course of the 1st century AD a pattern of trade was established between the coasts of Arabia and East Africa. Dhows sailed on the northeast monsoon winds (November to February) from the Kingdom of Saba, or Sheba, bringing beads, porcelain and Chinese silks, and returned with the southwest monsoon winds (April to September) laden with gold from Sofala, slaves and spices, ebony, ivory, indigo and tortoiseshell from the lands of 'Zinj el Barr', as the coast was called. The name is thought to have been derived from the Persian words *zangh* for black and *bar* referring to the coast – 'black coast'. The Greek astronomer Ptolemy described the 'Zenj' people in his 2nd century AD *Geography* as tall, dark and fearsome. The 19th-century English explorer Richard Burton held a more romantic notion that 'Zanzibar' was derived from the Arabic *Zayn za'l barr*, meaning 'Fair is this isle' – although the name was used until the late 15th century to describe the whole East African coast.

Word of the travels of sailors and traders spread far and wide: it is likely that the 9th-century legend of Sinbad the Sailor, as told in *The Thousand and One Nights*, was inspired by tales circulating of the land of Zinj. The distant, abundant lands became attractive to those seeking a new life abroad, and the population of the land of Zinj

When to Go

The climate of Zanzibar is hot, with temperatures between 21 and 29°C, and becomes increasingly humid from **mid-Nov to March**. The long rains – *masika* – fall between **April and May**, although showers often continue through June, so finishing later than on the mainland. **Early July to Oct** is coolest and driest, with an average temperature of 21°C in Aug. The 'short rains' – *vuli* – should fall in Nov, as intermittent showers followed by sunshine. It is hot and dry and humid between Dec and March, when the island is subject to the northeast monsoon wind – *kaskazi* – and is slightly cooler during the months of the southwest monsoon – *kusi* – between **April and Nov**.

Getting There

Although Zanzibar and the mainland are a United Republic, the Zanzibaris continue to enforce **immigration controls**, even from the mainland, and you will be required to show your passport with current visa.

NB: **Departure tax** from Zanzibar Airport is $5, or T.shs 5,000, payable in cash. There is also a $5 **port departure service charge**, whch must be paid in cash too, though most airlines include tax in the cost of the ticket. International departure tax is $25, also usually included; if not, make sure you have $25 cash.

By Air

International

Most international visitors arrive by air or boat from the mainland after flying into Dar es Salaam (*see* p.214 for airline details). There are, however, some international flights:

Air Kenya flies via Nairobi from London daily. **Air Tanzania** runs direct from Nairobi and Mombasa. Its service is much improved since a takeover by South African Airlines, and schedules now tie in with SAA flights.

Domestic: From the Mainland

There are reliable **scheduled** internal connections from many points on the mainland with **Coastal Travels, Precision Air, Zanair** and **Air Tanzania**. Coastal Travels alone flies six times daily from **Dar es Salaam** to Zanzibar. The cost is roughly $60 one way and the flight takes 20mins. Coastal Travels, Zanair, Precision Air and Air Tanzania fly from **Arusha** or **Kilimanjaro** to Zanzibar twice daily for $190. Coastal fly from **Selous** to Zanzibar, daily, for $130; Ruaha to Zanzibar, three times per week, $300. Zanair fly from **Sadani** and **Pangani** to Zanzibar four times a week.

Private charters can also be arranged from most locations on the mainland with Coastal.

Domestic: To and From Pemba and Mafia

Zanair and **Coastal Travels** have scheduled daily flights between Zanzibar and Pemba and Zanzibar and Mafia. Tickets cost roughly $90.

Airline Offices

Kenya Airways, Mazsons Hotel, Stone Town, t (024) 2232041–3/2234521.
Air Tanzania Corporation, Stone Town, Vuga Road, t (024) 2230297.
Coastal Travels, Zanzibar Airport, PO Box 992, Zanzibar, t (0741) 670815/t/f (024) 2233112; Stone Town, t (024) 2239664/t (0741) 412999; Upanga Road, PO Box 3052, Dar es Salaam, t (022) 2117959–60, f (022) 2118647/2117985, *aviation@coastal.cc, www.coastal.cc*.
Precision Air, Mazsons Hotel, Stone Town, Zanzibar, t (024) 2234521, f (024) 2234520,

began to be defined by a growing number of immigrants from different lands. A number of legends coincide with a mass emigration from Shiraz in Persia around AD 975, following religious upheavals sparked by the death of Prophet Mohammed in AD 632. A popular legend spread that the Persian king, Ali bin Sultan Hasan, was responsible for the first major Arabian civilizations along the East African coast. He is said to have had a dream in which a rat with iron jaws gnawed and destroyed the foundations of his palace, which he interpreted as a sign of the imminent disintegration of his dynasty. Despite the mockery of the court, he galvanized his six sons, each with his own entourage, into seven vast dhows – and set sail for Zinj el Barr. Each of

information@precisionairtz.com, www.precisionairtz.com.
Zanair, PO Box 2586, Zanzibar, t (024) 2233768/ t (0741) 321061/t/f (024) 2233670, zanair@zitec.org, www.zanair.com.

By Sea

Regular **ferries** operate between Dar es Salaam, Zanzibar and Pemba, with possible connections to Tanga. Various boat companies run from Dar to Zanzibar, which takes 70–90mins and costs c. $35. Their booking kiosks are dotted around the ports at both Dar and Zanzibar. The choice of ferry depends on the departure time. There are a number of boats going across every day (see timings below); the *Sea Express*, *Sea Star* and *Sea Bus* are all reliable. Beware of the *Flying Horse*, however; it may cost the least but will take an age to get there! The boats get quite full during July and August and sometimes over Christmas, when it is advisable to book tickets in advance. The seas can be rough, even on the short distance between Zanzibar and the mainland, and anyone prone to seasickness may find the crossing quite uncomfortable.

Azam Marine, Zanzibar, t (024) 2231655/ t (0741) 334884, or Dar, t (0741) 334347, azam@cats-net.com. Has two catamarans named *Sea Bus I* and *II*. Three sailings daily leave Dar at 10am, 2pm and 4pm, and Zanzibar at 7am, 10am and 1pm. The crossing takes 90mins and costs $30.

Sea Express Hydrofoil, Zanzibar, t (024) 2234690/t (0744) 278692. Departs Dar at 9.30, 12.30, 3.30, 4.30 and 6.

Sea Star Services, Zanzibar, t (0744) 310953/ t (0747) 411505. Two services a day, leaving Zanzibar at 7am and Dar at 10.30am.

Flying Horse, t (024) 2233031/2 or Dar, t (022) 2224504–7. The cheapest option, at $10, is

also a fairly hellish alternative, on this old catamaran, which takes 3–4hrs, departing for Dar at 10pm and returning from the mainland at 12.50pm. The 10pm boat sails overnight, reaching Dar in the early hours, although passengers cannot disembark until immigration opens at 6am. On a positive note, this at least saves on a night's accommodation costs.

To Pemba

Azam Marine, t (024) 2231655/t (0741) 334884. The old *Serengeti* crosses between Zanzibar and Pemba on Tues, Thurs and Sat, leaving at 10pm and arriving at 6am the following morning. The boat leaves Pemba on the following morning, on Wed, Fri and Sun, at 10am. The fare is cheap at $20 one-way, but the ancient craft makes a meal out of what should be a short hop.

Mega Speed Liners, on the *Sepideh* ferries, Zanzibar, t (0747) 411006/t (0748) 323699/ t (0741) 414343/t (0747) 415722/t (0741) 623355; Dar, t (0741) 453525/t (0741) 770286/ t (0741) 414343; Pemba, t (0747) 470344/ t (0747) 420243. Mega Speed is relatively slow. Prices depend on the route taken and whether you opt for first or standard class. 'Standard' is perfectly good, providing seats and comfort, and the extra dollars for a first class ticket generally just buy you a faster route up the gangplank. The *Sepideh* takes just over 1½hrs between Dar and Zanzibar Island (about $35–40) and 2½hrs between Zanzibar and Pemba. Dar to Pemba costs around $50–60. All fares include port tax.

Mon, Wed, Thurs and Sat: Dar–Zanzibar 7.30am; Zanzibar–Pemba 9.45am; Pemba–Zanzibar 12.15pm; Zanzibar–Dar 3.45pm.

Tues, Fri and Sun: Dar–Zanzibar 7.30am; Zanzibar–Dar 3.45pm.

The Religion of Zarathushtra
With many thanks to Vica Irani for this contribution.

Originating in Ancient Persia, the Zoroastrian faith was the very first of the great monotheist religions, founded by the Persian prophet Zarathushtra or Zoroaster in the 7th–6th centuries BC. It is believed that Zoroastrianism gave birth to the concept of heaven and hell, and the dual, conflicting forces of *spentamanus* (good) and *angramanus* (evil), as incarnated in **Ormazd**, the god of creation, light and goodness, and his arch enemy **Ahriman**, the spirit of evil and darkness, who jostle for supremacy among mankind. Zoroastrian lives are dedicated to the pursuit of good and the fulfilment of the three basic injunctions: **good thoughts**, **good words** and **good deeds**.

Ingrained in the Zoroastrian religion and teachings is a profound respect for the environment and the elements: **fire** has a great spiritual significance for the religion, and is its symbol of worship. Zoroastrians worship at fire temples, whose focal point is a constantly burning holy fire, consecrated and tended by priests.

The Zoroastrian concern for the environment is seen further in the method of disposing of the dead. Zoroastrians do not bury their dead, as this would contaminate the earth; nor do they cremate them, as this would contaminate fire and air. Instead, Zoroastrians are laid to rest in towers of silence, which are large, round, open structures, generally built on elevated ground and set in tranquil gardens on the outskirts of the city; in some places they are colonized by vultures.

Through the ages, Zoroastrians have sought to avoid political or military conflict. When Persia was invaded by Muslims in around AD 772, making it difficult for Zoroastrians to practise their religion freely, some fled to India where they were granted 'political asylum'. These Zoroastrians, now known as Parsees, have adopted elements of Hindu culture: their dress, language, food and customs resemble Hindu practice rather than that of their Zoroastrian counterparts in Persia. Others sailed further, following trade routes to the shores of Zanzibar, bringing with them the customs of their religion. In some areas these were taken on even before the advent of Islam; they still play a part in festivals today, notably **Mwaka Kogwa** (*see* p.316).

Worldwide Zoroastrian migration has continued over the centuries, and even today Zoroastrians are emigrating from their homes in search of greater prosperity and stability. Although there are still Zoroastrians in Iran, the majority have scattered around the Indian subcontinent, the USA, Canada, Europe, Australia and Africa.

the dhows landed at a different point along the coast, including Zanzibar, Kilwa, Tongoni, Mombasa and the Comoros – all known to be early Shirazi settlements.

The rise of Islam across the Arabian peninsula during the 7th century AD did bring war and unrest throughout Persia and Arabia, and there was a gradual influx of fleeing Omani and Shirazi settlers. The mix was not always peaceful, as the settlers battled for land ownership. Wars elsewhere on the African continent were also causing tribes on the mainland to seek new land, and throughout the 10th century Bantu tribes moved east and settled along the coast. They began to call themselves 'Sahil', from an Arabic word meaning coast – the beginning of the the mix of African, Arabic and Persian languages and people on the coastline that evolved into the

Swahili civilization and language. The foundations of the first mosque on Unguja can still be seen at Kizimkazi. The mihrab, or alcove facing Mecca to which prayers are directed, bears a Kufic inscription of the date AM 500, equivalent to AD 1107.

Enter the Portuguese

By the 15th century, the Portuguese were eagerly seeking a sea route to India and were charting routes around the irritatingly large continent that stood in the way. In 1498, the notorious seafarer Vasco da Gama rounded the Cape of Good Hope and made his presence known along the East African coast. The islands of Zanzibar and the port of Mombasa proved an invaluable base to prepare for the long trip to the Far East; the Portuguese sailors built garrisons that were soon followed, in 1503, by a push for Portuguese rule of the coastline. Capturing 20 Swahili dhows, shooting a number of islanders and forcing the local Mwinyi Mkuu – the island chief or 'Great Lord' of Zanzibar – to become a Portuguese subject, they reduced Zanzibar to one of the new Portuguese territories. By 1509 the colonists had occupied the whole of the Zanzibar archipelago. The Zanzibaris responded with hostility and resistance, until a truce was agreed so that the two sides could resist further Arab invasions together. The fort at Chake Chake on Pemba was built by the Portuguese in 1594, along with other fortifications along the coast, but they were not enough. Gradually the Portuguese territories were lost: Hormuz to the Persians in 1622, and Muscat to the Omanis in 1650. In 1652 the sultan of Oman mobilized his troops to the aid of the Mwinyi Mkuu – at his request – and the Omanis raided the Portuguese settlement on Zanzibar and burnt most of the garrison on Pemba. Following successive struggles, the Portuguese were forced to retreat as far south as Mozambique, and by 1698 the Omani Arabs had gained firm control, once more squeezing out the Mwinyi Mkuu. The islands entered a new phase as a protectorate of the Omani Empire. Portugal's legacy was not all bad: it left cassavas and cashews from Brazil, avocados and guavas – all now Zanzibari staples. It also encouraged the use of iron nails for boat building, a departure from the 'sewn boats' of yore, and showed how to use dung for cultivation. It was even indirectly responsible for the evolution of the kanga (see pp.350–51).

While the Portuguese became bogged down in Zanzibar, and were ultimately thrown out, the British were quietly doing what Vasco da Gama and his crew had originally set out to achieve in India. The first British ship, the *Edward Bonaventura*, dropped anchor at Zanzibar in 1591, under the command of Sir James Lancaster. The British befriended the Mwinyi Mkuu, who supplied them with water and food, and British ships began stopping at the island to restock en route to trade in India.

The Long Reign of the Sultans

The sultans of Oman originally ruled from Muscat, appointing governors to rule the islands and ordering fortifications to be built on the old Portuguese foundations on Unguja to strengthen his position. Oman was a powerful trading nation, relying on dates as a major crop export. In need of cheap labour, but forbidden by Islam to use Muslims as slaves, the Omanis started importing Africans from the mainland – the roots of the slave trade. Most trade along the East African coast began to be routed through Zanzibar, and during the 1820s Sultan Sayyid Said bin Sultan – sultan at the age of 15 – built the first stone buildings of what would later become Stone Town. Sultan Said was excited by this profitable island investment. He made a couple of visits before deciding to transfer the seat of his Sultanate from the contentious capital of Muscat to the breezier climes of Zanzibar in 1832, where he founded clove plantations and a well-established trade in ivory and slaves. He strongly encouraged all trade possibilities and signed commercial treaties with a number of Western powers – the first, in 1833, with the United States – and in 1837 allowed the United States to open the first foreign consulate, followed by the British; the sultan's ambition was to centralize all the trade of East Africa through the little island of Zanzibar.

When Sultan Said (1806–1856) arrived in Zanzibar for the first time in 1828, he recorded that the territories of Unguja Island were broadly divided between two distinct local tribes. The north of the island, including Tumbatu Island, was inhabited by the WaTumbatu – 'the people of Tumbatu'– ruled by a matrilineal queen, the Mwana wa Mwana – 'daughter of a daughter'. The south was occupied by the Hadimu, a name that seems to be derived from an Arabic word meaning 'slave' – although the Arabs who employed this name failed to conquer the islanders or to take them as slaves. In fact, it seems that the Hadimu employed their own slaves from the mainland, and were converts to Islam, claiming descent from the Shirazi immigrants who had settled on the southern shores of the island nearly a thousand years earlier. Whatever their true origins – probably mixed – the Hadimu had one ruler, of Shirazi origin, known as Mwinyi Mkuu – the 'Great Lord'.

When Sultan Said transferred the sultanate he had to acknowledge the local chief and negotiate terms of power. He employed the most likely method for success: extravagant promises of a generous pension – which was, in fact, never paid – although the Mwinyi Mkuu did manage to hang on to some rights of sovereignty. The Mwinyi Mkuu known to Sultan Said was Hassan bin Ahmed, the ruler and owner of the stone palace at Dunga, whose impressive ruins can still be visited. Hassan promised to share half of his labour force and collect taxes on the sultan's behalf, although he soon got wise, compensating for his unpaid pension by keeping half the profits for himself. With the cultivation of cloves, however, the demand for Hadimu labour grew.

Relations between sultan and chief did not improve with successive generations. Sultan Said's successor, Sultan Sayyid Majid bin Said (1856–1870), imprisoned Mwinyi Mkuu Muhammad bin Ahmed, commonly referred to as Sultan Hamadi. According to legend Sultan Hamadi was imbued with greater powers than most, and, following his exile or escape to the mainland, the islands suffered a terrible drought. The drought lasted three years, until the islanders petitioned for the return of their chief; bowing to pressure, or needing an ally to enforce tax collection and labour demands, Sultan Majid reinstated Sultan Hamadi, and the island was blessed again with rain. On his return the Mwinyi Mkuu fortified the fine palace at Dunga and pulled off an impressive political manoeuvre by marrying the queen of the Tumbatu tribe, the powerful Mwana wa Mwana – so uniting the 'kingdoms' of the Zanzibar archipelago.

In effect, the Mwinyi Mkuu became a nominal leader for all local matters, while the Omani Sultan looked after trade and international affairs. The transfer of the

The Slave Trade and Anti-Slavery Campaigns

Dingy, windowless cellars beneath the Anglican cathedral in Stone Town – the site of the central slave market on Zanzibar Island – serve as a reminder of the horrors of the trade in human lives. An underground tunnel leads from a deep, dark pit at Mangapwani to the sea, dating from the days of illegal trading. Slave-trading on the African continent was brutal and violent: thousands of slaves were rounded up on the mainland, where they were sold and shipped to Zanzibar Island. It was domination wrought by the power of arms – muskets and swords – controlled and carried out across the continent by caravans of slavers who opened routes into the interior. The effects of the trade were incalculable: tribes were destroyed and scattered as the caravans savagely plundered, and internecine wars broke out as some tribes raided each other to save themselves and profit from the trade too.

The anti-slavery campaign gained momentum after slavery was abolished in the British Empire in 1807 and became punishable by exile to Australia. The Americans followed suit in 1808, then France and Germany banned slavery too, but in East Africa slaves remained an important source of income. In 1839 the sultan agreed to an anti-slavery treaty that banned transport of slaves across the 'Moresby Line', a line on the map that led directly from the most southerly point of the sultan's domain in Mozambique to Diu Head in Gujarat, northern India. The treaty also banned the sale of slaves to Christians, and gave the British the right to confiscate any dhows carrying slaves in illegal waters. However the trade between Zanzibar and Oman continued unchanged; in fact demand seemed to increase, with dramatic effect across the mainland. Thousands of slaves continued to arrive on the shores of

sultanate from Oman to Zanzibar in 1832 brought an era of prosperity to the islands and the sultanate. The sultan capitalized on his new position at the centre of the slave and ivory trade, and then created his own vast plantations of coconuts and cloves to further increase his income; he decreed that every plantation owner must plant three clove trees to every coconut palm, or risk his land being confiscated.

Among the widespread estates and plantations the first sultan, Said, built impressive town and country palaces, reminiscent of Oman in its prime, and installed wives, advisors, eunuchs, slaves and a vast harem of concubines of different nationalities. The women were Arabian, Persian, Turkish, Circassian, Swahili, Nubian and Abyssinian, and their lives, languages and children mixed beneath the sultan's roof. The sultan divided his time between town and country; when in Stone Town he resided at Beit il Sahel, now the Palace Museum, which was later joined to a new palace called Beit al-Hukm by a suspension bridge that hung over the roofs of the Persian baths.

His daughter Princess Salme's *Memoirs of a Zanzibari Princess* give a colourful account of life among the harem and within the various palaces and residences of the sultans. The princess was christened Emily Reute when she converted to the Christian faith in order to marry her lover, a German merchant whose house in Zanzibar neighboured her own. Her memoirs are written from the perspective of her subsequent exile in Germany and span the reigns of the first three Zanzibari sultans. Salme was brought up in the oldest of the Zanzibari palaces, Beit il Mtoni, on the

Zanzibar. The sultan was anxious to protect his considerable interests – which covered more than 2.5 million square kilometres of the continent and provided a sizeable revenue – while the British shored up their efforts to diminish the trade. Both British and Omanis continued trying to secure their own advantage. In 1841 Sultan Said ceded a little to the first British consul, Captain Hamerton, in exchange for help fighting Mazrui Arabs in Mombasa and Oman. In return for their help, the British – keen to secure raw materials for industry from the African Continent – secured the first treaty limiting the slave trade. It was ineffective, and in 1845, under considerable pressure, the sultan signed a second treaty presented by Hamerton, reducing slave-trading to the region between the latitude lines of the sultan's dominion on the coast, preventing legal transport to Oman. But the illegal trade continued to flourish.

The death of anti-slavery campaigner Dr David Livingstone in 1873 was another milestone in the fight against slavery, leading the British to increase the pressure on Sultan Barghash by bringing in the Navy. The Navy struggled bitterly against the illegal trade, and there were many casualties: some of these are buried on Chapwani Island in Stone Town harbour. Barghash was forced to post a proclamation on the doors of the Customs House, officially ending the trade in slaves by sea and in all slave markets in East Africa. When journalist Henry Morton Stanley, who had pursued Livingstone across the continent, returned to the islands in 1874, he found the Zanzibar slave market had been abolished and designs were being drawn up for an Anglican cathedral in its place. Enforcement of abolition was often brutal as illegal trading continued into the 20th century; it was, however, the beginning of the end. With the decline of the slave trade, ivory became the main commodity.

seafront about 7km north of Stone Town. She describes the palace when its elegant balconies and rooms were filled with an entourage of courtiers and concubines, and the courtyards were home to an exotic menagerie of ostriches, peacocks and gazelles. When she returned to the palace in 1885, after 19 years of exile, she was aboard one of the five German warships that docked in Zanzibar harbour with their guns trained on the palace. Her Stone Town home of Mtoni was already in ruins, and to this day the dilapidated ruins of its walls are washed by the waves of the encroaching sea.

Sibling Rivalry Among Sultans

When Sultan Said died at sea in 1856, the population of Zanzibar was 25,000, rising to 40,000 during the northeast monsoon when the town became full of opportunistic merchants from the Persian Gulf. The succession was complex as the first sultan of Zanzibar left 36 children. Initially his son Majid took on the role of sultan, but his younger brother Barghash felt the sultanate should have been his: Barghash had been with his father on the boat from Oman to Zanzibar when the old sultan died, and resolved to overthrow his brother. This attempt was quashed, but Barghash again later conspired to usurp Majid. In fact the rightful heir was Said's eldest son Thuwain, sometimes called Tueni, alive and ruling in Oman. To keep the peace, the British helped to negotiate an annual payment by Majid to Thuwain. But one payment was enough for Majid, who resented being a vassal of Oman, and trouble flared again in 1859 when the belittled Sultan Sayyid Thuwain bin Said set sail to recoup his payments. He was met and pacified by a British cruiser on a single-minded mission to protect the British trade route to India. Two years later a British arbitrator, the Governor General of India, declared Zanzibar and Oman independent states. Together with the French, who also had a consul in Zanzibar, he drew up an Anglo-French agreement in recognition of Sultan Majid as independent sovereign over the East African territories. No sooner was Thuwain pacified, however, than Barghash popped up again, still plotting for the throne. Once again, the British intervened with a few well-timed shots fired from their gunboat, removing Barghash to Bombay in British India, where he remained for the duration of his brother's rule. On Majid's death, in 1870, the exiled prince at last took up the position he had so coveted.

While Sultan Sayyid Barghash bin Said suffered the indignity of seeing his hard-won dominion curtailed by the interests of foreign powers, he did at least build himself a fine collection of palaces. He had Chukwani Palace built eight miles south of the town in 1879, as a house in which to recuperate after illness – the air of Stone Town was fairly unpalatable at this time. The recuperation palace near Mtoni was followed by Marhubi Palace, an expression of sultanate opulence. Typically constructed in coral and wood, it was mainly destroyed by fire in 1899, although the ruins of the stone structure and bath houses remain. In 1883 Barghash built the House of Wonders as a ceremonial palace; it was designed by a British marine engineer, and was the tallest building in East Africa. The ornate fretwork of this four-storey palace shows the influence of Indian architecture that had impressed Barghash during his exiled years.

After the Slave Trade and the End of the Busaidi Dynasty

Among others, Henry Morton Stanley noted that the dominion and power of Sultan Barghash – now afflicted by elephantiasis, consumption and depression – were fast being diminished by political struggles. In 1877, Barghash attempted to 'lease' the mainland to Britain, but in the following decade British and German colonists simply grabbed the land and divided it up between them. In a fury, Barghash had one of his senior advisors poisoned for his friendliness to the German navy that was arrogantly floating in the sultan's harbour. Barghash himself died in March 1888 and was succeeded by his brother Khalifa. Despite claims that Khalifa was mentally unstable after six years locked in an underground chamber by his brother, the colonial powers championed his rights. They quickly drew up treaties, notably including the German East Africa Company's claim to a 50-year lease over the coastal territories. The Anglo-German agreement of 1890 defined mainland Tanzania as a part of German East Africa, and Zanzibar as a British protectorate with the sultan as sovereign.

The 'Shortest War in History' and the Demise of the Sultanate

Succession in the sultanate was never smooth, and in 1896 yet another scramble for power took place. The British intervened to make sure their man got the throne, bombarding the House of Wonders in what was later to become known as the 'shortest war in history' – 45 minutes of continuous bombing from the harbourfront that were enough to convince the rival candidate to desist. Despite his British

European Explorers in 'Stinkibar'

Zanzibar provided the ideal starting point for the hordes of European explorers and missionaries setting off on journeys into the interior in the 19th century (see p.11). The sultan was nominal sovereign of the uncharted lands beyond, and Zanzibar was the crucial trade centre for Arab trading caravans and ships. Here the travellers equipped for their expeditions, exchanging money for the beads and cloth that would be their currency on the mainland. The notes of these explorers are an interesting source of information about the island as seen through the eyes of Europeans.

On Stanley's first visit he noted that the sea was a startling 'cerulean blue', and the coastline variegated greens of mango, tamarind and coconut palms. He recorded that 'as [he] sailed along the coast...his nostrils were assailed by natural scents...but the sweet sensuousness of nature soon gave way to man-made pollution.' Livingstone's rather brutal observations of the island also note that it would be better named 'Stinkibar' for all the filth and pollution accumulated along the streets and beaches of Stone Town; not only was rubbish and sewage allowed to accumulate in the narrow streets, but it was common for the dead bodies of slaves to be dumped on the beaches. The decomposing mass became a haven for all number of vile diseases and ailments – no wonder Sultan Barghash built country palaces for his health.

Recently, local historian John da Silva has been collecting glassware found unearthed on the beach after seasonal monsoon tides: he has over 300 bottles and other artefacts dating from this 'stinki' period. Artefacts are found only at certain times of the year, when tide and monsoon are at a particular confluence. His private collection can be visited by appointment (see his contact details on p.332).

backing, Sultan Sayyid Hamud bin Muhammad (1902–1911) remained the absolute monarch and continued a lifestyle in the tradition of his predecessors: he retained four wives and a huge retinue of concubines and children, required his subjects to prostrate themselves in his presence and always had the final word. But he was the last to enjoy such an opulent lifestyle. His successors were forced to implement dramatic reforms, lessening their autonomy and introducing a constitution. The last sultan, Jamshid bin Abdullah (1963–4), was forced to flee Zanzibar within months of his coronation. He has since resided in England, tucked away in a suburb of Portsmouth, receiving a modest annual payment from the British government.

Post-War Zanzibar

Zanzibar's independent political development really began after 1956. There were two main political parties. The Zanzibar Nationalist Party (ZNP) was founded in 1955 as a continuation of the earlier National Party of Subjects of the Sultan of Zanzibar (NPSSZ); it developed rapidly from a league of rural African peasants into a radical Arab-led movement, which then failed to earn strong African support. A second party was formed in response to the plight of the ZNP, intended to represent the Shirazi and African majority – the Afro-Shirazi Party (ASP) led by Abeid Karume. After the first elections in July 1957, in which the ASP won five out of six seats and an independent candidate won the sixth, the parties continued to split and coalesce. A Shirazi splinter

Freddie Mercury

One of Zanzibar's most famous sons was Freddie Mercury, lead singer of the rock band Queen, born Farookh Bulsara in Zanzibar in 1946 to parents of Persian origin. The Bulsara family followed the Zoroastrian faith, into which Farookh was initiated at the age of eight in the traditional ceremony of Navjote. The rock star never forgot his Zanzibari roots: he included the Zanzibari Swahili exclamation *Bismillah* – meaning 'In the name of God' – in the lyrics of 'Bohemian Rhapsody', his most famous song. A lesser-known fact about Mercury was his passion for collecting Zanzibari stamps, a passion so great that he amassed a collection that sold on his death for $3 million. Bulsara and his family were forced to leave Zanzibar in 1963, along with many of Shirazi or Indian origin who were considered party to the supremacy of the sultan.

group of the ASP broke away to form the Zanzibar and Pemba People's Party (ZPPP), which formed a coalition with the ZNP in the 1961 elections, resulting in deadlock between the two opposing sides. Similar results were achieved in the 1963 elections, and, when Zanzibar was officially granted independence from Britain on 19 December 1963, it was as a constitutional monarchy under the sultan, with a coalition of the ZNP and the ZPPP in power. A militant splinter group of the ZNP, the progressive leftist Umma – meaning 'the masses' – later joined the ASP and supported the revolution, becoming a member of the Revolutionary Council of Zanzibar. Both blocs purported to represent the true African and Shirazi identity, exploiting the concept of domination by an Arab minority to gain power.

The Revolution

By January 1964 this perceived supremacy of the Arab minority had begun to pall, and a small band of Africans revolted against the supposed Arab domination. The uprising was incited by self-proclaimed 'Field Marshal' John Okello, an immigrant labourer from Uganda who told his African supporters they would be enslaved and their children slaughtered by the Arabs after Independence. At 3am on 12 January Okello and his followers carried out surprise attacks on the police station armoury, the army barracks, the radio station and the jail. The rebels planned to assassinate the sultan, but he fled with his family and a small entourage, ending up in England. For a while, there was widespread conflict on the islands: an estimated 12,000 members of the Arab community were killed, alongside 1,000 Africans; many fled.

Okello reigned briefly as leader of the Revolutionary Government, but was soon overthrown and expelled to the mainland. A new government was formed with the Afro-Shirazi Party, led by Abeid Karume as president of Zanzibar and chairman of the Revolutionary Government. An agreement was reached on 26 April 1964 that Zanzibar and Tanganyika would be officially joined and renamed the United Republic of Tanzania with Zanzibar, later abbreviated to the United Republic of Tanzania, but the islands would retain a great deal of autonomy. Even after the joint constitution was rewritten in 1965, officially determining the Republic as a one-party state, Zanzibar kept its ruling ASP alongside TANU, led by Julius Nyerere on the mainland. In 1977, however, President Nyerere merged TANU with the ASP to form a sole ruling party, the Chama Cha Mapinduzi party (CCM, or the Revolutionary Party of Tanzania). At this point Karume became first vice-president of the union and retained his position until he was assassinated seven years later, accused of wrongfully detaining a number of influential politicians and businessmen. Many felt that, having come to power undemocratically, Karume had not been the man to negotiate union with the mainland. He was succeeded by Aboud Jumbe, of the same political affiliations.

It was more than 30 years after the revolution before elections were held again, in 1980, when 40 candidates were elected to the Zanzibar House of Representatives. Jumbe resigned in 1984 and Ali Hassan Mwinyi took his place as president of Zanzibar, becoming president of the United Republic a year later.

Zanzibar has continued to struggle with democracy. The constitution was amended in 1992 to sanction multi-party elections, which were held in 1995, according to complex rules designed to prevent any one tribal, religious or ethnic group dominating. On Zanzibar the new opposition Civic United Front (CUF) party won a narrow lead over the ruling party – and a recount was demanded, which, unsurprisingly, put the government-sponsored CCM ahead. As a result the CUF boycotted the assembly. International observers monitoring the election declared it a shambles; the World Bank and the International Monetary Fund, among others, withdrew their funding from the islands in protest. In 1999 the two parties reached a grudging agreement to end the deadlock, giving Zanzibar greater autonomy to please the separatist CUF in exchange for its recognition of the CCM government.

Elections in October 2000 were nonetheless equally shambolic, pledges of renewed international aid clearly no sop to the political fervour of the opposing factions. While the electoral process on the mainland took place smoothly and without much altercation, on Zanzibar many of the estimated 750,000 voters found the polling stations closed, or open but with no ballot papers. Around 7,000 ballot papers mysteriously 'disappeared' from a car when the returning officer stopped to visit a lady friend. Extremes of mistrust between the two main parties, the CUF and the CCM, culminated in accusations of vote-rigging. After an outcry over the results, ballots were

Flag or Faith? Political Disturbance in 2004

Latent suspicions over the role of Islamic extremism in island life were compounded in 2004 following a spate of incendiary attacks. Some western governments issued travel warnings, though at the time of writing these had been rescinded. Islanders are disparaging about what they consider to be the West's intransigency and argue that such warnings are alarmist. They argue that any consequent downturn in the tourist trade is far more damaging to stability on the island than any Islamic extremist machinations. Given that the attacks were low-tech and its targets of purely domestic significance, it seems probable that the protest was motivated by a political rather than global religious agenda. Most likely, it was the work of a local Islamic separatist group. Nonetheless, the language of Islam in Zanzibari mosques has perceptibly altered over recent years, in line with worldwide developments. The Tanzanian government, mindful of the influence of the USA and its allies, has responded with strong counter-terrorism initiatives.

held again in some constituencies. The CCM candidate, Amani Abeid Karume, was instated as Zanzibar president, and the CUF once more publicly refused to recognize the government. There have been a number of localized acts of violence since the elections, mainly in the CUF stronghold of Pemba; in early 2001, however, clashes between police and opposition protesters on Unguja led to violence and loss of life.

Consequently, CUF members including 14 MPs exiled themselves to Kenya. The incident was embarrassing and seriously tarnished the union's claim to stability in the region. As an additional irritant, the CUF did well in the 2003 by-elections. The seeming disparity between the popular vote and the constitution of the legislature continues to cause concern. Discord stems ultimately from deep ambivalence over the future definition of Zanzibari sovereignty. For now, there is an insufficient drive for complete independence, so the issue will in all likelihood continue to be fudged. A conciliatory measure was made in April 2004 when Zanzibar was granted permission to hoist its own flag. Upcoming elections scheduled for late 2005 will determine to what extent the parties continue to engage with multi-party democracy.

Zanzibar Island

The island also known as Unguja is the largest of the Zanzibar archipelago, and Stone Town is its main settlement. It is possible to stay in the town and organize trips to Arabic palaces and spice farms and beach excursions from there, but most people

Diving Zanzibar

The Zanzibar archipelago is surrounded by thriving coral reefs and the gin-clear Indian Ocean, and is reputed to have some of the best diving in the world. The waters around the island teem with colourful marine life and have an average visibility of 20–60m. The water is warm – the average temperature is 27°C – and there are numerous colourful shallow sites to explore, which also make it a good spot for beginners. Visibility is generally better after the November rains, until March.

There are good shallow reefs around the north and northeast of Zanzibar Island, around the Mnemba Atoll and close to Stone Town, where conditions are varied enough to suit all abilities. Leven Banks in the north is a massive reef structure 10km out to sea, where depths vary from 14m at the shallowest point to deeper than 200m on the ocean bed. Mnemba Atoll has many clear shallow waters, with drops away to 40m, and one stunning 'great wall' plunging steeply from 35m to 70m. Dolphins and turtles are commonly seen on dives here. The waters around Zanzibar Island are generally shallower than those around Pemba, where channels more than 1,000m deep are renowned worldwide for excellent diving conditions and a variety suitable for more experienced divers. While reef, tiger, whale and nurse sharks are commonly spotted on dives around Zanzibar Island, the Pemba Channel is also visited by hammerhead sharks, manta rays and an assortment of extremely large fish. Wall dives and drift dives descend past superb coral formations.

See pp.334–5 for dive operators; 'Diving Nungwi', p.364; and 'Diving Pemba', p.380.

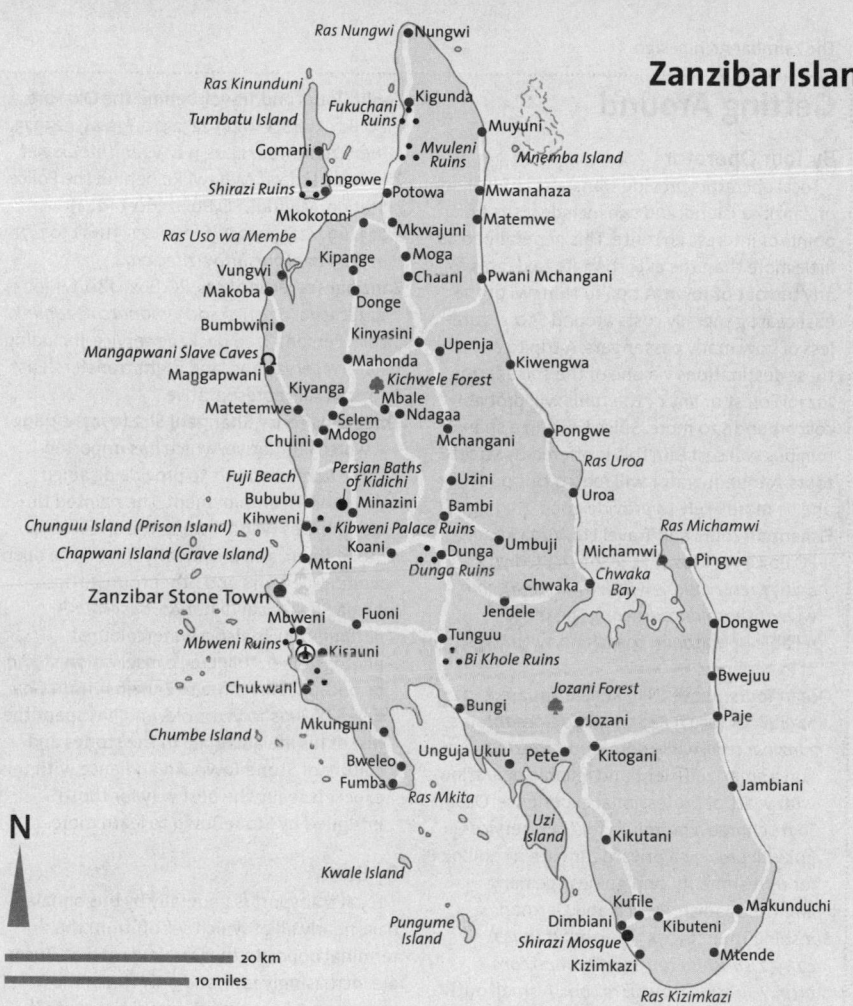

Zanzibar Island

Ras Nungwi • Nungwi
Ras Kinunduni
Fukuchani • Kigunda
Tumbatu Island   Ruins
Gomani   Muyuni
    Mvuleni • Mnemba Island
Shirazi Ruins   Ruins
Mkokotoni • Jongowe   Mwanahaza
Ras Uso wa Membe   Mkwajuni   Matemwe
Vungwi   Kipange • Moga
Makoba   Chaani   Pwani Mchangani
Bumbwini   Donge
Mangapwani Slave Caves   Kinyasini • Upenja
Maggapwani   Mahonda   Kiwengwa
    Kiyanga   Kichwele Forest
Matetemwe   Selem   Mbale
Chuini   Mdogo • Ndagaa   Pongwe
    Mchangani   Ras Uroa
Fuji Beach   Persian Baths   Uzini
Bububu   of Kidichi   Bambi   Uroa
Chunguu Island (Prison Island)   Kihweni   Minazini
Chapwani Island (Grave Island)   Kibweni Palace Ruins   Ras Michamwi
    Koani • Dunga   Umbuji   Michamwi • Pingwe
    Mtoni   Dunga Ruins   Chwaka   Chwaka
Zanzibar Stone Town   Jendele   Bay
    Mbweni   Fuoni   Dongwe
Mbweni Ruins   Tunguu   Bwejuu
    Kisauni   Bi Khole Ruins
Chukwani   Jozani Forest   Paje
    Bungi   Jozani
Chumbe Island   Mkunguni   Jambiani
    Bweleo   Unguja Ukuu   Pete • Kitogani
    Fumba   Ras Mkita
    Uzi   Kikutani
Kwale Island   Island
    Kufile   Makunduchi
Pungume   Dimbiani   Kibuteni
Island   Shirazi Mosque   Mtende
    Kizimkazi
    Ras Kizimkazi

N

20 km
10 miles

choose to do the opposite, heading out of town to stay on an idyllic beach, and seeing the city sights as a day's outing. The best beaches on the island are to the north and east, where the sun shines on clear sparkling waters in a range of striking turquoise blues, and the sand is fine. Beaches on the west coast are less inviting, as it shelters an industrial zone, but Mangapwani, Fuji, Mbweni and Kizimkazi remain clean and quiet enclaves on the western shore. All the islands are surrounded by rich coral reef, which protects the shoreline and also results in wide flat shallows that are subject to tidal extremes – although these are less extreme on much of Zanzibar's west coast.

Stone Town

The sun begins to dissolve into the horizon, perfecting a sweep of unknown orange against pure pale blue, and Stone Town stirs with the wakefulness of night. Muezzins in their different mosque towers call the faithful to prayers again, dogs bark and

Getting Around

By Tour Operator

Local operators provide transport to all areas of Zanzibar Island, and can include visits to points of interest en route. This generally costs little more than the extortionate taxi fares for any trip out of town. A taxi to Nungwi or the east coast generally costs around $50, regardless of how many passengers. A trip to any of these destinations via one of the spice farms, Jozani Forest or any of the ruins will probably cost around $20 more. Spice tours in a shared minibus will cost $10; this is offered by street touts. A tour operator will match this price and be more likely to provide good guiding.

Fisherman Tours and Travel Ltd, Vuga Road, PO Box 3537, t (024) 2238791–2/t (0747) 412677, *reservations@fisherman tours.com*, *www.fishermantours.com*. The most reliable operator on the island, with bags of experience.

Ocean Tours, above DHL, Kellele Square, t (024) 2238280/t (0747) 488500, *info@oceantours zanzibar.com*; *www.oceantourszanzibar.com*. Run a smart, efficient and reliable operation with years of professional experience. Ocean Tours charge a premium for their services, but will provide a private car with a coolbox for refreshments, and guides speaking English, Spanish, French and German.

Sunshine Tours, t (0747) 460052/t (0747) 423332, *sunshinetoursznz@yahoo.com*, *http:// sunshinetours.8m.com*. A small outfit operating out of the Old Fort. Friendly and organized, good for spice tours.

Zanzibar Hotels and Tanzania Safaris Company, Africa House Hotel, t (0747) 422677/t (0741) 422677/t (0744) 297486/ t (0747) 439340, *hotels@zanlink.com*. Offers comprehensive services for tourists, with friendly and well-informed staff. They promote their mainland safari tours, but it is advisable to do this with operators in Arusha or Dar. Offers a 24hr service.

Zenith Tours and Travel, behind the Old Fort, PO Box 3648, t (024) 2232320, f (024) 223973, *info@zenithtours.net*, *www.zenithtours.net*.

Zan Tours Ltd, off Malawi Rd behind the Police Station, Malindi, PO Box 2560, t (024) 2232692/2233042/t/f (024) 2233116/t (0747) 417279, *zantoursinfo@zitec.org*.

Zanzibar Travel Services, PO Box 1780, t/f (024) 2238220/t (0747) 414903, *monarch@zanlink. com*. Personalized package service, including hotel reservations and flight transfers. East African Air representative.

Three Legs Tours, Shangani St, t (0747) 431892. A worthy initiative, which has imported three rickshaw taxis to provide disabled drivers with employment. The painted tin-can vehicles wend around the streets of Stone Town, and are equally fun on the open road. Spice tours and other tourist trips.

John da Silva, local historian, *dasilvajb@ hotmail.com*, is also a watercolourist, photographer, collector, conservationist and raconteur. John came to Zanzibar from Goa when he was 10 years old, and has spent the rest of his life absorbed in the stories and culture of Stone Town. An audience with this expert is really the best way for those intrigued by Stone Town to learn more.

By Bus

Local transport is generally by bus or dala-dala, nearly all of which set off from the terminal opposite the Darajani market. **Buses** are increasingly rare, and only run in the morning and evening. A useful bus route is the no.309, which heads to the East Coast, Jambiani, Paje and Bwejuu. **Dala-dalas** are cheap, more frequent and worth considering if you are travelling light or making a day trip, and have plenty of time to spare. They tend to crawl along and get ridiculously overcrowded. But they do operate to all the main areas of the island and cost about $1. It is best to avoid the morning and evening 'rush hours'. All dala-dalas display their final destination on the

children shout as they play football in open corners or dive into the harbour waters with their friends. A crowd starts to gather along the harbourfront and in Forodhani Gardens, where smoke is beginning to rise from barbecues at the assorted food stalls and the curio markets are assembling by gaslight amid a hubbub of banter and chat.

front windscreen; ask anyone for help if you need it. Useful dala-dala routes include **506** to Amani Stadium, the football ground; **502** to Bububu; **505** to Uwanja wa Ndege, which translates as 'stadium of birds' – the airport.

By Bicycle

It is also possible to hire a bicycle through some tour companies and at the market on Creek Road for $5–6 a day. These are often ancient Chinese models, though decrepit mountain bikes are increasingly available for a few dollars more. Bear in mind that the roads are pretty terrible in places. If you are heading to the east coast, however, it is fun to hire a bike for a couple of days to explore the long beaches; this can be arranged through your hotel or with local boys on the beach. Fairly reliable models can be found at **Maharouky Bicycle Hire**, near the market.

By Car, *Pikipiki* Motorbike or Scooter

Not only are the roads pretty horrendous in places, but Zanzibari driving techniques and the abundance of chickens and children on the roads makes hiring a self-drive scooter, motorbike or car a serious consideration. There are a number of accidents involving tourists each year. When renting a vehicle or motorbike, ensure that it comes with valid road permit and insurance papers. You will need to show these at police posts at traffic junctions across the island. You must also have an international driver's licence, or a Zanzibari licence obtained from the traffic police office in the Malindi area at a cost of T.shs 6,000 per day. **Ally Keys**, in Coco de Mer Hotel, **t** (0747) 411797/ **t** (0741) 411797/**t** (0747) 419377, *allykeys786@ yahoo.com*. Reliably rents motorbikes, Suzuki jeeps and scooters, with insurance. His favourite greeting is 'Welcome, friend, I am not as dodgy as I look!' This is vouched for; his service has a very good reputation. **Nasor Aly Mussa's Scooter Service**, near the Anglican cathedral in Stone Town.

Motorbikes can be hired here, or from the selection outside the Tembo Hotel. **Chau** at **Malindi Lodge Annex**, **t** (024) 2234675. Four-wheel-drives and 250cc Hondas in good condition at reasonable prices.

Be sure to check your vehicle before setting off, as rental vehicles are often not in great condition and should always be test-driven. On average, cars cost $40–50 per day, motorbikes around $25 and scooters about $20.

Tourist Information

The **Zanzibar Tourist Authority** is found on Creek Road, just before the market entrance, on the same side of the road. It does not have a great deal of information, apart from a cabinet full of hotel brochures and leaflets about exotica such as seaweed-production. Much more can be gleaned on a walk around a few of the tour operators' offices in town, though be prepared for the sell.

Dress Code

Zanzibar is predominantly Muslim – about 96 per cent – although social mores have relaxed somewhat since the times when the Omani women were in purdah, venturing out only with a **veil** covering their entire faces except for the eyes. Today it is still unusual to see Zanzibari women without their **outer kangas**, or the flowing Arabic black *bui-bui*. A man and woman meeting alone still risk enforced marriage.

Traditional dress for a man is a *kanzu*, the Arabic-style long white dress, often worn with an **embroidered cap** and sometimes a jacket, over a shirt and long trousers or vest and loin cloth. Although the local people are progressively more used to the idiosyncrasies of Western dress, wearing revealing strappy T-shirts, mini-skirts and short shorts shows disrespect for the local culture and is regarded as provocative.

History

Zanzibar Stone Town is an extraordinary place. UNESCO recently declared the old town one of the world's historic cities, and efforts are at last being made to conserve it. The old quarter sits on a peninsula in the middle of the west coast of Zanzibar

Opening Hours

Shops open around 8.30am and generally close by 1–2pm; many reopen 4–6pm. **Office hours** are Monday to Friday 7.30am to 3.30pm. On Friday there is a break (12–2pm) for prayers. Banks open Mon–Fri 8–4 and Sat 8–1. Bureaux de Change open Mon–Sun 8–8.

Emergencies

Fahud Pharmacy, PO Box 3966, Creek Road, t (0748) 428888, *fahudpha@hotmail.com*.
Mnazi Mmoja Hospital, t (024) 2231071–3.
Ambulance, fire and police emergency, t 112.
Police head office, PO Box 237, t (024) 2231091. The main police station is in Malindi, opposite the petrol station. Traffic police are in the right side of the building, as obvious from the waving of hands and raising of voices; standard police in the left. The Zanzibar **police** force is affiliated with the mainland police, although it remains in some respects a separate entity. This force replaced the sultan's militia, and first received backing from the mainland force during the Independence struggle. Its miscellaneous duties include destroying crows and stray dogs and cats. Note that the Zanzibari police are not above asking for a *baksheesh* payment when a theft is reported. They may insist that the ink they use for the official stamp is prohibitively expensive and demand a payment of $10. If this happens, the most expedient response is to hand over the money.

Sports and Activities

Zanzibar Island is a paradise for **sailing**, **diving** and **fishing**, and Stone Town is often the best starting point for these activities. It is also a good base for **dolphin safaris**.

Dolphin Safaris, Dives and Boat Trips

There are **pods of bottle-nosed, humpback and spinner dolphins** all around Zanzibar and Pemba Island, commonly spotted on dives and boat trips. Resident pods are frequently seen around the **Fumba Peninsula**, just south of Stone Town, and around **Mnemba Island** off the northeast coast. The dolphins that receive most attention, however, are those around **Kizimkazi**, at the south of the island – the site of increasingly popular **dolphin safaris** (*see* p.377), which are basically a trip out in a local boat, spending about 2hrs scouting the waves for a sign of the resident pods. Dolphin trips elsewhere on the island range dramatically in quality and price. Offers for a $10 trip from Stone Town will probably buy you a quick trip down to Kizimkazi and back (sometimes on a bus) and a seat in a leaky wooden boat. Others offer a more elaborate day trip on a decent sailing dhow, and even having a good lunch on a shady sandbank, to find dolphins less plagued by the hordes. Try **Monarch Tours**, t (024) 2238220, *monarch@zanlink.com*, who also offer Stone Town tours and spice tours.

Diving

See also 'Diving Zanzibar', p.330, 'Diving Nungwi', p.364, 'Diving Pemba', p.380, and Pemba 'Sports and Activities' p.382.

Although prices vary, a single dive in Zanzibar waters costs approximately $40–50, and around $230–250 for a 10-dive package. Most dive schools can arrange introductory dives for anyone who has not previously completed a dive course. Night dives cost more, and should be booked in advance in order to coincide with the tides. PADI courses usually cost around $300 for a 5-day course.
The Zanzibar Dive Centre (aka **One Ocean Divers**), PO Box 608, t (024) 2238374/t (0742) 750161, *oneocean@zanlink.com*, *www.zanzibaroneocean.com*. Situated on the beach end of Kenyatta Road; widely considered the best and the only 5-star dive centre in Stone Town. Runs two dive trips every day, using only up-to-date equipment, including underwater cameras for $10 per day. The

Island, bordered by the sea on two sides and the Creek Road to the east. Beyond Creek Road, Stone Town rambles into Ng'ambo – 'the other side' – an expanse of modern blocks and tin-roofed housing that contains the growing population of modern Zanzibar. Attempts have been made to rename it Michenzani – 'the new city'. The old

Zanzibar Dive Centre staff are experienced and enthusiastic. Also has bases at the Blue Bay Beach Resort on the east coast, at Kiwengwa, and at Matemwe Beach Village on the northeast coast.

Mawimbini Watersports Ltd., PO Box 4226, t (0747) 418719, *info@mawimbini.com*. Very good service operating across Zanzibar.

Dive Africa Watersports, PO Box 2370, t (0741) 323096, f (0741) 230267, *zanzibar@ diveafrica.com*. Located on Mizingani Road.

There are dive shops around the island where divers can complete PADI or SSI courses, enjoy diverse packages for experienced divers or simply try to dive for the first time.

East African Diving and Watersports, operate from Amaan Bungalows on the west side of Ras Nungwi, in the northwest, and also run sailing charters to Pemba, with guests staying aboard overnight.

Paradise Dive Centre, t (024) 2231387/t 0747) 414129. A popular alternative amid the backpacker lodges that cluster around Nungwi Beach.

Scooby Doo Dive School operates from a dive shack near Kendwa Rocks.

Ras Nungwi Dive Centre at Ras Nungwi Beach Hotel, PO Box 1784, Zanzibar, t (024) 2232512. Excellent guidance and equipment is provided here, on the northeast aspect. Relaxed and experienced instructors provide regular PADI training courses, colourful introductory dives and dive packages for experienced divers, with specific focus on smaller groups and individual guidance.

Rising Sun Dive School, at Breezes Beach Club, in the southeast, *www.risingsun-zanzibar. com*. Run by SSI accredited instructors on a mission to discover a range of new, deeper dive sites on this little-dived stretch of coast, and to dispel the myth that the best diving is on the northeast aspect of the island. Offers SSI diving courses to beginners (around $300), as well as snorkelling and dives for more experienced underwater explorers. Dive courses and discovery dives are available on a one-to-one basis, and there is wide range of speciality dives including Aladin Computer dives. The attraction of this region is the number of uncharted sites that have been discovered since the centre was established here (presently 14), focusing on a deep drop-off beyond the eastern reef. These range from coral reefs gently sloping from 8–9m deep to a sandy bottom at 20m depth, to 40m sites beyond the barrier, including the 'Blue Wall', a perfectly vertical dropoff where everything you see is enormous – notably the turtles, but also sharks, including white-tips. Both hawksbill and green turtles are the stars of the Turtle Garden site and, as with elsewhere in Zanzibar, the months of November to January tend to afford the best visibility. Rising Sun provides tuition in English, Italian, German and French.

Fishing Trips

There are yet more alternatives for deep-sea fishing excursions. Serious fishermen may wish to contact the **East African Fishing Club**, PO Box 3870, t/f (024) 2233001.

Ras Nungwi Beach Hotel, PO Box 1784, Zanzibar, t (024) 2232512. Has a fully equipped deep-sea fishing boat for hire at about $650 for the boat per day, although shorter trips are charged for less.

Sailing

Sabran Jamil, PO Box 1759, Zanzibar, t (0747) 417279, *enquire@zanzibarunique.com*, *www.zanzibarunique.com*. Sabran Jamil is a traditional *jahazi*, a kind of large dhow, used for trips around the waters of Stone Town. Sunset cruises, island hops to Bawe, Chapwani and Prison islands, weddings and private charters are all available. Sunset cruises last 2hrs from 5pm, and cost $25.

city, however, remains a commercial centre and a living monument to the culture and history of its curious mix of East African, Arabian, Persian and European conquerors and seafaring traders. The ancient maze of narrow streets is a hotchpotch of old stone buildings, built close together for respite from the tropical island sun, and

The Impact of Tourism on Zanzibar

Tourism is a relatively recent development in Zanzibar, but the industry has been welcomed with gusto. The effects of it are both positive and negative. On the one hand there is a continually developing infrastructure with increasingly more reliable water and electricity supplies, a good central road system, some excellent hotels and transport services and a growing awareness of the need to preserve historical sites and develop conservation projects. Less heartening is the increased need for conservation as uninspiring hotel complexes spring up, catering to the package tourism market, and a potentially unsustainable demand for water and fish dinners surges.

Visitors to Zanzibar today can expect to find all the luxuries of the west. Needs are better catered to here than in most places on the mainland: hot running water is widely available, although sporadic power- and water-cuts render it unreliable at times – but most of the bigger hotels have their own generators which will take over when the mains lets you down. It is also possible to buy a variety of luxury Western goods such as photographic film, medicines and chocolate bars, but it is always worth checking the sell-by date beforehand. Communications and Internet connections are available, at a price, mainly around Stone Town.

Local attitudes have been strongly influenced by the influx of tourism. It is hard to reconcile the effects of hordes of wealthy foreigners spending their holiday money freely on the island, their children flaunting flashy Western toys in front of local children, with the island's widespread poverty. Many locals, however, look upon tourists as a potential source of economic progress and work hard to help foreigners enjoy their stay in exchange for the income. In return, a positive and friendly attitude does wonders for international relations, and a polite-but-firm manner is the best tactic for avoiding unwanted services. With a little effort, shared understanding is growing.

A surprising number of travellers to Zanzibar complain that the islands are not as they expected – not, as you might expect, because it is an impoverished, thriving, dirty market community where fish have their heads cut off in the street and the male population proudly pees in the harbour. The complaint, surprisingly, is that tourists in Zanzibar are asked to pay a 'fair' price, that bears more relation to Western prices than to the prices paid by tourists in places like India and Thailand. The islands do, however, remain relatively inexpensive by Western standards, and provide amply for a backpacker market. Those on a budget can expect to pay around $10 a night for a decent self-contained room with breakfast. There are also good hotels in the middle range, between $30 and $50 each a night, which provide good-value service for the price, although these are more difficult to find. At the upper end, accommodation generally succeeds in justifying rates by location and amenities. Generally hotels for all budgets are represented in all the main areas of Zanzibar Island.

Transport, other than the local bus system, often seems to be expensive, and if you are on a budget it is worth looking into the various shared minibuses, or getting to know the dala-dalas. Beers range from about $1 in a local bar to a $3 at some large resort hotels, where in some cases premiums seem to be added with shameless abandon. Wine is imported, and always expensive.

shaded by elegantly carved balconies, loggias and verandahs that appear to cling precipitously overhead – close enough to catch a whisper, or a kiss. These historic constructions now house homes and hotels, restaurants, guesthouses, offices and shops. The houses of the most wealthy and influential were built from coral stone, in the Arabic style, around a walled central courtyard accessed through one grand door. The elaborately carved door, all that could be seen from outside, was the outward expression of the wealth and standing of the household within. Many remain, with carvings of lotus flowers, fish and vines or dates; sometimes they are inscribed with passages from the Koran. In accordance with the customs of Persia many of the doors are also studded with impressive polished iron studs, sharply pointed to ward off marauding elephants – despite the lack of them on the shores of Zanzibar.

A Walk Around Stone Town

The best way to explore the old town is on foot. A walk around Stone Town may take a couple of hours' evening stroll, an afternoon, or all day, depending on how lost you wish to get. It is also possible to take guided walks with a tour operator or local guide: organized walks usually take 2–4 hours and cost $15–20 per person.

It is a town in which every old building tells a story of the past. The **Forodhani Gardens**, near the harbour, are a good place to get your bearings. Perhaps drink a soda here, consider the fact that these gardens were once a railway yard, and look back towards the panoramic vista of strange and beautiful architecture that stands behind. This area becomes the hub of activity of the town when the sun sets: crowds gather here to walk, talk and eat together and the harbour front is lined with rows of food stalls, illuminated by flickering gas lamps. The gardens have gone by many names: they started life as the Jubilee Gardens when they were officially laid out in 1936 to commemorate the silver jubilee of Sultan Khalifa bin Harub, whose rule continued for nearly another 25 years until 1960. After the Revolution in 1964 they were renamed Jamituri, the People's Gardens, before getting today's name, which means 'place of the customs'. The bandstand in the middle was used by the sultan's army band to entertain the people. The white arch was built for the arrival of Princess Margaret of Britain in 1956; unfortunately she arrived at the dhow harbour instead, and the arch has never been used in its official capacity.

Directly behind the gardens, across Mizingani Road is the **Arab Fort**, also called the **Old Fort** – 'Ngome Kongwe' in Swahili – or Gereza, meaning prison. It is one of the oldest buildings in Stone Town. The present two-storey crenellated structure was built by the Busaidi Omani Arabs between 1698 and 1701 after they defeated and ousted the Portuguese, and served as the base for their continuing defence against the vanquished Europeans and against the Mazrui, a rival Omani group, who occupied Mombasa at the time. They chose the site of an old Portuguese church as the site for the stronghold, and parts of this original building, dating from 1598–1612, can still be distinguished in the inside wall. In the 19th century the fort became a prison; prisoners were brutally punished and executed outside the east wall. In the early 1900s it was converted to gentler use as a railway workshop for the **Bububu Railway steam train**. The track ran 11km between Stone Town and Bububu, never making it the

Getting There and Around

For 'Getting There' *see* pp.319–20 – all air and sea routes to Zanzibar Island arrive in Stone Town. All visitors arriving at the airport or by sea will be invariably greeted by a throng of over-helpful touts. The best approach, if you have not pre-arranged to be met, is to calmly state your destination, look horrified at the first price, and await the best price.

The **roads** of Stone Town are not built for traffic. The few driveable roads are barely wide enough to accommodate the hefty **4x4 vehicles** that squeeze through them. It is possible to hire a **bicycle** (*see* p.333), and there are a handful of squeaky rickshaws rattling about, but **walking** is generally the safest and most fun option. However, there are plenty of **taxis** available for a quick route across town, which should cost no more than T.shs 2,000 for all trips within Stone Town.

Tourist Information

The **Zanzibar Tourist Information Office** is on Creek Road, in Darajani. The office holds a dusty collection of pamphlets and has a reasonably useful enquiries desk. If you have no joy here, try the **Zanzibar Commission for Tourism**, the authority that deals with the tourist industry, at PO Box 1410, Amaan Rd, nr Amaan Stadium, t (024) 2233485–6, f (024) 2233448, *zanzibartourism@zanzibartourism. net, www.zanzibartourism.net*.

The **post office** is off Kenyatta Road in Shangani Street; its complex includes the central telephone exchange. **Phone calls** from here are a serious business, involving form-filling, a deposit and patience. All calls are expensive, but for local calls it is now possible to buy phone cards that occasionally work in the phone booth outside. Phone calls can also be made from the larger hotels, which is easier but even more expensive.

Internet connections are everywhere. The servers and the phone connections can be frustratingly slow and unreliable but they are improving. The cheapest and best place for connection is at the local service provider, **Internet Zanzibar**, in a poky little office behind the Majestic Cinema on Vuga Road, which charges T.shs 2,000 per half-hour on line. The **Internet Café**, Zanzki Street, t (0741) 333453, shows no sign of food or drink but provides Internet access and secretarial services at fairly good rates. The **Serena Inn** has a **business centre**, providing e-mail, fax and photocopying. Otherwise try the **Shangani Business Centre** on Kenyatta Road.

Changing money is easier than it has ever been. Most **hotels** will exchange travellers' cheques and hard currency, although you will get a better rate from the *bureaux de change* in town. Cash (especially dollars) is rarely available on credit card, even if a sign to the contrary is displayed in the window. It is possible at **World Vision Bureau de Change** on Kenyatta Road, for a 5% charge (*open Mon–Fri 8am-10pm, Saturdays and bank holidays 8am–2.30pm*). **Credit cards** are accepted at larger hotels and restaurants, and the odd shop. There is a 'Visa and Mastercard Assistance Point' near the Serena Inn (*open Mon–Sat 8.30–5.30*). The most central **ATM** is opposite the Radha Food Hall, while Barclays have one with Visa and MasterCard access at the ZSTC building on Malawi Road. Nearby, the **Malindi Bureau de Change**, opposite Cinema Afrique on Malawi Road, is open every day.

Shopping

Zanzibar Stone Town is shoppers' heaven. **Contemporary Makonde carvings** are available throughout Stone Town and in the markets in Forodhani Gardens at night. These are often run-of-the-mill items mass-produced for tourists. Beware of being tricked into buying 'authentic ebony', as it is frequently made from lightweight wood, though these pieces can be attractive, and the wood certainly comes from a more renewable source than ebony. Among the masses there are often some quirky little pieces that have individual character. Look out for impossibly thin match-stick men carved in ebony – almost impossible to replicate ad infinitum on account of their delicacy. If you want to avoid paying ebony prices for a substitute, check the weight; ebony is almost implausibly heavy.

Traditional **Zanzibari wooden chests** are made all over town, but there are a couple of particularly good shops around the crossroads of Cathedral and Gizenga Streets, with varying sizes, styles and designs ranging from the ornately embellished in filigree gold to a simple lock box. For a good range of **antique chests**, doors, clocks and other items it might be worth having a look in Abeid's Curio Shop opposite St Joseph's Cathedral. It is also possible to commission contemporary pieces from artisans in their workshops.

Shops of the highest league – selling crafts and clothing at a good quality and cost – have opened on the **Kenyatta Road**. Among them is **The Gallery**, PO Box 3181, **t** (024) 2232721/ 2236734, *gallery@swahilicoast.com*, a combination of curio shop, gratifyingly well-stocked bookshop, art gallery and boutique in a fantastic warren of rooms and courtyards. It is run by the family of popular local photographer Javed Jafferji, who also publishes the excellent and informative local magazine, *Swahili Coast*. He maintains a wealth of backdated images, articles and information from past and present editions online, at *www.swahilicoast.com*. OneWay, *www.bundu.cc*, makers of well-stitched T-shirts, have a shop here too. **Real Art**, Kenyatta Road, **t** (0748) 460419, *anitasita@hotmail.com*, *bogaertpascal@hotmail.com*, stocks a wide selection of Tinga Tinga and other paintings by important East African artists. The Belgian co-owner teaches at the art school in Dar. Real Art will ship paintings to the rest of the world. **Mwanakwerekwe Art School**, outside Stone Town, welcomes visitors by prior arrangement; to visit the school and see exhibited pieces and work in progress, enquire at the Real Art shop for further details.

One of the best streets for shopping is **Gizenga Street**, which runs from Kenyatta Road to behind the Arab Fort. Look out for unusual and beautiful **hand-appliquéd cushion covers** in fluid Arabic styles at **Sasik**. **Moto Womens' Co-operative**, PO Box 152, **t** (0747) 466304, *www.solarafrica.net/moto*, is a fairtrade shop selling plaited baskets and good-quality textiles. Cheaper **textiles, batiks** and **baskets** can be bought from the craft market on the ground floor of the House of Wonders and around the outside of it. Cheap batiks are ubiquitous, often showing colourful cartoon-like images of people or animals. These are invariably sold alongside the now traditional **Tinga Tinga paintings** with a

distinct style of animal painted in bold industrial paints. Good-quality artwork is produced and sold in the form of large batik paintings and watercolours of the town. Try **Suraka Arts Studio**, Gizenga Road. Peruse Kiponda Road for **clocks**, **antiques** and bits of **silver jewellery** from India. Or find bits of **gold** at the stall in the Old Arab Fort, or Gold Souk in Mkunzini St.

If a pair of colourful **kangas** (*see* pp.350–51) appeals, find the street that sells nothing but: **Mchangani Street**, off Creek Road; look out for the Suma Store. They are always sold as two pieces to be divided after purchase, and are good value at just $5 a pair.

For all types of **camera paraphernalia**, **Musammil's** on the Creek Road is good.

Where to Stay

Stone Town

Very Expensive

Serena Inn, PO Box 4151, **t** (024) 2233587/ 2233567, **f** (024) 2233019, *reservations@ serena.co.tz*, *www.serenahotels.com*. The most upmarket luxury accommodation and service in Stone Town, operated by the Serena Hotel Group and owned by the Aga Khan. The Aga Khan's Fund for Economic Development has carried out a loving restoration of the old British-built Extelcoms building and the older, neighbouring Chinese Doctor's Residence, preserving the buildings in keeping with the surroundings. The whole has been grandly decked out with antiques and artefacts, in an attempt to recreate the opulence of Zanzibar's heyday. It occupies a prime location on the waterfront near the town centre, with a sparkling swimming pool that is unfortunately for residents' use only. Service and ocean-view dining in the restaurant are reliably good. In 2005 it opened 38 more suites/prime rooms, carefully renovating an adjacent 500-yearold building. It is a member of the Small Luxury Hotels of the World.

Expensive

Emerson and Green, 236 Hurumzi Street, PO Box 3417, **t** (024) 2230171/**t** (0747) 423266, **f** (0747) 429266, *anything@emerson-green. com*, *emersonandgreen@zitec.org*, *www*.

emerson-green.com. Home to possibly 'the
richest man in the Swahili Empire' during
the 1870s, when part of the present building
was the residence of Sir Tharia Thopan, head
of customs and financial advisor to the
sultan. It was originally the administrative
building for the customs offices, and then
during the 1880s and '90s it was used by the
British to pay for the release of slaves.
Contrived as a haven of opulent style and
panache in the centre of the old town,
Emerson and Green is a small hotel that
does not feel like a hotel at all. Choosing a
room or suite is not easy, as each is designed
with individual character and charm. New
additions include the enormous ball room,
with two vast double beds – said to be the
largest hotel room in Zanzibar – the
lavender room and the gallery. The suites are
the newest development; tucked high in the
eaves of neighbouring buildings, they are
reached via a confusion of stairs. These
eyries are big, and lovely, but since space is
hardly an issue in this hotel the top choice
has got to be one of the old favourites,
named after points of the compass: 'south' is
accessible over a high wooden bridge, and
provides a semi-open-air bathroom with
views over Stone Town, separated from the
bedroom by a small private verandah; 'west'
also has good views, and a kidney-shaped
bath for romantic soaks, while in 'east' a
lattice-work wall provides an atmospheric
dappled light and catches the breeze. All
guests should be warned, however, that the
open rooms that are so elegant during
waking hours are also infernally noisy
during the Zanzibari night; they enjoy the
languishing choirs of cats, cockerels and
children through the early hours after
midnight and the distinctive awakening of
the Muslim faithful at prayer times. The
months from late November to March are
usually very hot and humid, and you feel it
here at the heart of the old town. The
rooftop restaurant, however, provides wide
and airy views of the town and harbour, and
excellent multi-course meals in ethnic style.
Guests sit cross-legged on cushions and tiny
portions of the set menu are brought one
after another. Book at least on the day that
you wish to dine.

Africa House Hotel, PO Box 3246, Shangani,
Stone Town, t (0747) 432340, f (0747) 439340,
theafricahotel@yahoo.com. The recent
overhaul of this hotel has successfully
recaptured some of its colonial-era chic in
the public areas. This, however, is mostly due
to the judicious architectural design of its
halls and walkways. The owners have
worked in private aviation for years, and
have collected a vast mismatch of furnishings from around Asia and the Middle East
to fill the cramped rooms. The rooms are
vastly overpriced and facilities are woefully
lacking. The terrace bar remains the best
spot from which to view the sunset, but is
this hotel's only redeeming feature.
Beyt al Chai, PO Box 4236, t (0748) 515408,
reservations@stonetowninn.com. Also
known as the **Stone Town Inn**. The pretty
town house was at one time a tea house
belonging to a wealthy Zanzibari merchant.
Situated directly opposite the Serena Inn,
personal service and a rare sense of tranquillity away from the bustle of street life make
Beyt al Chai a fantastic choice. With just six
en suite rooms, the Inn has an intimate and
private atmosphere and rivals Emerson and
Green. Horsehair sofas, bold batiks and
finely crafted Zanzibari furnishings comple-
ment a rich palette to create a convincingly
authentic traders' house. All rooms are air-
conditioned, and a couple have wide stone
baths. The Red Room 'Ajab' is unquestionably
the best. Offers bed and breakfast only, but
its location on Kelele Square is convenient
for several very good restaurants.

Moderate
Tembo House Hotel, on Forodhani Street, PO
Box 3974, t (024) 2233005/2232069, f (024)
2233777, *tembo@cats-net.com*, *www.tembo
hotel.com*. Less ostentatious than the
Serena, the Tembo Hotel is also located in an
impressive old building right on the waterfront, in the midst of the fishermens' bustle.
It is designed around a central courtyard
with a swimming pool and beachfront
terrace. As a result, the Tembo has a breezy,
cool and pleasant atmosphere, with good
rooms facing the sea – an especially worthwhile aspect during the hotter months.
Rooms are furnished with antique Zanzibari

furniture and sunken Persian baths with showers, and have fridge, telephone, satellite TV, hairdryer and air-conditioning. Nevertheless it remains an elegant, authentic choice – to the extent that it is also Muslim-run and serves no alcohol. The Dharma Bar is opposite, and there is plenty of choice for sundowners nearby. The price is good value for such decent rooms, but staff seem reluctant to go out of their way.

Dhow Palace Hotel, in the Shanghani area, PO Box 3974, **t** (024) 2233012/2230304, **f** (024) 2233008, *dhowpalace@zanlink.com*, *www.zanzibar.net/dhow*, *www.tembohotel.com/dhowpalace.html*. Tucked away in the maze of Stone Town streets just a short distance from the harbourfront. The hotel is set around a cool indoor courtyard and deep tiled swimming pool. It is well run and decorated with authentic Zanzibari antiques, similar in style and atmosphere to its sister hotel, the Tembo. Without the benefit of the sea breeze and views, the Dhow Palace is marginally less expensive, but the good rooms are much larger, especially on the second floor, with some beds so tall that they come equipped with steps. The dining room serves only breakfast, but can prepare lunch and dinner with notice.

Chavda Hotel, on Baghani Street, **t** (024) 2232115/2231931, *chavda@zanzinet.com*. Newly renovated with Zanzibari charm, the Chavda is great value for money for clean and elegant accommodation. All rooms have air-conditioning, although be sure to ask for one with windows. The open dining room and pleasant rooftop café (*open all day*) are recommended in their own right. The hotel will arrange free transport from the airport and seaport.

Clove Hotel, behind the Palace Museum on Hurumzi Street, PO Box 1117, **t** (0747) 484567, *clovehotel@zanlink.com*, *www.zanzibarhotel.nl*. The best moderately priced hotel in Stone Town, with an excellent location in a quiet side street behind the House of Wonders. A neat and clean building decked out in cool Californian pastels rises far from the dust of the street. A vertiginous climb takes you to the high rooftop seating area overlooking the towers of the Hindu temple and the faraway boats of the harbour. There is a well

stocked fridge from which guests are trusted to serve themselves. Once the sun begins to set it is a lovely spot to rest, listen to the wail of the muezzin and watch the light fade. Early in the evening guests can even enjoy the sounds of performances from the nearby rooftop restaurant at Emerson and Green. As with all Stone Town hotels, make sure you pack your earplugs.

Beyt al Amaan, **t** (0747) 414364/411362, *www.houseofpeace.com*, or via Monsoon restaurant. The 'House of Peace' is well named; the townhouse is highly recommended for those travellers jaded by hotel stays, or who prefer a low-key 'at-home' service. Guests are given keys so that they can come and go as they please, while a discreet housekeeper is on hand to help. If you can't find him when you arrive, just call out. There is a small kitchen so that drinks and simple food can be prepared. Breakfast is literally a movable feast; in all likelihood the most expansive in East Africa and eaten as late or early as you desire. Throughout the house exquisite Zanzibari antiques sit on polished wood floors; while aged Persian rugs hang next to Makonde figurines. Small but well-tended public gardens opposite are a burst of colour; in the evenings they echo with the sounds of children at play.

Bhagani House Hotel, PO Box 609, **t** (024) 235654, **f** (024) 233030, *baghani@zanzinet.com*, *www.zanzibarhotels.net/baghani*. Next door to the Dhow Palace, it has an old-fashioned charm and good-value rooms.

Narrow Street Annex II, PO Box 3784, **t** (024) 2233006/2232620, **f** (024) 2230052. Another small, clean and characterful choice.

Coco de Mer, PO Box 2363, **t** (024) 2230852, *cocdemer_znz@yahoo.com*. Excellently located off Gizenga Street, this hotel has a fun bar at street level and its ornate window dressing is reminiscent of a Montmartre back-street bar. Inside, it is less engaging, though it has a reasonable standard of accommodation. A decent breakfast is served in a kitsch side room, though the restaurant is not especially recommended.

Cheap

Garden Lodge, PO Box 3413, Kaunda Road, Stone Town, **t** (024) 2233298, *gardenlodge@*

zanlink.com. The best mid-range accommodation in Stone Town; offers amenable service and clean rooms, as well as a breezy rooftop restaurant and bar serving decent continental meals. It's a little out of town too, so offers solace from the dusty streets, and it has a *baraza* for outdoor socializing.

Hotel Kiponda, on Nyumba ya Moto in Kiponda, PO Box 3446, **t** (024) 2233052, **f** (024) 2233020. Originally built to house the overflow of the sultan's harem, but the ancient old house is now a small, quiet and charismatic hotel with comfortable double rooms and a rooftop restaurant. Sadly, both now look in need of a revamp.

Vuga Hotel, located on a crumbly old side street off Vuga Road Roundabout, PO Box 3904, **t** (024) 2233613. The accommodation is clean and comfortable: a number of large self-contained rooms around a small courtyard are furnished with kanga-covered Zanzibari beds. The atmosphere is congenial and welcoming, and a simple breakfast is served each morning in the central area. A couple of the rooms house a number of beds, to suit small groups.

Pyramid Guest House, Kokoni Street, PO Box 254, **t** (024) 2233000, **f** (024) 2230045. A selection of fairly good rooms with old beds, and a rooftop restaurant for breakfast, which is served with verve and style. This family-run guesthouse has a jovial atmosphere and friendly staff – and a tendency to keep the satellite TV in the lobby on constantly. Unfortunately the nearby mosque has a rather brusque and insistent muezzin who favours a distinctly peevish morning call.

Malindi Guest House, PO Box 609, **t** (024) 2230165, **f** (024) 2233030, *riz@africaonline. co.tz*. In the old European quarter of town and popular with travellers, although the location is not ideal, being very close to dubious night-time action around the port. There is a distinctly bohemian air, with only a few self-contained rooms; the dining room is filled with a sociable crowd of travellers.

Manch Lodge, off Vuga Road, PO Box 3060, **t** (024) 2231918. A very well-run and friendly family guesthouse, immaculately looked after, with gardens, a wide book-filled balcony and some self-contained rooms. Manch Lodge excels on provision of breakfast: fruit, pancakes and spicy tea are all included in the price.

St Monica's Hostel, **t** (024) 2230773, a development of the old St Monica's Missionary Hospital for the University Mission to Central Africa established by Livingstone before 1880, it now provides good budget accommodation with an unusually spacious design and situation. Decent self-contained doubles, with cold running water, or much cheaper rooms without. The hostel is also a reliable choice for a good breakfast.

South of Stone Town

Expensive

Mbweni Ruins Hotel, PO Box 2542, **t** (024) 2235478–9, *hotel@mbweni.com*, *www. mbweni.com*, *sales@adventurecamps.co.tz*, *www.adventurecamps.com*. Also with a strong religious history, the Mbweni Ruins is a good choice for naturally beautiful and unusual accommodation outside the town, situated in grounds that encompass the impressive ruins of St Mary's School for Girls', *see* p.352. The hotel has 13 very pleasant whitewashed apartment-style rooms, each with its own private balcony with sea views, some facing the swimming pool. Rooms are all air-conditioned. The pool is almost on the beachfront, with views across the sea at sunset, prettily enclosed on three sides by gardens. The gardens here are worth a visit on their own account, as they have developed over the years into a mature and fragrant botanical garden. The paths also eventually find their way up to a very spacious and breezy outdoor dining room and bar, both laid out beneath a generous *makuti* structure. Boats to Chumbe Island leave from this beach, a private hotel bus trundles to and from town five times each day, and airport and harbour transfers cost $10 per car, for up to four persons. Bed and breakfast, half board or full board.

North of Stone Town

Moderate

Mtoni Marine Centre, PO Box 992, **t** (024) 2250117/2250140, **f** (024) 2250496, *www.*

mtoni.com. 4km north of Stone Town, easily accessible from town by taxi or dala-dala. Mtoni Marine Centre is a great alternative to staying in Stone Town, and offers the nearest beach, and a poolside bar with massage centre. Recommended (*see* p.361).

Maruhubi Beach Villas, PO Box 3088, t (0747) 451188/451177, *maruhubi@zanlink.com*, *www.maruhubibeachvillas.com*. A family atmosphere presides at this newly built shorefront resort. *See* p.361.

Eating Out

Most of Zanzibar's specialities are the fruit of the wide Indian Ocean that surrounds it: lobster, kingfish, prawns, octopus, crabs and squid. At their best, these might be subtly flavoured with local spices or fresh coconut. A range of regional country dishes are also available. Dining has almost come of age in Stone Town in recent years; the choice is wide, and the quality good. Eating out is better here than anywhere on the mainland.

Moderate

Serena Inn, t (024) 2233587/2231015/2233567, *www.serenahotels.com*. Perhaps the finest international restaurant on the beachfront with some good tables overlooking the ocean. The food and service are excellent, and the restaurant provides a reliable environment for expensive, romantic nights out, although not necessarily an authentic Zanzibari experience. The Serena Hotel Group also run an excellent beachside restaurant at Mangapwani, about half an hour from the centre of Stone Town on the west coast. The romantic design of **Mangapwani Seafood Grill and Watersports**, t (024) 2233587, sets diners on a series of small wooden terraces overlooking an idyllic sandy cove (*see* p.361). This is an excellent lunch spot, specializing in sumptuous barbecues. A shuttle bus leaves the Serena Inn at 8.30am and 11.30am each day, returning from Mangapwani at around 4pm. Snorkelling ($5), boat rides, dhow cruises and fishing trips ($40) are all available from the beach here, making it a full day out.

Pagoda Chinese Restaurant, PO Box 976, in Shangani, t (024) 2234688/t (0747) 411168, *pagoda888@hotmail.com*. Extremely popular with expats and attracts a remarkable Chinese contingent to its tables. The atmosphere within is smart and cool, more to do with the air-conditioning than the racy management – a welcoming and friendly family. Meals are of a high quality, and include a number of innovative seafood dishes with Asian spices, ostensibly delicious Chinese dishes with a Zanzibari twist. A very high standard is provided for the price.

La Fenice, close to Africa House Hotel, t (024) 2250368. The newest arrival for fine dining in town, which has opened up a wide, spacious terrace in Shangani, with views of the sea and sunset over the waters. The joy of La Fenice is its range of dishes, all provided in small portions and usually served as a combination – a sort of Italian *tapas*. Two or three dishes is a good meal.

Mercury's, PO Box 3435, Zanzibar, t (024) 2233076, *mercury's@zanlink.com*, at the northern end of the harbour. It is strangely fitting that Freddie Mercury was Zanzibar-born; the rock singer somehow perfectly encapsulates the streak of baroque campery that is a part of island life. This restaurant is dedicated to his memory, but there is little that conjures up the rock and roll firestorm of his life. However, the harbour wall location is fab, and evenings are atmospheric, especially at low tide when a beach pyre is lit, throwing shadows across the water. The food is very good; fresh seafood is served in a variety of ways; with curry, baked or pan-fried, though it is really so good that it is best eaten unadulterated. Lighter meals and other meats are available. The vegetarian selection is, as usual, limited, though the chef has cleverly divined Freddy's preferred lettuce-tomato combo to create 'Freddy's favourite house salad'.

Africa House Hotel, PO Box 3246, Shangani, Stone Town, t (0747) 432340, *theafricahotel@yahoo.com*. Africa House is the phoenix of Stone Town; it has risen from decades of neglect to become the most elegant drinking hole around. The colonials bagged the best place on the beach to build an English Club where they could enjoy a sundowner or three after a hard day being beastly. The terrace bar has been painstakingly renovated, with an Arabic flavour. Turkish leaded light lanterns illuminate potted plant exotica and Willy Wonka-designed *shisha* scattered around the airy, open room. The refit feels a little homespun, but no matter, this is absolutely the best place to be at sunset. There is a frisson of excitement as the sun sinks into the sea; and the click-whirr of a host of cameras. The machismo of the Top Gun-esque 80s soundtrack feeds the sense of occasion. Table service is attentive even when the bar is busy. The cocktail list is of biblical proportions, though they are expensive and rather weak. Top tip: the alcohol content improves dramatically if you keep your beady eye on the concoction as it is put together! Also, the food cannot be recommended, which is a shame. The portions are small, poorly put together and the menu an unimaginative assortment of burgers, luminous chilli sauce and coagulated chips. Perhaps all will improve over time, as the hotel becomes more established.

Monsoon Restaurant, Forodhani Gardens, t (0747) 411362/410410, *www.monsoon.com*. An excellent restaurant with regular music and dance performances. In the traditional African way, diners loll on scattered cushions and thick-weave mikeka mats, eating the delicious Swahili food with fingers and supping spiced chai. *A la carte* and set meals are available. Mellow Swahili curry predominates, with the creamy flavours of coconut and cassava, yam and cumin. The legendary Bi Kidude is rumoured to make the odd guest appearance here; something not to be missed since Bi is said to have invented the hugely popular Swahili *taarab*. In the 1920s she was the first to popularize the élite Arabic *taarab* by singing ditties in Swahili. Due to her advanced years she may not perform much in the future, though others have enthusiastically carried on the tradition. Kilua dance troupes and traditional taarab players also appear regularly.

Spices Rendez-Vous, on Kenyatta Road, t (0747) 410707/413062. Another popular choice for its sumptuous array of small dishes, formerly the Maharaja Restaurant. The menu, as the name suggests, provides a delicious range of spicy Indian-style delicacies, with chapatis and mountains of rice. It also specializes in seafood. The restaurant is dimly lit with a distinguished but relaxed atmosphere and is a good spot for a fun night out, with a 'super top show' of local singing and dancing every Tuesday night.

Sweet Eazy Restaurant and Lounge, Beach Front Forodhani, Stone Town, opposite NBC, t (0747) 416736. This place has single-handedly raised the bar for restaurants in Stone Town, and is reputed to be better than its sister restaurant in Dar es Salaam. The menu is extensive, and offers beautifully cooked African and Thai dishes. A choice of cooking sauces for meat and fish allows you to prepare your own dishes. The bar is a destination in itself, its air-condtioned interior adding to an ambience of studied cool.

Emerson and Green Rooftop Restaurant, t (024) 2230171. Remains an institution for Stone Town dining, despite the fact that it is no longer the only option for such an elevated, breezy aspect. The evening meal here is a set menu, but includes such a wealth of courses as to appeal to all. Most of the small dishes served are seafood or vegetarian, and all are superbly spiced and flavoured. The atmosphere aims to be thoroughly bohemian: diners languish on piles of floor cushions. This evening of taste sensations is usually around $30 per person, but a premium of $5 is added on the occasional weekends when traditional dancers entertain, and most diners fall prey to the lure of the expensive house cocktails.

Kidude, t (0747) 423266, a comfortable and air-conditioned retreat from the crowded thoroughfares leading to its doors, Emerson and Green's latest venture offers a self-assured modern take on African cooking. Recommended. Happy hours 6–7pm and 9.30–10.30pm. There is no danger of losing the place in the labyrinthine alleyways of the old town; an escort will meet guests at their hotels and walk with them to the restaurant (call the number above).

Fisherman Restaurant, opposite Tembo Hotel, t (024) 2233658 (*moderate*). Locally run, but becoming a more expensive choice for a fine fish supper. It remains nonetheless a good choice if you crave spicy prawns, curried crab or lobster Thermidor, which tops the price list at $25. While the prices rise, the décor and overall atmosphere have barely altered over the years. The service can be surly and slow, but the charm of the surroundings adds to the appreciation of good fresh fish.

Mtoni Marine Restaurant, 4km north of the old town, t (024) 2250117/t (0742) 740443. A fine location to enjoy *à la carte* dining in a beachfront restaurant, looking back over the twinkling lights of Stone Town. Just a short taxi ride from the town centre; *see* p.361.

Moderate–Cheap

Archipelago Café and Restaurant, PO Box 4156, t (024) 2235668/t (0747) 462311, seafront end of Kenyatta Road, Shangani. A canteen-style eaterie in a great balcony location, with good-value African and Western dishes. Service is slow; the café opens late and is filled with lively groups of young people drinking excellent spice-infused coffee.

Plaza ETC, opposite La Fenice on the square, near Tippu Tip House, t (0747) 410987. Climb up runaway stairs to the top of this spindly house for great views and decent food. Relaxed and welcoming, the menu is a mixture of Spanish, Italian and Swahili flavours.

Chavda Hotel, t (024) 2232115. Rooftop dining is recommended here, although whether it is really a rooftop could be disputed as a small all-day café occupies the highest level. The restaurant is nevertheless open on two sides, high enough to afford twinkling views over the town, and the menu is fabulously varied and well prepared, with a choice of Indian, Tandoori, Chinese or European dishes, and a focus on local fresh seafood.

Amore Mio, opposite La Fenice, on the seafront, t (024) 2233666, *walz@yahoo.it*. More of a café than a restaurant, this great seaside eaterie serves home-made ice-cream and pizzas, under the shade of waving palm fronds. Well worth a visit in the late afternoon, to watch the sun go down.

Old Fort Restaurant, t (0744) 278737/t (0747) 498135, *oldfort9@hotmail.com*. Pleasantly located under a large baobab at the Old Fort. Has a superb menu of 'local delights', including ugali in different guises, green bananas and Zanzibari spiced grilled fish.

The food is basic but good and cheap; the restaurant has suffered some neglect since it was the Neem Tree Café and is most worth visiting when a dance or music performance is scheduled. The restaurant is relatively cheap, and opens all day. It sits next to an impressive coral rock amphitheatre, which is becoming popular for local drumming and musical events. It looks ancient, but was constructed recently on top of the British-built Ladies' Tennis Club. During the tourist season there is a drumming and traditional dance display every Tues, Thurs and Sat, with a mouthwatering buffet barbecue.

Cheap

Two Tables Restaurant, close to Victoria House, off Vuga Road, t (024) 2231979. A popular choice for a taste of a range of local specialities and non-alcoholic drinks. The husband-and-wife team used to provide just two tables on the verandah, but have recently upgraded to three. Book in advance (put your head around the door early in the day).

Cafés

Chit Chat Restaurant, Kenyatta Street – look out for signs around St Joseph's Cathedral, t (024) 2232548. For good spicy fare, an old favourite with both locals and tourists, which serves good-value, quality dishes in Zanzibari and Goan style. *Open every night except Mon, 6–10*. Ring bell on door.

Camlurs, Kenyatta Road, t (024) 2232548. Another tiny but fun family-run enclave specializing in dishes with a spicy Goan flair.

Radha Food House, near the underground bridge, t (024) 2234808. A simple local choice for spicy vegetarian Indian dishes in a Zanzibari style. Try the mixed *thali*. Look out for signposts beside the bridge.

Dolphin Restaurant, on Kenyatta Road, t (024) 2231987. The large, blue-painted Dolphin serves a variety of seafood and curries.

Every night is a barbecue extravaganza at the **Forodhani Gardens** on the seafront: local stalls lay out an array of seafood and cook by the light of their fires. A cheap feast of delicious fresh **chapatis**, **kebabs** and **burgers** is also available alongside an array of Zanzibari specialities, such as the much-publicized **Zanzibari pizza** or *mantabali* – a strange concoction more like a an omelette than pizza, made with an egg-based dough and containing mince, onion, tomatoes and peppers. A good vegetarian alternative can be made to order. *Katlesi* is a deep-fried ball of potato mash and meat filling. *Kachori* is the same without the meat. **Zanzibar mix** or *miksi* is a tasty hotchpotch of potato, tamarind, cassava strips, salad and pilipili sauce. *Pilipili hoho* – a popular and dangerous hot chilli sauce – is available with all of the above. **Samosas** and **chapatis** and delicious **African doughnuts** called *mandazi* are available from stalls and cafés around the Cinema Afrique.

All through the old town you will come across Zanzibari **coffee barazas**, a sociable convention for outdoor get-togethers.

Entertainment and Nightlife

Bars and Discos

Good night-time drinking spots include the **Dharma Lounge**, opposite the Tembo Hotel, c/o Mercury's, *open Wed–Mon, 5pm till late*. The only air-conditioned bar in town; karaoke night is Thurs. It gets busy most evenings, and at weekends is the pre-club bar for The Garage, upstairs. **Sweet and Eazy**, next door to the One Dive School, is a grown-up drinking bar with measured music and excellent cocktails. In a town that once would not have allowed it, there are now plenty of places to party the night away: the hottest place is still **The Garage**, t (0747) 416374, opposite the Tembo Hotel, *open Wed–Mon, 10pm till late*. Security is a priority; escorts will walk visitors back to hotels, and a taxi service runs all night. During high season plenty of the restaurants catering to the tourist trade lively up into sociable dancing bars. The **Komba Disco** at Bwawani Hotel in Malindi is very popular with local youth (*open weekends only; no smoking*).

Music

Live bands often play to the packed amphitheatre at the **Old Fort** at weekends and on public holidays; bigger gigs are held at the **Amaan Stadium**, a couple of km from the Shangani. Look out for drumming and traditional dance displays at the **Old Fort**

Restaurant. The **Serena** and **Emerson and Green** also host regular performances.

Taarab music is the great Zanzibari tradition, descended from the sultans' preference for the sounds of Arabia. The name derives from the Arabic *tariba*, 'to be moved', and has swayed the hearts of Zanzibaris since the start of the *taraab* clubs, advocated by Sultan Sayyid Hamud bin Muhammad in the early 1900s. **Akhwan Safaa** in the Malindi area was among the first of these, and now the **Culture Music Club** on Vuga Road is regarded with equal respect. A group usually has a large number of musicians playing a combination of instruments including flute, drums, tambourines, violins and the distinctive *kanun*, rather like a harp on a backing board and played flat across the knees. Electric guitars, organs and cellos might be added to the ensemble, but every band also has at least one singer, who will perform long solos.

One of the most revered of the Zanzibari *taarab* artists is **Siti binti Sadi**, the eternally popular ancient singer fondly known as **Bi Kidude**, meaning 'little granny'. She originally started out as a daughter of a slave, and with a wonderful voice and sheer endeavour she accomplished the singing of courtly *taarab*, singing in Arabic in praise of the palace and sultan. She started from the Ng'ambo district of Stone Town, later performing and distributing her recordings throughout East Africa; her popularity was so widespread that she is even attributed with assisting the spread of Swahili language to the regions. Now in her late 80s, Bi Kidude still occasionally performs, accompanied by the highly acclaimed group the **Twinkling Stars**; their recordings enliven numerous Zanzibari weddings.

Zanzibar Flava is the current music craze sweeping the handful of discos of Stone Town. It is a peculiarly Zanzibarian take on the music of the mainland known as Bongo Flava (*see* p.224). Zanzibar Flava is more relaxed even than its Dar counterpart; and can be recognized by its more laidback beat. Well known favourites such as **2 Beery** often play at **Komba Disco**, in Malindi. The **Irie Sound Studio** at PO Box 706, Creek Rd, Stone Town sells a good range of local Bongo Flava as well as having an excellent supply of reggae. CDs are burned from originals while you wait.

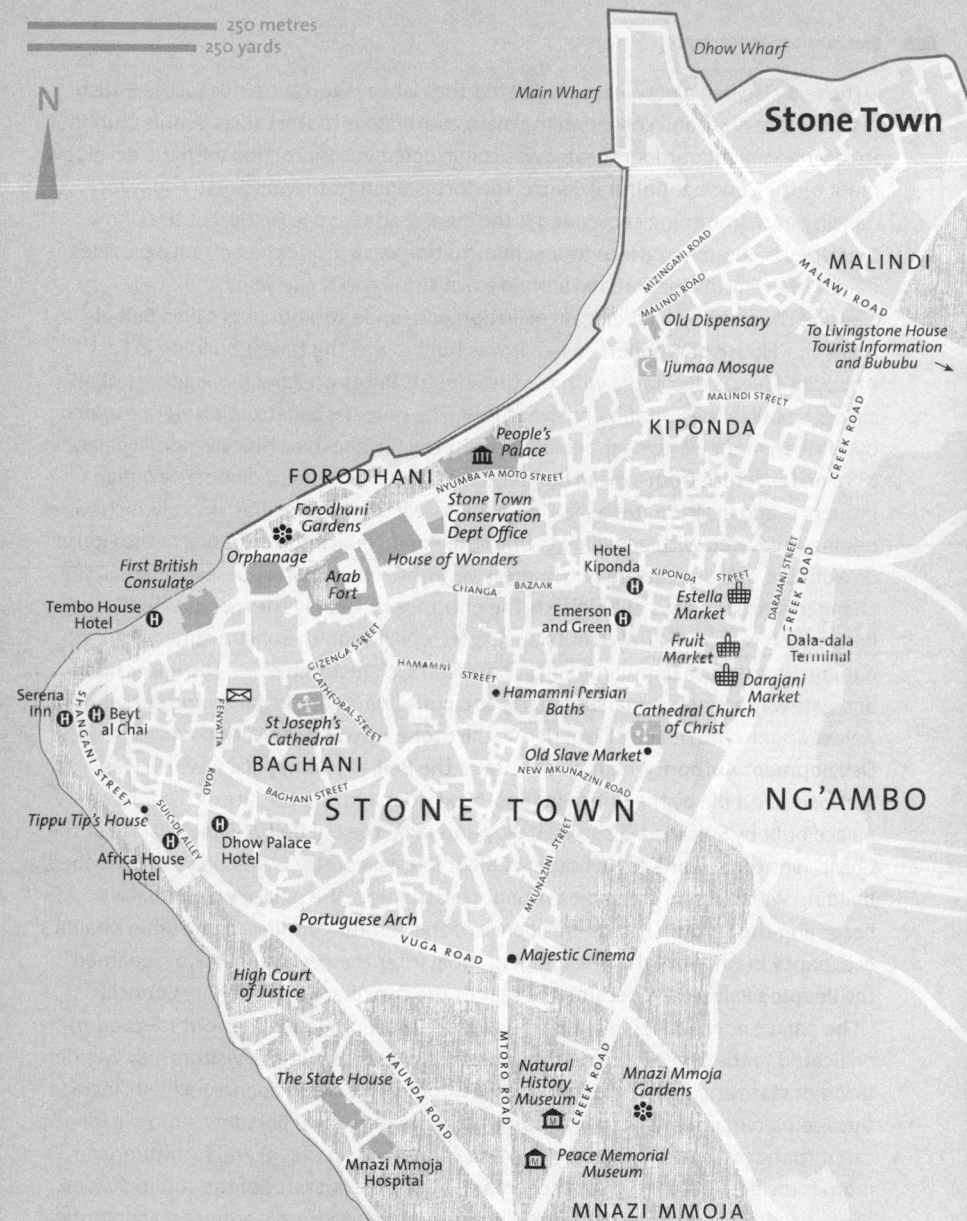

Stone Town

250 metres
250 yards

N

Dhow Wharf

Main Wharf

MALINDI

Old Dispensary

To Livingstone House
Tourist Information
and Bububu →

MIZINGANI ROAD

MALINDI ROAD

MALAWI ROAD

Ijumaa Mosque

MALINDI STREET

KIPONDA

CREEK ROAD

People's
Palace

FORODHANI

NYUMBA YA MOTO STREET

Stone Town
Conservation
Dept Office

Forodhani
Gardens

Orphanage

House of Wonders

Hotel
Kiponda

KIPONDA   STREET

CHANGA   BAZAAR

Estella
Market

First British
Consulate

Arab
Fort

Emerson
and Green

Fruit
Market

Dala-dala
Terminal

Tembo House
Hotel

GIZENGA STREET

CATHEDRAL STREET

HAMAMNI   STREET

Darajani
Market

DARAJANI STREET

CREEK ROAD

Serena
Inn

Beyt
al Chai

FENI ATIA   ROAD

St Joseph's
Cathedral

Hamamni Persian
Baths

Cathedral Church
of Christ

SHANGANI STREET

BAGHANI

BAGHANI STREET

STONE TOWN

NG'AMBO

Old Slave Market

NEW MKUNAZINI ROAD

Tippu Tip's House

SUICIDE ALLEY

Dhow Palace
Hotel

Africa House
Hotel

MKUNAZINI STREET

Portuguese Arch

VUGA ROAD

Majestic Cinema

High Court
of Justice

KAUNDA ROAD

MTORO ROAD

CREEK ROAD

The State House

Natural
History
Museum

Mnazi Mmoja
Gardens

Mnazi Mmoja
Hospital

Peace Memorial
Museum

MNAZI MMOJA

last 24 miles to Mkokotoni as originally planned – perhaps a good thing, as it passed so close to the houses that pedestrians were forced to duck into doorways at its approach. The railway did, however, become the principal means of transport for people, livestock and produce between rural areas and the market. At the end of the First World War, the railway was extended to transport sand and stone from a quarry at Chukwani for the construction of a new port by land reclamation – on the present site. When the work was completed, the railway finally closed in August 1929, and the railway yard in front of the port was landscaped.

The fort also had a new lease of life after the railway workshop closed: the British restored it in 1949, and converted the main courtyard into the Ladies' Tennis Club. In 1994, an excellent outdoor theatre was constructed in conjunction with the development of the **Zanzibar Cultural Centre**. The fort is open from Monday to Friday for dancing and drumming shows, and is the ideal arena for the Festival of the Dhow Countries in July (*see* p.316). A tourist information desk inside the entrance provides details of events at the fort and around town throughout the year.

Beside the fort, the pale, elegant elevation with wide verandahs is called **Beit al-Ajaib**, the '**House of Wonders**'; when it was built it was the tallest building in East Africa, and it was decorated with the first electric lights on Zanzibar, leading British sailors to call it 'the Sultan's Christmas Tree'. The unusual construction was designed by a British marine engineer, and built for Sultan Barghash as his ceremonial palace in 1883, on his return from exile in Bombay; the architecture has a distinctive Indian influence, and incorporates a lift. Fine, elaborately carved Zanzibari doors, which were originally covered with gilded texts from the Koran, guard the entrance to the House of Wonders, and outside are two impressive 16th-century **Portuguese cannons**. Little changed since the days of Barghash, the entrance lacks only the menagerie of caged lions which was once arrayed outside its gates. Although the palace suffered great damage in the 1896 bombardment, it has been well restored since. The lower floor and gateway are now a **market** for arts and crafts, particularly batiks and basketwork.

Next door to the House of Wonders is the **Stone Town Conservation and Development Authority**, built on the site of the **Beit al-Hukm** palace, which was bombed to rubble by the British in 1896. Next door again is the site of the former palace built by Sultan Said between 1827 and 1834: the old **Beit al-Sahel**, 'Palace at the Coast', was the sultan's town house, by all accounts a pretty two-storey whitewashed building with red and green tiles. After its destruction, the palace was rebuilt, becoming the **Sultan's Palace** – residence of the sultans' families from Sultan Khalifa's occupancy in 1911 until the Revolution in 1964. After the Revolution it was renamed the **People's Palace**, and became the seat of the Zanzibar Revolutionary Council.

The palace now houses an interesting **Palace Museum** (*open Tues–Sat 10–6; adm*) dedicated to the opulent reign of the Busaidi dynasty of sultans. Visitors may wander through state and private rooms on three floors of the old residence; exhibits include the ageing parchments of international trade treaties, royal portraits, a room dedicated to the fascinating runaway Princess Salme (*see* pp.324–5) and furniture. One room is divided in two to show the remarkably different tastes of the sultans' wives; the bedrooms display a dubious taste in formica wood-effect wardrobes, apparently favoured by the last sultan, Jamshid bin Abdullah, overthrown during the Revolution.

It is sometimes possible to visit the adjoining **Royal Cemetery**, which contains a half-finished tomb of Sultan Said and his sons Khaled, Barghash and Khalifa. The mausoleum was started by Sultan Majid, but left unfinished after puritans of the Ibadhi sect complained. Continuing northeast along **Mizingani Road**, the wide, flat-faced buildings that look slightly as if they have had too much sun are soon to be given a facelift by a luxury hotel chain. Next door is the **Old Customs House**, with fine carved doors and green frescoed walls.

Further along Mizingani Road towards the port stands the elegantly restored **Ithna'sheri Dispensary**, commissioned by Sir Tharia Thopan, a wealthy accountant to the sultans, as a charitable dispensary for the poor. The foundation stone was laid in 1885, although the honourable Thopan was not alive to see it and his wife continued the work. It faced directly out to sea until the 1920s, when the New Harbour was built on reclaimed land in front of it. Frederick Portage, the consulting engineer who oversaw the final completion of the building in 1894, commended the craftsmen for their fine workmanship on the ornate balconies (inside and out), elaborate stucco work and stained-glass windows, which withstood a harsh test of time during the following years. The dispensary housed a doctor and pharmacy until its occupants were forced to flee during the 1964 Revolution, when the building fell into the hands of a new government that had neither the money nor the incentive to maintain it. Twenty-five years of neglect later, the Old Dispensary was restored by the Aga Khan Trust for Culture with techniques that remained true to the original materials and design. The three-storey structure combines an external appearance of elegance and ornate detail with an internal sense of solidity created from thick wooden floors and balustrades and solid walls surrounding a light, airy courtyard. A small craft market and a good bookshop operate on the ground floor. The upper floors house offices, though, incongruously enough, there is a plan to open a grand aquarium showcasing indigenous marine life, giving local lobsters the best office space in town.

Continuing along the harbour road, past the old European quarter of Malindi, or turning left through the port gates (into a hectic pell-mell of boat ticket salesmen), brings you to the **Dhow Wharf**, where local fishermen dock to unload their catch. It has a particularly lively atmosphere in the mornings, but is always a vibrant place to stop and watch the activity on the large dhows, called *jahazi*, that dock here.

A good 10 minutes' walk along the Malawi Road, past Cinema Afrique, brings you to **Livingstone House**, the base used by the missionary and explorer in 1866 to prepare for his final arduous journey into the interior. The house now contains the offices of the Zanzibar Tourist Corporation, which is not apparently willing to show you around or offer advice, but it is occasionally possible to find someone at the desk and catch a brief glimpse of the cavernous stone interior. If this extra walk for possibly little reward does not appeal, turn right off Malawi Road and head back into the labyrinthine heart of Stone Town.

To the left of the Old Dispensary is **Mtini**, the Big Tree, planted by Sultan Khalifa in 1911. This huge old fig hanging with vines is as much a feature of the old city as the finest architecture: there is always a crowd gathered in its shade, either building or working on repairs to small dhows, or simply sitting, contemplating passers-by. Just behind the tree is the Friday or **Malindi Ijumaa Mosque**. It is an impressively modern construction: although a mosque was originally built on this site by Muharmi Arabs, and enlarged by the Mwinyi Mkuu in 1839, it was fully renovated in 1994 in modern arabesque style. There are around **48 mosques** within the boundaries of Stone Town, but many are unostentatious and practically indistinguishable from nearby buildings.

From the Friday Mosque keep heading straight, taking a left-hand kink but not actually turning left, into Mchangani Street and the blaze of colour that is the

Cloth with Attitude: Kangas

No visitor to mainland Tanzania or Zanzibar Island could fail to notice that women everywhere are swathed in seemingly infinite variations and combinations of coloured 'kangas' – traditional brightly printed, patterned cotton wraps. Kangas have become the signature and expression of East Africa, bringing colour and life to an already vivid land. Every Tanzanian and Zanzibari woman possesses at least one, which most are in the habit of wearing over their ordinary clothes outside. During the 1970s, kanga-wearing became a national requirement when laws were passed to dissuade all people from following the Western example of wearing their skirts too short or their trousers too tight – an era in which the police had authority and instruction to insert a bottle in a man's trousers to prove they were baggy enough.

Kangas are everywhere, and are highly and fondly regarded. Pairs of kangas are traditionally exchanged as gifts, often as the first wrap for a newborn child, as presents between husbands and their wives and from children to their mothers, or a pair might be shared between a couple of friends, as they always come in twos. In fact kangas have become a currency for relationships, often requested as an important part of a dowry: not giving enough kangas to your wife is grounds for divorce.

It is hard to imagine East Africa before kangas, but they are a relatively recent phenomenon that has developed since the middle of the 19th century. It is said that they originated from cloth known as *leso*, which had been brought to Africa by the Portuguese. Leso was printed with square designs intended to be cut into individual squares, but Zanzibari women became the trailblazers for a new trend, sewing two lengths of cloth with three squares of pattern across; in a further development the cloth was cut and the designs varied by sewing them together in different patterns. Soon the spirit of commercial enterprise prevailed, and shopkeepers began to order lengths of cloth in the appropriate size, already printed with distinctive designs.

From the 1850s to the 1950s kangas were imported from India, Europe and the Far East, and generally had a border and a pattern of white spots on a dark background. It is said that this is what earned them the name of 'kanga', after the Swahili word for guinea fowl – the handsomely white-speckled birds of the bush.

Kangas have developed into an intricate form of communication themselves, and are often bought and worn on account of their endless different messages. These have become popular, developing since the turn of the 20th century, when they were first printed with Swahili sayings or slogans written in Arabic script. Now they are more commonly written in the Roman alphabet. New designs, with different sayings, expressions and aphorisms continue to roll off the printing presses, communicating a range of meanings that reflect the social and political identity of the nation.

Kanga Bazaars. If you do turn left from here you will enter into the hubbub of **Darajani Market**, which assails the senses with a profusion of colour, chatter and the wafting scent of spices from the stalls along the roadside. Fruit and vegetables are piled in precarious pyramids; carts sell sugar cane or prickly bunches of bright red rambutan. Under the covered market on the eastern side a wide assortment of sea creatures is spread on huge slabs of stone, and meat is carved from hanging

This unusual form of 'outerwear' has evolved into an acutely revealing insight into the popular Swahili psyche as the prints on an ever-increasing variety of kangas have developed into an amusing collection of slogans and instructions, often expressed in metaphors. Kanga messages and meanings are often carefully chosen in order to convey a distinct opinion or argument. These are often worn around the family home, where they might be directed at co-wives or mothers-in-law, with such classic messages across your *wowo kubwa* (big buttocks) as 'You can say and do what you like, I have him in my bed!' Often, though, the meaning is less direct, hidden in more obscure sayings, such as *Pilipili iko mtini yakuwashia nini?*, 'How can a chilli pepper on its plant make you hot?' – meaning how can you be affected by things that don't concern you? Husbands or wives who show an inclination to stray might be given the instruction *Usiache mbachao kwa msala upitao*, which translates as 'Don't abandon your old rug for a passing mat'. Alternatively, *Usinione nasinzia uyasemayo nayasikia* means 'You see me dozing but I hear whatever you say', implying that the wearer is well aware of things going on behind her back.

Often kanga sayings are moralistic or instructive. They can be about the nature of work, such as *Tamu ya mua kifundo* meaning 'A sugar cane is sweetest at the joint' – telling how the things that are hardest to attain are often the most worthwhile. Many kangas emphasise the necessity of hard work in order to achieve, such as *Mcheza kwao hutunzwa. Ukiona vyaelea vimeundwa*, meaning, 'When you see vessels afloat, somebody made them'. Concerning destiny, *Usisafirie nyota ya mwenzio* warns 'Don't set sail using somebody else's star', meaning that each person must find their own route to success. A kanga might try to alleviate jealousy: *Mso hili ana lile* – 'A person missing this has that', or no one has it all!

Since the 1950s cloths have been printed with all manner of coloured abstract patterns, with familiar and homely themes showing fruit, crops, chickens, or images of famous national attractions such as mountains, monuments and wildlife. Particularly in Tanzania, kangas have been used as a vehicle for political slogans, rallying support for government issues and policies and strengthening the national identity. In the month following the death of President Julius Nyerere in 1999 a mass of new prints showing the face, head and dates of the first president appeared in every tiny duka and village, alongside others commemorating new President Mkapa.

Kanga sayings are frequently ambiguous or obscure in their meanings, and anyone having trouble translating can often ask a number of Swahili speakers and find themselves with just as many interpretations. With this in mind, kanga wearers should choose their cloth with care, and then be sure to choose a good position in which to wear their motto!

carcasses. Although it was once the duty of the men to shop while their wives and daughters kept out of sight, it is now more common to see women picking their way among the stalls and buying food for the table. The fresh fruit and vegetables are both delicious and cheap, but the old adage is a good one: boil it, peel it or forget it – in this case peeling is probably your best option; there are knife stalls nearby selling very cheap knives.

The market faces onto the **Creek Road**, a main road into and out of town and a central point for transport. The dala-dala terminal is opposite the market. Turn right from the market onto Creek Road and walk a short distance south to the wide **New Mkunazini Road** on the right-hand side, which leads back into town. A short distance down is another major right-hand turn, leading to the Anglican **Cathedral Church of Christ**. The cathedral, built on the site of the last open slave markets in the world, is a mixture of Gothic and Arabic styles. Bishop Steer (1874–84), the first man to translate the Bible into Swahili, supervised its construction. A mission was established as a result of Steer's pleas to Oxford University, and a speech by Dr David Livingstone at Cambridge University describing his personal experience of the horrors of the slave trade. The Universities Mission in Central Africa (UMCA) united the efforts of Britain's four most important universities at that time. The first service took place on Christmas Day 1877, four years after the slave market was finally closed by a reluctant Sultan Barghash and a year before the cathedral was finished.

The **slave chambers** still exist below. A guide from the church can take you down and regale you with tales of the injustices suffered, although the dimensions of the cells speak for themselves. A **red circle** in the floor before the altar marks the spot where slaves were tied to a post and whipped. All around are reminders of those who dedicated their lives to ending the abominable trade: a central **crucifix** is made from the tree beneath which Dr Livingstone's heart was buried in Zambia and a stained-glass window is dedicated to his memory; another **stained-glass window**, behind the font, remembers those men who died on the Indian Ocean while fighting the slave trade; **plaques** on the walls remember missionaries and servicemen who died in action. The altar is decorated with **mosaics** by Miss Caroline Thackeray, who reigned as head teacher at **St Mary's School for Girls** for more than 25 years. Established in 1871 by the Universities Mission to Central Africa, the school was dedicated to educating freed girl slaves, or the daughters of freed slaves, and children of the mission workers, and was originally built around an old Arab merchant house that still stands at the centre of the ruins. A village of freed slaves grew up around the school, and the mission grew to cover 60 hectares of land tended by the new settlement. The girls at the school were divided according to their intelligence and willingness to learn, with most being trained in reading, writing, history and Bible studies so that they could go on to become mission teachers on the mainland. Others were taught more mundane but equally necessary skills in cooking, cleaning and growing and tending crops. An impressive two-storey chapel was later built close to the main school, with finely wrought stone arches designed to an Islamic trifoliate finish. The ruins of the old school and its chapel can still be seen in the extensive grounds of Mbweni Ruins Hotel (*see* 'Where to Stay', p.342), surrounded by a fine botanical garden.

Continue west along Mkunazini Road towards the heart of Stone Town; at its end turn right onto Katificheni Street and take the first right again onto Hamamni Street, to find the **Hamamni Persian Baths** on the right-hand side. The large and elaborate Persian-style steam baths were donated to the public by the royal bathing enthusiast Sultan Barghash, and built by Hadj Gulamhussein in the 1880s. They have not been in use since the 1920s, but have been restored to allow visitors today to gain a fair impression of how they must have been when they held water and functioned. Numerous rooms surround a central fountain courtyard, with areas for steam baths, plunge pools, shaving and ablutions. To visit, look for the caretaker, Hakim Wambi, in the building opposite. He will give you a guided tour and extract an entrance fee.

From the Hamamni or 'Place of the Baths', it is a short distance to the Catholic **St Joseph's Cathedral**, on Cathedral Street (which can be reached by turning left, left and right, right). The cathedral was completed in 1906, built by French missionaries and designed in the Romanesque style by the same architect who designed the basilica of Marseilles. Many of the first Christian converts were freed slaves; a very mixed Catholic community now uses the cathedral regularly for Mass. Occasionally the building is open to see the badly restored murals and the cracked stained glass inside. There is a concerted effort under way to restore the building.

Turning left from this cathedral brings you to the crossing of **Gizenga Street**, a popular shopping street packed with stalls and artisans proffering their wares. If you can resist the urge to shop (the carpenters are very good just here), and continue instead along **Cathedral Street**, the road ends in an area at the back of the Arab Fort that was once the fruit and vegetable market, and is the site of the last public execution (beheading by sword), in 1889. Heading left and left again from the cathedral, or right and right again, should bring you on to **Kenyatta Road**, one of the main streets running through this part of Stone Town and a reliable point of reference. Following Kenyatta Road to the left brings you into **Shangani Street**.

Tucked between Shangani Street and the delightfully named **Suicide Alley** are the large and dusty remains of the **Africa House Hotel** (*see* p.340), the English Club from 1888 to Independence, and one point in the old town where sundowners on the seaside verandah have become something of an institution. It is without doubt the best spot to watch the sun fall through the sky and into the sea, and has recently been restored to something of its former glory. Climb the marble stairs – inlaid with plundered stone from the sultan's palace – to reach the first-floor terrace bar. Original photographs and prints of Zanzibari life adorning the walls lend the climb the spirit of a visit to a museum. The original library is on the ground floor and worth a visit; dusty tomes attest to the worthy interests of English colonials. In a nice touch, Internet access is now possible in the library.

The house where the infamous Arab slave trader known as 'Tippu Tip' (*see* box, p.354) enjoyed his old age in wealth and comfort can also be seen in Shangani Street, behind the dilapidated Africa House Hotel. **Tippu Tip's House** has now been converted into flats and is a private residence.

Emerging from the back of Tippu Tip's house brings you back onto Shangani Street and from there onto Kelele Square, which means 'noise' in Swahili on account of the incessant barking of the dogs belonging to the European residents. This is the location of the Serena Inn, which has been redesigned and redeveloped on the site of the old **Extelcoms Building** and the next door **Chinese Doctor's House**. The hotel still houses some of the ancient telephone equipment in the reception area. The **Beyt al Chai**, the Stone Town Inn, is found here in a refurbished townhouse that served formerly as the home of a wealthy trader and as a tea house.

Tippu Tip

The most notorious of all slave-traders, Hamed bin Mohammed el Murjebi was born in 1840 to a Muscat Arab merchant, although he also had African blood and it is said that his grandmother was a slave. This fearsome and powerful merchant warlord was widely known as **Tippu Tip** or Tippoo Tib, a nickname said in one story to have come from the sound of his muskets firing. In his autobiography he says, apparently with some pride, 'the name Tip Tip had been given me by the locals who said this man's guns went "tiptip" in a manner too terrible to listen to.' Another story says it refers to his nervous tic of blinking his eyes very rapidly – a local bird with distinctive blinking eyes is, apparently, also known locally as tippu tib.

Tippu Tip, Chief Mirambo and Mutesa were the three most powerful potentates of interior during the 19th century, ruling vast tracts of land by force and fear. Tippu Tip took control of the previously uncharted forest west of Lake Tanganyika, and developed his bush 'empire' over 25,000 square kilometres with the fire power of his muskets. He is said to have transformed the currency of the interior from barter to cash: initially exchange, were made in cowry beads and then in Maria Theresa dollars.

Although nominally subject to the sultan, to whom he would bow whenever he returned to the island on which his fortune was accumulating, Tippu Tip was an independent ruler of land that few others could navigate. The sultan was happy that trade from the interior was routed through Zanzibar, whoever controlled it, and even those who deplored the nature of the slave-trader's wealth were forced to turn to him for assistance. Most famously, David Livingstone, the British missionary and explorer of the African interior, found that his survival depended on the assistance of the slave merchants whose trade he abominated. Journalist Henry Morton Stanley enlisted the help of Tippu Tip when he sought to follow Livingstone, and again later when he carried out a near-fatal expedition with King Leopold of Brussels to rescue and resupply Emin Pasha in 1867.

Explorers and missionaries provided the old warrior with a means to a pension in his latter years, exchanging a free rein to exploit the interior's natural resources for Tippu Tip's promise to abstain from capturing slaves in the Free State established by the Belgians. Tippu Tip complained bitterly, however, about Stanley's unfulfilled promises of payment when he returned to Europe at the end of his trans-African trip – with which the old slave-driver had helped him considerably. 'When he gets to Europe he will send my money. Yet when he arrived, not even greetings did he send. Of my money he gave me only 3,000 of the 7,000 dollars he had promised me.'

Turning back on to Shangani Street, towards the Forodhani Gardens, on the corner after the Tembo House Hotel you can still see the original building of the first **British Consulate**, now covered with advertising boards and housing an inglorious Internet centre. To your right, over and around the bridge and tunnel, is the sad site of the **Zanzibar Orphanage**. Continuing southeast along Kenyatta Road and then Kaunda Road, parallel to the waterfront, brings you to the **Peace Memorial Museum**, opposite the park called **Mnazi Mmoja** ('One Coconut Tree' – although there are lots), on Creek Road. The museum building is designed in an impressive, symmetrical classical-cum-

Arabic style, and was built in 1925 by the British architect John Sinclair. He had quite a monopoly on major building design in this part of town; the long road out to the museum also passes his other works along the way. One is the **British Residency**, just past the Portuguese Arch at Vuga Roundabout and up Kaunda Road past the **High Court of Justice**, also designed by Sinclair. The museum houses an eclectic collection of memorabilia from all eras of Zanzibari history: an interesting although dusty and dishevelled array of items related to slave-traders and sultans, the Mwinyi Mkuu and early European explorers and missionaries – including Livingstone's old medicine chest. There is also a translation of the *Periplus of the Erythraean Sea* – the famous 1st century AD traders' guide – and a number of ancient black and white photographs showing Zanzibar during the colonial period – mainly the damage done by the British to the palace complex in 1896. Opposite the Peace Memorial Museum is the **Zanzibari Natural History Museum**, home to a dusty collection of stuffed birds and animals – apparently including the bones of a dodo. *Both museums open daily 9–6; joint adm.*

Day Trips and Excursions from Stone Town

Stone Town is the place to plan and arrange all excursions around the island. There are a number of trips to visit ruins, beaches, forests or spice plantations; these may be planned as a day out or an afternoon, or included en route to the coast. Do not be too quick to dismiss the following options if the concept of a planned excursion rings alarm bells of horror. With the exception of Chunguu or Prison Island and some dolphin tours, they can be a low-key arrangement involving just you and a guide with transport. The choice between an established tour operator and a ubiquitous 'tour tout' – without a valid ID card – is that the latter invariably fails to inform you of extra prices that will be incurred as entrance fees, or the fact that you are joining a group of twenty students in a dangerously overloaded vessel. Also, if so-and-so's brother's friend has a taxi, there is no guarantee that it can make it there and back without breaking down for three hours on the way. At least the tour operators tend to have a wheel jack, spare tyre and some means of fixing it.

The most usual trips offered by tour operators, and seemingly by every single boy in the streets, include the following. Prices range from $10 to $100, and are per person, based on two people travelling; they decrease for a group and become slightly ridiculous for a single person, who may consider joining with others.

City Tour

Usually a half-day walking tour with a bilingual guide, which can be arranged to include a guided tour of the Anglican Cathedral and slave chambers. It is worth noting that Zanzibar currently does not include history in its educational syllabus; so, while there are many willing guides to show you around, if you are interested in the real history of the place, it may be better to hire a guide from a reputable tour operator. **Omar Musso**, at the shop **Sasik** on Gizenga Street, is a recommended guide, **t** (0747) 418185. If you still have time on your hands in Stone Town, it is also possible to arrange excellent Swahili cooking lessons at the Arab Fort ($15–20).

Spice Farms Tour

Usually takes about half a day. Following your nose and tasting a variety of brightly coloured fruit is a fun way to spend a morning. It proves an invigorating educational experience as you see how a multitude of different pods, blossoms and barks turn into the aromatic coloured powders that may be more familiar in the kitchen at home, and taste hundreds of new and familiar fruits (around 57 varieties are grown in all!). The 'lipstick pod' is used both as the colouring for tandoori meals and as a vibrant lip-colour. The tour can be combined with a slap-up spicy lunch cooked and prepared on a farm, and can also include a visit to the Persian baths at Kidichi or a stop at Mangapwani Beach en route. All the tour operators will organize trips to spice farms; usually each has a deal with a different farm. Many tours include other activities along the way. Lunch stops are becoming more popular. The well-known individual tour leader **Mr Mitu** is highly recommended for group trips, organizing a full-day tour including lunch and a trip to the beach for a very reasonable price. His son, who grew up on a spice farm, has joined the operation and is an excellent guide. His offices are signposted just behind Malawi Road, near the old Cinema Afrique. Tours cost $10–30, depending on the size of the group. **Island Discoveries** guide similar tours at the same price, and use local dala-dala transport for an authentic experience. Both tours often stop at Mangapwani, to visit the slave caves and beach.

Jozani Forest Tour

For anyone missing the safari action, or just seeking a bit of natural seclusion, Jozani Forest is an unusual little nature reserve halfway between Stone Town and the southeast coast. The Jozani Forest Reserve has various nature trails to explore through different natural habitats that include a mangrove boardwalk, a botanical nature trail and a monkey-sighting site. Each of these provide opportunities to catch a glimpse of a number of interesting rare species, such as the rare and handsome **red colobus monkey** (*Piliocolobus kirkii*) endemic to Zanzibar. These fiery-coloured primates sport a dashing white mane and seem unfazed by passing tourists. Despite instructions to tourists not to get too close for fear of passing on infections, the monkeys are strangely keen to demonstrate extraordinary jumping skills at very close proximity. Back in the 1970s conservationists suggested issuing a series of promotional stamps featuring the island's exotic flora and fauna. At this time the monkeys were a great deal more reticent, and one had to be temporarily caught in order for a photographer to take a shot. Duly caged, the monkey blinked bemusedly while a Polaroid portrait was snapped. A long, agile arm reached out and a paw grabbed the photo, the marks of which could clearly be discerned on the eventual image on the stamp.

The mangrove boardwalk may provide a sighting of the rare **Zanzibari coconut crab** (*Birgus latro*), which is also found on Chumbe Island. Thought to have descended from a hermit crab, this lumbering old crustacean grows up to half a metre long, and can weigh 2.5–3kg. It eats coconuts and climbs trees, giving rise to the old belief that it could scale a palm to claw coconuts down to eat. Its nasty nickname is the 'robber crab', due to its ingenious ability to pilfer food. The crabs have been known to slice through tin cans, pots and pans to get to the food inside. The dry, seasonal woodlands are also inhabited by the less rare but perhaps more endearing **Zanzibari bushbaby** (*Galagoides zanzibaricus*). This small, long-tailed woolly primate has a distinctive 'whoop whoop!' call, but its nocturnal habits make daytime sightings rare. **Sykes monkeys**, **small buck** and **bushpigs** are often seen too in the forest.

All walks should be accompanied by a guide; the $8 entry fee allows visitors to cover all walks at their leisure. Tours cost around $15 from town, $15 entrance, or about $35 if combined with a full day trip to the east coast.

Mangapwani Slave Caves Tour

A half-day tour ($15) to Mangapwani Slave Caves takes a scenic route about 11km north of Stone Town up the coast road to a natural cave that may or may not have been used for holding slaves, and a man-made chamber that definitely was. The sites are close to a good beach overlooked by the Aga Khan's new restaurant, which provides a good seafood and meat grill for $25 per person in an idyllic setting – a welcome distraction from the grisly past of the place.

Tour operators Monarch **t** (024) 2238220, *monarch@zanlink.com*, run tours to the caves, and you can also get there using the shuttle bus from the Serena Inn in Stone Town (see p 339) and the Serena Restaurant and watersports facility at Mangapwani. A full day tour to the north coast ($35) can include a spice tour or a stop at Mangapwani Slave Caves. Some tour operators include lunch in the price.

Island-hopping around Stone Town

The closest island to Stone Town is called **Changuu**, Swahili for 'tortoise', in reference to its unusual residents. The island is also known as **Prison Island**, and is said to have been owned by a wealthy Arab, who used it to hold slaves. A prison proper was built on the island by General Lloyd Matthews, Welsh commander of the British-influenced Sultan's Army, in 1893. Matthews spent much of his time in Zanzibar apprehending ruffian slave smugglers and insurrectionists, but the prison was never used. Instead it became a quarantine station for immigrants entering coastal East Africa. Frangipani trees were planted for the 'inmates' to enjoy a fragrant night-time stroll.

A 30-minute boat ride from Stone Town port now brings you to this small, pretty island surrounded by coral reefs and clear sea – making it a popular spot for **snorkelling**. Snorkels can be hired beforehand or on the island for T.shs 1,000 a day. Most swimmers set off from a sandbank beach facing the town that gets smaller and smaller as the tide comes in and more excursion boats stop to moor alongside it.

The island itself is picturesque, and provides a rare opportunity to sunbathe. A path circumnavigates it, taking around 15 minutes to walk. Along the way it passes large pits in the ground, which were quarries for the coral rag that was used to build some of the original stone houses in Stone Town and Dar es Salaam.

Changuu's main attraction, however, is its resident population of **giant tortoises**, four of which were brought to the island from Aldabra in the Seychelles in 1919 as a gift to the British Regent. They used to roam the island freely, and thrived; in 1956 a visiting sailor claimed to have seen 200 animals. However, their population declined

Getting There

Transfers to Changuu, Chapwani and Chumbe Islands are best arranged through the ZTC, the individual lodges listed below or Stone Town tour operators.

Tourist Information

The **Zanzibar Tourist Corporation** (ZTC) has a small office that you have to visit on arrival on **Changuu Island** to pay an entrance fee of $5, or T.shs 3,000.

Where to Stay and Eat

Chapwani Island

Chapwani Private Island, PO Box 3248, t (0747) 433102/t (0744) 858111 *chapwani@zitec.org*, *www.chapwaniisland.com*, also *www.house ofwonders.com* (*expensive*). Twenty bunga- lows on Chapwani Island, accessible from Fuji Beach near Salme's Garden. The local contact for the island is not the easiest person to communicate with, and a trip to the island is worth the bother only in the unlikely event that you don't have time to travel to the coastlines of the main island. It

is possible to visit the lodge as a day trip; simply charter one of the many trip boats from the harbour. Expect to pay $10 per person for the ride. The island management levy a $5 charge to deter the hordes, waived if visitors eat at the restaurant; which is recommended despite the relative expense, since the chef is formerly of the Emerson and Green restaurant.

Chumbe Island

Chumbe Island Coral Park and Lodge, PO Box 3203, t/f (024) 2231040/t (0747) 413582, *chumbe@zitec.org*, *chumbe.island@raha.com*, *www.chumbeisland.com* (*expensive*). Seven two-storey beach *bandas* are built from coconut leaf thatch on bamboo and mangrove poles, with a smooth plaster base in the lower- level living area decorated with mosaics and coloured designs. The overall effect gives a delightfully virtuous sensation of non-impact barefoot luxury, which can be enjoyed from the perspective of hammock or carved wooden sofa until the gong sounds for a fine supper of deliciously prepared Arab, Indian and African dishes. Full-board accommodation is in calming eco-*bandas* and the price includes transfers, soft drinks, snorkelling and all guides through the reef and forest.

following a trend for visitors to steal the pocket-sized babies; they are now contained within a vast pen. Visitors can climb inside and feed these prehistoric-looking reptiles with oranges, mango peel and greenery – for which they are always grateful. Riding the tortoises, though they can withstand the weight, is not allowed since it causes them distress. There is a plan to free the massive creatures again, while continuing to protect the now thriving young; in a recent three-month period, 16 new babies were born. In the meantime, there is little hope of casually pocketing a fully grown male, as their body weight is several tonnes.

A short distance further north, the less-visited **Chapwani (Grave) Island** is the site of an old Christian naval cemetery dating from 1879, marking the lives lost in the suppression of slavery. During the Kusi monsoon, the winds carried the dhows away from Zanzibar laden with ivory, mangrove poles and slaves. British sailing cutters gave chase to those dhows suspected of harbouring slaves. But the work was perilous; stokers laboured in boiler rooms at temperatures of over 100 degrees, and the men suffered from disease and died while fighting the dhow crews. The last burial in the Chapwani cemetery was in 1905, after which time another site nearer Stone Town was used. The island also has a tiny stand of war graves commemorating the lives lost after the routing of the HMS *Pegasus*. The ship was at anchor off Shangani point when it was attacked by the German cruiser SMS *Konigsberg* on 20 September 1914, during the opening days of the First World War. Day-trippers are allowed to visit the graves, and the island, but they must either pay a $5 fee or eat a meal in the lodge restaurant (*see* box, left). The restaurant is pleasant and it is possible to spy the odd dik dik skittering through the tangled undergrowth.

Chumbe Island Coral Reef is the first **marine sanctuary** created in Zanzibar. It's a colourful little island surrounded by a shallow reef alive with 90 per cent of all the coral species ever recorded in East Africa – estimated to be around 200 species. It is said to be one of the most spectacular coral gardens anywhere in the world. The fronds and shadows of this wide coral garden are home to more than 350 species of fish, sea turtles and lobsters. A small coral rag island rises up at the centre with a host of other living creatures in its protective embrace. Most of the island is forested, and knitted with curious twisting **nature trails** that lead past the haunts of rare and endangered coconut crabs and a host of doves, rare roseate terns and other birds. The paths emerge on to prickly coral cliffs with clear and peaceful views over the ocean. Chumbe Island is open all year round, and despite its proximity to Zanzibar Island it receives significantly less rainfall. Migrating humpback whales pass westwards in October–November, and dolphins occasionally pass throughout the year.

There are five rangers on the island, all former fishermen who once would have contributed to the demise of marine life that they now work to protect and teach their old colleagues to preserve. Education was the original purpose of the marine park when it was established, through the grit and determination of a Dr Sybille Riedmiller, in 1991, for the purpose of educating local children and fishermen. It has only since become an **eco-resort** as a means of preserving the integrity of her lease and ensuring that the park, which is the first privately managed marine park in the world, can afford to pay for its education programmes. So while schoolchildren still make day trips to the island, and young Muslim girls are provided a rare opportunity to swim, the island has been transformed to cater to tourists, with stress-free snorkelling using innovative teaching aids, such as the impressively named 'Floating Information Module' – a wide inflatable ring with illustrated colour plates for under-water identification.

In the centre a historic old gas-powered **lighthouse** built by the British in 1904 still stands tall, commanding superb views of the island and Zanzibar Town if you can endure the precarious climb to the top. Beside the visitors' centre a 100-year-old **mosque** in a state of quiet dilapidation is still used by the staff and rangers for prayers. Lovingly tended and beautifully designed, the **eco-lodge** is centred around a dining room and education centre created from a lofty *makuti* thatch, yet strangely reminiscent of the Sydney Opera House – just a bit smaller. This area was built on the foundations of the house of the old lightkeeper, an old Zanzibari who tended the lighthouse for 30 years and has now retired to live with his family. Two-storey beach bandas for guests all adhere to the ecologically friendly premise. Each uses only rain-water stored in huge tanks beneath the floor, and all water waste is channelled into filter systems and recycled. Composting toilets ensure that no sewage is directed into the sea, and electricity and hot water are solar-powered. The island, lodge and marine park has won accolades and awards for its approach to tourism, and may well become a blueprint for future developments.

Chumbe Island Coral Park can be visited as a day trip from Zanzibar Island, $70 inclusive of transfers and lunch, bookable through **Fisherman Tours** and other local tour operators, and through **Mbweni Ruins Hotel**, from where the boat leaves; it is worth staying overnight if at all possible. Call t (024) 2231040/t (0747) 413232/t (0744) 485659. The price is inclusive of boat transport, lunch, use of bungalow for showering, non-alcoholic drinks, boat trips to reef, guidance on the reef and forest trails, use of snorkelling and tuition. Departures 10am from Mbweni Ruins Hotel, near the airport; returns 5.15–5.30pm. Advance booking necessary; minimum 24hrs in advance.

West Coast: Stone Town to the North of the Island

The west coast north of Stone Town is the main area for industrial and fuel depots, military bases and government buildings: it is advisable not to take photographs or wander too close to any of the properties. But the coast road also wends its way past the ruins of historic palaces and some surprisingly good beaches, interesting caverns and caves. The best parts of the coast are all accessible as day trips from Stone Town.

Sultan Said, the Omani Sultan who transferred his capital to Zanzibar in the 1820s, and his sons appreciated the joys of a fine country residence in easy reach of Stone Town, and chose to build palaces beside the sea on this northern stretch of coast. About 3km along the coast road you reach the ruins of **Maruhubi Palace** on the left-hand side. Sultan Barghash built the palace in 1882 to contain his extensive harem, reputed to consist of 99 concubines and one true wife. The sultan was not renowned for his kind heart, and there are many stories about this palace and its grounds, in which it is said he spilt the blood of any offending concubine or wife. Stories tell how the autocratic sultan would pick six concubines at a time, who would all risk death if he was not satisfied by their performance, to be replaced in order to keep the harem at the statutory figure of 99. Concubines were also generously put at the disposal of any passing Arab guests, but would then have to be killed so that they would not bear the fruit of other Arab tribes.

The palace burned down in 1899: the ornate wooden verandahs and craft work that once surrounded it were destroyed, leaving only the supporting stone pillars standing. The Peace Memorial Museum in Stone Town has a photograph of the intact palace at the end of the 19th century; this same photograph is published in *Historical Zanzibar, Romance of the Ages*, a book of photographs from the Zanzibar Archives. Since its demise the surviving marble has been stolen from the once fine baths, but both the sultans' baths and all the women's cubicles can still be explored. The remaining stone structure gives an eerie impression of what once was; the extensive mango and coconut palm groves and round ponds give a sense of the environment in which the concubines and eunuchs once whiled away their days.

A little further north is the less well-preserved ruin of **Mtoni Palace**, built between 1828 and 1834 for Sultan Said, and said to be his favourite residence. This palace had

Getting There

The **502 dala-dala** goes frequently to
Bububu, and will stop at any point along the
way. Otherwise **taxi**, **tour operator**, **bicycle** or
motorbike, all of which can be arranged in
Stone Town, are the best options.

Where to Stay and Eat

Salme's Garden, accessible from Fuji Beach, for
details and bookings contact the House of
Wonders in Stone Town, **t** (024) 2250050/
t (0747) 429189/**t** (0742) 750557, *info@
houseofwonders.com* (*expensive*). One of the
most unusual places to stay on this stretch
of coast is the romantic old palace of
Princess Salme, tucked away down a bumpy
earth track with views over a scenic stretch
of rocky fishing beach. It's a five-bedroom
house with wonderful Zanzibari beds and a
quirky nostalgic air, available for rent in its
entirety or shared with others. It has a
private atmosphere, with a rambling,
unkempt garden that gives a sense of a true
ancient hideaway, and is flanked by a very
antique-looking mosque. Mainly recommended for young groups of friends or
travellers who have backpacking experience.
The communal kitchen is clean, although
dimly lit, and the housekeepers can assist in
preparing meals. Private transport is really
required to make the most of the location.

Mtoni Marine Centre, PO Box 992, **t** (024)
2250117/2250140/**t** (0741) 323226/**t** (0747)
430117, **f** (024) 2250496, *mtoni@zanzibar.cc*,
www.mtoni.com (*moderate*). Situated in
luxuriant gardens on a peaceful bay just a
few kilometres north of Stone Town, with
views back on the old town. Easily accessible
from town by taxi or dala-dala, it is a great
retreat from Stone Town, and the nearest
place for sunbathing and swimming. The
swimming pool and beach are open to all
comers, though visitors should be aware
that they are expected to spend at least
some money in the bar or restaurant.
Damtu, a local woman, has set up a lovely
massage, aromatherapy and braiding centre
on the beach that offers treatments using
oils made from island spices. Its beachside
restaurant is well situated and convenient

to visit from Stone Town, or if visiting
Marahubi Ruins or the west coast. The
restaurant has a choice of light lunches, but
really comes into its own in the evenings,
with a popular *à la carte* menu and fine
beach dining most nights, with a sumptuous beach barbecue on Tues and Sat. The
Mcheza sports bar and bistro is a lively place
to drink and the food is cheaper. Pizza is
prepared in fire wood ovens. Major rugby
and football games are screened. The Palm
Court has the best rooms; 20 smaller rooms
are to be built in the same 'sultan' style.
There is a terrace of five club rooms, hidden
away in the midst of flowering gardens.
Three-bedroom bungalows are available and
ideal for groups. Mtoni Marine can arrange
diving, dhow sailing and fishing trips.

Maruhubi Beach Villas, PO Box 3088, **t** (0747)
451188/451177, *maruhubi@zanlink.com*,
www.maruhubibeachvillas.com (*moderate*).
This newly built shorefront resort just 3km
north of Stone Town offers villas, some with
well-equipped kitchens for self-catering.
Guests can use the facilities – swimming
pool, massage centre, restaurant and sports
bar – at next-door Mtoni Marine Centre. The
ambience is peaceful and quiet, and the
large *makuti* restaurant is a fantastically
laid-back spot to watch the sun dip into the
sea at sundowner time. It is open to non-
residents who may want to sample the
simple seafood cooking.

Mangapwani Seafood Grill, close to the old
slave chambers at Mangapwani, **t** (024)
2233587 (*moderate*). The first instalment of a
new development taking place under the
auspices of the Aga Khan and the Serena
Hotel Group. Plans are afoot to build a hotel
in 2005, but so far only the restaurant and
watersports centre is complete. Above a
truly beautiful beach with white sands and
clear turquoise seas worthy of the northern
beaches, the Mangapwani Seafood Grill is
spread over a succession of small 'private'
verandahs, each with views of the fishermen
working their *ngalawa* outriggers and
dhows and out to the far horizon. The
restaurant has recently developed facilities
for watersports, including sailing, fishing
and snorkelling. Lunch is around $25 a head.
There is no accommodation in Mkokotoni.

two storeys and several surrounding buildings, including a mosque, bath houses and an elegant tower that served as an ornate verandah for private meetings and contemplation. Said's daughter, Princess Salme, grew up as a daughter of one of his concubines and describes her childhood at Mtoni in her *Memoirs* (*see* pp.324–5). She describes how the palace was always busy with innumerable staff, visitors, wives and concubines of all nationalities, and the courtyards home to elegant tame birds such as peacocks, ostriches and flamingos. Mtoni Palace has been in ruins since a fire destroyed it in 1914, although for a while the mosque escaped the fire damage and remained in good condition. All this changed when it was used as a warehouse in the First World War. After the war the remains were cleared to make way for the oil depot. To visit the ruins, take the narrow track to the left just before the oil depot.

Soon after Mtoni the northward journey brings you to the curiously named small village of **Bububu** in a quiet rural coastal region. The stories of why Bububu is called Bububu are fun to relate, if only to repeat its name. Some say that the name came about as a result of two boys who lived in the area who were both mute – *bubu* in Swahili. A slightly less absurd explanation relates to the Bububu Railway that ran between 1904 and 1929, covering the seven miles from the edge of the clove planta- tion to the Old Fort in Stone Town. The locomotive was a steam engine, and it is said the name is the sound of the chuffing train: 'Bu-bu-bu-Bu-bu-bu'. However, it seems that the name might have been in use even before the steam train, and some suggest it comes instead from the freshwater spring that bubbles nearby, from which most of the island receives its water supply.

From Bububu a small track leads west and onto a pretty, popular but very unspoilt beach, **Fuji Beach,** a good place to rest halfway up the coast, or an easy day trip from Stone Town. A small local restaurant and bar serves inexpensive meals and drinks on the beach. The road also branches east at Bububu and heads inland to the spice plantations, where the tours take place. About 4km along this road are the old **Persian Baths** at **Kidichi** and about 3km further inland some similar but less accessible **ruins** at **Kizimbani**. The baths were built for Sultan Said's second wife, Binte Irich Mirza, known as Schesade (or Scheherazade) – a granddaughter of the Shah of Persia – to remind her of home. Schesade was a strong-willed woman who loved game-hunting on horseback, and these baths were designed to be visited after riding.

A few kilometres further north is the turning to **Mangapwani**, the site of two strange **caverns** near the beach. To the right-hand side of the track lies chilling evidence of the determination of slave traders to carry on trading illegally after the trade was abolished by the British in a treaty with Sultan Barghash in 1845. Here is a deep subterranean stone chamber, its hipped roof just jutting above ground level and broken at the centre by a rough stone entrance. Illegally held slaves were led across a drawbridge and down into the darkness, and then imprisoned by a heavy wooden door overhead. A path carved through the coral rock between the chambers and the beach, so that prisoners could be transported to the sea without being seen, has since been blocked by falling rock.

On the left-hand side of the track to Mangapwani there is a path to another cavern, a natural limestone cave containing a cool, dark pool of fresh spring water. Stories tell how this spring was discovered by the young slave of a wealthy Arab named Hamed bin Salim El-Harthy. The boy was herding his master's goats when one disappeared; its cries seemed to come from under a bush. The boy searched beneath the bush and discovered the cave, which has since provided good water to nearby villagers. The cave is also thought to have spiritual powers, and, along with a number of natural caves around the island, it is used by some as a place to leave offerings to spirits that might dwell there and provide help in times of sickness or need.

Further north, on the road leading up towards the northernmost peninsula of Ras Nungwi, another spring is found in the northeast corner of the ruins of a coral rag house at **Mvuleni**. These ruins ostensibly date from the 16th century, although it is thought that there was a Shirazi settlement here before this time, and what remains of the present structure was probably constructed by the Portuguese. The house had simple pointed stone arches and the appearance of a fortified domestic dwelling, with thin gun slits evident in the gatehouse. Across the road at **Fukuchani** are the remains of a similar construction, almost certainly built over a much older building dating from the 9th century.

Mkokotoni and Tumbatu Island

The western coast road to the north comes to a natural end at **Mkokotoni**. Mkokotoni looks out on to **Tumbatu Island**, whose aloof and proud inhabitants do not much welcome visitors. The Tumbatu Island royal family had a long history, until its reign was ended by an attack by piratical Arabs. The Mwana Mwena of Tumbatu was traditionally considered queen of all of northern Zanzibar, but made a bit of a political blunder when she gave the island to the Portuguese and set off to Goa to become a Christian. She never regained her popularity; even when she came back and tried to smooth things over, her son took on the rule. The people of the island, known as WaTumbatu, speak their own dialect of Swahili and are famous throughout East Africa for their skill in seafaring. At **Makutani**, at the southeastern end of the island, there are ruins of a substantial Shirazi settlement, with remains of a large mosque and houses, thought to have been founded in 1204 by Yusef bin Alawi. In the 13th century an Arab geographer named Yakut travelled to Tumbatu and recorded that the inhabitants were Muslims who had withdrawn to the island following an attack elsewhere. A local chronicler records that a leader of the royal family of Tumbatu, probably Yusef, ruled until the town at Makutani was destroyed by piratical Arabs and the importance of his reign diminished in the 15th century. But the people did not flee, instead starting a new settlement on the northern shores of the island.

To visit Tumbatu Island today you are obliged to first visit the Mkokotoni police post to obtain a pass, and then find a dhow or boatman to carry you over. The trip can be arranged from the port at Mkokotoni; due to the reputation of the people of Tumbatu it is advisable to find someone who can make an introduction for you on arrival.

Tumbatu may have been one of the earliest Shirazi settlements in the Zanzibar archipelago, but the people of the island have also traditionally held very strong beliefs in African magic – *shetani*. Superstitions concerning boat travel are especially strong: one enduring belief is that all visitors to Tumbatu should be clean. Men who have not washed their body since sleeping with a woman put a boat at risk, and any woman who has her period is certain to be responsible for the death of all on board if she dares to cross the waters before it is over. While many admit that this magic is losing its power, a dhow that overturned recently, drowning 12 people, is widely thought to have sunk because a woman passenger pretended she was 'clean', but lied.

Mkokotoni is a rural fishing village with a bustling market and rows of dusty dukas selling a motley assortment of fruit and random 'essential' imported goods. A wide, dark beach reaches down beyond the marketplace and forms a harbour for the dhows and outriggers and their assorted cargoes that pass between here and Tumbatu Island. There are echoes of colonial order and administration as you enter the village through its sleepy police post; to the eastern side of the market and beach a few grand buildings are dotted among the trees, a legacy of the British station here. In 1984, some ancient Chinese coins were found on the beach, themselves a legacy of a much older age of trade between Zanzibar and India, Arabia and China.

North Coast: Nungwi

The northern peninsula of Zanzibar is stunning: for anyone with a passion for beaches it has all the elements of paradise. It is hard to imagine any traveller arriving on a fine day without a gasp of admiration for the translucent waters washing over fine coral sands and the wide views across the Indian Ocean. Here, on the northern-most tip of Zanzibar Island, the air feels fresh from its wide sea crossing, the water susceptible to the slightest nuance and reflection as the sun rises and sets. The sand shores up against the land in impossibly fine, pale drifts, and the beach makes its changing way around the headland, depending on the tide. When the tide is out the way is open to walk the long distances exposed. Crabs scuttle among the odd flotsam of shells and shapely coral. Colourful women sing and chatter together as they gather around their wide fishing nets, fully clothed and knee-deep in pale turquoise waters, to survey the day's catch. Tin pots worn on their heads – for convenience – catch and

Diving Nungwi

For anyone seeking an opportunity to see turtles swim in wider waters, along with the possibility to glimpse a dolphin, and the certainty of seeing a mass of reef fish, there are PADI certificate dive centres at Nungwi on either side of the peninsula. Diving is also good around coral reefs off the northeast of the island and skirting the Mnemba Atoll. Resident pods of dolphins here are frequently seen on dives or on the way to or from the dive sites, and are fun to swim with if they are in the mood to do so. There is plenty for experienced divers also, if they dream of wall dives, night dives and drift dives (advise the dive centre in advance), or wish to explore deeper waters where lush coral gardens extend as far as the eye can see. In deeper channels wahoo, barracuda, kingfish and tuna hunt together with large Napoleonic wrasse, graceful manta rays and sharks, whereas in the shallows a huge variety of Indo-Pacific coral gardens are the playground of colourful tropical fish. *See* pp.334–5 for dive operators.

Getting There

The **road** to Nungwi disintegrates into a **potholed coral track** at the northern end, which adds to its sense of glorious isolation. It takes more than an hour to get to the northern beaches from Stone Town. **Taxis** cost around $50, **buses** and **dala-dalas** are much cheaper, but more of a struggle if you are travelling with bulky luggage as they may drop you some way from your destination.

Where to Stay and Eat

It is advisable to book accommodation in advance here.

Ras Nungwi

Expensive
Ras Nungwi Beach Hotel, Box 1784, Zanzibar, t (024) 2233767/2232512, f (024) 2233098/ 2233039, info@rasnungwi.com, www. rasnungwi.com. The best choice for accommodation in Nungwi, the Beach Hotel aspires to be an idyll: it's both relaxed and simple, while still providing conscientious service. Rooms are comfortably designed, with immaculate, newly tiled bathrooms and furniture. There is a choice of three types of room: lodge or 'garden' rooms towards the back of the hotel, and deluxe chalets or super-deluxe beach chalets with sea views. The terraced lodge rooms are all self-contained and each has its own verandah; of these, rooms 32 and 33 have excellent views of the sea and a huge shared verandah with an adjoining door that make them a perfect choice for families, or a pair of couples. The chalets are all detached or semi-detached, all have private balconies and all have views across the bay and a choice of air-conditioning or a fan. Super-deluxe rooms are newer, larger and afford even greater privacy on the far western side

of the hotel. Fitted mosquito nets in all rooms are not only essential but give a romantic feel; the atmosphere and aspect of the hotel make it a popular choice for honeymooning couples. As well as these, the hotel's separate **Ocean Suite** (*very expensive*) is among the finest accommodation on the island; the detached suite ranges over 200 sq m and has its own gardens, plunge pool and private path to the beach. It has a magnificent roof terrace and open-air sitting room, and guests use the hotel's facilities. The hotel spreads out across floral and sandy garden paths on a beautiful stretch of unspoilt and breathtaking beach. A spacious thatched restaurant and bar provide 180° views of the horizon beneath a makuti thatch, and numerous little 'hideaway' areas create atmospheric places for guests to relax and enjoy their surroundings with a semblance of privacy and peace. Local chefs make the most of fresh local spices and produce, and provide a fine daily menu that relies heavily on abundant fruit and seafood. The wine list is the most extensive in the region, with over 60 South African wines available. A fantastic swimming pool is the centrepiece of the garden, raised on an elegant platform, with views out to sea. Artfully blended into the sedate surroundings is a games area with a table tennis and pool table, a little boutique shop and even a concealed television room. Ras Nungwi Beach Hotel is also ideally located for diving the northeast coast and Mnemba Atoll, and the popular **dive centre** provides equipment and guides for all abilities. Deep-sea fishing, windsurfing and dhow cruises are available too, and there are table tennis and beach volleyball for action enthusiasts.

Moderate
Nungwi Village Beach Resort, t (022) 224049/ t (0747) 4159751, f (022) 2240491/f (024) 2232531, nungwi@nungwivillage.com, www.

reflect the gleam of the sun, as their songs rise and fall on the wind. These beaches are the life force of the nearby local villages: children, too, scour the shoreline gathering shellfish for suppers while women fish in the shallows.

The northernmost headland is named **Ras Nungwi** – Ras means headland and Nungwi means north in Swahili – and its coves and beaches stretch around the *nungwivillage.com*. A recently completed grand thatched affair, set away from the backpacker centre. This vast new centre has been well designed in parts, with fine two-storey accommodation overlooking the beach and smaller 'lodge' rooms behind.

Amaan Beach Bungalows, at the centre of the action, PO Box 2750, t (024) 2240026/t (0741) 327747/337453, *amaanbungalows@yahoo. com, www.amaanbungalows.com*. The most obviously successful of all the enterprises on this popular beach are the ever-increasing and lively Amaan Beach Bungalows, originally a collection of small cottages with balconies, fans and nets; a new two-storey wing has been developed. It boasts the most atmospheric restaurant, with slatted woodwork and dappled light creating a 'castaway island' atmosphere, and a well-stocked bar. The extensive rooms are immaculately managed by a German couple. The adjoining **dive centre** is popular and well equipped.

Moderate–Cheap

The less expensive hotels are mainly centred around the northwestern aspect of the peninsula, and form a village-like cluster along the seashore. Privacy and peace are not well catered for, but the accommodation in the following is the best value for tranquillity. Other, even cheaper, options do exist.

Baobab Beach Bungalows, t (024) 2236315/ t (0747) 494321/416964/429391, f (024) 2230475, *baobabnungwi@zanzinet.com, www.baobabbeachbungalows.com*. A solid-looking new development of stone cottages at the northwesterly tip of Nungwi Bay. The common areas are lively, with a generic sports-bar atmosphere, catering to the tastes of middle-aged European men. The kitchen claims to stock 20 different types of mango, and emphasis is on lavish buffets. Organizes tours, diving and fishing.

Baracka Bungalows, PO Box 3502, t (024) 2240412. Set in leafy gardens tucked away behind Paradise Beach, run entirely by local villagers. All rooms have wide balconies with coir rope beds, and a colourful atmosphere. There is a real sense of pride in the place; it's a quiet oasis in the midst of the mayhem. The gardens are well tended and becoming mature, but there are no direct sea views from the rooms. Baracka also has a good restaurant with masses of choice from cheap snacks to more elaborate dishes. As an additional bonus, there is a flourishing turtle sanctuary in the grounds of the resort.

Cholo's Beach Bar. Alongside all of these, Cholo's continues to develop its unusual reputation as the most laid-back evening hang-out on the island. Curiously inspired design flair has developed this bar inside a broken down *jahazi* dhow, filling it with a strange selection of *objets trouvés*. Lit by dripping candles, enlivened by local characters and a juke box, this is the coolest drinking spot on the island.

Banana Willies. A pretender to Cholo's title, 'Willies' is the newest and best-placed joint for whiling the sunset hours away. High up on stilts on a curving spit, with views over the bay, the bar has maximized its horizontal ambience with every conceivable design for reclining. The staff here are not so idiosyncratic as Cholo's, and the emphasis on the very good pizza makes this a more grown-up option than its neighbour.

Kendwa Beach

Whether the song of Kendwa should remain unsung remains to be seen. For the time being this westerly stretch of the Nungwi Peninsula provides a haven for simple, idyllic beach accommodation, with a reputation for lively beach parties at the full moon, and well-danced sands. To get to Kendwa, ask around at Nungwi beach for a boat at high tide, or more prosaically, take the road. When the tide is out it is possible to walk along the beach all the way, but en route you will pass a new Italian-

rambling sprawl of Ras Nungwi village. The land here is essentially coral rock, affording few possibilities for farming; life on the peninsula can be tough, despite its natural beauty. The people of Nungwi have developed a reputation as a rural population with a head for politics. The Nungwi people's affiliation with the opposition party has made the ruling party reluctant to provide them with basic amenities such as built Renco hotel, known locally as 'The Prison'. Its vastness and its glaring mirrored windows cannot be anything but an eyesore; fortunately you cannot currently see it from the low-key lodges. To return to Nungwi, the lodges will send you back by boat.

Kendwa Rocks, PO Box 3939, t (0747) 415527, *kendwarocks@hotmail.com, www.kendwa rocks.com* (*moderate–cheap*). The first place to open here, in 1995, remains arguably the best of the handful of small resorts along this fabulous stretch of beach. Since its opening the lodge has provided just a few basic palm shelters and bungalows in mature gardens. Over the last few years, however, it has improved dramatically, and there are now a few great rooms down on the beach fetching $50 a night. It's owned and run by a Zanzibari-Finnish husband-and-wife team, with simple, quiet attention to detail. Kendwa Rocks has the first Internet café in Kendwa. Plans are afoot to convert a large dhow into rooms for 3 or 4 and to anchor it offshore. Euros are accepted here.

Kendwa Amaan Bungalows, PO Box 132, t (024) 2240026, *kendwa@amaanbungalows.com, www.amaanbungalow.com/kendwa.htm* (*moderate*). Good, locally run, managed by the German couple responsible for Amaan Beach Bungalows. The lodge provides 17 simple bungalows set in pretty gardens; ask for the rooms furthest from the generator.

Kendwa Sunset, t (0747) 413818, *sunsetbunga low@hotmail.com* (*cheap*). Another place with a generator is the small Kendwa Sunset, which provides nice, comfortable *bandas* with concrete floors and bathrooms, set back some distance from the beach and sea. The generator is oddly situated in the middle and often doesn't work, so the rooms have lamps, but no electricity. The Sunset's disco, however, is gaining in popularity and their **dive centre** and restaurant are reliable.

Whitesands, PO Box 732, t (0747) 480987, *Zanzibar_ws_beachhotel@hotmail.com*, next door (*cheap*). Bags of character and new *bandas* high up on the ridge. The bar is a funky cavern with sunken seating and playful swings. The *bandas* are attractive and good value, and the owner is a seriously laid-back individual. At low season it is possible to take over the kitchen and cook for yourself with local ingredients.

Sports and Activities

Nungwi is not just a pretty beach, it is also popular for diving, snorkelling and fishing around the close offshore reefs.

Diving

There are PADI certificate dive centres at Nungwi on either side of the peninsula, including Kendwa. The dive centre at Ras Nungwi Beach Hotel is well equipped to train beginners and runs regular PADI courses, which should be booked in advance (*see* pp.334–5 for Zanzibar dive operators, and p.364 for details of 'Diving Nungwi').

Beach- and Reef-walking

The tidal extremes of the beaches here as all around Zanzibar Island make for stunning walks around the headland at low tide. The beaches at Nungwi are especially beautiful – mainly wide expanses of sand dotted with numerous translucent pools. At low tide it takes just 30mins to walk from the backpacker lodges to the eastern beaches, or around to Kendwa Rocks (about 3km southwest of Nungwi village), where there is usually still a beach at high tide and some fine reefs for snorkelling.

The unspoilt natural delights of Kendwa Rocks can also be reached on the daily boat taxi from Amaan Beach Bungalows and by road (*see* above). Boat trips are also possible from Kendwa to Tumbatu Island, and kayaks are available on the beach.

water (a precious commodity on the island), electricity and roads. As a result the headland remains largely undeveloped, despite a sudden spurt of tourist popularity.

The most upmarket accommodation in this area, Ras Nungwi Beach Hotel, is situated on a wild and unspoilt stretch of beach on the northeast of the peninsula, with acres of low bush extending to the far horizon in a westerly stretch. Between 30 and

40 minutes' walk west around the headland leads past Nungwi lighthouse and brings you to the increasing sprawl of budget lodges, a popular 'backpacker village' clustered around a good but crowded beach. A wide choice of restaurants, bars and dive centres attracts an excitable party crowd; if you're keen to party too, the atmosphere here is an attraction, especially after sundown. Continuing westwards, a further 30-minute walk around the headland brings you to the less-visited haven of **Kendwa Rocks**, hitherto a haven of natural calm, but now threatened with new development.

The **villages around Ras Nungwi** are primarily fishing villages, and to the northwest of the peninsula is one of the main centres for Zanzibar's traditional dhow-building industry. On a beach just beyond the village boat-builders still create the 'sewn boats' that so perplexed Marco Polo, weaving wide planks together with rope made from coconut husks. The crafts are constructed from natural materials close at hand: the hardwood timbers of the trees that grow nearby.

Further on, where the road forks, a pretty natural rock pool in a coral inlet has been turned into the **Mnarani Turtle Sanctuary**, a haven for small, shiny-shelled green and hawksbill turtles. The colourful pool forms a protected aquarium, watched and tended by local people whose livelihood has been threatened by the project: sea turtles have traditionally been regarded as a food source, and their shells sold for ornaments. The locals now make some money from donations, however, so there is a chance that turtle preservation will continue. Zanzibari turtles are desperately endangered, and further threatened by onshore developments that confuse their sense of time with lights that look to them like a full moon, so they are lured onto the beach to lay their eggs at the wrong times of the month. There are signs of giant sea turtles on the Nungwi beaches, leaving a trail as wide as a caterpillar tractor in the sand as they leave the sea in the early dawn to lay and bury their eggs on the beach; they are frequently encountered swimming by divers. Tourists can play a part in the attempt to preserve the species around these islands by taking care not to buy goods made with tortoiseshell, and watching out for buried eggs. The sanctuary has recently been enclosed within the grounds of the Baracka Beach Bungalow Annex, open to visitors.

Northeast Coast: Matemwe to Chwaka

The east coast of Zanzibar has a superb succession of long, windswept, palm-fringed beaches. As you go further south, the beaches become progressively more wild and strewn with flotsam than their northern neighbours. Many of the hotels sweep their beach areas, but these regions are prone to fluctuations of seaweed early in the year. The sand is nevertheless remarkably fine and clean, with knee-high drifts to relax into under the palms; these shining beaches seem to stretch on and on. The east coast is naturally divided into northern and southern regions by the formation of the coastline, which is followed by the roads. One route leads from the island's central main road to the northern reaches of **Matemwe** (Pwani Mchangani), **Kiwengwa** and **Chwaka**, another to the southern beaches of Paje, Bwejuu and Jambiani. There is a wide choice of accommodation along this coastline, although it is highly favoured by the Italian club hotels, many of which cater exclusively to Italian package tours. These

Getting There and Around

The villages of Matemwe and Kiwengwa are accessible by **car** from the main road that leads through the centre of the island. The beach hotels straggle along the rather more bumpy and dishevelled coastal road with its tyre-threatening masses of coral rag rock. It's slow going in anything other than a 4x4, especially after the rains.

Dala-dalas travel back and forth from Matemwe Beach Village, and can usually be persuaded to continue on to Matemwe Bungalows for a small extra charge. Another dala-dala route heads to Chwaka Bay along the east road out of Stone Town past the Dunga Palace towards the southeast coast.

It may be possible to take a **bus** to the coast; check at the Creek Road bus station.

Where to Stay

Mnemba Island

Mnemba Island Lodge, PO Box 1200, t (022) 2232572, *information@ccafrica.com, www.ccafrica.com* (UK agent: Tanzania Odyssey, t (020) 7471 8780, *info@tanzaniaodyssey.com*) (*very expensive*). Just off the northeast coast but visible from it, Mnemba Island is a tiny dream island of coral atolls. Its sandy shores are surrounded by a rich, colourful reef brimming with fish, little and large – dolphins, barracuda, tuna and shark-like swimmers are often seen. At the island's centre is a cool pine forest; the eastern coastal aspect is wild and unkempt. The lodge is stylishly run by the South African hotel chain, Conservation Corporation Africa, as a retreat for island-hoppers seeking an exclusive idyll. It targets 'barefoot luxury' in desert island style. Accommodation is in eight roomy thatched beach *bandas* with bathrooms along a corridor of woven coconut palm. Each *banda* is set back from the beach in a private clearing in the forest. All bedrooms, verandahs and central living areas are designed with light cotton nets, African prints and cushions. If you can afford to pay the astronomical rates, tropical cocktails, diving expeditions, watersports and fishing trips are included. The lodge runs a professional **dive school** and traditional wooden dhows from which to explore the warm clear waters and coral reefs. Guests return to the island to enjoy feasts of fresh fruit, vegetables, seafood and meat, all fabulously prepared and presented. Visitors may find themselves sharing cocktails with Mnemba-fan Bill Gates: he might be the only visitor who doesn't blanch at the rates.

Matemwe

Matemwe Bungalows, PO Box 3257, reception t (0747) 414834, bookings t (027) 2502799/ t (0748) 763338, *matemwebungalows@ zanzinet.com, www.matemwebungalows. com*, hookings. *info@asilialodges.com, www.asilialodges.com* (*expensive*). A remote and scenic choice, tucked behind a sandy palm-fringed fishing village on a windswept beach on the east coast. Twelve thatched and whitewashed bungalows extend along a grassy stretch on a private, pale sandy beach, linked by flower-covered walkways to a highly recommended restaurant – among the best on the island – specializing in seafood with an original and diverse menu. It has views over the Indian Ocean and faces a second beach, where children play and fishermen go in and out with the tides, which are extreme all along this coastline. A 2005 refurbishment of this gem of a lodge has seen all the rooms upgraded into suites and the introduction of a much-needed split-level swimming pool. The rooms are some of the best on Zanzibar, playing host to hand-crafted elegance with sprung mattress beds, now built on raised plinths to ensure lazy ocean views. All the rooms have king-sized beds and are en suite, with solar power for hot water, and a hammock on the verandah. Matemwe aims to be as harmonious with its situation as possible, and to promote low-impact tourism. Guests are encouraged to join trips to local food and fish markets and are discouraged from buying and collecting shells and corals. By July 2006 families will be well catered for once the two bedroom self-contained villas are built nearby. These will have separate cooking arrangements, though families will be able to eat in the restaurant also.

Activities include sailing in traditional *ngalawa* outriggers, snorkelling, diving and big-game fishing, as well as reef walks across the reef in front of the bungalows, bicycle hire and day trips with picnics.

Matemwe Beach Village, PO Box 3481, **t** (024) 2239340/**t** (0741) 622391/330349, *matemwe beachvillage@zitec.org* (*moderate*). The only budget accommodation in the area is at Matemwe Beach Village, which provides 10 simple cottages close to the beach, each with en-suite bathroom and cold water showers – the place has gone from strength to strength in recent times, and lives up to the cheerful motto placed over the entrance gate: 'no shoes; no news'. Most rooms have views of the garden rather than of the wide, sandy public fishermen's beach, which is prone to seaweed. The central restaurant is almost entirely constructed of canvas, which opens out to let the breeze in during the hotter months of the year, and the menu is reasonable (T.shs 2–3,000). Perhaps the greatest attraction of this spot is the branch of the **One Ocean Dive Centre** office that has opened here for dives at sites around Mnemba Atoll. Air-conditioning is extra; children aged 7–12 get very good rates.

Kiwengwa

Kiwengwa Beach is a stretch of sand trailing down the middle of the east coast. The sand is fine, but this coastline does attract seaweed at the beginning of the year. The whole stretch is occupied by a range of hotels, from the brand new Kempinski to the older cluster of Italian 'club' hotels in the northern reaches and some smaller alternatives further south. The Italian package hotels also tend to keep themselves to themselves, providing extensive in-house entertainment that dissuades guests from wandering further afield. If this is for you, you may be able to book direct with Stone Town tour operators, who may squeeze you into **Bravo Club**, PO Box 4095, **t** (0741) 339961/2, **Vera Club**, PO Box 2529, **t/f** (0741) 330345, or **Kiwengwa Club Village**, PO Box 4095, **t** (0741) 326205. For the more individual alternatives, *see below*.

Zamani Kempinski Resort, **t** 0800 426 313 55 (Europe and UK) or **t** 800 426 3135 (North

America), *www.kempinski-zanzibar.com* (*very expensive*). Kempinski is opening Zanzibar's first international 5-star hotel. The resort will have 110 spacious rooms and suites, each with their own private terrace and sea views. Each will have an outdoor shower in a private tropical courtyard. Room service will be 24hrs, and the resort will have two restaurants, an all-day café and two bars. The health and beauty spa will be 'the most luxurious in Zanzibar' and the outdoor pool will be a whopping 60m long.

Mapenzi Beach Village, PO Box 100, **t** (0741) 325985, **f** (0741) 333739, *resa@mapenziplan hotel.com*, *info@planhotelzanzibar.com*, *www.planhotel.com*, *www.mapenziplan hotel.com* (*expensive*). The Mapenzi Beach Village in Kiwengwa also caters mainly for Italian package tourists, but does provide a fine standard of luxury accommodation. The all-inclusive package includes drinks and activities such as tennis, canoeing, archery, billiards, darts and table tennis as well as a large central pool with Jacuzzi spa and cyber café. Its one-storey rooms, set in maturing tropical gardens, give Mapenzi a more relaxing atmosphere than its nearest competitors.

Blue Bay Beach Resort, PO Box 3276, **t** (024) 2240240/1/2/4/**t** (0741) 338171/2, **f** (024) 2240245, *mail@bluebayzanzibar.com*, *www.bluebayzanzibar.com* (*expensive*). The largest and newest hotel to grace the sands of Kiwengwa Beach, although it seems that many of its European guests find its huge swimming pool more enticing than the ocean. Accommodation is in a series of stone 'cottages', with eight rooms in each, designed with a nod to traditional Zanzibari style. These are stepped up from the beach, quite a distance from it. The resort is set in spacious gardens inter-linked with shady tree-lined paths, and has a wide range of facilities to keep guests amused: a tennis court, fitness centre and diving centre, wind-surfing and sailing equipment, table tennis, pool and music theatre – to name but a few. There is also a choice of restaurants. Food is surprisingly excellent for a resort of this scale. The Blue Bay regularly receives awards and accolades, particularly for its environmental record. The beach and the diverse atmosphere make this a popular choice for children. Rates are highest between Christmas and March.

La Villa, PO Box 3156, t (0747) 422137, *direction lavill@zanzinet.com, www.zanzibarlavilla.it.* This very lovely resort of just 14 rooms is next door to Blue Bay, and will probably benefit from direct access to its facilities if a planned merger happens. Both *makuti*-roofed stone huts and more substantial 'suite' rooms share a small kidney-shaped plunge pool amid wild, colour-burst gardens. A games room and lounging space with guitars and scatter cushions has been built above the suite rooms, while a smart restaurant serves up delicious seafood nearer to the beach. The wooden hulls of tiny boats have been up-ended and cleverly converted into tables on the sand. A row of flags posted around the bar flutter in the sea breeze, making a lovely backdrop to sip cocktails.

Ocean Paradise, PO Box 106, Kijangwani, t (0747) 439990/1/2/3/t (0747) 476040, *reservations@oceanparadisezanzibar.com, www.oceanparadisezanzibar.com* (*expensive*). A seriously grandiose affair, newly opened, which has the starched atmosphere of a luxury hotel with bellboys and the like. The 100 bungalows have been built 'in the native style' but provide high standards of comfort, with air-conditioning, minibar and hairdryers. The suites have a separate living room with TV, bar and phone. The swimming pool is truly fantastic, with a wide and elegant poolside bar serving everything from milkshakes to cocktails. An animation team organizes events and there is a watersports centre. The impressive facilities – the place even has its own disco and a resident band – make this a good place for families with older children, or groups of travellers seeking laid-on fun, but its vastness and too-slick service is off-putting.

Shooting Star, on Kiwengwa Beach, PO Box 3076, t (0747) 419984/414166, *star@zanzibar. com, star@zanzibar.org, www.zanzibar.org/ star* (*expensive*). A little gem of a small hideaway hotel – utterly different from the international resort-style Ocean Paradise.

Choose between a few large, well-scrubbed *makuti*-thatched, semi-detached bungalows (with adjoining doors for families), or smaller lodge rooms with private verandahs. The accommodation in both is clean, neat and comfortable. Soon, air-conditioning will be available in all the rooms. Local dhow trips, snorkelling, diving, fishing trips and massage therapies are available. This tiny family-run lodge is set high on a cliff, with steep steps down to the sand, where there is a lovely bar elevated over the beach. A swimming pool will soon be built on the cliff, with infinity views to the reef. The restaurant (*moderate*) and bar serve excellent food, including lobster, on a semi-gardened terrace, and the atmosphere is peaceful, quiet and relaxed. Beach dining can be arranged for special occasions.

Reef View, Kiwengwa, PO Box 3215, t (0747) 413294, *reefviewzanizibar@hotmail.com, www.reefview.com* (*cheap*). A highly recommended beach hideaway for anyone seeking peace and seclusion at minimal cost, focusing on the beach and sea in a simple style. A good 1km south of all the larger Italian hotels clustered further up this stunning stretch of beach, the Reef View provides a quiet sanctuary of *makuti*-thatched *bandas* a few metres from the beach. The attraction here is its 'back to basics' approach: there is no electricity, so lamps are distributed each night, water is supplied to the nearby bathroom *banda* through a hosepipe, and guests enjoy the thrills of long-drop toilets – making the whole thing more ecologically friendly than the vast resort hotels. There is a book exchange, snorkels for rent and the possibility of a boat as well. Helen and Haroub, the English and Zanzibari couple who run Reef View, have faithful clients who return year after year. It is worth spending a few days here to relax into the pace of life. Return trips to Stone Town take about an hour each way on the dala-dala, or may be negotiated to coincide with the shopping run. If the peace and quiet is too much for you, night-time excitement can be found further up the beach at a disco built on a long jetty by one of the Italian club hotels

($10 per person). Reef View's in-house cooking is delicious, with excellent options for vegetarians, and special dietary requirements catered for with advance warning.

Pongwe Beach

Pongwe Beach Resort, Pongwe Beach, south of Kiwengwa and north of Chwaka, PO Box 2937, t (0747) 413 973, *www.pongwe.com* (*moderate*). With 10 comfortable en-suite bungalows overlooking a beautiful stretch of sandy beach which extends back to the heart of the property, the lodge is in a wide area generously shaded with palm trees – creating good private areas – and all overlooking the clear, sparkling sea. The lodge has a number of boats available for fishing, diving and snorkelling excursions and a good, laid-back atmosphere throughout. Meals *cheap*, usually a choice of fish with chips or rice, or local-style cuisine.

Uroa

Zanzibar Safari Club Resort, PO Box 1561, t (024) 2238553, *www.zanzibarsafari.co.tz* (*expensive*). Neither a 'club resort' with exclusive clientele nor a small and simple place, the 'ZSCR' has assembled all the facilities required to earn its 3-star rating and yet retains a quaint, idiosyncratic style. All 40 rooms have the outward appearance of a Disney village: rows of small, clean and comfortable red-tiled bungalows, all air-conditioned and facing the sea, although the first row obviously get the best view. With two bars, two restaurants, conference facilities, tennis courts and a superb central swimming pool, the Safari Club manages to provide most of the amenities of a large hotel while retaining a relatively exclusive feel; it specializes in kitsch comfort. Safari Club staff speak German and Dutch – reflecting the nationality of their guests. The resort also provides a range of diving and watersports facilities.

Tamarind Beach Hotel, south of Uroa Village, PO Box 2206, Zanzibar, t (024) 2237154, *tamarind@zanzinet.com* (*moderate*). Among the first places to open on this coast, it has recently been entirely refurbished. Its Norwegian-Zanzibari management has taken it from strength to strength: the hotel has gained good reports for food and service, and rooms are commonly reported to be clean and comfortable.

Chwaka

Chwaka Bay is a less visited region for tourism, despite being the spot chosen by the colonial government for beachside repose. A few old two-storey structures with balconies and verandahs from the colonial era stand in dilapidated evidence today – long since taken over by the Zanzibari government as 'rest houses' for ministers to entertain guests, and subsequently allowed to fall into disrepair. The sandy roads and paths at this rural junction between north and south are rarely travelled, and the ocean here is millpond-smooth, protected by the sandy peninsula that extends across the bay. This area of the island has a rather wild, windswept atmosphere – slightly barren and deserted.

Chwaka Bay Hotel, PO Box 1480, t (024) 2240289 (*moderate*). It is in this atmosphere of strange quiet and reserve that the Chwaka Bay Hotel stands among the palm trees, a collection of 10 round whitewashed bungalows set in tropical gardens around a central *makuti* restaurant and bar. The hotel is run by a Swedish-Zanzibari management, and is popular with a mixed European clientele – especially catering to groups. The rooms are comfortable, clean and well appointed with private bathrooms, hot running water and fans. All areas are pervaded by an idiosyncratic atmosphere of Swahili decorative flair. The walls of the restaurant and central reception are brightly muralled with maps of Zanzibar island, and adorned with the faces of presidents past and present hung in shabby frames. The restaurant serves seafood in local and international styles, and is pleasantly open-sided, although sea views are limited. Perhaps its one drawback is that the hotel is oddly arranged behind the main road that divides it from the beach. The staff are laid-back, sometimes appearing perturbed by visitors, but it's a quiet and private location providing decent accommodation.

tend to be very insular: at least they do not generally stray far from the in-house facilities. A few welcome direct international bookings.

Southeast Coast

Stone Town to Paje

This stretch of coastline has until recently remained the most undeveloped; some parts of it still feel quite wild, increasingly so further south. The main road leads to **Paje** village, about halfway along the coast, and then splits, turning either north to new, big, resort hotels such as Breezes, the Italian Venta Club Resort, Sultan's Palace and Karafuu, or south to small, rural villages and clusters of guesthouses.

The route to the southeast coast from Stone Town travels down a long avenue of mature **mango trees**, providing shade along the road, which at this point is straight and narrow, as it was designed for carriages in the days of the sultans. The avenue of trees was planted by one of Sultan Said's most beautiful daughters, Princess Bi Khole, and has generated many stories about its conception. One tells how the princess had such an unquenchable desire for beautiful young men that she made sure each tree was planted by a different one of the slaves she desired. She intended to extend the avenue all the way to Stone Town, but ran out of mangoes – or men. No two neighbouring mango trees in the avenue are the same species, creating a fantastic spread of colour and fruit through most of the year.

Further along are the ruins of **Dunga Palace**, the old home of the Swahili Great Lord and now designated a 'Gazetted Monument of the Mwinyi Mkuu' by the Zanzibari government. Enough remains to make it an evocative place to stop – the ancient stone thrones and fountains are convincing proof that the Mwinyi Mkuu enjoyed an opulent dotage. The Mwinyi Mkuu system of rule originated in Zanzibar in the 13th century, and continued unhindered until the arrival of the Omani Arabs. Doubts remain over the Mwinyi Mkuus' origins, although it is known that the first recorded Mwinyi Mkuu was Hassan bin Abubakar. The most famous of these 'Great Lords' was Ahmed bin Mohammed (1785–1865), who built this great palace between 1845 and 1856. It is said of the Mwinyi Mkuu that his 'rule was felt in every part of Unguja', although areas such as Tumbatu Island had their own subordinate rule. The domain of the Mwinyi Mkuu was, however, diminished by the advent of the Omani sultans; by the reign of Sultan Barghash, the traditional Great Lord of Zanzibar's stature was reduced to that of a village governor. Relics of the glory days remain in the ruins of this palace: a hand-painted porcelain bowl that may be of oriental origin is among the few items from this period in the National Museum.

Bwejuu, Paje and Jambiani

The sleepy fishing village of **Paje** and flanking settlements of **Bwejuu** and **Jambiani** once enjoyed 'top spot' popularity with budget backpackers seeking to get back to basics on sun-drenched beaches, but more recently Nungwi has somewhat eclipsed the southeast coast. These beaches are much wilder than Nungwi, palm-fringed, with

Getting There

A good tarmac **road** to the east coast continues for about 50km from Stone Town; the last 8km deteriorates to a wide, bumpy, rough earth road. **Taxis** tend to charge upwards of $40 for a journey from Stone Town to this stretch of coast. A **dala-dala** goes to Michamwi, and another route heads to Chwaka Bay along the east road out of Stone Town to the Dunga Palace on the way to the southeast coast.

Where to Stay

Dongwe Village

The Palms, PO Box 1298, t (0747) 437007, f (0748) 203093, *info@palms-zanzibar.com*, *www.palms-zanzibar.com* (*very expensive*). The first island retreat on a par with the more luxurious safari lodges, Palms is a triumph. Six stone *bandas* are set apart from each other in riotously blooming gardens. The interior is generously spacious; with an open-plan bedroom and living area with a bar. A heavy and serene quietness fills the air: this is an ultimate retreat space. Each *banda* has a private verandah with a carved Zanzibari day bed and deep Jacuzzi screened by a sailcloth curtain. Fabrics and furnishings are from all corners of the world, but have been chosen by a talented eye. Behind the doors of a carved cabinet there is a widescreen TV with DVD player: the resort has its own DVD library. A low-slung colonial-style building with a wide and long verandah is the centrepiece of the resort. The piped classical music is grating, but is at such a low level that it is easy to ignore. Dining is at private tables, while lunch is served in the poolside bar. The pool is a delight but, like the compound itself, is rather small, and, with no grounds to speak of, any leg stretching must be done down on the beach. Here the sense of exclusivity is compromised somewhat by the presence of Breezes, the resort's sister resort. Guests can benefit from Breezes' impressive watersports facility. The resort has its own spa, The Sanctuary, inside a shaded *makuti* hut, with a full-time Thai masseur.

Breezes Beach Club, t (0747) 415049, f (0741) 333151, *info@breezes-zanzibar.com*, *breezes@africaonline.tz*, *www.breezes-zanzibar.com* (*expensive*). Widely well regarded. Luxurious beach accommodation with entertainment. The rooms are in spacious and comfortable stone apartments with air-conditioning, and are categorized as 'luxury' or 'special deluxe' depending whether they are at ground level with balconies or on the upper floor with bougainvillaea trailing over the verandahs. You can have your bed laid out beneath the stars on the verandah, with mosquito nets. A small restaurant on stilts above the beach caters to anyone who might wish to pay a little extra and enjoy a more extravagant *à la carte* menu than in the large central restaurant, although it too is well designed to diminish the impression of size, and its meals are sumptuous and imaginative. The beach is wild and endlessly long, with soft coral sand in thick drifts shaded by coconut palms. It is, however, prone to tidal extremes and has a tendency to build up seaweed during January and February. The waters are shallow, making it especially popular with beachcombers and children. Many guests spend their stay gathered around the swimming pool and beach bar. Despite its vast complex the hotel does try to lessen the 'holiday camp' atmosphere by keeping organized activities low-key and out of view: the well-equipped dance and fitness centre and the disco are some distance from the central area, beyond a fine ornamental garden flanked by a number of tennis courts. The Frangipani Spa was the first in East Africa, and Breezes is rightly proud of it; treatments are of the highest quality, in scented and candlelit surroundings. The 'Apres-safari Treatment' promises rejuvenation after the rigours of life in the bush. Half-board includes huge buffet breakfasts and 4-course dinners; you can pay more for a deluxe room with a private balcony. **Rising Sun Dive School and Watersports Centre** is situated on the beach (*see* p.335).

Pingwe

Karafuu Hotel Beach Resort, PO Box 71, t (0747) 413647–8, f (0747) 419915, *karafuuhotel@zanzinet.com* (*expensive*). At the northern tip of this southeastern corner of the island is a vast hotel complex with 89 rooms lined up in serried ranks set back from the beach. Those with front-row views of the sea are, clearly, far more desirable than those with views of everyone else's air-conditioning systems. They are linked by straight concrete paths, quite out of character with the large central restaurant and bar, which is an impressive *makuti* structure. The atmosphere is that of a resort hotel, with a disco, flood-lit tennis courts, fitness sessions around the pool, watersports and PADI certificate dive centre. It also employs a number of animators to organize entertainment and games, and has the random attraction of a fake Maasai village constructed within a purpose-built enclosure, including real Maasai inhabitants and at least one cow. There is a kindergarten, well strewn with toys. The staff, speaking a range of European languages but specializing in Italian and French, have coined the appropriate catchphrase '*Karafuu – C'est fou!*' A motley European and South African crowd drifts between the bars and restaurants; elaborate cocktails and expensive soft drinks are served in the bar, poolside or beach. The beach is coral beyond the first few metres of sand, but a walkway has been constructed out to a deep sandy natural pool beyond the reef.

Bwejuu

Sultan's Palace, PO Box 4047, t (0741) 335828, f (0741) 323496, *sultanzanzibar@zanlink.com* (*very expensive*). A curious place, full of promise for opulent accommodation, but built on such a grand scale that guests rattle around its cavernous halls. The two huge floors of the central living area and reception are wonderfully constructed in dark, heavy teak wood, and there are numerous sunlit stone balconies leading off its circular structure for breakfast, sundowners, coffee and lounging. The coffee terrace is a low-slung cushioned area that brings Arabic seriousness back into the coffee-drinking ritual. The bedrooms are vast, with fine Arabic beds and grand marbled bathrooms. Each opens out onto a private flower-filled garden, complete with hammock slung between the

trees. The hotel is well designed, rising up from the seashore in impressive white crenellated battlements and gardens. The views are superb and the shore is sandy, the sea is fairly shallow, rocky and tidal in the main here, but a path has been constructed to a wide and deep natural lagoon, described as 'God's own swimming pool'. It is an atmospheric choice, particularly recommended for those who prefer their own company. This unusual hotel is run by a friendly English/Kenyan couple.

Sunrise Hotel and Restaurant, PO Box 3967, Zanzibar, t/f ((024) 2240270, *sunrise@ zanlink.com, www.sunrise-zanzibar.com* (*moderate*). A small choice with character, providing pleasant accommodation in terraced bungalows set back from the beach in gardens. The beach here is windswept, wild and timeless, and the atmosphere of the Sunrise Hotel parallels it; the Belgian management have developed it since the days of no electricity or running water when it was the ultimate secret hideaway; now the hotel provides electricity and both hot and cold running water. The restaurant, famous for its cooking even in the more primitive days, retains its reputation for good meals in its pleasant beachside location. It specializes in fantastic sauces and rich and delicious puddings. This is an ideal spot to get away from the world and relax in a very quiet and laid-back environment. The situation of Sunrise allows for easy walks to Breezes Beach Club nearby (for watersports), the village of Paje or backpacker lodges.

Palm Beach Inn, contact Suna Tours, t (024) 2233385, in Zanzibar Stone Town for reservations (*cheap*). The best budget option along this stretch is this welcoming locally run guesthouse, with comfortable laid-back atmosphere. Staff are fun and attentive and the round restaurant serves excellent local food. It benefits from its proximity to the village. All 15 rooms have en-suite bathrooms with hot water, and mosquito nets, and most have air-conditioning and fridges. Four have a sea view, while others are set in quiet gardens behind. Air-conditioning extra.

Twisted Palm (*cheap*). Just between Paje Village and Sunrise is a small establishment greatly favoured by the backpackers who find it, situated beside the unusual twisted tree that gives it its name. This is a very relaxed and sandy haven providing simple but good backpacker accommodation with nets and fans, and some bathrooms en suite. A breezy restaurant has been constructed on a second level, providing ultimate back-packer-style heaven with views of the sea and plenty of beer. The lodge is run by a local family, presided over by a wonderfully efficient mama, and has a welcoming and very laid-back atmosphere.

Twisted Palm Bungalows, a few metres further south (*cheap*). Capitalizing on the name and reputation of its predecessor.

Paje

Paradise Beach Bungalows, PO Box 2346, t (024) 2231387, *paradisebb@zanlink.com*, *saori@cats-net.com*, *www.geocities.jp/ paradisebeachbungalows* (*moderate*). The tiny and unusual Paradise Beach Bungalows was established in 1992 by Saori Miura, an impressive Japanese woman with a flair for her native cooking. Her restaurant specializes in a combination of Japanese and Zanzibari seafood, using the finest Tanzanian ingredients. Sushi and sashimi are also freshly prepared. The seven white-washed bungalows are thatched and decorated with local materials, with hand-crafted doors, beams and beds. They appeal to travellers who prefer this basic style as it is, without electricity or mod cons. The atmosphere is interesting, with opportuni-ties to study Swahili, do a course in local cooking or cultural village work, or visit a seaweed plantation alongside the boat trips, fishing, diving and snorkelling.

Sun and Sea View Hotel, t (0747) 420774, *ssvresort@zanjcom.com* (*cheap*). Halfway between Bwejuu and Paje, this simple resort offers a quiet beach retreat for the traveller who is content with basic amenities. Five well built stone cottages provide 10 rooms. Minimally furnished, the rooms have no fan, but have been built to benefit from the ocean breeze. Mellow African pop music floats through the beachside restaurant, which is furnished with bleached driftwood. The cottages are run by locals and the atmosphere is friendly and low-key.

Paje By Night, t (0747 460710, *info@pajeby night.net*, *www.pajebynight.net* (*cheap*). A little treasure of a resort, one of the original backpacker stop-offs in Paje village. Its bohemian feel and sense of fun more than make up for the fact that newer, less characterful resorts have blocked the sea view. The bar stretches languidly out onto the sand, its alcove seating perfect to while away the hours. Chess, backgammon and Bao are played by a friendly mix of villagers and visitors. Pizza is very good here, and can be eaten in the restaurant or by the fire, where dance and music performances are sometimes held. The management are Italian and the romantic sort; they will happily prepare special meals and beach dining on request. Rooms are frequently improved, and facilities upgraded. Beds are wide and made from coconut wood, and draped with cotton throws. Decoration has been done with more exuberance than style, but the overall feel is well cared for. The Internet is free, and there is a satellite TV.

Jambiani

Shehe Guest House, PO Box 398, t (024) 2240149, *shehebungalows@hotmail.com* (*cheap*). The best accommodation in Jambiani, run by Mr and Mrs Fatih Shehe. It used to be one of the great backpacker favourites, set around a fantastic two-storey building on a wide stretch of beach. Sadly recent reports have suggested that extensive, expensive modifications have destroyed the simple charm of the place, but the rooms are comfortable, there's a TV, and food is available. Most importantly, the management are friendly and experienced in ensuring that guests are well catered for at a budget price.

Gomiani Guesthouse (*cheap*). One of the nicest choices here, set back off the beach on low coral cliffs, providing great sea views from most of its clean, quiet doubles. Welcoming and unassuming.

Jambiani Beach Hotel, PO Box 2213, t (024) 2240155 (*cheap*). Despite its name, it's not on the beach, but is close enough for good sea views from the pleasant, simple bungalows. All include en-suite bathrooms and have a quiet side. Good meals.

tides that go out for miles. Owing to the area's diminished popularity, they now provide a quiet budget alternative. **Jambiani** is the most southerly and inaccessible of these southeastern villages, sprawling languidly along this last long stretch of beach.

Southwest Coast: Kizimkazi

This remote region in the far south of the island has found itself a focal point for tourist hordes as a result of its resident pods of **dolphins**. Schools of bottlenose

Where to Stay and Eat

Makowezi Guesthouse, PO Box 1523, t (0747) 410252 (*cheap*). The oldest and most respected establishment at Kizimkazi, formerly the Kizimkazi Beach Villa, where guests are ensured a clear view of the sea, a comfortable room and good local cooking. Rooms are very basic but clean, and most share bathrooms; just one self-contained room is available. Although it's a little dog-eared, there is a good atmosphere here and the proximity to the village and dolphin sites makes it easy to get around and meet people. The nearby beach is private and good for swimming, alongside women coming to collect coconut coir from where they have buried it under rocks. The management here is extremely friendly and helpful, with years of experience in welcoming strangers. The price is good too.

Dolphin Shadow (*cheap*). Quite a distance further from the action of the village, but it has the advantage of having been recently established and in much better condition throughout. The local management here are much younger, and there is generally a fresh air of upbeat commercialism. The rooms are again well priced at $15 per person.

Dolphin View, PO Box 3781 (*moderate–cheap*). Even further out, but provides smarter accommodation in just two bungalows. The atmosphere here is rather less friendly and welcoming, with a more down-to-earth approach to providing clean and essential accommodation for a price. The private swimming beach is good.

Cabs Restaurant, Kizimkazi Dimbiani. A large restaurant, pleasantly shaded with thatch, good sea views and an extensive 'book' menu, which includes a number of hot European or local dishes with chips or rice.

Dolphin Safaris

Dolphin 'safaris' can be arranged directly with local fishermen from either Kizimkazi village, where the rates are around T.shs 10,000 or $15 per person for two people in a boat, or from Kizimkazi Dimbiani where you will pay around T.shs 25,000 for a place in a boat carrying any number up to 10 people.

Trips are usually around 2hrs long, but if you are nice to your boatman and there is a successful sighting he might be persuaded to stay out for an extra half an hour.

All the dolphins are wild, so sightings of any species are never guaranteed, and the humpback variety are generally much shyer than their co-species. If they don't want to play they don't hang around, and they can swim much faster than any flipper-clad swimmer.

The dolphin-watching industry that has sprung up around Kizimkazi has benefited the Stone Town tour operators more than the people of the village, and the tourists more than the dolphins. Tourists, however, get the most satisfaction out of the whole business: around nine out of 10 return home satisfied, having had a close-up view of these exceptional animals. It is also possible to do a 'swim with the dolphins' trip, in which case you have a roughly 30 per cent chance of seeing them. It's worth negotiating for snorkelling gear. The best time to see dolphins is between September and February. The sea is often rougher from June to September.

It cannot, however, be overstressed that these dolphins are wild animals, and need to be treated with consideration. Leave them alone if there are any signs of distress, and do not chase or surround them. Recently there have been reports of overcrowding around Kizimkazi, posing a severe environmental risk to the dolphins.

dolphins – an estimated 150 of them – may be seen all year, and are frequently joined by 50 or so of the shyer humpback dolphins. The region is divided into two villages about 2km apart. The main village, **Kizimkazi Mkunguni**, is the site of most of the 'action' – closest to the dolphin safaris and guesthouses. **Kizimkazi Dimbiani** is the site of the oldest Shirazi **mosque** on the island, dated AD 1107. It is not much to look at from the outside, presenting a fine corrugated iron roof and plain-walled face to the elements. The mosque is open to non-Muslims, including women, but you have to find the caretaker first to let you in. Make sure you are properly covered to avoid causing offence. The inscription and date of the building is in the mihrab, the niche facing Mecca at the eastern end.

Pemba

Pemba makes up the other, smaller half of the Zanzibar archipelago. The island lies a full 40km north of its sister, Unguja (Zanzibar Island), and has a very distinct character. Unlike its southern sister, Pemba has, so far, remained virtually unknown to the hordes of beach tourists. Just a couple of tourist destinations have opened up recently on its rural shores. Pemba has a fascinating reputation among mainland Tanzanians and Zanzibaris, in part for its reputation for black magic, in part as a hotbed of political activism – the majority of the island's population supports the opposition Civic United Front party, which continues to fight for full democracy on the archipelago. Travellers intent on discovering Pemba's charms may be discouraged by the reactions of Unguja inhabitants, who generally consider travelling the distance to Pemba as far more daunting than flying halfway around the world to reach Zanzibar in the first place. Pemba was in fact a major destination for travellers in past years, when it was known as 'Al Khudra' – the green island – and today it remains green and picturesque, coloured by the greens of 10 types of mango and the hundreds of clove trees that have traditionally supported the fortunes of this spice island.

The now-tranquil island of Pemba is renowned along the East African coast for the powers and abilities of its Waganga, or witch doctors. Belief in witch doctors and sorcery is still strong in Tanzania; it remains prevalent alongside the more recent

Pemba Wildlife: Birds and Land Beasts

Pemba is a green island, with masses of unusual wildlife to excite nature-lovers. This tiny island has four endemic bird species: the **Pemba white-eye** and the **Pemba sunbird** are common throughout the island; Ngezi Forest Reserve, a tall tropical forest filled with slanting sunlight and unusual wildlife, is the best place to spot the **Pemba green pigeon** and **Pemba scops owl**. Here you may also see the unusually squat, endemic **Pemba palm tree** (*Cressolido dibsis pembanus*), and might catch a glimpse in the gathering dusk of the island's endemic **fruit bat**, also known as the flying fox, and the endemic **Galago bushbaby**. Keen bird-watchers will enjoy the ferry trip across from Zanzibar Island, with likely possible sightings including the **masked booby**, **common noddy** and **bridled tern**.

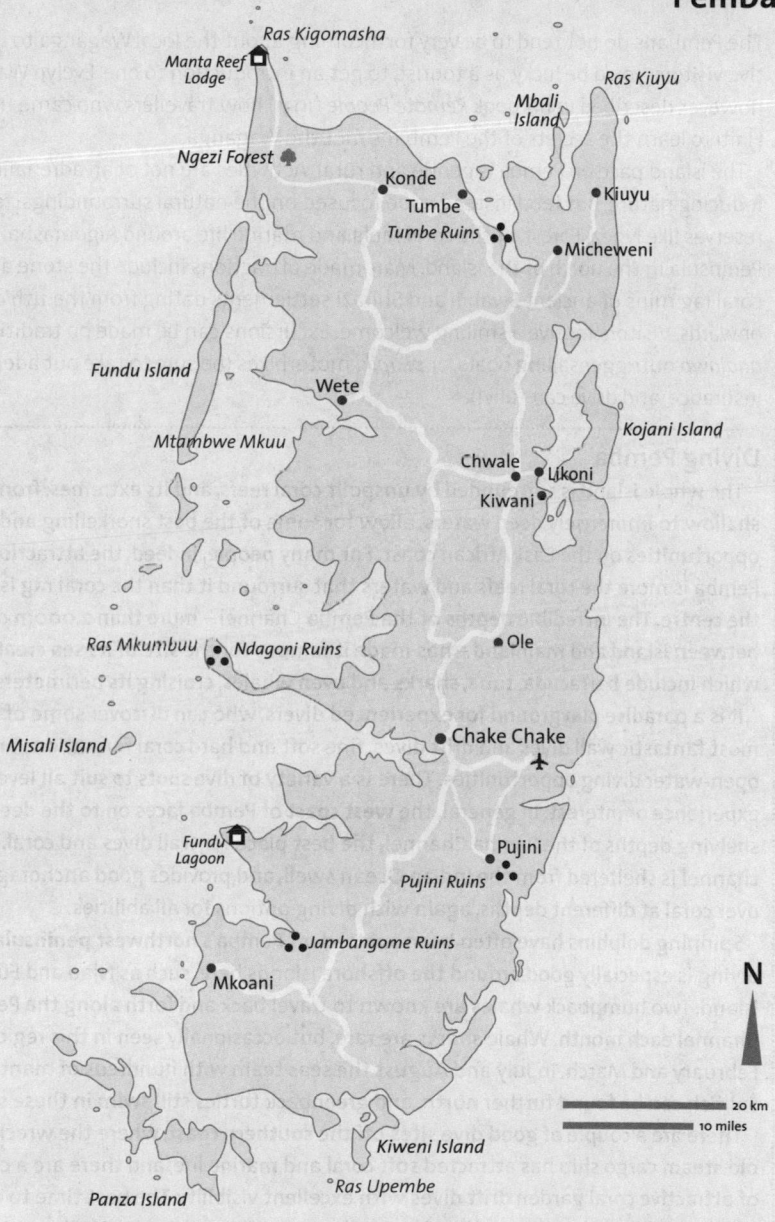

Pemba

Ras Kigomasha

Manta Reef
Lodge

Ras Kiuyu

Mbali
Island

Ngezi Forest

Konde

Tumbe

Tumbe Ruins

Kiuyu

Micheweni

Fundu Island

Wete

Mtambwe Mkuu

Kojani Island

Chwale

Likoni

Kiwani

Ras Mkumbuu

Ndagoni Ruins

Ole

Misali Island

Chake Chake

Fundu
Lagoon

Pujini

Pujini Ruins

Jambangome Ruins

Mkoani

N

20 km

10 miles

Kiweni Island

Ras Upembe

Panza Island

religious beliefs introduced in the last 2,000 years. Tanzanians travel to Pemba – as to the Usambara Mountains (*see* pp.181–4) – to find appropriate Waganga to cure, or cause, ills through acts of sorcery known as *uchawi*; the *uchawi* might originally be caused by unruly spirits or by evil intent against an individual. The most common reasons for bewitching are – perhaps unsurprisingly – jealousy, envy or sexual affairs.

The Pembans do not tend to be very forthcoming about the local Waganga to inquisitive visitors; you'd be lucky, as a tourist, to get an introduction to one. Evelyn Waugh, however, described in his book *Remote People* (1931) how travellers who came from Haiti to learn the secrets of the Pembans met the Waganga.

The island pace on Pemba is gentle and rural. Activities are not of an adrenaline-inducing nature, but tend instead to be focused on the natural surroundings: forest reserves like Ngezi Forest, or the coral reefs and marine life around Kigomasha Peninsula in the north of the island. Man-made attractions include the stone and coral rag ruins of ancient Swahili and Shirazi settlements dating from the 11th century onwards. Visitors receive a smiling welcome. Excursions can be made on traditional *ngalawa* outrigger sailing boats, or *pikipiki* motorbikes (be sure to take out adequate insurance, and drive carefully!).

Diving Pemba

The whole island is surrounded by unspoilt coral reefs, and its extremes, from very shallow to immensely deep waters, allow for some of the best snorkelling and diving opportunities on the East African coast. For many people, indeed, the attraction of Pemba is more the coral reefs and waters that surround it than the coral rag island at the centre. The incredible depths of the Pemba Channel – more than 2,000m deep between island and mainland – has made it famous for the size of its sea creatures, which include barracuda, tuna, sharks and even whales, cruising its perimeters.

It is a paradise playground for experienced divers, who can discover some of the most fantastic wall dives and drift dives, fine soft and hard coral formations and open-water diving opportunities. There is a variety of dive spots to suit all levels of experience or interest. In general, the **west coast** of Pemba faces on to the deep-shelving depths of the Pemba Channel, the best place for wall dives and coral. The channel is sheltered from the Indian Ocean swell, and provides good anchorage spots over coral at different depths, again with diving options for all abilities.

Spinning dolphins have often been spotted off Pemba's **northwest peninsula**; the diving is especially good around the offshore islands here, such as Njao and Fundu Island. Two humpback whales are known to travel back and forth along the Pemba Channel each month. Whale sharks are rare, but occasionally seen in this region in February and March. In July and August the seas teem with hundreds of manta rays. Sailfish can be found further north, and greenback turtles still swim in these seas.

There are a couple of good dive sites off the **southern coast**, where the wreck of an old steam cargo ship has attracted soft coral and marine life, and there are a couple of attractive coral garden drift dives with excellent visibility. The best time to dive the south coast is during the north monsoon, between December and April.

The **east coast** remains the preserve of experienced divers, who are fit enough to brave the swell of the Indian Ocean. This is the true domain of the big fish, and those that wish to find them should be certified to dive depths of at least 30m.

Offshore islands, such as Misali Island in the southwest, accessible from Chake Chake, also have excellent reefs and remote beaches for day trips.

See box, p.382, for dive operators and schools.

Getting There

For details of **air** and **sea** routes to Pemba from Zanzibar and Tanzania, *see* pp.319–20.

Getting Around

All visitors to Pemba arrive by sea or air; most land at Mkoani Port in the south of the island, or at the airport just south of Chake Chake in the middle. Those arriving at Mkoani will find themselves on a quietly bustling street corner where some **dala-dalas**, a couple of **taxis** and a few **private 4x4 vehicles** wait to take people in either direction along the two forks of the road.

To the right, the road to Chake Chake has been recently renovated and now links the main port and the town in less than 30mins' drive. There is also a new road from Chake Chake to Wete in the north of the island. To the left the road curves up around the cliff to reach the budget hotels in Mkoani.

By Car or *Pikipiki* Motorcycle

There are one or two **cars for hire** from local operators or guesthouses such as Jondeni in Mkoani, who also arrange tours. Vehicles are also available to show guests around the island at the smarter lodges such as Fundu Lagoon, Manta Reef Lodge or the Star Inn at Chake Chake.

Pikipiki **motorbikes** are available for hire too through **Partnership Travel**, PO Box 192, Chake Chake, Pemba, **t** (024) 2452278.

By Bus or Dala-Dala

A number of **buses**, **dala-dalas** and **shared taxis** roar around the island. Dala-dala drivers can often be persuaded to cover the extra distance between the end of their route and a nearby beach or more remote spot. The following are the most frequent and central routes, all of which are more often travelled in the mornings.

Bus no.3 between Chake Chake and Mkoani.
Bus no.6 between Chake Chake and Wete.
Bus no.24 between Wete and Konde.

A bus to Ngezi Forest leaves twice a day from Chake Chake, via Konde and Ngezi. Other buses go as far as Konde, from where it is a 4km walk to the gate house.

Tourist Information

Pemba Commission For Tourism: PO Box 250, Chake Chake.
Zanzibar Tourist Corporation, PO Box 18, Chake Chake, **t** (024) 2452124.
Foreign exchange. Currency can be exchanged at the **People's Bank of Zanzibar**, which has branches at Mkoani, Chake Chake and Wete, and is open Mon, Thurs and Sat 8.30–12.30, Fri 8.30–11, or at the **National Bank of Commerce** in Chake Chake, whose more generous opening hours are Mon–Fri 8.30–4, Sat 8.30–12.30.

The central town of Chake Chake is one of the best places for fully independent travellers to arrange travel itineraries around the island. **Partnership Travel**, PO Box 192, Chake Chake,

In December and July, when all the crops are harvested and stored, the people of Pemba organize **bullfights**, a legacy of their one-time Portuguese colonialists.

History

The early history of Pemba is similar to that of Unguja. It is thought that Pemba was originally inhabited by migrating African tribes in search of a life away from the growing mêlée of mainland habitation, that could be sustained by seasonal fishing. It is likely that the island was inhabited before the 1st century AD, and these first settlers became a tribe known as the Pemba, much like the Hadimu and Tumbatu people of Zanzibar Island. A small group of the Tumbatu also formed a community in the south of Pemba. Separate villages were internally governed and developed into mini-monarchies, entirely independent of each other, a lack of unity that provided an easy target for sailors seeking to move in. After years of trade with foreign visitors the African

Pemba, t (024) 2452278, is a reliable local tour operator providing English-speaking guides and assistance with transport and itineraries all around the island. In Mkoani, **Faizin Tours and Travel Agency**, PO Box 70, t (024) 2456102/ t (0744) 366489, are very helpful.

Sports and Activities

Cat-diving Ltd, PO Box 3203, t (0742) 781376, *a.martinkat@t-online.da*. Probably the best option for boating and diving excursions around Pemba, aboard the catamaran *Inula*. The catamaran is equipped for adventures; the company makes the most of many years' personal experience enjoying the wilderness of the Pemba reefs. The German owner has made this option a classic choice.

Pemba Afloat, Njao Inlet, Pemba Island, c/o Maruhubi Beach Villas, PO Box 3088, t (0747) 451188, *maruhubi@zanlink.com*. Lying off the Pemba coast, the *Karibu*, a 60ft ketch, and her sister yacht *Sitra* can accommodate up to 10 people. With speedboats, dinghies and a small sailing boat, the yachts are the perfect retreat from which to explore the open waters and inland creeks of Pemba. Both yachts are fully equipped with dive gear, and waterskiing is available. Back on land it is possible to enjoy barbecues on isolated beaches, tours through spice plantations and bird-watching while walking through the Ngezi Forest.

Where to Stay and Eat

There are just a few **international holiday hotels** that are geared up to cater to an international tourist market for visitors to Pemba. A couple of these have character and charm enough to alone make the trip to Pemba worthwhile.

Fundu Lagoon, just north of Mkoani Port on Wambaa Beach, in the southwest of the island, t (024) 2232926, *fundu@africaonline. co.tz, www.fundulagoon.com* (*expensive; less for non-divers*) stands out as the best accommodation on Pemba. Since its opening in 2000, the lodge has gained a reputation of a stylish and smart beach hotel with fantastic accommodation under canvas, set against a backdrop of steep forested hillside. Fundu Lagoon fills a niche for top-quality accommodation and food in an upmarket but environmentally sympathetic style. All 14 rooms are huge, private safari tents under *makuti* thatch, either on the beach or on a hilltop position; all are decked out with hand-finished chunky wooden décor and teak floors and connected with 'nature-trail'-style wooden rope-banister walkways. Two of the rooms are suites with their own private chillout decks and plunge pools. The open restaurant and bar at the centre are the height of casual elegance – billowing white nets and *makuti*, filled with a fine aroma of fresh coffee. Here guests enjoy a sumptuous international menu, while enjoying views of the beach and sea. Staff are immaculately dressed and friendly. Only near to the designer gift shop and reception does the hotel have the atmosphere of a glitzy big hotel. From here guests look out over the long wooden jetty towards the open-air bar where lunches and sundowners are an absolute must; gaze out over the dark golden beach, and watch Pemba fishermen unloading the catch of the day while the sun burns into the sea. Fundu Lagoon has a fleet of more modern boats for diving, snorkelling and watersports, and a

population became familiar with newcomers, and perhaps barely noticed when some began to settle. Later the Pemba were conquered by an Arab colonial regime. The Swahili word meaning 'to be civilized' is still *ustaarabu*, literally 'like an Arab', after the grandeur and refinement of the Arabs. An adventurous sailor and Arab writer called Abu'l Hasan 'Ali al-Mas'udi recorded an account of his travels to Zanj at the end of the 10th century AD, and told how the civilization of Pemba, then called Quanbalu, minted its own coins. When refugees were driven from their homes by religious upheavals and persecution around the Persian Gulf between the 8th and 11th centuries, they catamaran that can take guests out for full-day sailing and fishing, and has a show for sunset cruises. The highlight of staying at Fundu, however, is their daily trips to Misali Island, Pemba's only marine sanctuary, *see* pp.386–7. Not only are the beaches wonderful but this area has been voted as one of the top 10 dive spots in the world. Charters can also be arranged to Zanzibar Island and Stone Town.

Manta Reef Lodge, Kigomasha Peninsula, on the northern tip of Pemba, t (0747) 423930, *reservations@mantareeflodge.com, www. mantareeflodge.com (expensive)*. A superbly situated beach haven, especially good for divers keen to experience the best dive sites that Pemba has to offer. Non-divers can just as easily appreciate the natural side of the lodge, which has 12 wooden cabins facing the ocean and a line of vibrant tropical forest. It's close to Ngezi Forest, with plenty of superb rural walks and wildlife action. Bushbabies scamper and chatter in the night, while guests enjoy the fresh evening air from the comfort of their own room. The large central living area is comfortably decorated, and designed so that outside verandah tables benefit from their aspect to enjoy fresh breakfasts and evening meals beneath the stars. Its position and design, with a wide archway open to east and west, allows for full appreciation of sunrise and sunset, and is focused on easy access to the new beach bar and dive centre. Food is good and freshly prepared, served with broad smiles. The lodge overlooks a superb northern stretch of Panga ya Watoro Beach and is very close to the hidden coral caves here, and walks to nearby beaches or Ras Kigomasha lighthouse are easy, interesting and enjoyable. The original concept of Manta Reef was as accommodation for divers, and the Kenyan **One Earth** diving operation makes the most of its northernmost situation on Pemba by shipping in clients just as easily from Shimoni in southern Kenya (2hrs' drive from Mombasa, then 1hr by speedboat), as from Zanzibar or Dar. It takes 2hrs to drive to Manta Reef from Mkoani Port at the south of the island. All information and guidance is knowledgeable, experienced and reliable, with PADI courses available and different day-trips individually priced and for all levels of experience. For example, a colourful three-dive day trip to see the corals and fish at Uvinge, near Misali, diving at Manta Point and including a barbecue in Fundu will cost guests around $20 each extra. Open-sea dives on the east coast among barracuda, tuna and grey and hammerhead sharks are for experienced divers only; a day out with a lunchbox on the beach costs around $15 extra per person. Dives generally cost around $35 for two to three dives a day. All equipment is available for rent individually or as a complete set. The lodge can also organize deep-sea fishing trips, kayaking and snorkelling. The situation of the lodge is such that it is impossible not to be aware of prolific local wildlife, especially in the surrounding seas. The lodge has a number of large diving boats and speedboats.

Kiweni Marine Resort, on Kiweni Island (shown on some maps as Shamiani Island) in the south of the island; for information contact **Liria** in Dar es Salaam, t (022) 2600901. On a small island just off the southernmost coast of Pemba, 14 beach *bandas* are under construction. This is a beach resort still very much in the development stages, but the site is pervaded by an air of creativity that extends to a fine dining area and numerous rock, wood and cactus

sailed down the east coast of Africa; one of the places these Shirazi people settled was Pemba. Ruins around the island illustrate the lavish lifestyle of these settlers, who developed a renowned port and community. The site at Ras Mkumbuu has pillar tombs inlaid with china, and ruins of other palaces nearby show intricate irrigation systems, wells and mosques, now silted up and sinking into the sands. Yet little is known about these settlers beyond a handful of bizarre legends.

More is known about the Portuguese invasion in the 15th century. After rounding the Cape of Good Hope in 1498, the Portuguese returned in 1502 with 20 extra ships, gardens, a shop selling unusual handicrafts and even its own little natural history museum. All of this is positioned on a very fine coral sand beach and lapped by a superbly blue sea. The greatest difficulty is getting there and away. When the accommodation is completed, an ox cart is planned to take transfers between the nearest dhow port and the resort. The hotel plans to be self-sufficient as far as possible, supplying its own fruit and vegetables, chickens and milk, and works closely with the local community to involve local women and the community in building projects. A nature trail is also being devised for guests to enjoy the surrounding island. The restaurant's numerous menu plans seem promising. The *bandas* all overlook a deep swimming pool, designed for diving tuition. Bungalows will probably be *expensive* to stay in, but there are also cheaper tents available for divers. Diving and fishing excursions should also be available.

Pemba Afloat, *pembaafloat@pembaisland.com,www.pembaisland.com* (*moderate*) is an operation that runs three live-aboard dive boats that are permanently mored at Njao Lagoon. Although primarily a diving operation Pemba Afloat also has easy access to some fabulous beaches as well as the surrounding Ngezi Forest.

Pemba also has some excellent **guest houses**, and although these are a little more expensive than those on Zanzibar Island they provide a very high standard of clean, comfortable, welcoming accommodation. Power cuts are common, so don't base your stay on hairdryers and electric razors.

Mkoani
Jondeni Guest House, PO Box 111, Mkoani, **t** (024) 2456042, *pembablue@hotmail.com*
(*cheap*). The best budget accommodation near Mkoani Port, the Jondeni has a homely backpacker-style atmosphere and an excellent outdoor dining room terrace with superb views over palm tree tops to the sea. The management is extremely capable and well organized; it can arrange day trips on dhows with engines, or in Land Cruisers, and also diving trips (for experienced divers) to Misali, Fundu, Njao or the wreck. Excursions come with lunch and a guide; all kinds of *chai* are provided too. The terrace restaurant has a mouthwatering menu, with a wide choice of seafood, meat and vegetarian dishes, reasonably priced. Signposted from the port. There is also a dormitory with cheaper beds.

Mkoani Guest House (*cheap*). Cheaper and less atmospheric accommodation is available even closer to the port at a dimly lit but friendly establishment with decent rooms and very basic facilities. Guests may cook their own meals, or meals can be provided if ordered in advance. The guesthouse is only a few metres from the port, and the owner promises the utmost in security and safety for guests – including bars on the windows.

Chake Chake
The Tavern, PO Box 144, Chake Chake, **t** (024) 2452660 (*cheap*). The cleanest and newest place, which has just six very fine new rooms on the first floor, all immaculately clean and well presented. Situated at the centre of town, it is convenient for early morning starts and a taste of urban Pemba's not terribly racy nightlife. The family serves excellent food on request; it's your best bet for a decent, wholesome meal anywhere in Chake town, although you are likely to be subjected to satellite TV throughout. All are subjected to the cries of roosters at dawn.

fully prepared for invasion. They conquered Pemba in 1505, three years after their accession in Kilwa. Evidence of their military rule is cast in stone at Chake Chake fortress, which is was originally constructed by the Portuguese, later rebuilt by Mazrui Arabs. The fortress became a jail after Independence, and then a police barracks, but in the last years of the 20th century a European Union aid donation built a new hospital on the site, knocking down much of the old ruin.

Portuguese domination earned so little popularity that the Omanis in Muscat responded to pleas from the East African coast in 1698 and sent a naval force against

Swahili Divers, in the old Quaker Mission building, t (024) 2452786, *www. swahili drivers.com, swahilidrivers@intafrica.com, swahilidivers@superonline.com* (*cheap*). A bit more character in a serious divers' haunt. Its fine old colonial location gives this place charm, along with excellent views over the town and sunset over the creek. This haven for divers on a budget attracts a diverse and interesting clientele, occasionally united by a desire to dive the Pemba Channel. The lodge is excellently run by its charismatic Turkish owner, who creates an open, friendly atmosphere and encourages all his guests to feel as passionate about this exceptional island as he evidently does.

Comfortable accommodation in friendly settings is available just north of Chake town at slightly lower rates, although it's a short dala-dala or taxi ride from town. These places are near the fine new sports stadium, home of the local football team.

Venus Lodge, PO Box 183, Chake Chake, t (0744) 312484 (*cheap*). Spacious and clean. Guests can lounge in the comfortable and airy central sitting room, complete with TV, video and music systems, and enjoy supper laid on a long table outside. Meals must be pre-ordered but are delicious.

Star Inn, PO Box 109, t (024) 2252190 (*cheap*). The nearby Star Inn also has a good reputation and provides a similar standard of home-style comfort, good food and security for similar prices. Friendly staff will assist with trips around the island. Evening meals available.

Evening entertainment in Chake revolves around a few **roadside food stalls** and a **mini duka** for cigarettes and soggy sweets. Beers are available in the grungy but amusing bar attached to the **Chake Hotel**, or otherwise at the **Policeman's Mess**.

Wete

There are two good guesthouses to choose from in Wete. Both provide a good service, although the prices are notably higher than you might expect to pay for similar accommodation on the mainland or Zanzibar island.

Sharook Guest House, PO Box 117, Pemba, t (024) 2454386 (*cheap*). Closer to Wete Port, where cheery sailors returning from Mombasa and Tanga unload their maize meal, tomatoes, and vegetable crops, the Sharook is clean, friendly and run with enthusiasm. It claims to be 'small in size but big in hospitality', and offers five double rooms, two of which are self-contained. Lunch and supper are available on advance request. The Sharook can also organize boat trips to the offshore islands and trips to Ngezi Forest. Free viewing of the family satellite television in the central sitting room. Sharook is the meeting point for visitors bound for the yachts of Pemba Afloat (*see* p.384).

Super Guest House, PO Box 60, Pemba, t (024) 2454332 (*cheap*). The small but cosy family-run 'Super' has just three double rooms, one of which is self-contained. All rooms have mosquito nets and clean, decent-sized beds. There is cold running water, but no hot. Supper must be pre-ordered, and comes at a standard rate of T.shs 2,500.

Wete Guest House, PO Box 66, Wete, t (024) 2454301 (*cheap*). The cheapest accommodation is at the local state-run hotel, which has eight rooms for rent. The accommodation was once colourful, but is now very dilapidated with plenty of damp spots and peeling wallpaper to gladden the senses.

them, successfully recapturing Mombasa, Kilwa and Zanzibar and Pemba in 1699, and finally ousting the Portuguese administration. Subsequently these regions fell under the jurisdiction and control of Oman; its sultan sent *liwalis* (governors) to all towns and settlements. Once again the locals found themselves strictly governed, so much so that by the 1740s communities were begging the Portuguese to come back and rid them of the Arabs. It was too late, but in 1744 the Yorubi dynasty in Oman was overthrown by the Omani Busaidi dynasty, which would soon give way to the succession of Sayyid Said bin Sultan (1806–56), the first Sultan of Zanzibar and the man responsible for rebuilding the fortunes of Pemba Island. Sultan Said developed Zanzibar's and Pemba's trade potential, and implemented a massive clove-planting initiative on Pemba, an undertaking that transformed the character of this previously forested island for ever. Of Zanzibar's estimated 3.5 million clove trees, the majority are on Pemba, where the air is scented with their spice as families lay their crops to dry in front of their houses. Crops are harvested twice a year, and Zanzibar State Trading Company is the sole buyer and exporter. The cloves from these islands are still considered to be of the highest quality and finest aroma. The Pemba Essential Oil Distillery at Chake Chake was established in 1982 to extract the essential oil from cloves locally and increase the local revenue. Guests are welcome to visit the factory, which also presses lemongrass and cinnamon oils.

Beaches

Although Pemba is surrounded by fine coral reef and pristine seas its shores are also thick with dense mangrove forests; the best beaches take a bit of finding and getting to. The Zanzibar archipelago's beaches are in general subject to tidal extremes, and the tides around Pemba expose coral reefs and sea grass at low tide. The reefs can then be explored on foot, but suitable footwear is advised!

There are wonderfully clean and translucent clear beaches at the north of the island. The best expanses of sand stretch for 3km at **Vumawimbi**, just north of Ngezi Forest; the more sheltered and shining sands of **Tondooni** and **Verani** to the west of the peninsula, and **Panga ya Watoro** further north are also exceptional. On the opposite side of the peninsula you can find remote sands that are inaccessible by car – you may be able to reach them on a bicycle, *pikipiki* or motorbike – at **Mbuyu Kambaa**, **Ras Kiuyu** and **Mbuyuni** beaches.

Just east of Vitongoji are three bays that are easily reached from Chake Chake, passing the essential oil factory en route, and provide good swimming when the tide is high, and reef walking when it is low; **Liko la Ngezi**, the southernmost of the three, is also known as the site of the 'lonely tomb of Vitongoji'. On the west coast, there are long stretches of golden sandy beach at **Wambaa**, the site of the Fundu Lagoon Hotel – a long way from the main road, and currently reached only by bike or boat.

Offshore Islands and Islets: Misali Island

Some of the best beaches worth making an extra effort to reach are those around **Misali Island**, off the coast to the west at the same latitude as Chake Chake . Swimming here is a real pleasure, especially for snorkelling and diving over coral reefs straight off the beach, and you can walk all around the island at low tide. The island has a 'shiver-me-timbers' reputation as the hiding place for the notorious Scottish privateer, pirate and murderer Captain Kidd's treasure, which he is reputed to have buried here in 1698. The island is known to have been popular with 17th-century pirates as a safe place to stash their booty.

The island forest is home to a dazzling green forest bird, the rare Fischer's muraco, and to vervet monkeys and 'flying fox' fruit bats. The waters around the island are a marine conservation area: fishing is strictly controlled, and totally forbidden on the western reefs. Conservationists are petitioning for it to be made a fully recognized national marine park. Trips to Misali can be arranged from each of the three central ports of Pemba – Mkoani, Chake Chake and Wete, and through larger hotels. The Jondeni Guest House at the top of the hill at Mkoani can arrange boats to Misali, and at Wete boats can be arranged through the Sharook Guest House (see p.385).

There is another stretch of sandy beach on the northern peninsula of **Kojani Island** (see p.391), barely detached from Pemba just to the east of Chwale: you can drive to Likoni on the east coast and then hire a boat to **Fumbi la Kiua**, then a 1km walk.

Chake Chake

The central town of Chake Chake forms the hub of Pemba business and commerce. It is situated in an elevated position at the head of Chake Chake creek, once a thriving channel for boat trade but now so silted up that just a few dhows venture back and forth along it when the tides are high. Shops and dukas are crowded together in the old town centre, filled with the stuff of life – all kinds of hardware supplies that are most necessary to the people of Pemba, alongside tour guides and photographers.

Evidence of the antiquity of Chake Chake is still just about apparent in the stone remains at the top of the town, although sadly the construction of a fine new hospital incurred the near-absolute demolition of the **Old Fort**, thought to date from the Portuguese era between 1499 and 1698. Barely enough is left to determine the origins of this fine defence, which 19th-century records describe as having two round and two square towers, with thatched roofs between. The round towers are a typically Arabic construction, and much of the decorative stonework also points to Arabic influences, but the stone towers seem to indicate earlier Portuguese origins.

Chake Chake developed near the site of a much older settlement in the area, the ancient trading post of **Ras Mkumbuu**, which was located on the peninsula just to the north of Chake Chake creek, overlooking Misali Island and across the ocean to the mainland. Excavations of the site have revealed the remains of a mosque dating from the 10th century. Most of the standing remains date from the 13th and 14th centuries, when the settlement featured in records kept by the 13th-century Arabic geographer Yakut bin Abdulla al Rumi. The ruins include the remains of an obviously once elaborate mosque, constructed on pillars, and also a number of tombs inlaid with porcelain, illustrating Arab trading connections with China. It is thought that Ras Mkumbuu was inhabited until the 16th century; it is not clear why it was abandoned, but the site now lies some way from any habitation and is difficult to access by land, except on a motorbike or on foot. Most visitors reach the site by boat from Chake Chake, often combining a visit with a trip to Misali Island.

More ruins of 13th century Pemba can be seen at **Pujini**, a short drive out of Chake Chake (around 10km), on the southeast coast. Here the remains of a vast fortress and creek harbour are said to have been the domain of Mohammad bin Abdulrahman, now better known as Mkame Ndume – 'the milker of scrotums' – on account of his despotic practices. He was notorious along the Indian Ocean coast as a merchant, boat-builder, mosque-builder – and pirate; the milker's name was known from Kenya to the Comoros even before he amassed the wealth to build his empire in Pujini on Pemba. He was reputed to have built his fortress – with some walls more than a metre thick – by forcing his people to carry stones while shuffling on their buttocks. While these ruins are among the most easily accessible, a perfect sunny walk on a quiet afternoon, they are in a very poor state of repair and bear little resemblance to their glorious original state; the archaeological site is fighting the demands of nature to reclaim it. Among a mass of brambles and sand, visitors can still see the deep well that was unusually divided into two chambers with a wall between, designed to prevent Mkame Ndume's two wives from meeting.

Wete

The port town of Wete lies about 40 minutes' drive northwest of Chake Chake, beyond a fertile agricultural stretch of fields and coconut palms. Despite being the central dhow port for the import and export of fruit, vegetable and crop supplies from Kenya and the mainland, Wete has a quiet atmosphere around its single-storey housing, which extends back from the main road along sandy tracks.

Archaeological excavations on the flat hilltop of the peninsula opposite the harbour have revealed the remains of the 11th-century settlement of **Matambwe Mkuu**, the 'Great Peninsula', which was also described by the Arabic geographer Yakut al Rumi. These remains extend over an impressive 215 hectares and were the site of the discovery of a handful of tiny silver coins, almost the the only coins minted in sub-Saharan Africa in the Middle Ages, along with those found at Kilwa. Matambwe Mkuu was a secondary settlement to Ras Mkumbuu, and was abandoned earlier, probably during the 14th century. Little is left standing on this island peninsula today.

Kigomasha Peninsula

The northernmost peninsula is a good place for invigorating walks and day trips. The distance from Ngezi Forest Reserve to the endless sands of Vumawimbi Beach can be covered on foot in less than an hour. The region is rural and unspoilt, with a maze of paths and tracks leading through fields where locals tend their seasonal crops, or pile the fruit of their labours onto ox carts to take them to market. As with anywhere in Pemba, it can be worthwhile walking with a guide, who can be arranged through individual hotels and guesthouses, or local tour companies.

Ngezi Forest Reserve

The superbly peaceful and unusual rich tropical rainforest at Ngezi Forest Reserve remains one of the last pockets of the original Pemba landscape as it was just a few hundred years ago, before the population growth and the 1850s clove-planting project transformed much of the fertile island land. Visitors pay a $5 charge at the warden's hut at the entrance to explore the nature trails, one of which covers around

2km and can be easily walked in an hour, although longer walks are also possible. The office is open between 7.30am and 4pm; when it is closed you can usually find a ranger at the first house south. The guides, Juma Tanfik and Suliman, are enthusiastic, fluent and informative walking companions. Their quick and familiar eyes are good at spotting unusual wildlife – the flicker of a cicada, the trail of an ant – although your chances of spotting a flying fox – the endemic Pemba fruit bat – are rare. Anyone wishing to stake out the forest for fruit bats or the shy, miniature scops owl can negotiate with the guides for an evening or night walk, at a charge of around $10 per person, less for a group. They will also keep a beady eye open for any local amphibians and reptiles, such as the Mozambique spitting cobra, boomslangs or spotted wood snakes, and all manner of different geckos, and speckle-lipped skinks.

Ngezi Forest is especially unusual in that it is made up of lots of highland species such as *Olea oleanna* and *Tifandara* (Madagascar), and yet it is lowland forest. Orchids are blown to seed in any nook and tree arm or among the highest branches, flowering in December and January, when the sunlit glades are filled with butterflies dancing. Around 130 tree species have been identified in the forest, although there has been very little study of the local flora generally. Visitors can hardly fail to notice the tall, skinny features of the 35m-high bombax tree, with seed pods full of kapok. Important species endemic to Pemba, such as the Pemba palm tree (*Cressolida dibsis pembanus*) can be seen along the road through the forest, as can the odd endangered species of wild banana palm, which provide the favourite food for resident Galago bushbabies, vervet monkeys and the famous fruit bats. Most of the forest mammals are quite undersized: among the largest is the tiny, shy and very rare duiker antelope; Zanzibar tree hyraxes and marsh mongooses are common and Jevan civet cats also live in the forest, although they are not endemic but were introduced by Arabs who bred them for musk for perfume. Red colobus monkeys were introduced at one stage, but no study has yet been undertaken to see if they still live here.

Keen bird-watchers have every chance of catching a glimpse of endemic Pemba birds such the Pemba scops owl, green pigeon or white eye, the Pemba sunbird, or masses of other colourful equatorial species such as the sisticola, violet-breasted starling or crowned hornbill. The lake area at the centre of the forest attracts a range of water birds, such as the breadbill ibis, mangrove kingfishers, white-face or whistling ducks, pygmy kingfishers and pygmy geese, while red-eye doves, sparrow hawks and harrier hawks fly the air between.

Beyond the Forest

All around this area you will see houses which have vast covered ovens outside to dry coconuts for copra. Beyond the forest, the road leads through abandoned **rubber plantations** left to grow wild and go to seed, the smooth trunks of the rubber trees still in orderly rows. This region of Pemba is rural and fresh, with a startling clarity of sunlight. There are a number of country tracks through coloured grasses and shamba fields, mainly used by local farmers collecting crops for sale at the market with the help of an ox and cart. These also lead up to the northernmost **Kigomasha Lighthouse** whose kerosene lamp is lit nightly by the diligent lighthouse keeper and

Chwale and the 'Game of the Cow'

At the central intersection at the middle of the island, the village of Chwale is famous in Pemba for being the site of the annual bullfight, the ***Mchezo ya ngombe***, or 'game of the cow'. This is a source of great amusement, and is held when the weather is hot and dry, the cloves have been harvested, and the farmers have no urgent jobs. So before the short rains in October and November and sometimes in July the islanders of Pemba gather in the empty fields and bet on their favourite bull. They require three bulls for each fight, each tethered at the end of a very long rope. The following action generally involves local boys posing as matadors in front of a moody-looking bull, until the animal charges and the 'matadors' jump aside. It can also involve local wide-boys racing around hitting the animals with sticks, and lots of shouting, squealing and general encouragement from the women. The bulls always win, and are led through the streets in triumph, decked with flowers. A popular favourite in recent years has been Resasi, a name meaning 'bullet'. Bullfights also take place in the villages of Pujini, Mchangamdogo, Ole, Wingwi and Kengeja.

his family; they will sometimes allow you to climb the scary stairs to the top (for a couple of dollars) to appreciate views in all directions. Nearby, on the eastern side of the peninsula, there are small, sheltered beaches, which are good for swimming although subject to extreme tides. Slightly further south, **Vumawimbi Beach** ('vuma' for sound plus 'wimbi' meaning waves, so 'sound of waves' beach) curves around the shore, extending for an impressive 3–4km of unspoilt sands. It's a renowned market point for local fishermen, who can often be found gathered in a close huddle here while the catch is dragged up the beach and auctioned to the highest bidder.

Eastern Pemba

Continuing eastwards around the northern side of Pemba brings you to **Tumbe**, predominantly a farming and fishing village lined with coconut palms, just off the main road between Konde and Mapufo. This region has become a central port for fishermen to sell their fish and for women to harvest seaweed. The market here is more central and accessible than the auction at Vumawimbi, and attracts a crowd of locals from around Tumbe and Mbali Island, just over the water, in the mornings. The people hold a popular annual boat race here to celebrate the New Year.

Further south, just off the road beyond the tiny village of Chwaka are seven **Mazrui Ruins** that again illustrate the elaborate living standards on Pemba between the 15th and 18th centuries. A guide can usually be found among the nearby cassava plantations to lead you southwards along a sandy path to find the remains of a large Mazrui mosque and six tombs, all abandoned in the early 19th century when Sultan Said and the Busaidi Arabs overthrew the Mazrui rule. These ruins are in an advanced state of decline, with paw paws and roots dilapidating what is left.

A narrow path continues through the cassava plantations to the edge of a valley and the site of a second **15th-century town**, which was ruled by a harsh prince called

Harouni bin Ali, who remains immortalized in one of the 10 glazed and decorated tombs that surround the largest mosque here. The town seems to have been quite substantial in its day, covering 20 hectares and including a fortress, iron works, at least two mosques and grand reception halls all arranged around a small harbour. Legend tells how Prince Harouni was known as Mvunja Pau – 'the breaker of the pole'. His reputation for ruling with violence is so similar to that of the tyrant Mkana Ndune at Pujini, south of Chake Chake, that many suggest Harouni was his son.

Another nature reserve is defined on the northeastern peninsula, called **Msitu Mkuu**. Antelopes and monkeys are said to live here, although sightings are rare.

The people of nearby **Kojani Island** are fishermen of considerable repute. They work in groups of 10 or so men, using a traditional technique known only to them. They traditionally leave Pemba and fish commercially around Mombasa, then return home to support their women and children. It is thought that Kojani Island has a population of as many as 80,000 people; onlookers from Pemba mainland see a number of fine-looking houses clustered together on the opposite shore.

Still thriving, well-tapped, sun-dappled **rubber plantations** extend inland along the Chwale-Mzambaraoni Road; you can stop to visit the processing factory at the side of the road. The rubber is tapped in December, and during this time the sap is collected from the trees and poured into a giant outdoor bath. From here it is weighed and dried, squashed and squared, and then pressed and hung out to dry. Rubber squares are taken into a smoke house, with huge coal burners beneath each, where they are heated to vast high temperatures to make them malleable and easily manipulated. The factory has a capacity to produce approximately 5,000–6,000kg per day. The final material is exported for latex bandages and other rubber uses. The surviving rubber trade in Pemba is, however, precarious, with crisis constantly anticipated.

The Mafia Archipelago

The Mafia archipelago is at the mouth of the Rufiji River Delta, and consists of **Mafia**, **Jibondo**, **Juani** and **Chole Islands**. These islands' position as the most southerly islands on the Tanzanian coast has made them strategically covetable throughout the country's long history of wrangling for rule. Visitors today find rural farming and fishing communities whose day-to-day lives continue in much the same pattern as they have for millennia – with little indication that this was once a strategic trading post, battled over by Arab factions and Portuguese, Kua and Kisimani people, Germans and British. Mafia Island and the surrounding archipelago have a great deal to offer as an unspoilt, little-visited alternative to other Indian Ocean locations around Zanzibar and along the coast, although options for accommodation and seafaring navigation are relatively expensive. Budget travellers will find it harder to reach and to stay on Mafia, unless they are fully self-sufficient with camping equipment.

The archipelago provides excellent opportunities for diving and snorkelling, and for discovering deserted beaches and offshore islands of natural and historic interest. The deeper channels around the islands are also renowned for world-class deep-sea

Getting There

By Boat

Mafia used to be served by the ancient *Canadian Spirit* ferry service between Dar es Salaam and Mtwara, but it no longer stops here, making arrival on the islands by public boat tricky. The only means of approach by boat is now on a motorized or sailing dhow: cargo dhows operate from Kisiju Beach, around 80km south of Dar es Salaam; the fare is cheap – $3–6 – but the journey is long – about 12hrs with a motor or 24hrs under sail – and travellers travel at their own risk.

By Air

Coastal Travels, Mafia Airport, **t** (023) 2402522, or 107 Upanga Road, PO Box 3052, Dar es Salaam, **t** (022) 2117959, *aviation@coastal.cc*, *www.coastal.cc*, flies daily from Dar.

Precision Air, PO Box 70770, Dar es Salaam, **t** (022) 2121718, **f** (022) 2113036, or Mazsons Hotel, Zanzibar Stone Town, **t** (024) 2234521, **f** (024) 2234520, *information@precisionairtz. com*, *www.precisionairtz.com*, now runs a scheduled flight to Mafia on a 19-seater aircraft three times a week from Dar es Salaam via Zanzibar. The trip from Dar takes an hour, and the fare is around $100 return.

Kinasi Lodge operates its own light aircraft and will arrange transfers for its guests to and from Dar es Salaam or Zanzibar ($130 per person each way). Be prepared for a $3 departure tax from Mafia Airport.

Getting Around

There are no tarmac roads on Mafia Island, and only two major graded roads, one running north to south and one west to east; all roads meet at Kilindoni, the central town and site of the airstrip. The rest of the island is linked by narrow sandy paths and tracks, just wide enough to walk, bicycle or manoeuvre a cow. Longer-distance local transport relies on the tides, as it is generally by dhow. Private motorized vehicles are limited to those owned by the hotels and conservation organizations; visitors are advised to pre-arrange transport through their accommodation – Kinasi Lodge will organize all transfers as a matter of course. Otherwise it is possible to arrange a **taxi service** on arrival at Kilindoni, which charges around $15 for a transfer to Utende and Chole Bay. **Bicycles** can be hired from Lizu's Hotel in Kilindoni, and from Kinasi Lodge in Utende.

Tourist Information

The **bank** and **post office** are both on the airport road in Kilindoni. The bank is open Mon–Fri 8.30am–3pm, Sat 8.30–12.30.

Where to Stay

Kinasi Lodge, PO Box 3052 Dar es Salaam, **t** (022) 2843501/2843495, *kinasi@intafrica. com* (UK representative: Tanzania Odyssey, **t** (020) 7471 8780, *info@tanzaniaodyssey. com*, *www.tanzaniaodyssey.com*) *(expensive)*. By far the best choice, a small and elegant option for a luxurious stay on Mafia Island. High standards of accommodation and service are consistent. The lodge was built by its owner, who has now managed it for many years. Fourteen palm-thatched bungalows are set around a hilly, palm-filled garden, each with its own hammock slung in the shade of its own private verandah. Guests enjoy views over the Chole Pass and Chole Island, and are lulled to sleep by the whispering palms. Great attention to detail has been paid to all areas of the lodge, with an eye for comfort and artisan style throughout. The open-sided sitting room around the bar is comfortable and well furnished, complete with cushions, magazines and a reference library for all local

fishing, and home to at least two greatly endangered species: the docile dugong (manatee or sea cow) is still thought to find refuge cruising the seagrass between Mafia and the Rufiji River Delta, and the small islands around the archipelago remain a popular breeding ground for giant and green turtles. Under the RAMSAR convention Tanzania has now declared Mafia, the Rufiji Delta and the coastline to Kilwa a new interests. The swimming pool has recently been redesigned to include a poolside barbecue and bar, and is surrounded by flower beds. The main focus of any stay at Kinasi is likely to be based around making the most of the fleet of boats, which include a number of traditional lateen sailing dhows, two small dive boats and a vast 85-horsepower gamefishing and diving boat. Kinasi now has a very smart spa-relaxation therapy centre. The closest beach is not the best, but guests tend to spend their days out exploring the pristine waters, islands and sandbanks that surround Mafia Island, returning to the lodge each night for devastatingly delicious cocktails and supper. Kinasi prides itself on its cooking, and prepares lavish picnics and meals, with excellent seafood, home-made breads and yoghurts and an endless variety of soups.

Dolphin Island Pole Pole Bungalow Resort, PO Box 198, Mafia Island, for bookings t (022) 2601530, f (022) 2600140, *www.polepole.com* (*expensive*). Italian-run accommodation in just a couple of very fine wooden cabins on stilts. These are comfortable, with a surprising Swiss chalet-style feel. Each has a wide balcony overlooking the Chole Channel. The dining area is also on woodern decking, raised on stilts near the water's edge, and the cooking is reputedly fine. Pole Pole ('slowly slowly' in Swahili) is so small that it would be a good choice for a couple of couples, or a small group, who would practically have the run of the place. Boats are available for trips, snorkelling and fishing, but there are no diving facilities or swimming pool.

Chole Mjini, PO Box 20 Mafia Island, *2chole@ bushmail.net*, *www.cholemjini.com* (*expensive*). Mafia-bound travellers with an intrepid sense of adventure and taste for unusual eco-experiences are well advised to spend a couple of nights here. There are five huge tree houses each with two levels, one for sleeping and the other a lounge. Construction of the tree houses has been slow, as it has been conscientiously held in line with community projects to build and develop a hospital, clinic and school on the island, and to ensure that the hotel is integral and not intrusive to island life – the management has a keen interest in the ecological surroundings. There is no beach at the lodge; however, diving, sailing, fishing and walking around the area can be organized. Along the ecological lines there is no electricity and only bucket showers.

Mafia Island Lodge, PO Box 2, Mafia, *info@ mafialodge.com, reservations@mafialodge. com, www.mafialodge.com* (*moderate*). New owners have spent some money rehabilitating what used to be a state-owned enterprise. Changes were ultimately cosmetic, and did not efface the fundamental 1970s feel. Regardless, the lodge is soundly run, and since prices have been lowered since the bad old days is good value for money. It is an excellent place to go if your concern is to be in and under the water as much as humanly possible, rather than the aspect and style of the accommodation. It is situated in rambling seaside palm gardens on the best beach around. Accommodation is in box-like air-conditioned terraced cabins with sliding glass doors onto the garden. The restaurant and bar are vaguely reminiscent of an airport lounge, but the Western food is decent, views are good, and the concrete and glass structure is softened by the scent of frangipani. There are two suites/family rooms.

Lizu's Hotel, t (022) 2116223 (*cheap*). At Kilindoni, around 5mins' walk from the airport, a simple but comfortable establishment with double rooms, either en suite or sharing a bathroom. The restaurant provides simple but decent local-style meals and the bar is usually adequately stocked with cold beers and spirits.

protected wetland ecosystem. These islands are an idyllic natural haven for birds and wildlife, with more than 120 different species of birds sighted and recorded, including five types of sunbird (*see* p.395). The whole area is best explored from the deck of a traditional sailing dhow.

The Mafia Archipelago

Ras Mkumbi

Bweni

Kirongwe

Mafia Island

Baleni

Kilindoni

Kinasi Lodge · Chole Bay

Mafia Island Lodge · Chole Island

Mwera · Utende

Chole Mjini

Ruins of Kua · Juani Island

Jibondo Island

Rufiji River Delta

N

20 km
10 miles

History

Debate continues as to whether the wide Rufiji River Delta is the site of the lost metropolis of **Rhapta**, a thriving trade port described in the *Periplus of the Erythraean Sea*. Rhapta was said to be 'beside and to the east of a cape with a river', and about 30km from the island of Menouthias, 'a low-lying island covered with trees in which there are rivers'. While many scholars believe that Menouthias may have been Pemba or Zanzibar and the port town Bagamoyo, others think the description fits Mafia and that Kilwa was the port of Rhapta. 'Two days' sail beyond the island lies the last mainland market town of Azania, which is called Rhapta,' the guide says, adding, 'Men of the greatest stature, who are all pirates, inhabit the whole coast.' The legendary island and port have never, however, been finally identified, and if the ancient civilization was in fact near Mafia Island it now lies well buried beneath the ebb and flow of the silted Rufiji River Delta.

Similarly to Zanzibar, the first millennium AD of Mafia history remains mysterious. It is likely that the islands were first settled by iron-working Bantu farmers from the mainland. Towards AD 1000 they were joined by the first settlers to arrive on the northeast monsoon winds from Arabia, who called the islands **Morfieyeh** – an Arabic word meaning group, or archipelago. Legends tell how Mafia was settled by one of the sons of Ali bin al-Hasan, the famous sultan of Kilwa who bought his territory from the ruling chief for a length of cloth in AD 975. His son Bashat, who was posted up to Mafia to govern the wider realms of the sultanate, was perhaps responsible for establishing the earliest civilizations here – the stone towns of Ras Kisimani on Mafia Island and Kua on Juani Island.

The early Arab settlers were especially attracted by the safety of the islands of Zanzibar, Pemba and Mafia, which were large enough to be self-sufficient, far enough from the mainland to be out of reach of marauders in dug-out canoes and too far from anywhere for slaves, concubines and wives to escape by swimming. The islanders were also easy to convert to Islam: while the entire African continent was too great to persuade of a new faith, the few islanders were impressed and cowed by the grand new mosques erected in their midst. The settlers could also trade with the mainland from the island staging posts, bringing with them exotica including glass-ware and pottery from Persia, porcelain and painted plates from Tang-dynasty China, and ornaments, phials and brass lamps from across the Arabian Sea, which they exchanged for gold, ivory and slaves, leopard skins, rhinoceros horn and the highly prized ambergris – a waxy substance excreted from the stomachs of the many sperm whales that then cruised the Indian Ocean, desired for its aphrodisiac properties and for 'fixing' perfumes and scents (and subsequently found to be pure cholesterol). Many of these ancient luxury goods ended up buried beneath the ruins of the old Arab settlements; locals of the Mafia archipelago sometimes still discover gold inlaid china, pottery and coins from as early as the 9th century, as well as the more common shards from the 12th to 14th centuries, when the Mafia settlement was at its height.

The good life of the settlers was doomed to end: Vasco da Gama sailed his Portuguese fleet around the Cape of Good Hope, rounded Mozambique and on 4 April 1498 sighted Mafia to starboard on his northbound course. It was not until 1505 that the first viceroy returned to the islands to depose Arab rule, marking the islands of 'Monfiyah' on his maps – a misinterpretation of the Arabic 'Morfieyeh'. Mafia was subjected to a 16th- and 17th-century power struggle between the Omani Arabs and the Portuguese, until the Omanis trounced the Portuguese in Mombasa in 1698 and the sultan of Oman took control of the coast from Lamu to Kilwa.

In the end it was the citizens of Mafia who destroyed their own civilization, after the island settlements of Kisimani and Kua became enemies. It all began when the people of Kisimani, who were called the Dibri but were also Sacklava people from Madagascar, invited the townsfolk of Kua to celebrate the launch of a huge new ship with them. The Kua people were delighted to accept the invitation: they arrived and gathered around the boat in good faith, awaiting the signal for the launch. They were utterly taken aback when the Kisimanis snatched their children, laid them out on the sand and launched the ship over their bodies. The Kuans mulled over their revenge for

Mafia Archipelago Wildlife and Birds

The islands are inhabited by a great diversity of wildlife, with **hippos** residing in a pool at the centre of the island, **Sykes** and **vervet monkeys**, **Galago bushbabies**, **blue duiker**, **genets** and **wild pigs** in the forests and bush. There are also plenty of giant fruit bats (*Pteropus*), a colony of which can be seen roosting on Chole Island.

Mafia Island also provides a relaxed and unspoilt spot for bird-watching, with more than 120 species noted on the lists assiduously kept by Kinasi Lodge of birds observed by residents and visitors. Some of the best areas for bird-watching are the woodlands and forests that run along the Kua Channel, and the northern reaches of Mafia Island. A wide variety of bird species can also be spotted from the balconies and gardens of hotels around Chole Bay, and on the offshore islands.

Diving Mafia

The reefs that make up the **Mafia Island Marine Park** provide a range of possibilities for diving to suit all abilities. The archipelago has some of the finest and most diverse diving and snorkelling along this coastline, with the best conditions between December and March. Anyone keen to take specialist adventure dives or beginners' courses is advised to book in advance at one of the hotels, and thus ensure that the tide, moon and instructor are all prepared for your arrival! It has richly varied and sheltered reefs in **Chole Bay** that provide opportunities for learners and beginners, with more advanced diving and drift diving through **Kinasi Pass**, where the current is stronger, and even more advanced possibilities in the outer channels. Most of the best diving here is at depths of less than 30m, where there is a stunning diversity of marine life, including over 50 types of coral and 400 species of fish so far identified. Local dives around Chole Bay reveal excellent examples of giant table corals and huge blue-tipped staghorn corals; the coral outcrops or 'bommies' behind the Kinasi and Chole walls provide colourful photo-opportunities and snorkelling at low tide.

Kinasi Lodge can arrange all kinds of 'adventure' dives, including night dives, wall dives, reef dives and drift dives; the drift dives carry through Kinasi Pass and often pass shoals of barracuda. On a spring tide the current can be very strong and fast, so that divers cover a couple of kilometres in 30 to 35 minutes. These drifts are not necessarily deep, but divers need to be experienced; and those with less experience should time their dive for a more gentle current. The **Kinasi Wall** and **Chole Wall** are also popular, varying in depth between 8 and 21m. Coral variations are excellent, with shoaling and reef fish and turtles commonly sighted.

The Pinnacle is a 12m spire of coral rock close to the rock island in the Kinasi Pass, which provides an unusual dive site in the channel for its mixture of pelagic and reef fish. Old regulars often encountered here are a large moray eel in his rock home on the western side of the stack, and an equally sizeable potato cod, nicknamed Charlie.

Outside the bay there are fine deep dives at **Dindini North Wall** and **Forbes Bay**, where larger fish such as sharks, tuna and mid-sized groupers and shoals of red-toothed triggerfish are found, and there is also a chance of encountering rare species of butterflyfish, including Meyers', black pyramid and longnose. The boat ride to these sites is exciting enough in itself, and provides seasonal opportunities to trawl for gamefish on the way. Kinasi Lodge can arrange excursion dives for a full day trip or including overnight camping, and keeps a copy of *The Guide to Diving Mafia Island: An Unexplored Paradise*, put together by the volunteer research group Frontier during their years of research here, in its reference library.

seven years, until the wedding of their king's daughter: this time it was their turn to issue the invitation, asking the people of Kisimani to celebrate the marriage with them. As the guests arrived they were ushered into a specially prepared underground room. The hosts slipped away one by one, leaving just one old man entertaining. He did his job so well that no one noticed the door being bricked up – and it is said that their bodies remain there to this very day.

As a result of these bitter internecine struggles the town of Kisimani was sunk beneath the waves – or so the legend goes – and the people of Kua suffered a further vendetta from an army of Sacklava cannibals from Madagascar, who returned in a fleet of 80 canoes in 1829 to sack the town. Those who did not escape were eaten or kept as slaves. The sultan of Zanzibar heard of the destruction of this major settlement and sent a regiment of his own personal Baluchi troops to the island to restore order, but, although they captured the offending pirates and brought them back to Mafia as slaves, the town of Kua was never rebuilt. Instead, Sultan Said established a new settlement on Chole Island; among those living around Kitoni near Kisimani on the west coast are said to be descendants of the Pakistani regiment. Chole was the name of one of the numerous daughters of Sultan Said, greatly favoured by her father and described by her sister Salme: 'There was, indeed, no one to equal her in our whole house, as there was, indeed, no one to equal her in our whole family, and the fame of her beauty spread far and wide.'

The Omani Arabs developed an unusually orderly settlement at Chole, which appealed greatly to the German occupants when they were awarded Mafia under the treaty of 1890, in exchange for the territory between Lake Nyasa and Tanganyika, which the British took. Germany paid Sultan Sayyid Ali bin Said of Oman 4 million marks for Mafia and a chunk of the mainland coast, and the German flag was raised over the island. The first German resident arrived in 1892 with a number of Sudanese troops, and began construction of what later developed into a grand ensemble of buildings on Chole Island. The original two-storey boma and a thick-walled gaol can both still be seen, now twined with roots and rubble. The colonial town at Chole lost importance around 1913, when the administrative capital was moved to its present site at Kilindoni on the Mafia channel and the route of the coastal steamship service.

In January 1915, British troops took Mafia as a strategic base for an air and sea assault on the German cruiser *Konigsberg*, which lay concealed in the Rufiji River

Fishing Mafia

The waters around Mafia are famed for their fishing potential, with world records for big game fish caught here. The main season runs from August to March. For those interested in partaking in the size-driven sport the best season is between July and November, as this is when the northeast monsoon brings in the greatest variety of fish, with kingfish, barracuda and tuna among the favourite big catches. A 57kg yellow-fin tuna holds at least one record, and a 34.2kg dorado caught here in 1950 by mystery spinner 'Sir Arthur Conan Doyle' still holds the record for all of Africa. The best fishing for billfish, sailfish and marlin is between December and March. Fly-fishing in the saltwater creeks and light and heavy tackle fishing in the reef and channels is good at any time of year; all fishermen who successfully fight a big fish on their line can be assured of popularity with other guests when they supply supper.

Kinasi Lodge is a member of the International Game Fishing Association and provides weighing facilities, rods and tackle, although serious fishermen prefer to bring their own. Kinasi also hold a Mafia Channel Fishing Tournament each New Year.

Delta for repairs. The British put the ship out of action (although the Germans salvaged the guns), and continued to rule under martial law until late 1922, when Mafia finally became the territory of Tanganyika.

Today, all the four main islands that make up the archipelago are inhabited, with farming and fishing villages and homesteads. Smallholder farmers grow a variety of crops including rice, cassava, pineapple, paw paw and beans, and most households have cashew, coconut and mango trees. This area of the coast is dense with coral reefs and marine life; diving these waters is rewarding for divers of all abilities. A government protection order has been granted to preserve the diversity of the reefs, in response to the extensive work done by conservation groups such as Frontier and the Worldwide Fund for Nature. Mafia Island Marine Park has been created.

Mafia Island

The crossroads town of **Kilindoni** provides a colourful introduction to Mafia today. Although the German colonialists made it their centre for administration and their main harbour in 1913, there is little sign of them now. The town is essentially a small, bustling fish, fruit and vegetable market, with an enjoyable Swahili flavour. Anyone requiring supplies should certainly try to find them here: fishing tackle – hook, line and sinker – can be found in the market, as can food supplies, kangas and so on. A local café behind the market serves simple dishes of fish, rice and ugali, and sodas are available from the new Pirates Bar opened by Kinasi in the town square, Mwisheha Shop, the Peace and Love Shop and the Market General Supply Store.

About half an hour's drive south of Kilindoni brings you to **Kisimani** on the south-west peninsula. This is the site of probably the earliest settlement on Mafia, which was already flourishing by the 11th century and continued to do so into the 14th century. At this time there was a great palace here. After the completion of the palace orders were given for the amputation of the hands of the chief builder – a slave – so that he could never recreate his work elsewhere in rival constructions. There is no longer much to see, although the journey is worthwhile for the wide and beautiful palm-fringed beaches. Kisimani means 'place of the well' in Swahili: part of the original well can still be made out on the beach. But, while the ruins have suffered badly from sea erosion, early pottery and coins are often tossed up here by the waves. There is a tiny island just west of Ras Kisimani called Bwejuu – a small coral outcrop surrounded by sandy beaches.

Chole Island

Boats to Chole can be arranged from your hotel, or you can jump aboard the local **dhow ferry** from the beach at Utende, just in front of the Mafia Island Beach Hotel. This ferries back and forth regularly all day until 4pm, and the wait on the beach is pleasant as the boat is always in view. The fare is about T.shs 200, and the ferryman and crew are welcoming and friendly as long as you are decently dressed.

The overgrown ruins of the German administration on Chole provide an eerie sense of the imposing power of colonialist rule. The old stone edifices stand grandly aligned along a wide, straight central path, the old stone gaol and boma now exposed to nature. There are also less distinct remains of older Arab settlements here. The island is home to a sizeable roost of giant fruit bats, signposted along a path past a chirruping Koran school; the racket of the roost at dawn and dusk is guide enough. The beach at Chole is a good spot to see traditional boat-building and sail-making, all materials impressively fashioned by hand. The tiny island, only a kilometre across, is a natural haven to wander at leisure. The local people are friendly, and it is interesting to see their smart mud and pole houses, decorated with pebbles to add colour and style. The paths around the island follow fine lines between garden plots in which cassava and beans grow, and past the new school and clinic.

Juani Island and Jibondo Island

The remains of the legendary civilization at **Kua** are on the west coast of **Juani Island**, a 20-minute boat-ride from Mafia Island and accessible only at high tide. The overgrown ruins cover a huge area; enough stands to give an impression of the fine civilization that once existed here. The ruined mosques date from the 14th century, while the other visible ruins are from the 18th century. A vast two-storey structure still stands, the largest ruin, with stone stairs and a maze of anterooms – although the state of the ruins make it hard to get around; crumbling coral stone steps lead up to the second storey; beneath the stairs a small room is said to have been a confinement chamber for badly behaved slaves. The ruins maintain a strange aura of bygone grandeur. Local people deem parts of them spiritual sanctuaries, leaving offerings here for gods and spirits. An extremely old but remarkably lithe caretaker lives in a small hut just beyond the ruins, and is grateful for contributions; if you feel he has not merited your donation, remember that you have to squelch through his cassava plantations to reach the ruins, and that the house in front of his hut is said to be the very place where the townspeople of Kisimani met their untimely fate. Nearby, surrounded by cavernous stone tombs, the ancient central mosque stands, roofless, but complete with vast internal pillars and sculpted mirhab. Potsherds and beads can be found all around, glinting among the shingle on the beach.

The island of Juani also has a reputation for its medicinal powers: the milk from the island was said to have curative properties and the seawater pool that fills one of its caves was widely believed to cure aching rheumatic joints. The effectiveness of this natural saline bath is, however, dependent on the quality of sweet offerings brought by the afflicted for the custodian of the cave, who is partial to dates and honey.

Explorers might like to range through the undergrowth to find the **'Green Lagoon'** of the Kua Channel, a shady swimming hole where a huge and apparently friendly grouper fish bids you welcome. The lagoon, about halfway along the channel, is most easily accessible from a boat.

Another 20 minutes' sail from Juani, **Jibondo Island** has a sizeable community, with great prowess as boat-builders and fishermen. Their building methods are entirely reliant on simple hand tools, with hand-made nails to hold the vessels together. The women of Jibondo are unusually adept sailors and fishers too. The community is organized into immaculate grids of streets at one end of the island, with fields for cultivation at the other.

Dhow Trips around the Archipelago

It is also possible to arrange dhow trips to other areas around Mafia Island and the smaller islands of the archipelago, discovering small, deserted beaches and rural fishing communities. **Bweni**, on the northernmost tip of Mafia Island, is stunningly beautiful, peaceful and unspoilt. **Dinidini Beach** on the eastern peninsula north of Chole Bay is also worth visiting, although only accessible at high tide. There is a large coral rock pool behind the beach, surrounded by small dunes, which makes a good lunch stop after a diving expedition to the Dinidini Wall. **Dimidizi Beach**, to the south of Chole Bay, is another fine beach, about 4km from Kinasi Lodge. Offshore islands such as **Barakuni**, 12km northwest of Mafia, and **Nororo Island**, 12km north of the main island, are quiet, natural hideaways used by fishermen.

These northern islands and the wonderful beaches and estuaries on this side of Mafia can now be included in excursions and picnics from the new camp at Ras Bweni, 'La Lua Cheia', opened by Kinasi in August 2005. Nororo has a resident community, and a couple of local restaurants where you can get fish and rice dishes. You should, however, go well prepared with fresh water and refreshments for all excursions. Kinasi Lodge can arrange camping trips to heavenly deserted beaches on the northern peninsula, and to **Okuza** and **Nyuni Islands** south of Mafia, complete with tents, mattresses and lavish cool-box supplies.

Language

Swahili developed as the language used by Bantu speakers and Arabic traders along the Indian Ocean coast. Its linguistic base is Bantu, but it has incorporated Arabic, Farsi, Hindi, Portuguese, German and English words. There are many dialects; that of Zanzibar Stone Town is the one that has become the lingua franca of many parts of East Africa and is used in government and schools.

Verbs

Swahili verbs always carry with them the subject (and sometimes the object) and the tense. For example, *Ninakula* is a complete sentence, meaning 'I am eating'.

The *Ni...* prefix stands for the subject 'I'; *...na...* stands for 'am', showing the tense (present continuous); *...kula* is the infinitive form of the verb 'to eat'.

When looking up words in a dictionary, the infinitive of the verb is shown, so, if translating from Swahili to English, be sure to identify and look up the right part.

Only the central part of the word changes to indicate the tense:
NiLIkula I ate (*LI* indicates the past tense)
NiMEkula I have eaten (*ME* indicates the perfect tense)
NiNAkula I am eating (*NA* indicates the present continuous tense, as above)
NiTAkula I will eat (*TA* indicates the future tense)
A prefix indicates the person:
Ni (-nakula) I am eating
U (-nakula) You (singular) are eating
A (-nakula) S/he is eating
Tu (-nakula) We are eating
M(w) (-nakula) You (plural) are eating
Wa (-nakula) They are eating
No distinction is made between he or she, him or her in Swahili, which often results in confusion when Swahili speakers try to remember which is which in English!

Personal Pronouns
I *mimi*
you (singular) *wewe*
s/he *yeye*
you (plural) *nyinyi*
we *sisi*
they *wao*

Greetings
How are you? *Habari?*
Well *Nzuri*
Very well *Nzuri sana*

The basic greeting *Habari?*, which literally means 'What news?' can be extended to ask more specific questions:
What news of...? *Habari za...?*
What news of work? *Habari za kazi?*
What news about you? *Habari gani?*
What news of you? *Habari yako?*
What news about your journey?
  Habari za safari?
What news since I last saw you?
  Habari za siku nyingi?

Alternatively you can ask *Hujambo?* – 'How are you?', which is usually answered *Sijambo* – 'I'm fine'.
Welcome! *Karibu!*
Goodbye *Kwaheri*
Goodbye for now *Kwaheri sasa*
Sleep well *Lala salama*

A more polite greeting in coastal society is *Shikamoo*, a term of great respect most frequently employed when greeting an elder; the expression literally means 'I clasp your feet', and the reply given is *Marahabaa*, which shows acknowledgement of respect.

The younger generations of Zanzibar prefer popular slang expressions like *Mambo?* – 'How's it going?' The reply is most often *Poa* – 'Cool', or *Safi* – 'Fresh'.
Do you speak English? *Unasema kiingereza?*
I speak Swahili *Ninaweza kusema Kiswahili*

I speak a little Swahili *Ninasema Kiswahili kidogo*
I can't speak Swahili *Siwezi kusema Kiswahili*
Say that again *Sema tena*
I don't understand *Sielewi*
Thank you (very much) *Asante (sana)*
Please *Tafadhali*
What is your name? *Jina lako nani?*
My name is... *Jina langu (ni)...*
Sorry *Samahani/Pole*
Excuse me, please *Samahani*
I am (very) happy *Nimefurahi (sana)*
I am angry *Nimekasirika*
Help me, please *Nisaidie, tafadhali*
sawa *okay*
where? *wapi?*
when? *lini?*
how? *vipi?*
what? *nini?*
who? *nani?*
which? *ipi?*
friend *rafiki*
thief *mwizi*
danger *hatari*
cold *baridi*
hot/fire *moto*

Transport

Where are you going? *Unakwenda wapi?*
I am travelling *Ninasafiri*
car *gari*
bicycle *baiskeli*
motorcycle *pikipiki*
shared minibus or taxi *dala-dala*
taxi *teksi*

Accommodation

Where is there a guesthouse? *Ipo wapi nyumba ya wageni/gesti?*
Do you have a room? *Nafasi zipo?*
toilet *choo*

Time

Swahili time counts the hours from sunrise to sunset and from sunset to sunrise each day, rather than from midnight to midday and from midday to midnight. It can do this as,

being so close to the equator, dawn is always at 6am, *saa kumi na mbili asubuhi* – 12 hours in the morning Swahili time; 7am, *saa moja asubuhi*, is one hour, and so on until *saa kumi na mbili jioni*, 12 hours again – at 6pm. To work out Swahili time quickly, the trick is to wear your watch upside down.

time/hour *saa*
minute *dakika*
watch/clock *saa*
What time is it? *Saa ngapi?*
8 o'clock in the morning (Swahili time) *saa mbili asubuhi*
noon *saa sita mchana*
early morning *alfajiri*
morning *asubuhi*
afternoon *mchana*
late afternoon *alasiri/jioni*
dusk *magharibi*
evening *jioni/usiku*
night *usiku*
late night *usiku wa manane*
today *leo*
yesterday *jana*
tomorrow *kesho*
day before yesterday *juzi*
day after tomorrow *kesho kutwa*
now *sasa*
day *siku*
week *wiki*
month/moon *mwezi*
year *mwaka*
century *karne*

Days of the Week

Sunday *Jumapili*
Monday *Jumatatu*
Tuesday *Jumanne*
Wednesday *Jumatano*
Thursday *Alhamisi*
Friday *Ijumaa*
Saturday *Jumamosi*

Numbers

one *moja*
two *mbili*
three *tatu*
four *nne*

five *tano*
six *sita*
seven *saba*
eight *nane*
nine *tisa*
ten *kumi*
eleven *kumi na moja*
twelve *kumi na mbili*
thirteen *kumi na tatu*
twenty *ishirini*
twenty-one *ishirini na moja*
thirty *thelathini*
forty *arobaini*
fifty *hamsini*
sixty *sitini*
seventy *sabini*
eighty *themanini*
ninety *tisini*
hundred *mia*
one hundred and twenty-one *mia moja na
   ishirini na moja*
thousand *elfu*
one thousand nine hundred and ninety-nine
   elfu moja mia tisa na tisini na tisa
half *nusu*
one and a half *moja na nusu*
quarter *robo*

Proverbs

Hurry hurry has no blessing (more haste, less
   speed) *Haraka haraka haina baraka*
No problem *Hakuna matata*
No worries *Hamna matatiso*

Animals

leopard *chui*
lion *simba*
cheetah *duma*
elephant *tembo* / *ndovu*
rhinoceros *kifaru*
buffalo *nyati*
baboon *nyani*
monkey *kima*
chimpanzee *sokwe*
zebra *punda*
giraffe *twiga*
impala / deer *swala* / *paa*
hyena *fisi*
warthog *ngiri*
hippo *kiboko*
python *chatu*
snake *nyoka*
dog *mbwa*
wild dog *mbwa mwitu*
pig *nguruwe*
boar *nguruwe mwitu*
cat *paka*
goat *mbuzi*
cow / ox *ng'ombe*
sheep *kondoo*
ostrich *mbuni*
bird *ndege*

Further Reading

Photographs

Jafferji, Javed, photographs, Mercer, Graham, text, *Tanzania, African Eden* (Gallery Publications, Zanzibar, 2001).

Jafferji, Javed, photographs, Rees Jones, Bethan, text, *Images of Zanzibar* (HSP Publ'ns, 1996).

Joynson-Hicks, Paul, *Tanzania: Portrait of a Nation* (Quiller Press Ltd, 1998).

Reader, John, *Kilimanjaro* (Elm Tree Books, Penguin Group, 1982).

Smith, A., *The Great Rift: Africa's Changing Valley* (BBC, 1988).

Van Lawick, Hugo, *Savage Paradise* (Collins, 1977). Images of the Serengeti.

Van Lawick, Hugo, *Among Predators and Prey* (Elm Tree Books, Penguin Group, 1986).

Van Lawick, Hugo and Goodall, Jane, *Innocent Killers* (Houghton Mifflin, 1971).

Wildlife

The Tanzanian National Parks Agency, TANAPA, produces information booklets for all the national parks, published by the African Publishing Group, Harare. It is best to get them direct from the park gates.

Estes, Richard, illus. by Otte, Daniel, *The Safari Companion – A Guide to Watching African Mammals* (Chelsea Green Pub'ns, 1999).

Estes, Richard Despard, *Behaviour Guide to African Mammals* (Univ. of Calif. Press, 1991).

Helm, Christopher, *Birds of Kenya and Northern Tanzania* (Turner and Zimmerman, 1996).

Hoskings, David and Withers, Martin B., *Larger Animals of East Africa* (HarperCollins, 1996).

Kingdon, Jonathon, *The Kingdon Field Guide to African Mammals* (Academic Press, 1999).

Von Perlo, Ber, *Collins Illustrated Checklist of the Birds of East and Southern Africa.*

Goodall, Jane, *Through a Window – My Thirty Years with the Chimpanzees of Gombe* (George Weidenfeld and Nicolson, 1990).

History

French-Sheldon, Mary 'Bebe Bwana', *Sultan to Sultan – Adventures Among the Masai and Other Tribes of East Africa* (Manchester University Press, 1892).

Hall, Richard, *Empires of the Monsoon – A History of the Indian Ocean and its Invaders* (HarperCollins, 1998).

Packenham, Thomas, *The Scramble for Africa, 1876–1912* (1991).

Stephenson, James, *The Language of the Land: Living Among the Hadzabe in Africa* (St Martins Press, 2000).

Reute, Emily, *Memoirs of an Arabian Princess from Zanzibar – An Autobiography of Emily Reute, born Salme, Princess of Oman and Zanzibar (1886)* (Gallery Publications, Zanzibar, 1998).

Dundas, Charles, *Kilimanjaro and its People* (1924).

Gilman, C., *An Ascent of Kilimanjaro.*

Selous, Frederick C., *African Nature Notes and Reminiscences.*

Sykes, Laura and Waide, Uma, *Dar es Salaam – A Dozen Drives Around the City* (Mkuki na Nyota Publishers, PO Box 4246, Dar, 1997).

Adams, Jonathon S. and McShane, Thomas O., *The Myth of Wild Africa – Conservation without Illusion* (University of California Press, 1996).

Fair, Laura, *Pastimes and Politics: Culture, Community and Identity in Post Abolition Urban Zanzibar, 1890–1945* (James Currey, 2001).

Leguin, Colin and Mmari, Geoffrey, *Mwalimu – The Influence of Nyerere* (James Currey, 1995).

Spear, Thomas and Walter, Richard (eds.), *Being Maasai – Ethnicity and Identity in East Africa* (James Currey, London, 1993).

Tip, Tippu, translated by Whitely, W.H., *Autobiography of Tippu Tip* (East African Literature Bureau, 1966).

Tanzanian Fiction

Gurnah, Abdulrazak, *Paradise* (Penguin 1994).

Gurnah, Abdulrazak, *Admiring Silence* (Penguin).

Vassanji, M.G., *Uhuru Street* (Heinemann, 1991).

Vassanji, M.G., *The Book of Secrets* (Macmillan, 1995).

Index

Main page references are in **bold**. Page references to maps are in *italics*.

RUAHA
NATIONAL PARK

Perhaps Tanzania's best kept secret, Ruaha is Africa as it once was generations ago; a spectacular and hauntingly beautiful paradise of the natural world and one of the finest National Parks on the African continent!

MWAGUSI SAFARI CAMP

Situated in an unique transition zone where East and Southern African fauna and flora overlap, and with its vast, unspoilt wilderness protecting a variety of species virtually unequalled in East Africa, Ruaha's diversity offers a richly rewarding wildlife experience.

Amid sculpted rolling hills, plateaux and riverine and legendary, majestic baobab trees, more than 80 species of animal can be found within 45 minutes drive from the camp, including Lion, Leopard, Cheetah, the enigmatic African Hunting Dog, Warthog, Roan & Sable Antelope, Greater & Lesser Kudu, Hippo and Crocodile, huge herds of Buffalo and large concentrations of Zebra, Giraffe and Elephant. And the diversity of bird life in Ruaha – around 460 species, including visits by northern and southern migrants – is extraordinary.

Perfectly located deep inside Ruaha, nestled into the banks of the Mwagusi Sand River where the wildlife is most concentrated, lies this small tented safari camp, owner-run by Chris Fox, a guide of renown, born and bred in the region. Thatched 'bandas', in keeping with traditional African style, enclose comfortably furnished tents and en suite facilities.

Experience quality wildlife viewing: in open Landcruisers, without the disturbance of lots of other vehicles; from the seclusion of your own verandah; during walks, accompanied by a skilled guide.

From the moment you touch down at the local airstrip, the adventure begins!

For further information and booking enquiries, please contact:
TROPICAFRICA   14 Castelnau, London SW13 9RU, England
Phone: **+44 (0)20 8846 9363**   E-mail: **tropicafrica.uk@virgin.net**

Remote Ruaha